America

The Essential Learning Edition

America

The Essential Learning Edition

VOLUME ONE

DAVID EMORY SHI

GEORGE BROWN TINDALL

W. W. Norton & Company, Inc.
New York • London

W. W. Norton & Company has been independent since its founding in 1923, when William Warder Norton and Mary D. Herter Norton first published lectures delivered at the People's Institute, the adult education division of New York City's Cooper Union. The firm soon expanded its program beyond the Institute, publishing books by celebrated academics from America and abroad. By mid-century, the two major pillars of Norton's publishing program—trade books and college texts— were firmly established. In the 1950s, the Norton family transferred control of the company to its employees, and today—with a staff of four hundred and a comparable number of trade, college, and professional titles published each year—W. W. Norton & Company stands as the largest and oldest publishing house owned wholly by its employees.

Editor: Jon Durbin
Developmental Editors: Lisa Moore and John Elliott
Associate Editor: Justin Cahill
Project Editor: Melissa Atkin
Editorial Assistant: Penelope Lin
Marketing Manager, History: Sarah England
Manuscript Editor: Mike Fleming
Managing Editor, College: Marian Johnson
Managing Editor, College Digital Media: Kim Yi
Production Manager: Andy Ensor
Media Editor: Lisa Moore
Media Project Editor: Penelope Lin
Media Editorial Assistant: Chris Hillyer
Design Director: Hope Miller Goodell
Photo Editor: Nelson Colón
Permissions Manager: Megan Jackson
Composition: Graphic World, Inc.
Manufacturing: Courier, Kendallville

The Library of Congress has cataloged the full edition as follows:

Tindall, George Brown.
    America : a narrative history / George Brown Tindall,
David Emory Shi.—9th ed.
        p.   cm.
    Includes bibliographical references and index.
    ISBN 978-0-393-91262-3 (hardcover)
    1. United States—History—Textbooks.   I. Shi, David E.   II. Title.
E178.1.T55 2013   2012034504
973—dc23
    This edition:
    ISBN 978-0-393-93802-9

W. W. Norton & Company, Inc., 500 Fifth Avenue, New York, NY 10110-0017
wwnorton.com
W. W. Norton & Company Ltd., Castle House, 75/76 Wells Street, London W1T 3QT
1 2 3 4 5 6 7 8 9 0

For Jon Durbin, editor and friend

About the Authors

DAVID SHI is a professor of history and the president emeritus of Furman University. He is the author of several books on American cultural history, including the award-winning *The Simple Life: Plain Living and High Thinking in American Culture* and *Facing Facts: Realism in American Thought and Culture, 1850–1920*.

GEORGE TINDALL recently of the University of North Carolina, Chapel Hill, was an award-winning historian of the South with a number of major books to his credit, including *The Emergence of the New South, 1913–1945* and *The Disruption of the Solid South*.

Lead authors for media and pedagogy

JON LEE (San Antonio College, Texas) served on the American Historical Association/Lumina Tuning Project and educational commissions in the state of Texas to establish discipline-wide historical learning outcomes. He received the "Most Inspirational Professor" award from Phi Theta Kappa Beta Nu. He is the coordinator of the Honors Academy at San Antonio College.

ERIK ANDERSON (San Antonio College, Texas) teaches American history and is involved with the Honors Academy. He also serves as the academic liaison with the Travis Early College High School program at San Antonio College. Anderson earned his doctorate at Brown University.

Contents
in Brief

Contents

PART FOUR | A House Divided and Rebuilt   415

Maps

What's It All About?

Thinking Like A Historian

Preface

The Essential Learning Edition builds upon *America*'s long-established emphasis on history as a storytelling art. It features colorful characters and anecdotes informed by balanced analysis and social texture, all guided by the unfolding of key events. But this Essential Learning Edition, a new addition to the *America* family, includes innovative pedagogical features and tools to help students better understand the most important aspects of American history, to learn how historians study, interpret, and debate the past, and to assess their own progress.

To guide my efforts in crafting the Essential Learning Edition, I asked students and professors at a variety of colleges what they most needed in an introductory survey textbook. Their answers varied, but overall there was a strong consensus on several key points: students want a manageable, inexpensive textbook that focuses on the essentials of American history while telling the dramatic story of the nation's past in vivid but simple language. They stressed that many textbooks overwhelm them, either by flooding them with too much information or by taking too much for granted in terms of the knowledge that students bring to the introductory course. Students also asked for a textbook that would help them more easily identify the most important developments or issues to focus on (and remember) as they read.

To address these student concerns, I have streamlined and compressed the Brief Ninth Edition of *America* to build the Essential Learning Edition. It has 30 chapters as compared to 34 in the Brief Ninth Edition, which means that it nicely fits the chapter per week model for most courses. Moreover, I have trimmed the narrative text of the Brief Ninth Edition by about fifteen percent to focus on the most essential elements of *America*'s past. Finally, because I assumed little or no background knowledge on the part of the student reader, I sought to ensure that the major topics in each chapter are easily grasped and all key terms are clearly identified.

When asked about their needs in a survey text, instructors said much the same as their students, but they also asked for a textbook that introduced students to the nature of historical research, analysis, and debate. Many professors also mentioned the growing importance to them and their institutions of assessing the success of their classes in meeting the learning goals established by their department. Accordingly, I have aligned the Essential Learning Edition with specific learning outcomes for the introductory American history survey course approved by various state and national organizations, including the American Historical Association. To help me make those changes, my innovative editor, Jon Durbin, recruited a talented multi-disciplinary group of professors, pedagogical specialists, developmental editors, instructional designers, reviewers, and copy editors. In particular, Erik Anderson and Jon Lee of San Antonio College in Texas served as the pedagogical specialists and lead media authors for this project. They are both widely recognized as superb teachers and innovative leaders in assessment and community-college instruction. The new pedagogical features in the Essential Learning Edition were a direct outgrowth of their efforts teaching the survey course and working closely with students in a dynamic, collaborative, community-based learning environment in the Honors College at San Antonio College. Moreover, the new pedagogical features of this book and its accompanying media components—including the new Norton InQuizitive program, an adaptive online tool designed to guide student learning—make it much easier for professors to assess their students' performance on a variety of learning levels.

These and other suggestions from students and professors have shaped this Essential Learning Edition. Each of the 30 chapters begins with a list of five or six Core Objectives, carefully designed to help students understand—and remember—the major developments in each period. To make it easier for students to grasp the major developments, I have reorganized every chapter to ensure that the narrative aligns sequentially with the objectives. Each Core Objective appears at the beginning of each major section in the chapter for which it is relevant. Core Objective Flags, unique to this edition, appear in the page margins to highlight topics in the narrative that are essential to understanding the broader Core Objective. Key terms, chosen to reinforce the major concepts, are bolded in the text and defined in the margin, helping students appreciate and remember their significance. At the end of each chapter, new review features are designed to reinforce the Core Objectives, including clear chapter summaries, lists of key terms, and chapter chronologies.

This book breaks new ground by incorporating several new instructional features designed to improve student learning. Maps, for example, are essential to history textbooks, but in this version I have taken the additional step of listing questions underneath each map to help students analyze the implications embedded in maps in a way that promotes active learning.

Interactive maps are but just one example of the innovative elements in this book designed to deepen student learning. Each chapter in the Essential Learning Edition also includes a **What It's All About** feature, which visually summarizes in a graphical format major issues such as:

- Chapter 3: Comparative examination of how different regions of the English colonies were settled and developed.
- Chapter 9: Analyzes sectional conflicts and the role the economic policies of Henry Clay and Andrew Jackson played in those conflicts.
- Chapter 12: Abolitionist versus pro-slavery arguments on slavery.
- Chapter 15: Tracing the legal and legislative road from slavery to freedom for African Americans in the former Confederate States.
- Chapter 23: The First New Deal compared to the Second New Deal.

Another unique new feature, called **Thinking Like a Historian**, helps students better understand—and apply—the research techniques and interpretive skills used by historians. Through carefully selected examples the

Thinking Like a Historian feature highlights the essential role of primary and secondary sources as the building blocks of history and illustrates the ways in which historians have differed in their interpretations of the past. There is one Thinking Like a Historian feature for each major period of American history; each feature takes on a major interpretive issue in that era. In Part I of the activity, students first read excerpts from two original secondary sources that offer competing interpretive views framing that period. In Part II, students then read some of the original primary sources that those same historians used to develop their arguments. Finally, students are asked to answer a series of questions that guide their reading and analysis of the sources.

As always, this new edition also includes new content. As I created the Essential Learning Edition, I have complemented the political narrative by incorporating more social and cultural history into the text. Key new discussions include:

- Chapter 3, Colonial Ways of Life, 1607–1750, includes a new portrait of Antonio, an enslaved African brutalized by his Dutch owner in Maryland in the mid-seventeenth century. There is also new material on the competition among American colonists for British luxury goods in the 1760s and 1770s.
- Chapter 4, From Colonies to States, 1607–1776, has enriched material on the non-importation efforts (boycotts of British goods) led by grassroots Americans prior to the Revolutionary War. It also includes new material about the conversion of American farmers into soldiers after the clash of arms at Lexington and Concord.
- Chapter 5, The American Revolution, 1776–1783, includes more material about slaves who took advantage of the war to escape or join the British forces, and about the ways in which women, Native Americans, and slaves became engaged in the war effort.
- Chapter 6, Creating a "More Perfect Union," 1783–1800, elaborates on Shays's Rebellion and other expressions of agrarian discontent across the nation after the Revolution, and there is also more discussion about how women, Native Americans, and slaves figured into the thinking of the Founding Fathers during the Constitutional Convention in 1787.
- Chapter 7, The Early Republic, 1800–1815, has new material on the way in which the War of 1812 affected slavery/blacks.
- Chapter 8, The Emergence of a Market Economy, 1815–1850, offers new discussions of the emergence of the cotton culture in the South and the plight of the Irish fleeing the famine at home and heading to America.
- Chapter 9, Nationalism and Sectionalism, 1815–1828, more fully discusses the role of labor advocates and unions in forging what would become the Jacksonian movement.
- Chapter 10, The Jacksonian Era, 1828–1840, describes the effect of the Panic of 1837 and the ensuing depression on the working poor.
- Chapter 11, The South and Slavery, 1800–1860, boasts substantial new material related to slavery and African American culture. There is also

a new discussion of a New Orleans slave revolt led by Charles Deslondes in 1811, the largest slave revolt in American history.

- Chapter 12, Religion, Romanticism, and Reform, 1800–1860, includes enriched treatment of the revivalism of the Second Great Awakening, and a completely rewritten discussion of Mormonism.
- Chapter 14, The War of the Union, 1861–1865, adds new material about the social history of the Civil War, including more material on common soldiers, rioting in opposition to the military draft, and backwoods violence rarely included in discussions of the war, such as the summary of the execution of thirteen Unionists in Madison County, North Carolina.
- Chapter 15, Reconstruction, 1865–1877, highlights the circumstances of former slaves—from their perspective. It also includes new examples of the ways in which the Freedmen's Bureau helped negotiate labor contracts between white planters and freedmen.
- Chapter 16, Big Business and Organized Labor, 1860–1900, discusses the emergence of a new middle class during the Gilded Age, and includes substantially revised material on women's and labor history.
- Chapter 17, The South and the West Transformed, 1865–1900, offers a newly rewritten section on the emergence of new racial segregation in the South, and also new material about the everyday realities of Western expansion.
- Chapter 20, The Progressive Era, 1890–1920, provides new sections the attitudes of Theodore Roosevelt and Woodrow Wilson's attitudes and policies concerning race.
- Chapter 21, America and the Great War, 1914–1920, now highlights the war's social effects in the United States, with special attention to women, blacks, and Mexican Americans.
- Chapter 22, A Clash of Cultures, 1920–1929, incorporates new material on the consumer culture, women's history, and revised material on the Harlem Renaissance with a new profile of Zora Neale Hurston.
- Chapter 24, The Second World War, 1933–1945, includes new material about the wartime experience of Mexican Americans.
- Chapter 25, The Cold War and the Fair Deal, 1945–1952, benefits from new coverage of women industrial workers, and also the efforts of Latinos to gain equal rights in the aftermath of World War II.
- Chapter 27, New Frontiers, 1960–1968, showcases a new portrait of Fannie Lou Hamer, a black Mississippi activist, in the section on the early civil rights movements.
- Chapter 28, Rebellion and Reaction, the 1960s and 1970's, includes new material on the women's movement, Mexican Americans, and Native Americans.

In sum, this new *Essential Learning Edition* includes the most dramatic changes ever made in a resilient book that is celebrating its thirtieth year in print.

Media Tools for Students and Instructors

New lead authors for media and pedagogy Jon Lee and Erik Anderson have ensured that the Essential Learning Edition of *America* is supported by an array of digital media with tools faculty need to meet course goals—in the classroom and online—and activities for students to develop core skills in reading comprehension, writing, and analysis.

The Essential Learning Edition Team

I have already introduced you to Erik Anderson and Jon Lee, but our talented team of innovative support authors also includes Brandon Franke (Blinn College), Cathy Parzynski (Montgomery County Community College), Melissa Weinbrenner (Northeast Texas Community College), Brian Cervantez (Tarrant County College), and Laura Farkas (Ivy Tech College–West Lafayette), who have contributed to all of the enriching learning materials we can offer students and instructors for support:

⚖ INQUIZITIVE
Quizzing to Learn

InQuizitive, Norton's new adaptive quizzing platform, uses interactive questions and guided feedback to motivate students to read and understand the text. Varied question types—featuring images, maps, and sources—prompt critical and analytical thinking on each of the chapter's Core Objectives. Robust grading functionality helps instructors track their students' progress on learning outcomes.

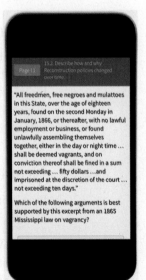

Student Site

This free site offers students access to additional primary source documents and images, Office Hour videos with author David Shi, and iMaps. It is ideal for instructors interested in granting students access to additional material without creating or administering online assignments.

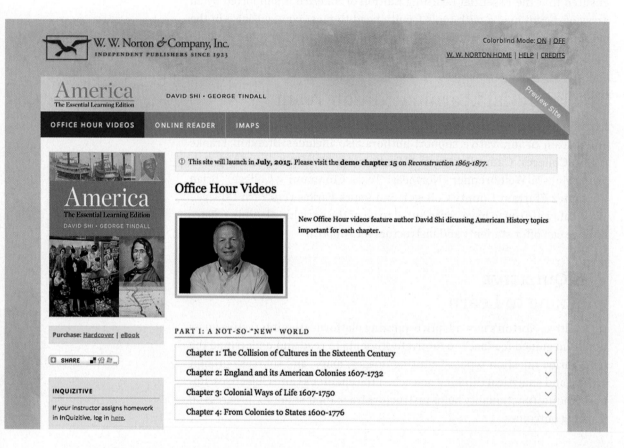

Norton Ebooks

Norton Ebooks let students access the entire book and much more: they can search, highlight, and take notes with ease, as well as collaborate and share their notes with instructors and classmates. Ebooks can be viewed on any device—laptop, tablet, phone, even a public computer—and will stay synced between devices.

Norton Coursepacks

Free Norton Coursepacks (downloadable in Blackboard, WebCT, D2L, and Moodle; additional formats can be provided upon request), include:

- **NEW Gradable Assignments** allow you to assign quizzes based on questions from the text including Assessing the Core Objectives, What's It All About?, and Thinking Like a Historian.

- **NEW Primary Source Exercises** include several primary sources from across cultures with a brief multiple choice exam and a short answer question.
- **Guided Reading Exercises**, keyed to each chapter's Core Objectives, instill the three-step Note-Summarize-Assess pedagogy. Each chapter has one exercise built around passages from the text.
- **Review Quizzes** include targeted feedback that highlights Core Objective, page reference, and difficulty. *Chrono-Quizzes* end each chapter quiz with a matching question.
- **Online Reader** provides over 100 primary-source documents and images.
- **Map Resources** include *iMaps*, where students can peel back each layer to highlight the information they want to see, and *American History Tours*, powered by Google Earth that are dynamic, interactive primary sources that trace geographical developments over time. *Map Worksheets* provide each map without labels for offline relabeling and quizzing.
- **Forum Prompts** for online and hybrid courses are a set of topics that can be used to launch discussions.
- **Key Term Flash Cards** allow students to self-study historical vocabulary.
- Links to **InQuizitive** for each chapter.

Classroom Presentation Tools

- **Lecture PowerPoints** and **Art PowerPoints** feature photographs and maps from the book, retouched for in-class presentation.

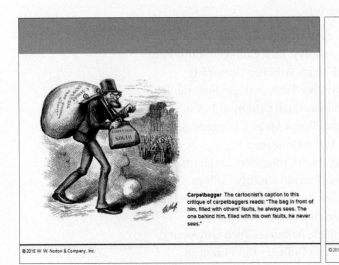

Carpetbagger The cartoonist's caption to this critique of carpetbaggers reads: "The bag in front of him, filled with others' faults, he always sees. The one behind him, filled with his own faults, he never sees."

©2015 W. W. Norton & Company, Inc.

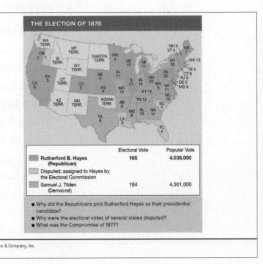

©2015 W. W. Norton & Company, Inc.

- The **Norton American History Digital Archive** includes over 1,700 images, audio and video files that are arranged chronologically and by theme, available online or on DVD.

Instructor's Manual (Melissa Weinbrenner, Northeast Texas Community College)

The Instructor's Manual for The Essential Learning Edition has everything instructors need to prepare lectures and classroom activities: chapter summaries, suggestions for teaching Core Objectives, as well as lecture ideas, classroom activities, and lists of recommended books, films, and websites.

Test Bank (Brandon Franke, Blinn College; Cathy Parzynski, Montgomery County Community College; and Melissa Weinbrenner, Northeast Texas Community College)

The Test Bank features multiple-choice, true/false, and essay questions aligned with the chapter's Core Objectives and classified according to level of difficulty, Bloom's Taxonomy, and the American Historical Association's guidelines for student learning outcomes, offering multiple avenues for content and skill assessment. All Norton test banks are available with Exam-View Test Generator software, allowing instructors to easily create, administer, and manage assessments.

Acknowledgments

The quality and range of reviews on this project were truly exceptional. The book and its accompanying media components benefited from the insights of numerous instructors.

Erik Anderson, San Antonio College
Milan Andrejevich, Ivy Tech College–South Bend
Evan Bennett, Florida Atlantic University
Laura Bergstrom, Ivy Tech College–Sellersburg
Keith Berry, Hillsborough Community College
Albert Broussard, Texas A&M, College Station
Blanche Brick, Blinn College
Cory Burger, Ivy Tech College–Terre Haute
Brian Cervantez, Tarrant County College–Northwest Campus
Michael L. Collins, Midwestern State University
Lee Cowan, Tarrant County College
Thomas A. DeBlack, Arkansas Tech University
Scott Derr, Ivy Tech College–Bloomington
S. Matthew DeSpain, Rose State College
Michael Downs, Tarrant County College–Northeast Campus
Shannon Duffy, Southwest Texas State University

Karen Dunn-Haley, University of California, Davis
Stephen D. Engle, Florida Atlantic University
Laura Farkas, Ivy Tech College–West Lafayette
David Haney, Austin Community College
Andrew Hollinger, Tarrant County College–Southeast Campus
Frances Jacobson, Tidewater Community College
Jon Lee, San Antonio College
Robert MacDonald, Ivy Tech College–Lafayette
Richard McCaslin, University of North Texas–Denton
Suzanne McFadden, Austin Community College
Joel McMahon, Kennesaw State University
Greg Miller, Hillsborough Community College
Catherine Parzynski, Montgomery Community College
R. Lynn Rainard, Tidewater Community College
Hazel Ramos, Glendale Community College
Nicole Ribianszky, Georgia Gwinnett College
Allen Smith, Ivy Tech College–Indianapolis
Bruce Solheim, Citrus College
Mark Stanley, University of North Texas–Denton
Melissa Weinbrenner, Northeast Texas Community College

Once again, I thank my friends and colleagues at W. W. Norton for their consummate professionalism and good cheer, especially Jon Durbin, Justin Cahill, Penelope Lin, Lisa Moore, Chris Hillyer, Melissa Atkin, John Elliott, Mike Fleming, Nelson Colón, Hope Miller Goodell, Debra Morton-Hoyt, Andy Ensor, and Sarah England. In addition, my talented friends Charles Cornwell and Jim Stewart read drafts of numerous chapters, helping me to clarify my descriptions and prune my prose.

Finally, I have dedicated this new version of *America* to Jon Durbin, my tireless editor at W. W. Norton, who is a marketing genius and so much more.

America

The Essential Learning Edition

An Old "New" World

History is filled with ironies. The unexpected and unplanned—luck and accidents—often shape events more than intentions. Long before Christopher Columbus happened upon the Caribbean Sea in his effort to find a westward passage to the Indies (a term then used to refer to east Asia), the native peoples he mislabeled *Indians* had occupied and transformed the lands of the Western Hemisphere (also called the Americas—North, Central, and South). The first residents in what Europeans came to call the "New World" had migrated from northeastern Asia nearly 20,000 years ago. By 1492, when Columbus began his famous voyage west from Spain, there were millions of Native Americans living in the Western Hemisphere. Over the centuries, they had developed diverse and often highly sophisticated societies, some rooted in agriculture, and others focused on trade or conquest. The New World was "new" only to the Europeans who began exploring, conquering, and exploiting the region at the end of the fifteenth century.

The Native American peoples were profoundly affected by the arrival of Europeans and Africans. Very different societies collided, each having its own distinct heritage and world view. Indian peoples were exploited, infected, enslaved, displaced, and exterminated. Yet the conventional story of tragic conquest oversimplifies the complex process by which Indians, Europeans, and Africans interacted in the Western Hemisphere. The Native Americans were more than passive victims of European power; they were also trading partners and both allies and rivals of the transatlantic newcomers. They became neighbors and advisers, converts and spouses. As such they participated jointly in the creation of the new society known as America.

The Europeans who risked their lives to settle in the Western Hemisphere were a diverse lot. Young and old, men and women, they came from Spain, Portugal, France, the British Isles, the Netherlands (Holland), Scandinavia, Italy, and the German states (Germany would not become a united nation until the mid–nineteenth century). A variety of motives inspired them to undertake the dangerous transatlantic voyage. Some were adventurers and fortune seekers eager to gain glory and find gold and silver. Others were passionate Christians eager to create kingdoms of God in the New World. Still others were prisoners, debtors, servants, landless peasants, and political or religious exiles. Many were simply seeking a piece of land, higher wages, and greater economic opportunity. A settler in Pennsylvania noted that "poor people (both men and women) of all kinds can here get three times the wages for their labor than they can in England."

Yet such wages did not attract enough workers to keep up with the rapidly expanding colonial economies, so the Europeans early in the seventeenth century turned to Africa for their labor needs. European nations— especially Portugal and Spain—had long been transporting captive Africans to the Western Hemisphere, from Chile to Canada. In 1619 a Dutch warship brought twenty captured Africans to Jamestown, near the coast of Virginia. The Dutch captain exchanged the slaves for food and supplies. This first of many transactions involving enslaved people in British America would transform American society in ways that no one at the time envisioned. Few Europeans during the colonial era saw the contradiction between the promise of freedom in America for themselves and the expanding institution of race-based slavery.

The intermingling of people, cultures, and ecosystems from the continents of Africa, Europe, and the Western Hemisphere gave colonial

American society its distinctive vitality and variety. In turn, the diversity of the environment and the varying climate spawned quite different economies and patterns of living in the various regions of North America. As the original settlements grew into prosperous and populous colonies, the transplanted Europeans had to create new communities and political systems to manage dynamic growth and control rising tensions.

At the same time, bitter rivalries among the Spanish, French, English, and Dutch triggered costly wars fought in Europe and around the world. The monarchs of Europe struggled to manage often-unruly colonies, which, they discovered, played crucial roles in their frequent European wars. Many of the colonists had brought with them to America a feisty independence, which led them to resent government interference in their affairs. A British official in North Carolina reported that the settlers were "without any Law or Order. Impudence is so very high, as to be past bearing." The colonists and their British rulers maintained an uneasy partnership throughout the seventeenth century. But as the royal authorities tightened their control during the mid–eighteenth century, they met resistance from colonists, which exploded into revolution.

DE SOTO AND THE INCAS This 1596 color engraving shows Spanish conquistador Hernando de Soto's first encounter with King Atahualpa of the Inca Empire. Although artist Theodor de Bry never set foot in North America, his engravings reflect travelogues of explorers and Spanish perceptions of Native Americans in the sixteenth century.

The Collision of Cultures

in the 16th Century

D ebate continues about when and how the first humans arrived in North America. Until recently, archaeologists had assumed that ancient peoples from northeast Asia, some 12,000 to 15,000 years ago, were the first arrivals in the Western Hemisphere. Those Asian wanderers ("nomads") who hunted the massive woolly mammoths and other big game animals had journeyed 600 miles across the Bering Strait on what was then a treeless land bridge connecting northeastern Siberia with Alaska, when the oceans were much lower than today.

Archaeologists call these first peoples Paleo-Indians ("Old Indians"). Over hundreds of years, as the climate warmed and the glaciers melted, a steady stream of small groups fanned out southward across the entire Western Hemisphere, from the Arctic Circle to the tip of South America. They were skilled "hunter-gatherers" (as well as tool-makers and warriors) whose food consisted of large mammals and edible wild plants, berries, and seeds gathered as they searched for game. As the isolated bands of hunters trekked across the prairies and the plains, they encountered animals unlike those found there today: mastodons, giant sloths, camels, bison, lions, saber-toothed tigers, cheetahs, and massive wolves, beavers, and bears. Recent archaeological discoveries in Pennsylvania, Virginia, and Chile suggest that prehistoric humans may have arrived much earlier than assumed (perhaps 18,000 to

CORE OBJECTIVES INQUIZITIVE

1. Explain why there were so many diverse human societies in the Americas before Europeans arrived.

2. Summarize the major developments in Europe that enabled the Age of Exploration.

3. Describe how the Spanish were able to conquer and colonize the Americas.

4. Assess the impact of the Columbian Exchange between the "Old" and "New" Worlds.

5. Analyze the legacy of the Spanish form of colonization on North American history.

THE FIRST MIGRATION

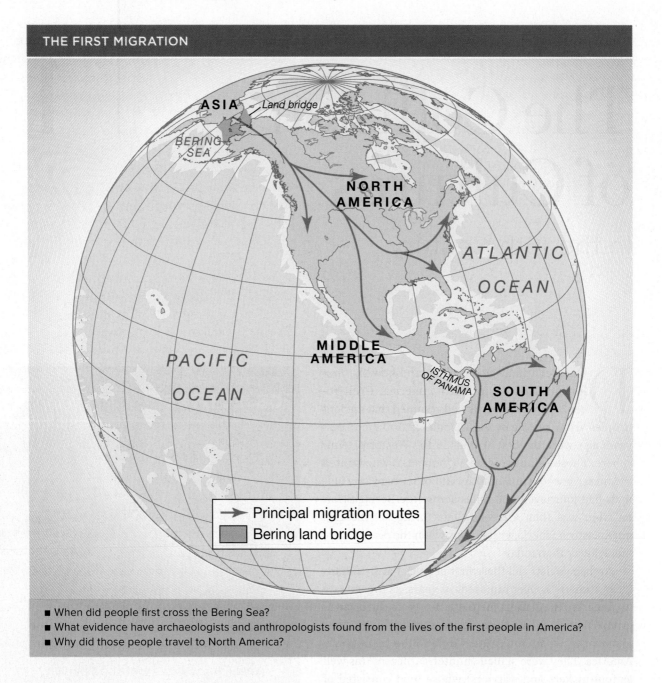

- When did people first cross the Bering Sea?
- What evidence have archaeologists and anthropologists found from the lives of the first people in America?
- Why did those people travel to North America?

40,000 years ago) from various parts of Asia—and some may even have crossed the Atlantic Ocean from southwestern Europe.

Regardless of when ancient humans first set foot on the North American continent, the region eventually became a crossroads for various peoples from around the globe: Europeans, Africans, Asians, and others—all of whom brought with them distinctive backgrounds, cultures, technologies, and motivations that, taken together, helped form the American mosaic.

Early Cultures in the Americas

CORE **OBJECTIVE**

1. Explain why there were so many diverse human societies in the Americas before Europeans arrived.

For at least 15,000 years before the arrival of Europeans, Native Americans had occupied the vastness of North America undisturbed by outside invaders. By the time Christopher Columbus happened upon the Western Hemisphere, the hundreds of Indian societies living in North America may have numbered over 10 million people. They had developed a diverse array of communities in which more than 300 languages were spoken.

Archaeologists have labeled the earliest arrivals in North America the Clovis peoples, named after a site in New Mexico where ancient hunters around 9500 B.C.E. killed tusked woolly mammoths (fourteen feet tall) using distinctive "Clovis" spear points. Clovis people lived in small bands of five to ten families. Over many centuries, as the post–Ice Age climate warmed, sea levels rose, growing seasons lengthened, and snowfall and rainfall lessened, leading many lakes to dry up into deserts. The largest mammals—mammoths, mastodons, giant bison, single-hump camels, huge beavers, sabre-toothed tigers—eventually died out. Hunters shifted from stalking mammoths and mastodons to smaller, yet more abundant mammals: deer, antelope, elk, moose, and caribou.

Global warming diminished grasslands and stimulated forest growth, which provided plants and small animals for human consumption. The ancient Indians adapted to the diverse new environments—coastal forests, grassy plains, southwestern deserts, eastern woodlands—by developing new ways to survive and flourish. Some continued to hunt large animals; others fished and trapped small animals; some gathered wild plants and herbs and collected acorns and seeds; others would farm. Many did some of each. Contrary to the romantic myth of early Indian civilizations living in perfect harmony with nature and one another, indigenous peoples often engaged in warfare and exploited the environment by burning large wooded areas in order to plant fields. They also developed their own nature-centered religions, mastered the use of fire, and improved technology such as spear points, basketry, and pottery.

Global warming, and climatic and environmental diversity

By about 5000 B.C.E., Native Americans in Mexico had adapted to the warmer climate by transforming themselves into farming societies. They became expert at growing the plant foods that would become the primary crops of the hemisphere: chiefly **maize (corn)** to be ground into flour, beans, and squash, but also chili peppers, avocados, and pumpkins. The annual cultivation of such crops enabled Indian societies to grow larger and more complex, with their own distinctive social, economic, and political institutions.

Agricultural revolution

maize (corn) The primary grain crop in Mesoamerica yielding small kernels often ground into cornmeal. Easy to grow in a broad range of conditions, it enabled a global population explosion after being brought to Europe, Africa, and Asia.

The Mayas, Incas, and Mexica

Around 1500 B.C.E., farming towns first appeared in Mexico, enabling people to live in one place rather than move with the seasons. The more settled life in turn provided time for the cultivation of religion, art and crafts,

Mayan society A fresco depicting the social divisions of Mayan society. A Mayan lord, at the center, receives offerings.

science, governmental administration—and frequent warfare. Agriculture supported the development of densely populated cities complete with gigantic pyramids, temples, and palaces in Middle America (Mesoamerica, what is now Mexico and Central America). The Mayas, who dominated Central America for more than 600 years, also developed an elaborate written language and used sophisticated mathematics and astronomy to create a yearly calendar more accurate than the one the Europeans were using at the time of Columbus.

> Vast empires and monumental cities

Farther south, as many as 12 million people speaking at least twenty different languages made up the Inca Empire. By the fifteenth century, the Incas' vast realm stretched some 2,500 miles along the Andes Mountains in the western part of South America, transforming their mountainous empire into a flowering civilization with fertile farms fed by irrigation systems, enduring stone buildings, and interconnected networks of paved roads.

> Tribute and trade

During the late thirteenth century, the **Mexica** (Me-SHEE-ka)—whom Europeans later called Aztecs ("People from Aztlán," the place they claimed as their homeland)—began drifting southward from northwest Mexico. They eventually took control of the sweeping valley of central Mexico, where they built the city of Tenochtitlán in 1325 on an island in Lake Tetzcoco, the site of present-day Mexico City. Tenochtitlán would become the largest city in the Western Hemisphere by the end of the fifteenth century.

Mexica Otherwise known as "Aztecs," a Mesoamerican people of northern Mexico who founded the vast Aztec Empire in the fourteenth century, later conquered by the Spanish under Hernán Cortés in 1521.

Warfare was a sacred ritual for the Mexica. Gradually, they expanded their control over neighboring societies in central Mexico, forcing them to pay tribute in goods and services each year and developing a thriving

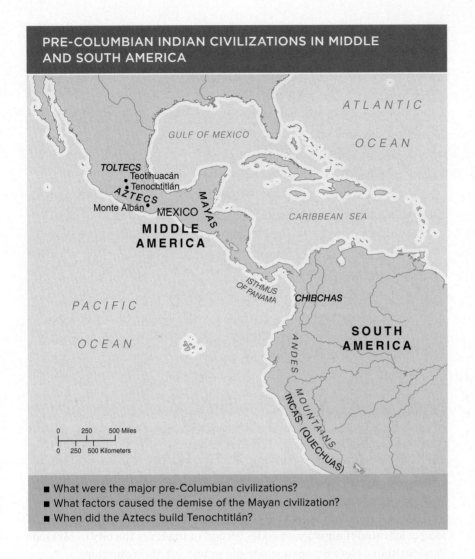

PRE-COLUMBIAN INDIAN CIVILIZATIONS IN MIDDLE AND SOUTH AMERICA

- What were the major pre-Columbian civilizations?
- What factors caused the demise of the Mayan civilization?
- When did the Aztecs build Tenochtitlán?

trade in gold, silver, copper, and pearls as well as agricultural products. Towering stone temples, broad paved avenues, thriving markets, and some 70,000 adobe huts dominated the dazzling capital city of Tenochtitlán. When the Spanish invaded Mexico in 1519, they found a sprawling **Aztec Empire** connected by a network of roads, connecting 371 city-states organized into 38 provinces.

Like most agricultural peoples, the Mexica were intensely spiritual. Their religious beliefs focused on the interconnection between nature and human life and the sacredness of natural elements—the sun, moon, stars, rain, mountains, rivers, and animals. To please the gods and bring good harvests and victory in battle, the Mexica, like most Mesoamericans, regularly offered live human sacrifices—captives, slaves, women, and children. In elaborate weekly rituals, priests used stone knives to cut out the beating hearts of the victims. The need for more sacrificial victims fed the Mexica's relentless warfare against other indigenous groups. A Mexica

Religion, war, tribute, and trade

Aztec Empire A network of more than 300 city-states and upwards of 30 provinces, established in the fourteenth century under the imperialistic Mexica, or Aztecs, in the valley of Mexico.

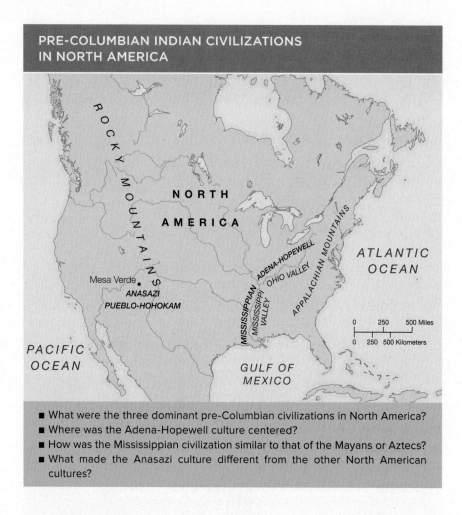

PRE-COLUMBIAN INDIAN CIVILIZATIONS IN NORTH AMERICA

- What were the three dominant pre-Columbian civilizations in North America?
- Where was the Adena-Hopewell culture centered?
- How was the Mississippian civilization similar to that of the Mayans or Aztecs?
- What made the Anasazi culture different from the other North American cultures?

song celebrated their warrior code: "Proud of itself / is the city of Mexico-Tenochtitlán / Here no one fears to die in war. / This is our glory. . . ."

North American Civilizations before 1500

| Diverse regional societies

North of Mexico, numerous indigenous civilizations existed in the present-day United States. They shared several fundamental spiritual myths and social beliefs, especially the sacredness of nature, the necessity of communal living and collective effort, and respect for elders, but they developed in different ways at different times and in different places. In North America alone, there were probably 240 different societies of native peoples speaking many different languages when the Europeans arrived.

| Southwest pueblo cultures

The dry Southwest (what is now Arizona, New Mexico, Nevada, and Utah) hosted corn-growing societies, elements of which exist today and heirs to which (the Hopis, Zunis, and others) still live in the multi-story adobe cliffside villages (called *pueblos* by the Spanish) erected by their ancestors. About 500 C.E., the native Hohokam people from present-day

Mexico migrated to southern and central Arizona, where they constructed hundreds of miles of irrigation canals to water their crops. They also crafted decorative pottery and turquoise jewelry, and they constructed temple mounds (earthen pyramids used for sacred ceremonies) similar to those in Mexico. Perhaps because of prolonged drought, the Hohokam society disappeared during the fifteenth century.

The most widespread and best known of the Southwest pueblo cultures were the Anasazi (Ancient Ones). In ancient times they developed extensive settlements in the "Four Corners" region where the modern-day states of Arizona, New Mexico, Colorado, and Utah meet. Anasazi society was remarkable for *not* having a rigid class structure. The religious leaders and warriors worked much as the rest of the people did. And the Anasazi engaged in warfare only as a means of self-defense. (*Hopi*

Cliff Dwellings Ruins of Anasazi cliff dwellings in Mesa Verde National Park, Colorado.

means "Peaceful People.") Environmental factors shaped Anasazi culture and eventually caused its decline. Toward the end of the thirteenth century, a lengthy drought and the pressure of Indian peoples migrating from the north led to the disappearance of Anasazi society.

Along the heavily forested northwest Pacific coast, where shellfish, salmon, seals, whales, deer, and edible wild plants were abundant, there was little need for farming. In fact, many of the Pacific Northwest peoples needed to work only two days to provide enough food for a week. Because of plentiful food, the Native American population along the Pacific coast was larger and more concentrated than in other areas. Such social density enabled the Pacific peoples to develop intricate religious rituals and sophisticated woodworking arts, such as those displayed on totem poles. For shelter, they built large, earthen-floored, cedar-plank houses twenty-five to a hundred feet long, where whole bands of families lived together. They also built sturdy, oceangoing canoes carved out of red cedar tree trunks; some were large enough to carry fifty people. Socially, the Indian bands along the Northwest Pacific coast were hierarchical, divided into slaves, commoners, and chiefs. Seashells were used as money. An abundance of food, a mild climate, and a prosperous trading network made the Pacific coast the most densely populated of all the regions in North America.

> Pacific Northwest forest and fishing cultures

The peoples living on the Great Plains (Plains Indians), a vast, flat land of cold winters and hot summers west of the Mississippi River, and in the

> Plains bison-hunting cultures

Great Basin (present-day Utah and Nevada) include the Arapaho, Blackfeet, Cheyenne, Comanche, Crow, Apache, and Sioux. They were nomadic hunter-gatherers, following on foot enormous herds of bison across a sea of grassland, collecting seeds, nuts, roots, and berries as they roamed. At the center of most hunter-gatherer religions is the idea that the hunted animal is a willing sacrifice provided by the gods ("spirits"). To ensure a successful hunt, these peoples performed sacred rites of gratitude beforehand. Once a buffalo herd was spotted, the hunters would set fires to drive the stampeding animals over cliffs.

Eastern "mound builders"

East of the Great Plains, in the vast woodlands from the Mississippi River to the Atlantic Ocean, several "mound-building" cultures flourished as predominantly agricultural societies. First the Adena and later the Hopewell peoples (both names derive from the archaeological sites) developed communities along rivers in the Ohio Valley between 800 B.C.E. and 400 C.E. The Adena-Hopewell cultures focused on agriculture, including tobacco. They left behind enormous earthworks and 200 elaborate **burial mounds** shaped like great snakes, birds, and other animals, several of which were nearly a quarter mile long. Evidence from the mounds reveals a complex social structure featuring a specialized division of labor, whereby different groups performed different tasks for the benefit of the society as a whole. Some were fisher folk; others were farmers, hunters, artists, cooks, and mothers.

Like the Adena, the Hopewell also developed an extensive trade network from the Gulf of Mexico to Canada, exchanging exquisite carvings, metalwork, pearls, seashells, copper ornaments, and jewelry. By the sixth century, however, the Hopewell culture disappeared, giving way to a new phase of

burial mounds A funereal tradition, practiced in the Mississippi and Ohio Valleys by the Adena-Hopewell cultures, of erecting massive mounds of earth over graves, often shaped in the designs of serpents and other animals.

Great Serpent Mound At over 1,300 feet in length and three feet high, this snake-shaped burial mound in Adams County, Ohio, is the largest of its kind in the world.

Native American development east of the Mississippi River, the Mississippian culture, which flourished from 800 to 1500 C.E. The Mississippians, centered in the southern Mississippi Valley, were also mound-building and corn-growing peoples led by chieftains. They cleared vast tracts of land in order to grow maize, beans, squash, and sunflowers, and they built substantial towns around central plazas and temples. The Mississippi peoples developed a far-flung trading network extending all the way to the Rocky Mountains. Their ability to grow large amounts of corn each year in the fertile flood plains of rivers spurred rapid population growth.

The largest of these advanced regional centers, called "chiefdoms," was **Cahokia** (950–1250 C.E.), in southwest Illinois, just a few miles across the Mississippi River from what is now St. Louis, Missouri. There the Mississippians constructed a huge, intricately planned farming settlement with pole-and-thatch houses, temples (where humans were sacrificed to the gods), monumental public buildings, spacious ceremonial plazas, and over a hundred flat-topped earthen pyramids with thatch-roofed temples on top. At the height of its influence, prosperous Cahokia hosted 15,000 people on some 3,200 acres, making it the largest city north of Mexico. Outlying towns and farming settlements ranged up to fifty miles in all directions.

Cahokia mysteriously vanished after 1400. What caused its collapse remains a mystery, but the most likely reason was environmental. The overcutting of trees may have set in motion ecological changes that doomed the community when a massive earthquake struck around 1200 C.E. The loss of trees led to widespread flooding and the erosion of topsoil that finally forced people to look for better lands for corn growing elsewhere. As Cahokia disappeared, however, its former residents carried with them its cultural traditions, thereby spreading its advanced ways of life to other areas across the Midwest and into the South.

Eastern Woodlands Peoples and European Contact

After the collapse of Cahokia, the **Eastern Woodlands peoples** rose to dominance along the Atlantic seaboard from Maine to Florida and along the Gulf coast to Louisiana. They included three regional groups distinguished by their different languages: the Algonquian, the Iroquoian, and the Muskogean. These are the societies the Europeans would first encounter when they arrived in North America in the sixteenth and seventeenth centuries.

The hundreds of Algonquian-speaking peoples stretched from the New England seaboard to lands along the Great Lakes and into the Upper Midwest and south to New Jersey, Virginia, and the Carolinas. The Algonquians along the coast were skilled at fishing; the inland Algonquians excelled at hunting. All of them practiced agriculture to some extent, regularly burning dense forests to improve soil fertility and provide browsing room for deer. They used canoes made of hollowed-out tree trunks ("dugouts") or made

Cahokia The largest chiefdom and city of the Mississippian Indian culture located in present-day Illinois, and the site of a sophisticated farming settlement that supported up to 15,000 inhabitants.

Eastern Woodlands peoples Various Native American peoples, particularly the Algonquian, Iroquoian, and Muskogean regional groups, who once dominated the Atlantic seaboard from Maine to Louisiana.

Algonquian chief in warpaint
From the notebook of English settler John White, this sketch depicts Native American chief.

Warfare and rivalries

from birch bark to travel down rivers and across lakes. Most Algonquians lived in small, round shelters called *wigwams*. Their villages typically ranged in size from 500 to 2,000 inhabitants, but they often moved their villages with the seasons.

West and south of the Algonquians were the Iroquoian-speaking peoples (including the Seneca, Onondaga, Mohawk, Oneida, and Cayuga nations, as well as the Cherokee and Tuscarora to the south), whose lands spread from upstate New York southward through Pennsylvania and into the upland regions of the Carolinas and Georgia. The Iroquois built no great mounds or templed pyramids. They were farmers who lived together in extended family groups ("clans"), sharing bark-covered "long houses" in towns of 3,000 or more people. The most important crops were corn and squash, both of which figure prominently in Iroquois mythology.

Unlike the patriarchal Algonquian culture, in which men were dominant, in the Iroquoian culture women held the key leadership roles (hence such cultures are called "matriarchal"). As an Iroquois elder explained, "In our society, women are the center of all things. Nature, we believe, has given women the ability to create; therefore it is only natural that women be in positions of power to protect this function." Men and women were not treated as equals. Rather, the two genders operated in two separate social domains. No woman could be a chief; no man could head a clan. Women selected the chiefs, controlled the distribution of property, and planted as well as harvested the crops. After marriage, the man moved in with the wife's family. In part, the Iroquoian matriarchy reflected the frequent absence of Iroquois men, who as skilled hunters and traders traveled extensively for long periods, requiring women to take charge of domestic life in their absence.

War between rival groups of Native Americans, especially the Algonquians and Iroquois, was commonplace, usually as a means of settling feuds or gaining slaves. Success in fighting was a warrior's highest honor. As a Cherokee explained in the eighteenth century, "We cannot live without war. Should we make peace with the Tuscororas, we must immediately look out for some other nation with whom we can engage in our beloved occupation."

The third major Native American group in the Eastern Woodlands included the southern peoples along the Gulf coast who spoke the Muskogean language: the Creeks, Chickasaws, and Choctaws. Like the Iroquois, they were often matrilineal societies, meaning that ancestry was traced only through the mother's line, but they had a more rigid class structure. The Muskogeans lived in towns arranged around a central plaza. In the Lower South, many of their thatch-roofed houses had no walls because of the heat.

Over thousands of years, the native North Americans had displayed remarkable resilience, adapting to the uncertainties of frequent warfare, changing climate, and varying environments. They would display similar resilience in the face of the challenges created by the arrival of Europeans. In the process of adapting their heritage and ways of life to unwanted new realities, the Native Americans played a significant role in shaping America.

The Expansion of Europe

The European exploration of the Western Hemisphere resulted from several key developments during the fifteenth century that transformed Europe by 1492. Dramatic intellectual changes and scientific discoveries affected religion, warfare, family life, and the economy. In addition, the resurgence of the old vices—greed, conquest, exploitation, oppression, racism, and slavery—would help fuel European expansion abroad.

A severe population decline caused by warfare, famine, and plagues (the "Black Death") meant that once-great noble estates no longer had enough agricultural workers to maintain them. By the end of the fifteenth century, medieval feudalism's static agrarian social system, whereby serfs worked for local nobles in order to live on and farm the land, had largely died out. People were no longer forced to remain in the same locality and keep the same social status in which they were born. A new "middle class" of profit-hungry bankers, merchants, and investors emerged, men who were committed to a more dynamic commercial economy driven by innovations in banking, currency, accounting, and insurance.

The growing trade-based economy in Europe freed monarchs from their dependence on feudal nobles, enabling them to unify the scattered cities ruled by princes ("principalities") into large kingdoms with stronger, more centralized governments. The rise of towns, cities, and merchants provided kings and queens with new tax revenues, and lesser agrarian-based nobles were displaced by the emergence of powerful new commercial *nations* governed by these centralized bureaucracies with the power to collect taxes.

At the same time, the rediscovery of ancient Greek and Roman texts spurred an intellectual revolution known as the *Renaissance* (rebirth). Educated people throughout Europe began to challenge prevailing beliefs as well as the absolute authority of rulers and priests. They discussed controversial new ideas about politics, religion, and science, engaged in scientific research, and unleashed their artistic creativity.

This "rebirth" of learning also involved the practical application of new ideas that enabled the Age of Exploration. New knowledge and new technologies made possible the construction of stronger, larger sailing ships armed with cannons and capable of oceanic voyages. The development of more-accurate magnetic compasses, maps, and navigational instruments such as *astrolabes* and *quadrants* enabled sailors to determine their location by reference to the sun or stars. The fifteenth and sixteenth centuries also witnessed the invention of gunpowder, cannons, and firearms—and the printing press.

CORE **OBJECTIVE**
2. Summarize the major developments in Europe that enabled the Age of Exploration.

The rise of a middle class

Powerful new nations

Innovations in shipbuilding, navigation, and weaponry lead to global revolution in maritime trade

By the end of the fifteenth century, trade between western European nations and across the seas became more important than ever. The Portuguese, blessed with expert sailors and fast new three-masted ships called *caravels*, took the lead in the Age of Exploration during the fifteenth century. Portuguese sailors roamed down the west coast of Africa in search of grains, gold, ivory, spices, and slaves. Eventually, they continued all the way around Africa in search of the fabled Indies (India and Southeast Asia), as well as China and Japan, rich with spices, silk cloth, and other exotic trade goods.

By the end of the fifteenth century, four powerful nations had emerged in western Europe: England, France, Portugal, and Spain. The marriage of King Ferdinand of Aragon and Queen Isabella of Castile in 1469 unified Spain into a single nation. Both monarchs were Christian expansionists. By 1492, they had forcibly expelled all Muslims and Jews from Spain and were making plans for exploring west across the Atlantic Ocean.

The Voyages of Columbus

These were the circumstances that led Christopher Columbus to pursue his own dream of finding an Atlantic route to the Indies. Born in Genoa, Italy, in 1451, the son of a weaver, Columbus took to the sea at an early age, teaching himself geography, navigation, and Latin. By the 1480s he was eager to spread Christianity across the globe. Columbus also wanted to win glory and riches by discovering what he hoped would be a shorter way to the "Indies" by sailing west across the Atlantic Ocean. The tall, red-haired Columbus eventually persuaded Ferdinand and Isabella to finance his voyage in exchange for awarding him a tenth share of any riches he gathered. The legend that the queen had to sell the crown jewels to finance the voyage is as false as the fable that Columbus set out to prove the earth was round rather than flat. Most educated Europeans knew that the earth was round.

On August 3, 1492, Columbus and ninety men and boys, mostly from Spain but from seven other countries as well, set sail on three ships, the *Santa María*, the *Pinta*, and the *Niña*, respectively about sixty, fifty-five, and fifty feet long. From Spain, this little squadron of tiny ships sailed first to Lisbon, Portugal, and then headed west. For weeks they journeyed across the open sea, hoping to sight land at any moment, only to be disappointed. By early October, the worried sailors grew rebellious at the "madness" of sailing blindly and threatened to take over the ships and turn back. Columbus had little choice but to promise that if they did not find land within three days, they would turn back.

Then, at dawn on October 12, a sailor stationed at the masthead yelled, "Tierra! Tierra!" ("Land! Land!"). He had sighted an island in the Bahamas east of Florida that Columbus named San Salvador (Blessed Savior). Columbus mistakenly concluded that they must be near the Indies, so he called the island people *Indios*. At every encounter with these native people, known as Tainos or Arawaks, his first question was whether they had any gold. If they

Christopher Columbus A portrait by Sebastiano del Piombo, ca. 1519.

Lust for gold

COLUMBUS'S VOYAGES

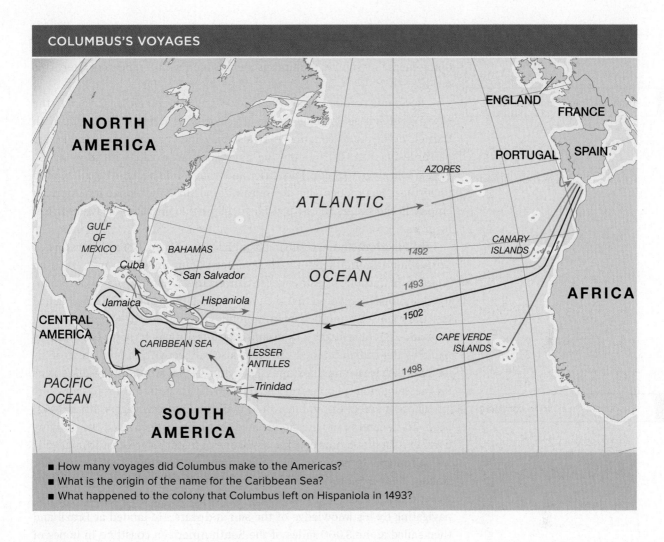

■ How many voyages did Columbus make to the Americas?
■ What is the origin of the name for the Caribbean Sea?
■ What happened to the colony that Columbus left on Hispaniola in 1493?

had gold, the Spaniards seized it; if they did not, the Europeans forced them to search for it.

After leaving San Salvador, Columbus continued to search for a passage to the Indies through the Bahamas and westward to Cuba. There, Columbus went ashore, sword in one hand, cross in the other, exclaiming that this was the "most beautiful land human eyes have ever beheld." Columbus then sailed eastward to the island he named Hispaniola (now Haiti and the Dominican Republic). There he found indigenous people who wore gold jewelry and introduced him to smoking tobacco.

At the end of 1492, Columbus, still convinced he had reached an outer island of Japan, sailed back across the Atlantic after leaving about forty men on Hispaniola and capturing a dozen Arawaks to present as gifts to the Spanish king and queen. Upon reaching Spain, Columbus received a hero's welcome, which he encouraged through his inflated claims of what he had discovered. Thanks to the newly invented printing press, news of his westward voyage spread rapidly across Europe. The Spanish monarchs,

Ferdinand and Isabella, told Columbus to prepare for a second voyage, instructing him to "treat the Indians very well and lovingly and abstain from doing them any injury." Columbus and his men would repeatedly defy this order.

Treaty of Tordesillas (1494)

The Spanish monarchs also wanted to strengthen their legal claim to the New World in case Portugal decided to send ships across the Atlantic. With the help of the pope (a Spaniard), rivals Spain and Portugal signed the Treaty of Tordesillas (1494), dividing the non-Christian world, with most of the New World given to Spain, and Africa and what would become Brazil granted to Portugal. In practice, this meant that while Spain developed its American empire in the sixteenth century, Portugal provided it with enslaved African laborers.

Flush with the fame resulting from his first voyage, Columbus returned across the Atlantic in 1493 with seventeen ships and 1,400 men. Also on board were Catholic priests eager to convert the native peoples to Christianity. Columbus discovered that the men he had left behind on Hispaniola had lost their senses, raping women, robbing villages, and, as Columbus's son later added, "committing a thousand excesses for which they were mortally hated by the Indians." The Europeans also carried with them a range of infectious diseases—smallpox, measles, typhus—that would prove disastrous for the indigenous peoples, for they had no natural immunities to them.

Vespucci's New World continent

Before he died, Columbus would make two more voyages to the Caribbean. To the end of his life, he insisted that he had discovered the outlying parts of Asia, not a new continent. By one of history's greatest ironies, this led Europeans to name the New World not for Columbus but for another Italian sailor-explorer, Amerigo Vespucci, a talented astronomer. In 1499, with the support of Portugal's monarchy, Vespucci sailed across the Atlantic, navigating by his knowledge of the sun and stars. He landed at Brazil and then sailed along 3,000 miles of the South American coastline in hopes of finding Asia. In the end, Vespucci reported that South America was so large that it must be a *new* continent rather than Asia, as Columbus still believed. In 1507, a German mapmaker paid tribute to Vespucci's navigational skills by labeling the New World using a variant of his first name: America.

Religious Conflict in Europe

At the same time that the voyages of Vespucci and Columbus were prompting other explorers to cross the Atlantic, powerful religious conflicts were tearing Europe apart in ways that would greatly influence settlement in the New World.

When Columbus sailed west in 1492, all of Europe acknowledged the thousand-year-old supremacy of the Roman Catholic Church and its pope in Rome. The brutal efforts of the Spanish to convert native peoples to **Roman Catholicism** illustrated the murderous intensity with which Europeans embraced religious life in the sixteenth century. Spiritual concerns inspired, comforted, and united people. People believed in heaven and hell, devils and

Roman Catholicism The Christian faith and religious practices of the Roman Catholic Church, which exerted great political, economic, and social influence on much of Western Europe and, through the Spanish and Portuguese Empires, on the Americas.

witches, demons and angels, magic and miracles. And Christians were willing to kill and die for their beliefs.

The enforced unity of Catholic Europe began to crack in 1517, however, when Martin Luther (1483–1546), a German priest who taught at the University of Wittenburg, rebelled against the Catholic Church and in the process launched the **Protestant Reformation**. Luther undermined the authority of the Catholic Church by showing that many of its officials were corrupt. He called the pope "the greatest thief and robber that has appeared or can appear on earth." Luther especially criticized the sale of *indulgences* (whereby priests would forgive sins in exchange for money or goods). God alone, through Christ, he insisted, offered people salvation; people could not earn it or buy it. Salvation, in other words, resulted from *belief*. As Luther exclaimed, "By faith alone are you saved!"

Luther tried to democratize Christianity by urging believers to read the Bible themselves rather than blindly follow the dictates of Catholic priests and the pope. The people themselves represented a "priesthood of all believers," perhaps his most revolutionary idea. To enable people to be their own "priests," Luther produced the first Bible in a German translation.

> Protestant Reformation

Catholic officials lashed out at Luther's "dangerous doctrines," calling him a "wild boar" and "a leper with a brain of brass and a nose of iron." Luther fought back with equal fury, declaring that he was "born to war." When the pope expelled Luther from the Catholic Church in 1521 and sentenced him to death, civil war erupted throughout the German principalities (the various German states did not become a united nation until 1871). A powerful German prince protected Luther from the Church's wrath. What had begun as a religious movement now became a political reformation, too. Luther was no longer simply an outspoken priest; he was a spiritual revolutionary, a folk hero, and a political prophet, encouraging German princes and dukes to separate themselves from the Italian papacy. A settlement between warring Lutherans and Catholics did not come until 1555, when each prince was allowed by the Treaty of Augsburg to determine the religion of his subjects.

> Wars and upheavals

Soon after Martin Luther began his revolt against the shortcomings of Catholicism, Swiss Protestants also challenged papal authority. In Geneva, the movement looked to John Calvin (1509-1564), a brilliant French scholar who had fled to that city and brought it under the sway of his powerful beliefs. In his great theological work, *The Institutes of the Christian Religion* (1536), Calvin set forth a stern doctrine. All people, he taught, were damned by Adam's original sin, but the sacrifice of Christ made possible the redemption of those whom God had "elected" and thus had predestined to salvation from the beginning of time.

Intoxicated by godliness, Calvin insisted upon strict morality and hard work, values that especially suited the rising middle class. Moreover, he taught that God valued every form of work, however menial it might be. Calvin also permitted lay members a share in the governance of the church

Protestant Reformation
Sixteenth-century religious movement initiated by Martin Luther, a German monk whose public criticism of corruption in the Roman Catholic Church, and whose teaching that Christians can communicate directly with God, gained a wide following.

through a body of elders and ministers called the presbytery. Calvin's doctrines formed the basis for the German Reformed Church, the Dutch Reformed Church, the Presbyterians in Scotland, some of the Puritans in England (and eventually America), and the Huguenots in France. Through these and other groups, John Calvin exerted a greater effect upon religious belief and practice in the English colonies than did any other leader of the Reformation. His insistence on the freedom of individual believers, as well as his recognition that monarchs and political officials were sinful like everyone else, helped contribute to the evolving ideas in Europe of representative democracy and the importance of separating church power from state (governmental) power.

Catholic Counter-Reformation

Even though the Catholic Church launched a "Counter-Reformation" that reaffirmed basic Catholic beliefs while addressing some of the concerns about priestly abuses raised by Luther, Calvin, and others, the Protestant Reformation spread rapidly across Europe during the sixteenth century. Most of northern Germany, along with Scandinavia, became Lutheran, often calling themselves the "Protesting Estates," from which derived the label "Protestants." The Reformation thus became in part a theological dispute, in part a political movement, and in part a *catalyst* for social change, civil strife, and imperial warfare. Throughout the sixteenth and seventeenth centuries, Catholics and Protestants persecuted, imprisoned, tortured, and killed each other in large numbers in Europe—and in the Americas. Every major international conflict became, to some extent, a religious holy war between Catholic and Protestant nations. Equally important, the Protestant world view, with its emphasis on the freedom of the individual conscience and personal Bible-reading, would play a major role in the colonization of America and the development of the American character.

CORE **OBJECTIVE**

3. Describe how the Spanish were able to conquer and colonize the Americas.

The Spanish Empire

During the sixteenth century, Catholic Spain created the world's most powerful empire. At its height, it encompassed much of Europe, most of the Americas, parts of Africa, and various trading outposts in Asia. But it was the gold and silver looted from the Americas that fueled the engine of Spain's "Golden Empire." By plundering, conquering, and colonizing the Americas and enslaving the native peoples, the Spanish planted Christianity in the Western Hemisphere and gained the resources to rule the world.

Spanish foothold in the Caribbean

The Caribbean Sea served as the funnel through which Spanish power entered the Americas. After establishing colonies on Hispaniola, including Santo Domingo, which became the capital of the West Indies, the Spanish proceeded eastward to Puerto Rico (1508) and westward to Cuba (1511–1514). Their motives, as one soldier explained, were "to serve God and the king, and also to get rich."

Many of the Europeans in the first wave of settlement in the New World died of malnutrition or disease. But the Native Americans suffered far more casualties, for they were ill equipped to resist the European invaders. Disunity everywhere—civil disorder, rebellion, and tribal warfare—left them vulnerable to division and foreign conquest. Attacks by well-armed soldiers and deadly germs from Europe overwhelmed entire native societies.

A Clash of Cultures

The often-violent encounter between Spaniards and Native Americans involved more than a clash between different peoples. It also involved contrasting forms of technological development. The Indians of Mexico used wooden canoes for water transportation, while the Europeans crossed the seas in much larger, heavily armed sailing vessels. The Spanish ships not only carried human cargo, but also steel swords, firearms, explosives, and armor. The wood-tipped arrows and tomahawks used by Native Americans were no match for guns, cannons, smallpox, and warhorses. "The most essential thing in new lands is horses," reported one Spanish soldier. "They instill the greatest fear in the enemy and make the Indians respect the leaders of the army."

> Lethal weapons and warhorses

Cortés's Conquest

The most dramatic European conquest of a major Indian civilization on the North American mainland occurred in Mexico. On February 18, 1519, Hernán Cortés, driven by dreams of gold and glory, set sail for Mexico from Cuba. His fleet of eleven ships carried nearly 600 soldiers and sailors. Also on board were 200 indigenous Cubans, sixteen horses, and cannons. After the Spanish landed on the coast of the Gulf of Mexico, Cortés convinced the local Totomacs to join his assault against the Mexica, their hated rivals. To prevent any of his soldiers, called **conquistadores** (conquerors), from deserting, Cortés had the ships burned, sparing one vessel to carry the expected gold back to Spain. With his small army, cannons, and Indian allies, Cortés brashly set out to conquer the sprawling Mexica (Aztec) Empire, which extended from central Mexico to what is today Guatemala. The nearly 200-mile march of Cortés's army through the mountains to the magnificent Mexica capital of Tenochtitlán took nearly three months.

> Rivals collaborate against the Mexica

Spanish Invaders

As Cortés and his army marched across Mexico, they heard fabulous accounts of Tenochtitlán. With some 200,000 inhabitants, it was the largest city in the Americas and much larger than most European cities. Graced by wide canals, stunning gardens, and formidable stone pyramids, the lake-encircled capital seemed unconquerable. But Cortés made the most of his assets. Through a combination of threats and deceptions, Cortés and his Indian allies entered Tenochtitlán peacefully and captured the emperor,

conquistadores Spanish term for "conquerors," applied to Spanish and Portuguese soldiers who conquered lands held by indigenous peoples in central and southern America as well as the current states of Texas, New Mexico, Arizona, and California.

Cortés in Mexico Page from the *Lienzo de Tlaxcala*, a historical narrative from the sixteenth century. The scene, in which Cortés is shown seated on a throne, depicts the arrival of the Spanish in Tlaxcala.

Montezuma II. Cortés explained to the captive Montezuma why the invasion was necessary: "We Spaniards have a disease of the heart that only gold can cure."

After taking the Mexicas' gold and silver, the Spanish forced them to mine more of the precious metals. Then, in the spring of 1520, disgruntled Mexica decided that Montezuma was a traitor. They rebelled, stoned him to death, and, armed with stone-bladed wooden swords and wicker shields, attacked the Spaniards. Forced to retreat to the mainland, the Spaniards lost about a third of their men. Their 20,000 Indian allies remained loyal, however, and Cortés regrouped his forces. For months, sporadic fighting continued. In 1521, having been reinforced with horse-borne troops (cavalry) from Cuba and thousands more Native Americans eager to defeat the despised Mexica, he surrounded the imperial city for eighty-five days, cutting off its access to water and food and allowing a smallpox epidemic to devastate the inhabitants. For three months, the Mexica bravely defended their capital. Then the siege came to a bloody end. The ravages of smallpox and starvation, as well as the support of 75,000 anti-Mexica Indian allies, help explain how such a small force of determined Spaniards was able to vanquish a proud nation of nearly 1 million people. After 15,000 Mexica were slaughtered, the others surrendered. A merciless Cortés ordered the leaders hanged and the priests devoured by fighting dogs. In two years, Cortés and his disciplined army had conquered a fabled empire that had taken centuries to develop. Cortés became the first governor of New Spain and began a systematic process of replacing the Mexica leaders with Spanish bureaucrats and church officials.

Cortés's conquest of Mexico established the model for waves of plundering conquistadores to follow. Within twenty years, Spain had established a vast empire in Mexico and the Caribbean, which Cortés called "New Spain," based on a pattern of ruthless violence and enslavement of the native

Cortés conquers the Mexica, and Pizarro invades the Inca

SPANISH EXPLORATIONS OF THE MAINLAND

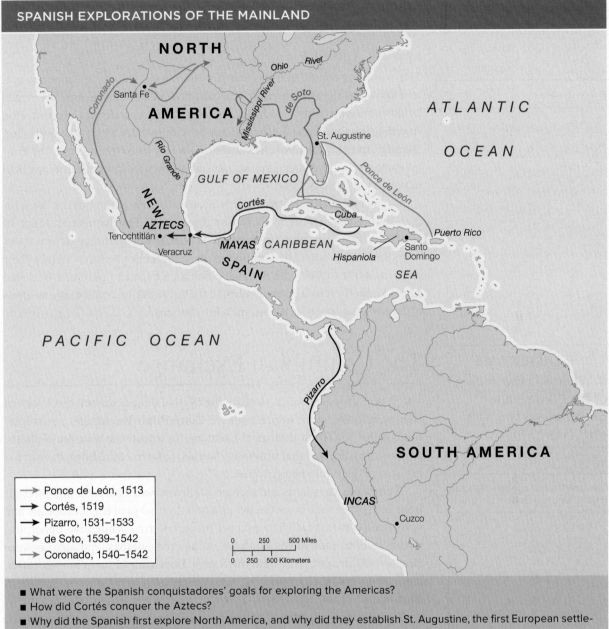

■ What were the Spanish conquistadores' goals for exploring the Americas?

■ How did Cortés conquer the Aztecs?

■ Why did the Spanish first explore North America, and why did they establish St. Augustine, the first European settlement in what would become the United States?

peoples followed by oppressive rule over them—just as the Mexica had done in forming their own empire.

In 1531 another Spaniard, Francisco Pizarro, led a band of soldiers down the Pacific coast from Panama toward Peru, where they brutally subdued the Inca Empire. The Spanish invaders seized the Inca palaces and looted the empire of its gold and silver. From Peru, Spain extended its control southward through Chile by about 1553 and north, to present-day Colombia, by 1538.

Spanish America

Encomienda

The crusading conquistadores transferred to America a socioeconomic system known as the **encomienda**, whereby favored officers became privileged landowners who controlled Indian villages. As *encomenderos*, they protected the villages in exchange for the Indians providing them with goods and labor. Spanish America therefore developed a society of extremes: wealthy conquistadores and *encomenderos* at one end of the spectrum and Indians held in poverty at the other end.

By the mid-1500s, Native Americans were nearly extinct in the West Indies, reduced even more by European diseases than by Spanish brutality. In all of New Spain's empire, the indigenous population plummeted from about 50 million at the outset to 4 million in the seventeenth century. To take their place, as early as 1503 the Spanish colonizers began to purchase enslaved Africans, the first in a wretched traffic that eventually would carry millions of captive people across the Atlantic into bondage.

The Columbian Exchange

CORE OBJECTIVE

4. What was the impact of the Columbian Exchange on the "Old" and "New" Worlds?

New plants and animals lead to a global food revolution

The first European contacts with the Native Americans of the Western Hemisphere began an unprecedented **Columbian Exchange**, now sometimes called the Great Biological Exchange—a worldwide transfer of plants, animals, and diseases that ultimately worked in favor of the Europeans at the expense of the indigenous peoples.

If anything, the plants and animals of the two worlds were more different from each other than were the peoples and their ways of life. Europeans had never seen creatures such as iguanas, bison, cougars, armadillos, opossums, sloths, and hummingbirds. Turkeys, guinea pigs, llamas, and alpacas were also new to Europeans. Nor did the Native Americans know of horses, cattle, pigs, sheep, goats, chickens, and rats, which soon arrived from Europe in abundance.

The exchange of plant life between the Americas and Europe/Africa transformed the diets of both hemispheres. Before Columbus's voyage, three foods were unknown in Europe: maize (corn), potatoes (sweet and white), and many kinds of beans (snap, kidney, lima, and others). The white potato, although commonly called Irish, is actually native to South America. Explorers brought it back to Europe, where it thrived. The "Irish potato" was eventually transported to North America by Scots-Irish immigrants during the early eighteenth century. Other Western Hemisphere food plants included peanuts, squash, peppers, tomatoes, pumpkins, pineapples, sassafras, papayas, guavas, avocados, cacao (the source of chocolate), and chicle (for chewing gum). Europeans in turn introduced rice,

encomienda A land-grant system under which Spanish army officers (conquistadores) were awarded large parcels of land taken from Native Americans.

Columbian Exchange The transfer of biological and social elements, such as plants, animals, people, diseases, and cultural practices, among Europe, the Americas, and Africa in the wake of Christopher Columbus's voyages to the New World.

wheat, barley, oats, wine grapes, melons, coffee, olives, bananas, "Kentucky" bluegrass, daisies, and dandelions to the Americas.

Population growth in Europe

The beauty of the biological exchange was that the food plants were more complementary than competitive. Corn, it turned out, could flourish almost anywhere in the world. The nutritious food crops exported from the Americas, especially the potato, thus helped nourish a worldwide population explosion probably greater than any since the invention of agriculture. The new food crops helped spur a dramatic increase in the European population that in turn provided the restless, adventurous young people who would colonize the New World.

By far, however, the most significant aspect of the biological exchange was the transmission of **infectious diseases**. During the three centuries after Columbus's first voyage, Europeans and Africans brought with them deadly diseases that Native Americans had never experienced: smallpox, typhus, malaria, and measles. The results were catastrophic. Far more native people—tens of millions—died from smallpox than from combat. By 1568, just 75 years after Columbus's first voyage, 90 percent of the Indian population had been killed—the greatest loss of human life in history. Unable to explain or cure the diseases, Native American chieftains and religious leaders often lost their stature—and their lives, as they were usually the first to meet the Spanish and thus were the first infected. As a consequence of losing their leaders, the indigenous peoples were less capable of resisting the European invaders.

Spanish Exploration in North America

CORE **OBJECTIVE**

5. Analyze the legacy of Spanish colonization on North American history.

Three centuries of Spanish domination and Hispanic influence

Throughout the sixteenth century, no European power other than Spain held more than a brief foothold in the New World. Spain had the advantage not only of having arrived first but also of having stumbled onto those regions that would produce the quickest profits. While France and England were preoccupied with political disputes and religious conflict, Spain had forged an intense national unity that enabled it to dominate Europe as well as the New World. The treasures seized from Mexico and Peru added to Spain's military and economic power, but the single-minded focus on gold and silver also tempted the Spanish government to live beyond its means. Between 1557 and 1662, the kings of Spain were forced to declare bankruptcy ten times.

For most of the colonial period, much of what is now the United States belonged to Spain, and Spanish culture etched a lasting imprint upon American ways of life. Spain's colonial presence lasted more than three centuries, much longer than either England's or France's. New Spain was centered in Mexico, but its frontier outposts extended from Florida to

infectious diseases Also called contagious diseases, illnesses that can pass from one person to another by way of invasive biological organisms able to reproduce in the bodily tissues of their hosts. Europeans unwittingly brought many such diseases to the Americas, devastating the Native American peoples.

Alaska. Hispanic place-names—San Francisco, Santa Barbara, Los Angeles, San Diego, Santa Fe, San Antonio, Pensacola, and St. Augustine—survive to this day, as do Hispanic influences in art, architecture, literature, music, law, and cuisine.

Juan Ponce de León, then governor of Puerto Rico, made the earliest known exploration of Florida in 1513. Meanwhile, Spanish explorers skirted the Gulf of Mexico coast from Florida to Veracruz, scouted the Atlantic coast all the way to Canada, and established a short-lived colony on the Carolina coast.

In 1539, Hernando de Soto and 600 conquistadores landed on Florida's west coast, traveled north as far as western North Carolina, and then moved westward beyond the Mississippi River and up the Arkansas River, looting and destroying Indian villages along the way. In the spring of 1542, de Soto died near Natchez, Mississippi; the next year, the survivors among his party floated down the Mississippi River, and 311 of the original adventurers found their way to Spanish Mexico. In 1540, Francisco Vásquez de Coronado, inspired by rumors of gold, traveled northward from Mexico into New Mexico and northeast across Texas and Oklahoma as far as Kansas.

The Spanish established provinces in North America not so much as commercial enterprises but as defensive buffers protecting their more lucrative empires in Mexico and South America. In 1565 a Spanish outpost on the Florida coast, St. Augustine, became the first European town in the present-day United States. It included a fort, church, hospital, fish market, and over one hundred shops and houses—all built decades before the first English settlements at Jamestown and Plymouth. While other early American outposts failed, St. Augustine survived as a defensive base perched on the southern edge of a continent.

The Spanish Southwest

The Spanish eventually established other permanent settlements in what are now New Mexico, Texas, and California. Missionaries established Catholic missions, where they imposed Christianity on the Indians and treated them like slaves. After about ten years, a mission would be secularized: its lands would be divided among the converted Indians, the mission chapel would become a parish church, and the inhabitants would be given full Spanish citizenship—including the privilege of paying taxes. The soldiers who were sent to protect the missions were housed in *presidios*, or forts; their families and the merchants accompanying them lived in adjacent villages.

New Mexico A region in the American Southwest, originally established by the Spanish, who settled there in the sixteenth century, founded Catholic missions, and exploited the region's indigenous peoples.

The land that would later be called **New Mexico** was a center of Catholic missionary activity in the American Southwest. In 1598, Juan de Oñate, the rich son of a Spanish mining family in Mexico, received a land grant for the territory north of Mexico above the Rio Grande. He then recruited soldiers and hundreds of Mexican Indians and *mestizos* (the offspring of Spanish fathers and Indian mothers), including women, children, and priests. The caravan of colonists, including animals and carts carrying supplies, began moving north from the mountains above Mexico City. After walking over 800 miles in seven months, they established the colony of "New Mexico" near present-day Santa Fe ("Holy Faith" in Spanish), and sent out expeditions to search for gold and silver. Oñate told the local Indians, called Pueblos, that they now belonged to Spain, but he promised that the Spaniards would bring them peace, justice, prosperity, and protection. If they embraced Christianity, Oñate added, the Indians would receive "an eternal life of great bliss" instead of "cruel and everlasting torment."

Some Indian peoples welcomed the Spanish missionaries as "powerful witches" capable of easing their burdens. Others tried to use the European invaders as allies against rival Indian groups. Still others saw no alternative but to submit. The Indians living in Spanish New Mexico were required to pay tribute to their *encomenderos* and perform personal tasks for them, including sexual favors. Soldiers and priests flogged disobedient Indians.

Before the end of New Mexico's first year as a colony, in December 1598, the Pueblos revolted, killing several soldiers. During three days of relentless fighting, vengeful Spanish soldiers killed 500 Pueblo men and 300 women and children. Survivors were enslaved. Pueblo men over the age of twenty-five had one foot cut off to frighten the others and keep them from escaping or resisting. Children were taken from their parents into a Catholic mission, where, Oñate pledged, they would "attain the knowledge of God and the salvation of their souls."

Cultural conflict This Peruvian illustration, from a 1612–1615 manuscript by Felipe Guaman Poma de Ayala, shows a Dominican Catholic friar forcing a native woman to weave.

Spanish New Mexico expanded very slowly. The hoped-for deposits of gold and silver were never found, and a lack of rain for farming blunted the interest of potential colonists. In 1608 the government decided to turn New Mexico into a royal province. The following year it dispatched a royal governor, and in 1610, as the first English settlers were struggling to survive at Jamestown, in Virginia, the Spanish moved the province's capital to Santa Fe, the first permanent seat of government in the present-day United States. By 1630 there were fifty Catholic churches and monasteries in New Mexico, as well as some 3,000 Spaniards.

Roman Catholic missionaries in New Mexico claimed that 86,000 Pueblos had been converted to Christianity during the seventeenth century. In fact, however, resentment among the Indians increased with time. In 1680 a powerful Indian leader named Popé organized a massive rebellion against the Spanish. The Native Americans burned Catholic churches;

Catholicism in New Spain and the Pueblo Revolt (1680)

tortured, mutilated, and executed priests; and destroyed all relics of Christianity. Popé then established Santa Fe as the capital of his confederacy. The Pueblo Revolt of 1680 was the greatest defeat that Indians ever inflicted on European efforts to conquer the New World. It took fourteen years and four military campaigns for the Spanish to reestablish control over New Mexico.

Horses and the Great Plains

Another major consequence of the Pueblo Revolt was the opportunity it gave Indian rebels to get hundreds of Spanish horses (Spanish authorities had made it illegal for Indians to own horses). The Pueblos in turn established a thriving horse trade with Navajos, Apaches, and others. By 1690, horses were in Texas, and they soon spread across the Great Plains, the vast rolling grasslands extending from the Missouri Valley in the east to the base of the Rocky Mountains in the west.

Horses and bison

Prior to the arrival of horses, Indians hunted on foot and used dogs as their beasts of burden. But dogs are carnivores, and it was always difficult to find enough meat to feed them. The introduction of the **horse** changed everything, though, providing the Plains Indians with a new source of mobility and power. Horses are grazing animals, and the vast grasslands of the Great Plains offered plenty of forage. Horses could also haul up to seven times as much weight as dogs, and their speed and endurance made the indigenous people much more effective hunters and warriors.

In the short run, the horse brought prosperity and mobility to the Plains Indians. Yet the Indians on horseback eventually killed more bison than the herds could replace. Further, horses competed with the bison for food, often depleting the prairie grass. And as Indians on horses traveled greater distances and encountered more people, infectious diseases spread more widely.

French and Dutch Exploration of America

Spanish rivals for New World wealth

The success of Spain in conquering much of the Western Hemisphere spurred Portugal, France, England, and the Netherlands (Holland) to begin their own exploration and exploitation of the New World. The French were the first to pose a serious threat. Spanish treasure ships sailing home from Mexico, Peru, and the Caribbean islands offered tempting targets for French privateers (privately owned warships) and pirates. The French also began looking for a passage to Asia through the Americas. In 1524, the French king sent the Italian Giovanni da Verrazano westward across the Atlantic. Upon sighting land (probably at Cape Fear, North Carolina), Verrazano ranged along the coast as far north as Maine. On a second voyage, in 1528, he was killed in the West Indies by Carib Indians.

Unlike the Verrazano voyages, those of Jacques Cartier, beginning in the next decade, led to the first French effort at colonization in North America. During three voyages, Cartier explored the Gulf of St. Lawrence

horse The Spanish introduced horses to the Americas, eventually transforming many Native American cultures.

The Columbian Exchange and the Spanish Empire in North America

The following chart lists examples of organisms and foods exchanged between the Old and New Worlds during the Columbian Exchange that ensued as the Spanish created a vast empire in the Americas. As you review the chart, consider the role that these exchanges played in the Spanish conquest and colonization of North America.

	Old World ⟶ New World	New World ⟶ Old World
Animals	horses, cattle, pigs, sheep, goats, chickens	llamas, turkeys, alpacas, guinea pigs
Food	rice, wheat, barley, oats, wine grapes, melons, coffee, olives, bananas, Kentucky bluegrass, daisies, dandelions	maize, potatoes, snap beans, kidney beans, lima beans, peanuts, squash, peppers, tomatoes, pumpkins, pineapples, sassafras, papayas, guavas, avocadoes, cacao, chicle
Diseases	smallpox, typhus, diphtheria, bubonic plague, malaria, yellow fever, cholera	syphilis

Impact on the Old and New Worlds

1. New foods revolutionized diets in both worlds.
2. The spread of corn in particular led to an explosion of the worldwide population.
3. Infectious diseases, especially smallpox, decimated Native American populations and ways of life, enabled the Spanish to take control over many societies in the Americas, and also led to the beginning of slave importation from Africa.

QUESTIONS FOR ANALYSIS

1. How did the biological organisms (plants, animals, and microbes) brought by the Spaniards complement the technological advantages they possessed over Native Americans?

2. How did this biological exchange allow the Spanish to establish political and economic control over many societies in North America?

3. How were food diets revolutionized?

and ventured up the St. Lawrence River, now the boundary between Canada and New York. Twice he got as far as present-day Montreal, and twice he wintered at or near the site of Quebec, near which a short-lived French colony appeared in 1541–1542. From that time forward, however, French kings lost interest in Canada for over half a century.

Greater threats to Spanish power arose from the Dutch and the English. The United Provinces of the Netherlands, which had passed by inheritance

ENGLISH, FRENCH, AND DUTCH EXPLORATIONS

■ Who were the first European explorers to rival Spanish dominance in the New World, and why did they cross the Atlantic?

■ Why was the defeat of the Spanish Armada important to the history of English exploration? What was the significance of the voyages of Gilbert and Raleigh?

to the Spanish king but had become largely Protestant, rebelled against Spanish Catholic rule in 1567. A long, bloody struggle for independence ensued in which Protestant England aided the Dutch. Spain refused to recognize the independence of the Dutch republic for a hundred years, in 1648.

Almost from the beginning of the Protestant Dutch revolt against Catholic Spain, the Dutch plundered Spanish treasure ships in the Atlantic and carried on illegal trade with Spain's colonies. While England's Queen

Elizabeth, a Protestant, steered a tortuous course to avoid open war with Spain, she secretly encouraged both Dutch and English privateers ("sea dogs") to attack Spanish ships and their colonies in the Americas.

The Defeat of the Armada

The English raids on Spanish shipping continued for twenty years before open war erupted between the two nations. Determined to conquer England, Philip II, the king of Catholic Spain who was Queen Elizabeth's brother-in-law and fiercest opponent, assembled in 1588 the massive **Spanish Armada**: 132 warships, 8,000 sailors, and 18,000 soldiers—the greatest invasion fleet in history. On May 28, 1588, the Armada sailed north, determined to conquer the English and restore them to Catholicism. English warships, smaller but faster than those of the Spanish fleet, were waiting for them. As the battle unfolded, the larger Spanish warships could not compete with the speed and agility of the smaller English ships. The English chased the Armada through the English Channel before a terrible storm swept the Spanish fleet into the North Sea, destroying dozens of the world's finest warships. The stunning defeat of Catholic Spain's fearsome Armada greatly strengthened the Protestant cause across Europe.

> The English defeat the Spanish Armada (1588)

The great naval victory was the climactic event of Queen Elizabeth's long reign. England at the end of the sixteenth century was surging with new power and optimism, filled with a youthful zest for exploring new worlds. The defeat of the Spanish Armada marked the beginning of England's global naval supremacy and cleared the way for English colonization of America. English colonists could now make their way to North America without fear of Spanish interference.

English Exploration of America

English efforts to colonize America began a few years before the great battle with the Spanish Armada. In 1578, Queen Elizabeth had given Sir Humphrey Gilbert permission to establish a colony in the "remote heathen and barbarous lands" of America. Gilbert's group set out in 1583, intending to settle near Narragansett Bay (in present-day Rhode Island). He instead landed in fogbound Newfoundland (Canada). With winter approaching and his largest vessels lost, Gilbert and the colonists headed home. On the way back, Gilbert's ship vanished, and he was never seen again.

The next year, Queen Elizabeth asked Sir Walter Raleigh, Gilbert's half-brother and a favorite of the queen, to organize a colonizing mission. Raleigh's expedition discovered the Outer Banks of North Carolina and landed at Roanoke Island. Raleigh named the area Virginia, in honor of childless Queen Elizabeth, the presumably "Virgin Queen," who herself chose the name. After several false starts, Raleigh in 1587 sponsored another expedition of about one hundred colonists, including twenty-six women and children, led by Governor John White. White spent a month on Roanoke Island and then returned to England for supplies, leaving behind his

> The lost Roanoke colony

Spanish Armada A massive Spanish fleet of 130 warships that was defeated at Plymouth in 1588 by the English navy during the reign of Queen Elizabeth I.

The English in Virginia The arrival of English explorers on the Outer Banks, with Roanoke Island at left.

daughter Eleanor and his granddaughter Virginia Dare, the first English child born in the New World. White's journey back to Virginia was delayed because of the naval war with Spain. When he finally returned to America in 1590, he discovered that the Roanoke outpost had been abandoned and looted.

No trace of the "lost colonists" was ever found. Indians may have killed them, or hostile Spaniards—who had certainly planned to attack—may have done the job. The most recent evidence indicates that the "Lost Colony" suffered from a horrible drought that prevented them from growing enough food to survive. While some of the colonists may have gone south, the main group of them appears to have gone north, to the southern shores of Chesapeake Bay, where they lived for some years until they were killed by local Indians.

There was not a single English colonist in North America when the great Queen Elizabeth died in 1603. The Spanish controlled the only colonial outposts on the continent. But that was about to change. Inspired by the success of the Spanish in exploiting the New World, and emboldened by their defeat of the Spanish Armada in 1588, the English—as well as the French and the Dutch—would soon develop American colonial empires of their own, quite different from that of the Spanish.

New Spain at its Height

During the two and a half centuries after 1492, the Spanish developed the most extensive empire the world had ever known. It would span southern Europe and the Netherlands, much of the Western Hemisphere, and parts of

Asia. Yet the Spanish Empire grew so vast that its sprawling size and complexity eventually led to its disintegration.

During the sixteenth century, Spanish America (called New Spain) gradually developed into a settled society. From the outset, the Spanish in the Americas behaved more like occupying rulers than permanent settlers, carefully regulating every detail of colonial administration and life. They were less interested in creating self-sustaining colonial communities than they were devoted to taking gold and silver, and to enslaving the indigenous peoples and converting them to Christianity. Between 1545 and 1660, the Spanish forced Native Americans and Africans to mine 7 million pounds of silver in the New World, twice as much silver as existed in all of Europe in 1492.

The legacy of New Spain is, therefore, decidedly mixed. While connecting the cultures of Europe and the Americas, the Spanish explorers, conquistadores, and priests imposed on the native peoples Catholicism as well as a cruel system of economic exploitation and dependence. That system created terrible disparities in wealth, education, and opportunity that would trigger repeated revolts and political instability. Bartolomé de Las Casas, a courageous Spanish priest in Mexico who tirelessly called for humane treatment of the native peoples, concluded, "The Spaniards have shown not the slightest consideration for these people, treating them (and I speak from firsthand experience, having been there from the outset) . . . as piles of dung in the middle of the road. They have had as little concern for their souls as for their bodies."

New Spain's legacy

■ **Native American Societies** Asian hunter-gatherers came across the Bering Strait by foot and settled the length and breadth of the Americas, forming groups with diverse cultures, languages, and customs. Global warming enabled an agricultural revolution, particularly the growing of *maize*, that allowed former hunter-gatherer peoples to settle and build empires, such as that of the *Mexica*, whose *Aztec Empire* included many subjugated peoples and a vast system of trade and tribute. Some North American peoples developed an elaborate continental trading network and impressive cities like *Cahokia*; their *burial mounds* reveal a complex social organization. The *Eastern Woodlands peoples* that the Europeans would first encounter included both patriarchal and matriarchal societies as well as extensive language-based alliances. The Algonquian, Iroquoian, and Muskogean were among the major Indian nations. Warfare was an important cultural component, leading to shifting rivalries and alliances among indigenous communities and with European settlers.

■ **Age of Exploration** By the 1490s, Europeans were experiencing a renewed curiosity about the world. Warfare, plagues, and famine undermined the old agricultural feudal system in Europe, and in its place arose a middle class that monarchs could tax. Powerful new nations replaced the land estates and cities ruled by princes. A revival of interest in antiquity led to the development of modern science and the creation of better maps and navigation techniques, as well as new weapons and ships. Navies became the critical component of global trade and world power. When the Spanish began to colonize the New World, the conversion of Indians to *Roman Catholicism* was important, but the search for gold and silver was primary.

The national rivalries sparked by the *Protestant Reformation* in Europe shaped the course of conquest in the Americas.

■ **Conquering and Colonizing the Americas** Spanish *conquistadores* such as Hernán Cortés used their advantages in military technology, including steel, gunpowder, and domesticated animals such as *horses,* in order to conquer the powerful Aztec and Inca Empires. European diseases, first introduced by Columbus's voyages, did even more to ensure Spanish victories. The Spanish *encomienda* system demanded goods and labor from the indigenous peoples. As the Indian population declined, the Spanish began to import enslaved Africans.

■ **Columbian Exchange** Contact between the Old World and the New resulted in a great biological exchange, sometimes called the *Columbian Exchange*. Crops such as *maize*, beans, and potatoes became staples in the Old World. Native peoples incorporated into their culture such Eurasian animals as the *horse* and pig. But the invaders also carried *infectious diseases* that set off pandemics of smallpox, plague, and other illnesses to which Indians had no immunity. The Americas were depopulated and cultures destroyed.

■ **Spanish Legacy** Spain left a lasting legacy in the borderlands from California to Florida. Catholic missionaries contributed to the destruction of the old ways of life by exterminating "heathen" beliefs in the Southwest, a practice that led to open rebellion in *New Mexico* in 1598 and 1680. Spain's rival European nation-states began competing for gold and glory in the New World. England's defeat of the *Spanish Armada* cleared the path for English dominance in North America.

KEY TERMS

CHRONOLOGY

by 12,000 B.C.E.	Humans have migrated to the Americas
5000 B.C.E.	Agricultural revolution begins in Mexico
1050–1250 C.E.	The city of Cahokia flourishes in North America
1325	Mexica (Aztec) Empire founded in Central Mexico
1492	Columbus makes his first voyage of discovery in the Americas
1503	Spaniards bring first enslaved Africans to the Americas
1517	Martin Luther launches the Protestant Reformation
1519	Cortés begins the Spanish conquest of Mexico
1531	Pizarro subdues the Inca Empire in South America for Spain
1541	Spaniards build fort at St. Augustine, the first permanent European outpost in the present-day United States
1584–1587	Raleigh's Roanoke Island venture
1588	The English navy defeats the Spanish Armada
1680	Pueblo Revolt

INQUIZITIVE

Go to InQuizitive to see what you've learned—and learn what you've missed—with personalized feedback along the way.

OLD VIRGINIA As one of the earliest explorers and settlers of the Jamestown colony, John Smith put his intimate knowledge of the region to use by creating this seventeenth-century map of Virginia. In the upper right hand corner is a warrior of the Susquehannock, whom Smith called a "G[i]ant-like people."

England and Its American Colonies

1607–1732

The England that Queen Elizabeth governed at the beginning of the seventeenth century was a unique blend of elements. The Church of England mixed Protestant theology with Catholic rituals to produce the Anglican form of Christianity. England was also distinctive in that English rulers shared considerable power with Parliament, the legislature, unlike the absolute monarchs of France and Spain. Even English monarchs took pride in the civil liberties that were born from this evolution of royal power.

The English settlers who poured into coastal America and the Caribbean during the seventeenth century found not a "virgin land" of uninhabited wilderness but a developed region populated by tens of thousands of Indians. As was true in New Spain and New France, European diseases overwhelmed the Native Americans. Smallpox epidemics left the coastal areas "a widowed land." Governor William Bradford, the leader of the Plymouth colony in Massachusetts, reported that the Indians "fell sick of the smallpox, and died most miserably . . . like rotten sheep."

Native Americans dealt with Europeans in different ways. Many resisted, others retreated, and still others developed thriving trade relationships with the newcomers. In some areas, land-hungry colonists quickly

CORE OBJECTIVES InQuizitive

1. Identify the economic, religious, and political motivations for the establishment of England's diverse American colonies.

2. Describe the political, economic, social, and religious characteristics of English colonies in the Chesapeake region, the Carolinas, the Middle Colonies, and New England prior to 1700.

3. Analyze the ways by which English colonists and Native Americans adapted to each other's presence.

4. Analyze the role of indentured servants and the development of slavery in colonial America.

5. Explain how the English colonies became the most populous, prosperous, and powerful region in North America by 1700.

displaced or decimated the Indians. In others, Indians found ways to live in cooperation with English settlers—if they were willing to adopt the English way of life. In Massachusetts, a young John Adams, who would one day become the second president of the United States, occasionally visited a neighboring Indian family, "where I never failed to be treated with whortleberries, blackberries, strawberries or apples, plums, peaches, etc."

After creating the Virginia and Maryland colonies in the Chesapeake Bay region and the New England colonies during the first half of the seventeenth century, the English would go on to conquer Dutch-controlled New Netherland, settle Carolina, and eventually fill out the rest of the thirteen original American mainland colonies. In the middle Atlantic region between New England and Maryland, four new colonies taken from the Dutch emerged: New York, New Jersey, Pennsylvania, and Delaware. The diverse American colonies had one thing in common: to one extent or another, they all took part in the enslavement of other peoples, either Native Americans or Africans or both. Slavery, a dreadful practice throughout the world in the seventeenth and eighteenth centuries, enriched a few, corrupted many, and compromised the American dream of equal opportunity for all.

The English Background

> **CORE OBJECTIVE**
> **1.** Identify the economic, religious, and political motivations for the establishment of England's diverse American colonies.

People and Profits

Like other European countries, England envied the riches taken from the New World by Spain, especially the enormous amounts of gold and silver. However, the English colonies in America were different from the Spanish colonies. Spanish settlements were royal expeditions; most of the wealth they found became the property of the monarchs who funded the conquistadores. In contrast, English colonization in the Americas was led by two different groups that sometimes overlapped: those seeking freedom from religious persecution in England, both Protestants and Catholics, and those seeking land and profits.

> Joint-stock companies

English colonies were thus private business ventures rather than government enterprises. And they were expensive. Few individuals were wealthy enough to finance a colony over a long period. Those interested in colonization thus decided to band together and share the financial risks of starting colonies in the "American wilderness." Investors purchased shares of stock to form "**joint-stock companies**." That way, large amounts of money could be raised and, if a colony failed, no single investor would suffer the whole loss. If a colony succeeded, the profits would be shared among the investors in the joint-stock companies. While Queen Elizabeth and her successors did not fund the colonial expeditions, they did grant the royal charters needed to launch them. The joint-stock companies represented the most important organizational innovation of the

joint-stock companies Businesses owned by investors, who purchase shares of stock and share all the profits and losses.

Age of Exploration, and they provided the first instruments of English colonization in America.

The English settlements in America differed in other respects from Spain's far-flung colonies throughout the Western Hemisphere and France's far-reaching trade outposts across Canada and down the Mississippi Valley. The mainland English colonies were more compact, adjoining one another in concentrated geographical areas. England's American empire, therefore, did not focus on conquering sprawling Native American empires as Spain had done in Mexico and Peru. The native peoples along the Atlantic coast of America were less numerous, more scattered, and less wealthy than the Mexica and the Incas.

Unlike the male-dominated French and Spanish colonies, where fur traders and Spanish conquistadores often lived among the Indians and intermarried, most English settlers viewed the Indians as an impediment to be removed as they created family-based agricultural and trading communities. By 1750, English colonists (male and female) outnumbered the French in North America (mostly male) nearly twenty to one—1.3 million to 70,000—while in what became Texas, New Mexico, Arizona, Florida, and California, there were only 20,000 Spaniards.

The English had two primary goals for their American colonies: 1) to provide the mother country with valuable raw materials such as timber for shipmaking, tobacco for smoking, and fur pelts for hats and coats; and, 2) to develop a thriving consumer market in America for English manufactured goods and luxury items. To populate their new colonies, the English encouraged social rebels (including convicts), religious dissenters, and the homeless and landless to migrate to America, thereby reducing social and economic tensions at home.

> Provide raw materials and develop consumer markets

By far, the best way to entice people to become settlers in America was to offer them land and the promise of a better way of life: what came to be called the American dream. Land, plentiful and cheap, was English America's miraculous treasure—once it was taken from the Native Americans.

> Massive immigration

Political Traditions

English colonists brought to America their own political institutions and social folkways. Over the centuries, the island nation of England had developed political practices and principles quite different from those on the continent of Europe. The English rulers shared power with the nobility and a lesser aristocracy called the *gentry*. Their representatives formed the legislature known as the **Parliament**, made up of the hereditary and appointed House of Lords and the elected House of Commons. The most important power allocated to Parliament was the authority to impose taxes. By controlling government tax revenue, the legislature exercised great leverage over the monarchy.

> Parliament, civil rights, and liberties

Parliament Legislature of Great Britain, composed of the House of Commons, whose members are elected, and the House of Lords, whose members are either hereditary or appointed.

England's parliamentary monarchy was unique in sixteenth-century Europe. It began with the Magna Carta (Great Charter) of 1215, a statement of basic rights and liberties that nobles had forced the king to approve. The Magna Carta established the basic principle that everyone was equal before the law and no person—not even a king or a queen—was above the law.

Religious Conflict and War

When Queen Elizabeth, who never married, died in 1603 without a child of her own to inherit the throne, James VI of Scotland, a distant cousin of Elizabeth, became King James I of England. While Elizabeth had ruled through constitutional authority, James claimed to govern by "divine right," by which monarchs answered only to God.

A divided Church of England

King James I confronted a divided Church of England, with the reform-minded **Puritans** in one camp, and the Anglican establishment, headed by the archbishop and bishops, in the other. In seventeenth-century England, those who criticized or abandoned the official Anglican Church were called *Dissenters*. The Puritans were conservative dissenters who believed that the Church of England needed further "purifying." They demanded that all "papist" (Roman Catholic) rituals be eliminated. No use of holy water. No organ music. No elegant robes (vestments). No jeweled gold crosses. No worship of saints. No kneeling for communion. No tyrannical bishops and archbishops. The Puritans wanted to simplify religion to its basics: people worshipping God in plain, self-governing congregations without all the formal trappings of Catholic and Anglican ceremonies and wealth. They had hoped the new king would support their efforts to "purify" the Church of England. But James I instead sought to banish the Puritans from England.

Religious persecution

Some of the Puritans eventually decided that the Church of England should not be fixed but abandoned, so they created their own congregations separate from the Anglican churches, thus earning the name *Separatists*. Such rebelliousness infuriated the leaders of the Church of England, who required people by law to attend Anglican church services. During the late sixteenth century, the Separatists (also called *Nonconformists*) were "hunted & persecuted on every side." English authorities imprisoned Separatist leaders, three of whom were hanged. In 1604, King James I vowed to "make them conform or I will hurry them out of the land or do worse." Many Separatists left England to escape persecution, and some, who would eventually be known as Pilgrims, decided to sail for America.

James's son, Charles I, succeeded his father as king in 1625, and proved to be an even more stubborn defender of absolute royal power. He took the shocking step of disbanding Parliament from 1629 to 1640; he raised taxes without consulting Parliament; and, he persecuted the Puritans. Some fled to Europe; others went to islands in the West Indies. Most of them, however, went to America.

But the monarchy went too far when it tried to impose Anglican forms of worship on Presbyterian Scots. In 1638, Scotland rose in revolt against English tyranny, and in 1640 King Charles, desperate for money to fund his army and save his skin, revived Parliament, ordering its members to raise taxes for

Puritans English religious dissenters who sought to "purify" the Church of England of its Catholic practices.

the defense of his kingdom against the Scots. The Parliament refused, going so far as to condemn to death the king's chief minister. Militant Puritans took the lead in Parliament, insisting that all bishops in the Church of England be eliminated. In 1642, when the king tried to arrest five members of Parliament, a bloody civil war erupted between Royalists and Parliamentarians. In 1646 parliamentary forces captured King Charles and convicted him of high treason, labeling him a "tyrant, traitor, murderer, and public enemy." He was beheaded in 1649.

Oliver Cromwell, the skilled Puritan commander of the parliamentary army, operated like a military dictator. He extended religious toleration to all Britons except Roman Catholics and Anglicans, but his dictatorship fed growing resentment. After Cromwell's death in 1658, the army allowed new elections for Parliament and in 1660 supported the Restoration of the monarchy under young Charles II, son of the executed king.

Unlike his father, King Charles II agreed to rule jointly with Parliament. His younger brother, the Duke of York (who became James II upon succeeding to the throne in 1685), was less flexible. He openly embraced Catholicism, had political opponents murdered or imprisoned, defied Parliament, and appointed Roman Catholics to key positions.

Execution of Charles I Flemish artist John Weesop witnessed the execution and painted this gruesome scene from memory. He was so disgusted by "a country where they cut off their king's head" that he refused to visit England again.

The English people could bear James II's rule only so long as they expected one of his Protestant daughters, Mary or Anne, to succeed him. In 1688, however, the birth of a royal son who would be reared in the Roman Catholic tradition brought matters to a crisis. Determined to avoid a Catholic monarch, political, religious, and military leaders invited the king's Protestant daughter, Mary Stuart, and her Protestant husband, the ruling Dutch prince William III of Orange, to displace King James II and assume the English throne as joint monarchs. When William landed in England with a Dutch army, his father-in-law, King James II, not wanting to lose his head, fled to France. Amid this dramatic transfer of power, which soon became known as the "Glorious Revolution," Parliament reasserted its right to counterbalance the authority of the monarchy. Kings and queens could no longer suspend Parliament, create armies, or impose taxes without Parliament's consent. The monarchy would henceforth derive its power not from God but from the people.

CORE **OBJECTIVE**
2. Describe the political, economic, social, and religious characteristics of English colonies in the Chesapeake region, the Carolinas, the Middle Colonies, and New England prior to 1700.

Settling the American Colonies

During these tumultuous years in English political and social history, all of England's North American colonies except Georgia were founded. The first waves of colonists were energetic, courageous, and often ruthless, even violent, people willing to risk their lives in hopes of improving them. Many of those who were jobless and landless in England would find their way to America, already in the early seventeenth century viewed as a land of opportunity. Yet what many of them found instead was disease, drought, starvation, warfare, and death.

The Chesapeake Region

In 1606, King James I chartered a joint-stock enterprise called the Virginia Company, owned by merchant investors (including the wealthiest merchant in London) seeking to profit from the gold and silver they hoped would be found. He also gave the Virginia Company a religious mission by ordering the settlers to bring the "Christian religion" to the Indians, who "live in darkness and miserable ignorance of the true knowledge and worship of God." But as was true of many colonial ventures, such missionary activities were quickly dropped in favor of making money. No one foresaw what the first permanent English colony in America would actually become: a place to grow tobacco.

Jamestown

A fragile Jamestown

In 1607, the Virginia Company sent to America three tiny ships carrying about a hundred men and boys, many of them from prominent English families. In May they reached Chesapeake Bay after five storm-tossed months at sea. They chose a river with a northwest bend—in the hope of finding a passage to Asia—and settled about forty miles inland, to avoid Spanish raiders. They called the river the James, in honor of the king, and named their first settlement James Fort, later renamed Jamestown.

On a marshy peninsula fed by salty water and swarming with mosquitoes, the sea-weary colonists built a fort with thatched huts and a church. They struggled to find enough to eat, for most of the colonists were either townsmen unfamiliar with farming or "gentleman" adventurers who despised manual labor. Starvation led them to desperate measures. One hungry man killed, salted, and ate his pregnant wife. His fellow colonists then tortured and executed him. Of the original settlers, only thirty-eight survived the first nine months.

John Smith saves Jamestown

Fortunately for the Virginia colonists, they found an effective leader in Captain John Smith, a twenty-seven-year-old mercenary (a soldier for hire). With the colonists on the verge of starvation, Smith imposed strict military discipline and forced all to work if they wanted to eat. When no gold or silver

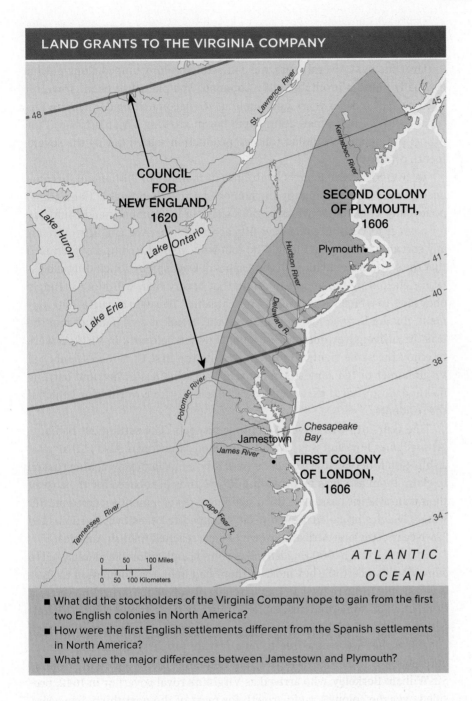

LAND GRANTS TO THE VIRGINIA COMPANY

COUNCIL FOR NEW ENGLAND, 1620

SECOND COLONY OF PLYMOUTH, 1606

Plymouth

St. Lawrence River

Kennebec River

Lake Huron

Lake Ontario

Lake Erie

Hudson River

Delaware R.

Potomac River

Tennessee River

Cape Fear R.

James River

Jamestown

Chesapeake Bay

FIRST COLONY OF LONDON, 1606

ATLANTIC OCEAN

0   50   100 Miles

0   50   100 Kilometers

■ What did the stockholders of the Virginia Company hope to gain from the first two English colonies in North America?

■ How were the first English settlements different from the Spanish settlements in North America?

■ What were the major differences between Jamestown and Plymouth?

was discovered, the Virginia Company shifted its focus to the sale of land, which would rise in value as the colony grew in population. The company recruited more settlers by promising that Virginia would "make them rich." Hundreds of new settlers nearly overwhelmed the infant colony. A new charter also appointed an all-powerful governor. The company then lured new investors and attracted new settlers by promising to give them land after seven years.

Over the next several years, the Jamestown colony limped along until it gradually found a profitable crop: **tobacco**. The plant had been grown on Caribbean islands for years, and smoking had become a popular habit in Europe. In 1612 Englishman John Rolfe began growing Virginia tobacco for export to England. Virginia's tobacco production soared during the seventeenth century.

Land and liberty

In 1618 Sir Edwin Sandys, a prominent member of Parliament, became head of the Virginia Company and launched a new "**headright**" (land grant) policy: any Englishman who bought a share in the company and could pay for passage to Virginia could have fifty acres upon arrival, and fifty more for any servants he brought along. The following year, the company promised that the settlers would have all the "rights of Englishmen," including a legislature elected by the people, arguing that "every man will more willingly obey laws to which he has yielded his consent." This was a crucial development, for the English had long enjoyed the broadest civil liberties and the least intrusive government in Europe. Now the colonists in Virginia were to enjoy the same rights. On July 30, 1619, the first General Assembly of Virginia met in the Jamestown church, "sweating & stewing, and battling flies and mosquitoes," as it assumed responsibility for governing on behalf of the residents.

The first enslaved Africans

The year 1619 was eventful in other respects. The settlement had outgrown James Fort and was formally renamed Jamestown. Also in that year, a ship with ninety young women aboard arrived in Jamestown. Men rushed to claim them as wives by providing 125 pounds of tobacco for the cost of their transatlantic passage. A third significant development occurred in 1619 when a Dutch ship called the *White Lion* stopped at Jamestown and unloaded "20 Negars," the first Africans known to have reached English America.

By 1624, some 14,000 English men, women, and children had migrated to Jamestown since 1607, but most of them had died; the population in 1624 was still only 1,132. In 1624 an English court dissolved the struggling Virginia Company, and "weak and miserable" Virginia became a royal colony. No longer would the settlers be mere laborers toiling for a distant joint-stock company; they were now free to own private property and start business enterprises. But their governors would thereafter be appointed by the king. Sir William Berkeley, who arrived as Virginia's royal governor in 1642, presided over the colony's rapid growth for most of the next thirty-five years. Tobacco prices surged, and the wealthiest planters began to dominate the social and political life in the colony.

Maryland

In 1634, ten years after Virginia became a royal colony, a neighboring settlement appeared on the northern shore of Chesapeake Bay. Named Maryland in honor of English queen Henrietta Maria, it was granted to Sir George

tobacco A "cash crop" grown in the Caribbean as well as the Virginia and Maryland colonies, made increasingly profitable by the rapidly growing popularity of smoking in Europe after the voyages of Columbus.

headright A land-grant policy that promised fifty acres to any colonist who could afford passage to Virginia, as well as fifty more for any accompanying servants. The headright policy was eventually expanded to include any colonists—and was also adopted in other colonies too.

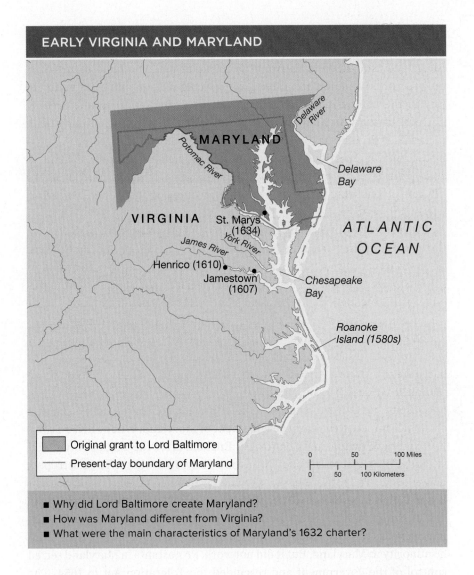

EARLY VIRGINIA AND MARYLAND

MARYLAND

Delaware River

Delaware Bay

Potomac River

VIRGINIA   St. Marys (1634)

ATLANTIC OCEAN

York River

James River

Henrico (1610)

Jamestown (1607)

Chesapeake Bay

Roanoke Island (1580s)

Original grant to Lord Baltimore

Present-day boundary of Maryland

0   50   100 Miles

0   50   100 Kilometers

- Why did Lord Baltimore create Maryland?
- How was Maryland different from Virginia?
- What were the main characteristics of Maryland's 1632 charter?

Calvert, Lord Baltimore, by King Charles I and became the first *proprietary* colony—that is, it was owned by an individual, not by a joint-stock company. Calvert had created a stir in 1625 when he converted from Anglicanism to Catholicism, which meant he had to resign from his government position as the king's secretary of state. To compensate him for his losses, Calvert asked the king to grant him a charter for an American colony to the north of Virginia. However, Calvert died before the king could act on his request, so the charter was awarded to his son, Cecilius Calvert, the second Lord Baltimore, who actually founded the colony. He wanted Maryland to be a refuge for English Catholics, a persecuted minority in Anglican England. But he also wanted his new colony to be profitable and to avoid antagonizing Protestants, so he instructed his brother, Leonard, the colony's first governor, to ensure that the Catholic colonists worship in private and remain "silent upon all occasions of discourse concerning matters of religion."

Maryland: The first proprietary colony and a refuge for English Catholics

In 1634, Cecilius Calvert and his brother, Leonard, planted the first settlement in coastal Maryland at St. Marys, near the mouth of the Potomac River. They sought to learn from the mistakes made at Jamestown. First, they recruited a more committed group of colonists—families intending to stay in the colony rather than single men seeking quick profits. Second, Calvert did not want Maryland to be a colony of scattered farms and settlements like Virginia, or to become dependent solely on tobacco. He wanted instead to create fortified towns, carefully designed to promote social interaction. Third, Calvert wanted to avoid the extremes of wealth and poverty in Virginia by ensuring that the government would "do justice to every man" without partiality.

The charter from the king gave Cecilius Calvert power to make laws with the consent of the freemen (that is, all property holders). But the Calverts discovered that they could not attract enough Roman Catholics to develop a self-sustaining economy. The majority of the servants who came to the colony were Protestants, both Anglicans and Puritans. In addition, to recruit servants and settlers, the Calverts had to offer them small farms, most of which grew tobacco. Unlike Virginia, which struggled for its first twenty years, Maryland succeeded more quickly because of its focus on growing tobacco from the start. And its long coastline along the Chesapeake Bay gave planters easy access to shipping.

Toleration Act (1649)

Despite the Calverts' caution "concerning matters of religion," sectarian squabbles impeded the early development of Maryland. When Oliver Cromwell and the Puritans took control in England after the English Civil War, Cecilius Calvert feared he might lose the colony. To avoid such a catastrophe, he wrote the Toleration Act (1649) which welcomed all Christians, regardless of their denomination or beliefs (it also promised to execute anyone who denied the divinity of Jesus). Lord Baltimore convinced the Maryland legislature to pass the Toleration Act in the hope that it would protect the Catholic minority in Maryland. But it did not work. Protestants in Maryland seized control of the government and rescinded the Toleration Act in 1654. The once-persecuted Puritans had become persecutors themselves, at one point driving Lord Baltimore out of his own colony. Were it not for the colony's success in growing tobacco, Maryland may well have disintegrated. In 1692, following the Glorious Revolution in England, Catholicism was banned in Maryland. Only after the American Revolution would Marylanders again be guaranteed religious freedom.

New England

Very different English settlements were emerging far to the north of the Chesapeake Bay colonies. Unlike the Jamestown settlers, the New England colonists were often middle-class families that could pay their own way across the Atlantic. There were relatively few servants, and no elite plantation owners. Most male settlers were small farmers, merchants, seamen, or fishermen. New England also attracted more women than did the southern colonies.

Although its soil was not as fertile as that of the Chesapeake region and its growing season was much shorter, New England was a much healthier place to live. Because of its colder climate, settlers avoided the infectious diseases like malaria that ravaged the southern colonies and killed so many during the first waves of settlement. During the seventeenth century, only 21,000 colonists arrived in New England, compared with the 120,000 who went to the Chesapeake Bay colonies. But by 1700, New England's thriving white population exceeded that of Maryland and Virginia. Over several generations, New Englanders had larger families and relatively fewer diseases than their southern counterparts.

Plymouth

The first permanent English settlement in New England was established by a group of ungodly adventurers and pious farm families who were forced to leave England because of their refusal to worship in Anglican churches. (Accordingly, in their own time they were known as Separatists; only much later would this particular group of Separatists be remembered as "the Pilgrims.") They first moved to Holland, only to worry that their children were becoming Dutch. So in September 1620, about a hundred women, men, and children crammed aboard the tiny *Mayflower*, a vessel only 100 feet long, and headed across the Atlantic bound for the Virginia colony, where they had obtained permission to settle. It was hurricane season, and storms blew the ship off course to Cape Cod, just south of what became Boston, Massachusetts. Since they were outside the jurisdiction of any organized government, the forty-one Separatists on board the *Mayflower* signed the **Mayflower Compact**, a formal agreement to abide by the laws made by leaders of their own choosing.

The colonists, both "strangers and pilgrims," as William Bradford wrote in his journal, settled in a deserted Indian village and named their colony Plymouth, after the English port from which they had embarked. Unlike the Jamestown colonists, the Separatists at Plymouth were motivated primarily by religious ideals. The Pilgrims wanted to create a model Christian society living strictly according to God's commandments. This meant "purifying" their church of all Catholic and Anglican rituals and enacting a code of laws and a government structure based upon biblical principles. Such a holy settlement, they hoped, would provide a living example of righteousness for a wicked England to imitate.

Throughout its existence, until it was absorbed into Massachusetts Bay Colony in 1691, the Plymouth colony governed itself on the basis of the Mayflower Compact, which was a covenant (that is, a group contract) to form a church. Thus the civil government grew out of the church government, and the members of each were identical. The signers of the Mayflower Compact at first met as the General Court, which chose the governor

> The Pilgrims at Plymouth and the Mayflower Compact (1620)

Mayflower Compact (1620)
A formal agreement signed by the Separatist colonists aboard the *Mayflower* to abide by laws made by leaders of their own choosing.

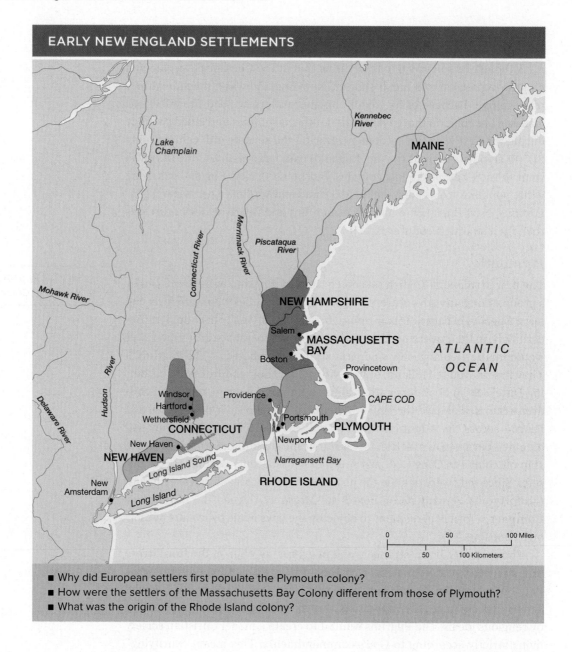

EARLY NEW ENGLAND SETTLEMENTS

- Why did European settlers first populate the Plymouth colony?
- How were the settlers of the Massachusetts Bay Colony different from those of Plymouth?
- What was the origin of the Rhode Island colony?

and his assistants (or council). Others were later admitted as members, or "freemen," but only church members were eligible. Eventually, as the colony grew, the General Court became a legislative body of elected representatives from the various towns.

Massachusetts Bay

Massachusetts Bay Colony
English colony founded by Puritans in 1630 as a haven for persecuted Congregationalists.

The Plymouth colony's population never rose above 7,000, and after ten years it was overshadowed by its much larger neighbor, the **Massachusetts Bay Colony**. That colony, too, was intended to be a holy commonwealth. The

Massachusetts Bay Puritans, however, were different from the Pilgrims. They were non-separating Congregationalists who wanted to purify the Church of England from within. They were called *Congregationalists* because their churches were governed by their congregations rather than by an Anglican bishop in distant England. Their self-governing churches limited membership to "visible saints"—those who could demonstrate receipt of the gift of God's grace.

In 1629, the same year that King Charles I shut down Parliament, the monarchy gave a royal charter to a joint-stock company called the Massachusetts Bay Company. It consisted of a group of Puritans led by John Winthrop, a prosperous lawyer with intense religious convictions. Winthrop wanted the colony to be a haven for persecuted Puritans and a model Christian community—"a city on the hill," as Winthrop declared. To that end, he shrewdly took advantage of an oversight in the company charter: it did not require that the joint-stock company maintain its home office in England. Winthrop's group took its royal charter with them, thereby transferring government authority from London to Massachusetts, where they hoped to govern themselves.

John Winthrop The first governor of the Massachusetts Bay Colony, in whose vision the colony would be as "a city upon a hill."

Puritan New England

It is hard to exaggerate the crucial role Winthrop played in establishing the Massachusetts Bay Colony, centered on Boston. He was a strong leader who prized stability and order and hated the idea of democracy—the people ruling themselves. Like many Puritan leaders, Winthrop believed that the role of government should be to enforce religious beliefs and ensure social stability. Ironically, the same Puritans who had fled persecution in England did not hesitate to persecute people of other religious views in New England. Catholics, Anglicans, Quakers, and Baptists had no rights in Puritan New England; they were punished, imprisoned, banished, or even executed.

The transfer of the Massachusetts Bay Colony's royal charter, whereby an English trading company evolved into a provincial government, was a unique venture in colonization. Unlike "Old" England, New England had no powerful lords or bishops, kings or queens. The Massachusetts General Court, wherein power rested under the royal charter, consisted of all the shareholders, called freemen. At first, the freemen had no power except to choose "assistants," who in turn chose the governor and deputy governor. In 1634, however, the freemen turned themselves into the General Court, with two or three deputies to represent each town. A final stage in the democratization of the government came in 1644, when the General Court organized itself like the Parliament with a House of Assistants, corresponding roughly to the House of Lords, and a House of Deputies, corresponding to the House of Commons. All decisions had to be ratified by a majority in each house.

Thus, over a period of fourteen years, the joint-stock Massachusetts Bay Company evolved into the governing body of a holy commonwealth in which freemen were given increasing power. Puritans had fled not only religious persecution but also political repression, and they ensured that their

Rights and representation in New England

liberties in New England were spelled out and protected. Over time, membership in a Puritan church replaced the purchase of stock as the means of becoming a freeman, or voter, in Massachusetts Bay.

Rhode Island

More by accident than design, the Massachusetts Bay Colony became the staging area for other New England colonies created by people dissatisfied with Puritan control. Young Roger Williams (1603–1683), who had arrived from England in 1631, was among the first to cause problems, precisely because he was the purest of Puritans—a Separatist. He criticized Puritans for not completely cutting their ties to the "whorish" Church of England. Where John Winthrop cherished strict governmental and clerical authority, Williams stubbornly championed individual liberty and criticized the way the Indians were being shoved aside. The combative Williams posed a radical question: If one's salvation depends solely upon God's grace, why bother to have churches at all? Why not give individuals the right to worship God in their own way?

In Williams's view, true *puritanism* required complete separation of church and state and freedom from all coercion in matters of faith. "Forced worship," he declared, "stinks in God's nostrils." According to Williams, governments should be impartial regarding religions. Such radical views led the General Court to banish Williams to England. Williams, however, slipped away during a raging blizzard and found shelter among the Narragansett Indians. In 1636 he bought land from the Indians and established the town of Providence at the head of Narragansett Bay, the first permanent settlement in Rhode Island and the first in America to allow complete freedom of religion.

From the beginning, Rhode Island was the most democratic of the colonies, governed by the heads of households rather than by church members. Newcomers could be admitted to full citizenship by a majority vote, and the colony welcomed all who fled religious persecution in Massachusetts Bay. For their part, Puritans came to view Rhode Island as a refuge for rogues. A Dutch visitor reported that Rhode Island was "the sewer of New England. All the cranks of New England retire there." Thus the colony of Rhode Island and Providence Plantations, the smallest in America, began as a sanctuary for those who insisted that governments had no right to impose religious beliefs.

Williams was only one of several prominent Puritans who clashed with Governor John Winthrop's stern, unyielding governance of the Bay Colony. Another, Anne Hutchinson, quarreled with Puritan leaders for different reasons. The strong-willed, intelligent wife of a prominent merchant, Hutchinson raised thirteen children and hosted meetings in her Boston home to discuss sermons. Soon, however, the discussions turned into large gatherings (of both men and women) at which Hutchinson shared her strong feelings about religious matters. According to one participant, she "preaches better Gospel than any of your black coats [male ministers]." Blessed with vast biblical knowledge and a quick wit, Hutchinson claimed to know which of her neighbors had truly been saved and which were damned, including ministers.

A pregnant Hutchinson was hauled before the all-male General Court in 1637 for trying to "undermine the Kingdom of Christ," and for two days she sparred on equal terms with the Puritan leaders. Her ability to cite chapter-and-verse biblical defenses of her actions led an exasperated Governor Winthrop to explode: "We are your judges, and not you ours. . . . We do not mean to discourse [debate] with those of your sex." He told Hutchinson that she had "stepped out of your place" as a woman in a man's world. As the trial continued, an overwrought Hutchinson was eventually lured into convicting herself by claiming direct revelations from God—blasphemy in the eyes of Puritans.

In 1638 the General Court banished Hutchinson as a "leper" not fit for "our society." She initially settled with her family and about sixty followers on an island in Narragansett Bay south of Providence. But the hard journey took its toll. Hutchinson grew sick, and her baby was stillborn, leading her critics in Massachusetts Bay to claim that the "monstrous birth" was God's way of punishing her. Hutchinson's spirits never recovered. After her husband's death, in 1642, she moved just north of New Amsterdam (New York City), then under Dutch control. The following year, she and six of her children were massacred by Indians. Her fate, wrote a spiteful John Winthrop, was "a special manifestation of divine justice."

The Trial of Anne Hutchinson In this nineteenth-century wood engraving, Anne Hutchinson stands her ground against charges of heresy from the all-male leaders of Puritan Boston.

Connecticut, New Hampshire, and Maine

Connecticut had a more conventional beginning than Rhode Island. In 1636, the Reverend Thomas Hooker led three church congregations from Massachusetts Bay to the Connecticut Valley, where they organized the self-governing colony of Connecticut. In 1639, the Connecticut General Court adopted the Fundamental Orders, a series of laws that provided for a "Christian Commonwealth" like that of Massachusetts, except that voting was not limited to church members. The Connecticut constitution specified that the Congregational churches would be the colony's official religion. The governor was commanded to rule according to "the word of God."

New England expands

To the north of Massachusetts, most of what are now the states of New Hampshire and Maine was granted in 1622 to Sir Ferdinando Gorges and Captain John Mason. In 1629, Mason and Gorges divided their territory, with Mason taking the southern part, which he named the Province of New Hampshire, and Gorges taking the northern part, which became the Province of Maine. During the early 1640s, Massachusetts took over New Hampshire and in the 1650s extended its authority to the scattered settlements in Maine. This led to lawsuits, and in 1678 English judges decided against Massachusetts in both cases. In 1679, New Hampshire became a royal colony, but Massachusetts continued to control Maine. A new Massachusetts charter in 1691 finally incorporated Maine into Massachusetts.

The Carolinas

From the start, the Carolina colony consisted of two widely separated areas of settlement, which eventually became two different **Carolina colonies**. The northernmost part, long called Albemarle, had been settled in the 1650s by colonists who had drifted southward from Virginia. For half a century, Albemarle remained a remote scattering of farmers along the shores of Albemarle Sound. The eight nobles, called lords proprietor, to whom the king had given Carolina neglected Albemarle and instead focused on more promising sites to the south. They recruited experienced English planters from the Caribbean island of Barbados to bring to southern Carolina the profitable West Indian sugar-plantation system based on the hard labor of enslaved Africans. In a reference to Barbados and the other English colonies in the Caribbean, an English colonist pointed out in 1666 that "these Settlements have been made and upheld by Negroes and without constant supplies of them cannot subsist."

> **Slavery in the Carolinas**

The first English colonists arrived in southern Carolina in 1669 at Charles Town (later named Charleston). Over the next twenty years, half the southern Carolina colonists came from Barbados and other English island colonies in the Caribbean such as Nevis, St. Kitts, and Jamaica. Most of them brought African slaves with them, putting them to work clearing land, cutting wood, planting gardens, and herding cattle. In 1712, the Carolina colony was formally divided in two: North and South.

> **Religious tolerance**

The government of Carolina rested upon one of the most curious documents of colonial history, the Fundamental Constitutions of Carolina, drawn up by one of the eight proprietors, Lord Anthony Ashley Cooper, with the help of his secretary, the renowned philosopher John Locke. Its provisions for a formal titled nobility had little effect in the colony except to encourage a practice of awarding large land grants to prominent Englishmen. From the beginning, however, smaller "headrights" (land grants) were given to every immigrant who could pay for passage across the Atlantic. The Fundamental Constitutions granted religious toleration as a means of encouraging immigration, which gave Carolina a greater degree of religious freedom (extending to Jews and "heathens") than England or any other colony except Rhode Island.

Carolina colonies English proprietary colonies comprised of North and South Carolina, whose semitropical climate made them profitable centers of rice, timber, and tar production.

After rebelling against the lords proprietors, South Carolina became a royal colony in 1719. North Carolina remained under the proprietors' rule for ten more years, until it too became a royal colony. Rice became as much the dominant commercial crop in coastal South Carolina as tobacco was in Virginia and Maryland. Planters discovered that the translucent grain was

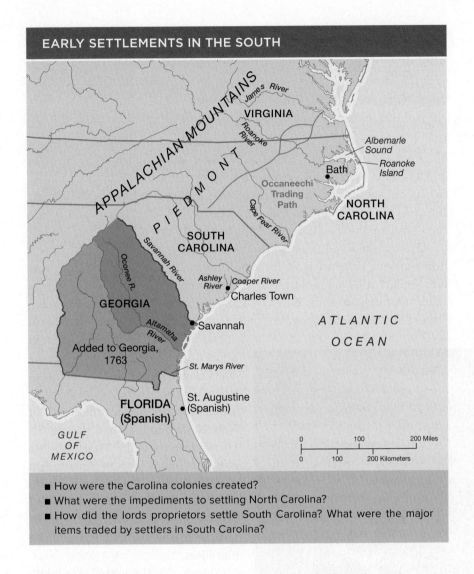

EARLY SETTLEMENTS IN THE SOUTH

- How were the Carolina colonies created?
- What were the impediments to settling North Carolina?
- How did the lords proprietors settle South Carolina? What were the major items traded by settlers in South Carolina?

perfectly suited to the growing conditions in the semitropical coastal areas known as the low country. Because rice, like sugarcane and tobacco, was labor-intensive, planters used enslaved Africans to work their rice plantations in the Carolinas. Both Carolinas also had huge forests of yellow pine trees that provided lumber and other key materials for shipbuilding. The resin from trees could be boiled to make tar, which was needed to waterproof the seams of wooden ships (which is why North Carolinians came to be called Tar Heels).

The Middle Colonies and Georgia

The area between New England and the Chesapeake—Maryland and Virginia—included colonies in New York, New Jersey, Delaware, and Pennsylvania. By 1670, the mostly Protestant Dutch had the largest merchant fleet in the world and the highest standard of living. They controlled northern

European commerce and had become one of the most diverse and tolerant societies in Europe—and England's most ferocious competitor in international commerce.

New Netherland Becomes New York

The Dutch in North America

In London, King Charles II decided to pluck out that old thorn in the side of the English colonies in America: **New Netherland**. The Dutch colony was older than New England. The Dutch East India Company (organized in 1602) had hired an English sea captain, Henry Hudson, to explore America in hopes of finding a northwest passage to the spice-rich Indies. Sailing along the coast of North America in 1609, Hudson discovered Delaware Bay and then sailed up the river named for him in what is now New York.

Profits and pluralism

Like Virginia and Massachusetts, New Netherland was created as a profit-making enterprise. In 1610 the Dutch established fur-trading posts on Manhattan Island and upriver at Fort Orange (later called Albany). In 1626 the Dutch governor purchased Manhattan (an Indian word meaning "island of many hills") from the Indians for 60 gilders, or about $1,000 in current values. The Dutch then built a fort at the lower end of the island. The village of New Amsterdam (eventually New York City), which grew up around the fort, became the capital of New Netherland. Unlike their Puritan counterparts in Massachusetts Bay, the Dutch in New Amsterdam were preoccupied more with profits and freedoms than with religion and restrictions. They promoted free enterprise as well as ethnic and religious pluralism.

Dutch settlements gradually emerged wherever fur pelts might be found. In 1638, a Swedish trading company established Fort Christina at the site of present-day Wilmington, Delaware, and scattered settlements up and down the Delaware River. The Dutch in 1655 took control of New Sweden. The chief contribution of the short-lived New Sweden to American culture was the idea of the log cabin, which the Swedes and a few Finnish settlers had brought from the woods of Scandinavia to Delaware.

Castello Plan of New Amsterdam A map of New Amsterdam in 1660, shortly before the English took the colony from the Dutch and christened it New York City.

New Netherland Dutch colony conquered by the English in 1667, out of which four new colonies were created—New York, New Jersey, Pennsylvania, and Delaware.

The New Netherland governors were mostly stubborn autocrats, either corrupt or inept, and especially clumsy at Indian relations. They depended upon a small army for defense, and the colonists, many of whom were not

Dutch, were hardly devoted to the government. New Amsterdam was one of the most ethnically diverse colonial cities—as is New York City today. Its residents included not only the Dutch but also Swedes, Norwegians, Spaniards, Jews, free and enslaved blacks, English, Germans, and Finns. In 1664, the diverse colonists showed almost total indifference when Governor Peter Stuyvesant called them to arms against a threatening English fleet. Stuyvesant blustered and stomped about on his wooden leg but finally surrendered the colony to the English without firing a shot.

The English conquest of New Netherland had been hatched by the Duke of York, who would become King James II. Upon the capture of New Amsterdam, his brother, King Charles II, granted the entire Dutch region to him, and the English promptly renamed both New Netherland and the city of New Amsterdam as New York, in honor of James, and they renamed Fort Orange, farther up the Hudson River, as Albany.

In September 1654, ten years before the English took control of New Netherland, a French ship arrived in New Amsterdam harbor. On board were twenty-three Sephardim, Jews of Spanish-Portuguese descent. Penniless and weary, they had come seeking refuge from Portuguese-controlled Brazil. They were the first Jewish settlers to arrive in North America.

> The first Jewish settlers

The Dutch officials embraced the homeless Jews, explaining that they wanted to "allow everyone to have his own belief, as long as he behaves quietly and legally, gives no offense to his neighbor, and does not oppose the government." But it would not be until the late seventeenth century that Jews could worship in public. Such restrictions help explain why the American Jewish community grew so slowly. In 1773, over 100 years after the first Jewish refugees arrived in New Amsterdam, Jews represented only one tenth of 1 percent of the entire colonial population. Not until the nineteenth century would the American Jewish community experience dramatic growth.

New Jersey

Shortly after the conquest of New Netherland, James Stuart, the Duke of York, granted the lands between the Hudson and Delaware Rivers to Sir George Carteret and Lord John Berkeley (brother of Virginia's governor) and named the territory for Carteret's native Jersey, an island in the English Channel. In 1676, by mutual agreement, New Jersey was divided into East and West Jersey, with Carteret taking the east, Berkeley the west. But neither Jersey colony prospered, so in 1702, East and West Jersey were united as the single royal colony of New Jersey.

Pennsylvania

The Quaker sect, as the Religious Society of Friends was called in ridicule (because they were supposed to "tremble at the word of the Lord"), became the most influential of many radical religious groups that emerged from the

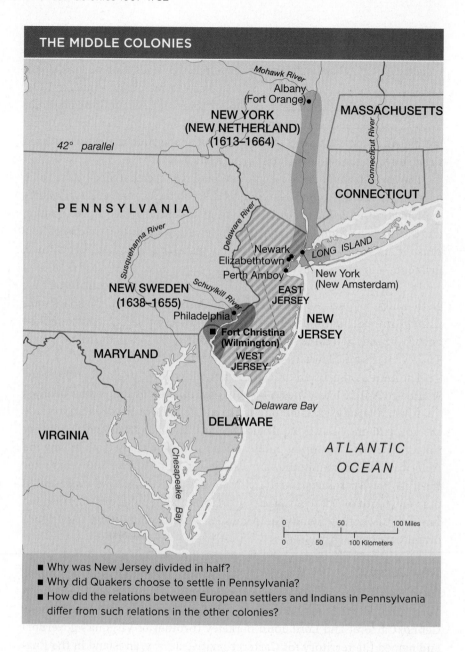

THE MIDDLE COLONIES

- Why was New Jersey divided in half?
- Why did Quakers choose to settle in Pennsylvania?
- How did the relations between European settlers and Indians in Pennsylvania differ from such relations in the other colonies?

turbulence of the English Civil War. Founded in England in 1647 by George Fox, a saintly roving preacher, the Quakers, like the Puritans, rejected the formalism of the Anglican Church. But they did more. The Quakers rebelled against *all* forms of political and religious authority, including salaried ministers, military service, and paying taxes. Quakers insisted that everyone, not just a select few, could experience a personal revelation from God, what they called the "Inner Light." Quakers discarded all formal religious rituals and even a formal ministry, and embraced a fierce pacifism. Some Quakers went barefoot, others wore rags, and a few went naked to demonstrate their "primitive" commitment to Christ. Quakers demanded complete religious freedom for everyone and promoted equality of the sexes, including the full participation of women in religious affairs.

Quakers suffered intense persecution. New England Puritans banned them, tortured them, and executed them. Often, the Quakers seemed to invite such abuse. In 1663, for example, Lydia Wardell, a Quaker in Newbury, Massachusetts, grew so upset with the law requiring everyone to attend Puritan religious services that she arrived at the church naked to dramatize her protest. Puritan authorities ordered her "to be severely whipped," after which she and her husband moved to West Jersey.

The settling of English Quakers in West Jersey encouraged other Friends to migrate, especially to the Delaware River side of the colony, where William Penn's Quaker commonwealth, the colony of Pennsylvania, soon arose. Penn, the son of Admiral Sir William Penn, had become a Quaker as a student at Oxford University. Upon his father's death, he inherited a substantial estate, including a huge tract of land in America. The land was named, at the king's insistence, for Penn's father—Pennsylvania (literally, "Penn's Woods"). Unlike John Winthrop in Massachusetts, Penn encouraged people of different religions to settle in his new colony. By the end of 1681, a town was emerging at the junction of the Schuylkill and Delaware Rivers. Penn called it Philadelphia ("City of Brotherly Love").

> A Quaker-controlled Pennsylvania

The colony's government, which rested on three Frames of Government drafted by Penn, resembled that of other proprietary colonies except that the freemen (taxpayers and property owners) elected the council members as well as the assembly. The governor had no veto, although Penn, as proprietor, did. Penn hoped to show that a government could operate in accordance with Quaker principles, that it could maintain peace and order, and that religion could flourish without government support and with absolute freedom of conscience.

Delaware

In 1682, the Duke of York also granted Penn the area of Delaware, another part of the former Dutch territory (which had been New Sweden before being acquired by the Dutch in 1655). At first, Delaware—taking its name from the Delaware River, which had been named to honor Thomas West, Baron De La Warr (1577–1618), Virginia's first colonial governor—became part of Pennsylvania, but after 1704 it was granted the right to choose its own legislative assembly. From then until the American Revolution, Delaware had a separate assembly but shared Pennsylvania's governor.

Georgia

Georgia was the last of the English colonies to be established—half a century after Pennsylvania. During the seventeenth century, settlers pushed southward into the borderlands between Carolina and Spanish Florida. They brought with them enslaved Africans and a desire to win the Indian trade from the Spanish. Each side used guns, gifts, and rum to court the Indians, and the Indians in turn played off the English against the Spanish.

Georgia established for the "worthy poor"

In 1732, King George II gave the land between the Savannah and Altamaha Rivers to twenty-one trustees appointed to govern the Province of Georgia, named in honor of the king. In two respects, Georgia was unique among the colonies: it was to provide a military buffer against Spanish Florida and also to serve as a social experiment bringing together settlers from different countries and religions, many of them refugees, debtors, or members of the "worthy poor." General James E. Oglethorpe, a prominent member of Parliament, was appointed to head the colony.

In 1733, a band of about 120 colonists founded Savannah on the Atlantic coast near the mouth of the Savannah River. Carefully laid out by Oglethorpe, the old town, with its geometric pattern of crisscrossing roads graced by numerous parks, remains a wonderful example of city planning. Protestant refugees from Austria began to arrive in 1734, followed by Germans and German-speaking Moravians and Swiss, who for a time made the colony more German than English. The addition of Welsh, Highland Scots, Sephardic Jews, and others gave the early colony a diverse character like that of Charleston, South Carolina.

As a buffer against Spanish Florida, the Georgia colony succeeded, but as a social experiment creating a "common man's utopia," it failed. Initially, landholdings were limited to 500 acres in order to promote economic equality. Rum was banned, and the importation of slaves was forbidden. But the idealistic rules soon collapsed as the colony struggled to

Savannah, Georgia The earliest known view of Savannah, Georgia (1734). The town's layout was carefully planned.

become self-sufficient. The regulations against rum and slavery were widely disregarded and finally abandoned. By 1759, all restrictions on land-holding had been removed.

In 1754, Georgia became a royal colony. It developed slowly over the next decade but grew rapidly in population and wealth after 1763. Georgians exported rice, lumber, beef, and pork, and they carried on a lively trade with the islands in the West Indies. Almost unintentionally, the colony had become an economic success and a slave-centered society.

Native Peoples and English Settlers

CORE **OBJECTIVE**

3. Analyze the ways by which English colonists and Native Americans adapted to each other's presence.

The process of creating English colonies in America did not occur in a vacuum: the Native Americans played a crucial role in their development. Most English colonists adopted a strategy for dealing with the Indians quite different from that of the French and the Dutch. Merchants from France and the Netherlands focused on exploiting the profitable fur trade. The thriving commerce in animal skins—especially beaver, otter, and deer—helped spur exploration of the vast American continent. It also enriched and devastated the lives of Indians. To get fur pelts from the Indians, the French and Dutch built trading outposts in upper New York and along the Great Lakes, where they established friendly relations with the Hurons, Algonquins, and other Indians in the region, who greatly outnumbered them. The Hurons and Algonquins also sought French support in their ongoing wars with the mighty Iroquois Nations. In contrast to the French experience in Canada, the English colonists were more interested in pursuing their "God-given" right to hunt and farm on Indian lands and fish in Indian waters.

Food and Land

The English settled along the Atlantic seaboard, where Indian populations were much smaller than those in Mexico or the islands in the Caribbean. Moreover, the various native peoples of North America were fragmented, often fighting among themselves over disputed land. There was no powerful Aztec or Inca Empire to conquer and exploit. In most cases, the English colonists established their own separate communities near Indian villages.

The Jamestown settlers, for example, had come to America expecting to find gold, friendly Indians, and easy living. Most did not know how to exploit the area's abundant game and fish. When some of the starving Jamestown residents tried to steal food from nearby Indian villages, the Indians ambushed and killed them. John Ratcliffe, the initial leader, was captured and skinned alive by women using oyster shells, then burned. Only the effective leadership of John Smith and timely trade with the Indians, who taught the

Agricultural exchanges

EUROPEAN SETTLEMENTS AND INDIAN TRIBES IN EARLY AMERICA

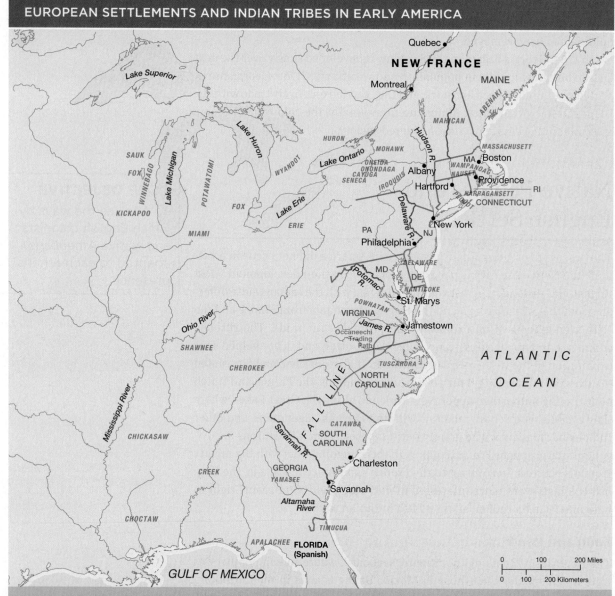

■ Why did European settlement lead to the expansion of hostilities among the Indians?

■ What were the consequences of the trade and commerce between the English settlers and the southern indigenous peoples?

■ How were the relationships between the settlers and the members of the Iroquois League different from those between settlers and tribes in other regions?

ill-prepared colonists to grow corn, enabled a remnant of the original colonists to survive. The short, stocky Smith, a seasoned soldier-for-hire, had himself been wounded in another battle and narrowly escaped execution when the young Indian princess known as Pocahontas convinced the warriors to exchange the Englishman for muskets, hatchets, beads, and trinkets.

Thereafter, the Native Americans around Jamestown fluctuated between exchanging goods with the English and trying to kill them.

By 1616, the discovery that tobacco flourished in Virginia intensified the settlers' lust for more land. English tobacco planters especially coveted the fields already cultivated by Indians because they had already been cleared and were ready to be planted. In 1622, the Indians tried to repel the land-grabbing English. As reported by Captain Smith, the "wild, naked natives" attacked twenty-eight farms and plantations along the James River, "not sparing either age or sex, man, woman, or childe," and killing a fourth of the settlers. Houses were burned, crops destroyed, equipment wrecked, and animals killed or scattered. The English retaliated by decimating the Indian peoples of Virginia. Smith said they were determined to "force the Savages to leave their Country or bring them in . . . fear and subjection."

> Battles over Indian lands

The Indian peoples of the Chesapeake region were dominated by the **Powhatan Confederacy**. Powhatan was the name for the supreme chief of several hundred villages (of about a hundred people each) organized into thirty chiefdoms in eastern Virginia. At the time, the Powhatan Confederacy may have been the most powerful group of native peoples along the entire Atlantic coast. Largely agricultural people focused on raising corn, they lived in oval-shaped houses framed with bent saplings and covered with bark or mats. Chief Powhatan (his proper name was Wahunsenacawh) forced the rival peoples he had conquered to give him most of their corn. He also traded with the English colonists, exchanging corn and hides for hatchets, swords, and muskets. But he realized too late that the newcomers wanted more than corn; they planned to seize his lands and enslave his people.

Bacon's Rebellion

The relentless stream of new settlers into Virginia exerted constant pressure on Indian lands and produced growing tensions. The largest planters bought up the most fertile land along the coast and rivers, forcing freed servants to become farm workers or try to claim less-fertile land inland. In either case, these landless farmers found themselves at a disadvantage. By 1676, a fourth of the free white men in Virginia were landless. They were forced to roam the countryside, squatting on private property, working at odd jobs, poaching game, or committing other petty crimes to survive.

> Intensified conflict with Indians

In the mid-1670s, simmering tensions caused by falling tobacco prices, rising taxes, and crowds of freed servants greedily eyeing Indian lands contributed to the tangled events that came to be called **Bacon's Rebellion**. The royal governor, William Berkeley, noted that "poor, indebted, discontented, and armed" Virginia colonists were ripe for rebellion. The discontent erupted when a squabble between a white planter and native people on the Potomac River led to the murder of the planter's herdsman and, in turn, to retaliation by frontier vigilantes, who killed some two dozen Indians. Frontiersmen then murdered five native chieftains who had sought to negotiate. Enraged Indians took revenge on frontier settlements. Scattered attacks continued

Powhatan Confederacy
An alliance of several powerful Algonquian tribes under the leadership of Chief Powhatan, organized into thirty chiefdoms along much of the Atlantic coast in the late sixteenth and early seventeenth centuries.

Bacon's Rebellion (1676)
Unsuccessful revolt led by planter Nathaniel Bacon against Virginia governor William Berkeley's administration, which, Bacon charged, had failed to protect settlers from Indian raids.

STRANGE NEWS

FROM

VIRGINIA;

Being a full and true

ACCOUNT

OF THE

LIFE and DEATH

OF

Nathanael Bacon Efquire,

Who was the only Caufe and Original of all the late
Troubles in that COUNTRY.

With a full Relation of all the Accidents which have
happened in the late War there between the
Chriftians and Indians.

LONDON,
Printed for *William Harris*, next door to the Turn-
Stile without *Moor-gate.* 1677.

News of the Rebellion A pamphlet printed in London provided details about Bacon's Rebellion.

Religious conversion and land confiscation

southward to the James River, where Nathaniel Bacon's farm manager was killed. In 1676, when Berkeley refused to take action against the Indian raiders, Bacon defied the governor's authority by assuming command of a group determined to terrorize the "protected and darling Indians." Bacon said he would kill all the Indians in Virginia.

The twenty-nine-year-old Bacon, a graduate of Cambridge University, had been in Virginia only two years. The rebellion he led quickly became a battle of landless servants, small farmers, and even slaves against Virginia's wealthiest planters and political leaders. But Bacon was also the spoiled son of a rich family with a talent for trouble. His ruthless assaults against peaceful Indians and his greed for power and land rather than any commitment to democratic principles sparked his conflict with the governing authorities and the planter elite.

For his part, Governor Berkeley opposed Bacon's plan to destroy the Indians not because he liked Native Americans but because he didn't want to disrupt the profitable deerskin trade with the Indians. Bacon, whose ragtag "army" now numbered in the hundreds, issued a "Declaration of the People of Virginia" accusing Berkeley of corruption and attempted to take the governor into custody. Berkeley's forces resisted—feebly—and Bacon's men burned Jamestown in frustration. Bacon, however, could not celebrate the victory long; he fell ill and died a month later. With Bacon dead, his rebellion gradually disintegrated. Governor Berkeley had twenty-three of the rebels hanged. For such severity, the king denounced Berkeley as a "fool" and recalled him to England, where he died within a year.

Native Americans and Christianity

In the spring of 1621 the Pilgrims in Plymouth were struggling with hunger and disease, just as the Jamestown settlers had before them. And as was true in Virginia, Indian peoples were crucial to their survival. Nevertheless, once they were established the New England Puritans aggressively tried to convert Native Americans to Christianity and "civilized" living. They insisted that Indian converts abandon their religions and languages, their clothes, long hair, names, and villages, forcing them to move to what were called "praying towns" to separate them from their "heathen" brethren.

One reason that Roger Williams of Rhode Island was considered so radical by the Puritan leaders was his insistence that all faiths—including those of the Indians—should be treated equally. He labeled efforts by governments to impose Puritanism on everyone "soul rape."

The relations between the Indians and the Quakers in Pennsylvania were friendly from the beginning, in part because of William Penn's careful policy of purchasing land titles from the Native Americans rather than simply seizing their lands. Penn, like Roger Williams, also took the trouble to learn the

Algonquian ceremony celebrating harvest As with most Native Americans, the Algonquians' dependence on nature for survival shaped their religious beliefs.

local Indian language, something few colonists ever attempted. For some fifty years, the Pennsylvania settlers and the neighboring Indian peoples lived in peace.

The Pequot War

Generally, Indians in the English colonies who fought to keep their lands were forced out. In 1636, settlers in Massachusetts accused a Pequot of murdering a colonist; they took revenge by setting fire to a Pequot village. As the Indians fled the flames, the Puritans killed them—men, women, and children. The militia commander declared that God had guided his actions "to smite our Enemies . . . and give us their land for an Inheritance." Sassacus, the Pequot chief, organized the survivors and counterattacked. During the ensuing Pequot War of 1637, the colonists and their Narragansett allies killed hundreds of Pequots in their village near West Mystic, in the Connecticut Valley. Under the terms of the Treaty of Hartford (1638), the Pequot Nation was dissolved. Only a few colonists regretted the massacre. Roger Williams warned that the lust for land would become "as great a God with us English as Gold was a God with the Spanish."

> The Pequot Nation destroyed

King Philip's War

After the Pequot War, relations between colonists and Indians improved somewhat, but the continuing influx of English settlers and the decline of the beaver population eventually reduced the Native Americans to poverty. By 1675, the Indians and English settlers had come to fear each other deeply.

> Bloody war between Puritans and Wampanoags

King Philip's War A 1772 engraving by Paul Revere depicts Metacomet (King Philip), leader of the Wampanoags.

The era of peaceful coexistence came to a bloody end during the last quarter of the seventeenth century. Native American leaders, especially the chief of the Wampanoags, Metacomet (known to the colonists as King Philip), resented the English efforts to convert Indians to Christianity. In the fall of 1674, John Sassamon, a Christian Indian who had graduated from Harvard College, warned the English that the Wampanoags were preparing for war. A few months later, Sassamon was found dead in a frozen pond. Colonial authorities convicted three Wampanoags of murder and hanged them. Enraged Wampanoag warriors then burned Puritan farms on June 20, 1675. Three days later, an Englishman shot a Wampanoag, and the Wampanoags retaliated by ambushing and beheading a group of Puritans.

The gruesome violence soon spun out of control. Both sides suffered severe losses in what came to be called **King Philip's War**, or Metacomet's War. The brutal fighting killed more people and caused more destruction in New England in proportion to the population than any American conflict since. Vengeful bands of warriors destroyed fifty towns while killing and mutilating hundreds of men, women, and children. Atrocities occurred on both sides. And Indians fought on both sides.

Within a year, the Narragansetts, after suffering a surprise attack by colonists that killed 300 warriors and 400 women and children, retaliated by destroying Providence, Rhode Island, and were threatening Boston itself, prompting a prominent minister to call this "the saddest time with New England that was ever known." The situation grew so desperate that the colonies passed America's first conscription laws, drafting into the militia all males between the ages of sixteen and sixty.

In the end, staggering casualties as well as shortages of food and ammunition wore down the Indians. Some surrendered, many succumbed to disease, and others fled to the west. Those who remained were forced to move to villages supervised by English officials. Metacomet initially escaped, only to be hunted down and killed. The victorious colonists marched his severed head to Plymouth, where it was displayed atop a pole for twenty years, a gruesome reminder of the English determination to ensure their dominance over Native Americans, once and for all.

Enslaving Indians in Carolina

King Philip's War (1675–1678) A war in New England resulting from the escalation of tensions between Native Americans and English settlers; the defeat of the Native Americans led to broadened freedoms for the settlers and their dispossessing the region's Native Americans of most of their land.

The quickest way to raise money in the early years of Carolina's development was through trade with Indians, not unlike what the French were doing in Canada. In the late seventeenth century, English merchants began traveling southward from Virginia into the Piedmont region of Carolina, where they developed a prosperous trade with the Catawba Indians. By 1690, traders from Charles Town had made their way up the Savannah River to arrange deals with the Cherokees, Creeks, and Chickasaws. Between 1699 and 1715, Carolina exported to England an average of 54,000 deerskins per year. Europeans, in turn, transformed the valuable hides into leather gloves, belts, hats, work aprons, and book bindings. The growing trade in deerskins entwined

Indians in a dependent relationship with Europeans that would prove disastrous to their traditional way of life. Beyond capturing and enslaving Indians, English traders began providing them with goods, firearms, and rum as payment for their capturing rivals to be sold as slaves.

The eight English proprietors of Carolina, meanwhile, wanted the colony to focus on producing the most profitable crops. Such production took time to develop, however. Land had to be cleared and then crops planted, harvested, transported, and sold. These activities required laborers. Some Carolina planters had brought enslaved Africans and white servants with them from the English-controlled islands in the West Indies, but slaves and servants were expensive to purchase and support.

Native American slave traders

The profitability of captive Indian workers, on the other hand, prompted a frenzy of slaving activity among English settlers. As many as 50,000 Indians, most of them women and children, were sold as slaves in Charles Town between 1670 and 1715. More enslaved Indians were exported during that period than Africans were imported, and thousands more captured Indians were sold to "slavers" who took them to islands in the West Indies through New England ports. The growing trade in enslaved Indians triggered bitter struggles between rival nations, ignited unprecedented colonial warfare, and generated massive internal migrations across the southern colonies.

The Iroquois League

One of the most significant effects of European settlement in North America during the seventeenth century was the intensification of warfare among Indians. The same combination of forces that wiped out the Indian populations of New England and the Carolinas affected the native peoples around New York City and the lower Hudson Valley. The inability of various Indian groups to unite against the Europeans, as well as their vulnerability to infectious diseases, doomed them to conquest and exploitation.

Iroquois relations with French and English

In the interior of New York, however, a different situation arose. There, sometime before 1600, the Iroquois Nations had forged an alliance so strong that the outnumbered Dutch and, later, English traders were forced to work with them in order to acquire beaver pelts. By the early seventeenth century, some fifty sachems (chiefs) governed the 12,000 members of the **Iroquois League**, known to its members as the *Haudenosaunee*. Its capital was Onondaga, a bustling town a few miles south of what later became Syracuse, New York.

The League was governed by a remarkable constitution, called the Great Law of Peace, which had three main principles: peace, equity, and justice. Each person was to be a shareholder in the wealth or poverty of the nation. The constitution established a Great Council of fifty male *royaneh* (religious-political leaders), each representing one of the female-led clans of the Iroquois Nations. The Great Law of Peace gave essential power to the people. It insisted that every time the *royaneh* dealt with "an especially important matter or a great emergency," they had to "submit the matter to the decision of their people," both men and women, for their consent.

Iroquois League An alliance of the Iroquois Nations, originally formed sometime between 1450 and 1600, that used their combined strength to pressure Europeans to work with them in the fur trade and to wage war across what is today eastern North America.

Wampum belt Woven to certify treaties or record transactions, the white squares likely denote nations and alliances, while the purple often conveys apprehension.

The search for furs and captives led Iroquois war parties to range widely across what is today eastern North America. They gained control over a huge area from the St. Lawrence River south to Tennessee and from Maine west to Michigan. For more than twenty years, warfare raged across the Great Lakes region between the Iroquois (supported by Dutch and English fur traders) and the Algonquians and Hurons (and their French allies). In the 1690s, the French and their Indian allies destroyed Iroquois crops and villages, infected them with smallpox, and reduced the male population by more than a third.

Facing extermination, the Iroquois made peace with the French in 1701. During the first half of the eighteenth century, they stayed out of the struggle between the two rival European powers, which enabled them to play the English off against the French while creating a thriving fur trade for themselves.

CORE **OBJECTIVE**

4. Analyze the role of indentured servants and the development of slavery in colonial America.

Slavery and Servitude in the Colonies

Indentured Servitude

Indentured servitude solves labor shortage

During the seventeenth century, the English colonies, especially Virginia and Maryland along the Chesapeake Bay, grew so fast that they needed more workers than there were settlers. As early as 1619, the connection between growing tobacco and the need for laborers was clear. If "all our riches for the present do consist in Tobacco," explained a Jamestown planter, then it followed that "our principal wealth . . . consisteth in servants." The colonies needed what another planter called "lusty laboring men . . . capable of hard labor, and that can bear and undergo heat and cold."

indentured servant Settler who signed on for a temporary period of servitude to a master in exchange for passage to the New World.

To solve the labor shortage, the planters at first recruited **indentured servants** from England, Ireland, Scotland, and continental Europe. The term derived from the *indenture*, or contract, which enabled a person to pay for passage to America by promising to work for a fixed number of years (usually between three and seven). As tobacco production soared during the seventeenth century, indentured servants did most of the work. Of the 500,000 English immigrants to America from 1610 to 1775, 350,000 came as indentured servants, most of them Protestants. Not all the servants went voluntarily. Many homeless children in London were "kidnapped" into servitude in America. In addition, Parliament in 1717 declared that convicts could avoid the hangman by relocating to the colonies.

Once in the colonies, servants were provided food and a bed by their employer, but their rights were limited. As a Pennsylvania judge explained in 1793, indentured servants occupied "a middle rank between slaves and free men." They could own property but could not engage in trade. Marriage required the master's permission. Masters could whip servants and extend their length of service for bad behavior. Once the indenture ended, usually after four to seven years, the servant could claim the "freedom dues" set by custom and law: money, tools, clothing, food, and occasionally small tracts of land. Indeed, some former servants did very well for themselves. In 1629, seven members of the Virginia legislature were former indentured servants. Such opportunities for servants to assume leading roles in society were much less common in England or Europe, giving people even more reasons to opt for America.

Indentured servants An advertisement from the *Virginia Gazette*, October 4, 1779, for indentured servants.

Slavery in North America

In 1700 there were enslaved Africans in every one of the American colonies, and they made up 11 percent of the total population (slaves would comprise more than 20 percent by 1770). But slavery in English North America differed greatly from region to region. Africans were a tiny minority in New England (about 2 percent). Because there were no large plantations in New England and fewer slaves were owned, "family slavery" prevailed, with masters and slaves usually living under the same roof.

Slavery was much more prevalent in the Chesapeake colonies and the Carolinas, where the economy was increasingly dominated by large plantations. By 1730, the black slave population in Virginia and Maryland had become the first in the Western Hemisphere to achieve a self-sustaining rate of population growth. By 1750 about 80 percent of the slaves in the Chesapeake region, for example, had been born there.

Growth of slavery in the colonies

African Roots

The transport of African captives, mostly young, across the Atlantic to the Americas was the largest forced migration in world history. Over ten million people eventually made the terrifying journey, the vast majority of whom were taken to Brazil or the Caribbean sugar islands.

Enslaved Africans came from very different places in Africa, spoke as many as fifty different languages, and worshipped many different gods. Some had lived in large kingdoms and others in dispersed villages. Africans had preyed upon other Africans for centuries. Warfare was constant, as rival tribes conquered, kidnapped, enslaved, and sold one another. Slavery in Africa, however, was less brutal than the culture of race-based slavery that developed in the Americas. In Africa, slaves lived with their captors, and their

Different Beginnings, Common Trends: The English Colonies in North America, 1600–1700

The English government oversaw the development of numerous colonies on the Atlantic seaboard of North America in the seventeenth century. By 1700, most of the English colonies were attracting a diverse European population, had eliminated Native American threats to their domain (often through violence), were growing an export trade to other regions in the Atlantic World, and had developed self-governing traditions including elected legislative assemblies. The English colonies were the most prosperous, powerful, and populous region of the continent. Yet, they were a diverse lot.

THE FIRST COLONIES

	Chesapeake Colonies: Virginia and Maryland	New England Colonies: Plymouth, Massachusetts Bay, Rhode Island, Connecticut, New Hampshire	Carolina Colonies and Georgia: North and South Carolina	Middle Colonies: New York, Pennsylvania, New Jersey, Delaware, Georgia
Foundation and Government	Virginia was originally a joint-stock company with an elected assembly; it later became a royal colony. Maryland was the first proprietary colony.	Plymouth Puritans at first were independent, but later absorbed into Massachusetts Bay, a joint-stock company, royally chartered as a self-governing entity with legislative bodies elected by church members.	Proprietorships that later became royal colonies	Proprietorships
Religion	Virginia was officially Anglican. Catholic Maryland also welcomed Protestants.	Puritan New England did not tolerate dissent, but Rhode Island challenged Puritan control as the first colony to establish freedom of religion.	Carolina colonies tolerated many religious communities.	New York inherited a diverse religious community from the previous New Netherland colony. Quaker Pennsylvania also welcomed other religious groups.

	Chesapeake Colonies	New England Colonies	Carolina Colonies and Georgia	Middle Colonies
Economy and Trade	The region primarily cultivated tobacco, using indentured servants and, increasingly, African slaves, who were also exported to England.	New England colonists thrived as small farmers, merchants, seamen, and fishermen.	Colonists brought slaves from the West Indies and created rice plantations. Early on, Carolinians profited from lumber, deerskin trade, and Native American slave trade. Georgia exported rice, lumber, beef, and pork, traded with the West Indies, and became a slave-centered society.	Middle colonists exported furs secured through trade with Native Americans. Many small farmers emerged as well.
Relations with Indians	English colonists traded with the Indians for furs, but also fought several bloody wars with Indians to gain more land for English settlers.	Colonists tried to convert Indians to Christianity without assimilating them into their society. When Indians showed resistance, colonists used force to gain control of Indian lands and to remove them from the region.	The Indian slave trade decimated much of the Indian population, led to devastating wars among various societies, and generated massive internal migrations.	The Pennsylvania government sought peaceful relations with Indians through legally purchased land titles. The Iroquois League maintained its independence from English and French domination in northern New York.

QUESTIONS FOR ANALYSIS

1. Which colonies were founded by joint-stock companies? Which were founded by proprietors? How were the others founded? How did this contribute to self-rule in the colonies?

2. What were the religious distinctions among the colonies? Which colonies were more religiously tolerant than others?

3. Which colonies were more involved with slavery and why? What were the main exports of the different slave-centered regions? What characterized the economies of the other colonies?

4. Which colonies had better relations with Indians?

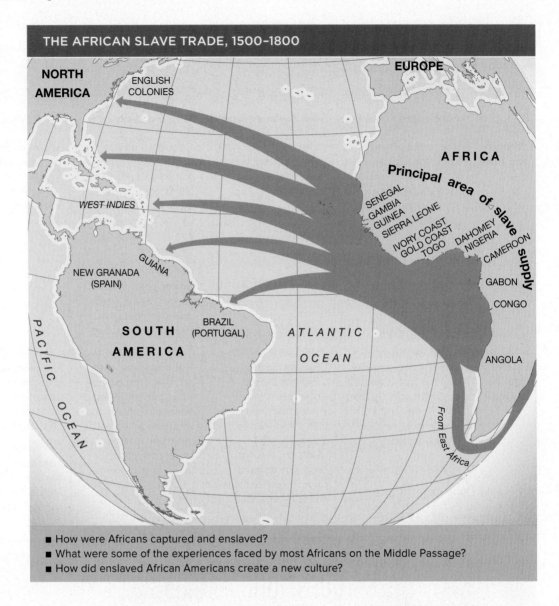

THE AFRICAN SLAVE TRADE, 1500–1800

■ How were Africans captured and enslaved?
■ What were some of the experiences faced by most Africans on the Middle Passage?
■ How did enslaved African Americans create a new culture?

Middle Passage The hellish and often deadly middle leg of the transatlantic "triangular trade" in which European ships carried manufactured goods to Africa, then transported enslaved Africans to the Americas and the Caribbean, and finally conveyed American agricultural products back to Europe.

children were not automatically enslaved. The involvement of Europeans in transatlantic slavery, whereby captives were sold and shipped to other nations, was much worse.

During the seventeenth and eighteenth centuries, African slave traders brought captives to dozens of "slave forts" along the West African coast, where they were sold to European slave traders. Once purchased, the millions of people destined for slavery in the Americas were branded on the back or buttocks with a company mark, chained, and loaded onto horrific slave ships, most of them British-owned, where they were packed as tightly as livestock in the constant darkness below deck. They then were subjected to a four-week to six-month transatlantic voyage, known as the **Middle Passage** (because it was the middle leg of the so-called "triangular trade" that carried European manufactures to Africa, African slaves to America, and American produce and lumber to Europe). One in six captives died along the way. Almost one in every ten of these floating prisons experienced a revolt during the crossing. Some captives committed suicide by jumping off the ships. Yet many of the whites engaged in slave trafficking considered their work highly respectable. "What a glorious and advantageous trade this is," wrote James Houston, who worked for a slave-trading firm. "It is the hinge on which all the trade of this globe moves."

The rapid growth of slavery in the Western Hemisphere was driven by high profits and justified by a widespread racism that viewed Africans as beasts of burden rather than human beings. Once in America, Africans were treated as property ("chattel"), herded in chains to public slave auctions, and sold to the highest bidder. Once purchased, their most common roles were to cook and clean, care for the owner's babies and children, dig ditches, drain swamps, clear, plant, and tend fields, and feed livestock. On large southern plantations that grew tobacco, sugar cane, or rice, groups of slaves were organized into work "gangs" supervised by black "drivers" and white overseers. The slaves were often quartered in barracks, fed like livestock, and issued ill-fitting work clothes and shoes so uncomfortable that many slaves preferred to go barefoot. Colonial laws allowed whites to use brutal means to discipline slaves. They were whipped, branded, shackled, castrated, or sold away, often to the Caribbean islands, where few survived the brutal working conditions of harvesting sugar cane.

> High profits and widespread racism

Slave ship One in six Africans died while crossing the Atlantic in ships like this one, from an American diagram ca. 1808.

African cultural heritage in the South The survival of African culture among enslaved Americans is evident in this late-eighteenth-century painting of a South Carolina plantation. The musical instruments and pottery are of African (probably Yoruban) origin.

Slave resistance

Enslaved Africans, however, found ingenious ways to resist being "mastered." Some rebelled against their captors by resisting work orders, sabotaging crops and stealing tools, faking illness or injury, or running away. If caught, runaways faced certain punishment—whipping, branding, and even the severing of an Achilles tendon. Runaways also faced uncertain freedom. Where would black runaways run *to* in a society ruled by whites and governed by racism?

Slave Culture

African and American cultural exchange

Africans who were transported to America brought with them powerful kinship ties. Even though most colonies outlawed slave marriages, many whites believed that slaves would work harder and be more stable if they were allowed to form families. Though families were often broken up when members were sold to different owners, slave culture retained its powerful sense of domestic ties. It also developed gender roles distinct from those of white society. Most enslaved women were field workers as well as wives and mothers responsible for child-rearing and household affairs.

In the process of being forced into lives of bondage in a new world, Africans from diverse homelands forged a new identity as African Americans. At the same time, they wove into American culture many strands of their African heritage, including new words that entered the language, such as *tabby*, *tote*, *goober*, *yam*, and *banana*, as well as the names of the Coosaw, Pee

Dee, and Wando Rivers in South Carolina. More significant are African influences upon American music, folklore, and religious practices. Slaves often used songs, stories, and religious preachings to circulate coded messages expressing their distaste for masters or overseers. The fundamental theme of slave religion, adapted from the Christianity that was forced upon them, was deliverance: God would eventually free African Americans and open the gates to heaven's promised land.

Thriving Colonies

CORE **OBJECTIVE**
5. Explain how the English colonies became the most populous, prosperous, and powerful region in North America by 1700.

By the early eighteenth century, the English colonies in the New World had outstripped those of both the French and the Spanish as tensions among the three major European powers grew. English America, both the mainland colonies and those in the Caribbean, had become the most populous, prosperous, and powerful of the European empires. American colonists were better fed, clothed, and housed than their counterparts in Europe, where a majority of the people lived in landless poverty. But the English colonization of North America included failures as well as successes. Many settlers found hard labor, desperation, and an early death in the New World. Others flourished only because they were able to exploit Indians, indentured servants, or Africans.

The English created self-governing and profitable American colonies because of crucial advantages they had over their European rivals. The tightly controlled colonial empires created by the monarchs of Spain and France stifled innovation. By contrast, the English organized colonies as profit-making enterprises with a minimum of royal control. Where New Spain was dominated by wealthy men who controlled vast estates and often intended to return to Spain, many English colonists ventured to America because, for them, life in England was intolerable. The leaders of the Dutch and non-Puritan English colonies, unlike their rivals the Spanish and French, welcomed people from a variety of nationalities and religions who came in search of a new life. Perhaps most important, the English colonies enjoyed a greater degree of self-government, which made them more dynamic and creative than their French and Spanish counterparts.

Organized for profit and self-governing, with widespread land ownership

Throughout the seventeenth century, geography reinforced England's emphasis on the concentrated settlements of its colonies. No one great river offered a highway to the interior. The farthest western expansion of English settlement stopped at the eastern slopes of the Appalachian Mountains. To the east lay the wide expanse of ocean, which served not only as a highway for the transport of people, ideas, commerce, and ways of life from Europe to America, but also as a barrier that separated old ideas from new, allowing the English colonies to evolve in a "new world"—while developing new ideas about economic freedom and political liberties that would flower later in the eighteenth century.

■ **English Background** England's colonization of North America differed from that of its European rivals and reflected its unique traditions and developments in the seventeenth century. While chartered by the Crown, English colonization was funded by *joint-stock companies* or groups of proprietors eager for profits derived from the productive activity of English settlers. Their colonial organization and governments reflected the governmental model of a two-house *Parliament* and long-held English views on civil liberties and representative institutions. The colonization of the eastern seaboard of North America occurred at a time of religious and political turmoil in England, strongly affecting colonial culture and development.

■ **English Settlers and Colonization** The early years of Jamestown and Plymouth were grim. The Virginia Company used the *headright* system of granting fifty acres to any Englishmen who bought passage, and in time *tobacco* flourished but this success also laid down roots for a slave-based economy in the South. Sugar, and later rice, plantations developed in the proprietary *Carolina colonies*, which operated with minimal royal intrusion. Family farms and a mixed economy characterized the middle and New England colonies. Religion was the primary motivation for the founding of several colonies. *Puritans* drafted the *Mayflower Compact* and founded *Massachusetts Bay Colony* as a Christian commonwealth outside the structure of the English government and the Anglican Church. Rhode Island was established by Roger Williams, a religious dissenter from Massachusetts. Maryland was founded as a refuge for English Catholics. William Penn, a Quaker, founded Pennsylvania and invited Europe's persecuted religious sects to his colony. The Dutch, with their policy of toleration, allowed members of all faiths to settle in *New Netherland*, but commercial rivalry between the Dutch and the English led to war, during which the Dutch colony of *New Netherland* surrendered to the English in 1664.

■ **Indian Relations** Settler–Indian relations were complex. Trade with the *Powhatan Confederacy* in Virginia enabled Jamestown to survive its early years, but brutal armed conflicts such as *Bacon's Rebellion* occurred as settlers invaded Indian lands. Puritans retaliated harshly against Indian resistance in the Pequot War of 1637 and in *King Philip's War* from 1675 to 1676. Among the chief colonial leaders, only Roger Williams and William Penn treated Indians as equals. The powerful *Iroquois League* played the European powers against each other to control territories from Tennessee into Canada.

■ **Indentured Servants and Slaves** The colonies increasingly relied on *indentured servants* for their labor supply. European immigrants looking for a better life could pay for passage to America by signing contracts (indentures) that required them to work for several years upon arriving in America. By the end of the seventeenth century, enslaved Africans had replaced indentured servants as the primary form of labor to produce tobacco in the Chesapeake. The demand for slaves in the sugar plantations of the West Indies drove European slave traders to organize the transport of Africans via the dreaded *Middle Passage* across the Atlantic. With the supply of slaves seemingly inexhaustible, the Carolinas soon adopted African slavery to cultivate rice. African cultures fused with others in the Americas to create a native-born African American culture.

■ **Thriving English Colonies** By 1700, England had become a great trading empire. English America was the most populous and prosperous region of North America. Minimal royal interference in the proprietary for-profit colonies and widespread landownership encouraged settlers to put down roots for a sustainable future. Religious diversity attracted a variety of investors. By relying increasingly on slave labor, the southern colonies provided England with tobacco and other plantation crops.

KEY TERMS

CHRONOLOGY

1603	James I takes the throne of England
1607	The Virginia Company establishes Jamestown, the first permanent English colony
1612	John Rolfe begins growing tobacco for export in Virginia
1614	The Dutch charter the New Netherland Company
1619	First Africans arrive in English America
1620	The Plymouth colony is founded by Pilgrims; Pilgrims agree to the Mayflower Compact
1622	War between Indians and colonists begins in Virginia
1630	Massachusetts Bay Colony is founded by Puritans
1634	Settlement of Maryland begins
1637	The Pequot War in New England
1642–1651	The English Civil War (Puritans vs. Royalists)
1649	The Toleration Act in Maryland
1660	Restoration of English monarchy
1669	Charles Town is founded in the Carolina Colony
1675–1676	King Philip's War in New England
1676	Bacon's Rebellion erupts in Virginia
1681	Pennsylvania is established
1733	Georgia is founded

INQUIZITIVE

Go to InQuizitive to see what you've learned—and learn what you've missed—with personalized feedback along the way.

THE ARTISANS OF BOSTON (1766) While fishing, shipbuilding, and maritime trade dominated New England economies, many young men entered apprenticeships under master craftsmen in the hopes of becoming blacksmiths, carpenters, gunsmiths, printers, candlemakers, leather tanners, and more.

Colonial Ways of Life

1607–1750

The process of carving a new civilization out of an abundant "New World" involved sometimes-violent encounters among European, African, and Indian cultures. Warfare, duplicity, displacement, and enslavement were often the tragic results. Yet on another level the process of transforming the American continent was not simply a story of conflict but also one of blending and accommodation, a story of diverse peoples and resilient cultures engaged in the everyday tasks of building homes, planting crops, trading goods, raising families, enforcing laws, and worshipping gods. Those who colonized America during the seventeenth and eighteenth centuries were part of a massive social migration occurring throughout Europe and Africa. Everywhere, it seemed, people were in motion—moving from farms to villages, from villages to cities, and from homelands to colonies.

People moved for various reasons. Most English and European settlers were responding to rapid population growth and the rise of commercial agriculture, which squeezed poor farm workers off the land. Many of the landless and jobless rural poor drifted into cities like London, Edinburgh, Dublin, and Paris, where they struggled to survive in growing urban ghettos. That most Europeans in the seventeenth and eighteenth centuries were desperately poor helps explain why so many were willing to risk their lives by migrating to the American colonies. Others journeyed to America in search of political security or

CORE
OBJECTIVES INQUIZITIVE

1. Explain the major factors that contributed to the demographic changes that took place in the English colonies during the eighteenth century.

2. Describe women's various roles in the English colonies.

3. Compare the societies and economies of the southern, middle, and New England colonies.

4. Describe the creation of race-based slavery during the seventeenth century and its impact on the social and economic development of colonial America.

5. Analyze the impact of the Enlightenment and Great Awakening on American thought.

religious freedom. A tragic exception was the Africans, who were captured and transported to new lands against their will.

Those who initially settled in colonial America were mostly young (more than half were under twenty-five years old), male, and poor. Almost half were servants or slaves, and during the eighteenth century, England would transport more than 50,000 convicts to the North American colonies as a way to relieve overcrowded jails and provide needed workers in the colonies. Only about a third of the settlers came with their families. Once in America, many of the newcomers kept moving within and across colonies in search of better lands or new business opportunities, such as trading with the native peoples who controlled the profitable fur trade. This extraordinary migration of adventurous people created many of America's enduring institutions and values, as well as its distinctive spirit and restless energy.

The Shape of Early America

CORE **OBJECTIVE**

1. Explain the major factors that contributed to the demographic changes that took place in the English colonies during the eighteenth century.

Population Growth

The early months and years of England's colonies in America exacted a fearsome toll: many in the first wave of settlement died of disease, starvation, or warfare with Native Americans. But once colonial life became more settled and secure, the colonies grew rapidly. On average, the American population doubled every twenty-five years during the colonial period. By 1750, the number of colonists had passed 1 million; by 1775, it approached 2.5 million. By comparison, the combined population of England, Scotland, and Ireland in 1750 was 6.5 million.

Plentiful land, scarce labor, and better living conditions

The extraordinary increase of the colonial population, explained Philadelphia's Benjamin Franklin, a keen observer of many things, resulted from two facts: land in America was plentiful and cheap, and laborers were scarce and expensive. The opposite conditions prevailed in Europe. There, the "enclosure movement" had led nobles—who had traditionally opened their estates to all farmers for common purposes, such as grazing animals—to fence their lands and focus on large-scale commercial ("cash") crops and herds, such as sheep. Many surrounding landless farmers were thus displaced, creating widespread unemployment, homelessness, and starvation. As a result, America's plentiful lands lured migrants eager to have their own farms. Once in the colonies, the settlers tended to have large families, in part because farm children could lend a hand in the fields; once grown, they could find new land for themselves, if need be.

Birth and Death Rates

Rapid population growth

Colonists tended to marry and start families at an earlier age than in Europe. In England, the average age at marriage for women was twenty-six; in America, it dropped to twenty. Men in the colonies also married at a younger age. The **birth rate** rose accordingly, since women who married younger had time for about two additional pregnancies during their childbearing years.

Equally responsible for the fast-growing colonial population was a much lower **death rate** than that in Europe. By the middle of the seventeenth century, infants had a better chance of reaching maturity in New England than in England, and adults lived longer in the colonies. Lower mortality rates in the colonies resulted from several factors. Since fertile land was plentiful, famine seldom occurred after the early years of colonization, and, although the winters were more severe than in England, firewood was abundant. Being younger—the average age in 1790 was sixteen—Americans on the whole were less susceptible to disease than were Europeans. That they were more scattered than in Europe also meant they were less exposed to infectious diseases. That began to change as colonial cities grew larger and more dense. By the mid–eighteenth century, the colonies experienced levels of disease much like those in the cities of Europe.

Colonial farm This plan of a newly cleared American farm shows how trees were cut down with axes and the stumps left to rot.

"Women's Work" in the Colonies

CORE **OBJECTIVE**
2. Describe women's various roles in the English colonies.

In contrast to the colonies of New Spain and New France, English America had far more women, which largely explains the difference in population growth rates among the European empires competing in the Americas. But higher numbers of women did not mean greater equality. Most European colonists brought to America deeply rooted convictions about the inferiority of women. As one New England minister stressed, "the woman is a weak creature not endowed with [the] strength and constancy of mind [of men]." Women, as had been true for centuries, were expected to obey and serve their husbands, nurture their children, and do the hard daily work required to maintain their households ("domestic" life). Women in most colonies could not vote, hold office, attend schools or colleges, bring lawsuits, sign contracts, or become ministers.

In the eighteenth century, "**women's work**" typically involved activities in the house, garden, and fields. Yet the scarcity of workers in the colonies created new opportunities for women. In the towns, women commonly served as tavern hostesses and shopkeepers and occasionally also worked as doctors, printers, upholsterers, painters, and silversmiths. Often, these

birth rate Proportion of births per 1,000 of the total population.

death rate Proportion of deaths per 1,000 of the total population; also called *mortality rate*.

women's work Traditional term referring to routine tasks in the house, garden, and fields performed by women; eventually expanded in the colonies to include medicine, shopkeeping, upholstering, and the operation of inns and taverns.

The First, Second, and Last Scene of Mortality **(ca. 1776)** Prudence Punderston's needlework shows the domestic path, from cradle to coffin, followed by most colonial women.

women were widows carrying on their dead husbands' trade or business. Such working widows became accustomed to some measure of social authority in the "man's world" of eighteenth-century economic life.

One woman who exercised leadership outside the home was South Carolinian Elizabeth Lucas Pinckney (1722–1793). After her father, a British army officer, was called back to the Caribbean island of Antigua (where the family had come from), fifteen-year-old Eliza cared for her ailing mother and younger sister in Charleston, South Carolina, while managing three plantations worked by enslaved Africans. She decided to grow a West Indian plant called *indigo*, which provided a much-coveted blue dye for coloring fabric. Indigo made her family a fortune, as it did for many other plantation owners on the Carolina coast.

The shortage of women in the first years of colonial settlement at times made them more highly valued than they were in Europe. In addition, the Puritan emphasis on a well-ordered family life led to laws protecting wives from physical abuse and allowing for divorce. In addition, colonial laws gave wives greater control over the property they contributed to a marriage or that was left after a husband's death. But such exceptions did not change the basic status of women: the age-old notions of women being subordinate to men remained firmly entrenched in colonial America. As a boy in Massachusetts claimed in 1662, the superior aspect of life was "masculine and eternal; the feminine inferior and mortal."

> Overall inferior status but new opportunities and greater property rights for women under the law

Society and Economy in the Colonies

CORE **OBJECTIVE**
3. Compare the societies and economies of the southern, middle, and New England colonies.

In the early eighteenth century, England and Scotland merged. The Act of Union in 1707 announced a new name for the joint monarchies: Great Britain. Its colonies—now referred to as the British American colonies—were part of a complex North Atlantic commercial network, trading sugar, wheat, tobacco, rum, rice, and many other commodities, as well as African and Indian slaves, with Great Britain and its highly profitable island colonies in the West Indies such as Bermuda, Barbados, and Jamaica. In addition, American merchants also traded ("smuggled") with Spain, France, Portugal, Holland, and their colonies, which were often at war with Britain and therefore officially off limits to Americans. Out of necessity, the colonists were dependent on Britain and Europe for manufactured goods and luxury items such as wine, glass, and jewelry.

The colonies were blessed with abundant natural resources, but they struggled to find enough laborers for their rapidly expanding economy. The primary solution to the shortage of workers in the colonies was indentured servitude. This practice, whereby servants agreed to work for four to seven years in exchange for their "master" paying for their travel to America, accounted for probably half the white settlers (mostly from England, Ireland, Scotland, or Germany) in all the colonies outside New England. These unfree workers brought their own cultures to the regions where they lived, creating a diverse ethnic mix, especially in the southern and middle colonies. During the late seventeenth and eighteenth centuries, however, the southern colonies turned from using indentured servants to purchasing life-long Indian or African slaves to satisfy the growing demand for agricultural workers on vast tobacco and rice plantations.

A rapidly expanding economy

The Southern Colonies

Rising inequality and a slave-based economy in the South

As the southern colonies matured, inequalities of wealth became more visible and social life grew more divided by marked differences in status. The use of enslaved Indians and Africans to grow tobacco, sugar cane, rice, and indigo created enormous wealth for a few large landowners and their families. Socially, the planters and merchants increasingly became a class apart. They dominated the colonial legislatures, bought luxury goods from London and Paris, and built brick mansions with formal gardens like those in England—all the while looking down upon their social "inferiors," both white and black.

Warm weather and plentiful rainfall enabled the southern colonies to grow the **staple crops** (most profitable) valued by the mother country: tobacco, rice, sugar cane, and indigo. In the Chesapeake region of the Upper South, Virginia, as King Charles I put it, was "founded upon smoke." Tobacco

staple crop A profitable market crop, such as cotton, tobacco, or rice, that predominates in a given region.

Virginia plantation wharf Southern colonial plantations were often constructed along rivers, with easy access to oceangoing vessels, as shown on this 1730 tobacco label.

production soared during the seventeenth century. "In Virginia and Maryland," wrote a royal official in 1629, "tobacco . . . is our All, and indeed leaves no room for anything else." The same was true for rice cultivation along the South Carolina coast. Over time, the rice planters became the wealthiest group in the British colonies, forcing their slaves to "work for hours in mud and water." Using only hand tools, slaves transformed the landscape of coastal South Carolina and, eventually, Georgia, removing trees from swamps and wetlands infested with snakes, alligators, and mosquitos. They then created a system of floodgates to allow workers to drain or flood the rice fields as needed.

As plantations grew in size, the demand for enslaved laborers, first male Indians and later Africans, rose dramatically. Almost 90 percent of the Africans transported to the American mainland went to the southern colonies. South Carolina had a black majority throughout the eighteenth century. As one visitor observed, "Carolina looks more like a negro country than like a country settled by white people."

New England

New England townships

There was remarkable diversity among the American colonies during the seventeenth century and after. Few New England colonists, for example, owned huge tracts of land, as was common in Carolina, Virginia, Maryland, and Dutch New Netherland. In New England, settlers, often already gathered into a church congregation, would ask the general court for a township and then divide its acreage in roughly equal parcels: those who invested more or had larger families or greater status might receive more land. Over time, as the population grew, the land was divided into separate farms more distant from the original village.

Religion

Church and state

Whenever towns were founded, the first public structure built was usually a church. The New England Puritans believed that God had created a *covenant*, or contract, in which people formed a congregation for common worship. This led to the idea of people joining together to form governing bodies too, but "democracy" was not part of Puritan political thought.

Housing in colonial New England This frame house, built in the 1670s, belonged to Rebecca Nurse, one of the women hanged as a witch in Salem Village in 1692.

Puritan leaders sought to do the will of God, not to follow the will of the people, and the ultimate source of authority in Puritan New England was not majority rule but the Bible as interpreted by ministers and magistrates (political leaders). By law, every town had to collect taxes to support a church. And every resident—whether a church member or not—was required to attend midweek and Sunday religious services. The average New Englander heard 7,000 sermons in a lifetime.

Over time, Puritan New England experienced a gradual erosion of religious commitment. More and more children and grandchildren of the original "visible saints" could not give the required testimony of spiritual conversion. In 1662, a group of Boston ministers created the "Half-Way Covenant," whereby baptized children of church members could be admitted to a "halfway" membership, but they could neither vote in church nor take communion. A further blow to Puritan ideals came with the Massachusetts royal charter of 1691, which required toleration of religious dissenters (such as Quakers) and based the right to vote in public elections on property ownership rather than church membership.

The strains accompanying Massachusetts's transition from Puritan utopia to royal colony reached a tragic climax in the witchcraft hysteria at Salem Village (now the town of Danvers) in 1692. Belief in witchcraft was widespread throughout Europe and the colonies in the seventeenth century. Prior to the dramatic episode in Salem, almost 300 New Englanders (mostly middle-aged women) had been accused of practicing witchcraft, and more than 30 had been hanged.

The Salem episode was unique in its scope and intensity, however. During the winter of 1691–1692, several adolescent girls became fascinated with the fortune telling and voodoo practiced by Tituba, a West Indian slave. The

Salem witch trials

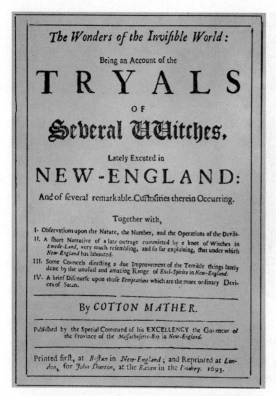

The Wonders of the Invisible World Title page of the 1693 London edition of Cotton Mather's account of the Salem witchcraft cases. Mather, a prominent Boston minister, warned his congregation that the devil's legions were assaulting New England.

entranced girls began to behave oddly—shouting, barking, crawling, and twitching for no apparent reason. When asked who was tormenting them, the girls claimed that three women—Tituba, Sarah Good, and Sarah Osborne—were Satan's servants. Authorities then arrested the three accused women. They were tried and two were hanged. Within a few months, the village jail was filled with townspeople—men, women, and children—all accused of practicing witchcraft. As the accusations multiplied, leaders of the Massachusetts Bay Colony began to worry that the witch hunts were out of control. The governor finally intervened when his own wife was accused of serving the devil. He disbanded the special court in Salem and ordered the remaining suspects released. Nineteen people had been hanged—all justified by the Biblical verse that tells believers not to "suffer a witch to live." More than 100 others had been jailed. A year after it had begun, the witchcraft frenzy was finally over.

What explains Salem's hysteria? It may have represented nothing more than theatrical adolescents trying to enliven the dreary routine of everyday life. Some historians have stressed that most of the accused witches were women, many of whom had in some way defied the traditional roles assigned to females. Still another interpretation suggests that the witchcraft accusations may have reflected the hysteria caused by frequent Indian attacks occurring just north of Salem, along New England's northern frontier. Whatever its actual causes, the witchcraft controversy reflected the peculiar social tensions of Salem Village. Nothing quite like it occurred anywhere else in the colonies.

Economy

Early New England farmers and their families led hard lives. Simply clearing the many rocks from the glacier-scoured soil might require sixty days of hard work per acre. The growing season was short, and, unlike in the southern colonies, no staple crops like tobacco or rice grew in the colder climate. The crops and livestock were those familiar to rural England: wheat, barley, and oats; cattle, pigs, and sheep.

Fishing and farming

Not all New England towns were founded as religious communities. In coastal towns, residents were often more devoted to catching fish and engaging in trade or operating taverns than worship. After a Puritan minister delivered his first sermon to a congregation in the port of Marblehead, a crusty fisherman scolded him for being so spiritual: "You think you are preaching to the people of the Bay. Our main end is to catch fish." Cod, a tasty fish that can weigh hundreds of pounds, had been a regular element of the European diet for centuries, and the waters off the New England coast had the heaviest concentrations of cod in the world. Whales, too, were numerous in New England waters and supplied oil for lighting and lubrication. The waters off New England, unlike the farms, supplied plenty of cod for export to Europe, with lesser grades of fish going to the West Indies as food for slaves. The fishing and whaling activities spurred shipbuilding, which in turn facilitated a profitable trade with Europe and other colonies.

The system of trade in New England and the middle colonies differed from that in the South in two respects: the lack of staple crops—tobacco, rice, and indigo—to exchange for English goods was a relative disadvantage, but New England's shipbuilding, fishing, and maritime trading were very profitable enterprises. After 1660, in order to protect England's own agricultural and fishing economies, the government in London placed high duties (taxes) on certain colonial exports— fish, flour, wheat, and meat—while leaving the door open to timber, furs, whale oil, tobacco, and indigo, products in great demand in the home country.

Profitable fisheries Fishing for, curing, and drying cod in Newfoundland in the early 1700s. The rich fishing grounds of the North Atlantic provided New Englanders with a prosperous industry for centuries.

The New England colonies eventually specialized in shipping goods to foreign markets through what came to be called the "**triangular trade**," in which New Englanders shipped rum to the west coast of Africa, where they exchanged it for slaves; ships then took the enslaved Africans to sell in the West Indies; they then returned home with various Caribbean commodities, including molasses, from which they manufactured more rum. In another version of the trading triangle, they shipped products such as meat and fish to the West Indies, where they acquired sugar and molasses, which they then transported to England, and returned to America with manufactured goods and luxury items from Britain and Europe.

The Middle Colonies

Both geographically and culturally, the middle colonies (New York, Pennsylvania, New Jersey, Delaware, and Maryland) stood between New England and the South, including aspects of both regions. As such, they more completely reflected the diversity of colonial life and more fully foreshadowed the pluralism of America.

The primary crops in the middle colonies were those of New England but more plentiful, owing to more fertile soil and a longer growing season. The middle colonies harvested crop surpluses for export to the slave-based plantations of the South and the West Indies: wheat, barley, oats,

> "Triangular" trade networks

triangular trade A network of trade in which exports from one region were sold to a second region; the second sent its exports to a third region that exported its own goods back to the first country or colony.

ATLANTIC TRADE ROUTES

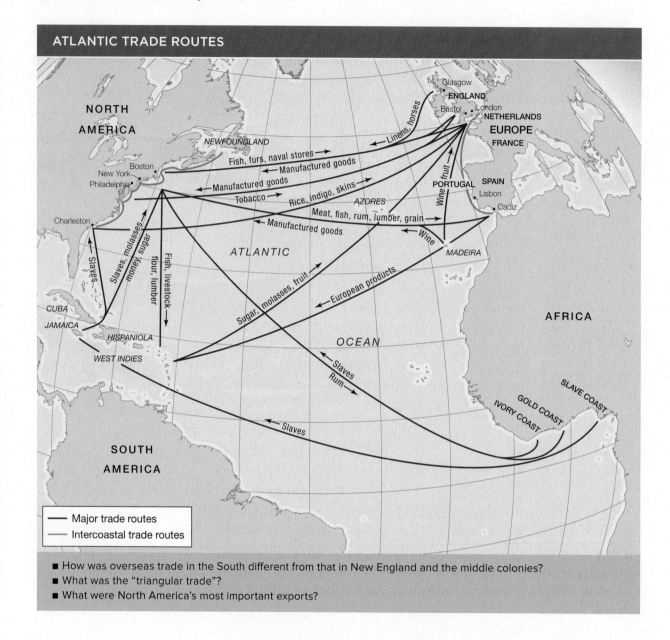

- How was overseas trade in the South different from that in New England and the middle colonies?
- What was the "triangular trade"?
- What were North America's most important exports?

as well as livestock. Three great rivers—the Hudson, the Delaware, and the Susquehanna—and their tributaries gave the middle colonies access to the backcountry of Pennsylvania and New York, which opened up a rich fur trade with Native Americans. As a consequence, the region's bustling trade, centered in New York City, Philadelphia, and Baltimore, rivaled that of New England.

Dutch *patroonship*

Land policies in the middle colonies followed the *headright* system in distributing fifty acres to any settler who had paid his own passage and fifty more if the settler brought servants. In New York, the early royal governors continued the Dutch practice of the *patroonship*, whereby influential men (called *patroons*) were granted vast estates on Long Island and throughout the Hudson and Mohawk River valleys north of New York City. The *patroons* controlled self-contained estates farmed by tenants (renters) who paid fees to use the landlord's mills, warehouses, and docks.

In the makeup of their population, the middle colonies differed from both New England's Puritan settlements and the biracial plantation colonies to the south. In New York and New Jersey, for instance, Dutch culture and language lingered. Along the Delaware River near Philadelphia, the first settlers—a small number of Swedes and Finns—were overwhelmed by an influx of English and Welsh Quakers, followed in turn by other European ethnic groups of Germans, Irish, and Scots-Irish. By the mid-eighteenth century, the middle colonies were the fastest growing region in North America.

Ethnic diversity in the middle colonies

The Germans came to America (primarily Pennsylvania) mainly from the Rhineland region of Europe that suffered from brutal religious wars that pitted Protestants against Catholics. William Penn's recruiting brochures in German translation circulated throughout central Europe, and his promise of religious freedom in Pennsylvania appealed to many persecuted sects, especially the Mennonites, German Baptists whose beliefs resembled those of the Quakers.

In 1683, a group of Mennonites founded Germantown, near Philadelphia. They were the first among a surge of German migration in the eighteenth century, a large proportion of whom paid their way to America as indentured servants, or "redemptioners," as they were commonly called. The waves of German immigrants during the eighteenth century alarmed many British colonists. Benjamin Franklin worried that the Germans "will soon . . . outnumber us."

Throughout the eighteenth century, the feisty Scots-Irish moved still farther out into the Pennsylvania backcountry. ("Scotch-Irish" is the more common but inaccurate name for the Scots-Irish, a mostly Presbyterian population transplanted from Scotland to northern Ireland by the English government a century earlier in order to give Catholic Ireland a more Protestant tone.) There were so many Scots-Irish streaming into Pennsylvania during the eighteenth century that the colony could not contain them all, so they kept moving southwest into the fertile valleys in central Virginia and western Carolina.

Land was the great magnet attracting the Scots-Irish. They were, said a recruiting agent, "full of expectation to have land for nothing" and were "unwilling to be disappointed." In most cases, the lands they "squatted on" were claimed by Native Americans. In 1741 a group of Delaware Indians protested to Pennsylvania authorities that the Scots-Irish intruders were taking "our land" without giving "us anything for it." If the colonial government did not stop the flow of whites, the Delawares threatened, then they would "drive them off."

The Scots-Irish and the Germans became the largest non-English ethnic groups in the colonies. Other ethnic minorities also enriched the population

A tradition of social tolerance

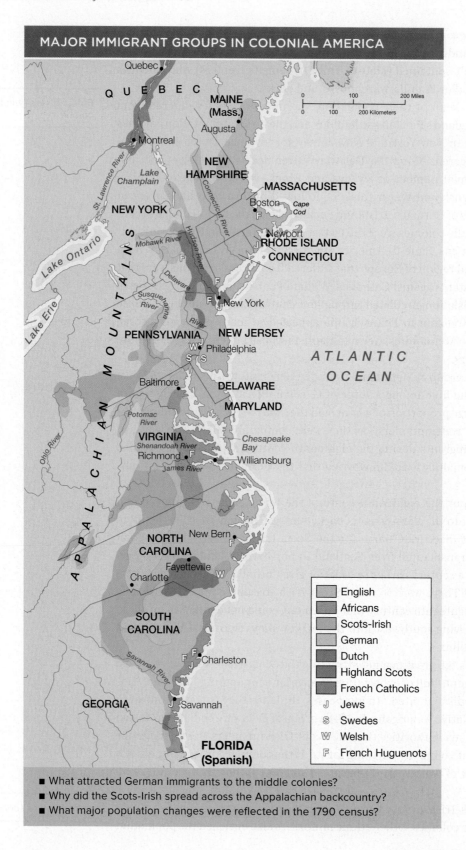

MAJOR IMMIGRANT GROUPS IN COLONIAL AMERICA

Legend:
- English
- Africans
- Scots-Irish
- German
- Dutch
- Highland Scots
- French Catholics
- J Jews
- S Swedes
- W Welsh
- F French Huguenots

- What attracted German immigrants to the middle colonies?
- Why did the Scots-Irish spread across the Appalachian backcountry?
- What major population changes were reflected in the 1790 census?

in the middle colonies: Huguenots (French Protestants whose religious freedom had been revoked in 1685, forcing many to leave France), Irish, Welsh, Swiss, and Jews. New York had inherited from the Dutch a tradition of ethnic and religious tolerance, which had given the colony a diverse population before the English conquest: French-speaking Walloons (a Celtic people from southern Belgium), French, Germans, Danes, Portuguese, Spaniards, Italians, Bohemians, Poles, and others, including some New England Puritans. The Sephardic Jews who landed in New Amsterdam in 1654 quickly founded a synagogue there.

The eighteenth century saw soaring population growth in British North America, during which the colonies grew even more diverse. In 1790, the white population was 61 percent English; 14 percent Scottish and Scots-Irish; 9 percent German; 5 percent Dutch, French, and Swedish; 4 percent Irish; and 7 percent "unidentifiable," a category that included people of mixed origins as well as "free blacks." If one adds to the 3,172,444 whites in the 1790 census the 756,770 nonwhites, without even considering the almost 100,000 Native Americans that went uncounted, only about half the nation's inhabitants, and perhaps fewer, could trace their origins to England.

Race-Based Slavery in the Colonies

CORE **OBJECTIVE**
4. Describe the creation of race-based slavery during the seventeenth century and its impact on the social and economic development of colonial America.

By the eighteenth century, the economy in the southern colonies had become utterly dependent on enslaved workers, either Indians or Africans. The profound economic, political, and cultural effects of African slavery in the Americas would be felt far into the future. Most Europeans during the colonial period viewed **race-based slavery** as a normal aspect of everyday life in an imperfect world; few considered it a moral issue. They instead believed that God determined one's "station in life." Slavery was thus considered a "personal misfortune" dictated by God rather than a social evil. It was not until the late eighteenth century that large numbers of white Europeans and Americans began to raise ethical questions about slavery.

Initially, during the early seventeenth century, many of the first Africans in America were treated like indentured servants, with a limited term of service. Those who finished their term of indenture gained their freedom, and some of them, as "free blacks," themselves acquired black slaves and white servants. Gradually, however, life-long slavery for African Americans became the custom—and the law—of the land. Slaves cost more than did indentured servants, but they served for life, so they were an increasingly shrewd investment. By the 1660s, colonial legislatures had begun to legalize the institution of race-based slavery, with strict slave codes regulating their lives. During the colonial era, slavery was legal in all the colonies but was most prevalent in the South.

Legalization of lifelong slavery

race-based slavery Institution that uses racial characteristics and myths to justify enslaving a people by force.

Racial Prejudice

As slavery in the American colonies grew more widespread, the role of race grew more prominent. Did a deep-rooted color prejudice lead to race-based slavery, or did the practice of slavery over time produce the racial prejudice? More than a century before the English arrived in America, the Portuguese and Spanish had established a global trade in enslaved Africans—the word "negro" is Spanish for "black." English settlers often enslaved Indian captives, as had the Spanish and Portuguese before them. However, the Europeans did not enslave other Europeans who were captured in warfare. Color was the crucial difference, or at least the crucial rationalization used to justify the institution of slavery and its brutalities.

Deep-rooted color prejudice

The English in the seventeenth century associated the color black with darkness and evil; they considered the different appearance, behavior, and customs of Africans, as well as the indigenous peoples of America, as representing "savagery" and "heathenism." The colonial Virginians justified slavery by convincing themselves that blacks (and Indians) were naturally lazy, treacherous, and stupid, among other shortcomings. Throughout history, dominant peoples have repeatedly assigned ugly traits to those they enslaved. And in the seventeenth and eighteenth centuries, American colonists readily justified enslaving Africans because they were deemed both "heathens" and "aliens."

African Slavery in North America

African slave trading networks

The continent of Africa during the sixteenth and seventeenth centuries experienced almost constant civil wars among competing groups and kingdoms. Africans kidnapped and sold each other into slavery in large numbers. Slave-trading networks crisscrossed the African continent. Eventually, over 10 million Africans made the forced journey into slavery across the Atlantic, most of them destined for the Spanish and Portuguese colonies. Their great ethnic diversity is often overlooked. Some came from lands as remote from each other as Angola and Senegal, thousands of miles distant, and they spoke many different languages. Many of the Africans taken to North America came in ships built in New England and owned by merchants in Boston and Newport. Most of the enslaved were young—twice as many men as women—between the ages of fifteen and thirty.

Virginia and Maryland plantation owners favored slaves from West Africa, where the cultivation of yams (sweet potatoes) was similar to the cultivation of tobacco. Fulani from West and Central Africa were prized as cattle herdsmen. South Carolina rice planters preferred slaves from Africa's "Rice Coast," especially Gambia, where rice cultivation was commonplace. Owners of slaves from the lowlands of Africa used their talents as boatmen in the coastal waterways. In a new colonial society, many slaves became skilled workers: blacksmiths, carpenters, coopers (barrel makers), bricklayers, and the like. Many enslaved women worked as household servants and midwives, helping to deliver babies.

Colonial Race Relations

Enslaved workers were eventually used in virtually every activity within the expanding colonial economy. To be sure, the vast majority were agricultural workers, often performing strenuous labor from dawn to dusk in oppressive heat and humidity. Jedidiah Morse, a prominent minister in Charleston, South Carolina, admitted in the late eighteenth century that "no white man, to speak generally, ever thinks of settling a farm, and improving it for himself, without negroes." In 1750, the vast majority of slaves in the American colonies were in Virginia and Maryland, numbering about 150,000, compared with 60,000 in South Carolina and Georgia, and only 33,000 in all the northern colonies.

Most slaves in the northern colonies lived in towns or cities, which gave them more opportunities to circulate within the larger society than

Slavery in New Amsterdam (1642) African slaves had become a mainstay of the economy so early on in American history that they appear hefting tobacco in this early and rare engraving of the Dutch colony New Amsterdam, later known as New York.

their southern counterparts living on large plantations distant from town. By 1740, New York City was second only to Charleston in the percentage of slaves in colonial cities. Most of the enslaved blacks in New York City came from the Caribbean sugar islands rather than directly from Africa. As the number of slaves increased in the congested city, racial tensions mounted and occasionally exploded. In 1712, several dozen slaves revolted; they started fires and then used swords, axes, and guns to kill whites who rushed to fight the fires. Called out to restore order, the militia captured twenty-seven slaves. Six committed suicide, and the rest were executed; some were burned alive.

New York officials thereafter passed a series of ordinances—a "black code"—strictly regulating slaves. Any slave caught with a weapon, for example, would be whipped, and owners could punish their slaves as they saw fit, as long as they did not kill them. New York and other states modeled their **slave codes** after those in South Carolina—which had been written in 1691 and allowed whites to abuse blacks verbally and physically. In 1680 the Virginia legislature had ordered thirty lashes with a whip "if any negro or other slave shall presume to lift up a hand in opposition against any Christian." Even the enlightened Thomas Jefferson, who owned almost three hundred slaves, ordered that runaways be "severely flogged."

At its most basic level, slavery is a system in which the powerless are brutalized by the powerful. Slaves who ran away in colonial America faced

Slave codes

slave codes Ordinances passed by a colony or state to regulate the behavior of slaves, often including severe punishments for infractions.

ghastly punishments when caught; many were hanged or burned at the stake. Antonio, a west African man shipped as a slave to New Amsterdam and then to Maryland during the first half of the seventeenth century, worked in the tobacco fields alongside indentured servants and enslaved Native Americans. Antonio tried to escape several times. After his last attempt, in 1656, his owner, a young Dutch planter named Syman Overzee, recaptured Antonio (a "dangerous Rogue"), whipped his "bare back" with branches from a pear tree, poured hot grease into his wounds, then tied him to a ladder where he slowly died. Overzee was charged with murder—and acquitted.

> Stono Rebellion

In a few cases, as had happened in New York City, slaves organized armed rebellions, stealing weapons, burning and looting plantations, and occasionally killing their masters. In 1739, some twenty slaves attacked a store in Stono, South Carolina, south of Charleston. They killed the owner, seized weapons, and headed toward freedom in Spanish-controlled Florida, gathering more recruits along the way. Within a few days, the slaves participating in the **Stono Rebellion** had killed twenty-five whites, whereupon the militia caught up with them. Most of the rebels were killed, and in the weeks that followed, some sixty more were captured by enraged planters who "cut off their heads and set them up at every Mile Post."

Slavery in the Western Hemisphere was a rapidly growing phenomenon by the time of the American Revolution. It was driven by high profits and justified by a pervasive racism. Although race-based slavery entailed the dehumanization of an entire class of human beings, white Europeans believed they were justified in doing so because of the supposed "backwardness" of Africans and Indians. Not even the American Revolution's ideals of freedom and equality (for whites) would change that attitude.

CORE **OBJECTIVE**

5. Analyze the impact of the Enlightenment and the Great Awakening on the colonies.

First Stirrings of a Common Colonial Culture

By the middle of the eighteenth century, the thirteen colonies were rapidly growing and maturing. Schools and colleges were springing up, and the standard of living was rising as well. More and more colonists were able to read about the latest ideas circulating in London and Paris while purchasing the latest consumer goods from Europe.

During the eighteenth century, prosperous Americans became addicted to buying the latest "baubles" from Britain. The rage for British luxury goods, especially fine clothing and beaver hats, heightened social inequality, especially in the cities. Many ministers and laymen complained that wealthy Americans were so preoccupied with buying luxury goods from London that they were ignoring their religious commitment to Christian ideals. In 1714, a Bostonian regretted the "great extravagance that people are fallen into, far

Stono Rebellion (1739) A slave uprising in South Carolina that was brutally quashed, leading to executions as well as a severe tightening of the slave codes.

beyond their circumstances, in their purchases, buildings, families, expenses, apparel—generally in their whole way of living."

English merchants required Americans to buy their goods only with *specie* (gold or silver coins). This left little "hard money" in the colonies themselves. American merchants tried various ways to get around the shortage of specie. Some engaged in *barter*, using commodities such as tobacco or rice as currency in exchange for manufactured goods and luxury items from England. The issue of money—what kind and how much—would become one of the major subjects of dispute between the colonies and Britain leading to the Revolution.

> Commerce and culture

Colonial Cities

The American colonies were mostly populated by farmers or farm workers. Colonial cities hugged the coastline or, like Philadelphia, sprang up on rivers large enough to handle oceangoing vessels. Never comprising more than 10 percent of the colonial population, the large coastal cities had a disproportionate influence on commerce, politics, society, and culture. By the end of the colonial period, Philadelphia, with some 30,000 people, was the largest city in the colonies. New York City, with about 25,000, ranked second; Boston numbered 16,000; Charleston, 12,000; and Newport, Rhode Island, 11,000.

The urban social elite was dominated by wealthy merchants and property owners served by a middle class of shop owners, innkeepers, and skilled craftsmen. Almost two thirds of the urban male workers were artisans, people who made their living at handicrafts. They included carpenters and coopers (barrel makers), shoemakers and tailors, silversmiths and blacksmiths, sailmakers, stonemasons, weavers, and potters. At the bottom of the social order were sailors, manual laborers, servants, and slaves.

> An urban elite and city problems

Colonial cities were busy, crowded, and dangerous. The use of open fireplaces for heating led to frequent fires that in turn led to the development of fire companies. Rising crime and violence required increased policing of neighborhoods by sheriffs and local militias. Colonists also were concerned about the poor and homeless. The number of Boston's poor receiving assistance from colonial authorities rose from 500 in 1700 to 4,000 in 1736; in New York City, the number rose from 250 in 1698 to 5,000 in the 1770s. In colonial America, those designated "helpless" among the destitute poor, especially the disabled, elderly, widows, and orphans, were often provided money, food, clothing, and firewood by the county, town, or city. In some towns, "poorhouses" were built to house the homeless poor and provide them with jobs.

***The Rapalje Children* (1768)** John Durand painted the children of a wealthy Brooklyn merchant wearing clothing typical of upper-crust urban society.

Comparing the Three English Colonial Regions

The following charts highlight some important social, cultural, and economic characteristics of the three regions of colonial America: the southern, middle, and New England colonies.

The Southern Colonies	
Colonies (and Cities)	Virginia, Maryland, North Carolina, South Carolina, Georgia (Charleston, Baltimore)
Economy and Climate	Warm and wet, best suited for staple crops: tobacco, rice
Religious Character	Anglicanism in Virginia, the Carolinas, and Georgia; Catholicism in Maryland with religious toleration
Immigrant Groups	Mostly biracial: English and Africans
Equality/Inequality	High rates of inequality: many slaves, indentured servants, landless whites at one extreme and wealthy gentry at the other

The Middle Colonies	
Colonies (and Cities)	New York, Pennsylvania, Delaware, New Jersey (Philadelphia, New York)
Economy and Climate	Commercial crossroads with mixed economy: foodstuffs for export and trade, fur trade with Native Americans; temperate climate with longer growing season
Religious Character	Pluralistic: Anglican, Protestant, and Jewish, with freedom of religion in Pennsylvania
Immigrant Groups	Diverse: Dutch, Swedes, Scots-Irish, Finns, English, Germans, Swiss, French, Welsh, Africans
Equality/Inequality	Moderate inequality: more small-farm ownership and extensive trade with Native Americans

Travel and taverns: The circulation of new ideas

The Urban Web

The first American roads were Indian trails that were widened with frequent travel, then made into roads. Overland travel was initially by horse or by foot. The first public stagecoach line opened in 1732. Taverns and inns were important in the colonial era, since travel at night was treacherous. (During this period it was said that when the Spanish settled an area, they would first

The New England Colonies	
Colonies (and Cities)	Massachusetts, Rhode Island, Connecticut, New Hampshire (Boston, Newport)
Economy and Climate	Mixed economy: fishing, shipbuilding, shipping and trade, small farms; triangular trade of slaves and rum; cold and harsh climate with short growing season
Religious Character	Largely Puritan Congregationalists with limited religious toleration, except Rhode Island
Immigrant Groups	Mostly English
Equality/Inequality	Greatest level of equality in the colonies: Congregational faith–based towns with few slaves

QUESTIONS FOR ANALYSIS

1. Which region had the largest cities, and why?

2. How did geography and climate contribute to the different economies of each region?

3. Which region was the most religiously diverse, and why? Which was the least diverse, and why?

4. Which region appeared to be the most ethnically diverse, and why? Which was the least diverse, and why?

5. What factors help explain the different level of social inequality in the various colonies?

build a church; the Dutch, in their settlements, would first erect a fort; and the English, in theirs, would first construct a tavern.) By the end of the seventeenth century, there were more taverns in America than any other business. Colonial taverns and inns were places to eat, drink, relax, read a newspaper, play cards, gossip about people or politics, learn news from travelers, or conduct business.

Tavern culture A tobacconist's business card from 1770 captures men talking in a Philadelphia tavern while they drink ale and smoke pipes.

A postal system

Taverns served as a forum for conversation and social interaction, but long-distance communication was more complicated. Postal service in the seventeenth century was almost nonexistent—people gave letters to travelers or sea captains in hopes they would be delivered. Under a parliamentary law of 1710, the postmaster of London named a deputy in charge of the colonies, and a postal system eventually encompassed most of the Atlantic seaboard. Benjamin Franklin, who served as deputy postmaster for the colonies from 1753 to 1774, sped up the service with shorter routes and night-traveling mail riders.

Freedom of the press

More reliable mail delivery gave rise to newspapers in the eighteenth century. Before 1745, twenty-two newspapers had been started: seven in New England, ten in the middle colonies, and five in the South. An important landmark in the progress of freedom of the press was John Peter Zenger's trial for publishing criticisms of New York's royal governor in his newspaper, the *New-York Weekly Journal*. Zenger was imprisoned for ten months and brought to trial in 1735. English common law held that one might be punished for "libel," or criticism that fostered "an ill opinion of the government." Zenger's lawyer startled the court with his claim that the editor had published the truth—which the judge ruled an unacceptable defense. The jury, however, held the editor not guilty. The libel law remained standing as before, but editors thereafter were emboldened to criticize officials more freely.

The Enlightenment in America

Enlightenment A revolution in thought begun in Europe in the seventeenth century that emphasized reason and science over the authority and myths of traditional religion.

The most significant of the new European ideas circulating in eighteenth-century America grew out of a burst of innovative intellectual activity known as the **Enlightenment**. The Enlightenment celebrated rational inquiry, scientific research, and individual freedom. Enlightened people were those who sought the truth, wherever it might lead, rather than remain content with believing dogmas passed down through the ages or taken from the Bible. Curious, well-educated, and well-read people were no longer willing simply to accept biblical explanations of the universe as sufficient and complete. Immanuel Kant, the eighteenth-century German philosopher, summed up the Enlightenment point of view by saying: "Dare to know! Have the courage to use your own understanding." He and others used the power of reason to analyze the workings of nature. To do so, they employed new tools like microscopes and telescopes to engage in close observation, scientific experimentation, and precise mathematical calculation.

The Enlightenment, often called the Age of Reason, was triggered by a scientific revolution in which the ancient view that the earth was at the center of the universe was overthrown in the early sixteenth century by the controversial heliocentric (sun-centered) solar system described by Nicolaus Copernicus, a Polish astronomer who was also a Catholic priest. His theory in 1533 that the earth orbits the sun was scorned by Catholic officials before it was later confirmed by other scientists.

The scientific revolution

The climax to the scientific revolution came in 1687 when Englishman Isaac Newton (1642–1727) announced his controversial theory of the earth's gravitational pull. Newton challenged biblical notions of the world's workings by depicting a mechanistic universe moving in accordance with natural laws that could be grasped by human reason and explained by mathematics. He implied that natural laws rather than God's actions govern all things, from the orbits of the planets to the science of human relations: politics, economics, and society.

Some enlightened people believed in **Deism**, which carried Newton's scientific outlook to its logical conclusion, claiming that God created the world and designed its "natural laws," and these laws, not God directly, govern the operation of the universe. In other words, Deists insisted that God planned the universe and set it in motion, but no longer interacted directly with the earth and its people. So the rational God of the Deists was nothing like the intervening God of the Christian tradition, to whom believers prayed for daily guidance and direct support. Evil in the world, according to the Deists, resulted not from humanity's inherent *sinfulness* as outlined in the Bible but from human *ignorance* of the rational laws of nature. Therefore the best way to improve both society and human nature, according to Deists such as Thomas Jefferson and Benjamin Franklin, was by cultivating Reason, which was the highest Virtue (Enlightenment thinkers often capitalized both words). By doing so, by using education, reason, and scientific analysis, societies were bound to improve their knowledge as well as their quality of life. Faith in human progress was thus one of the most important beliefs of the Enlightenment.

Deism

Equally important was the enlightened notion of political freedom. Both Jefferson and Franklin were intrigued by the English political philosopher John Locke (1632–1704), who maintained that "natural law"

Deism Enlightenment thought applied to religion, emphasizing reason, morality, and natural law rather than scriptural authority or an ever-present God intervening in the daily life of humans.

called for a government resting on the consent of the governed and respecting the "natural rights" of all. It was not far from such an idea to finding justification for revolution against tyrannical monarchies, like those governing Great Britain and France.

The Age of Reason in America

Benjamin Franklin epitomized the Enlightenment in the eyes of both Americans and Europeans. Born in Boston in 1706, a descendant of Puritans, Franklin left home at the age of seventeen, bound for Philadelphia. There, before he was twenty-four, he bought a print shop where he edited the *Pennsylvania Gazette*, one of the leading newspapers in the colonies. When he was twenty-six, he published *Poor Richard's Almanack*, a collection of seasonal weather forecasts, puzzles, household tips, and witty sayings about success and happiness. Before he retired from business at the age of forty-two, Franklin had founded a public library, started a fire company, helped create the academy that became the University of Pennsylvania, and organized a debating club that grew into the American Philosophical Society.

Benjamin Franklin was devoted to scientific investigation. Skeptical and curious, pragmatic and irreverent, he was an inventive genius. His wide-ranging scientific experiments ranged across the fields of medicine, meteorology, geology, astronomy, and physics, among others. He developed the Franklin stove, the lightning rod, bifocal spectacles, and a glass harmonica.

Franklin's love of science and reason clashed with prevailing Christian beliefs. Although raised as a Presbyterian, he became a Deist who prized science and reason over orthodox religion. He questioned the divinity of Jesus and the assumption that the Bible was truly the word of God. Like the European Deists, Franklin came to believe in a God that had created a universe directed by natural laws, laws that curious people could discover through the use of reason and the scientific method. For Franklin and others in the eighteenth century, to be "enlightened" meant developing the confidence and capacity to think for oneself, to think critically rather than simply accepting what tradition dictated as truth.

Benjamin Franklin A champion of reason, Franklin was an inventor, philosopher, entrepreneur, and statesman.

The Great Awakening

The growing popularity of Enlightenment rationalism posed a direct threat to traditional religious life in Europe and America. But religious faith has always shown remarkable resilience in the face of challenging new ideas. This was certainly true in the early eighteenth century, when the American colonies experienced a widespread revival of spiritual zeal designed to restore the primacy of emotion in the religious realm.

Religious response to the Enlightenment

Between 1700 and 1750, when the controversial ideas of the Enlightenment were circulating among the best educated colonists, hundreds of new Christian congregations were founded. Most Americans (85 percent) lived in colonies with an "established" church, meaning that the colonial government officially endorsed—and collected taxes to support—a single official denomination. The Church of England, also known as Anglicanism, was the "established" church in Virginia, Maryland, Delaware, and the Carolinas. Puritan Congregationalism was the official faith in New England. In New York, Anglicanism vied with the Dutch Reformed Church for control. Pennsylvania had no single state-supported church, but Quakers dominated the legislative assembly. New Jersey and Rhode Island had no official denomination and hosted numerous Christian splinter groups.

Most colonies organized religious life on the basis of well-regulated local parishes, which defined their theological boundaries and defended them against people who did not hold to the same faith. In colonies with official religions, people of other faiths could not preach without the permission of the local parish. Then, in the 1730s and 1740s, the parish system was thrown into turmoil by the arrival of outspoken traveling evangelists, called *itinerants*, who claimed that most of the local parish ministers were incompetent. In their emotionally charged sermons, the itinerants, several of whom were white women and African Americans, insisted that Christians must be "reborn" in their convictions and behavior.

During the early 1730s, a widespread sense of religious decline and the need for "rebirth" helped spark a series of emotional revivals known as the **Great Awakening**. The revivals began in the southern colonies and quickly spread up the Atlantic coast to New England. Whole towns were swept up in the ecstasy of renewed spiritual passion. Unlike the Enlightenment, which affected primarily the intellectual elite, the evangelical energies unleashed by the Great Awakening appealed mostly to the masses. As a skeptical Benjamin Franklin observed of the Awakening, "Never did the people show so great a willingness to attend sermons. Religion is become the subject of most conversation." The Awakening was the first popular movement before the American Revolution that affected all thirteen colonies, and as such it helped create ties across the colonies that would later help coordinate revolutionary activities against the British government.

In 1734–1735, a remarkable spiritual transformation occurred in the congregation of Jonathan Edwards, a prominent Congregationalist minister in the western Massachusetts town of Northampton. One of America's most brilliant philosophers and theologians, Edwards had entered Yale College in 1716, at age thirteen, and graduated at the top of his class four years later. In 1727, Edwards was named minister of the Congregational church in Northampton. He was shocked at the town's lack of religious conviction. Edwards claimed that the young people of Northampton were preoccupied with sinful pleasures; they indulged in "lewd practices" that "corrupted others." Christians had also become obsessed with making and spending money. He also warned that the rebellious new ideas associated with the Enlightenment were eroding the importance of religious life. Edwards attacked Deists

Traveling evangelists and intense revivals

Great Awakening Emotional religious revival movement that swept the thirteen colonies from the 1720s through the 1740s.

Jonathan Edwards One of the foremost preachers of the Great Awakening.

for believing that "God has given mankind no other light to walk by but their own reason."

To counteract the secularizing forces of the Enlightenment, Edwards resolved to restore the emotional side of religion. "Our people," he said, "do not so much need to have their heads stored [with new scientific knowledge] as to have their hearts touched [with spiritual intensity]." His own vivid descriptions of the sufferings of hell and the delights of heaven helped rekindle spiritual intensity among his congregants. By 1735, Edwards could report that "the town seemed to be full of the presence of God; it never was so full of love, nor of joy." To judge the power of the religious awakening, he thought, one need only observe that "it was no longer the Tavern" that drew local crowds, "but the Minister's House."

While Jonathan Edwards was promoting a revival of religious emotion in Puritan New England, William Tennent, an Irish-born Presbyterian revivalist, was stirring souls in Pennsylvania. He and his sons charged that many of the local ministers were "cold and sapless," afraid to "thrust the nail of terror into sleeping souls." Tennent's oldest son, Gilbert, defended their aggressive (and often illegal) tactics by explaining that he and other traveling evangelists invaded parishes only when the local minister showed no interest in the "Getting of Grace and Growing in it." The Tennents caused great anxiety because they preached to those at the bottom of the social scale— farmers, laborers, sailors, and servants. By promoting a passionate piety, urging people to renounce their ministers, and attacking the luxurious excesses of the wealthiest and most powerful colonists, the radical evangelists threatened to disrupt the social order in the colonies. Competition was emerging in colonial religious life. Worried members of the colonial elite charged that the radical revivalists were spreading "anarchy, levelling, and dissolution."

The most celebrated promoter of the Great Awakening was a young English minister, George Whitefield, whose reputation as a spellbinding evangelist preceded him to the colonies. Congregations were lifeless, he claimed, "because dead men preach to them." Too many ministers were "slothful shepherds and dumb dogs." Whitefield set out to restore the fires of religious intensity in American congregations. In the autumn of 1739, the twenty-five-year-old evangelist began preaching to huge crowds across the colonies. A disgusted Bostonian described a revival meeting's theatrics: "The meeting was carried on with . . . some screaming out in Distress and Anguish . . . some again jumping up and down . . . some lying along on the floor. . . . The whole with a very great Noise, to be heard at a Mile's Distance, and continued almost the whole night." Benjamin Franklin, who went to see Whitefield preach in Philadelphia, got so carried away by the fiery sermon that he emptied his pockets into the collection plate.

Jonathan Edwards took advantage of the energies stirred up by Whitefield to spread his own revival gospel throughout New England. The Great

Jonathan Edwards: "Sinners in the Hands of an Angry God"

Awakening reached its peak in 1741 when Edwards delivered his most famous sermon, "Sinners in the Hands of an Angry God." It was designed in part to frighten people into seeking salvation. Edwards reminded the congregation that hell is real and that God "holds you over the pit of hell, much as one holds a spider, or some loathsome insect, over the fire, abhors you, and is dreadfully provoked. . . . He looks upon you as worthy of nothing else, but to be cast into the fire." When Edwards finished, he had to wait several minutes for the agitated congregants to quiet down before he led them in a closing hymn.

The Great Awakening made religion intensely personal by creating both a deep sense of spiritual guilt and a yearning for redemption. Yet while the Great Awakening saved souls, it also undermined many of the established churches by emphasizing that individuals, regardless of wealth or social status, could receive God's grace without the guidance of their local ministers. It also gave people more religious choices. During the Great Awakening, the major denominations fractured: Presbyterians divided into "Old Side" critics of revivalism and "New Side" supporters; Congregationalists into "Old Light" and "New Light" factions. Jonathan Edwards regretted the emergence of warring factions. We are "like two armies," he said, "separated and drawn up in battle array, ready to fight one another." New England religious life would never be the same.

> Challenges to established churches

Individualism and Colonial Culture

The energies of the Great Awakening subsided by 1750, but like its very different counterpart movement, the Enlightenment, it set in motion powerful currents that still flow through American life. Ministers could no longer control the direction of religious life as more and more people took charge of their own spirituality and new denominations sprouted like mushrooms. The Great Awakening implanted in American culture the evangelical impulse and the emotional appeal of revivalism. By encouraging the creation of new denominations, the Awakening heightened the need for the toleration of many religious persuasions rather than just one's own.

In some respects, however, the conflict between the emotional forces unleashed by the Awakening and the rational analyses of the Enlightenment led by different roads to similar ends. Both movements cut across all of the colonies and thereby helped bind them together. Both movements emphasized that individuals should have the freedom to take responsibility for their own lives and salvation. By urging believers to exercise their own spiritual judgment, the revivals weakened the authority of the established churches and their ministers, just as colonial resentment of British economic regulations would later weaken the colonists' loyalty to the king. As such, the Great Awakening and the Enlightenment helped nurture an American commitment to individual freedom and resistance to authority that would play a key role in the rebellion against British tyranny in 1776.

> Emerging individualism

■ **Colonial Demographics** Cheap land lured most poor immigrants to America, and the initial shortage of women eventually gave way to a more equal gender ratio and a tendency to earlier marriage than in Europe, leading to higher *birth rates* and larger families. People also lived longer on average in the colonies than in Europe. The lower *death rates* led to rapid population growth in the colonies.

■ **Women in the Colonies** English colonists brought their traditional beliefs and prejudices with them to America, including convictions about the inferiority of women. Colonial women remained largely confined to *women's work* in the house, yard, and field. Over time, though, necessity created new opportunities for women outside their traditional roles.

■ **Colonial Differences** A thriving colonial trading economy sent raw materials such as fish, timber, and furs to England in return for manufactured goods. The expanding economy created new wealth and a rise in the consumption of European goods, and it fostered the expansion of slavery. Agriculture diversified: tobacco was the *staple crop* in Virginia, rice in the Carolinas. Plantation agriculture based on slavery became entrenched in the South. New England's prosperous shipping industry created a profitable *triangular trade* among Africa, America, and England. By 1790, German, Scots-Irish, Welsh, and Irish immigrants and other European ethnic groups had settled in the middle colonies, along with members of religious groups such as Quakers, Jews, Huguenots, and Mennonites.

■ **Race-Based Slavery** Deep-rooted color prejudice led to *race-based slavery*. Africans were considered "heathens" whose supposed inferiority entitled white Americans to use them for slaves. Diverse Africans brought skills from Africa to build America's economy. The use of African slaves was concentrated in the South, where landowners used them to produce lucrative *staple crops*, such as tobacco, rice, and indigo, but slaves lived in cities, too, especially New York. As the population of slaves increased, race relations grew more tense, and *slave codes* were created to regulate the movement and activities of enslaved people. Sporadic slave uprisings, such as the *Stono Rebellion*, occurred in both the North and South.

■ **The Enlightenment and the Great Awakening** Printing presses, higher education, and city life created a flow of new ideas that circulated via long-distance travel, tavern life, the postal service, books, and newspapers. The attitudes of the *Enlightenment* were transported along international trade routes. Sir Isaac Newton's scientific discoveries culminated in the belief that reason could improve society. Benjamin Franklin, who believed that people could shape their own destinies, became the face of the Enlightenment in America. *Deism* expressed the religious views of the Age of Reason. By contrast, during the 1730s, a revival of faith, the *Great Awakening*, swept through the colonies. New congregations formed as evangelists insisted that Christians be "reborn." Individualism, not orthodoxy, was stressed in this first popular religious movement in America's history.

KEY TERMS

CHRONOLOGY

1660s	Colonial assemblies legalize lifelong slavery
1683	German Mennonites arrive in Pennsylvania
1687	Sir Isaac Newton publishes his theory of universal gravitation
1691	South Carolina passes first slave codes; other states follow
1692	Salem witch trials
1712	Slave revolt in New York City; New York passes stricter laws governing slaves
1730	Chesapeake region's slave population achieves self-sustaining rate of population growth
1730s–1740s	The Great Awakening
1739	Stono Rebellion
1750	Colonial population passes 1 million
1775	Colonial population passes 2.5 million

INQUIZITIVE

Go to InQuizitive to see what you've learned—and learn what you've missed—with personalized feedback along the way.

BOSTON TEA PARTY Disguised as Native Americans, a swarm of Patriots seized three British ships and dumped more than three hundred chests of East India Company tea into the Boston harbor.

From Colonies to States

1607-1776

Four great naval European powers—Spain, France, Britain, and the Netherlands (Holland)—created colonies in North America during the sixteenth and seventeenth centuries as part of their larger fight for global supremacy. Throughout the eighteenth century, wars raged across Europe, mostly pitting the Catholic nations of France and Spain against Protestant Great Britain and the Netherlands, but at times the battle lines were complicated by other considerations of economics, alliances, and political opportunism. The tensions and fighting increasingly spread across the high seas to the Americas. By the middle of the eighteenth century, North America had become a primary battleground, involving both colonists and the Native Americans who were allied with different European powers.

Spain's sparsely populated settlements in the borderlands north of Mexico were small and weak compared to those in the British colonies. The Spanish in what is now the American Southwest as well as Texas and California failed to create settlements with self-sustaining economies. Instead, Spain emphasized the conversion of native peoples to Catholicism, prohibited manufacturing within its colonies, strictly limited trade with Native Americans, and searched—in vain—for gold.

The French and the British, however, developed a thriving trade with Native Americans (trade that included supplying Indians with firearms), but the fierce rivalry between the British and the French gradually shifted the balance of power in Europe. By the end of the eighteenth century, Spain would be in decline, leaving France and Great Britain to fight for supremacy. The nearly constant warfare around the globe led Great Britain to tighten its control over the American colonies in order to raise the funds needed to combat France and Spain and to fill the ranks of its military forces. Tensions over the British effort to preserve its empire at the expense of American freedoms would lead first to rebellion and eventually to revolution.

CORE **OBJECTIVE**

1. Compare how the British and French empires administered their colonies before 1763.

Troubled Neighbors

New France

The actual settlement of New France began in 1605, when the enterprising soldier-explorer Samuel de Champlain, the "Father of New France," founded Port-Royal in Acadia, along the Canadian coast. Then, three years later, Champlain established Quebec, to the west, along the St. Lawrence River (Quebec is an Algonquian word meaning "where the river narrows"). Champlain was the first European to explore and map the Great Lakes.

French fur trading companies, religious restrictions, and limited immigration

Until his death in 1635, Champlain governed New France on behalf of trading companies exploiting the fur trade with the Indians. The merchant-investors in the trading companies sponsored Champlain's voyages in hopes of creating a prosperous commercial colony. But in 1627 the French government ordered that only Catholics could live in New France. This restriction stunted its growth—as did the harsh winter climate. As a consequence, the number of French who colonized Canada was *much* smaller than the number of British, Dutch, and Spanish colonists in other North American colonies, and they were almost all men.

Coureurs des bois

Champlain knew that the greatly outnumbered French could survive only by befriending the native peoples. To that end, he dispatched young French trappers and traders to live with the indigenous peoples, learn their languages and customs, marry native women, and serve as ambassadors of New France. These hardy woodsmen, called *coureurs des bois* (runners of the woods) pushed into the forested regions around the Great Lakes and developed a thriving fur trade with the native peoples.

Royal control

In 1663, French king Louis XIV changed struggling New France into a royal colony led by a governor-general who managed an administrative structure modeled after that of the monarchy in France. New France was fully subject to the French king. The colonists had no political rights or representative government, and public meetings could not be held without official permission. Louis dispatched soldiers and new settlers, including shiploads of young women, known as the King's Daughters, to provide wives for the mostly male colonists. The king also awarded large grants of land, called *seigneuries*, as a lure to aristocratic settlers. The poorest farmers usually rented land from the *seigneur*.

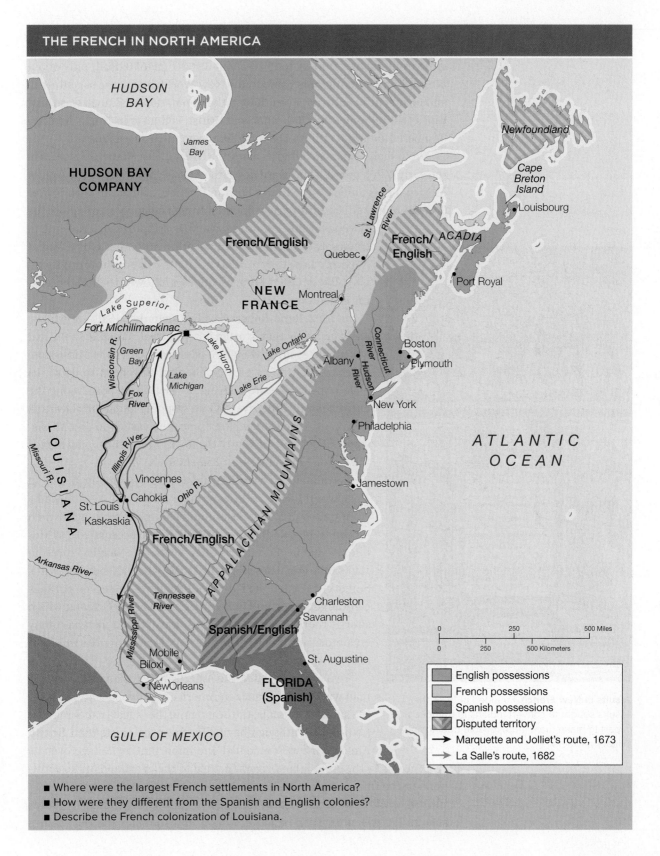

THE FRENCH IN NORTH AMERICA

HUDSON BAY

James Bay

HUDSON BAY COMPANY

Newfoundland

Cape Breton Island

Louisbourg

St. Lawrence River

French/English

ACADIA

French/English

Quebec

Port Royal

Lake Superior

NEW FRANCE

Montreal

Fort Michilimackinac

Wisconsin R.

Green Bay

Lake Huron

Lake Ontario

Connecticut River

Boston

Fox River

Lake Michigan

Lake Erie

Albany

Hudson River

Plymouth

Illinois River

New York

L O U I S I A N A

Philadelphia

Missouri R.

Vincennes

Cahokia

Ohio R.

ATLANTIC OCEAN

St. Louis

Kaskaskia

Jamestown

Arkansas River

French/English

A P P A L A C H I A N   M O U N T A I N S

Tennessee River

Charleston

Savannah

Spanish/English

Mobile

Biloxi

Mississippi River

St. Augustine

NewOrleans

FLORIDA (Spanish)

GULF OF MEXICO

| 0 | 250 | 500 Miles |
| 0 | 250 | 500 Kilometers |

English possessions
French possessions
Spanish possessions
Disputed territory
→ Marquette and Jolliet's route, 1673
→ La Salle's route, 1682

- Where were the largest French settlements in North America?
- How were they different from the Spanish and English colonies?
- Describe the French colonization of Louisiana.

But none of these efforts worked to transform New France from being essentially a fur trading outpost. The tiny French population of New France grew from about 4,000 in 1665 to about 15,000 in 1690. Still, only about 40,000 French immigrants came to the New World during the seventeenth and eighteenth centuries, even though the population of France was three times that of Spain. By 1750, when the British colonists in North America numbered about 1.5 million, the total French population was 70,000.

From their Canadian outposts along the Great Lakes, French explorers in the early 1670s moved southward down the Mississippi River to the Gulf of Mexico. Louis Jolliet, a fur trader born in Quebec, teamed up with Father Jacques Marquette, a Jesuit priest fluent in Indian languages, to explore the Wisconsin River south to the Mississippi River. Traveling in canoes, they paddled south to within 400 miles of the Gulf of Mexico, where they turned back for fear of encountering Spanish soldiers. Other French explorers followed their pathbreaking expedition.

In 1682, René-Robert Cavelier, sieur de La Salle, organized an expedition that started in Montreal, crossed the Great Lakes, and eventually made it all the way down the Mississippi River to the Gulf of Mexico, the first European to do so. La Salle hoped to create a string of fur trading posts along the entire length of the river. While stopping along the riverbank in Arkansas, he claimed for France the vast Ohio and Mississippi Valleys—all the way to the Rocky Mountains—and named the region Louisiana, after King Louis XIV.

Settlement of the Louisiana territory finally began in 1699, when Pierre Le Moyne, sieur d'Iberville, established a colony near Biloxi, Mississippi. The main settlement then moved to Mobile Bay and, in 1710, to the present site of Mobile, Alabama. For nearly fifty years, the driving force in Louisiana was Jean-Baptiste Le Moyne, sieur de Bienville. Sometimes called the Father of Louisiana, he served periodically as governor, and in 1718 he founded New Orleans, which shortly thereafter became the capital of the Louisiana colony encompassing much of the interior of the entire North American continent.

Jesuits in New France Founded in 1539, the Jesuits sought to convert Indians to Catholicism, in part to make them more reliable trading and military partners.

Two centuries later, the American historian Francis Parkman wrote that "France in America had two heads, one amid the snows of Canada, the other amid the [sugar] canebrakes of Louisiana." Although having far fewer colonists than British America, New France had one important advantage over its rival: access to the great inland rivers that led to the heartland of the continent. In the Illinois region, scattered French settlers began farming the fertile soil, while Jesuits established missions to convert the Indians at places such as Terre Haute ("High Land," in what is now Indiana) and Des Moines

("Of the Monks," in present-day Iowa—the name probably shortened from Rivière des Moines, or "River of the Monks"). Because of geography as well as deliberate policy, however, New France remained during the eighteenth century a vast wilderness traversed by a mobile population of traders, trappers, missionaries, and mainly Indians. By building closer bonds and encroaching far less upon Native American lands, the French won Native American allies against the more numerous British Americans. For well over a century, in fact, Native Americans would determine the military balance of power within North America.

Native American allies

The British System

The British colonies in North America were quite different from those of New France. Within the more diverse British colonies, governments typically included a governor and a legislative assembly. As chief executives, the governors of each colony were appointed by the king. Few of the royal governors were especially gifted administrators, but they could appoint and remove officials, command the militia, and grant pardons to people convicted of crimes.

However, the American colonists enjoyed some rights and powers absent in Britain—as well as in New France. The British colonies in America, unlike the Spanish, French, or Dutch colonies, had *elected* legislative assemblies. Whether called the House of Burgesses (Virginia), the House of Delegates (Maryland), or the House of Representatives (Massachusetts) or simply the Assembly, the "lower" houses in each colony were chosen by popular vote. Not all colonists could vote, however. Only adult males owning a specified amount of property could vote. Women, Native Americans, and African Americans were excluded from the political process. But because property holding was widespread in America, a greater proportion of the male population could vote in the colonies than anywhere else in the world.

Elected legislative assemblies

The most important political trend in eighteenth-century America was the growing power of the colonial legislatures. Like Parliament, the colonial assemblies controlled the budget, and they could pass laws and regulations. Most of the colonial assemblies also influenced the royal governors by controlling their salaries. Throughout the eighteenth century, the assemblies expanded their power and influence relative to the royal governors. Unlike the situation in New France, where the governor-general exercised almost absolute power and there were no legislative assemblies and an absence of ethnic and religious diversity, self-government in British America became first a habit, then a cherished "right."

Mercantilism

Throughout much of the seventeenth and eighteenth centuries, British officials exercised what one politician called a **salutary neglect** by not strictly enforcing the laws regulating the American colonies, especially those

salutary neglect Informal British policy during the first half of the eighteenth century that allowed the American colonies freedom to pursue their economic and political interests in exchange for colonial obedience.

involving trade restrictions. Smuggling was commonplace, a way to escape paying taxes on goods imported from other countries. The perpetual struggle between Parliament and the British kings made it difficult to develop either consistent colonial policies around the world or to create effective means of enforcing such policies. The English Civil War (1642–1646) sharply reduced the flow of money and people from Britain to America and created great confusion regarding Britain's colonial policies.

> From salutary neglect to mercantilism

The 1651 victory of Oliver Cromwell's Puritan army over Royalist forces in the English Civil War had direct effects in the colonies. As Britain's new ruler, Cromwell ended the tradition of "salutary neglect" in favor of **mercantilism**, a political and economic policy adopted by most of the European monarchs during the seventeenth century. In a mercantile system, the government would take control of all economic activities. Key industries were regulated, taxed, or "subsidized" (supported by payments from the government). People with specialized skills or knowledge of new industrial technologies, such as textile machinery, were not allowed to leave the country.

Mercantilism also supported the creation of global empires. Colonies, it was assumed, enriched their founding nation in several ways: (1) by providing silver and gold as well as the raw materials (furs, fish, grains, timber, sugar, tobacco, indigo, tar, etc.) needed to supply food and produce goods; (2) by creating a captive market of colonial consumers who would be forced to buy goods created in the home country; (3) by relieving social tensions and political unrest in the home country, because colonies could provide a new home for the growing numbers of poor, unemployed, and imprisoned; and (4) by prohibiting its colonies from producing goods that would compete with manufacturers in the "mother country."

Navigation Acts

mercantilism Policy of Great Britain and other imperial powers of regulating colonial economies to benefit the mother country.

Navigation Acts (1650–1775) Restrictions passed by the British Parliament to control colonial trade and bolster the mercantile system.

Such mercantilist assumptions prompted Oliver Cromwell to adopt the first in a series of **Navigation Acts** intended to increase Britain's colonial revenues. The Navigation Act of 1651 required that all goods imported to or exported from Britain be carried *only* in ships built in Britain and owned by Britons. The law was intended to hurt the rival Dutch—but because the Dutch controlled New Netherland (New York, West and East Jersey, and Delaware) and because the law applied not only to Britain but also to Britain's American colonies, the Navigation Act of 1651 thus had tremendous effect in North America. American merchants resented such a regulation because the Dutch shippers charged much less to transport American goods than the British. By 1652, Britain and the Netherlands were at war, the first of three naval conflicts that erupted between 1652 and 1674 as a result of the intense economic competition between the two Protestant European rivals.

After the British monarchy was restored in 1660, the new royalist Parliament passed the Navigation Act of 1660, which specified that certain colonial products such as tobacco were to be shipped *only* to Britain or to other

British colonies, not European nations. The Navigation Act of 1663, also known as the Staples Act, required that *all* shipments of goods from Europe to America stop first in Britain, be offloaded, and be taxed before their re-shipment to the colonies.

In 1664, a British fleet of warships conquered New Netherland, removing the Dutch rival from North America. Over time, the Navigation Acts worked as planned: by 1700, the British had surpassed the Dutch as the world's leading maritime power. Virtually all of the products sent to and from America from Europe and Africa were carried in British ships. What the British government did not predict or fully understand was that the mercantile system would arouse growing resentment in the colonies.

> Navigation Acts target Dutch

Resentment in the British Colonies

Colonial merchants and shippers loudly complained about the Navigation Acts. New England, which shipped 90 percent of all American exports, was particularly hard hit. In 1678, a defiant Massachusetts legislature declared that the Navigation Acts had no legal standing in the colony. Six years later, in 1684, King Charles II tried to teach the rebellious colonists a lesson by revoking the royal charter for Massachusetts.

The following year, in 1685, King Charles II died and was succeeded by his brother, the Duke of York, now crowned King James II. The new king reorganized all of the New England colonies into a single royal colony called the Dominion of New England. In 1686, the newly appointed royal governor, Sir Edmund Andros, arrived in Boston to take control. Andros imposed new taxes as well as the Anglican religion, ignored the authority of town governments, strictly enforced the Navigation Acts, and punished American smugglers who tried to avoid regulation altogether.

> Dominion of New England

The Glorious Revolution

In 1688, the Dominion of New England added the former Dutch provinces of New York, East Jersey, and West Jersey to its control, just a few months before the **Glorious Revolution** erupted in Britain in December. When news reached Boston that the Catholic King James II had been forced to flee to France and that he would be replaced by his Protestant daughter Mary and her Protestant husband William III (the ruling Dutch Prince) as the new king and queen of Great Britain, Boston staged its own revolution. A group of merchants, ministers, and militiamen (citizen-soldiers) arrested Governor Andros and his aides and removed Massachusetts Bay Colony from the new Dominion. Within a few weeks, the other colonies that had been absorbed into the Dominion also restored their independence.

William and Mary, the new British monarchs, allowed all of the colonies to regain their former status except Massachusetts Bay and Plymouth, which after some delay were united under a new charter in 1691 as the royal colony of Massachusetts Bay. But William and Mary were also determined to crack

Glorious Revolution (1688)
Successful coup, instigated by a group of English aristocrats, that overthrew King James II and instated William of Orange and Mary, his English wife, to the British throne.

down on American smuggling and rebelliousness. They appointed new royal governors in Massachusetts, New York, and Maryland. In Massachusetts, the new governor was given authority to veto acts of the colonial assembly, and he removed the Puritans' religious qualification for voting.

The Glorious Revolution in Britain had significant long-term effects on American history in that the removal of King James II revealed that a hated monarch could be deposed. (The revolution was called "Glorious" because it took place with very little bloodshed, unlike the English Civil War a generation earlier; indeed, the long-standing geographical designation "Great Britain" for the island shared by England, Scotland, and Wales would soon be revived as the official name of the nation.) A powerful justification for revolution appeared in 1690 when the English philosopher John Locke published his *Two Treatises on Government*, which had an enormous impact on political thought in the colonies. Locke rejected the "divine" right of monarchs to govern with absolute power. He also insisted that people are endowed with **natural rights** to life, liberty, and property. After all, as Locke noted, it was the need to protect those "natural" rights that led people to establish governments in the first place. When rulers failed to protect the property and lives of their subjects, Locke argued, the people had the right—in extreme cases—to overthrow the monarch and change the government.

CORE OBJECTIVE

2. Analyze the effects of the French and Indian War and how the war changed relations among the European powers in North America.

natural rights An individual's basic rights (life, liberty, and happiness) that should not be violated by any government or community.

Warfare in the Colonies

The Glorious Revolution of 1688 transformed relations among the great powers of Europe. The Protestant William and Mary, the new British King and Queen, were passionate foes of Catholic France's Louis XIV. The new king William organized an alliance of European nations against the French in a transatlantic war known in the American colonies as King William's War (1689–1697). It was the first of four major wars fought in Europe and the colonies over the next seventy-four years. In each case, Britain and its European allies fought against Catholic France or Spain and their allies. By the end of the eighteenth century, the struggle between the British and the French would shift the balance of power in Europe.

The French and Indian War

By far, the most significant conflict between Britain and France in North America was the French and Indian War (1754–1763). Unlike the three previous wars between Britain and France and their allies, it ended with a decisive victory. Sparked by competing claims over the Indian lands in the vast Ohio Valley, the "most fertile country of America," the stakes were high. Both the British and the French governments believed that whoever controlled the "Ohio Country" would come to control the entire continent.

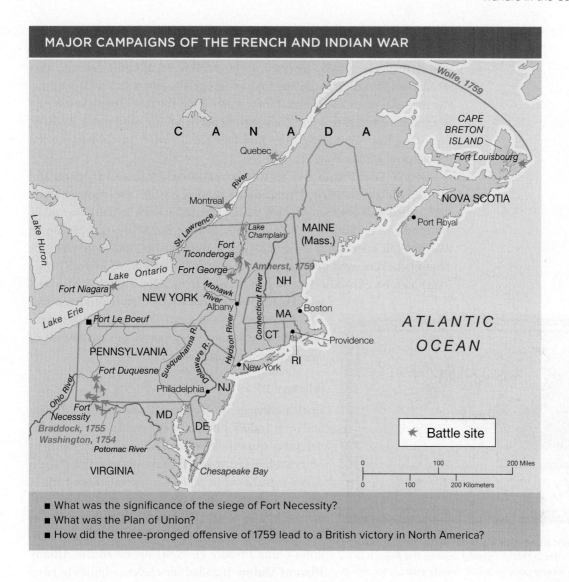

MAJOR CAMPAIGNS OF THE FRENCH AND INDIAN WAR

■ What was the significance of the siege of Fort Necessity?
■ What was the Plan of Union?
■ How did the three-pronged offensive of 1759 lead to a British victory in North America?

To defend their interests in the Ohio Valley, the French pushed south from Canada and built forts in upstate New York and western Pennsylvania. When the Virginia governor learned of the French forts, he sent a twenty-one-year-old Virginia militia officer, Major George Washington, to warn the French to leave the area. With an experienced guide and a few others, Washington made his way on foot and by horseback, canoe, and raft over 450 miles to Fort Le Boeuf (just south of Lake Erie, in northwest Pennsylvania) in late 1753. He demanded that the French withdraw from the Ohio Country; the French captain refused. A frustrated George Washington returned to Virginia through the deepening snow. A few months later, in the spring of 1754, George Washington went back to the Ohio Country. This time he led 150 inexperienced volunteer soldiers and Indian allies to build a fort where the Allegheny, Monongahela, and Ohio Rivers converged (where the city of Pittsburgh later developed). After two months of difficult travel through densely-forested, hilly terrain, Washington learned that French soldiers had beaten him to the strategic site and built Fort Duquesne. Washington made camp about forty miles from the fort. The next day, the Virginians ambushed a French scouting party, killing ten French soldiers, including the commander—the first fatalities in what would become the French and Indian War.

George Washington and his troops, reinforced by more Virginians and British soldiers dispatched from South Carolina, hastily constructed a crude fort, called Fort Necessity, which a large force of French soldiers attacked a month later, on July 3, 1754. After the day-long Battle of Great Meadows, Washington surrendered, having seen a third of his 300 men killed or wounded. France was now in undisputed control of the Ohio Country. George Washington's expedition not only had failed to oust the French; it also triggered a series of events that would ignite a massive world war. As a British politician exclaimed, "the volley fired by a young Virginian in the backwoods of America set the world on fire."

The first American political cartoon Benjamin Franklin's exhortation to the colonies to unite against the French in 1754 would become popular again twenty years later, when the colonies faced a different threat.

Albany Plan

British officials, worried about war with the French and their Indian allies, hastily organized a meeting of delegates from the northern colonies as far south as Maryland. Twenty-one representatives from seven colonies gathered in Albany, in upstate New York. It was the first time that a large group of colonial delegates had met to take joint action. At the urging of Pennsylvania's Benjamin Franklin, the Albany Congress (June 19–July 11, 1754) approved the **Albany Plan of Union**. It called for eleven colonies to band together, headed by a president appointed by the king. Each colonial assembly would send two to seven delegates to a "grand council," which would have legislative powers. The Union would have jurisdiction over Indian affairs.

But the Albany Plan of Union was too radical for the time. The colonial legislatures, eager to maintain their powers, and British officials, who wanted simply a military alliance against Indian attacks, rejected it. Benjamin Franklin later maintained that the 1754 Plan of Union, had it been adopted, may have postponed or eliminated the eventual need for a full-scale colonial revolution.

With the failure of the Albany Plan, the British government decided to force a showdown with the "presumptuous" French in North America. In June 1755, a British fleet captured the French forts protecting Acadia, a colony of New France along the Atlantic coast of Canada. The British then

Albany Plan of Union (1754)
A failed proposal by the seven northern colonies in anticipation of the French and Indian War, urging the unification of the colonies under one Crown-appointed president.

expelled 11,500 of the Catholic French residents, called Acadians. They were put on ships and scattered throughout the British colonies, from Maine to Georgia. Hundreds uprooted by the "Great Expulsion" eventually found their way to French Louisiana, where they became known as Cajuns (the name derived from *Acadians*).

Braddock's Defeat

In 1755, the British government also sent a thousand soldiers to Virginia to force the French out of the Ohio Country. The British commander, General Edward Braddock, was a stubborn, overconfident officer who had no experience fighting in the American wilderness. Braddock viewed Native Americans with contempt, and his ignorance of Indian warfare would prove fatal. With the addition of some American militiamen, including George Washington as a volunteer officer, Braddock's force hacked a 125-mile-long road west through the rugged Allegheny Mountains toward Fort Duquesne. The British were on the verge of success when, on July 9, 1755, six miles from Fort Duquesne, they were ambushed by French soldiers and Indians. Attacked on three sides, the British troops suffered horrific losses. General Braddock died from his wounds. Twenty-three-year-old George Washington, his coat riddled by four bullets, helped other officers lead a hasty retreat.

The French and Indians had killed 63 of 86 British officers, 914 out of 1,373 soldiers, and captured the British cannons, supplies, and secret papers. It was one of the worst British defeats in history. Twelve of the wounded British soldiers left behind on the battlefield were stripped and burned alive by Indians. A devastated George Washington wrote his brother that the British army had "been scandalously beaten by a trifling body of men." The vaunted redcoats "broke & run as sheep before hounds," but the Virginians "behaved like Men and died like Soldiers."

A World War

Braddock's stunning defeat sent shock waves through the colonies. Inspired by the news, Indians allied with the French attacked American families living on isolated farms throughout western Pennsylvania, Maryland, and Virginia. It was not until May 1756, however, that Britain and France formally declared war; the **French and Indian War** in America would become known as the Seven Years' War in Europe. A worldwide war between the Protestant and Catholic nations, it would eventually be fought on four continents and three oceans around the globe. In the end, it would redraw the map of the world.

In 1759, the French and Indian War reached its climax with a series of British triumphs on land and at sea around the world. The most decisive British victory was at Quebec, the gateway to French Canada. Thereafter, the war in North America dragged on until 1763. In the South, fighting flared up between the Carolina settlers and the Cherokee Nation. A force of British regulars and colonial militia broke Cherokee resistance in 1761.

From La Roque's *Encyclopédie des Voyages* An Iroquois warrior in an eighteenth-century French engraving.

The French and Indian War becomes the Seven Years' War

French and Indian War (Seven Years' War) (1756–1763) The last and most important of four colonial wars between England and France for control of North America east of the Mississippi River.

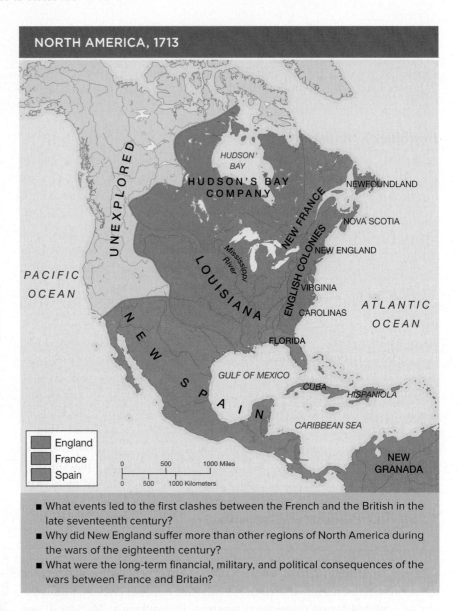

NORTH AMERICA, 1713

HUDSON BAY

HUDSON'S BAY COMPANY

UNEXPLORED

NEWFOUNDLAND

NOVA SCOTIA

NEW FRANCE

Mississippi River

NEW ENGLAND

ENGLISH COLONIES

VIRGINIA

CAROLINAS

LOUISIANA

PACIFIC OCEAN

ATLANTIC OCEAN

FLORIDA

NEW SPAIN

GULF OF MEXICO

CUBA

HISPANIOLA

CARIBBEAN SEA

NEW GRANADA

England
France
Spain

0   500   1000 Miles
0   500   1000 Kilometers

- What events led to the first clashes between the French and the British in the late seventeenth century?
- Why did New England suffer more than other regions of North America during the wars of the eighteenth century?
- What were the long-term financial, military, and political consequences of the wars between France and Britain?

George III The young king of a victorious empire.

Meanwhile, the much larger Seven Years' War played out around the globe, with skirmishes in South America, Africa, India, and the Philippines in addition to British gains in North America. Most of the fighting, though, was in Europe, where Great Britain's allies, especially Prussia, and the nations allied with France and Spain, primarily Austria, Sweden, and Russia, ravaged each other. Hundreds of towns and cities were plundered and destroyed and over a million people killed.

On October 25, 1760, King George II arose at 6 A.M., as was his habit, then drank his morning chocolate milk, and suddenly, unexpectedly, died on his toilet. His death shocked the nation, in part because the new twenty-two-year-old king, George III, was inexperienced and despised by his grandfather, George II. The boyish king turned into a strong-willed leader. He

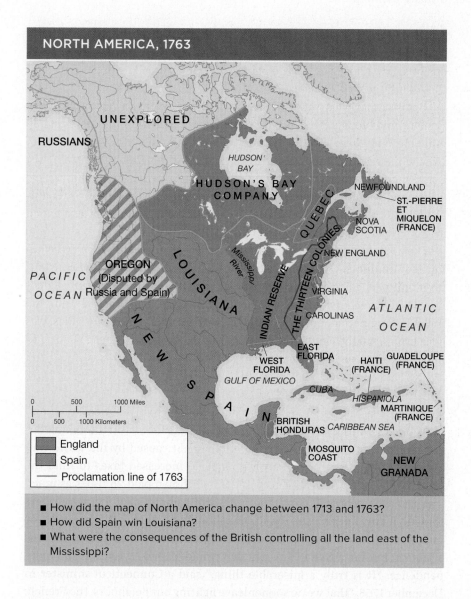

NORTH AMERICA, 1763

UNEXPLORED

RUSSIANS

HUDSON BAY

HUDSON'S BAY COMPANY

QUEBEC

NEWFOUNDLAND

ST.-PIERRE ET MIQUELON (FRANCE)

NOVA SCOTIA

NEW ENGLAND

Mississippi River

LOUISIANA

INDIAN RESERVE

THE THIRTEEN COLONIES

VIRGINIA

PACIFIC OCEAN

OREGON (Disputed by Russia and Spain)

CAROLINAS

ATLANTIC OCEAN

NEW SPAIN

EAST FLORIDA

WEST FLORIDA

GULF OF MEXICO

HAITI (FRANCE)

GUADELOUPE (FRANCE)

CUBA

HISPANIOLA

MARTINIQUE (FRANCE)

BRITISH HONDURAS

CARIBBEAN SEA

MOSQUITO COAST

NEW GRANADA

0   500   1000 Miles
0   500   1000 Kilometers

■ England
■ Spain
— Proclamation line of 1763

- How did the map of North America change between 1713 and 1763?
- How did Spain win Louisiana?
- What were the consequences of the British controlling all the land east of the Mississippi?

oversaw the military defeat of France and Spain, which made Great Britain the ruler of an enormous world empire and a united kingdom brimming with confidence and pride. Within three years of George III's ascension to the throne, Britain became the largest, richest, and most powerful empire in the world. And the American colonists celebrated the great British victories with as much excitement and pride as did the British themselves.

The Treaty of Paris (1763)

More territory was transferred from the vanquished to the victors as a result of the French and Indian War than any other war before or since. In the **Treaty of Paris**, signed in February 1763, victorious Britain took several profitable French "sugar island" colonies in the West Indies, most of the French colonies in India, and all of France's North American possessions east of the Mississippi River: all of Canada and all of what was then called

Treaty of Paris (1763) Settlement between Great Britain and France that ended the French and Indian War.

Spanish Florida (including much of present-day Alabama and Mississippi). The hugely profitable fur trade that the French had developed with the Indians was now transferred to the British, as were the rich fishing grounds off the Atlantic coast of Canada.

> The British gain most of North America; the Spanish gain the Louisiana Territory

British Americans were delighted with the outcome of the war. As a New England minister declared, Great Britain had reached the "summit of earthly grandeur and glory." The British now controlled most of the continent of North America. In compensation for its loss of Florida in the Treaty of Paris, Spain received from France the vast Louisiana Territory (including New Orleans and all French land west of the Mississippi River). The loss of Louisiana left France with no territory on the continent. British power reigned supreme over North America east of the Mississippi River.

But Britain's spectacular military success also created massive challenges. Humiliated France thirsted for revenge; a new war was a constant possibility. The British victory was also costly; Britain's national debt doubled during the war. The cost of maintaining the North American empire, including the permanent stationing of British soldiers in the colonies, was staggering. And the victory meant that Britain now had to manage half a *billion* acres of new colonial territory in North America.

Managing a New Empire

> Colonists taxed to pay staggering British debts

No sooner was the Treaty of Paris signed than young King George III and his cabinet began strictly enforcing economic regulations on the colonies as a means of reducing the crushing national debt caused by the world war. During the war, the British government had increased taxes to fund the military expenses. In 1763, the average Englishman paid 26 times as much in taxes each year as the average American colonist paid. British leaders thought it only fair that the Americans should pay more of the expenses for maintaining and defending the colonies. Many Americans disagreed, thus setting in motion a chain of events that would lead to revolution and independence. "It is truly a miserable thing," said a Connecticut minister in December 1763, "that we no sooner leave fighting our neighbors, the French, but we must fall to quarreling among ourselves."

Pontiac's Rebellion

Pontiac's Rebellion (1763) A series of Native American attacks on British forts and settlements after France ceded to the British its territory east of the Mississippi River, as part of the Treaty of Paris without consulting France's Native American allies.

Royal Proclamation of 1763 Proclamation drawing a boundary along the Appalachian Mountains from Canada to Georgia in order to minimize occurrences of settler–Native American violence; colonists were forbidden to go west of the line.

From the beginning, the colonists in America had always pushed westward, and the lust for new lands only increased after 1763. Tens of thousands of European immigrants arrived each year, lured by promises of free land, low taxes, and religious freedom. No sooner had the war with France ended than colonists began squabbling over Indian-owned land west of the Appalachian Mountains that the French had ceded to the victorious British in the Treaty of Paris. Native American leaders, none of whom attended the meetings leading to the Treaty of Paris in 1763, were shocked to learn that the French had "given" their lands to the British. They demanded to know "by what right the French could pretend" to transfer Native American lands to the British.

In a desperate effort to recover their lands, Indians fought back in the spring of 1763, capturing most of the British forts around the Great Lakes and in the Ohio Valley. They also raided colonial settlements in Pennsylvania, Maryland, and Virginia, destroying hundreds of farm cabins and killing several thousand people.

The widespread Indian attacks in the spring and summer of 1763 came to be called **Pontiac's Rebellion** because of the prominent role played by the inspiring Ottawa chief. The British government eventually negotiated an agreement with the Indians that allowed British troops to reoccupy the frontier forts in exchange for a renewal of the fur trade. Still, as Chief Pontiac stressed, the Indians denied British claims to their territory under the terms of the Treaty of Paris. He told a British official that the "French never conquered us, neither did they purchase a foot of our Country, nor have they a right to give it to you."

To help keep peace with the Indians, King George III issued the **Royal Proclamation of 1763**, which drew an imaginary "proclamation line" along the crest of the Appalachian Mountains from Canada in the north to Georgia in the south. White settlers ("our loving subjects") were forbidden to go west of the line in order to ensure that the Indians would not be "molested or disturbed" on their ancestral lands. For the first time, American territorial expansion was to be curtailed by royal officials. The British government sent 10,000 soldiers to enforce the new boundary line separating Indians and whites and to ensure that the former French colonists in Canada did not cause trouble. Yet in practice the Proclamation Line was impossible to enforce. Land-hungry settlers defied its boundaries and continued to push across the Appalachian ridges into Indian country. By 1767, an Indian chief was complaining that whites were "making more encroachments on their Country than ever they had before."

Tightening Control over the Colonies

CORE **OBJECTIVE**
3. Describe how, after the French and Indian War in the 1760s, the British tried to strengthen their control over the colonies and then summarize the colonial responses.

The Royal Proclamation of 1763 was the first of several efforts by the British government after the French and Indian War to increase control over the colonies. Little did the king and his ministers know that their efforts would spark a revolution.

Grenville's Colonial Policy

New taxes and regulations

Just as the Proclamation of 1763 was being drafted, a new British government led by George Grenville began to grapple with the huge debts the government had accumulated during the war—and the added expenses of maintaining large numbers of British troops in America. George Grenville's colonial policy declared that the Americans, whom he called the "least taxed

The Road to the American Revolution

The French and Indian War (1754–1763) redrew the map of the world. It was sparked by competing claims over the Native American lands in the vast Ohio Valley. The military defeat of France and Spain made Great Britain the ruler of an enormous world empire. American colonists celebrated the British victories with as much excitement and pride as did the British themselves. The British victory gave them control of most of the North American continent, although Native Americans still claimed most of it as their own. The following timeline highlights important features in the British government's attempts to manage its empire in North America after the French and Indian War, leading up to the American Revolution.

1763 Treaty of Paris; Royal Proclamation Line

■ In the Treaty of Paris, Britain acquires all of France's North American possessions east of the Mississippi River, as well as Spanish Florida (Florida, Alabama, and Mississippi), but Native Americans refuse to recognize the Treaty and fight for their lands.

■ King George III ends fighting with Native Americans and issues the Royal Proclamation of 1763 to prevent American colonists from settling west of the Appalachian Mountains; colonists ignore the Proclamation.

1764 American Revenue Act (Sugar Act); Currency Act

■ Sugar Act cuts the import tax on molasses in an attempt to deter colonial distillers from smuggling molasses from the French, but also imposes new import duties on textiles, wine, coffee, indigo, and sugar in order to raise new revenue from the colonists.

■ Currency Act prohibits colonies from printing more paper money in order to ensure the payment of colonial debt to British merchants in gold and silver coins.

1765 Stamp Act; Quartering Act

■ Stamp Act orders colonists to pay a tax on all printed materials.

■ Quartering Act requires colonies to feed and house British troops.

1766 Boycotts, Protests; Stamp Act Repealed; Declaratory Act

■ A humiliated Parliament repeals the Stamp Act after widespread colonial protests and boycotts of British goods but issues the Declaratory Act announcing that it has authority to pass any law regulating the colonies.

1767 Townshend Acts; Revenue Act

■ Townshend Acts shut down the New York colonial assembly in retaliation for its defiance of the Quartering Act (the assembly quickly yields).

■ A new Revenue Act imposes taxes on the colonies' glass, lead, paint, paper, and tea imports.

British warships target American smugglers

people in the world," must pay for the British troops defending them. Grenville also resented the large number of American smugglers who avoided paying taxes on imported goods. Americans after the war went on a buying binge, eager to purchase the latest fashionable items from Britain and France, and they preferred buying from smugglers—it was cheaper. So Grenville ordered colonial officials to tighten the enforcement of the Navigation Acts, and he sent warships to capture American smugglers.

1770 Revenue Act repealed; Boston Massacre

- Parliament repeals all taxes imposed by the Revenue Act except for that on tea.
- Tensions with British troops spark the Boston Massacre.

1773 Tea Act

- Parliament, in an effort to bail out the British East India Company, passes the Tea Act, which allows the company to sell its tea to the colonists without paying any taxes.

1774 Boston Tea Party; Coercive Acts

- Bostonians defy the Tea Act by destroying the British East India Company's tea at the Boston Tea Party.
- Parliament passes the Coercive Acts, which close the port of Boston, direct local authorities to house and feed British troops, repeal the right of Massachusetts colonists to elect many civic officials, and ban all town meetings held without the Royal Governor's permission.

1775 Continental Congress; Conciliatory Proposition; Continental Army; Olive Branch Petition

- The First Continental Congress meets to oppose the Coercive Acts and to assert the colonies' autonomy from Parliament.
- In response, British prime minister sends to each colony a Conciliatory Proposition to eliminate all of Parliament's revenue-generating schemes in any colony that volunteers to pay its share for the defense and governance of the colony.

- British soldiers clash with Massachusetts Minutemen at Lexington and Concord in Massachusetts.
- The Second Continental Congress appoints George Washington to lead a new Continental army.
- While suffering terrible losses, British forces defeat Americans at the Battle of Bunker Hill outside of Boston.
- King George III rejects the Continental Congress's Olive Branch Petition urging reconciliation.

1776 Declaration of Independence

- The Continental Congress authorizes all thirteen colonies to form independent state governments.
- The Continental Congress adopts the Declaration of Independence.

QUESTIONS FOR ANALYSIS

1. How did British citizens in Britain and in the American colonies respond differently to the British Empire's acquisition of Native American lands after the Treaty of Paris?

2. What were the overall goals of Britain's colonial policy after the French and Indian War?

3. How did British policy change in response to the colonists' opposition?

4. Judging from this timeline, were there opportunities for a compromise between the British and American colonists before the colonists' declaration of independence?

The Sugar Act

Grenville realized that his new effort to enforce the often-violated Molasses Act of 1733 posed a serious threat to New England's prosperity. Making rum in New England out of molasses, a sweet syrup made from sugarcane was quite profitable, especially if the molasses could be smuggled in from Caribbean islands controlled by the French. The tax on molasses, therefore, was not mainly intended to raise revenue for the British government but to force New England rum producers to buy molasses from the British islands in the Caribbean rather than from the French. To ease the burden of the tax on imported molasses, Grenville put through the American Revenue Act of 1764, commonly known as the Sugar Act, which cut the tax on molasses in half. Doing so, he believed, would reduce the temptation to smuggle molasses or to bribe royal customs officers. But the Sugar Act contained a catch: it also added new duties (taxes) on other goods (sugar, wines, coffee, spices) imported into America. The new revenues generated by the Sugar Act, Grenville estimated, would help pay for "the necessary expenses of defending, protecting, and securing, the said colonies and plantations."

The Sugar Act raised the stakes over British regulations in the colonies. For the first time, Parliament had adopted so-called external duties (taxes) designed to raise *revenues* from the colonies and not merely intended to *regulate* trade with other nations. As such, it was viewed as violating a basic British principle by taxing the colonists without their consent, since the colonies had no representatives in Parliament.

The Currency Act

Another of Grenville's new regulatory measures, the Currency Act of 1764, was equally hated in the colonies. It prohibited the colonies from printing more paper money, and stipulated that all payments for British goods must be in gold or silver coins or a commodity like tobacco. This caused the value of existing paper money to plummet and dried up much of American commerce. As a Philadelphia newspaper noted, "The Times are Dreadful, Dismal, Doleful, Dolorous, and DOLLAR-LESS."

The Quartering Act

Then, in 1765, Grenville persuaded Parliament to pass the Quartering Act as part of his new system of colonial regulations. The Quartering Act required the colonies to feed and house British troops. Such a step seemed perfectly appropriate to Grenville, since he and many others in Britain believed that the Americans should contribute to the expense of defending the colonies. In the view of many Americans, however, the Quartering Act was yet another form of tax as well as another form of repression. Many Americans saw no need for so many British soldiers in colonial cities. If the British were there to defend against Indians, why weren't they positioned closer to the Indians? Some colonists decided that the Quartering Act was actually an effort to use British soldiers to bully the Americans.

The Stamp Act

Britain's prime minister, George Grenville, excelled at doing the wrong thing—repeatedly. The Sugar Act, for example, did not produce more revenue for Great Britain; the cost of enforcing it, in fact, was four times greater than the additional revenue it generated. Yet Grenville worsened the situation by pushing through an even more controversial measure to raise money in America: a stamp tax. On February 13, 1765, Parliament passed the **Stamp Act**, which created special paper with tax stamps embossed on it. The colonists would have to purchase stamped paper for virtually every possible use: newspapers, pamphlets, bonds, leases, deeds, licenses, insurance policies, college diplomas, even playing cards. The requirement was to go into effect November 1, nine months later. The Stamp Act was especially important because it affected all the colonists, not just New England merchants and shippers, and it was the first effort by Parliament to place a direct—or "internal"—tax specifically on American goods and services rather than an "external" tax on imports and exports.

The Whig Point of View

Grenville's colonial policies outraged many Americans. Unwittingly, the prime minister had stirred up a storm of protest and set in motion a violent debate about the proper relationship between Great Britain and her American colonies. Slowly, more and more colonists began developing what could be called an American rather than a British point of view. It was not based on a common ancestry, a shared religion, or even a common culture. Rather, the American perspective involved taking for granted certain essential principles and practices: self-government, equality of economic opportunity, religious freedom, and territorial expansion. Now, all of those deeply embedded values seemed threatened by Parliament's determined efforts to tighten control over its colonies after 1763. In the late eighteenth century, the Americans who opposed British policies began to call themselves Whigs, a name earlier applied to British critics of royal power, and to label the king and his "corrupt" government ministers and Parliamentary supporters as "Tories," a word meaning friends of the king.

In 1764 and 1765, American Whigs decided that Grenville was violating their rights in several ways. A professional army was usually a weapon used by tyrants, and now, with the French defeated and Canada solidly under British control, thousands of British soldiers remained in the colonies. Were the troops there to protect the colonists or to scare them into obedience?

Other factors heightened colonial fears. British citizens had the right to be taxed only by their elected representatives in Parliament, but Americans had no such representatives. British leaders countered that the colonists were "virtually" represented in Parliament, whose members were sworn to represent not simply their own districts but Britons everywhere. After all, Grenville and other British authorities argued, Americans were like many individuals and groups in Britain that had no voice in elections to Parliament because of high property qualifications for voting. They were instead

Virtual representation

Stamp Act (1765) Act of Parliament requiring that all printed materials in the American colonies use paper with an official tax stamp in order to pay for British military protection of the colonies.

provided with **virtual representation** by all of the members of Parliament acting in the national interest.

William Pitt, a staunch supporter of American rights in Parliament, dismissed Grenville's concept of "virtual representation" as "the most contemptible idea that ever entered into the head of a man." Many others, in both Britain and America, agreed. Sir Francis Bernard, the royal governor of Massachusetts, correctly predicted that the new stamp tax "would cause a great Alarm & meet much Opposition" in the colonies.

Protests in the Colonies

George Grenville had assumed that, because a stamp tax had been in place in Britain for years, it would not create much resistance in the American colonies. He was wrong. The Stamp Act aroused fierce resentment among the colonists. A New Yorker wrote that "this single stroke has lost Great Britain the affection of all her colonies." In a flood of pamphlets, speeches, and resolutions, critics repeated a slogan familiar to all Americans: "No taxation without representation [in Parliament]."

Through the spring and summer of 1765, this simmering resentment boiled over at meetings, parades, bonfires, and other demonstrations. The protesters, calling themselves **Sons of Liberty**, emerged in every colony, often meeting beneath "liberty trees"—in Boston a great elm, in Charleston, South Carolina, a live oak. In New York City, the Sons of Liberty erected "liberty poles" as symbols of their resistance (British soldiers would tear them down almost as soon as they were put up). In Virginia, Patrick Henry convinced the assembly to pass the "Stamp Act Resolutions," which asserted yet again that the colonists could not be taxed without being consulted by the British government or represented in the British Parliament.

In mid-August 1765, nearly three months before the Stamp Act was to take effect, a mob of angry Bostonians plundered the homes of the royal lieutenant governor and the royal official in charge of enforcing the stamp tax. Thoroughly shaken, the Boston stamp agent resigned, and stamp agents throughout the colonies were hounded out of office. By November 1, its effective starting date, the Stamp Act was dead.

The Nonimportation Movement

Americans opposed to the Stamp Act knew that the most powerful form of leverage they had against the British was economic. To demonstrate their resolve and to put pressure on the British government, colonists by the thousands signed nonimportation agreements, promising not to buy any British goods. These boycotts of imported British products were an especially effective tactic because American consumers had become a major boon to the British economy during the eighteenth century. Now this was at risk, and many London merchants sided with the Americans against the

Stamp Act Resolutions

virtual representation The idea that the American colonies, although they had no actual representative in Parliament, were "virtually" represented by all members of Parliament.

Sons of Liberty First organized by Samuel Adams in the 1770s, groups of colonists dedicated to militant resistance against British control of the colonies.

Opposition to the Stamp Act
In protest of the Stamp Act, which was to take effect the next day, *The Pennsylvania Journal* printed a skull and crossbones on its masthead.

proposed Stamp Act, fearful of losing their profitable business with their overseas customers.

The nonimportation movement of the 1760s and 1770s enabled women to play a significant public role in the resistance against Britain's colonial policies. Calling themselves **Daughters of Liberty**, many colonial women quit buying imported British clothes and made their own. The Daughters of Liberty also participated in public "spinning bees," whereby groups of women would gather in the town square to weave and spin yarn and wool into fabric, known as "homespun."

Americans saw the effort to boycott British products not only as a means of exerting political pressure on Parliament but also as a way to restore their own virtue. A Rhode Islander declared that a primary cause of America's problems was the "luxury and extravagance" brought on by their freewheeling purchases of British goods. The nonimportation movement would help Americans restore "our frugality, industry, and simplicity of manners." Plain living soon became a sign of American patriotism. A Boston minister claimed that those who could not do without British luxury goods and be satisfied with "plainness and simplicity" did not deserve to be American citizens.

Boycotts

Colonial Unity

The surprisingly effective boycotts of British imported goods strengthened colonial unity as Americans discovered that they had more in common with each other than with their fellow British subjects in Great Britain. The Virginia assembly struck the first official blow against the Stamp Act with the Virginia Resolves, a series of resolutions inspired by the fiery young Patrick Henry. Virginians, Henry declared, were entitled to all the rights of Englishmen, and Englishmen could be taxed only by their own

Virginia Resolves

Daughters of Liberty Colonial women who protested the British government's tax policies by boycotting British products, such as clothing, and who wove their own fabric, or "homespun."

The Stamp Act Congress, and the Declaration of Rights and Grievances

elected representatives. Newspapers spread the Virginia Resolves throughout the colonies, and other colonial assemblies hastened to follow Virginia's example.

In 1765, the Massachusetts House of Representatives invited the other colonial assemblies to send delegates to meet in New York to discuss their opposition to the Stamp Act. Nine responded, and from October 7 to 25, 1765, the so-called Stamp Act Congress formulated a Declaration of the Rights and Grievances of the Colonies. The delegates insisted that they would accept no taxes being "imposed on them" without "their own consent, given personally, or by their representatives." Parliament, in other words, had no right to tax people who were unrepresented in that body. Grenville responded to the American slogan "No taxation without representation!" by denouncing his colonial critics as "ungrateful" for all of the benefits provided them by the British government.

Repeal of the Stamp Act

The storm had scarcely broken before Grenville was out of office in London and the Stamp Act was repealed. Grenville had lost the confidence of the king, who replaced him with Lord Rockingham in July 1765. Pressure from British merchants hurt by the colonial boycott convinced the Rockingham-led government that the Stamp Act was a mistake. In February 1766, a humiliated Parliament repealed the Stamp Act. To save face, it also passed the Declaratory Act, which asserted the power of Parliament to govern the colonies "in all cases whatsoever." The repeal of the Stamp Act set off excited demonstrations throughout the colonies. Perhaps the worst was over, they hoped.

The Townshend Acts Fan the Flames

In July 1766, King George III replaced Lord Rockingham with William Pitt, the former prime minister who had exercised heroic leadership during the French and Indian War. For a time in 1767, the guiding force in the Pitt ministry was the witty but reckless Charles Townshend, the treasury chief whose "abilities were superior to those of all men," said a colleague, "and his judgment [common sense] below that of any man."

More taxes under Townshend

In 1767, Townshend, determined like his predecessors to extract more revenue from the colonies in order to pay for the costs of governing and defending them, pushed his ill-fated plan through Parliament; a few months later he died at age forty-two, leaving behind a bitter legacy: the **Townshend Acts**. Among Townshend's new policies, the Revenue Act of 1767, which taxed colonial imports of glass, lead, paint, paper, and tea, was the most hated. The Revenue Act of 1767 posed an even more severe threat to colonial assemblies than Grenville's taxes had done, for Townshend planned to use the new tax revenues to pay the royal governors in the colonies and thereby release them from financial dependence upon the colonial assemblies.

Townshend Acts (1767) Parliamentary measures to extract more revenue from the colonies; the Revenue Act of 1767, which taxed tea, paper, and other colonial imports, was one of the most notorious of these policies.

The Crisis Grows

American Patriots

The Townshend Acts surprised and angered the colonists. As American rage bubbled over, loyalty to Britain waned. Firebrand Samuel Adams of Boston emerged as the most radical of American rebels. Early in 1768, he and the Boston attorney James Otis convinced the Massachusetts assembly to circulate a letter they had written to the other colonies. The letter's tone was polite and logical: it restated the illegality of taxation without colonial representation in Parliament and invited the support of other colonies. British officials ordered the Massachusetts assembly to withdraw the Adams-Otis letter. The assembly refused, and the king ordered the assembly dissolved.

In response to an appeal by the royal governor of Massachusetts, 4,000 British troops were sent to Boston in October 1768 to maintain social order. **Loyalists**, as the American Tories who supported the king and Parliament were often called, welcomed the soldiers; **Patriots**, the name for those rebelling against British authority, viewed the British troops as an occupation force intended to crush dissent. Meanwhile, in London the king appointed a new chief minister, Frederick, Lord North, in January 1770.

The Boston Massacre

By 1770, the American nonimportation agreements were strangling British trade with the colonies and causing unemployment in Britain. The impact of the colonial boycott of British products persuaded Lord North to modify the Townshend Acts—just in time to prevent tensions from getting out of hand. In Boston, the British soldiers (called "lobsterbacks" or "redcoats" because of their red uniforms) had become a constant source of irritation to Patriots. Crowds heckled the soldiers, many of whom earned the abuse by harassing and intimidating Americans.

On March 5, 1770, a group of rowdies began taunting and throwing icicles at a British guard. Soldiers rushed to his aid. Then someone rang the town fire bell, drawing a larger crowd to the scene. At their head, or so the story goes, was Crispus Attucks, a runaway African American slave. Attucks and others continued to bait the British troops. Finally, a soldier was knocked down; he rose to his feet and fired into the crowd, as did others. When the smoke cleared, five people lay dead or dying, and eight more were wounded.

The so-called **Boston Massacre** sent shock waves throughout the colonies and all the way to London. Late in April 1770, Parliament repealed all the Townshend duties except for the tea tax. Colonial discontent diminished for two years thereafter. The redcoats left Boston, but they remained stationed nearby in Canada, and the British navy still patrolled the New England coast chasing smugglers.

CORE OBJECTIVE

4. Explain the underlying factors amid the events in the 1770s that led the colonies to declare their independence from Britain.

Samuel Adams Adams was the fiery organizer of the Sons of Liberty.

British troops and the Boston Massacre

Loyalists Colonists who remained loyal to Britain before and during the Revolutionary War.

Patriots Colonists who rebelled against British authority before and during the Revolutionary War.

Boston Massacre (1770) Violent confrontation between British soldiers and a Boston mob on March 5, 1770, in which five colonists were killed.

The Bloody Massacre Paul Revere's engraving of the Boston Massacre.

The *Gaspée* Incident

Then in 1772, a naval incident further eroded the colonies' fragile relationship with the mother country. Near Warwick, Rhode Island, the HMS *Gaspée*, a British warship, ran aground while chasing suspected smugglers, and its hungry crew went ashore and seized local sheep, hogs, and chickens. An angry crowd from the town then boarded the ship, shot the captain, removed the crew, and set fire to the vessel.

The *Gaspée* incident symbolized the anti-British anger felt by growing numbers of Americans. When the British tried to take the suspects to London for trial, Americans organized in protest. Thomas Jefferson remembered that it was the threat of transporting Americans for trials in Britain that reignited anti-British activities in Virginia. Likewise, in response to the fallout from the *Gaspée* incident, Samuel Adams in Boston organized the **Committee of Correspondence**, which issued a statement of American rights and grievances and invited other towns to do the same. Similar committees sprang up across Massachusetts and in other colonies, forming a network of rebellion. A Massachusetts Loyalist called the committees "the foulest, subtlest, and most venomous serpent ever issued from the egg of sedition." The crisis was escalating. "The flame is kindled and like lightning it catches from soul to soul," reported Abigail Adams, the high-spirited and politically astute wife of future president John Adams.

The *Gaspée* incident

Committee of Correspondence Group organized by Samuel Adams in retaliation for the *Gaspée* incident to address American grievances, assert American rights, and form a network of rebellion.

The Boston Tea Party

The new British prime minister, Lord North, soon provided the colonists with the spark to ignite colonial resentment. In 1773, he tried to bail out the struggling East India Company, which had in its British warehouses some 17 million pounds of tea that it desperately needed to sell before the tea rotted. Under the Tea Act of 1773, the government would allow the grossly mismanaged company to send its tea directly to America without paying any taxes. British tea merchants could thereby undercut the prices charged by their American competitors, most of whom were smugglers who bought tea from the Dutch. At the same time, King George III told Lord North that his job was to "compel obedience" in the colonies; North ordered British authorities in New England to clamp down harder on American smuggling.

The Committees of Correspondence, backed by Boston merchants, alerted colonists to the new danger. The British government, they said, was trying to purchase colonial submission with cheap tea. They saw the reduction in the price of tea as a clever trick to make them accept taxation without consent. Before the end of the year, large shipments of tea left Britain for the major colonial ports. In Boston, enraged colonists decided that their passion for liberty outweighed their love for tea. On December 16, 1773, scores of Patriots disguised as Indians boarded three British ships in Boston harbor and dumped 342 chests of East India Company tea overboard—cheered on by a crowd lining the shore.

The **Boston Tea Party** pushed British officials to the breaking point. They had tolerated criticism, evasion, and occasional violence, but the destruction of so much valuable tea convinced the king and his advisers that a forceful response was required. "The colonists must either submit or triumph," George III wrote to Lord North, who decided to make an example of Boston to the rest of the colonies. "We are now to establish our authority [over the colonies]," North said, "or give it up entirely." In the end, his reassertion of royal control helped make a revolution that would cost Britain far more than three shiploads of tea.

> Boston Tea Party

The Coercive Acts

In 1774, Parliament enacted a cluster of harsh laws, called the **Coercive Acts** (referred to by Americans as the "Intolerable" Acts), to punish rebellious Boston. The Boston Port Act closed the harbor from June 1, 1774, until the city paid for the lost tea. A new Quartering Act ordered local authorities to provide lodging for British soldiers. Finally, the Massachusetts Government Act made all of the colony's officials appointive rather than elective and ordered that no town meeting could be held without the royal governor's consent. In May, Lieutenant-General Thomas Gage, commander in chief of British forces in North America, was named governor of Massachusetts and assumed command of the British soldiers in Boston.

Boston Tea Party (1773) Demonstration against the Tea Act of 1773 in which the Sons of Liberty, dressed as Indians, dumped hundreds of chests of British-owned tea into Boston Harbor.

Coercive Acts (1774) Four parliamentary measures that required the colonies to pay for the Boston Tea Party's damages: imposed a military government, disallowed colonial trials of British soldiers, and forced the quartering of troops in private homes.

Elsewhere, colonists rallied to help Boston, raising money, sending supplies, and boycotting, as well as burning, British tea. In Williamsburg, when the Virginia assembly met in May, a young member of the Committee of Correspondence, Thomas Jefferson, suggested that June 1, the effective date of the Boston Port Act, become an official day of fasting and prayer in Virginia. The royal governor responded by dissolving the assembly, whose members then retired to the Raleigh Tavern where they decided to form a Continental Congress to represent all the colonies.

The First Continental Congress

The First Continental Congress

On September 5, 1774, the fifty-five delegates making up the First Continental Congress assembled in Philadelphia. During seven weeks of meetings, the Congress endorsed the Suffolk Resolves, which urged Massachusetts to resist British tyranny with force. The Congress then adopted a Declaration of American Rights, which proclaimed once again the rights of Americans as British citizens and denied Parliament's authority to regulate internal colonial affairs.

Finally, the First Continental Congress adopted the Continental Association of 1774, which recommended that every colony organize committees to enforce a complete boycott of all imported British goods. These elected committees became the organizational network for the resistance movement. Seven thousand men across the colonies served on the committees of the Continental Association, and many more thousands of women put the boycotts into practice. The committees required colonists to sign an oath refusing to purchase British goods. Those who refused to sign were punished; some were tarred and feathered.

Such efforts to gain economic self-sufficiency helped unify the diverse colonies. Thousands of ordinary men and women participated in the boycott of British goods, and their sacrifices on behalf of colonial liberties provided the momentum leading to revolution. For all of the attention given to colonial leaders such as Samuel Adams and Thomas Jefferson, it was common people who enforced the boycott, volunteered in Patriot militia units, attended town meetings, and exerted pressure on royal officials in the colonies. As the people of Pittsfield, Massachusetts, declared in a petition, "We have always believed that the people are the fountain of power."

Last Minute Compromise

In London, King George fumed. He wrote Lord North that "blows must decide" whether the Americans "are to be subject to this country or independent." In early 1775, Parliament declared that Massachusetts was officially "in rebellion" and prohibited the New England colonies from trading with any nation outside the British Empire. On February 27, 1775, Lord North issued the Conciliatory Propositions, which offered to resolve the festering dispute by eliminating all taxes on any colony that voluntarily paid both its share for military defense and the salaries of the royal governors. In other words, North was asking the colonies to tax themselves. By the time the Conciliatory Propositions arrived in America, shooting had already started.

Bold Talk of War

While most of the Patriots believed that Britain would back down in the face of united colonial resistance, in Virginia Patrick Henry dramatically declared that war was unavoidable. He urged Americans to prepare for combat. The twenty-nine-year-old Henry, a farmer and storekeeper turned lawyer, claimed that the colonies "have done everything that could be done to avert the storm which is now coming on," but their efforts had been met only by "violence and insult." Freedom, the defiant Henry shouted, could be bought only with blood. If forced to choose, he supposedly shouted, "give me liberty"—then paused dramatically, clenched his fist as if it held a dagger, and plunged it into his chest—"or give me death." Loyalists shouted "Treason!" But even more of those present stood and applauded.

As Patrick Henry had predicted, events during 1775 quickly moved toward armed conflict. By mid-1775, the king and Parliament had effectively lost control of their colonies; they could neither persuade nor force the Patriots to accept new regulations and revenue measures. In Boston, General Gage warned his British superiors that armed conflict with the Americans would unleash the "horrors of civil war." Lord Sandwich, the head of the British navy, was not worried by the idea of warfare. He dismissed the rebels as "raw, undisciplined, cowardly men." Major John Pitcairn, a British army officer, agreed, writing home from Boston in 1775 that "one active campaign, a smart action, and burning two or three of their towns, will set everything to rights."

Patrick Henry of Virginia Henry famously declared "Give me liberty, or give me death!"

Lexington and Concord

Major Pitcairn soon had his chance to quash the rebel resistance. On April 14, 1775, the British army in Boston received secret orders to stop the "open rebellion" in Massachusetts. General Gage had decided to arrest rebel leaders such as Samuel Adams and seize the American militia's gunpowder stored at Concord, sixteen miles northwest of Boston. After dark on April 18, some 700 redcoats secretly boarded boats in Boston and crossed the Charles River after midnight, then set out westward on foot to Lexington. When Patriots got wind of the plan, Paul Revere and William Dawes mounted their horses for their famous "midnight ride" to warn the rebel leaders that the British were coming.

In the gray dawn light of April 19, the British advance guard of 238 redcoats found Captain John Parker, a veteran of the French and Indian War, and about seventy "Minutemen" (Patriot militia who could assemble at a "minute's" notice), lined up on the Lexington town square, while about a hundred villagers watched. Parker and his men intended only a silent

Shots fired at Lexington and Concord

protest, but Major Pitcairn of the Royal Marines rode onto the Lexington Green, swinging his sword and yelling, "Disperse, you damned rebels! You dogs, run!" The outnumbered militiamen had already begun backing away when someone, perhaps an onlooker, fired a shot, whereupon the British soldiers began wildly shooting at the Minutemen, then charged them with bayonets, leaving eight dead and ten wounded. Jonathan Harrington, a militiaman who was shot in the back, managed to crawl across the Green, only to die on his doorstep.

The British officers quickly brought their men under control and led them to Concord, announcing their arrival with fifes and drums. In Concord, they searched buildings for hidden military supplies, destroying what they found. While marching out of the town, they encountered American riflemen at the North Bridge. Shots were fired, and a dozen or so British soldiers were killed or wounded. More important, the short skirmish and ringing church bells alerted hundreds, then thousands, of rebel farmers, ministers, craftsmen, and merchants from nearby communities to grab their muskets.

By noon, the British began a ragged retreat back to Lexington. Less than a mile out of Concord, they suffered the first of many ambushes. The narrow road back to Boston turned into a gauntlet of death as hundreds of rebel marksmen fired on the British troops from behind stone walls, trees, barns, and houses. "It was a day full of horror," one of the soldiers recalled. "The Patriots seemed maddened." By nightfall, the redcoat survivors were safely back in Boston, having suffered three times as many dead and wounded as the Americans. A British general reported to London that the feisty Americans had earned his respect: "Whoever looks upon them as an irregular mob will find himself much mistaken."

LEXINGTON AND CONCORD, APRIL 19, 1775

★ Battle site

Concord River
North Bridge
Concord
Lexington
Mystic River
Americans
Sudbury River
Menotomy
Medford *British retreat*
British advance
Massachusetts Bay
Cambridge
Charlestown
Charles River
Boston
Brookline
Boston Harbor
Roxbury

0 — 2 — 4 Miles
0 — 2 — 4 Kilometers

- Describe the outbreak of shooting on Lexington Green.
- Why did the Americans' tactics along the road between Concord and Lexington succeed?
- Why did the British march on Concord in the first place?

Outright Rebellion

The colonial resistance movement had grown into an outright rebellion, but few Patriots in 1775 were yet calling for American independence. They still considered themselves British subjects whose rights had been repeatedly violated by an arrogant king and a misguided Parliament. When the Second Continental Congress convened at Philadelphia on May 10, 1775, the delegates gathered under a British flag. Most Americans in 1775 still wanted

The Battle of Lexington (1775) Amos Doolittle's impression of the Battle of Lexington as combat begins between the Royal Marines and the Minutemen.

Parliament to restore their rights so that they could go back to being loyal British colonists.

Meanwhile, the British army in Boston was encircled and under siege by American militia units and small groups of musket-toting men who had raced from all across New England to join in the rebellion. They were still farmers, not trained soldiers, and the uprising was not yet an army; it lacked an organized command structure and effective support system. The Patriots also lacked training, discipline, cannons, muskets, bullets, gunpowder, and blankets. They did not even have a name for their ragtag army. But they did have a growing sense of confidence and resolve. As a Massachusetts Patriot warned in urging Americans to join the revolt, "Our all is at stake. Death and devastation are the instant consequences of delay. Every moment is infinitely precious."

With each passing day in the spring of 1775, war fever infected more and more colonists. "Oh that I were a soldier!" John Adams wrote to his wife Abigail from Philadelphia. "I will be. I am reading military books. Everybody must, and will, and shall be a soldier." On the very day that Congress met, the British Fort Ticonderoga, on Lake Champlain in upstate New York near the Canadian border, fell to a Patriot force of "Green Mountain Boys" led by Ethan Allen of Vermont and Massachusetts volunteers under Benedict Arnold. Two days later, the Patriots captured a smaller British fort at Crown Point, north of Ticonderoga.

The Spreading Conflict

On June 15, 1775, the Second Continental Congress unanimously selected forty-three-year-old George Washington to lead a new national professional army. Washington's service in the French and Indian War had made him one of the few experienced American officers. And he *looked* like a leader. Tall and strong, he was a superb horseman and fearless fighter. Washington humbly accepted the new responsibility but refused to be paid.

The Battle of Bunker Hill

On Saturday, June 17, the very day that George Washington was named commander in chief, Patriot militiamen engaged British forces in their first major clash, the Battle of Bunker Hill (adjoining Breed's Hill was the battle's actual location).

The First Battle: Bunker Hill

Twenty-four hundred British troops advanced up the hill in tight formation through waist-high grass and across pasture fences as Americans watched from behind their earthworks. The militiamen, mostly farmers, waited until the redcoats had come within thirty paces, then loosed a volley that shattered the front British ranks. The British re-formed their lines and attacked again, but the Patriot riflemen forced them to retreat a second time. During the third British assault, the colonials ran out of gunpowder and retreated in panic and confusion. "I jumped over the walls," Peter Brown remembered, "and ran for about half a mile while [musket] balls flew like hailstones and cannons roared like thunder."

The British took the high ground but were too tired to pursue the rebels. Victory came at a high price. The British suffered 1,054 casualties, over twice the American losses. "A dearly bought victory," reported British general Henry Clinton; "another such would have ruined us." The two armies, American and British, settled in for a nine-month stalemate around Boston, each hoping for a negotiated end to the crisis.

"Open and Avowed Enemies"

Olive Branch Petition rejected

Three weeks after the Battle of Bunker Hill, on July 6 and 8, 1775, the Continental Congress sent the king the Olive Branch Petition, urging him to negotiate with his angry colonies. When the Olive Branch Petition reached London, however, King George refused even to look at it. On August 22, he declared the American rebels "open and avowed enemies."

Independence

Common Sense (1776) Popular pamphlet written by Thomas Paine attacking British principles of hereditary rule and monarchical government, and advocating a declaration of American independence.

The Revolutionary War was well underway in January 1776 when Thomas Paine, a recent English emigrant to America, provided the Patriot cause with a stirring pamphlet titled ***Common Sense***. Until it appeared, colonial grievances had been mainly directed at the British Parliament; only a few colonists then considered independence an option. Paine, however, directly attacked the British monarchy. The "common sense" of the matter, he

The coming revolution The Continental Congress votes for independence, July 2, 1776.

stressed, was that King George III had caused the rebellion. Americans, Paine urged, should abandon the British monarchy and declare their independence: "The blood of the slain, the weeping voice of nature cries, 'tis time to part." Only by declaring independence, Paine predicted, could the colonists gain the crucial support of France and Spain: "The cause of America is in great measure the cause of all mankind." Paine added that the "sun had never shone on a cause of greater worth."

Within three months, more than 150,000 copies of Paine's stirring pamphlet were circulating throughout the colonies, an enormous number for the time. "*Common Sense* is working a powerful change in the minds of men," George Washington reported. Paine's *Common Sense* inspired the colonial population from Massachusetts to Georgia, helping to convince British subjects still loyal to the king to embrace the radical notion of independence. The momentum for independence was building. In Congress, the Pennsylvanian John Dickinson, perhaps the most underrated of the "Founding Fathers," urged delay. On June 1, he warned that independence was a dangerous step since America had no national government or European allies. But his was a lone voice of caution.

In June 1776, one by one, the colonies authorized their delegates in the Continental Congress to take the final step. On June 7, Richard Henry Lee of Virginia moved "that these United Colonies are, and of right ought to be, free

Declaration of Independence

Declaration of Independence The Declaration in its most frequently reproduced form, an 1823 engraving by William J. Stone.

Declaration of Independence (1776) Formal statement, principally drafted by Thomas Jefferson and adopted by the Second Continental Congress on July 4, 1776, that officially announced the thirteen colonies' break with Great Britain.

and independent states." Lee's resolution passed on July 2, a date that "will be the most memorable epoch in the history of America," John Adams wrote to his wife, Abigail. The more memorable date, however, became July 4, 1776, when the Congress formally adopted the **Declaration of Independence**.

Jefferson's Declaration

In June 1776, thirty-three-year-old Thomas Jefferson wrote a first draft of a statement of independence that was submitted to the Congress. Others then edited and polished Jefferson's document. The resulting Declaration of Independence was crucially important not simply because it marked the creation of a new nation but because of the ideals it expressed. It insisted that "all men are created equal" in having the right to maintain governments of their own choosing. Governments, in Jefferson's words, derive "their just Powers from the consent of the people," who are entitled to "alter or abolish" those governments when they deny citizens their "unalienable rights" to "life, Liberty, and the pursuit of Happiness." Because King George was trying to impose "an absolute Tyranny over these States," the "Representatives of the United States of America" therefore declared the thirteen "United Colonies" to be "Free and Independent States."

News of the Declaration of Independence so excited New Yorkers that they toppled a statue of King George and had it melted down to make 42,000 bullets for the war. General George Washington ordered the Declaration read to every unit in the Continental army. Benjamin Franklin acknowledged how high the stakes were: "Well, Gentlemen," he told the Congress, "we must now hang together, or we shall most assuredly hang separately."

The Contradictions of Slavery

George Washington had declared that Boston's fight against British tyranny "now is and ever will be considered as the cause of America (not that we approve their conduct in destroying the Tea)." The alternative, Washington warned, was to become "tame and abject slaves, as the blacks we rule over with such arbitrary sway [absolute power]." Washington and other American slaveholders, such as Thomas Jefferson, were in part so resistant to "British tyranny" because they witnessed every day what actual slavery was like—for the blacks under their control. Jefferson acknowledged their moral hypocrisy. "Southerners," he wrote to a French friend, are "jealous of their own liberties but trampling on those of others." The contradiction between American slaveholders demanding liberty from British oppression was not lost on other observers at the time, either. Phillis Wheatley, the first African American writer to see her poetry published in America, highlighted the "absurdity" of white colonists claiming their freedom while continuing to exercise "oppressive power" over enslaved Africans.

"We Always Had Governed Ourselves"

In explaining the causes of the Revolution, historians have highlighted many factors: the clumsy British efforts to tighten their regulation of colonial trade, the restrictions on colonists eager to acquire western lands, the growing tax burden, the mounting debts to British merchants, the lack of American representation in Parliament, and the role of revolutionary agitators such as Samuel Adams and Patrick Henry in stirring up anti-British feelings.

I am very affectionately your Friend
Phillis Wheatley
Boston March 21. 1774.

Phillis Wheatley An autographed portrait of America's first African American poet.

Each of those factors (and others) helped ignite the Revolutionary War. Yet colonists sought liberty from British tyranny for many reasons, not all of which were selfless or noble. The Boston merchant John Hancock embraced the Patriot cause in part because he was the region's foremost smuggler. Paying more British taxes would have cost him a fortune. Likewise, South Carolina's Henry Laurens and Virginia's Landon Carter, wealthy planters, worried that the British might abolish slavery in the future.

The difficult decision to declare independence from Great Britain was not simply about "taxation without representation." A larger issue had emerged by 1776. Many Americans had become determined to develop their own society in the ways they wished. Yes, most American "Patriots" still spoke the same language and worshipped the same God as the British, but they no longer thought the same way about things that mattered. Rebellious Americans wanted to trade freely with the world and to expand what Jefferson called their "empire of liberty" westward, across the Appalachians.

Perhaps the last word on the complex causes of the Revolution should belong to Levi Preston, a Minuteman from Danvers, Massachusetts. Asked late in life about the British efforts to impose new taxes and regulations on the colonists, Preston responded by asking his young interviewer, "What were they? Oppressions? I didn't feel them." He was then asked, "What, were you not oppressed by the Stamp Act?" Preston replied that he "never saw one of those stamps . . . I am certain I never paid a penny for one of them." What about the tax on tea? "Tea-tax! I never drank a drop of the stuff; the boys threw it all overboard." His interviewer finally asked why he decided to fight for independence. "Young man," Preston explained, "what we meant in going for those Redcoats was this: we always had governed ourselves, and we always meant to. They didn't mean we should."

■ **British and French Colonies** New France followed the model of absolute power in governing its far-flung trading outposts. Few French colonists settled in the vast geography of Canada and the Louisiana territory, but friendships with Native Americans and a profitable fur trade kept the balance of power in North America. On the other hand, the British policy of *salutary neglect* allowed the British colonies a large degree of self-government, until the British government's decision to rigidly enforce its policy of *mercantilism*, as seen in such measures as the *Navigation Acts*, became a means for Britain to enrich its global empire. The *Glorious Revolution* in Great Britain inspired new political philosophies that challenged the divine right of kings with the *natural rights* of free men.

■ **The French and Indian War** Four European wars affected America between 1689 and 1763 as the British and French, joined by their allies, fought each other throughout the world. Worried colonies joined together to create the *Albany Plan of Union*, which was ultimately rejected but formed an early blueprint for an independent American government. The *Seven Years' War* (1754–1763), known as the *French and Indian War* in the American colonies, was the first world war, eventually won by the British. In the *Treaty of Paris* in 1763, France lost all its North American possessions, Britain gained Canada and Florida, and Spain acquired the vast Louisiana territory. With the war's end, Native Americans were no longer regarded as essential allies and so had no recourse when settlers squatted on their lands. They fought to regain control in *Pontiac's Rebellion*, and Great Britain, weary of war, negotiated peace in the *Royal Proclamation of 1763*. But land-hungry settlers ignored the Proclamation Line intended to protect Indian lands. The 1763 Treaty of Paris also set the stage for conflict between the mother country and the American colonies as Britain tried to make the colonies pay for their own defense.

■ **British Colonial Policy** After the French and Indian War, the British government was saddled with an enormous national debt. To reduce that burden, George Grenville's colonial policy tried to implement various taxes to compel colonists to pay for their own defense. Colonists resisted, claiming that they could not be taxed by Parliament because they were not represented in Parliament. Colonial reaction to the *Stamp Act* of 1765 was the first sign of real trouble for British authorities. Conflicts between Whigs and Tories intensified when the *Townshend Acts* imposed additional taxes. The *Sons of Liberty* and the *Daughters of Liberty* mobilized resistance, particularly through nonimportation agreements. The boycotts of British goods were successful, helping convince Parliament to repeal the Stamp Act.

■ **Road to the American Revolution** But the crisis worsened. Spontaneous resistance led to the *Boston Massacre*; organized protesters later staged the *Boston Tea Party*. The British response, called the *Coercive Acts*, sparked further violence between *Patriots* and *Loyalists*. The First Continental Congress formed *Committees of Correspondence* to organize and spread resistance. Thomas Paine's pamphlet *Common Sense* helped kindle revolutionary fervor as well as plant the seed of independence, and conflicts over trade regulations, taxes, and expansion now erupted into war. In the heat of battle, compromise became less likely, and finally impossible, and the Continental Congress delivered its *Declaration of Independence*.

KEY TERMS

CHRONOLOGY

INQUIZITIVE

Go to InQuizitive to see what you've learned—and learn what you've missed—with personalized feedback along the way.

DEBATING the Origins of the American Revolution

History is more than just the memorization of *what* happened. It also involves interpreting *why* the past unfolded as it did. In seeking to understand *why*, historians often find themselves disagreeing. This happens for many reasons. Historians themselves are influenced by their own outlook and the society they live in. Historians can revise their thinking in light of fresh information from newly discovered *primary sources*. They can also interpret previously examined sources in new ways by applying new methodologies and theories. The study of how interpretations of history have changed is called *historiography*. It is the history of the field of history! For Part 1, *A Not-So-"New" World*, the case study of the origins of the American Revolution demonstrates how historians can disagree because they use different types of sources. Thus it is an excellent topic for sharpening your historiographical skills.

For this exercise you have two tasks:

PART 1: Compare the two secondary sources on the American Revolution.

PART 2: Using primary sources, evaluate the arguments of the two secondary sources.

PART I Comparing and Contrasting Secondary Sources

Below are excerpts from two prominent historians of the American Revolution who are at odds over its origins. The first piece comes from Bernard Bailyn of Harvard University, who has explored how the American Revolution was shaped by *ideology*—the system of ideas, ideals, and beliefs that undergird political and economic theory and practice. Bailyn focuses on the way that ideas from the English Whigs, who argued that the English constitution limited the power of the king (see page 125), influenced American Revolutionaries. The author of the second excerpt, Gary Nash of the University of California, Los Angeles, has studied the role that common people, as well as the economic forces that affected their lives, played in the American Revolution. Nash seeks to uncover not just the Whig ideology that is the focus of Bailyn's work, but also the ideas and forces that motivated the masses to participate in this great struggle. While Bailyn and Nash agree on much, their work illustrates how different methodologies lead to different historical interpretations. On the one hand, Bailyn looks at the ideas and writings of the Revolutionary elite—their ideas and arguments—to explain what people actually did. On the other hand, Nash examines the actions and economic circumstances of Revolutionaries who produced no written records in order to understand their motivations. So while Bailyn seeks to understand the causes of the Revolution through the writing of the colonial elite, Nash looks at the actions of common people to understand why they participated in this struggle.

Compare the views of these two historians by answering the following questions. Be sure to find specific examples in the text to support your answers.

■ What is the topic of each excerpt?

■ Are there any similarities between these two excerpts?

■ According to each author, what role did ideology play in the origins of the American Revolution?

■ According to each author, what role did economics and material conditions play in the origins of the Revolution?

■ What type of primary sources does each author mention?

■ What might account for the differences (if any) in interpretation between the authors?

Secondary Source 1

Bernard Bailyn, *The Ideological Origins of the American Revolution* (1992)

Study of the pamphlets [thin booklets] confirmed my rather old-fashioned view that the American Revolution was above all else an ideological, constitutional, political struggle and not primarily a controversy between social groups undertaken to force changes in the organization of the society or the economy. It confirmed too my belief that intellectual developments in the decade before Independence led to a radical idealization and conceptualization of the previous century and a half of American experience, and that it was this intimate relationship between Revolutionary thought and the circumstances of life in eighteenth-century America that endowed the Revolution with its peculiar force and made it so profoundly a transforming event. But if the pamphlets confirmed this belief, they filled it with unexpected details and gave it new meaning.

. . . I began to see a new meaning in phrases that I, like most historians, had readily dismissed as mere rhetoric and propaganda: "slavery," "corruption," "conspiracy." These inflammatory words were used so forcefully by writers of so great a variety of social statuses, political positions, and religious persuasions; they fitted so logically into the pattern of radical and opposition thought; and they reflected so clearly the realities of life in an age in which monarchical autocracy flourished, in which the stability and freedom of England's "mixed" constitution was a recent and remarkable achievement, and in which the fear of conspiracy against constituted authority was built into the very structure of politics, that I began to suspect that they meant something very real to both the writers and their readers: that there were real fears, real anxieties, a sense of real danger behind these phrases, and not merely the desire to influence by rhetoric and propaganda the inert minds of an otherwise passive populace. The more I read, the less useful, it seemed to me, was the whole idea of propaganda in its modern meaning when applied to the writings of the American Revolution. . . . In the end I was convinced that the fear of a comprehensive conspiracy against liberty throughout the English speaking world—a conspiracy believed to have been nourished in corruption, and of which, it was felt, oppression in America was only the most immediately visible part—lay at the heart of the Revolutionary movement.

Source: Bailyn, Bernard. *The Ideological Origins of the American Revolution.* Cambridge, Mass.: Belknap Press of Harvard University Press, 1992. xx–xxiii.

Secondary Source 2

Gary Nash, "Social Change and the Growth of Prerevolutionary Urban Radicalism" (1976)

One of the purposes of this essay is to challenge these widely accepted notions that the "predicament of poverty" was unknown in colonial America, that the conditions of everyday life among "the inarticulate" had not changed in ways that led toward a revolutionary predisposition, and that "social discontent," "economic disturbances," and "social strains" can generally be ignored in searching for the roots of the Revolution. I do not suggest that we replace an ideological construction with a mechanistic economic interpretation, but argue that a popular ideology, affected by rapidly changing economic conditions in American cities, dynamically interacted with the more abstract Whig ideology borrowed from England. These two ideologies had their primary appeal within different parts of the social structure, were derived from different sensibilities concerning social equity, and thus had somewhat different goals. The Whig ideology, about which we know a great deal through recent studies, was drawn from English sources, had its main appeal within upper levels of colonial society, was limited to a defense of constitutional rights and political liberties, and had little to say about changing social and economic conditions in America or the need for change in the future. The popular ideology, about which we know very little, also had deep roots in English culture, but it resonated most strongly within the middle and lower strata of society and went far beyond constitutional rights to a discussion of the proper distribution of wealth and power in the social system. It was this popular ideology that undergirded the politicization of the artisan and laboring classes in the cities and justified the dynamic role they assumed in the urban political process in the closing decades of the colonial period.

To understand how this popular ideology swelled into revolutionary commitment within the middle and lower ranks of colonial society, we must first comprehend how the material conditions of life were changing for city dwellers during the colonial period and how people at different levels of society were affected by these alterations. We cannot fathom this process by consulting the writings of merchants, lawyers, and upper-class politicians, because their business and political correspondence and the tracts they wrote tell us almost nothing about those below them in the social hierarchy. But buried in more obscure documents are glimpses of the lives of both ordinary and important people—shoemakers and tailors as well as lawyers and merchants. The story of changing conditions and how life in New York, Philadelphia, and Boston was experienced can be discerned, not with perfect clarity but in general form, from tax, poor relief, and probate records. . . .

The crescendo of urban protest and extralegal activity in the prerevolutionary decades cannot be separated from the condition of people's lives. . . . The willingness of broad segments of urban society to participate in attacks on narrowly concentrated wealth and power—both at the polls where the poor and propertyless were excluded, and in the streets where everyone, including women, apprentices, indentured servants, and slaves, could engage in action—should remind us that a rising tide of class antagonism and political consciousness, paralleling important economic changes, was a distinguishing feature of the cities at the end of the colonial period. It is this organic link between the circumstances of people's lives and their political thought and action that has been overlooked by historians who concentrate on Whig ideology, which had its strongest appeal among the educated and well-to-do.

Source: Nash, Gary. "Social Change and the Growth of Prerevolutionary Urban Radicalism." *The American Revolution: Explorations in the History of American Radicalism.* Ed. Alfred F. Young. Dekalb, Ill.: Northern Illinois University Press, 1976. 6–7.

PART II Using Primary Sources to Evaluate Secondary Sources

When historians are faced with competing interpretations of the past, they often look at *primary* source material as part of the process of evaluating the different arguments. Below are a selection of primary source materials relating to the origins of the American Revolution.

The first document is an excerpt from a series of letters by Pennsylvania Quaker John Dickinson that he published anonymously under the pen name "A Farmer." Dickinson wrote the first letter in 1767, following the British Parliament's suspension of the New York Assembly for failure to comply with the Quartering Act of 1765, which required the colonies to provide British troops with food and shelter.

The second document is an excerpt from a letter sent by Massachusetts Bay Governor Francis Bernard to British officials in London following the Stamp Act Riots in Boston during August of 1765. The riots begun on August 13 with an attack upon the house of Andrew Oliver, who was responsible for the collection of the tax. This act of destruction was widely celebrated by Samuel Adams and other Sons of Liberty. A few days later a mob ransacked and looted the house of the lieutenant-governor, Thomas Hutchinson. This mob acted without the support of Adams or other elite leaders.

Carefully read each of the following primary sources and answer the following questions. Decide which of the primary source documents support or refute Bailyn's and Nash's arguments about this period. You may find that some documents do both, but for different parts of each historians' interpretation. Be sure to identify which specific components of each historian's argument the documents support or refute.

■ Which of the two historians' *arguments* is best supported by the *primary source* documents? Or if you find that both arguments are well supported by the evidence, why do you think the two historians had such different interpretations about the period?

■ Based on your comparison of the two historians' arguments and your analysis of the primary sources, what have you learned about historiography and the ways historians interpret the past?

Primary Source 1

John Dickinson, "Letter from a Farmer in Pennsylvania" (1767)

My dear COUNTRYMEN,

I am a FARMER settled after a variety of fortunes, near the banks of the river *Delaware* in the province of *Pennsylvania*. . . . Being master of my time, I spend a good deal of it in a library. . . . I believe I have acquired a greater share of knowledge in history, and the laws and constitution of my country, than is generally attained by men of my class. . . . From my infancy I was taught to love humanity and liberty. Inquiry and experience have since confirmed my reverence for the lessons then given me, by convincing me more fully of their truth and excellence. . . . With a good deal of surprise I have observed, that little notice has been taken of an act of Parliament, as injurious in its principle to the liberties of these colonies, as the STAMP ACT was: I mean the act for suspending the legislation of New-York. . . . It [the Act] is a parliamentary assertion of the *supreme authority* of *the British legislature* over these colonies in *the part of taxation*; and is intended to COMPEL *New-York* into a submission to that authority. It seems therefore to me as much a violation of the liberty of the people of that province, and consequently of all these colonies, as if the parliament had sent a number of regiments to be quartered upon them till they should comply. For it is evident, that the suspension is meant as a compulsion; and the *method* of compelling is totally indifferent. It is indeed probable that the sight of red coats, and the beating of drums would have been most alarming, because people are generally more influenced by their eyes and ears than by their reason: But whoever seriously considers the matter, must perceive, that a dreadful stroke is aimed at the liberty of these colonies: For the cause of *one* is the cause of *all*. If the parliament may lawfully deprive *New-York* of any of its rights, it may deprive any, or all the other colonies of their rights; and nothing can possibly so much encourage such attempts, as a mutual inattention to the interests of each other. *To divide, and thus to destroy,* is the first political maxim in attacking those who are powerful by their union. He certainly is not a wise man, who folds his arms and reposes himself at home, viewing with unconcern the flames that have invaded his neighbour's house, without any endeavors to extinguish them.

Source: Dickinson, John. "Letters from a Farmer." *Letters from a Farmer in Pennsylvania, to the Inhabitants of the British Colonies.* Ed. R. T. H. Halsey. New York: The Outlook Company, 1903. 6–12.

Primary Source 2

Governor Francis Bernard, "Letter to the Lords of Trade" (1765)

The disorders of the town having been carried to much greater lengths than what I have informed your lordships of. After the demolition of Mr. Oliver's house was found so practicable and easy, and that the government was obliged to look on, without being able to take any one step to prevent it, and the principal people of the town publicly avowed and justified the act; the mob, both great and small, became highly elated, and all kinds of ill-humours were set on foot; everything that, for years past, had been the cause of any unpopular discontent, was revived; and private resentments against persons in office worked themselves in, and endeavored to exert themselves under the mask of the public cause. . . . Towards evening, some boys began to light a bonfire before the town-house, which is an usual signal for a mob. Before it was quite dark, a great company of people gathered together, crying 'Liberty and Property;' which is their usual notice of their intention to plunder and pull down a house.

. . .

The lieutenant-governor [Thomas Hutchinson] . . . was at supper with his family when he received advice that the mob was coming to him. . . . As soon as the mob had got into the house, with a most irresistible fury, they immediately looked about for him, to murder him, and even made diligent enquiry whither he was gone. They went to work with a rage scarce to be exemplified by the most savage people. Every thing moveable was destroyed in the most minute manner, except such things of value as were worth carrying off. . . . It was now becoming a war of plunder, of general leveling, and taking away the distinction of rich and poor: so that those gentlemen, who had promoted and approved the cruel treatment of Mr. Oliver, became now as fearful for themselves as the most loyal person in the town could be. When first the town took this new turn, I was in hopes that they would have disavowed all the riotous proceedings; that of the first night, as well as the last. But it is no such thing; great pains are taken to separate the two riots: what was done against Mr. Oliver is still approved of, as a necessary declaration of their resolution not to submit to the Stamp Act.

Source: Bernard, Francis. "Extract from a Letter to the Lords of Trade, dated August 31, 1765." *The Parliamentary History of England, from the Earliest Period to the Year 1803. From which Last-Mentioned Epoch It is Continued Downwards in the Work Entitled, "The Parliamentary Debates."* Vol. XVI. A. D. 1765–1771. London: Printed by T. C. Hansard, Peterborough-Court, Fleet-Street: for Longman, Hurst, Rees, Orme, & Brown; J. Richardson; Black, Parry, & Co.; J. Hatchard; J. Ridgway; E. Jeffery; J. Booker; J. Rodwell; Cardock & Joy; R. H. Evans; E. Budd; J. Booth; and T. C. Hansard, 1813. 129–131.

RNING *of the* FRIGATE PHILADELPHIA *in the* HARBOUR *of* TRIPOLI, *16.* Feb. 1804,

INHABITANTS OF AMERICA,

Building a Nation

The signing of the Declaration of Independence in early July 1776 thrilled the rebellious colonists and forced other Americans to make a life-or-death choice: to remain loyal subjects of King George III and thus traitors to the new United States of America, or to embrace the rebellion and become traitors to Great Britain. It was one thing for Patriot leaders to declare American independence and quite another to win it on the battlefield. The odds greatly favored the British; fewer than half of the colonists were Patriots who *actively* supported the Revolution, and many others—the Loyalists—fought against it. The political stability of the new nation was uncertain, and General George Washington found himself facing the world's greatest military power with a poorly supplied, often unpaid, and inexperienced army.

Yet the Revolutionaries would persevere and prevail. Washington and his lieutenants were skilled in taking advantage of geography. They knew the American landscape much better than the British. Even more important was the decision by the French to join the war against Britain. The Franco-American military alliance, negotiated in 1778, was the decisive event in the war. In 1783, after eight years of sporadic fighting and heavy human and financial losses, the British gave up the fight and their American colonies.

While fighting the British, the Patriots also had to create new governments for themselves. Colonies suddenly became co-equal states. The deeply ingrained resentment of British imperial rule led the Americans to give more power to the individual states than to the new national government. As Thomas Jefferson declared, "Virginia is my country." Such powerful local ties help explain why the Articles of Confederation, the original American constitution organizing the thirteen states into a nation, provided only minimal national authority when it was ratified in 1781. Final power to make and execute laws remained with the states. After the Revolutionary War, the flimsy political bonds authorized by the Articles of Confederation could not meet the needs of the new nation. This realization led to the calling of the Constitutional Convention in 1787. The process of drafting and approving the new constitution prompted a heated debate about the respective powers granted to the states and the national government, a debate that became the central theme of American political thought ever since.

The Revolution also unleashed social forces that would help reshape American culture. What would be the role of women, African Americans, and Native Americans in the new nation? How would the different economies of the various regions of the new United States be developed? Who would control access to the vast Native American lands to the west of the original thirteen states? How would the United States of America relate to the other nations of the world?

These questions gave birth to the first national political parties in the United States. During the 1790s, the Federalist party, led by George Washington and Alexander Hamilton, and the first Republican party, led by Thomas Jefferson and James Madison, furiously debated the political and economic future of the new nation. With Jefferson's election as president in 1800, the Republicans gained the upper hand in national politics and would remain dominant for the next quarter century. In the process, they presided over a maturing republic that aggressively expanded westward at the expense of the Native Americans, embraced industrial development, engaged in a second war with Great Britain, and witnessed growing tensions between North and South over slavery.

THE DEATH OF GENERAL MERCER AT THE BATTLE OF PRINCETON (CA. 1789–1831) Hot on the heels of the American victory in Trenton, New Jersey, was another unexpected win for George Washington (center, on horseback) and his men in the Battle of Princeton. One of the casualties, however, was Washington's close friend General Hugh Mercer (bottom), who became a rallying symbol for the revolution.

The American Revolution

1776–1783

Few foreign observers thought the upstart American revolutionaries could win a war against the world's richest and most powerful empire—and, indeed, the Americans did end up losing most of the battles in the Revolutionary War. But they outlasted the British, eventually forcing them to grant independence to the United States of America. This stunning result reflected the tenacity of the Patriots as well as the difficulties the British faced in fighting a transatlantic war thousands of miles from home.

What began as a war for independence became both a civil war between Americans (Patriots versus Loyalists), joined by their Indian allies, and a world war involving numerous "allied" European nations. The crucial development during the war was the ability of the United States to forge military alliances with France, Spain, and the Netherlands, all of which were eager to humble Great Britain and seize its colonies around the world. Those nations provided the American revolutionaries desperately needed money, supplies, soldiers, and warships. Ninety percent of the gunpowder used by American soldiers came from Europe.

Wars, of course, affect civilians as well as combatants. America's War of Independence unleashed unexpected social and political changes, as the effort to win the war required "common people" to take a more active role in governments at all levels, local, state, and national.

CORE
OBJECTIVES INQUIZITIVE

1. Explain the challenges faced by both British and American military leaders in fighting the Revolutionary War.

2. Identify key turning points in the Revolutionary War, and explain how they changed the direction of the war.

3. Describe the ways in which the American Revolution was also a civil war.

4. Examine how the Revolutionary War was an "engine" for political and social change.

5. Compare the impact of the Revolutionary War on African Americans, women, and Native Americans.

After all, as the Declaration of Independence asserted, governments derive "their just powers from the consent of the governed." And the "common people" readily took advantage of the new opportunities provided by republicanism. In Virginia, voters in 1776 elected a new state legislature that, as an observer noted, "was composed of men not quite so well dressed, nor so politely educated, nor so highly born" as had been the case in the past.

Mobilizing for War

British Military Power

CORE **OBJECTIVE**

1. Explain the challenges faced by both British and American military leaders in fighting the Revolutionary War.

The British Empire sent some 35,000 soldiers and half of its huge navy across the Atlantic to put down the American rebellion. To aid their war effort, the British also hired foreign soldiers (mercenaries). Almost 30,000 Germans served in the British armies in America. Most of them were from the German state of Hesse-Cassel—thus they became known to Americans as *Hessians*. The British also recruited American Loyalists, Native Americans, and African Americans to fight on their behalf, but there were never as many as British leaders had hoped. Further, it was a formidable challenge for the British to keep their large army in America supplied. They initially assumed that there would be enough food for their troops and forage for their horses in America. But they quickly realized that most of the supplies would have to come from Britain. It took two to three months for ships to make the Atlantic crossing, depending upon the weather, and the war in America soon became terribly expensive.

American challenges: Massive British forces

The British government under Lord North led Great Britain into a faraway war without a clear strategy for waging it. Initially, the British focused on blockading New England's seaports in order to strangle American trade and eventually force the Americans to give up. When that failed, the British military leaders sought to destroy George Washington's Continental army in New York. Despite their initial success in driving the Americans out of the city, the British generals failed to pursue the retreating Continental army. The British next tried to drive a wedge between New England and New York, splitting the colonies in two. That too would fail, leading to the final British strategy: moving their main army into the southern colonies in hopes of rallying Loyalists in that region to beat back the Revolutionaries. Although victorious in most conventional battles against the Americans, the British never fastened upon an overall strategy to defeat the Patriot cause. Ultimately, the Americans—fighting in their homeland for their independence and generously aided by the French—were able to outlast the British in a war of endurance.

The Continental Army

American challenges: Finance and supply for the military, citizen-soldiers

While the Patriots had the advantage of fighting on their home ground—the American commanders knew the terrain and the people—but they also had to create an army and navy from scratch, and with little money.

Recruiting, supplying, equipping, training, and paying soldiers and sailors were monumental challenges for the new nation. At the start of the fighting, there were no uniforms, and American weapons were "as various as their costumes."

The Patriot army that encircled the British in Boston in 1775 was little more than a poorly trained militia made up of lightly armed volunteers who had enlisted for six months. Unlike the professional soldiers in the British army, these part-time **citizen-soldiers** were mostly poor American farmers or recent immigrants who had been indentured servants. They often came and went as they pleased, gambled frequently, and drank liquor freely. The states rarely provided their share of the war's expenses, and the Continental Congress reluctantly had to allow the Patriot armies to take supplies directly from farmers in return for promises of future payment.

Before the war for independence, American militiamen (citizen-soldiers) were primarily a home guard—civilians called out from their farms and shops on short notice to defend their local communities. To repel an attack, the militiamen somehow mustered themselves; once the danger was past, they disappeared, for there were chores to do at home. Many of the local militiamen were unreliable and ungovernable. They "come in, you cannot tell how," General Washington said in exasperation, "go, you cannot tell when, and act you cannot tell where, consume your provisions, exhaust your stores [supplies], and leave you at last at a critical moment." Once the war started, American leaders knew that they could not win against veteran British and German soldiers using only militiamen. They needed a professional army of their own, with full-time soldiers enlisted from all thirteen colonies. As he recruited such an army, General Washington was pleased to see that the men from different colonies were developing a national (or "continental") viewpoint, in which they thought of themselves as fighting for a new *nation*, not just protecting their particular communities like militiamen. Washington thus decided to call it the *Continental army*. What the Continental army needed most were capable officers, intensive training, strict discipline, and multi-year enlistment contracts. He soon began whipping his new army into shape. Recruits who violated army rules were jailed, flogged, or sent packing. Some deserters were hanged.

George Washington at Princeton
Commissioned for Independence Hall in Philadelphia, this 1779 painting by Charles Willson Peale portrays Washington as the hero of the Battle of Princeton.

Native Americans and the Revolution

Both the British and Americans recruited Indian allies to "take up the hatchet" and fight with them, but the British were far more successful, because they promised to protect Indian lands. The peoples making up the Iroquois League split their allegiances, with most Mohawks, Onondagas, Cayugas, and Senecas, led by Mohawk Joseph Brant and Seneca Old Smoke, joining the British, and most Oneidas and Tuscaroras supporting the Patriots. The Cherokees also joined the British in hopes of driving out American settlers who had taken their lands. Most Indians in New England tried to remain neutral or sided with the Patriots. The Stockbridge Indians in Massachusetts, mostly Mahicans, formed a company of Minutemen who fought alongside Patriot

American and British challenges: Recruiting Native Americans

citizen-soldiers Part-time non-professional soldiers, mostly poor farmers or recent immigrants who had been indentured servants, who played an important role in the Revolutionary War.

units. They pledged that "wherever your armies go, there we will go; you shall always find us by your side; and if providence calls us to sacrifice our lives in the field of battle, we will fall where you fall, and lay our bones by yours. Nor shall peace ever be made between our nation and the Red-Coats until our brothers—the white people—lead the way." But however much the British or Americans claimed Native Americans as allies, most Indians engaged in the war as a means of protecting themselves and their own interests.

Disaster in Canada

In July 1775, the Continental Congress authorized an ill-fated attack against Quebec, in the vain hope of rallying support for the American rebellion among the French inhabitants in Canada. One Patriot detachment, under General Richard Montgomery, headed toward Quebec by way of Lake Champlain along the New York–Canadian border; another, under General Benedict Arnold, struggled westward through the dense Maine woods. The American units arrived outside Quebec in September, exhausted and hungry. A silent killer then ambushed them: smallpox. As the deadly virus raced through the American camp, General Montgomery faced a brutal dilemma. Most of his soldiers had signed up for short tours of duty, and many of them were scheduled for discharge at the end of the year. He could not afford to wait until spring for the smallpox to subside. Seeing little choice but to fight, Montgomery ordered a desperate attack on the British forces at Quebec during a blizzard, on December 31, 1775.

The assault on New Year's Eve was a disaster. Montgomery was killed early in the battle and Benedict Arnold was wounded. Over 400 Americans were taken prisoner. The rest of the Patriot force retreated to its camp outside the walled city and appealed to the Continental Congress for reinforcements. The smallpox virus spread throughout the American army. As fresh troops arrived, they too fell victim to the deadly virus. General Benedict Arnold warned George Washington in February 1776 that the runaway disease would soon lead to "the entire ruin of the Army." The British, sensing the weakness of the American force, attacked and sent the ragtag Patriots on a frantic retreat up the St. Lawrence River to the American-held city of Montreal and eventually back to New York and New England.

Quebec was the first military setback for the Revolutionaries. It would not be the last. By the summer of 1776, Americans knew that their quest for independence would be neither short nor easy, for King George and the British government were determined to crush the revolt and restore their Empire. To do so, they were willing to gather the most powerful fighting force in the world.

Washington's Narrow Escape

On July 2, 1776, the day the Continental Congress voted for independence, British redcoats landed on undefended Staten Island, across New York City's harbor from Manhattan. They were the first wave in a determined effort to smash the American Revolution. During the summer of 1776, a massive British fleet of 427 warships carrying 32,000 British and German troops, 1,200 cannons, and 10,000 sailors began landing on Long Island near New York City. It was the largest seaborne military expedition in history. "I could not believe my eyes," recalled a Pennsylvania militiaman. "I declare that I thought all London was afloat."

Meanwhile, Washington could gather only about 19,000 poorly trained militiamen and recruits in the new Continental army. It was too small a force to defend New York, but the Continental Congress wanted to keep the city in Patriot hands. Although a veteran of frontier fighting, Washington had never commanded a large force or supervised artillery (cannon) units. As he confessed to the Continental Congress, he had no "experience to move [armies] on a large scale" and had only "limited . . . knowledge . . . in military matters." In 1776 he was still learning the art of generalship, and the British invasion of New York taught him some costly and painful lessons.

Short of weapons and greatly outnumbered, the American army suffered a humiliating defeat at the Battle of Long Island. Had the British moved more quickly, they could have trapped Washington's entire army as it fled across lower Manhattan. But the British rested as the main American force made a miraculous escape northward, crossed the Hudson River, and retreated into New Jersey and over the Delaware River into eastern Pennsylvania.

By December 1776, the American Revolution was near collapse as winter arrived. A British officer reported that many of the "rebels" were "without shoes or stockings, and several were observed to have only linen drawers . . . without any proper shirt. They must suffer extremely." Washington had only 3,000 men left under his command, as thousands of militiamen had simply gone home to sit out the winter or tend to their farms. Unless a new army could be raised quickly, Washington warned, "I think the game is pretty near up."

But help emerged from an unexpected source: Englishman Thomas Paine. Having opened the eventful year of 1776 with his inspiring pamphlet *Common Sense*, Paine now composed *The American Crisis*, in which he wrote these stirring lines:

> These are the times that try men's souls: The summer soldier and the sunshine patriot will, in this crisis, shrink from the service of his country; but he that stands it NOW deserves the love and thanks of man and woman. Tyranny, like Hell, is not easily conquered. Yet we have this consolation with us, that the harder the conflict, the more glorious the triumph.

Paine's rousing pamphlet boosted Patriot morale. Soon the Continental Congress's decision to offer army recruits cash, land, clothing, and blankets would provide further support for what Paine's pamphlet inspired.

Thomas Paine's *Common Sense*
Thomas Paine's inspiring pamphlet was originally published anonymously because the British viewed its content as evidence of treason.

In December 1776, General William Howe, commander in chief of the British forces, settled down with his married Loyalist mistress (twenty-five-year-old Elizabeth Loring) to wait out the winter in New York City. (Eighteenth-century armies rarely fought during the winter months.) By not pursuing the Americans as they retreated from Long Island and later Manhattan, Howe had lost a great opportunity to end the Revolution. In coming months, he would continue to miss chances to destroy the struggling Continental army, leading one American general to conclude that Howe "shut his eyes, fought his battles, drank his bottle and had his little whore."

A Desperate Gamble

George Washington, however, was not ready to hibernate for the winter. He decided that the morale of his men and the hopes of the nation required "some stroke" of good news after the devastating defeats they had suffered around New York City. So he launched a desperate gamble to achieve a much-needed victory before more of his soldiers decided to return home. On Christmas night 1776, Washington led some 2,400 men, packed into forty-foot-long boats, from Pennsylvania across the icy, swollen Delaware River into New Jersey. Near dawn at Trenton, the Americans surprised 1,500 sleeping Hessians. It was a total rout, from which only 500 Hessians escaped. Just two of Washington's men were killed and four wounded, one of whom was James Monroe, the future president. A week later, the Americans again crossed the Delaware River and won another battle at Princeton before taking shelter in winter quarters at Morristown, in the hills of northern New Jersey. A British officer grumbled that the Americans had "become a formidable enemy." The American victories at Princeton and Trenton saved the cause of independence. A wave of Americans signed up to serve in Washington's army.

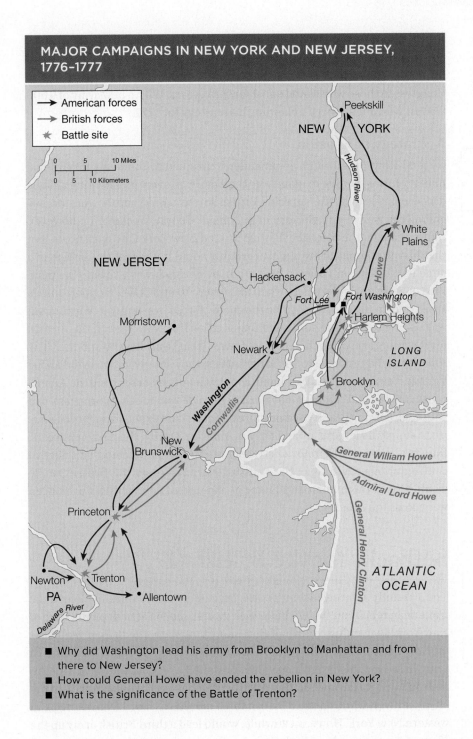

MAJOR CAMPAIGNS IN NEW YORK AND NEW JERSEY, 1776–1777

- → American forces
- → British forces
- ✳ Battle site

- ■ Why did Washington lead his army from Brooklyn to Manhattan and from there to New Jersey?
- ■ How could General Howe have ended the rebellion in New York?
- ■ What is the significance of the Battle of Trenton?

Winter in Morristown

During the winter at Morristown in early 1777, George Washington's army nearly disintegrated as six-month enlistment contracts expired and deserters fled the brutal weather, inadequate food, and widespread disease. One soldier recalled that "we were absolutely, literally starved. . . . I saw several of the men roast their old shoes and eat them."

American challenges: Demoralized troops

Only about a thousand Continental soldiers and a few militiamen stuck out the Morristown winter. With the spring thaw, however, recruits began arriving to claim the $20 and 100 acres of land offered by the Continental Congress to those who would enlist for three years. With a new army of 9,000 troops, Washington began planning his strategy for 1777.

A Strategy of Evasion

British challenges: American evasion and selective confrontation, and high supply costs

General Howe, the British commander, continued to think in conventional military terms, hoping to maneuver the American army into fighting a single decisive battle that the superior British forces would surely win, thereby ending the war in one glorious engagement. George Washington, however, refused to take the bait. The fighting around New York City had shown him that his outmanned army almost certainly could not defeat the British in a large battle. The only way to beat them, he decided, was to evade the main British army, carefully select when and where to attack when opportunities arose, and, in the end, wear down the enemy forces in a long war. Washington was willing to concede control of major cities like New York to the British, for it was his army, "not defenseless towns, [that] they have to subdue." The Americans did not have to win large battles; they simply had to avoid losing the war. Britain, on the other hand, could win only by destroying the American will to resist. Victory would come to the side that fought the longest, and with each passing year it became more difficult—and expensive—for the British to supply its large army and navy in America. During the next eight years, the Americans would follow a strategy of evasion punctuated by selective confrontations. Over time, the British government and the British people would tire of the human and financial expense of conducting a prolonged war across the Atlantic.

CORE **OBJECTIVE**

2. Identify key turning points in the Revolutionary War, and explain how they changed the direction of the war.

Setbacks for the British (1777)

The carefully conceived but poorly executed British plan to defeat the "American rebellion" in 1777 involved a three-pronged assault on the state of New York. By gaining control of that important state, the British would cut off New England from the rest of the colonies. The plan called for a British army, based in Canada and led by General John Burgoyne, known as "Gentleman Johnny," to advance southward from Quebec via Lake Champlain to the Hudson River, while another British force moved eastward from Oswego, in western New York. Howe, meanwhile, would lead a third British army up the Hudson River from New York City. As often happens with ambitious, complicated war plans, however, the British failed in their execution—and in their communications with one another. At the last minute, Howe changed his mind and decided to move his army south to attack the Patriot capital, Philadelphia. General Washington withdrew most of his men from New Jersey to meet the British threat in Pennsylvania. On September 11, 1777, at

Brandywine Creek, southwest of Philadelphia, the British overpowered the Americans and then occupied Philadelphia, the largest and wealthiest American city. The members of the Continental Congress were forced to flee the city. Washington and his army had to withdraw to winter quarters twenty miles away at Valley Forge, while Howe and his men remained in the relative comfort of Philadelphia.

The Campaign of 1777

Meanwhile, an overconfident General Burgoyne (nicknamed "General Swagger") led his mistress and army (including 225 women and 500 children) southward from Canada through dense forests and across rivers and creeks toward New York's Lake Champlain in June 1777. The heavily laden army struggled to cross the wooded, marshy terrain in upstate New York.

The American army commander in New York facing Burgoyne's redcoats was General Horatio Gates. In 1745, Gates and Burgoyne had joined the same British regiment. Now they were commanding opposing armies. As Patriot militiamen converged from across central New York, Burgoyne pulled his dispirited forces back to the village of Saratoga, where the reinforced American army surrounded the outnumbered and now-stranded British army, which was desperate for food.

In the ensuing, three-week-long **Battles of Saratoga**, Gates's army surrounded the outnumbered British forces, cutting off their supply lines. Desperate to retreat back to Canada, the British twice tried—and failed—to break through the encircling Americans. On October 17, 1777, Burgoyne surrendered his outnumbered and nearly starving army, turning over 5,800 troops, 7,000 muskets, and forty-two brass cannons to Gates. Burgoyne's shocking surrender prompted former British prime minister William Pitt to tell Parliament, "*You cannot conquer America.*" King George was devastated by the news, falling "into agonies on hearing the account" of Burgoyne's defeat.

Alliance with France

The surprising American victory at Saratoga was a strategic turning point because it convinced the French, who had lost four wars to the British in the previous eighty years, to sign two crucial treaties in early 1778 that created an American **alliance with France**. Under the Treaty of Amity and Commerce, France officially recognized the new United States and offered trade concessions, including important privileges to American shipping. Next, under the Treaty of Alliance, both parties agreed, first, that if France entered the war, both countries would fight until American independence was won; second, that neither would conclude a "truce or peace" without "the formal consent of the other"; and third, that each would guarantee the other's possessions in America "from the present time and forever against all other powers." France further bound itself to seek neither Canada nor other British possessions on the mainland of North America. In the end, it

General John Burgoyne
Commander of Britain's northern forces. Burgoyne and most of his troops surrendered to the Americans at Saratoga on October 17, 1777.

Battles of Saratoga (1777)

Battles of Saratoga (1777)
Decisive defeat of 5,000 British troops under General John Burgoyne in several battles near Saratoga, New York, in October 1777; the American victory helped convince France to enter the war on the side of the Patriots.

alliance with France Critical diplomatic, military, and economic alliance between France and the newly independent United States, codified by the Treaty of Amity and Commerce and the Treaty of Alliance (1778).

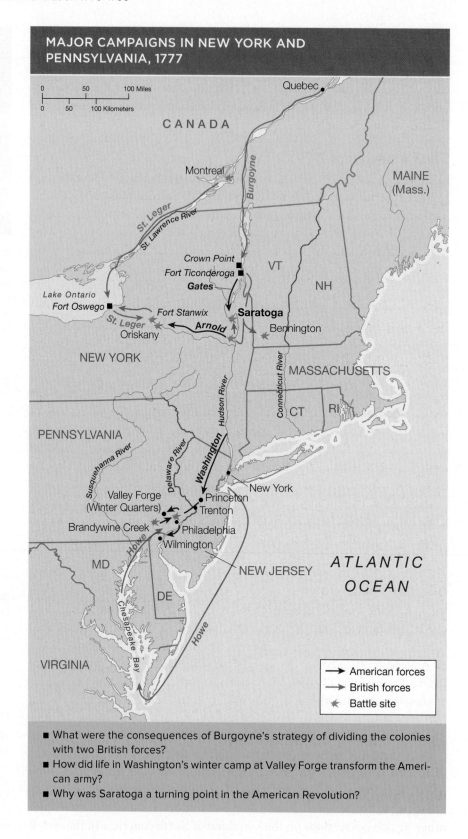

MAJOR CAMPAIGNS IN NEW YORK AND PENNSYLVANIA, 1777

- What were the consequences of Burgoyne's strategy of dividing the colonies with two British forces?
- How did life in Washington's winter camp at Valley Forge transform the American army?
- Why was Saratoga a turning point in the American Revolution?

was the intervention of the French army and navy on behalf of the struggling Americans that determined the outcome of the war. By June 1778, British vessels had fired on French ships and the two nations were at war once again. The Americans would also form alliances with the Spanish (1779) and the Dutch (1781), but neither of those allies provided as much support as the French.

After the British defeat at Saratoga and the news of the French alliance with the United States, the British Parliament tried to end the war by granting all the demands that the American rebels had made before they declared independence. But the Continental Congress would not negotiate until Britain recognized American independence and withdrew its forces. King George refused.

Valley Forge and Stalemate

For George Washington's army at **Valley Forge**, near Philadelphia, the winter of 1777–1778 was a time of intense suffering. The American forces endured unrelenting cold, hunger, and disease. Some soldiers lacked shoes and blankets, and their makeshift log-and-mud huts offered little protection from the howling winds and bitter cold. By February, 7,000 troops were too ill for duty. More than 2,500 soldiers died at Valley Forge; another 1,000 deserted. Fifty officers resigned on one December day. Several hundred more left before winter's end.

Desperate for relief, Washington sent troops across New Jersey, Delaware, and the Eastern Shore of Maryland to confiscate horses, cattle, and hogs in exchange for "receipts" promising future payment. By March 1778 the once-gaunt troops at Valley Forge saw their strength restored. Their improved health enabled Washington to begin a rigorous training program, designed to bring unity to his ragtag array of soldiers. Because few of the regimental commanders had any formal military training, their troops lacked leadership, discipline, and skills. To remedy this defect, Washington turned to an energetic Prussian soldier of fortune, Friedrich Wilhelm, baron von Steuben, who used an interpreter and frequent profanity to instruct the troops in the fundamentals of close-order drill: how to march in formation and how to handle their weapons properly.

Steuben was one of a number of foreign volunteers who joined the American army at Valley Forge. Another European was a twenty-year-old red-haired Frenchman named Gilbert du Motier, Marquis de Lafayette. A wealthy idealist excited by the American cause, Lafayette offered to serve for no pay in exchange for being named a general. General Washington was initially skeptical of the young French aristocrat, but Lafayette soon became the commander in chief's most trusted aide. The French general also proved to be a courageous soldier and able diplomat.

The Continental army's morale rose when the Continental Congress promised extra pay and bonuses after the war. The good news from France

> Winter of 1777–1778 at Valley Forge

Valley Forge (1777–1778) American military encampment near Philadelphia, where more than 3,500 soldiers deserted or died from cold and hunger in the winter.

about the formal military alliance also helped raise the Patriots' spirits. In the spring of 1778, British forces withdrew from Pennsylvania to New York City, with the American army in hot pursuit. Once the British were back in Manhattan, Washington's army encamped at nearby White Plains. From that time on, the major campaigns and battles in the North settled into a long stalemate.

War in the West

Terror tactics in Indian country

The one significant American military success of 1778 occurred in the west. The Revolution had created two wars. In addition to the main conflict between British and American armies in the east, a frontier guerrilla war of terror and vengeance pitted Indians and Loyalists against isolated Patriot settlers along the northern and western frontiers. In the Ohio Valley as well as western New York and Pennsylvania, the British urged frontier Loyalists and their Indian allies to raid farm settlements and offered to pay bounties for American scalps.

To end the English-led attacks, early in 1778 young George Rogers Clark took 175 Patriot frontiersmen on flatboats down the Ohio River. On the evening of July 4, the Americans captured English-controlled Kaskaskia (in present-day Illinois). Then, without bloodshed, Clark took Cahokia (in present-day Illinois across the Mississippi River from St. Louis) and Vincennes (in present-day Indiana). After the British retook Vincennes, Clark marched his men (almost half of them French volunteers) through icy rivers and flooded prairies, sometimes in water neck deep, and prepared to attack the astonished British garrison. Clark's men, all hardened woodsmen, captured five Indians carrying American scalps. Clark ordered his men to kill the Indians in sight of the fort. After watching the terrible executions, the British surrendered.

While Clark's Rangers were in the Indiana territory, a much larger American military expedition moved through western Pennsylvania to attack Iroquois strongholds in western New York, where Loyalists ("Tories") and their Indian allies had been terrorizing frontier settlements throughout the summer of 1778. Led by Mohawk chief Joseph Brant, the Iroquois had killed hundreds of militiamen along the Pennsylvania frontier. In response, George Washington sent 4,000 men under General John Sullivan to crush "the hostile tribes" and "the most mischievous of the Tories." At Newton, New York, on August 29, 1779, Sullivan's soldiers burned about forty Seneca and Cayuga villages, together with their orchards and food supplies, leaving many of the Indians homeless and without enough food to survive. The campaign broke the power of the Iroquois Confederacy for all time, but sporadic fighting continued until the end of the war.

In the Kentucky territory, Daniel Boone and his small band of settlers repeatedly clashed with the Shawnees and their British and Loyalist allies. In 1778, Boone and some thirty men, aided by their wives and children,

Joseph Brant This 1786 portrait of Thayendanegea (Joseph Brant) by Gilbert Stuart features the Mohawk leader who fought against the Americans in the Revolution.

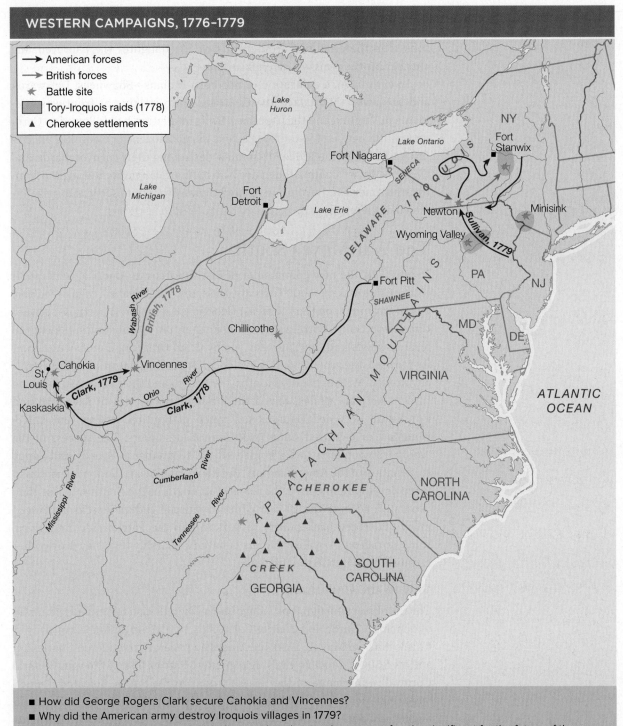

WESTERN CAMPAIGNS, 1776–1779

→ American forces
→ British forces
✳ Battle site
▨ Tory-Iroquois raids (1778)
▲ Cherokee settlements

- How did George Rogers Clark secure Cahokia and Vincennes?
- Why did the American army destroy Iroquois villages in 1779?
- Why were the skirmishes between Indians and settlers on the western frontier significant for the future of the trans-Appalachian frontier?

held off an assault by more than 400 Indians at Boonesborough. Later, Boone himself was twice shot and twice captured. Indians killed two of his sons, a brother, and two brothers-in-law. His daughter was captured, and another brother was wounded four times.

In early 1776, a delegation of northern Indians—Shawnees, Delawares, and Mohawks—had talked the Cherokees into striking at frontier settlements in Virginia and the Carolinas. Swift retaliation had followed as Carolina militiamen led by Andrew Pickens burned dozens of Cherokee villages just east of the Blue Ridge Mountains, destroying their corn, orchards, and livestock. By weakening the major Native American nations along the frontier, the American Revolution cleared the way for white settlers to seize Indian lands after the war.

The War Moves South

In late 1778, the new commander of British forces in America, General Sir Henry Clinton, sent 3,000 redcoats, Hessians, and Loyalists to take the port city of Savannah, on the southeast Georgia coast, and roll northeast toward Charleston, South Carolina gathering momentum by enlisting support from local Loyalists and the Cherokee, led by Chief Dragging Canoe, who promised to leave the ground "dark and bloody." Initially, Clinton's southern strategy worked. Within twenty months, the British and their allies had defeated three American armies, seized the strategic port cities of Savannah and Charleston occupied Georgia and much of South Carolina, and killed, wounded, or captured some 7,000 American soldiers. The success of the "southern campaign" led a British official to predict a "speedy and happy termination of the American war." But his optimistic prediction fell victim to three developments: first, the Loyalist strength in the South was less than estimated; second, the British effort to unleash Indian attacks convinced many undecided backcountry settlers to join the Patriot side; and, third, some British and Loyalist soldiers behaved so harshly that they drove other Loyalists to switch to the rebel side.

War in the Carolinas

The Carolina campaign took a major turn when British forces, led brilliantly by generals Clinton and Charles Cornwallis, bottled up an American army in Charleston. On May 12, 1780, the American general surrendered Charleston and its 5,500 defenders, the single greatest Patriot loss of the war. General Cornwallis, in charge of the British troops in the South, defeated a much larger American force at Camden, South Carolina. Cornwallis had Georgia and most of South Carolina under British control by 1780. Much of the fighting in the Carolinas was a civil war pitting Americans against Americans, Patriots fighting Loyalists, and both sides looted farms and plantations and tortured, scalped, and executed prisoners.

The Battle of King's Mountain

Cornwallis's two most ruthless cavalry officers, Sir Banastre Tarleton and Major Patrick Ferguson, who were in charge of training Loyalist militiamen, eventually overreached themselves. In a war without mercy, the British officers often let their men burn Patriot farms, liberate slaves, and destroy livestock. Major Ferguson sealed his doom when he threatened to march over the Blue Ridge Mountains, hang the mostly Scots-Irish Presbyterian frontier Patriot leaders ("backwater barbarians"), and destroy their farms. Instead, the feisty "overmountain men" from southwestern Virginia and western North and South Carolina (including "Tennesseans") went hunting for Ferguson and his army of Carolina Loyalists.

On October 7, 1780, the two sides clashed near King's Mountain, a heavily wooded ridge along the North Carolina border with South Carolina. There, in a ferocious hour-long battle, Patriot sharpshooters devastated the Loyalist troops. Major Ferguson, the only British soldier in the battle, had boasted beforehand that "all the rebels in hell could not push him off" King's Mountain. His body was riddled with seven bullet holes. Seven hundred Loyalists were captured, twenty-five of whom were later hanged. "The division among the people is much greater than I imagined," an American officer wrote to one of General Washington's aides. The Patriots and Loyalists, he said, "persecute each other with . . . savage fury."

As with so many confrontations during the war in the South, the Battle of King's Mountain was like an extended family feud. Seventy-four sets of brothers fought on both sides, and twenty-nine sets of fathers and sons. After the battle, Patriot captain James Withrow refused to help his Loyalist brother-in-law, who had been badly wounded. "Look to your friends for help," he said, leaving him to die on the battlefield. When Withrow's wife learned how her husband had treated her brother, she asked for a separation. Five brothers in the Goforth family from Rutherford County, North Carolina, fought at King's Mountain; three were Loyalists, two were Patriots. Only one of them survived. Two of the brothers, Preston and John Preston, both excellent riflemen fighting on opposite sides, recognized each other during the battle, took deadly aim as if in a duel, and fired simultaneously, killing each other.

The Battle of King's Mountain was a crucial American victory, for it undermined the British strategy in the South. Thomas Jefferson later said that the Battle of King's Mountain was "the turn of the tide of success." After King's Mountain, the British forces under Cornwallis retreated back into South Carolina and found it virtually impossible to recruit more Loyalists. By proving that the British and their Loyalist supporters could be beaten, the Battle of King's Mountain inspired farmers to join Patriot units under colorful leaders such as Francis Marion, "the Swamp Fox," and Thomas Sumter, "the Carolina Gamecock."

The Battle of King's Mountain (1780)

The Tide Turns in the South

In late 1780, the Continental Congress chose a new commander for the American army in the South: General Nathanael Greene, "the fighting Quaker" of Rhode Island. A former blacksmith blessed with unflagging patience, he was George Washington's ablest general—and well suited to the drawn-out war against the British forces. From Charlotte, North Carolina, where Greene arrived in December 1780, he moved his army eastward while sending General Daniel Morgan, one of the heroes of the Battle of Saratoga, with about 700 men on a sweep to the west of Cornwallis's headquarters at Winnsboro, South Carolina.

American victory at Cowpens

On January 17, 1781, Morgan's force took up positions near Cowpens, an area of cattle pastures in northern South Carolina, and lured Tarleton's army into an elaborate trap. Tarleton, long celebrated for his bravery but hated for his brutality, rushed his men forward, only to be ambushed by Morgan's cavalry. Tarleton himself escaped, but 110 British soldiers were killed and more than 700 were taken prisoner. Cowpens was the most complete tactical victory for the American side in the Revolution (Morgan called it a "devil of a whipping") and was one of the few times that Americans won a battle in which the two sides were evenly matched. When British general Cornwallis learned of the American victory, he snapped his sword in two, saying that the news "broke my heart."

After the victory at Cowpens, Morgan's army moved into North Carolina and linked up with Greene's troops. Greene lured Cornwallis's starving army north, then attacked the redcoats at Guilford Courthouse (near what became Greensboro, North Carolina) on March 15, 1781. The Americans lost the battle but inflicted such heavy losses that Cornwallis left behind his wounded and marched his men off toward Wilmington, on the North Carolina coast, to rest and take on supplies from British ships. The British commander reported that the Americans had "fought like demons." Greene then resolved to go back into South Carolina in the hope of drawing Cornwallis after him, or forcing the British to give up the state. Greene joined forces with local guerrilla bands led by Francis Marion and Thomas Sumter. Together they worked to win the war by using hit-and-run tactics that prolonged the fighting.

A War of Endurance

The Revolutionary War had become a contest of endurance, and the Americans held the advantage in time, men, and supplies. They knew they could outlast the British as long as they avoided a catastrophic defeat in any single battle. "We fight, get beat, rise, and fight again," General Greene said. By September 1781, the Americans had narrowed British control in the South to Charleston and Savannah, although local Patriots and Loyalists would continue to battle each other for more than a year in the backcountry, where there was "nothing but murder and devastation in every quarter," Greene said.

Meanwhile, General Cornwallis had pushed his British army northward from Wilmington, reasoning that before the Carolinas could be subdued, Virginia must be eliminated as a source of American reinforcements and supplies. In May 1781, the British marched into southeastern Virginia. There, the former American general Benedict Arnold, who had switched sides in the war, was eager to strike at the American forces. Arnold had earlier plotted to sell out his former American command of West Point, a critically important fortress on the Hudson River north of New York City. Only the lucky capture of a British spy, Major John André, had exposed Arnold's plot. Warned that his plan had been discovered, Arnold had joined the British in New York City, while the Americans hanged André as a spy.

Yorktown

When Cornwallis and his army joined up with Arnold's at Petersburg, Virginia, their combined British forces totaled 7,200 men. As the Americans approached, Cornwallis picked York-

MAJOR CAMPAIGNS IN THE SOUTH, 1778–1781

- Why did the British suddenly shift their military campaign to the South in 1778?
- Why were the battles at Savannah and Charleston major victories for the British?
- How did Nathanael Greene undermine British control of the Carolinas?

town, Virginia, a small tobacco port between the York and James Rivers on the Chesapeake Bay, as his base of operations. He was not worried about an American attack, since General Washington's main force seemed preoccupied with attacking New York, and the British navy controlled American waters. In July 1780, the French had finally managed to land 6,000 soldiers at Newport, Rhode Island, which the British had given up in order to concentrate on the South, but the French army had been bottled up there for a year, blockaded by the British fleet. As long as the British navy maintained supremacy along the coast, the Americans could not hope to win the war.

In May 1781, however, the elements for a combined Franco-American action suddenly fell into place. Indeed, it is impossible to imagine an American victory in the Revolution without the assistance of the French. As Cornwallis's army moved into Virginia, Washington persuaded the commander of the French army in Rhode Island to join in an attack on the British army in New York. The two armies linked up in July, but before they could strike, word came from the West Indies that Admiral François-Joseph-Paul de Grasse

> Yorktown: French forces tip the balance and British surrender

was headed for the Chesapeake Bay with his large French fleet and some 3,000 soldiers. The unexpected news led General Washington to change his strategy. He immediately began moving his army south toward Yorktown. At the same time, French ships slipped out of the British blockade at Newport, Rhode Island, and also headed south.

On August 30, Admiral de Grasse's fleet reached Yorktown, and French troops landed to join the Americans confronting Cornwallis's army. On September 6, the day after a British fleet appeared, de Grasse attacked and forced the British navy to abandon Cornwallis's army, leaving them with no way to get fresh food and supplies. De Grasse then sent ships up the Chesapeake to ferry down the soldiers who were marching south from New York, bringing the total American and French armies to 16,000 men—more than double the size of Cornwallis's army.

The **Battle of Yorktown** commenced on September 28, 1781. The combined American and French troops soon closed off Cornwallis's last route of escape and began bombarding the besieged British troops with artillery. On October 17, 1781, a glum Cornwallis surrendered. Two days later, the British force of more than 7,000 marched out and laid down their weapons. Cornwallis himself claimed to be too ill to participate. His report to the British commander in chief was brief: "I have the mortification to inform your Excellency that I have been forced to surrender the troops under my command."

The Treaty of Paris (1783)

Any lingering British hopes of victory vanished at Yorktown. In London, Lord North reacted to the news of the surrender as if he had "taken a ball [bullet] in the breast." The prime minister exclaimed: "Oh God, it is all over." In December 1781, King George decided to send no more troops to America. On February 27, 1782, Parliament voted to end the war, and on March 20, Lord North resigned. In part, the British leaders chose peace in America so that they could concentrate on their continuing global war with France and Spain.

Upon learning of the British decision to negotiate, the Continental Congress named a group of prominent Americans to go to Paris to discuss terms with the British. The commissioners included John Adams, who was then representing the United States in the Netherlands; John Jay, minister (ambassador) to Spain; and Benjamin Franklin, already in France. The cranky John Adams was an odd choice since, as Thomas Jefferson said, "He hates [Benjamin] Franklin, he hates John Jay, he hates the French, he hates the

YORKTOWN, 1781

Battle of Yorktown (1781) Last major battle of the Revolutionary War; General Cornwallis, along with over 7,000 British troops, surrendered to George Washington at Yorktown, Virginia, on October 17, 1781.

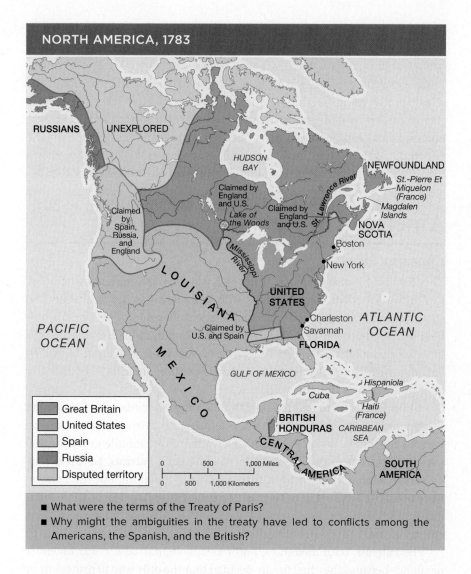

NORTH AMERICA, 1783

RUSSIANS UNEXPLORED

HUDSON BAY

NEWFOUNDLAND

Claimed by England and U.S.

St.-Pierre Et Miquelon (France)

Magdalen Islands

Lake of the Woods

Claimed by England and U.S.

St. Lawrence River

Claimed by Spain, Russia, and England

NOVA SCOTIA

Mississippi River

Boston

New York

UNITED STATES

Charleston

ATLANTIC OCEAN

PACIFIC OCEAN

Claimed by U.S. and Spain

Savannah

FLORIDA

M E X I C O

L O U I S I A N A

GULF OF MEXICO

Hispaniola

Cuba

Haiti (France)

BRITISH HONDURAS

CARIBBEAN SEA

C E N T R A L A M E R I C A

SOUTH AMERICA

- ◼ Great Britain
- ◼ United States
- ◼ Spain
- ◼ Russia
- ◼ Disputed territory

0   500   1,000 Miles
0   500   1,000 Kilometers

- ■ What were the terms of the Treaty of Paris?
- ■ Why might the ambiguities in the treaty have led to conflicts among the Americans, the Spanish, and the British?

English." In the end, Franklin and Jay did most of the work leading to the peace treaty.

The negotiations with the British dragged on for months until, on September 3, 1783, the Treaty of Paris was signed. Its provisions were quite favorable to the United States—Franklin, Jay, and Adams had done very well. Great Britain recognized the independence of the thirteen former colonies and—surprisingly—agreed that the Mississippi River was America's western boundary, thereby more than doubling the territory of the new nation. The boundaries of the United States created by the treaty covered some 900,000 square miles, most of which were *west* of the Proclamation Line of 1763, a vast region long inhabited by Indians and often referred to as *Transappalachia*. Native American leaders were given no role in the negotiations, and Indians were by far the biggest losers in the final treaty.

The treaty's unclear references to America's northern and southern borders would be a source of dispute for years. Florida, as it turned out, passed back to Spain from Britain. As for the prewar debts owed by Americans to British merchants, the U.S. negotiators promised that British merchants should "meet with no legal impediment" in seeking to collect money owed them. And on the tender point of the thousands of Loyalist Americans whose homes, lands, and possessions had been seized by state governments, the negotiators agreed that the Continental Congress would "earnestly recommend" to the states that the confiscated property be restored.

CORE **OBJECTIVE**

3. Describe the ways in which the American Revolution was also a civil war.

American Society at War

Choosing Sides

The Revolution was as much a brutal civil war among Americans (including the Native American peoples allied with both sides) as it was a prolonged struggle against Great Britain. The necessity of choosing sides divided families and friends, towns and cities. Benjamin Franklin's illegitimate son, William, for example, was the royal governor of New Jersey. An ardent Loyalist, he sided with Great Britain during the Revolution, and his Patriot father later removed him from his will.

Colonists divided

The colonists were divided into three groups: Patriots, who formed the Continental army and fought in state militias; Loyalists, or Tories, as the Patriots mockingly called them; and a less committed middle group swayed mostly by the better organized and more energetic Patriots. Loyalists may have represented 20 percent of the American population, but the Patriots were probably the largest of the three groups. Some Americans (like Benedict Arnold) switched sides during the war, and there were numerous deserters, spies, and traitors on both sides.

The Patriots, both moderates and radicals, supported the war for independence because they had finally decided that the only way to protect their liberty was to separate themselves from British control and also from the British monarchy and aristocracy. Patriots also wanted to establish an American republic, a unique form of government in the late eighteenth century that would convert them from being *subjects* of a king to being *citizens* with the power to elect their own government and pursue their own economic interests. "We have it in our power," wrote Thomas Paine, "to begin the world over again. . . . The birthday of a new world is at hand."

Loyalists oppose independence

The Loyalists, also called Tories, Royalists, or "King's Men," had no desire to "dissolve the political bands" with Britain, as the Declaration of Independence demanded. Instead, as some 700 of them in New York City said in a petition to British officials, they "steadily and uniformly opposed" this "most unnatural, unprovoked Rebellion." Where the Patriots rejected the monarchy, the Loyalists staunchly upheld royal authority and appreciated being defended by British soldiers. The British Empire, they felt, had

Four Soldiers (ca. 1781) This illustration by a French lieutenant captures the varied appearances of Patriot forces in the war (left to right): a black soldier (freed for joining the 1st Rhode Island Regiment), a New England militiaman, a frontiersman, and a French soldier.

long championed Protestantism, commerce, and liberty. Loyalists believed that the British constitution was more likely to protect their rights and liberties than the American aristocrats parading as revolutionaries. They viewed the Revolution as an act of treason and were horrified by the idea of independence.

Loyalists were most numerous in the seaport cities, especially New York City and Philadelphia, as well as the Carolinas, but they came from all walks of life. Governors, judges, and other royal officials were almost all Loyalists; most Anglican ministers also preferred the mother country, as did many Anglican worshippers. In the backcountry of New York and across the Carolinas, many small farmers who had largely been unaffected by the controversies over British efforts to tighten colonial regulations rallied to the British side. More New York men joined Loyalist regiments than the Continental army. Many Loyalists calculated that the Revolution would fail or feared that it would result in mob rule. In few places, however, were there enough Loyalists to assume control without the support of British troops.

The Loyalists Flee

The Loyalists suffered greatly for their stubborn support of King George and for their refusal to pledge allegiance to the new United States. During and after the Revolution, their homes, farms, and lands were confiscated, and many were assaulted and executed by Patriots (and vice versa). After the American victory at Yorktown, tens of thousands of panicked Loyalists headed to seaports to board British ships to flee the new United States. Thousands of African Americans, mostly runaway slaves, also flocked to New York City, Charleston, and Savannah, with many of their angry owners in hot pursuit.

The Fate of the Loyalists (1783)
After the Revolution, many Loyalists fled to British colonies in the Caribbean and Canada. This British cartoon shows Patriots, depicted as "savages let[ting] loose," mercilessly hanging and scalping the Loyalists.

Loyalist, African American, and Native American refugees

Some 80,000 desperate refugees—white Loyalists, free blacks, freed slaves, and Indians who had allied with the British—scattered throughout the British Empire, transforming it in the process. The largest number of Loyalist exiles landed in Canada, including 3,500 former slaves who had been given their freedom in exchange for joining the British army.

The departure of so many Loyalists from America was one of the most important social consequences of the Revolution. Their confiscated homes, vast tracts of land, and vacated jobs created new social, economic, and political opportunities for Patriots.

CORE **OBJECTIVE**

4. Examine how the Revolutionary War was an "engine" for political and social change.

War as an Engine of Change

Like all major wars, the Revolution had unexpected effects on political, economic, and social life. It not only secured American independence and created a unique system of self-governance, but it also began a process of societal change that has remained a defining element in the American experiment in representative democracy. The turmoil of eight years of war upset traditional social relationships and affected the lives of people who had long been discriminated against—African Americans, women, and Native Americans. In important ways, then, the Revolution was much more than simply a war for independence. It was an engine for political experimentation and social change.

A Political Revolution

Debating the forms of government

The Americans had won their War of Independence. Had they experienced a political revolution as well? Years later, former President John Adams insisted that the Revolution had begun long before the shooting started: "The Revolution was in the minds and hearts of the people. . . . This radical change in the principles, opinions, sentiments, and affections of the people, was the real American Revolution." Yet Adams's observation notwithstanding, the war itself ignited a prolonged debate about what new forms of government would best serve the new American republic.

Republican Ideology

American revolutionaries embraced a **Republican ideology** instead of the monarchical outlook that had long dominated Europe. The new American republic was not a democracy in the purest sense of the word. In ancient Greece, the Athenians practiced *direct democracy*, which meant that the citizens voted on all major decisions affecting their society, not unlike the town meetings in New England villages today. The new United States, rather, was technically a *representative democracy*, in which property-holding white men governed themselves through the concept of republicanism, whereby they elected representatives, or legislators, to make key decisions on their behalf. As Thomas Paine observed, representative democracy had many advantages over monarchies, one of which was greater transparency: "Whatever are its excellencies and defects, they are visible to all."

To preserve the delicate balance between liberty and power in the new American republic, the Revolutionary leaders believed that their new governments must protect the rights of individuals and states from being violated by the national government. The war for independence thus sparked a wave of new **state constitutions** that remains unique in history. Not only was a new nation coming into being, but also new state-level governments were also being created, all of which were designed to reflect the principles of the "republican ideology" limiting the powers of government so as to protect the people's rights.

> Representative democracy and individuals' rights

State Governments

Most of the political experimentation between 1776 and 1787 occurred at the state level in the form of written constitutions in which the people granted limited authority to their governments. The first state constitutions created governments much like the colonial governments, but with *elected* governors and senates instead of royally *appointed* governors and councils. Most of the constitutions also included a bill of rights that protected the time-honored rights of freedom of speech, trial by jury, freedom from self-incrimination, and the like. Most of them limited the powers of governors and strengthened the powers of the legislatures.

The Articles of Confederation

Once the American colonies had declared their independence in 1776, the Patriots needed to form a *national* government as well as thirteen *state* governments in the midst of the war. Before March 1781, the Continental Congress had exercised emergency powers without any legal or official authority. Plans for a permanent form of government emerged quickly,

Republican ideology Political belief in representative democracy in which citizens govern themselves by electing representatives, or legislators, to make key decisions on the citizens' behalf.

state constitutions Charters that define the relationship between the state government and local governments and individuals, also protecting their rights from violation by the national government.

however. As early as July 1776, a committee appointed by the Continental Congress had produced a draft constitution called the *Articles of Confederation and Perpetual Union*. When the **Articles of Confederation** finally were ratified (approved by the states) five years later, in March 1781, they essentially legalized the way things had been operating since independence had been declared. The Confederation government reflected the long-standing American fears of monarchy by not even allowing for a president or chief executive. The Confederation Congress was given full power over foreign affairs and over disputes between the states. But the Confederation Congress had no courts and no power to enforce its resolutions and ordinances. It also had no power to levy taxes and had to rely for its own budgetary needs on requisitions from the states, which state legislatures often ignored.

> Limited government and states' rights

The states were in no mood to create a strong central government. The Confederation Congress, in fact, had less power than the colonists had once accepted in Parliament, since it could not regulate interstate and foreign commerce. For certain important acts, moreover, a "special majority" was required. Nine states had to approve measures dealing with war, treaties, coinage, finances, and the army and navy. Unanimous approval from the states was needed to levy tariffs (often called "duties," or taxes) on imports. Amendments to the Articles also required unanimous ratification by the states. The Confederation had neither an executive nor a judicial branch; there was no administrative head of government (only the president of the Confederation Congress, chosen annually) and no federal courts.

For all its weaknesses, however, the Confederation government represented the most practical structure for the new nation. After all, the Revolution on the battlefields had yet to be won, and an America besieged by British armies and warships could not risk divisive debates over the distribution of power that other forms of government might have entailed. The new state governments were not willing in 1776 to create a strong national government that might threaten their liberties.

Expansion of Political Participation

Participation in the Revolutionary army or militia excited men who previously had taken little interest in politics. The new political opportunities afforded by the creation of state governments led more ordinary citizens to participate than ever before. The property qualifications for voting, which already admitted an overwhelming majority of white men, were lowered after 1776. As a group of farmers explained, "no man can be free and independent" unless he possesses "a voice . . . in the most important officers in the legislature." In Pennsylvania, Delaware, North Carolina, and Georgia, any male taxpayer could vote. In addition, farmers, tradesmen, and shopkeepers were soon elected to state legislatures. In general, a higher percentage of American males could vote in the late eighteenth and early nineteenth century than their counterparts in Great Britain.

Articles of Confederation
The first form of government for the United States, ratified by the original thirteen states in 1781; weak in central authority, it was replaced by the U.S. Constitution drafted in 1787.

A Social Revolution

The Revolutionary War helped excite a sense of common nationality. American nationalism embodied a stirring idea. This new nation, unlike the Old World nations of Europe, was not rooted in antiquity. Its people, except for the Native Americans, had not inhabited it over many centuries, nor did they all share the same ethnic background. "The American national consciousness," one observer wrote, "is not a voice crying out of the depth of the dark past, but is proudly a product of the enlightened present, setting its face resolutely toward the future."

A social revolution

Political revolutions often spark social revolutions. What did the Revolution mean to those workers, servants, farmers, and freed slaves who participated? Many hoped that the Revolution would remove, not reinforce, the elite's traditional political and social advantages. Many wealthy Patriots, on the other hand, would have been content to replace royal officials with the rich, the wellborn, and the able—and let it go at that. The poor did not overthrow the rich during the American Revolution, but the new republic's social fabric was visibly different after the war. The energy created by the concepts of liberty, equality, and democracy changed the dynamics of American social and political life in ways that people could not have imagined in 1776. The Philadelphia doctor and scientist Benjamin Rush recognized that unexpected changes were on the way: "The American war is over: but this is far from being the case with the American Revolution. On the contrary, but the first act of the great drama is closed."

Freedom of Religion

The Revolution also tested traditional religious loyalties and set in motion important changes in the relationship between church and government. Before the Revolution, Americans *tolerated* religious dissent; after the Revolution, Americans insisted on complete *freedom* of religion as embodied in the principle of separation of church and state. The Anglican Church, established as the official religion in five colonies and parts of two others, was especially vulnerable to changes prompted by the

Religious development The Congregational Church developed a national presence in the early nineteenth century. Lemuel Haynes, depicted here, was its first African American preacher.

war. Anglicans tended to be pro-British, and non-Anglicans, notably Baptists and Methodists, outnumbered Anglicans in all states except Virginia. All but Virginia eliminated tax support for the church before the fighting was over, and Virginia did so soon afterward. Although Anglicanism survived in the form of the new Episcopal Church, it never regained its pre-Revolutionary stature.

Religious freedom

In 1776, the Virginia Declaration of Rights guaranteed the free exercise of religion, and in 1786 the **Virginia Statute of Religious Freedom** (written by Thomas Jefferson) declared that "no man shall be compelled to frequent or support any religious worship, place or ministry whatsoever" and "that all men shall be free to profess, and by argument to maintain, their opinions in matters of religion." These statutes, and the Revolutionary ideology that justified them, helped shape the course that religious life would take in the new United States: diverse and voluntary rather than monolithic and enforced by the government. Even religious life was revolutionized.

CORE **OBJECTIVE**

5. Compare the impact of the Revolutionary War on African Americans, women, and Native Americans.

Equality and Its Limits

The Paradox of Slavery

The sharpest irony of the American Revolution is that Britain offered enslaved blacks more opportunities for freedom than did the new United States. In November 1775, the British promised freedom to slaves, as well as indentured servants, who would fight for the Loyalist cause. Thousands of slaves took advantage of the offer. Harry Washington, for example, was born in Africa, became one of George Washington's slaves in 1763, escaped to join the British army, and served in the Revolutionary War as a corporal in one of the black regiments organized by the British army. The British recruitment of slaves outraged George Washington, Thomas Jefferson, and other white plantation owners in Virginia, where 40 percent of the population was black. Twenty-three slaves escaped from Jefferson's Monticello plantation. The man who drafted the Declaration of Independence eventually reclaimed six of them, only to sell them for their "disloyalty" in seeking liberty for themselves.

In the end, however, the British policy of recruiting slaves into the military backfired. The "terrifying" prospect of British troops arming slaves persuaded many southerners to join the Patriot cause, and for many whites, especially in Virginia, the Revolution became primarily a war to defend slavery. Edward Rutledge of South Carolina said that the British decision to arm slaves did more to create "an eternal separation between Great Britain and the colonies than any other expedient." Slaves accused of disloyalty faced terrible punishment. In 1775, Thomas Jeremiah, a free black, was convicted and executed in Charleston, South Carolina, for telling slaves that British troops were coming "to help the poor Negroes."

In response to the British recruitment of enslaved African Americans, at the end of 1775 General Washington authorized the enlistment of free blacks—but not slaves—into the American army. Southerners, however, convinced the Continental Congress to instruct Washington in February 1776 to enlist no more African Americans, free or enslaved. But as the American war effort struggled, some states ignored southern wishes. Massachusetts organized two all-black army units, and Rhode Island organized one, which also included Indians. However, two states, South Carolina and Georgia, refused

Virginia Statute of Religious Freedom (1786) A Virginia law, drafted by Thomas Jefferson in 1777 and enacted in 1786, that guarantees freedom of, and from, religion.

to allow any blacks to serve in the Patriot forces. About 5,000 African Americans fought on the Patriot side, and most of them were free blacks from northern states.

The white Belknap family of Framingham, Massachusetts, freed their African American slave Peter Salem so that he might enlist in the Massachusetts militia. Salem was with the Minutemen at Concord in 1775 and also fought alongside other blacks at the Battles of Bunker Hill and Saratoga. Another former slave who fought at Bunker Hill, Salem Poor, was commended after the battle for being a "Brave & gallant Soldier" who "behaved like an experienced officer, as well as an excellent soldier."

In the end, the British army, which liberated 20,000 enslaved blacks during the war, was a far greater instrument of emancipation than the American forces. Most of the newly freed blacks found their way to Canada or to British colonies on Caribbean islands.

While thousands of free blacks and runaway slaves fought in the war, the vast majority of African Americans did not choose sides so much as they chose freedom. Several hundred thousand enslaved blacks, mostly in the southern states, took advantage of the disruptions caused by the war to seize their freedom. In the North, which had far fewer slaves than the South, the ideas of liberty and freedom that inspired the Patriots led most states to end slavery, either during the war or shortly afterward. In other words, the ideals of the Revolution provided the impulse to end slavery in the North, while at the same time, many southerners were prompted to join the Revolution to keep the British from freeing their slaves. These paradoxical attitudes would continue to shape the political disputes of the young nation.

British recruit and free slaves, while slavery abolished in the North

The Status of Women

The idea of liberty spawned by the Revolution applied to the status of women as much as to that of African Americans. The legal status of women in the colonies was governed by British common law, which essentially treated them like children, limiting their roles to child-rearing and maintaining the household. Women could not vote or hold office. Nor could they preach. Few had access to formal education. Boys were taught to read and write; girls were taught to read and sew. Most New England women in the eighteenth century could not write their own names. Until married, women were subject to their fathers. Once a woman married, she essentially became the property of her husband, and her goods became his. A married woman had no right to buy, sell, or manage property. Technically, any wages a wife earned belonged to the husband. Women could not sign contracts or sue others or testify in court. A husband could beat and even rape his wife without fearing legal action. Divorces were extremely difficult to obtain; wives were required to obey their husbands.

Yet the Revolution offered women new opportunities to broaden their social roles. Women supported the armies in various ways. They handled supplies, served as messengers or spies, and worked as camp followers, cooking, cleaning, and nursing the soldiers. Wives often followed their

Abigail Adams Abigail Adams, wife of John Adams, in a 1766 portrait. Though an ardent Patriot, Adams and other women like her saw few changes in women's rights emerging in the new United States.

soldier-husbands to camp and on occasion took their place in battle. In 1777, some 400 armed women mobilized to defend Pittsfield, Vermont. The men of the town had gone off to fight when a band of Loyalists and Indians approached the village. In a day-long battle, the women held off the attackers until help arrived. A few women disguised themselves and fought as ordinary soldiers. An exceptional case was Deborah Sampson, who joined a Massachusetts regiment as "Robert Shurtleff" and served from 1781 to 1783 by the "artful concealment" of her gender. Ann Bailey did the same. In 1777 she cut her hair, dressed like a man, and used a husky voice to enlist in the Patriot army in New York as "Samuel Gay." Bailey performed so well that she was promoted to corporal, only to eventually be discovered and dismissed.

Early in the Revolutionary struggle, Abigail Adams, one of the most learned, spirited, and independent women of the time, wrote to her husband, John: "In the new Code of Laws which I suppose it will be necessary for you to make, I desire you would remember the Ladies. . . . Do not put such unlimited power into the hands of the Husbands." Since men were "Naturally Tyrannical," she wrote, "why then, not put it out of the power of the vicious and the Lawless to use us with cruelty and indignity with impunity." Otherwise, "if particular care and attention is not paid to the Ladies we are determined to foment a Rebellion, and will not hold ourselves bound by any Laws in which we have no voice, or Representation." Husband John responded that he could not help but "laugh" at her proposals. While surprised that women might be dissatisfied, he insisted on retaining the traditional privileges enjoyed by males: "Depend upon it, we know better than to repeal our Masculine systems." If women were to be granted equality, he warned, then "children and apprentices" and "Indians and Negroes" would also demand equal rights and freedoms.

Little progress for women

Thomas Jefferson shared Adams's stance. In his view, there was no place in the new American republic for female political participation. When asked about women's voting rights, he replied that "the tender breasts of ladies were not formed for political convulsion." Improvements in the status of women would have to wait. New Yorker Margaret Livingston admitted as much in 1776 when she wrote her daughter that "our Sex are *doomed* to be obedient [to men] at every stage of life so that we shan't be great gainers by this contest [the Revolutionary War]."

Native Americans and the Revolution

The war for American independence had lasting effects on the Indians in the southern backcountry and in the Old Northwest territory west of New York and Pennsylvania. Most Native Americans sought to remain neutral in the war, but both British and American agents urged the chiefs to fight on their side. The result was the disintegration of the alliance among the six nations making up the Iroquois League. Most Mohawks, for example, accepted British promises to protect them from encroachments by American settlers on their lands. The Oneidas, on the other hand, fought with the Patriots. Indians on both sides attacked villages, burned crops, and killed civilians.

From Subjects to Citizens

The concepts of liberty, equality, and democracy changed the dynamics of American social and political life. As Americans won their War of Independence, they began to re-define their relationships with one another and develop new systems of government that reflected their view of themselves as independent citizens, not the subjects of any king.

Ideology	Americans embraced republicanism where political power was exercised by officials elected by citizens. They rejected all forms of monarchism or aristocracy. White men who owned certain amounts of property could vote in elections and enjoyed full rights as citizens.
Religion	Many state governments moved from the principle of religious tolerance to complete religious freedom for all citizens.
African Americans	During and after the Revolution, northern states began implementing policies to end slavery, concluding that the institution was incompatible with liberty. Southern states did not follow suit. Many slaveholders there had joined the Revolutionary side because they feared a British victory would result in freedom for their slaves.
Gender	Although women made significant contributions to the war for independence, men maintained control of politics, dismissing many women's appeals for political participation and voting rights.
Native Americans	While some Native Americans sided with the American Revolutionary cause, most did not. After independence, Americans continued to view them as a threat to future expansion and opportunity in the West.

QUESTIONS FOR ANALYSIS

1. Did Americans experience a *political* revolution after they won independence from Britain?

2. What was at the heart of the experiment in self-rule for the states?

3. How did the Revolution lead to broader political rights and expand civil liberties?

4. What were the ironies of the Revolution for African Americans, women, and Native Americans? Were there victories?

The new American government assured its Indian allies that it would respect their lands and their rights. But the American people adopted a very different goal: they used the disruptions of war to destroy and displace many Native Americans. Once the war ended and independence was secured, there was no peace for the Indians. The new U.S. government turned its back on most of the pledges made to Native Americans. By the end of the eighteenth century, land-hungry whites were again pushing into Indian territories on the western frontier. Independence for Americans would bring growing exploitation of Native Americans.

Displacement and destruction of Native Americans

■ **Military Challenges** In 1776 the British had the mightiest army and navy in the world. The Americans had to create an army—the Continental army—and sustain it. To defeat the British, George Washington realized that the Americans had to turn unreliable *citizen-soldiers* into a disciplined fighting force. He decided to wage a long, costly war, wagering that the British army was fighting thousands of miles from its home base and would eventually give up in order to cut its losses.

■ **Turning Points** The French were likely allies for the colonies from the beginning of the conflict because they resented their losses to Britain in the Seven Years' War. After the British defeat at the *Battles of Saratoga* the first major turning point, France agreed to fight with the colonies until independence was won. Washington's ability to hold his ragged forces together despite daily desertions and two especially difficult winters in Morristown and *Valley Forge,* the second and third major turning points. The British lost support on the frontier and in their southern colonies when terrorist tactics backfired. The Battle of King's Mountain drove the British into retreat, and the *alliance with France* meant that French supplies and the French fleet would tip the balance and ensure the American victory at the *Battle of Yorktown,* which were the final turning points.

■ **Civil War** The American Revolution was also a civil war, dividing families and communities. There were at least 100,000 Loyalists in the colonies. They included royal officials, Anglican ministers, wealthy southern planters, and the elite in large seaport cities; they also included many humble people, especially recent immigrants. After the hostilities ended, many Loyalists, including slaves who had fled their plantations to support the British cause, left for Canada, the West Indies, or Great Britain.

■ **A Political and Social Revolution** The American Revolution disrupted and transformed traditional class and social relationships. American revolutionaries embraced a *Republican ideology* in contrast to a monarchy, and more white men gained the right to vote as property requirements were removed. But fears of a monarchy being re-established led colonists to vest power in the states rather than a powerful national government under the *Articles of Confederation.* The states wrote new *state constitutions* that instituted more elected positions. Most included bills of rights that protected individual liberties. The *Virginia Statute of Religious Freedom* led the way in guaranteeing the separation of church and state, and religious toleration was transformed into religious freedom for all, including Roman Catholics and Jews.

■ **African Americans, Women, and Native Americans** Northern states began to free slaves after the Revolutionary War, but southern states refused to do so. Although many women had undertaken nontraditional roles during the war, afterward they remained largely confined to the domestic sphere, with no changes to their legal or political status. The Revolution had catastrophic effects on Native Americans, regardless of which side they had embraced during the war. During and after the Revolution, American settlers seized Native American land, often in violation of existing treaties.

KEY TERMS

CHRONOLOGY

1776   British forces seize New York City

General Washington's troops defeat British forces at the Battle of Trenton

States begin writing new constitutions

1777   American forces defeat British in a series of battles at Saratoga, New York

1778   Americans and French form a crucial military alliance

George Rogers Clark's militia defeats British troops in the Mississippi Valley

American forces defeat the Iroquois Confedercy at Newtown, New York

British seize Savannah and Charleston

1780   Patriots defeat Loyalists at the Battle of King's Mountain

1781   British invasion of southern colonies turned back at the Battles of Cowpens and Guilford Courthouse

American and French forces defeat British at Yorktown, Virginia

1781   Articles of Confederation are ratified

Continental Congress becomes Confederation Congress

1783   Treaty of Paris is signed, formally ending Revolutionary War

1786   Virginia adopts the Statute of Religious Freedom

INQUIZITIVE

Go to InQuizitive to see what you've learned—and learn what you've missed—with personalized feedback along the way.

WASHINGTON AS A STATESMAN AT THE CONSTITUTIONAL CONVENTION (1856) This painting by Junius Brutus Stearns is one of the earliest depictions of the drafting of the Constitution, capturing the moment after the convention members, including George Washington (right), decided to present the Constitution to the public.

Creating a "More Perfect Union"

1783–1800

The unlikely American victory in the Revolutionary War stunned the world, but the Patriots had little time to celebrate, for they faced the overwhelming task of creating the world's first large republic. The transition from war to peace was neither simple nor easy. Forging a new nation out of thirteen rebellious colonies posed huge challenges during and after the war. The period from the drafting of the Declaration of Independence in 1776, through the creation of the new Constitution in 1787, and ending with the election of Thomas Jefferson as president in 1800 was an especially turbulent time during which the new nation experienced growing political divisions, foreign troubles, and courageous statesmanship.

During the so-called Critical Period between 1783 and 1787, Americans developed sharp differences of opinion about national economic policies, international relations, and the proper relationship of the states to the national government. In the end, differences over those key issues created powerful tensions that gave birth to the nation's first political parties and, to this day, continue to complicate the American experiment in federalism (the sharing of power among national, state, and local governments).

CORE OBJECTIVES INQUIZITIVE

1. Identify the strengths and weaknesses of the Articles of Confederation and explain how they contributed to the creation of a new U.S. Constitution in 1787.

2. Describe the political innovations that the 1787 Constitutional Convention developed for the new nation.

3. Summarize the major debates surrounding the ratification of the Constitution and how they were resolved.

4. Compare the Federalists' vision for the United States with that of their Republican opponents during the 1790s.

5. Explain how attitudes toward Great Britain and France shaped American politics in the late eighteenth century.

CORE **OBJECTIVE**

1. Identify the strengths and weaknesses of the Articles of Confederation and explain how they contributed to the creation of a new U.S. Constitution in 1787.

The Confederation Government

During the 1780s, the widespread American distrust of centralized government power, originally directed at the British monarchy, was redirected toward the new American government under the Articles of Confederation. The union of states created in 1776 was a wartime alliance of necessity that, politically and economically, often functioned poorly. Riots and rebellions protesting government policies erupted with growing frequency after the Revolutionary War ended in 1783. The weaknesses of the Confederation government in dealing with such turmoil led political leaders to design a new national constitution and federal government in 1787, both of which proved to be more effective—and lasting—than the Confederation government.

A Loose Alliance of States

By design, the Articles of Confederation, drafted in 1776 and 1777 and approved by the states in 1781, had created not so much a united nation as a loose alliance ("confederation") of thirteen independent states. America's first national government under the Articles of Confederation had only one component, a one-house (unicameral) congress. There was no president, no executive branch, no separate national judiciary (court system). State legislatures appointed the members of the Confederation Congress; each state, regardless of size or population, had one vote. This meant that Rhode Island, with 68,000 people, had the same power in Congress as Virginia, with over 747,000 inhabitants. Altering the Articles of Confederation required a *unanimous* vote of both the Congress and the thirteen state legislatures; given this difficulty, they were never amended.

The Confederation Congress was weak by design, in order to ensure that it did not violate the rights of the thirteen states. It had little authority or resources, leading George Washington to call it "a half-starved, limping government, always moving upon crutches and tottering at every step." The Confederation Congress could neither regulate trade between the states or with other nations, nor pay off the country's large war debts; it could approve treaties with other nations but had no power to enforce their terms; it could call for the raising of an army but could not force men to fill the ranks. The Congress had no power to enforce its own laws and ran up a budget deficit every year of its existence. Because most of the states did not provide sufficient contributions to pay for the national government, the Confederation Congress resorted to printing paper money called Continentals, whose value plummeted as more were printed, leading to the joking phrase, "Not worth a Continental."

An Important Foundation

Yet in spite of its limitations, the weak Confederation Congress somehow managed to survive the war years and to lay important foundations for the new national government. The Articles of Confederation were crucially important in supporting the political concept of "republicanism," which meant that the American Republic would be governed not by kings or queens or nobles but "by the authority of the people."

The Confederation government also concluded the strategically important Treaty of Paris with Great Britain in 1783, ending the Revolutionary War. Perhaps most important, the Confederation established the basic principles of land distribution and territorial government that would guide America's westward expansion for decades to come.

> Successes: Support of "republicanism" and negotiation of Treaty of Paris (1783)

Land Policy

In ending the Revolutionary War and transferring Britain's North American colonies to America's Confederation government, the Treaty of Paris doubled the size of the United States. Between 1784 and 1787, the Confederation Congress issued three major policies, called *ordinances*, providing for the orderly development of the vast territories west of the thirteen original states in an effort to generate revenue for the national government. These documents—among the most important in American history—created the procedures that the United States would follow in its eventual expansion all the way to the Pacific.

In 1784 Thomas Jefferson drafted the first federal land ordinance, which urged states to drop their competing claims to Indian-held territory west of the Appalachian Mountains, north of the Ohio River, and east of the Mississippi River. That way, the vast, unmapped area could be divided into as many as seventeen *new* states. When a western territory's population equaled that of the smallest existing state (Rhode Island), the territory would be eligible for statehood. The Confederation Congress, after rejecting Jefferson's proposal that slavery be banned from the new territories, passed the Land Ordinance of 1784.

The next year, the Confederation Congress created the Land Ordinance of 1785, which outlined a plan of land surveys and sales that would stamp a rectangular pattern on what was called the Northwest Territory (the sprawling area that would become the states of Ohio, Michigan, Indiana, Illinois, and Wisconsin). Wherever Indian lands were purchased—or taken—they were divided into six-mile-square townships laid out along a grid of lines running east-west and north-south. Each township was in turn divided into thirty-six sections one mile square (640 acres), with each section divided into four farms. The 640-acre sections of "public lands" were to be sold at auctions, the proceeds of which went into the national treasury.

> Success: Creation of land ordinances

The Northwest Ordinance

The third major land policy created by the Confederation Congress was the **Northwest Ordinance** of 1787. It outlined two key principles: that the new western territories could become states that would be treated as equals rather than as colonies, and that slavery was banned from the western region (but slaves already there would remain slaves). The Northwest Ordinance

Northwest Ordinance (1787) Land policy for new western territories in the Ohio Valley that established the terms and conditions for self-government and statehood while also banning slavery from the region.

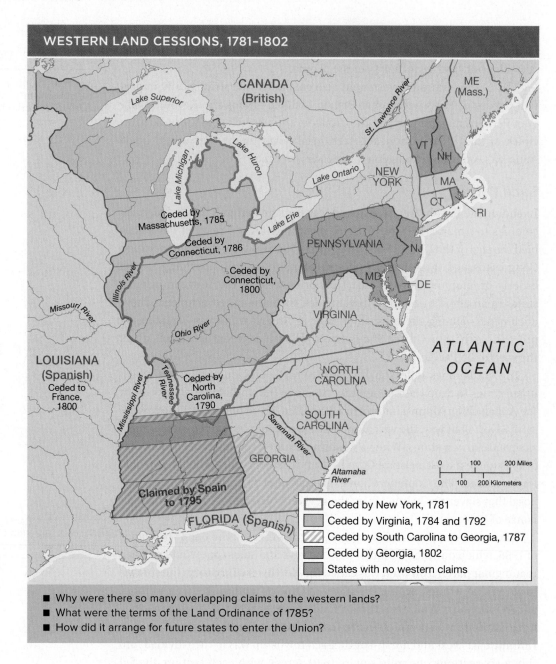

WESTERN LAND CESSIONS, 1781–1802

CANADA (British)

ME (Mass.)

Lake Superior

Lake Michigan

Lake Huron

Lake Ontario

St. Lawrence River

VT

NH

NEW YORK

MA

CT

RI

Ceded by Massachusetts, 1785

Lake Erie

PENNSYLVANIA

NJ

Ceded by Connecticut, 1786

Illinois River

Ceded by Connecticut, 1800

MD

DE

Missouri River

Ohio River

VIRGINIA

ATLANTIC OCEAN

LOUISIANA (Spanish)

Ceded to France, 1800

Mississippi River

Tennessee River

Ceded by North Carolina, 1790

NORTH CAROLINA

SOUTH CAROLINA

Savannah River

GEORGIA

Altamaha River

Claimed by Spain to 1795

FLORIDA (Spanish)

0   100   200 Miles

0   100   200 Kilometers

☐ Ceded by New York, 1781

▧ Ceded by Virginia, 1784 and 1792

▨ Ceded by South Carolina to Georgia, 1787

■ Ceded by Georgia, 1802

▨ States with no western claims

■ Why were there so many overlapping claims to the western lands?
■ What were the terms of the Land Ordinance of 1785?
■ How did it arrange for future states to enter the Union?

also included a promise (which would be repeatedly broken) that Indian lands "shall never be taken from them without their consent."

The Northwest Ordinance specified that a new territory would become a state through a three-stage process. First, Congress would appoint a territorial governor and other officials to create a legal code, keep the peace, and administer justice. Second, when the territorial population of adult males reached 5,000, a legislature would be elected. Third, when a territory's population reached 60,000 "free inhabitants," it could create a state constitution and apply to Congress for statehood. In 1803, Ohio was the first territory to be granted statehood in this way.

Foreign Tensions

After the Revolutionary War, the Confederation government confronted issues with Great Britain and Spain that it was powerless to resolve. Both European nations kept trading posts and forts on American soil, in violation of the Treaty of Paris (1783). Another major irritant in U.S.-British relations was the seizure of Loyalist property (homes, farms, plantations, slaves, businesses, etc.) by Patriots during and after the war. The British government demanded that the United States pay the Loyalists for their losses. With Spain, the chief issues were the disputed southern boundary of the United States along the Gulf of Mexico and the right of Americans to send boats or barges filled with their crops and products down the Mississippi River to the valuable Spanish-controlled port of New Orleans. In 1784 the Spanish governor in New Orleans closed the lower Mississippi River to American boats and barges, thus cutting off settlers in Tennessee and Kentucky from world commerce.

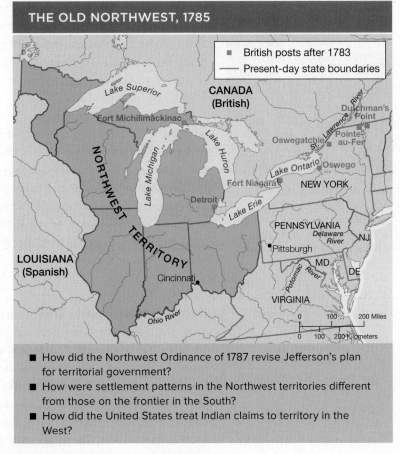

THE OLD NORTHWEST, 1785

- British posts after 1783
- Present-day state boundaries

- How did the Northwest Ordinance of 1787 revise Jefferson's plan for territorial government?
- How were settlement patterns in the Northwest territories different from those on the frontier in the South?
- How did the United States treat Indian claims to territory in the West?

The Spanish governor of Florida also provided firearms to Creeks who resisted American encroachment on their lands in south Georgia. Led by the powerful chief Alexander McGillivray, the son of a Scottish planter and trader and a half-French, half-Creek mother, the Creeks forced whites off their tribal lands. The Spanish argued that all of the land west of the Appalachian Mountains "belongs to the free and independent nations of Indians, and you [Americans] have no right to it." American frontiersmen disagreed violently with the Spanish position, but the Confederation Congress was powerless to help them.

Trade and the Economy

The Confederation government also struggled to manage complex economic issues. Seven years of warfare against Great Britain had nearly bankrupted the new nation. The plantation economies of the southern states were hard hit by the escape of tens of thousands of enslaved workers during and after

Failure: Regulation of interstate commerce and foreign relations

Domestic industry American craftsmen, such as this cabinetmaker, favored tariffs on foreign goods that competed with their own products.

the war. And the national economy was devastated by the loss of its trading network with the British Empire, which before the Revolution was the primary source of American prosperity. The British decision after the war to close its Caribbean island colonies such as Bermuda, Jamaica, and Barbados to American trade eliminated what had been a thriving market for timber, wheat, and farm products.

Merchants and shippers eager to revive the profitable trade relationships within the British Empire called for an economic war against Great Britain to force the government to end its restrictions on American commerce. Some state governments imposed special taxes on British vessels and special tariffs (taxes on imports) on British goods. The British responded by sending their ships to states whose tariffs were lower. In essence, the American states ended up competing against each other for foreign trade. By 1787, a clear need had emerged for the national government to regulate interstate trade and foreign relations.

Scarce Money

Failure: No national currency

Complex financial issues further threatened the stability of the new nation after 1783. There was no national currency and only a handful of banks. Farmers who had profited during the war now found themselves squeezed by lower crop prices and mounting debts and taxes. Creditors (people who loaned money to others) demanded that debtors (mostly farmers) pay back their loans or mortgages in gold or silver coins, which were always in short supply. By 1785, demands that states print new paper currency to supplement coins became the single most divisive issue in politics. Farmers saw adding paper currency as a simple way to raise prices for their crops and livestock and thereby help them pay their debts and taxes. In 1785–1786, seven states began issuing their own paper money to help farmers and to pay the cash bonuses promised to war veterans. The Rhode Island legislature issued so much paper money that creditors fled the state to avoid being paid in paper currency of such unstable value.

Shays's Rebellion

In neighboring Massachusetts, however, the legislature took a different stance. Hard-pressed farmers in the western part of the state, many of them military veterans who had not received their promised pay during the war, urged the state to issue new paper money and demanded more time to pay the taxes owed on their lands. When the Massachusetts legislature adjourned in 1786 without providing paper money or any other relief from taxes and debts, three rural counties erupted in revolt.

Led by thirty-nine-year-old Daniel Shays, who had served as a captain in the Revolutionary War, armed gangs of angry farmers forced judges to stop farm foreclosures. Shays urged them on, yelling "Close down the courts!" Shays and his followers wanted to use corn and wheat as money in paying their debts and taxes. The state government responded by sending 4,400 militiamen armed with cannons to suppress the rebellion. They scattered Shays's debtor army with a single volley that left four farmers dead. The farmers ran for the hills; Shays fled to Vermont.

The rebels nevertheless won a victory of sorts, as the state legislature decided to eliminate some of the taxes and fees on farmers. But the most important consequence of **Shays's Rebellion** was to spread panic among wealthy Americans. In Massachusetts, Abigail Adams dismissed Shays and his followers as "ignorant, restless desperadoes, without conscience or principles." In Virginia, George Washington was equally disturbed. "Good God!" he exclaimed. America needed a "government by which our lives, liberty, and properties will be secured." The events in Massachusetts, he feared, might tempt other angry debtor groups around the country to violate the law and disturb the peace.

Shays's Rebellion Shays and his followers demanded a more flexible monetary policy and the right to postpone paying taxes until the postwar agricultural depression lifted.

Creating the Constitution

In the wake of Shays's Rebellion, many public officials agreed with Virginian James Madison that the "crisis is arrived." It was time to empower the national government to bring order and stability to the new nation.

The Constitutional Convention

In 1787, the Confederation Congress called for a special convention to gather in Philadelphia's Old State House (now Independence Hall) for the "purpose of revising the Articles of Confederation." Twelve of the thirteen states eventually participated; tiny Rhode Island refused. Twenty-nine delegates began meeting on May 25, 1787 (altogether, fifty-five men served as delegates at one time or another). After four months of deliberations carried out in stifling heat behind closed windows and locked doors, thirty-nine delegates signed the new federal constitution on September 17. Only three refused to sign what has become the longest functioning written constitution in the world.

The durability of the ideas and institutions contained in the Constitution is a lasting testimony to the men who made it. The convention delegates were surprisingly young; their average age was forty-two, and the youngest was twenty-six. Most of the framers of the Constitution, later dubbed the "Founding Fathers," were members of the nation's political and economic elite (Thomas Jefferson and John Adams did not participate because they

> CORE **OBJECTIVE**
>
> **2.** Describe the political innovations that the 1787 Constitutional Convention developed for the new nation.

Shays's Rebellion (1786–1787) Storming of the Massachusetts federal arsenal in 1787 by Daniel Shays and 1,200 armed farmers seeking debt relief from the state legislature through issuance of paper currency and lower taxes.

were serving as diplomats in Europe). Twenty-six delegates were college graduates; two were college presidents. Thirty-four were lawyers. Nearly all were considered "gentlemen" or "natural aristocrats."

Yet they were also practical men of experience, tested in the fires of the Revolutionary War. Twenty-two had served in the military during the conflict (five were captured and imprisoned by the British), seven had been state governors, and eight had helped write their state constitutions. Most had been members of the Continental Congress, and eight had signed the Declaration of Independence. In the summer of 1787, they gathered in Philadelphia "to form a more perfect union," as the preamble to the new Constitution asserted.

Drafting the Constitution

George Washington served as presiding officer of the Constitutional Convention but participated little in the debates. The governor of Pennsylvania, eighty-one-year-old Benjamin Franklin, the oldest delegate, was in such poor health that he had to be carried to the meetings each day in a special chair, borne aloft by inmates from the Philadelphia jail. Like Washington, Franklin said little from the floor but provided a wealth of experience, wit, and common sense behind the scenes.

Most active in the debates was James Madison. He was the ablest political theorist in the group and the central figure at the convention. The thirty-six-year-old Madison, a Virginia attorney, had arrived in Philadelphia with trunks full of books about political theory and a head full of ideas about how to strengthen the Confederation. Barely five feet tall and weighing only one hundred thirty pounds (a colleague said he was "no bigger than half a piece of soap"), he was too frail to serve in the Revolutionary army. Although painfully shy and soft-spoken, Madison had an agile mind, a huge appetite for learning, and a lifelong commitment to public service. He was determined to create a new constitution that would ensure the "supremacy of national authority." The logic of his arguments—and his willingness to support repeated compromises—proved decisive in shaping the new constitution. "Every person seems to acknowledge his greatness," one delegate said of Madison.

Most delegates agreed with Madison that their young nation needed a stronger national government and less powerful state governments. A New Hampshire delegate explained that he "saw no more reason to be afraid of the central [national] government than of the state governments."

The two basic and interrelated assumptions of the Constitutional Convention were that the national government must have direct authority over the citizenry rather than governing the people only through the state governments, and that the national government must derive its "sovereignty" (powers) directly from the people rather than from the state governments. The insistence on the authority of "the people" was the most important political innovation since the Declaration of Independence, for by declaring

James Madison This 1783 miniature shows Madison at thirty-two years old, just four years before he would assume a major role in drafting the Constitution.

Innovation: All authority derived from "the people"

the Constitution to be the voice of "the people," the founders authorized the federal government to limit the powers of the individual states.

Experience with the Articles of Confederation had persuaded the delegates that an effective national government needed new authority to collect taxes, borrow and issue money, regulate commerce and international relations, fund an army and navy, and make laws binding upon individual citizens. Experience also suggested to them that the states must be stripped of certain powers: to print paper money, make treaties with other nations, wage war, and levy taxes (tariffs) on imported goods. This concept of dividing governmental authority between the national government and the states came to be called **federalism**, another major contribution of the new American republic to the rest of the world.

> Innovation: Federalism

The Virginia and New Jersey Plans

James Madison drafted the framework for the initial discussions at the Constitutional Convention. His proposals, called the Virginia Plan, started with a revolutionary suggestion: that the delegates scrap their original instructions to *revise* the Articles of Confederation and instead create an entirely *new* federal constitution. The Virginia Plan called for a new Congress divided into two houses: a lower House of Representatives and an upper house, to be called the Senate. States with larger populations, such as Virginia and Pennsylvania, would have more representatives in Congress than the smaller states.

Critics of the Virginia Plan submitted an alternative written by William Paterson of New Jersey. The New Jersey Plan sought to keep the existing structure of equal representation of the states in a unicameral (one-house) Congress but gave Congress the power to levy taxes and regulate commerce, and the authority to name a chief executive as well as a supreme court.

After intense debate over the two plans, the dispute was resolved by the Great Compromise (sometimes called the Connecticut Compromise), which used elements of both plans in creating a new legislative structure for the national government. The more populous states won apportionment (the number of delegates representing each state) by population in the proposed House of Representatives, while the delegates who sought to protect states' power won equality of representation in the Senate, where each state would have two members.

> Innovation: The Great Compromise

The Structure of the Federal Government

The delegates at the 1787 Constitutional Convention were preoccupied with *power*: who should have it and how it would be used and controlled. The new constitution created a "federal" structure in which each citizen is governed by both a state government and the national government. To prevent power from being abused, each branch of the new national government—executive, legislative, and judicial—was given a separate sphere of authority as well as

> Innovation: Separation of powers

federalism Concept of dividing governmental authority between the national government and the states.

the responsibility to counterbalance the other branches, called the **separation of powers**, to keep any one of the three branches of the government from growing too powerful.

Legislature (Congress)

As a result of the Great Compromise, the delegates at the Constitutional Convention embedded the concept of a separation of powers in the new Congress. It would have two "houses," each intended to counterbalance the other, with one (the House of Representatives) representing the voters at large and the other, the Senate, representing the state legislatures. The "lower house" of Congress, the House of Representatives, was designed to be closer to the voters, who elected its members every two years. Under the Articles of Confederation, none of the members of Congress had been chosen by popular vote; all of them had been elected by state legislatures. James Madison argued that allowing individual citizens to elect at least one part of the new legislature was "essential to every plan of free government." The upper house, or Senate, was intended to be a more elite group, elected for six-year terms, not by voters directly, but by state legislatures. The Senate was intended to be a conservative force, using its power, when necessary, to overrule either the House of Representatives or the president. The more prestigious Senate, explained Madison, would help "protect the minority of the opulent against the majority."

Executive (President)

The delegates at the Constitutional Convention struggled mightily over the design of a new executive branch of government. Most of them expected the Congress to be the dominant branch of the new national government. Some delegates urged that a board of three men, modeled after the *triumvirate* of ancient Rome, collectively serve as the nation's chief executive. But a majority of delegates soon opted for a single president. Alexander Hamilton, a delegate from New York who was a celebrated attorney and the former chief of staff for General George Washington during the Revolution, wanted the president to serve for life, but the delegates eventually decided that the president should be held accountable to the people by standing for election every four years. The president could veto acts of Congress, subject to being overridden by a two-thirds vote in each house. The president was named the nation's chief diplomat as well as the commander in chief of the armed forces, and was responsible for the execution of the laws.

But the powers of the new president were also to be limited in key areas. The chief executive could neither declare war nor make peace; those powers were reserved for Congress. Unlike the British monarch, moreover, the president could be removed from office. The House of Representatives could impeach the chief executive and other civil officers on charges of treason, bribery, or "other high crimes and misdemeanors." An impeached president could be removed from office if two-thirds of the Senate voted for conviction.

separation of powers Strict division of the powers of government among three separate branches (executive, legislative, and judicial) which, in turn, check and balance each other.

To preserve the separation of the three branches, the president would be elected not by the Congress, but by "electors" chosen by "the people" in local elections. The number of "electors" in each state would vary depending upon the combined number of congressional representatives and U.S. senators. This "Electoral College" was a compromise between those wanting the president elected by a vote in Congress and those preferring election by a popular vote of qualified citizens.

Judiciary (Court System)

The third proposed branch of government, the judiciary, sparked surprisingly little debate. The Constitution called for a national supreme court headed by a chief justice. The role of the national judiciary was not to make laws (which was reserved to Congress) or execute or enforce the laws (which was reserved to the presidency) but to interpret the law as applied to specific cases and to ensure that every citizen received equal justice under the law. The U.S. Supreme Court was given final authority in interpreting the U.S. Constitution as well as in adjudicating disputes arising from the various state constitutions. Furthermore, Article VI of the Constitution declared that the federal Constitution, federal laws, and treaties are "the supreme Law of the Land." That is, when federal laws and state laws conflicted, the federal law would triumph.

"We the People"

The men who drafted the new constitution claimed to be representing all of the American people. The Constitution begins with the words: "We the people." In fact, however, there were important groups of Americans left out of the Constitution's protections. Native Americans, for example, were not considered federal or state citizens unless they paid taxes, which very few did. The Constitution declared that Native American "tribes" were not part of the United States but instead were separate "nations." Only the U.S. Congress, not the states or individuals, could negotiate treaties with the Indian nations. Not until 1924 would Native Americans qualify for American citizenship.

Dealing with Slavery

Of all the issues that emerged during the Constitutional Convention, none was more explosive than the question of slavery. Many of the framers viewed slavery as an embarrassing contradiction to the principles of liberty and equality expressed in the Declaration of Independence and the new Constitution. A New Jersey delegate declared that slavery was "utterly inconsistent with the principles of Christianity and humanity."

By contrast, delegates from the southern states strenuously defended slavery. During the eighteenth century, the agricultural economies of Maryland, Virginia, the Carolinas, and Georgia had become dependent upon huge numbers of enslaved laborers, and delegates from those states were determined to protect the future of slavery. Caught in the middle were Virginia slaveholders like George Washington, Thomas Jefferson, and James Madison, who hated slavery but saw no way to eliminate it without civil war. Madison told the Convention that the "distinction of color" had created "the most oppressive dominion ever exercised by man over man."

Because the southern delegates would have walked out of the convention, the framers did not even consider abolishing slavery, nor did some of them view slaves as human beings whose rights should be protected. Such moral blindness to basic human dignities reflected the prevailing attitudes among most white Americans at the time.

But if the slaves were not to be freed or their rights to be acknowledged, how were they to be counted? Since the size of state delegations in the proposed House of Representatives was based on population, southern delegates argued that slaves should be counted along with whites. Northerners said it made no sense to count slaves for purposes of political representation when slaves were not treated as people but as property. The delegates finally agreed to a compromise proposed by James Wilson of Pennsylvania, whereby three-fifths of "all other persons" (that is, the enslaved) would be included in a state's population count as a basis for apportioning a state's congressional delegation.

Limitation: Failure to deal with slavery

By design, the original Constitution never specifically mentions the word *slavery*. Instead it speaks of "free persons" and "all other persons," and of persons "held to service of labor." The word *slavery* would not appear in the Constitution until the Thirteenth Amendment (1865) abolished slavery at the end of the Civil War. Under the 1787 Constitution, the national government had no authority to deal with slavery in the states. The success of southern delegates in getting slaves counted for purposes of calculating a state's representation in the House of Representatives and the Electoral College would give the southern states disproportionate power in the Congress by increasing the number of southern votes in the House of Representatives. This, in turn, increased southern influence in the Electoral College, since the number of each state's electors was to be the total of its senators and representatives. It was thus no accident that in the nation's first sixteen presidential elections, between 1788 and 1848, all but four chose a southern slaveholder. The pro-slavery nature of the Constitution prompted the fiery abolitionist William Lloyd Garrison to declare in the 1830s that the framers of the document had forged a "covenant with death and an agreement with hell."

***Charles Calvert and His Slave* (1761)**
In military regalia, the five-year-old descendant of Lord Baltimore towers over his slave, dressed as a drummer boy.

The Absence of Women in the Constitution

While the delegates found the debates over slavery contentious, they considered irrelevant any discussion of political rights for women. Yet not all women were willing to maintain their traditional subordinate role. During and after the Revolutionary War, there were many declarations of independence, many forms of resistance to old ways of doing things, indeed many personal "revolutions"—some successful, some not. Just as the experiences of the Revolutionary War led many African Americans to seize their freedom, some brave women demanded political equality for themselves.

Eliza Yonge Wilkinson, born in 1757 to a wealthy plantation family living on an island south of Charleston, South Carolina, lost her husband early in the war. In June 1780, after Wilkinson was assaulted and robbed by "inhuman" British soldiers during their forty-day siege of Charleston, she became a fiery Patriot who "hated Tyranny in every shape." Wilkinson's "saucy" personality led her to be openly critical of the British during their eighteen-month occupation of the city. She assured a friend that "We may be *led*, but we never will be *driven*!" And she showed great courage and resilience in helping American prisoners of war while managing her family's plantations during the war. Such unconventional experiences led Wilkinson to expect greater freedom for women after the war. "The men say we have no business [with politics]," she wrote to a friend. "It is not our sphere! I won't have it thought that because we are the weaker sex as to bodily strength, my dear, we are capable of nothing more than minding the dairy, visiting the poultry-house, and all such domestic concerns." Wilkinson demanded more. "They won't even allow us the liberty of thought, and that is all I want."

> Limitation: No political rights for women

With more and more women like Wilkinson calling themselves "perfect statesmen" and "great Politician[s]," Judith Sargent Murray, an essayist, playwright, and poet in Gloucester, Massachusetts, predicted the dawn of "a new era of female history" after the Revolution. She argued that the rights and liberties fought for by Patriots belonged not just to men but to women, too. In her essay "On the Equality of the Sexes," written in 1779 but not published until 1790, she, like Eliza Wilkinson, challenged the prevailing view that men had greater intellectual capacities than women. She insisted instead that whatever differences existed between the knowledge displayed by men and women resulted from prejudice and discrimination that prevented women from having access to formal education and worldly experience.

Like many other of the most radical voices of the Revolutionary era, Murray's support for gender equality was met largely by shock and disapproval among both men and women. At the Constitutional Convention in Philadelphia, there was never any formal discussion of women's rights, nor does the Constitution even include the word *women*. The "Founding Fathers" still defined politics and government as realms for men only. Writing from Paris, Thomas Jefferson expressed the hope that American "ladies" would be "contented to soothe and calm the minds of their husbands returning ruffled from political debate" rather than getting involved themselves. Neither Jefferson nor most Americans, he added, were "prepared" to support women holding elected office.

CORE **OBJECTIVE**
3. Summarize the major debates surrounding the ratification of the Constitution and how they were resolved.

The Fight for Ratification

The final draft of the Constitution was submitted to the states for approval (ratification) on September 28, 1787. Thus began the greatest public debate in world history up to that point. For the first time, the diverse peoples making up a large nation were able to discuss, debate, and decide by a peaceful vote how they would be governed. In the fierce ten-month-long debate, those supporting the new Constitution were called Federalists; their opponents became **anti-Federalists**. The two factions formed the seeds for America's enduring two-party political system.

A Fiery Debate

States' rights vs. expanding federal authority

Among the supreme legacies of the dramatic debate over the Constitution is *The Federalist Papers*, a collection of 85 essays published in 1787 and 1788. Written in support of the new Constitution by James Madison of Virginia and Alexander Hamilton and John Jay of New York, the essays defended the principle of a strong national government.

In perhaps the most famous Federalist essay, Number Ten, James Madison argued that the size and diversity of the expanding nation would make it impossible for any single faction to form a dangerous majority that could dominate the federal government. This contradicted the conventional wisdom of the time, which insisted that republics could survive only in small nations like Switzerland. Large republics, it was thought, would self-destruct as a result of warring factions. Not so, Madison insisted. Given a balanced federal government, a large republic could work better than a small one. "Extend the [geographic] sphere," he wrote, "and you take in a greater variety of parties and interests; you make it less probable that a majority of the whole will have a common motive to invade the rights of other citizens."

anti-Federalists Opponents of the Constitution as an infringement on individual and states' rights, whose criticism led to the addition of a Bill of Rights to the document. Many anti-Federalists later joined Thomas Jefferson's Democratic-Republican party.

The Federalist Papers Collection of eighty-five essays, published widely in newspapers in 1787 and 1788, written by Alexander Hamilton, James Madison, and John Jay in support of adopting the proposed U.S. Constitution.

Anti-Federalists v. Federalists

The anti-Federalists opposed the new Constitution by highlighting the dangers of placing more power in the hands of the central government. They predicted that the new federal government would eventually grow corrupt and tyrannical. Mercy Otis Warren of Massachusetts, the most prominent woman in the new nation to write regular political commentary, warned that the proposed constitution would put "shackles on our own necks." She and other anti-Federalists emphasized the absence of a bill of rights to protect individuals and states from the growing power of the national government.

The Federalists, also called nationalists, had several advantages in the prolonged national debate over the Constitution. First, they had a concrete proposal; their opponents had nothing to offer instead of the Constitution but criticism. Second, the Federalist leaders were on average 10–12 years younger than the anti-Federalists, and many of them had been members of the Constitutional Convention who were familiar with the disputed issues in the document. Third, the Federalists were more unified, better organized, and better able to manage the national debate.

By contrast, the anti-Federalist leaders—Virginians Patrick Henry, George Mason, Richard Henry Lee, and future president James Monroe; George Clinton of New York; Samuel Adams, Elbridge Gerry, and Mercy Otis Warren of Massachusetts; and Luther Martin and Samuel Chase of Maryland—were mostly older figures whose careers and reputations had been established well before the Revolution.

Regardless of the voices on each side, the tension between preserving states' rights and expanding federal authority at the center of the debate over ratification would not end in 1787; it became a defining drama of American politics thereafter.

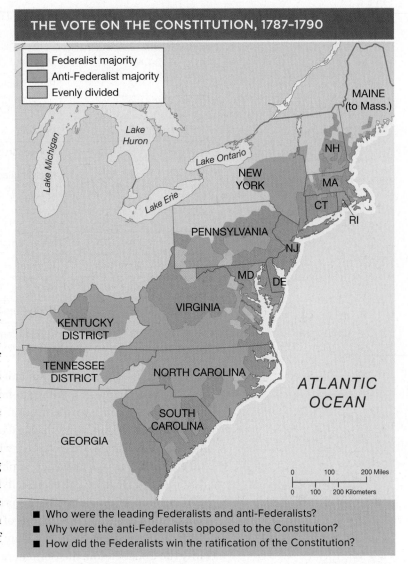

THE VOTE ON THE CONSTITUTION, 1787–1790

- Federalist majority
- Anti-Federalist majority
- Evenly divided

- Who were the leading Federalists and anti-Federalists?
- Why were the anti-Federalists opposed to the Constitution?
- How did the Federalists win the ratification of the Constitution?

The States Decide

The heated debate over ratification of the Constitution at times boiled over into violence. Riots erupted in several cities. Newspapers took sides, leading one New Englander to remark that the papers were being "read more than the Bible."

Amid the intense debate, ratification of the new Constitution gained momentum at the end of 1787. The state legislatures in Delaware, New Jersey, and Georgia voted unanimously in favor of ratification. Massachusetts, still sharply divided in the aftermath of Shays's Rebellion, was the first state legislature in which the outcome was close, approving the Constitution by a vote of 187 to 168.

RATIFICATION OF THE CONSTITUTION

Order of Ratification	State	Date of Ratification
1	Delaware	December 7, 1787
2	Pennsylvania	December 12, 1787
3	New Jersey	December 18, 1787
4	Georgia	January 2, 1788
5	Connecticut	January 9, 1788
6	Massachusetts	February 6, 1788
7	Maryland	April 28, 1788
8	South Carolina	May 23, 1788
9	New Hampshire	June 21, 1788
10	Virginia	June 25, 1788
11	New York	July 26, 1788
12	North Carolina	November 21, 1789
13	Rhode Island	May 29, 1790

On June 21, 1788, New Hampshire became the ninth state to ratify the Constitution, thereby meeting the minimum number of states needed for approval. But the new Constitution and the government it created could hardly succeed without the approval of Virginia, the largest, wealthiest, and most populous state, or New York, which had the third highest population and occupied a key position geographically. Both states included strong opposition groups who were eventually won over by the same pledge as had been made in Massachusetts—the promise of adding a bill of rights to the Constitution to specify protections of individual rights.

Upon notification that New Hampshire had become the ninth state to ratify the Constitution, the Confederation Congress selected New York City as the temporary national capital and fixed the date for the first national elections in 1788–1789.

The Bill of Rights

Protecting individual rights vs. the power of the state

The Constitution was adopted, but because of the spirited resistance it faced, in May 1789, James Madison proposed to the new Congress the cluster of constitutional amendments designed to protect individual rights from the power of the state. As Thomas Jefferson explained, a "bill of rights is what the people are entitled to against every government on earth, general or particular, and what no just government should refuse." After considerable discussion and debate, Congress approved twelve amendments in September 1789. By the end of 1791, the necessary three-fourths of the states had approved *ten* of the twelve proposed amendments, now known as the **Bill of Rights**.

Bill of Rights (1791) First ten amendments to the U.S. Constitution, adopted in 1791 to guarantee individual rights and to help secure ratification of the Constitution by the states.

The First Amendment declared that "Congress shall make no law respecting an establishment of religion or prohibiting the free exercise thereof." This statement has since become one of the most controversial principles of American government. The men who drafted and amended the Constitution made no direct mention of God, for they were determined to protect freedom of religion from government interference and coercion.

In the late eighteenth century, the United States was virtually alone among nations in not declaring a single "established" religion funded by the government. France and Spain, for example, were officially Roman Catholic nations; Great Britain was Anglican. In addition, when the Bill of Rights was ratified, most states still used tax revenues to support a single established religion. Dissenters, the members of other churches, were tolerated but forced to pay taxes for the state-supported religion, and they were often prohibited from voting or holding political office.

The First Amendment changed that at the national level. It prohibited the federal government from endorsing or supporting any religion or interfering with the religious choices that people make. As Thomas Jefferson later explained, the First Amendment erected a "wall of separation between Church and State."

The other original amendments to the Constitution provided safeguards for individual rights of speech, assembly, and the press; the right to own firearms; the right to refuse to house soldiers; protection from unreasonable searches and seizures; the right to refuse to testify against oneself; the right to a speedy public trial, with an attorney present, before an impartial jury; and protection against "cruel and unusual" punishment. The Tenth Amendment addressed the widespread demand that "powers not delegated to the United States by the Constitution, nor prohibited by it to the States, are reserved to the States respectively, or to the people."

The ten amendments constituting the Bill of Rights were written in broad language that seemed to exclude no one, but in fact, the first ten amendments technically applied only to property-owning white males. Whole groups of Americans were officially left out of its protections. Native Americans were entirely outside the constitutional system, defined as an "alien people" in their own land. Like the Constitution itself, the Bill of Rights gave no protections to enslaved Americans. Instead of constitutional rights, they were governed by state "slave codes" that regulated every aspect of their lives. They had no access to the legal system: they could not go to court, make contracts, or own property. Similar restrictions applied to women, who could not vote in most state and national elections.

A Flexible Framework

"Our constitution is in actual operation," Benjamin Franklin wrote to a friend in 1789; "everything appears to promise that it will last; but in this world nothing is certain but death and taxes." George Washington was even more uncertain about the nation's future under the new plan of government. He predicted that the Constitution would not "last for more than twenty years."

The Constitution has lasted much longer, of course, and in the process it has provided a model of resilient republican government whose features have been repeatedly borrowed by other nations. The Constitution, in other words, was not *completed* in 1787 but instead is a living experiment, just as the United States is a living experiment in republicanism. It was, however, flawed from the beginning, just as the nation was flawed, for by evading the issue of slavery, the framers of the Constitution unwittingly allowed growing tensions over the expansion of slavery to reach the point in 1861 where there could be no political solution—only civil war.

CORE **OBJECTIVE**

4. Compare the Federalists' vision for the United States with that of their Republican opponents during the 1790s.

The Federalist Era

It was one thing to ratify a new U.S. Constitution and quite another to make the new federal government run smoothly. During the 1790s, the debates between Federalists and anti-Federalists over the new government gave birth to the nation's first political parties: Federalists and Republicans (also called the Democratic Republicans or **Jeffersonian Republicans**).

The two political parties came to represent two very different visions of America's future development. In 1790, the United States was predominantly a rural society, and 80 percent of households were involved in agricultural production. Only a few cities—Philadelphia, New York City, and Boston—had more than 5,000 residents. The Republicans were mostly southerners like Thomas Jefferson and James Madison who wanted America to remain a nation of small farmers and few cities. The Federalists sharply disagreed. Led by Alexander Hamilton, they embraced urban and commercial growth. Hamilton became the champion of northern efforts to promote trade, banking, finance, and manufacturing as the most essential elements of America's future economy.

Jeffersonian Republicans
Political party founded by Thomas Jefferson in opposition to the Federalist Party led by Alexander Hamilton and John Adams; also known as the Democratic-Republican Party.

The Constitution provided a framework for nationhood but not a blueprint; it left unanswered many questions about the actual structure and conduct of the new government. As James Madison acknowledged, "We are in a wilderness without a single footstep to guide us." On the whole, the Jeffersonian Republicans promoted a strict interpretation of the Constitution, while Federalists believed that the language of the Constitution should be interpreted broadly to enable the new federal government to take decisive action when necessary. One of George Washington's greatest challenges as the nation's first president was to bridge the growing divides between Federalists and Republicans, northerners and southerners, merchants and planters.

A New Government

On March 4, 1789, the new Congress convened its first meeting in New York City. In April, the presiding officer of the Senate certified that George Washington, with 69 votes, was the unanimous choice of the Electoral College to be president. John Adams, with 34 votes, became vice president. George Washington was a reluctant first president, but he agreed to serve because he had been "summoned by my country." A self-made man who had lost his father at age eleven and had little formal education, he had never visited Europe. Vice President John Adams groused that Washington was "too illiterate, unlearned, unread for his station and reputation."

But George Washington had virtues that John Adams lacked. As a French diplomat commented after watching the inaugural ceremony, Washington "has the soul, look, and figure of a hero in action." He was a military hero who had married a wealthy young widow and become a prosperous planter. Washington brought to his new office a remarkable capacity for leadership that helped keep the young republic from disintegrating. Although capable of angry outbursts, Washington was remarkably self-disciplined; he possessed extraordinary stamina and patience, integrity and resolve, courage and resilience. Few doubted that he was the best person to lead the new nation.

Shaping a Federal Union

America's first president took charge of a tiny national government that faced massive challenges. George Washington had a larger staff at his plantation in northern Virginia than he did as president. During the summer of 1789, Congress created executive departments corresponding to those formed under the Confederation. To lead the Department of State, Washington named Thomas Jefferson, recently back from his diplomatic duties in France. To head the Department of the Treasury, Washington picked his brilliant thirty-four-year-old wartime aide, Alexander Hamilton, now a celebrated New York lawyer.

The Rise of American Capitalism

In 1776, the same year that Americans were declaring their independence from the British monarchy, Adam Smith, a Scottish philosopher, published a pathbreaking book titled *An Inquiry into the Nature and Causes of the Wealth of Nations*. It provided the first full description of a modern *capitalist* economy and its social benefits. Like the American Revolution, *The Wealth of Nations* was a declaration of independence from Great Britain's mercantilist system. Under mercantilism, national governments exercised tight controls over economic life in the contest for world power. In *The Wealth of Nations*, Smith argued for just the opposite. Instead of controlling economic activity, governments should allow energetic individuals and efficient businesses to compete freely for profits in the marketplace. Doing so would provide the best path to individual success and national prosperity. Smith also explained that modern capitalism involved diverse national economies in which all of the major sectors were flourishing: agriculture, trade, banking, finance, and manufacturing.

Alexander Hamilton greatly admired *The Wealth of Nations* and embraced the idea of a diverse capitalist economy in which the engine of competition drove prosperity. America's first secretary of the Treasury was determined to use the energies of capitalism to transform a weak cluster of states into a global economic power comparable to Great Britain. He also recognized, however, that the fragile American republic's economy required temporary government assistance to enable it to compete with the much more advanced economies of Europe. In addition, the federal treasury was virtually empty. Something had to be done quickly to generate enough cash for the new federal government to operate. To that end, Hamilton submitted to Congress a series of brilliant reports between January 1790 and December 1791. **Alexander Hamilton's economic reforms** outlined his bold vision for the new nation's economic development.

> Alexander Hamilton's economic reforms

Alexander Hamilton Secretary of the Treasury from 1789 to 1795.

Paying Debts

The United States was born in debt. And it fell to Alexander Hamilton to figure out how the debts should be repaid. In the first of two "Reports on Public Credit" sent to Congress, Hamilton outlined how the new federal government should absorb the massive debt that the states and the Confederation had incurred during the War of Independence. Some argued that the debts should not be repaid. Hamilton countered that not paying war debts was unjust and dishonorable. Only by paying its debts in full could the new nation gain credibility among the leading nations of the world. He also explained that the state debts from the Revolution were a *national* responsibility because all Americans had benefited from the war for independence. A federal debt, he claimed, would be a "national blessing," provide a "mechanism for national unity," and promote long-term prosperity.

James Madison led the opposition to Hamilton's "debt-funding" plan in Congress. Madison did not question whether the war-related debt should be paid; he was troubled, however, that far more debt was owed to northerners than to southerners. The gridlock over the debt issue ended in the summer of 1790 with a secret deal. In return for northern votes in favor of locating the permanent national capital on the Potomac River between Maryland and Virginia, Madison pledged to seek enough southern votes in Congress to pass Hamilton's debt-assumption plan. The Compromise of 1790 worked as planned. The national capital would be moved from New York City to Philadelphia for ten years, after which it would be settled at a new federal city (soon to be called Washington) on the Potomac River in the new federal District of Columbia. Once implemented, Hamilton's debt-financing plan was an immediate success. By making the United States

Alexander Hamilton's economic reforms Various measures designed to strengthen the nation's capitalist economy and generate federal revenue through the promotion of new industries, the adoption of new tax policies, the payment of war debts, and the establishment of a national bank.

financially solvent, he set in motion the greatest economic success story in history.

Raising Federal Revenue

Governments have three basic ways to raise money to pay their bills: they can impose taxes or fees on individuals, businesses, and specific products; they can borrow money by selling interest-paying government bonds to investors; and, they can print currency. To raise urgently needed funds, Congress in 1789, with the approval of Washington and Hamilton, imposed a 5 percent tariff tax on a wide variety of imported items.

The creation of federal tariffs marked but the beginning of Hamilton's ambitious effort to put the new capitalist republic on sound financial footing. His next effort, in 1791, was to convince Congress to impose federal taxes, called "excises," on specific items: carriages, sugar, salt, and alcoholic beverages. The new tax on whiskey outraged many frontier farmers because it taxed their most profitable commodity. During the eighteenth and early nineteenth centuries, nearly all Americans drank alcoholic beverages: beer, hard cider, ale, wine, rum, brandy, or whiskey. In the areas west of the Appalachian Mountains, the primary cash commodity was liquor distilled from grains (mostly corn and rye) or fruit (peaches and apples). It was far easier for western farmers to convert their crops to liquor and then take it across the mountains or down the Mississippi River than it was to transport the bulky grains or fruits. Unlike grain and fruit crops, distilled spirits could be easily stored, shipped, or sold—and at higher profits. A bushel of corn worth 25¢ could yield two and a half gallons of liquor, worth ten times as much.

| Hamilton's revenue plan: The first federal taxes |

A National Bank

After securing congressional approval for federal tariffs, Hamilton called for the establishment of a national bank modeled after the powerful Bank of England. Once again, Madison and Jefferson led the opposition, arguing that the Constitution said nothing about a national bank and therefore the government could not create one. Hamilton and his supporters countered that creating a bank was an "implied power" within the Constitution. Congress ended up agreeing with Hamilton, with virtually all northern Congressmen voting for the new bank while most southerners opposed it. But the fundamental debate between Jefferson and Hamilton over how to interpret the Constitution has continued to this day: should government officials be allowed to stretch the original language of the Constitution to adjust to new realities?

The **Bank of the United States** (B.U.S.) would have three primary responsibilities: (1) to hold government funds and make transfers of monies to other nations; (2) to provide loans to the federal government and to other banks to promote economic development; and (3) to manage the nation's money supply by regulating the power of state-chartered banks to issue paper currency (called banknotes). The B.U.S. could issue banknotes as needed to address the chronic shortage of gold and silver coins.

| Hamilton's National Bank |

Bank of the United States (1791) National bank responsible for holding and transferring federal government funds, making business loans, and issuing a national currency.

The Bank of the United States Proposed by Alexander Hamilton, the bank opened in Philadelphia in 1791.

Encouraging Manufactures

In the "Report on Manufactures," the last of his major proposals to Congress, Hamilton called for the federal government to help launch new industries that would reduce America's dependence on manufactured goods imported from Europe, especially Great Britain. Industrialization, Hamilton believed, would accomplish several goals: diversify an American economy overly dependent on agriculture; improve productivity through greater use of machinery; encourage immigration to entice skilled workers from abroad; and create more opportunities for economic expansion.

To encourage industrial development, Hamilton recommended that the federal government provide financial incentives to help people start new industries and spur inventors to create new technologies. He claimed that such government support was needed to enable new American companies to compete "on equal terms" with companies in the more advanced economies of Europe. Finally, Hamilton asked Congress to fund an improved transportation system across the young nation, including the development of roads, canals, and rivers for commercial traffic.

Hamilton's "Report on Manufactures"

Few of Hamilton's pro-industry proposals were enacted in the 1790s because of strong opposition among southerners. But his ideas were not forgotten. They provided an arsenal of arguments for the advocates of manufacturing and transportation improvements in years to come.

Hamilton's Achievement

Largely owing to the skillful Hamilton, the Treasury Department during the early 1790s accumulated a surplus that enabled it to begin paying off the Revolutionary War debts, and foreign capitalists began to invest heavily in the growing American economy. A Boston merchant reported in late 1790 that the United States had never "had a brighter sunshine of prosperity...."

Our agricultural interest smiles, our commerce is blessed, our manufactures flourish." Yet however beneficial Hamilton's policies were to the nation's long-term economic development, they continued to arouse fierce opposition among Republicans.

The Republican Alternative

By supporting industry and commerce as well as the expansion of federal authority at the expense of the states, Hamilton infuriated a growing number of people, especially in the agricultural South and western frontier. Because the southern states had virtually no manufacturing enterprises and much less varied commercial activity than New York and New England, Thomas Jefferson, James Madison, and other Republicans viewed Hamilton's economic policies as discriminating against them. The tax on whiskey infuriated frontier farmers in western Pennsylvania.

Regional economic differences

The increasingly bitter disputes between Secretary of the Treasury Hamilton and Secretary of State Jefferson soon fractured President Washington's cabinet. Hamilton was an intense American nationalist, but he very much admired the powerful British economy and its political system (a limited monarchy and a parliament governed by a constitution). The British government was, he observed, "the best model the world ever produced," and he wanted Great Britain to remain America's largest trading partner. He also remained devoted to a strong central government and a powerful national bank. By contrast, Jefferson was anti-British and pro-French; he loved French culture, cuisine, and wine. Unlike Hamilton, the Virginian hated banks and big cities. His dream for America was to preserve a decentralized agrarian republic made up primarily of small farmers. "Those who labor in the earth," he wrote, "are the chosen people of God, if ever he had a chosen people, whose breasts He has made His peculiar deposit for genuine and substantial virtue." Jefferson feared that Hamilton's campaign for American industries would produce a growing class of landless factory workers who were dependent upon others for their livelihood and therefore subject to political manipulation and economic exploitation.

Hamilton and Jefferson's conflicting visions

By mid-1792, Hamilton and Jefferson could no longer hide their hatred for each other. The two strongest members of the cabinet became mortal enemies—as well as the leaders of two emerging parties. Part of the opposition to Hamilton's financial proposals grew out of opposition to Hamilton himself. The brashly confident Hamilton acted as if he were President Washington's prime minister. As a Congressman said in 1791, Hamilton "is all powerful and fails in nothing which he attempts." Jefferson, twelve years older than Hamilton, told a friend that he and his rival "daily pitted [fought] in the cabinet like two cocks [roosters]." President Washington begged his chief officers to put an end to the "wounding suspicions and irritating charges." They did not. In September 1792, Jefferson told President Washington that "I was duped . . . by the Secretary of the Treasury, and made a fool for forwarding his [economic] schemes, not then sufficiently understood by

Thomas Jefferson A 1791 portrait by Charles Willson Peale.

me; and of all the errors of my political life, this has occasioned the deepest regret."

CORE **OBJECTIVE**

5. Explain how attitudes toward Great Britain and France shaped American politics in the late eighteenth century.

Foreign and Domestic Crises

In 1789, the same year that George Washington became president, frenzied violence erupted in France, as masses of enraged people, inspired in part by the example of the American Revolution, revolted against the monarchy and sent shock waves throughout Europe. By 1792, when Washington was unanimously reelected to serve a second term as president, the **French Revolution** was careening out of control. The radicals executed the king and queen as well as hundreds of aristocrats. On February 1, 1793, the revolutionary government declared war on archenemy Great Britain, as well as the Netherlands and Spain. Thereafter, the most violent of the French revolutionaries—called *Jacobins*—used guillotines to execute thousands of political prisoners and Catholic priests.

Secretary of State Thomas Jefferson, the former U.S. ambassador to France, called for the United States to aid revolutionary France in its war against the European monarchies. "To back away from France," he claimed, "would be to undermine the cause of republicanism in America." But President Washington (and Alexander Hamilton) wanted no part of the European conflict. On April 22, 1793, Washington announced that the United States would not take sides in the war; it would be "friendly and impartial toward the belligerent powers." Instead of settling matters, however, Washington's neutrality proclamation brought to a boil the ugly feud between Hamilton and Jefferson. In 1793, Jefferson urged his friend James Madison to "take up your pen" and cut Hamilton "to pieces" in the newspapers.

Neutrality proclamation

Citizen Genet

While not wanting the United States to get involved in the European war, President Washington did accept Jefferson's argument that the United States should recognize the new French revolutionary government (becoming the first nation to do so). The French government then sent its first ambassador to the United States—the impulsive thirty-year-old Edmond-Charles-Édouard Genet.

Citizen Genet, as he quickly became known (a nod to newly egalitarian France), landed at Charleston, South Carolina, to a hero's welcome. He then openly violated America's neutrality by recruiting four American privateers (privately owned warships) to capture English and Spanish merchant vessels. He also conspired with frontiersmen and land speculators to organize an attack on Spanish Florida and Louisiana.

As Genet made his way to Philadelphia, then America's capital, he was greeted along the way by large crowds cheering the French Revolution. Once in Philadelphia, Genet continued his reckless efforts to draw America into

French Revolution Revolutionary movement beginning in 1789 that overthrew the monarchy and transformed France into an unstable republic before Napoleon Bonaparte assumed power in 1799.

war on the side of France. When he threatened to go around President Washington and appeal directly to the American people, even Jefferson disavowed "the French monkey." In August 1793, President Washington demanded that the French government replace Genet.

Americans Take Sides

The war of the European monarchies against revolutionary France deeply divided public opinion in the United States. Republicans tended to support the French rebels; Federalists were more skeptical of their motives and methods and sided with the British. Thomas Jefferson was so disgusted by President Washington's refusal to support the French Revolution and Alexander Hamilton's economic policies and political scheming that he resigned as secretary of state at the end of 1793, eager to be rid of the "hated occupation of politics." Vice President John Adams greeted the news of Jefferson's departure by saying "good riddance." George Washington felt the same way. He never forgave Jefferson and James Madison for organizing networks of Republicans across the nation to oppose the administration's policies. After accepting Jefferson's resignation, Washington never spoke to him again.

> French Revolution divides Federalists and Republicans

Jay's Treaty

President Washington's challenges in leading the new nation only increased with time. During 1794, tensions between the United States and Great Britain threatened to renew warfare between the old enemies. The Treaty of Paris (1783) that ended the Revolutionary War had left the western and southern boundaries of the United States in dispute. In addition, in late 1793 British warships violated international law by seizing American ships that carried French goods or were sailing for French ports. By early 1794 several hundred American ships had been confiscated, and their crews were given the choice of joining the British navy or being imprisoned. At the same time, British troops in the Ohio Valley gave weapons to Indians, who in turn attacked American settlers.

Early in 1794, however, the British gave President Washington a timely opening. They stopped seizing American ships, and on April 16, 1794, Washington sent Chief Justice John Jay to London to settle the major issues between the two nations: getting the British out of their frontier forts and fur-trading posts near the Canadian-American border (as had been called for by the Treaty of Paris in 1783), and securing payment ("reparations") for the losses of American shipowners, compensation for southern slaves carried away by British ships in 1783, and a new commercial treaty that would reopen American trade with the British West Indies.

To win his objectives, Jay accepted the British argument that American products needed for the construction of French warships could not be shipped to French ports. Through Jay's negotiations, Britain also gained advantages in its trade with the United States and a promise that French privateers would not be outfitted in American ports. Finally, Jay conceded that the British need not compensate U.S. citizens for the enslaved African Americans who had escaped during the Revolutionary War and that the pre-Revolutionary American debts to British merchants would be paid by the U.S. government.

In return, the chief justice won *three* important promises from the British: they would evacuate their six forts in northwest America by 1796, reimburse Americans for the seizures of ships and cargo in 1793–1794, and grant American merchants the right to trade with the British West Indies.

But when the terms of **Jay's Treaty** were revealed, Americans were outraged that it favored Britain over France. The heated dispute over the treaty helped sharpen the differences between the Jeffersonian Republicans and the Federalists. Thomas Jefferson and the Republicans who supported France in its war with Britain were furious; they wanted no concessions to the hated British. Jefferson dismissed Jay's Treaty as an "infamous act." Another prominent Republican offered this toast to George Washington: "May he be damned if he signs Jay's Treaty."

The uproar over Jay's Treaty created the most serious crisis of George Washington's presidency. Some critics called for his impeachment. Yet Washington, while admitting that the treaty was imperfect, concluded that it was the only way to avoid a war with Britain, a war that America was bound to lose (the U.S. Army then had only 672 men, and there was no navy). In the end, Jay's Treaty barely won the necessary two-thirds majority in the Senate. Most of those voting against the treaty were southerners.

Frontier Tensions

Meanwhile, new conflicts erupted in the Ohio Valley between American settlers and Native Americans. President Washington named Revolutionary War hero General "Mad" Anthony Wayne to head a military expedition into the disputed region. In the fall of 1793, Wayne marched into the Northwest Territory's "Indian country" with some 2,600 men, built Fort Greenville in Ohio, and soon went on the offensive.

Jay's Treaty with Great Britain (1794)

Jay's Treaty (1794) Controversial agreement between Britain and the United States, negotiated by Chief Justice John Jay, that settled disputes over trade, prewar debts owed to British merchants, British-occupied forts in American territory, and the seizure of American ships and cargo.

TREATY OF GREENVILLE, 1795

- Why did General Wayne build Fort Greenville?
- What happened at the Battle of Fallen Timbers?
- What were the terms of the Treaty of Greenville?

In August of 1794, some 2,000 Shawnee, Ottawa, Chippewa, Delaware, and Potawatomi warriors, armed by the British and reinforced by Canadian militiamen, engaged Wayne's troops and Indian allies in the Battle of Fallen Timbers along the Michigan-Ohio border, near present-day Toledo, Ohio. The Americans decisively defeated the Indians, destroyed their crops and villages, and built a line of forts in northern Ohio and Indiana, one of which became the city of Fort Wayne, Indiana. The Indians finally agreed to the Treaty of Greenville, signed in August 1795, by which the United States bought most of the territory that would form the state of Ohio and the cities of Detroit and Chicago.

> Treaty of Greenville (1795)

The Whiskey Rebellion

Soon after the Battle of Fallen Timbers, the Washington administration displayed another show of strength in the backcountry—the sparsely populated hill country west of the Appalachian Mountains—this time against the so-called **Whiskey Rebellion**. Throughout the rural western region, from north Georgia up to western Pennsylvania, the whiskey tax of 1791 had ignited resistance. Some angry rebels, inspired by the example of the French Revolution, threatened to leave the Union.

In the summer of 1794, discontent exploded into open rebellion in western Pennsylvania. A mob burned the house of the federal tax collector. Other rebels threatened an assault on Pittsburgh. On August 7, 1794, Washington issued a proclamation ordering the rebels home. When they failed to respond, he led 13,000 militiamen from four states to Pennsylvania to suppress the rebellion. Washington was the first—and last—president to lead troops into battle while in office.

Whiskey Rebellion George Washington as commander in chief reviews the troops mobilized to quell the Whiskey Rebellion in 1794.

The massive show of federal force worked: the whiskey rebels vanished into the hills. The new federal government had made its point and showed its strength. But many critics claimed it had become tyrannical. The government's use of so many soldiers led those who sympathized with the frontiersmen to become Republicans, and Thomas Jefferson's party scored heavily in the next Pennsylvania elections.

Pinckney's Treaty

While these turbulent events were unfolding in western Pennsylvania, the Spanish began negotiations over their control of Louisiana and Florida, which they had gained from the British through provisions of the treaties

Whiskey Rebellion (1794)
Violent protest by western Pennsylvania farmers against the federal excise tax on corn whiskey, put down by a federal army.

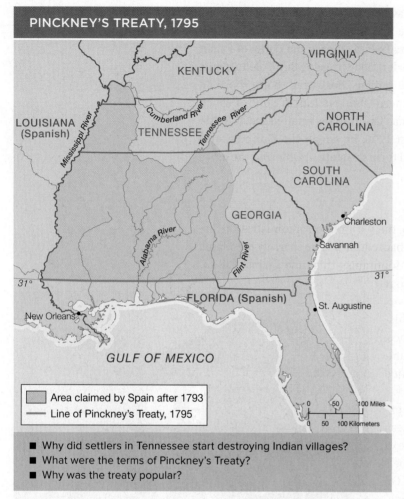

PINCKNEY'S TREATY, 1795

Area claimed by Spain after 1793
— Line of Pinckney's Treaty, 1795

- Why did settlers in Tennessee start destroying Indian villages?
- What were the terms of Pinckney's Treaty?
- Why was the treaty popular?

that ended the American Revolution. U.S. negotiator Thomas Pinckney, the former governor of South Carolina, pulled off a diplomatic triumph in 1795 when he convinced the Spanish to accept a southern American boundary at the 31st parallel in west Florida, along the coast of the Gulf of Mexico. The Spanish also agreed to allow Americans to ship goods down the Mississippi River to Spanish-controlled New Orleans. Senate ratification of Pinckney's Treaty (also called the Treaty of San Lorenzo) came quickly, for westerners were eager to use the Mississippi River to transport their crops to market.

Settlement of New Lands and the Wilderness Road

The important treaties with Great Britain and Spain negotiated by John Jay and Thomas Pinckney excited a new surge of Americans into the western territories. The lure of western lands led thousands of settlers to follow pathfinder Daniel Boone along the Wilderness Road he had helped cut into the territory known as Kentucky, or Kaintuck, from the Indian name Ken-Ta-Ke ("Great Meadow"). In the late eighteenth century, the Indian-held lands in Kentucky were a farmer's dream and a hunter's paradise; the vast area boasted fertile soil and abundant forests filled with buffalo, deer, and wild turkeys. Over the years, Boone and other whites bought or stole most of the Indians' ancestral lands in Kentucky.

Born on a small farm in 1734 in central Pennsylvania, Boone was a deadeye marksman by the age of twelve and would become an experienced farmer and an accomplished woodsman. After hearing about the fertile territory over the mountains, Boone set out alone in 1769 to find a trail into Kentucky. Armed with a rifle, tomahawk, and hunting knife, he found what was called the Warriors' Path, a narrow trail that buffalo, deer, and Indians had worn along the steep ridges. In 1773, Boone led the first group of settlers through the Appalachian Mountains at the Cumberland Gap. Two years later, he and thirty woodsmen used axes to widen the Warriors' Path into what became known as the Wilderness Road, a

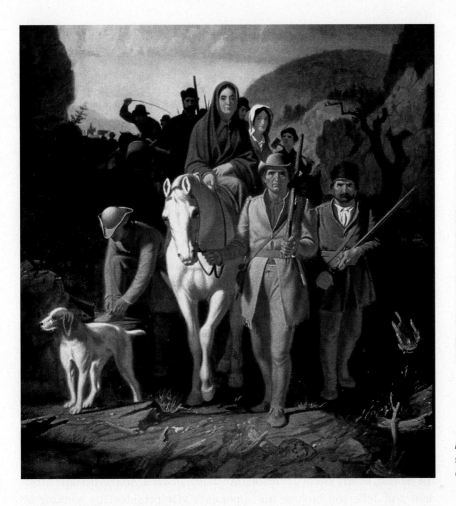

Daniel Boone Escorting Settlers through the Cumberland Gap by George Caleb Bingham.

passage that more than 300,000 settlers would use over the next twenty-five years.

Washington's Farewell

By 1796, George Washington had decided that two terms as president were enough. He was eager to retire to Mount Vernon, his beloved home in northern Virginia. He would leave behind a formidable record of achievement: the organization of a national government, a prosperous economy, the recovery of territory from Britain and Spain, a stable northwestern frontier, and the admission of three new states: Vermont (1791), Kentucky (1792), and Tennessee (1796).

On September 17, 1796, Washington delivered a farewell address to the nation in which he stressed that the United States should avoid getting involved in Europe's quarrels and wars. It was, he said, "our true policy to steer clear of permanent alliances with any portion of the foreign world." The key word here is *permanent*. Washington agreed that "temporary alliances for extraordinary emergencies" might be needed. His warning against permanent foreign entanglements would serve as a fundamental principle in U.S. foreign policy until the early twentieth century.

The Election of 1796

With George Washington out of the race, the United States had its first contested election for president in 1796. The logical choice of the Federalists would have been Alexander Hamilton. But since he had not been born in the United States, Hamilton could not be president. And his illegitimate birth, as well as his bold leadership within the cabinet, had created enemies, even among the Federalists. Vice President John Adams dismissed Hamilton as "a Creole bastard" who was "the incarnation of evil." So the Federalist "caucus," a group of leading congressmen, chose Adams as their presidential candidate. Thomas Pinckney of South Carolina, fresh from his diplomatic triumph in Spain, also ran as a Federalist candidate (at this time there were no candidates for the vice presidency; whoever came in second, regardless of party affiliation, became the vice president). As expected, the Republicans chose Thomas Jefferson. Aaron Burr, a brilliant young attorney and senator from New York, also ran as a Republican.

The campaign of 1796 was nasty. Republicans labeled Adams a closet monarchist because of his alleged elitism (Adams wanted people to refer to the President of the United States as "His Highness"). The Federalists countered that Jefferson was a French-loving atheist eager for another war with Great Britain. They also charged that the philosophical Jefferson was not decisive enough to be president. The increasing strength of the Republicans, fueled by the smoldering resentment of Jay's Treaty as far too lenient with the British, nearly swept Jefferson into office. Instead, Adams became president and Jefferson became his opponent's vice president by winning 68 electoral votes to Adams's 71.

The Adams Administration

Vain and prickly, opinionated and stubborn, John Adams had crafted a distinguished career as a Massachusetts lawyer, as a leader in the Revolutionary movement, as the hardest-working member of the Continental Congress, as a talented diplomat in France, Holland, and Great Britain, and as George Washington's vice president.

Adams lusted for the presidency, but he refused to compromise his principles to ensure his election. He was an independent thinker with a combative spirit and fiery temper who fought as often with his fellow Federalists as he did with his Republican opponents. Benjamin Franklin said Adams was "always an honest man, often a wise one, but sometimes . . . absolutely out of his senses."

Adams had many virtues, however. He was fiercely patriotic, intelligent, experienced, and conscientious. No one had served the new nation with as much dedication and energy. He had helped persuade the Continental

John Adams Political philosopher and politician, Adams was the first president to take up residence in the White House, in early 1801.

Congress to declare independence and assisted Jefferson in drafting the Declaration of Independence. Adams had also helped negotiate the Treaty of Paris, which ended the Revolutionary War in 1783.

The Quasi-War with France

As America's second president, Adams inherited a naval "quasi-war" with France, a by-product of revolutionary France's angry reaction to Jay's Treaty between the United States and Great Britain. When John Jay accepted the British insistence that food and military supplies being shipped from the United States to nations at war with Britain would be seized, the French announced that they would retaliate by confiscating American cargo headed for British ports. By the time of Adams's inauguration, in 1797, French naval vessels had plundered some 300 American ships and severed diplomatic relations with the United States.

> Quasi-war with France

President Adams immediately tried to restore good relations with France. In 1797, he sent three U.S. diplomats to Paris to negotiate a settlement of the dispute. But when the Americans arrived in Paris, they were accosted by three French officials (labeled "X," "Y," and "Z" by Adams in his report to Congress), who announced that negotiations could begin only if the United States paid a bribe of $250,000.

Such bribes were common eighteenth-century diplomatic practice, but the answer from the humiliated American side was "no, no, not a sixpence." When the so-called XYZ Affair was reported to Congress, American hostility toward France soared. Many Republicans—with the notable exception of Vice President Jefferson—joined the chorus crying for revenge. President

Conflict with France A cartoon indicating the anti-French sentiment generated by the XYZ affair. The three American negotiators (at left) reject the Paris Monster's demand for money.

Federalists vs. Republicans

With the ratification of the Constitution, the new federal government set out to address the challenges confronting the young nation and set a course for the future. Within President Washington's cabinet and the Congress, divisions quickly emerged as to what the federal government should do regarding financial and other economic matters, western expansion, and how to deal with the fallout from the French Revolution.

Competing Visions	Federalists	Republicans
The Federal Government	Federalists favored a strong national government that would rule the citizenry directly rather than through the states.	Republicans feared a strong national government would return the country to monarchy and trample on individual liberty.
The Constitution	Federalists favored an interpretation of the Constitution that included "implied powers" to give the national government the authority to address issues as they arose.	Jefferson and other Republicans feared excessive government power and favored a strict interpretation of the Constitution that limited the national government and protected individual and states' rights. They demanded a Bill of Rights.
The Economy	As secretary of the Treasury, Hamilton wanted to transform the United States into a global economic power comparable to Great Britain by promoting the growth of cities and commerce. Federalists did not engage issues of slavery and women's rights.	Jefferson and his Republican allies envisioned an egalitarian, agrarian nation. They championed farmers over bankers and feared that inequalities and corruption would arise from the growth of manufacturing and cities. Republicans also did not engage issues of slavery and women's rights.
Western Expansion	Hamilton and Federalists favored building up the population of the East Coast rather than encouraging rapid western expansion.	Republicans favored policies that promoted westward expansion and land ownership and farming rather than urban-industrial development.

The Convention of 1800

Adams asked Congress to authorize the construction of more warships and the expansion of the army. By the end of 1798, an undeclared naval war (a quasi-war) with France had begun in the West Indies. The success of the American navy in capturing nearly 100 French ships, combined with other French defeats around the world, now led the French government to ask for negotiations. In a treaty called the Convention of 1800, the Americans won the best terms they could from the French, including the end of the military alliance with the United States dating back to the Revolutionary War. The American government was eager to end the alliance to avoid being drawn into future European wars involving France. The Senate quickly ratified the agreement, which became effective on December 21, 1801.

Competing Visions	Federalists	Republicans
Debt and Revenue	Hamilton believed that it was the responsibility of the federal government to pay off all Revolutionary War debts, including those of the states, and promoted an ongoing national debt funded by taxes that would be used to continually invest in the economy.	Republicans agreed to the need for paying Revolutionary debts, but opposed an ongoing national debt and federal taxes.
The Bank of the United States	Hamilton favored the creation of a publicly chartered Bank of the United States to secure a sound currency, issue government bonds, and manage the federal government's revenue.	Republicans argued that the Constitution did not give the national government the authority to create a national bank and so opposed the creation of the Bank of the United States.
The French Revolution	Hamilton and Federalists were suspicious of the French Revolution, which they viewed as excessive, and were opposed to continuing the military alliance with France.	Republicans, while acknowledging the excesses of the French Revolution, welcomed its elimination of the monarchy and wanted the United States to support the new French Republic.

QUESTIONS FOR ANALYSIS

1. What were the major disputes between the Federalists and the Republicans?

2. How did their political competition influence the future direction of the United States?

3. What were the results of the Federalist and Republican battles in the 1790s?

The War at Home

The naval war with France sparked an intense debate between Federalists eager for war and the Republicans most sympathetic to France. Pro-French Thomas Jefferson told a French official that President Adams was "a vain, irritable, stubborn" man. In 1797, Vice President Jefferson secretly sponsored a vicious pamphlet that described Adams as a deranged monarchist intent upon naming himself king of the United States. Adams, who learned of his vice president's efforts to undermine his presidency, regretted losing Jefferson as a friend but "felt obliged to look upon him as a man whose mind is warped by prejudice."

Jefferson and other Republicans were convinced that the real purpose of the French crisis was to provide Federalists with an excuse to quiet their American critics. The infamous **Alien and Sedition Acts of 1798** seemed to confirm the Republicans' suspicions. These vengeful acts, passed amid the surge of patriotic war fever, limited freedom of speech and the press as well as the liberty of "aliens" (immigrants who had not yet gained citizenship). John Adams's support for the Alien and Sedition Acts would prove to be the greatest mistake of his presidency.

Three of the four Alien and Sedition acts reflected hostility to French immigrants, many of whom had become militant Republicans in the United States. The Naturalization Act lengthened from five to fourteen years the residency requirement for U.S. citizenship. The Alien Act empowered the president to deport "dangerous" aliens, and the Alien Enemies Act authorized the president in wartime to expel or imprison enemy aliens at will. Finally, the Sedition Act outlawed writing, publishing, or speaking anything of "a false, scandalous and malicious" nature against the government or any of its officers.

In response, Thomas Jefferson and James Madison drafted the Kentucky and Virginia Resolutions, passed by the legislatures of both states in 1798. The resolutions denounced the Alien and Sedition Acts as "alarming infractions" of constitutional rights and argued that the states should "nullify" (reject and ignore) acts of Congress that violated the First Amendment's guarantee of free speech. In attacking the Alien and Sedition Acts, Jefferson was suggesting something more dangerous: disunion. George Washington told Patrick Henry in Virginia that Jefferson was threatening to "dissolve the union or produce coercion."

Republican Victory in 1800

The furor over the Alien and Sedition Acts influenced the pivotal presidential election of 1800. The Federalists nominated John Adams for a second term and added Charles Cotesworth Pinckney to the ballot. But many leading Federalists continued to snipe at Adams and his policies, especially his refusal to declare war against France. New York's Alexander Hamilton, for example, publicly questioned Adams's fitness to be president, citing his "disgusting egotism."

Thomas Jefferson and Aaron Burr, the Republican candidates, represented the alliance of the two most powerful states, Virginia and New York, where Burr was a prominent political figure. The Federalists again attacked Jefferson for supporting the radical French Jacobin revolutionaries. His election, they claimed, would bring civil war and anarchy to America. Jefferson's supporters portrayed him as a passionate idealist and optimist who was the friend of farmers and the courageous champion of states' rights, limited government, and personal liberty.

In the **election of 1800**, Jefferson and Burr tied for the lead with 73 electoral votes each. Adams received only 65. The tie vote in the Elec-

Alien and Sedition Acts of 1798 Four measures passed during the undeclared war with France that limited the freedoms of speech and press and restricted the liberty of immigrants.

election of 1800 Presidential election involving Thomas Jefferson and John Adams; resulted in the first Democratic-Republican victory after the Federalist administrations of George Washington and John Adams.

THE ELECTION OF 1800

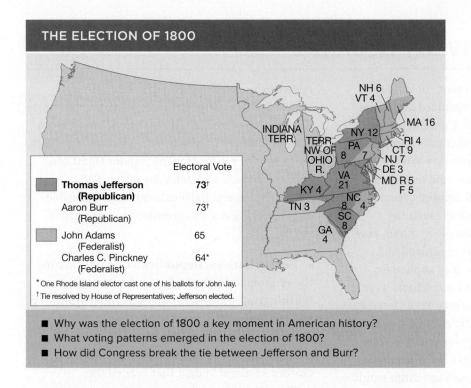

	Electoral Vote
Thomas Jefferson (Republican)	73†
Aaron Burr (Republican)	73†
John Adams (Federalist)	65
Charles C. Pinckney (Federalist)	64*

* One Rhode Island elector cast one of his ballots for John Jay.

† Tie resolved by House of Representatives; Jefferson elected.

■ Why was the election of 1800 a key moment in American history?

■ What voting patterns emerged in the election of 1800?

■ How did Congress break the tie between Jefferson and Burr?

toral College for Jefferson and Burr sent the choice of the president to the House of Representatives (a constitutional defect corrected in 1804 by the Twelfth Amendment). It took thirty-six ballots for the House of Representatives to choose Thomas Jefferson as the new president, making Burr the vice president.

Before the Federalists turned over power to the Jeffersonian Republicans on March 4, 1801, Congress passed the Judiciary Act of 1801. It was intended to ensure Federalist control of the judicial system by creating sixteen federal circuit courts with a new judge for each. Before he left office, Adams appointed Federalists to all the new positions. The defeated Federalists, in the words of Jefferson, "had retired into the judiciary as a stronghold." They would never again exercise political power.

A bitter John Adams refused to attend Thomas Jefferson's inauguration in the new federal capital in Washington, D.C. Instead, unnoticed and unappreciated, the ex-president boarded a stagecoach for the 500-mile trip to his home in Massachusetts. He and Jefferson would not communicate for the next twelve years. As Adams returned to his Massachusetts farm with his wife, Abigail, he told his eldest son, John Quincy, who would later become the nation's sixth president, that anyone governing the new United States faced "a hard, laborious, and unhappy life."

- **Confederation Government** Despite the weak form of government organized under the *Articles of Confederation*, the Confederation government managed to construct important alliances during the Revolutionary War, help win the War of Independence, and negotiate the Treaty of Paris (1783). It created executive departments and established through the *Northwest Ordinance* the process by which new western territories would be organized and governments formed before they applied for statehood. Postwar economic conditions were difficult because British markets were closed to American trade and the Articles of Confederation did not allow the national government to raise taxes to fund its debts. *Shays's Rebellion* made many Americans fear that such uprisings would eventually destroy the new republic unless the United States formed a stronger national government.

- **Constitutional Convention** Delegates gathered at the convention in Philadelphia in 1787 to revise the existing government, but almost immediately they decided to scrap the Articles of Confederation and start over. An entirely new document emerged, which created a system called *federalism* in which a strong national government with clear *separation of powers* between executive, legislative, and judicial branches functioned alongside state governments with clearly designated responsibilities. Arguments about how best to ensure that the rights of individual states were protected and also that "the people" were represented in the new Congress were resolved by establishing a Senate, with equal representation for each state, and a House of Representatives, the number of whose delegates was determined by population counts.

- **Ratification of the Constitution** Ratification of the Constitution was hotly contested, *Anti-Federalists* such as Virginia's Patrick Henry opposed the new structure of government because the absence of a bill of rights would lead to a loss of individual and states' rights. To sway New York State toward ratification, Alexander Hamilton, James Madison, and John Jay wrote *The Federalist Papers*. Ratification became possible only when Federalists promised to add a bill of rights.

- **Federalists vs. Republicans** Strengthening the economy was the highest priority of the Washington administration. Alexander Hamilton and the *Federalists*, wanted to create a diverse economy in which agriculture was balanced by trade, finance, and manufacturing. Hamilton crafted a federal budget that funded the national debt through tariff and tax revenues, and he created a national bank, the first *Bank of the United States*. Thomas Jefferson and others, known as the *Republicans* worried that Hamilton's plans violated the Constitution and made the federal government too powerful. They envisioned a nation dominated by farmers and planters where the rights of states would be protected against federal power.

- **Trouble Abroad** With the outbreak of war throughout much of Europe during the *French Revolution*, George Washington's policy of neutrality violated the terms of the 1778 treaty with France. At the same time, Americans sharply criticized *Jay's Treaty* with the British for giving too much away. French warships began seizing British and American ships and an undeclared war was underway. Federalists supported Washington's approach, whereas Republicans were more supportive of France. During the presidency of John Adams, the United States fought an undeclared naval war with the French, which led to the controversial *Alien and Sedition Acts* of 1798.

KEY TERMS

CHRONOLOGY

1781	Articles of Confederation take effect
1783	Treaty of Paris ends the war for independence
1784–1785	Land Ordinances
1786–1787	Shays's Rebellion
1787	Northwest Ordinance
	The Constitutional Convention is held in Philadelphia
1787–1788	*The Federalist Papers* are published
1789	President George Washington is inaugurated
1791	Bill of Rights is ratified
	Bank of the United States is created
1793	Washington issues a proclamation of neutrality
1794	Jay's Treaty is negotiated with England
	Whiskey Rebellion in Pennsylvania
	U.S. Army defeats Indians in the Battle of Fallen Timbers
1795	Treaty of Greenville
	Pinckney's Treaty is negotiated with Spain
1796	John Adams is elected president
1798–1800	Quasi-War with France
1798	Alien and Sedition Acts are passed
1800	Thomas Jefferson is elected president

INQUIZITIVE

Go to InQuizitive to see what you've learned—and learn what you've missed—with personalized feedback along the way.

WE OWE ALLEGIANCE TO NO CROWN (CA. 1814) The War of 1812 generated a renewed spirit of nationalism, inspiring Philadelphia sign-painter John Archibald Woodside to create this patriotic and iconic painting.

The Early Republic

1800–1815

When President Thomas Jefferson took office in early 1801, the United States and its western territories reached from the Atlantic Ocean to the Mississippi River. Nine of ten Americans lived on the land, with most of them growing enough food and raising enough livestock to maintain their households but rarely producing surpluses for sale outside the community. Nevertheless, Americans were rapidly developing a commercial economy, buying and selling goods with people around the world as well as with one another. The American desire to increase its trade and grow its economy was, according to Congressman Henry Clay, "a passion as unconquerable as any with which nature has endowed us. You may attempt to regulate [it]—[but] you cannot destroy it." Everywhere people were on the make and on the move, leading one newspaper to claim that what made America different from other nations was "the almost universal ambition to get forward."

The new president claimed that the United States was the "world's best hope" for social progress because it had the "strongest government on earth." The future was bright, Jefferson believed, for Americans could achieve anything they attempted. "Whatever they can, they will," he predicted. Everywhere he looked, Jefferson saw energetic Americans at work. Westward expansion, surging economic development, rapid population growth, and intense political activity preoccupied Americans at the start of the new century. As retiring president John Adams observed, "There is no

CORE OBJECTIVES INQUIZITIVE

1. Summarize the major domestic political developments that took place during Thomas Jefferson's administration.

2. Describe how foreign events impacted the United States during the Jefferson and Madison administrations.

3. Explain the primary causes of the American decision to declare war on Great Britain in 1812.

4. Analyze the most significant outcomes of the War of 1812 on the United States.

people on earth so ambitious as the people of America . . . because the lowest can aspire as freely as the highest."

In 1800 the United States, with 5.3 million people, was predominantly a rural society. Almost a million Americans were enslaved. The rapidly growing nation was also becoming younger. Two-thirds of American males in 1800 were under age twenty-five. Their prospects seemed unlimited, their optimism unrestrained.

The spirit of opportunistic independence affected free African Americans as well as whites. Free blacks represented the fastest-growing segment of the population during the early nineteenth century. Many had gained their freedom during the Revolutionary War by escaping, joining the British army, or serving in the American army. Every state except South Carolina and Georgia had promised freedom to slaves who fought the British. Afterward, anti-slavery organizations exerted increasing pressure on the South to end the degrading practice, as state after state in the North outlawed slavery. Massachusetts, for example, freed its slaves in 1780, during the Revolutionary War, citing Thomas Jefferson's phrase from the Declaration of Independence declaring that "all men are created equal."

Thomas Jefferson described the United States in the early years of the nineteenth century as an "empire of liberty" spreading westward across the continent. (He ignored the process by which Americans violated the liberty of Native Americans and Hispanics—people of Mexican or Spanish descent—in the process of moving west.) Native Americans fiercely resisted the invasion of their ancestral lands but ultimately succumbed to a federal government and a federal army determined to relocate them. Most whites, however, were less concerned about Indians than they were about seizing their own opportunities. A British visitor remarked that the Americans were a "restless people, always on the lookout for something better or more profitable." During the early years of the nineteenth century, the new nation set about forging its identity and earning its place among the great powers of the world. But it was not easy. It would take another war with Great Britain—the War of 1812—to ensure the independence of the rowdy American republic.

CORE OBJECTIVE

1. Summarize the major domestic political developments that took place during Thomas Jefferson's administration.

Jeffersonian Republicanism

The "People's President"

The 1800 presidential campaign between Federalists and Jeffersonian Republicans had been so fiercely contested that some had predicted civil war as the House of Representatives prepared to decide the outcome of the disputed election. But on March 4, 1801, the fifty-seven-year-old Thomas Jefferson was inaugurated without incident, leading some people to call his election "the peaceful revolution," for it was one of the first public elections in modern history that saw the peaceful transfer of power from one party to another.

Jefferson was the first president to be inaugurated in the new national capital named Washington, District of Columbia. The new city, still raw and unfinished, was crisscrossed with muddy avenues connecting a scattering of buildings clustered around two centers, Capitol Hill and the "President's Palace." Cows grazed along the Mall.

At his intentionally informal inauguration ceremony, Jefferson emphasized his sympathies for the plain style of the "common" people. Instead of wearing a ceremonial sword and riding in an elegant horse-drawn carriage, as George Washington and John Adams had done, the third president left his boarding house and rode his horse alone down stump-strewn Pennsylvania Avenue to the unfinished Capitol building. (Jefferson sold the presidential carriage.) He entered the Senate chamber, took the presidential oath, and then read his inaugural address in a barely audible voice. Jefferson's deliberate display of **Republican simplicity** set the tone for his administration. He wanted Americans to notice the difference between the monarchical trappings of the Federalists and the down-to-earth simplicity and frugality of the Republicans. He did not wear fancy clothes or host elegant parties. Jefferson often answered the door of the president's house himself, wearing a robe and slippers.

In his inaugural address, the tall, thin Virginian, his red hair now streaked with grey, imagined "a rising nation, spread over a wide and fruitful land, traversing all the seas with the productions of their industry, engaged in commerce with nations" across the globe. Although determined to overturn many Federalist policies and programs, he urged Americans to temper their political partisanship and work together. "We are all Republicans— we are all Federalists," Jefferson stressed, noting that "every difference of opinion is not a difference of principle." He asked Americans to "unite with one heart and one mind." It was a brilliant speech, but Jefferson's appeal for a united nation proved illusory, in part because he himself retained his own anti-Federalist prejudices. In a letter to a British friend, Jefferson described the Federalists as "insane" men: "Their leaders are a hospital of incurables."

Jefferson in Office

The inauguration of Thomas Jefferson ushered in a new, more democratic era in American life. An increasing proportion of white males gained the right to vote as state after state reduced or eliminated requirements that voters own property. In many northern states, the percentage of eligible voters went from 20 percent to 80 percent by eliminating or reducing the property requirements. Men of humble origins, some of whom were uneducated and illiterate, began to displace the social and political elite in the state legislatures. And over half of the members of the Republican-controlled Congress

> Expanded political participation

Republican simplicity
Deliberate attitude of humility and frugality, as opposed to monarchical pomp and ceremony, adopted by Thomas Jefferson in his presidency.

were newly elected. Unlike John Adams, George Washington, and the Federalists, Thomas Jefferson and the Republicans urged states to expand the electorate so that more men of simple means could vote and hold office. Diehard Federalists were horrified by the "democratization" of politics. "We are sliding down into the mire of a democracy," moaned Fisher Ames of Massachusetts.

Thomas Jefferson was a bundle of contradictions. On one hand, he was a wealthy, slave-owning planter with expensive tastes in food, wine, and furnishings. Charming and brilliant, he was an inventive genius of wide learning and many abilities. He designed the state capitol in Richmond, Virginia, as well as his thirty-three-room mountaintop mansion near Charlottesville called *Monticello* (Little Mountain). Yet while he lived the luxurious life of a slaveholding planter, Jefferson consistently championed the "honest heart" of the common people. His faith in expanding the number of eligible voters and his determination to reduce the power of the national government opened a more democratic era in American life in which the founding generation of aristocratic "gentlemen" such as John Adams and George Washington were gradually displaced in positions of power by men from more common backgrounds.

For all of his natural shyness and admitted weakness as a public speaker, Jefferson was the first president to pursue the role of party leader and political wheeler-dealer, openly cultivating congressional support at frequent dinner parties and elsewhere. In the new president's cabinet, the leading figures were Jefferson's best friend, neighbor, and political ally, Secretary of State James Madison, and Secretary of the Treasury Albert Gallatin, a Swiss-born Pennsylvania Republican whose financial skills had won him the

The Capitol building This 1806 watercolor was painted by its architect Benjamin Henry Latrobe and inscribed to Jefferson. The iconic dome would be added later, after the building was damaged in the War of 1812.

respect of the Federalists. To cultivate Federalist-controlled New England, Jefferson chose men from that region for the positions of attorney general, secretary of war, and postmaster general. In lesser offices, however, Jefferson often succumbed to pressure from the Republicans to remove Federalists. In one area—the judiciary—he removed the offices altogether.

Marbury v. Madison

In 1802, at Jefferson's urging, the Republican-controlled Congress repealed the Judiciary Act of 1801, which the Federalists had passed just before the transfer of power to the Jeffersonian Republicans on March 4, 1801. The Judiciary Act of 1801 was intended to ensure Federalist control of the judicial system by creating sixteen federal circuit courts and appointing—for life—a new Federalist judge for each. The controversy over rescinding the judgeships sparked the precedent-setting case of **Marbury v. Madison** (1803), the first in which the U.S. Supreme Court declared a federal law unconstitutional.

The case involved the appointment of Maryland Federalist William Marbury as justice of the peace in the District of Columbia. Marbury's "midnight" letter of appointment, or commission, signed by President Adams just two days before he left office, was still undelivered when Madison took office as secretary of state, and President Jefferson directed Madison to withhold it. Marbury then filed suit to force Madison to deliver his commission.

The Supreme Court's unanimous opinion, written by Chief Justice John Marshall, a brilliant Virginia Federalist and fierce critic of Jefferson, his cousin, held that Marbury deserved his commission but denied that the Court had jurisdiction in the case. The Federal Judiciary Act of 1789, which gave the Court authority in such proceedings, was unconstitutional, the Marshall court ruled, because the Constitution specified that the Court should have original jurisdiction only in cases involving foreign ambassadors or nations. The Court, therefore, could issue no order in the case. With one bold stroke, Marshall had reprimanded the Jeffersonian Republicans while avoiding an awkward confrontation with an administration that might have defied his order. More important, with the *Marbury* ruling the Court declared a federal law invalid on the grounds that it violated provisions of the Constitution.

Marshall stressed that the Supreme Court was empowered "to say what the law is." In other words, the Marbury decision granted to the Supreme Court a power not mentioned in the Constitution: the right of *judicial review*, or deciding whether acts of Congress were constitutional. So even though William Marbury never gained his judgeship, Marshall established that the Supreme Court decided constitutional interpretations. This was such an astonishing decision that the Court did not declare another federal law unconstitutional for fifty-four years. Since then, however, the Court has struck down over 150 acts of Congress and over 1,100 acts of state legislatures.

Marbury v. Madison (1803)

Marbury v. Madison **(1803)**
First Supreme Court decision to declare a federal law—the Judiciary Act of 1789—unconstitutional.

Jefferson's Economic Policies

Athough John Marshall got the better of Thomas Jefferson in court, the president's first term included a series of triumphs in domestic affairs. Jefferson did not set out to dismantle all of Alexander Hamilton's Federalist economic program, despite his harsh criticism of it. Instead, following the advice of Treasury secretary Gallatin, Jefferson, who like many other southern planters never understood the function of banks and hated them, learned to accept the national bank as essential to economic growth. He did, however, reject Hamilton's insistence that a federal debt was a national "blessing" because it gave bankers and investors who lent money to the government a direct financial stake in the success of the new republic. Jefferson believed that a large federal debt would bring high taxes and government corruption, so he set about paying down the debt by slashing the federal budget. If it were not eliminated, Jefferson told Gallatin, "we shall be committed to the English career of debt, corruption, and rottenness, closing with revolution. The discharge of the debt, therefore, is vital to the destinies of the government."

Shrinking the government

In his first message to Congress in 1801, Jefferson promised to reduce the size, expense, and power of the federal government ("too complicated, too expensive"), shrink the government bureaucracy, and restore the authority of the sovereign states. He fired all federal tax collectors and cut the military budget in half, saying that the state militias provided the nation with adequate protection. Jefferson's was the first government in history that intentionally reduced its scope and power.

Jefferson once admitted that he had a peculiar affection for the "men from the Western side of the mountains." To address the grievances of grain farmers and backwoods distillers, Jefferson repealed the federal whiskey tax that Alexander Hamilton had instituted in 1791. Fortunately for Jefferson, the prosperous economy enabled the federal budget to absorb the loss of the whiskey taxes. Revenues from federal tariffs on imports rose, and the sale of government-owned western lands soared. Continuing conflicts in Europe increased American shipping traffic to the nations at war and further padded the federal Treasury.

Western Expansion

Where Alexander Hamilton always faced east, looking to Great Britain for his model of national greatness, Thomas Jefferson looked to the west for his inspiration, across the mountains and even across the Mississippi River. Only by expanding westward, he believed, could America avoid the social turmoil and misery common in the crowded cities of Europe. Only by "enlarging the empire of liberty" could America remain a nation primarily of farmers.

To ensure westward settlement, Jefferson and the Republicans strove to reduce the cost of federal lands, and appreciative settlers flocked to buy property in the western territories. Ohio's admission to the Union in 1803 increased the number of states to seventeen. Land sales west of the Appalachian Mountains skyrocketed in the early nineteenth century as settlers shoved Indians aside and established homesteads.

The Louisiana Purchase

The **Louisiana Purchase** of 1803 was a brilliant diplomatic achievement that more than doubled the territory of the United States. The purchase included 875,000 square miles of land extending far beyond the boundaries of present-day Louisiana. It comprised the entire Mississippi Valley west of the river to the Rocky Mountains. Six states in their entirety, and most or part of nine more, would eventually be carved out of the Louisiana Purchase.

> The Louisiana Purchase (1803)

In 1801, soon after Jefferson learned that Spain had transferred the Louisiana Territory to Napoleonic France, he sent Robert R. Livingston to Paris to acquire the area. Spain in control of the Mississippi River outlet was bad enough, but the power-hungry Napoléon in control could only mean serious trouble for the United States. "The day that France takes possession of New Orleans," Jefferson wrote Livingston, "we must marry ourselves to the British fleet and nation"—an unhappy prospect for the French-loving Jefferson.

Early in 1803, Jefferson sent James Monroe, his trusted Virginia friend, to assist Livingston. Their initial goal was simply to acquire the city of New Orleans, strategically situated along the banks of the Mississippi River near its outlet at the Gulf of Mexico. Over the years, New Orleans under Spanish and French rule had become a dynamic crossroads community where people of all races and classes intermingled, reinventing themselves as Americans, while taking advantage of the city's control of the commerce floating down the mighty Mississippi. For years, Americans living in Tennessee and Kentucky had threatened to secede if the federal government did not ensure that they could send their crops and goods down the river to New Orleans.

No sooner had Monroe arrived in Paris than the French surprised him and Livingston by asking if the United States would buy not just New Orleans but *all* of France's immense Louisiana Territory. Livingston quickly snapped up the offer. Napoléon was willing to sell the Louisiana Territory because his army in Saint-Domingue (Haiti) had been decimated by a massive slave revolt and an epidemic of yellow fever. After losing 57,000 French soldiers to disease and warfare, Napoléon decided to cut French losses in the Americas by selling the Louisiana Territory—and thereby helping to finance his ongoing war with Great Britain. The transfer of the vast region, Napoléon said, "strengthens forever the power of the United States, and I have just given to England a maritime rival [the United States] that will sooner or later humble her pride."

By the Treaty of Cession, dated April 30, 1803, the United States obtained the Louisiana Territory for about $15 million. This surprising turn of events presented Jefferson with a "noble bargain"—as well as a constitutional dilemma. Nowhere did the Constitution mention the purchase of territory. Was such an action legal? Jefferson admitted that the purchase was not

Louisiana Purchase (1803)
President Thomas Jefferson's purchase of the Louisiana Territory from France for $15 million, doubling the size of U.S. territory.

authorized by the Constitution, but he allowed his desire to expand the American republic to trump his legal concerns. He hoped "that the good sense of our country will correct the evil of loose construction [of the Constitution] when it shall produce ill effects."

Jefferson and other Republicans supported the Louisiana Purchase for several reasons. Acquiring the territory, the president explained, would serve "the immediate interests of our Western citizens" and promote "the peace and security of the nation in general" by removing French control and creating a protective buffer separating the United States from the rest of the world. Besides, Jefferson and his supporters argued, if the nation waited to pass a constitutional amendment to enable the acquisition, Napoléon might change his mind.

New England Federalists, however, were not convinced. They worried that the growing numbers of Americans moving west were driving up wages on the Atlantic coast by reducing the workforce and lowering the value of real estate in their region. They also cringed at the prospect that new western states would likely be settled by southern slaveholders who were Jeffersonian Republicans. In a reversal that anticipated many more reversals on constitutional issues, Federalists found themselves arguing for strict construction of the Constitution in opposing the Louisiana Purchase. Jefferson and the Republicans brushed aside Federalist reservations; the opportunity to almost double the size of the United States outweighed any legal reservations.

Jefferson called a special session of Congress on October 17, 1803, whereupon the Senate ratified the treaty by an overwhelming vote of 26–6. On December 20, 1803, U.S. officials took formal possession of the sprawling Louisiana Territory. At first the Spanish kept West Florida, but in 1810 American settlers revolted against Spanish rule and proclaimed the Republic of West Florida, which was quickly annexed and occupied by the United States as far east as the Pearl River. In 1813, with Spain itself a battlefield for French and British forces, Americans took over the rest of West Florida, out of which the states of Mississippi and Alabama would emerge. Legally, as the U.S. government has claimed ever since, all these areas were included in the Louisiana Purchase, the most significant event of Jefferson's presidency. From Tennessee, Andrew Jackson wrote Jefferson to congratulate him on acquiring the Louisiana Territory. "Every face wears a smile, and every heart leaps with joy."

Lewis and Clark

In the American imagination, beginning with the first colonists, the West, first meaning the Appalachian Mountains, then the Ohio and Mississippi Valleys, then the part of the continent closer to the Pacific Ocean, was always a magical place where dreams could be fulfilled. Thomas Jefferson had long been fascinated by the mysterious region west of the Mississippi River. To

One of Lewis and Clark's maps In their journals, Lewis and Clark sketched detailed maps of unexplored regions.

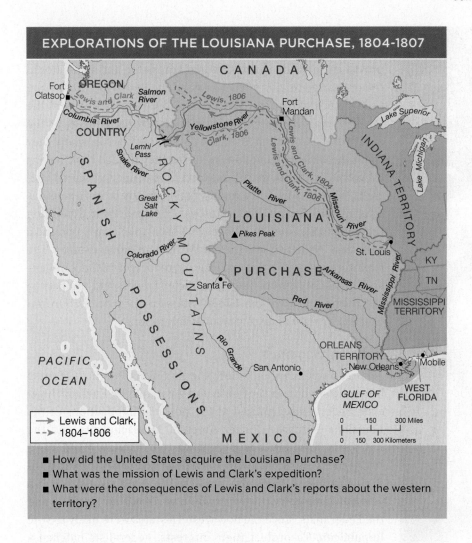

EXPLORATIONS OF THE LOUISIANA PURCHASE, 1804-1807

- How did the United States acquire the Louisiana Purchase?
- What was the mission of Lewis and Clark's expedition?
- What were the consequences of Lewis and Clark's reports about the western territory?

learn more about its geography, its flora and fauna, and its prospects for trade and agriculture, he asked Congress in 1803 to fund a scientific expedition to the territory. Congress approved, and Jefferson appointed former army officers Meriwether Lewis and William Clark, both Virginians, to lead what we now refer to as the **Lewis and Clark expedition**. Lewis was then serving as Jefferson's private secretary. Clark, it was said, was "a youth of solid and promising parts, and as brave as Caesar."

In 1804 the "Corps of Discovery," numbering nearly fifty men, set out from a small village near St. Louis to follow the muddy Missouri River northward through some of the most rugged wilderness in North America, in part to determine whether the river made its way to the Pacific Ocean. Six months later, near the Mandan Sioux villages in what would become North Dakota, they built Fort Mandan and wintered in relative comfort, sending downriver a barge loaded with maps, soil samples, and live specimens of creatures such as the prairie dog and the magpie, previously unknown in America.

Lewis and Clark expedition

Lewis and Clark expedition (1804) Led by Meriwether Lewis and William Clark, a mission to the Pacific coast commissioned for the purposes of scientific and geographical exploration.

In the spring, Lewis and Clark added to their main party a remarkable young Shoshone woman named Sacagawea, who proved an enormous help as a guide, translator, and negotiator in the uncharted territory. They crossed the Rocky Mountains and used canoes to descend the Snake and Columbia Rivers to the Pacific Ocean. Near the future site of Astoria, Oregon, at the mouth of the Columbia River, they built Fort Clatsop, where they spent the winter. The following spring they headed back, having overcome hunger by eating dogs and horses, and weathered blizzards, broiling sun, fierce rapids, raging grizzly bears, numerous injuries, and swarms of mosquitoes. The remarkable expedition returned to St. Louis in 1806, having been gone nearly two and a half years. No longer was the Far West an unknown country. The explorers' accurate maps and exciting reports of friendly Indians and abundant beavers quickly attracted traders and trappers to the region and gave the United States a claim to the Oregon Country by right of discovery and exploration.

Political Schemes

Jefferson's policies, including the Louisiana Purchase, earned him solid support in the South and West. In New England, however, Federalists panicked at the political implications of the Louisiana Purchase. Fisher Ames of Massachusetts said the Louisiana Territory was a great waste of money, for it was a "wilderness unpeopled with any beings except wolves and wandering Indians." Ames also predicted that the acquisition of a vast new empire in the West would weaken New England and the Federalists, since the new western states were likely to vote Republican. To protect their interests, Federalists hatched a scheme to link New York politically to New England by trying to elect Vice President Aaron Burr, a Republican rival of Jefferson, as governor of New York. Burr chose to drop his Republican affiliation and run for governor as an independent candidate. Several prominent Federalists opposed the scheme. Alexander Hamilton, for example, urged Federalists not to vote for Burr, calling him "a dangerous man, and one who ought not to be trusted with the reins of government." To his surprise, Burr ended up losing the election to the Republican candidate, who had been endorsed by Jefferson.

Hamilton was among those Burr blamed for his defeat. An angry Burr demanded that Hamilton make a public retraction of his critical remarks, and, when Hamilton refused to do so, Burr challenged him to a duel. At dawn on July 11, 1804, the two proud men met near Weehawken, New Jersey, across the Hudson River from New York City. Both men fired, but only Hamilton, whose son had been killed in an earlier duel at the same location, was hit. Mortally wounded, he died the next day. Upon learning that he had been

Sacagawea Of the many memorials devoted to Sacagawea, this statue by artist Alice Cooper was unveiled at the 1905 Lewis and Clark Centennial Exposition before another pioneering woman: feminist Susan B. Anthony.

charged with murder by New Jersey authorities, Burr, who was still the vice president, fled to South Carolina, where his daughter lived.

In the meantime, the presidential campaign of 1804 began when a congressional caucus of Republicans renominated Jefferson and chose George Clinton of New York as the vice presidential candidate. By then, to avoid the problems associated with parties running multiple candidates for the presidency, Congress had passed, and the states would soon ratify, the Twelfth Amendment, stipulating that the national electors use separate ballots to vote for the president and vice president. The Federalist candidates, Charles C. Pinckney and Rufus King, never had a chance. Jefferson and Clinton won 162 of the 176 electoral votes. It was the first landslide election in American history.

Divisions in the Republican Party

Freed from strong opposition—Federalists made up only a quarter of the new Congress—the dominant Republican majority began to fragment into warring factions. Fiery Virginian John Randolph (described by a colleague as "an object of admiration and terror") was initially a loyal Jeffersonian, but over time he emerged as the most colorful of the anti-Jefferson "Old Republicans"—mostly southerners who were more consistent than Jefferson in defending states' rights and strict construction of the Constitution. As the imperious Randolph admitted, "The *old* Republican party is already ruined, past redemption," but he tried to save it nonetheless. "I am an aristocrat," he declared. "I love liberty. I hate equality." He and other Old Republicans opposed any compromise with the Federalists, any expansion of federal authority at the expense of states' rights, any new taxes or tariffs, and any change in the nation's agrarian way of life. The Jeffersonian Republicans, on the other hand, were more moderate, pragmatic, and nationalistic in their orientation. As Jefferson demonstrated, they were willing to compromise their states' rights principles to maintain tariffs on imports and a national bank, and to stretch the "implied powers" of the Constitution to accommodate the Louisiana Purchase.

The Burr Conspiracy

Meanwhile, New Yorker Aaron Burr continued to plot and scheme. Sheer brilliance and opportunism had carried him to the vice presidency in 1800. He might easily have become the next president, but a taste for backroom deal-making was his tragic flaw. After the controversy over his duel with Alexander Hamilton subsided, Burr focused on a cockeyed scheme to carve out his own personal empire in the West. What came to be known as the Burr Conspiracy was hatched when Burr and General James Wilkinson plotted to get the Louisiana Territory to secede from the Union and declare itself an independent republic. Earlier, Burr had secretly sought British support for his scheme to separate "the western part of the United States in its whole extent."

Aaron Burr Burr graduated from what is now Princeton University, where he changed his course of study from theology to law.

In late 1806, Burr floated down the Mississippi River with 100 volunteers, only to be arrested and transported to Richmond, Virginia, to face trial for treason before Chief Justice John Marshall. President Jefferson became personally involved, urging the court to convict Burr. In the end, however, Burr was acquitted. With further charges pending, he skipped bail and took refuge in France. He returned in 1812 and resumed practicing law in New York.

Slave Trade Legislation

President Jefferson had little time to fret over the escapades of Aaron Burr; other pressing issues demanded his attention. On December 2, 1806, in his annual message to Congress, Jefferson deplored the "violations of human rights" caused by the continuing trafficking in enslaved Africans. He reminded the Congress that the Constitution stipulated that the international slave trade could be outlawed on January 1, 1808. Congress agreed, and in 1807 the president signed a landmark bill that stopped the importation of enslaved Africans into the United States. At the time, South Carolina was the only state that still permitted the foreign slave trade. The new law ending the importation of slaves did nothing to stop the buying and selling of slaves within the United States, however. In fact, the banning of slaves imported from Africa made the enslaved in America even more valuable, and the number of slave auctions actually increased.

CORE OBJECTIVE

2. Describe how foreign events impacted the United States during the Jefferson and Madison administrations.

War in the Mediterranean and Europe

The Barbary Pirates

Issues of foreign relations emerged early in Jefferson's first term, when events in the distant Mediterranean Sea gave him second thoughts about the need for American warships. On the Barbary Coast of North Africa, the Islamic rulers of Morocco, Algiers, Tunis, and Tripoli had for years specialized in piracy, preying upon European and American ships. After the Revolution, **Barbary pirates** continued to capture American vessels and enslave the crews. The U.S. government made ransom payments, first to Morocco in 1786, then to the others in the 1790s. In 1801, however, the pasha (ruler) of Tripoli upped his demands and declared war on the United States. Jefferson sent warships to blockade Tripoli. A naval war dragged on until 1805, punctuated in 1804 by the notable exploit of Lieutenant Stephen Decatur, who slipped into Tripoli Harbor by night and set fire to the frigate *Philadelphia*, which had been captured (along with its crew) after it ran aground. The pasha finally settled for a $60,000 ransom and released the *Philadelphia*'s crew, whom he had held hostage for more than a year. It was still ransom (called "tribute" in the nineteenth century), but far less than

Barbary pirates North Africans who waged war (1801–1805) on the United States after Jefferson refused to pay tribute (a bribe) to protect American ships.

Burning of the Frigate Philadelphia Lieutenant Stephen Decatur set fire to the captured *Philadelphia* during the United States' standoff with Tripoli over the enslavement of American sailors.

the $300,000 the pasha had demanded at first and much less than the cost of war.

Naval Harassment by Britain and France

In his first term, Jefferson had been able to avoid most foreign entanglements, particularly the new war in Europe pitting Napoleonic France against Great Britain. But during his second term, the expanding European war (1803–1815) forced him to take action to protect America's economic interests. In May 1806, Britain's desperate war with France led it to declare a naval blockade of the entire European coast to prevent merchant ships from making port in France. Because the United States was officially "neutral" in the war, its ships technically were allowed by international law to carry cargo from the islands in the French and Spanish West Indies through the British blockade to French ports. But the British quickly decided to end such commerce.

The tense situation posed a dilemma for American merchants. If they agreed to British demands to stop all trading with the French, they would be subject to seizure by the French navy, and vice versa. French and British efforts to control trade across the Atlantic soon brought Americans into the war. Hundreds of American ships were intercepted and their cargoes seized.

For American seamen, the danger was heightened by the British practice of *impressment*, whereby British naval personnel forcibly boarded American ships and captured sailors they claimed were British citizens who had deserted the British navy. American merchant ships paid seamen more than twice as much as did the Royal Navy, so thousands of British sailors had

"Impressment"

deserted the navy to work on American ships. Needing 12,000 new sailors each year to man its growing fleet of warships, the British wanted their deserters back, but they often did not bother to determine the citizenship of those they took off American vessels and "impressed" into service for the British navy. The British often "impressed" American citizens who had been born in Britain, claiming "once a British citizen, always a British citizen," even if the United States had granted citizenship.

To Americans, the British practice of impressment assaulted the honor and dignity of the newly independent nation. As Senator John Quincy Adams, the son of former president John Adams, groused, impressment was "kidnapping on the ocean." Between 1803 and 1811, some 6,200 American sailors were "impressed" into the British navy.

In early 1807, Napoléon responded to the British blockade of Europe by sending French warships to blockade the ports of Great Britain. The British then announced that they would no longer allow any foreign ships to trade with the French islands in the Caribbean.

The *Chesapeake* Incident (1807)

The United States was again caught in the crossfire between the two warring European powers. On June 22, 1807, the British warship HMS *Leopard* stopped a U.S. vessel, the *Chesapeake*, about eight miles off the Virginia coast. After the *Chesapeake*'s captain refused to allow the British to search his ship for British deserters, the *Leopard* opened fire, killing three Americans and wounding eighteen. The *Chesapeake* was forced to surrender. A British search party seized four men, one of whom was later hanged for desertion from the British navy.

Preparation for War to Defend Commerce Shipbuilders, like those pictured here constructing the *Philadelphia*, played an important role in the war efforts against America's many rivals.

The British attack on the *Chesapeake* was both an act of war and a national insult. The *Washington Federalist* editorialized: "We have never, on any occasion, witnessed . . . such a thirst for revenge." Public anger was so great that President Jefferson could have declared war on the spot. He later wrote that the *Chesapeake* incident "put war into my hand, I had only to open it and let havoc loose." In early July, Jefferson called his cabinet members to meet in Washington, D.C. He then issued a proclamation banning all British warships from American waters and called on state governors to mobilize their militia units. But like John Adams before him, Jefferson resisted war fever, in part because the United States was not prepared for war. Jefferson's caution outraged his critics. A politician eager for war called Jefferson a "dish of skim milk curdling at the head of our nation."

The Embargo

Not ready for war, President Jefferson convinced Congress to cut off all American trade with Europe. As Jefferson said, his choices were "war, embargo, or nothing." The unprecedented **Embargo Act** (December 1807) stopped all American ships from leaving for foreign ports. All trade with foreign nations was banned. Jefferson and his secretary of state, James Madison, assumed that the loss of trade with America would quickly force the warring nations of Europe to quit violating American rights—but Jefferson and Madison were sorely wrong, as neither Britain nor France yielded.

With each passing month, the embargo devastated the American economy, especially in New England, where merchants howled because the embargo cut off their primary industry: oceangoing commerce. The value of American exports plummeted from $48 million in 1807 to $9 million a year later. Shipbuilding declined by two-thirds, and prices for farm crops were cut in half. New England's once-thriving port cities—Boston, Salem, and Providence—were like ghost towns. Thirty thousand unemployed American sailors wandered the streets, drinking and cursing Jefferson's unpopular embargo. Meanwhile, smuggling grew rampant, especially along the border with Canada. While American merchant ships sat idle, the British gained a near monopoly on trade with Canada and the islands in the West Indies. Americans in every region but especially New England grew furious at "Jefferson's embargo." A Bostonian wrote the president to report that he was "in a starving condition" and accused Jefferson of being "one of the greatest tyrants in the whole world." Another told the president that he had paid $400 to four friends "to shoot you if you don't take off the embargo."

The embargo turned American politics upside down. Jefferson, the nation's leading spokesman for reducing the power of the federal government, now found himself expanding federal power into every aspect of the nation's economic life. The tiny U.S. Navy was deployed to enforce the embargo. In effect, the United States blockaded its own shipping, cutting off the profitable

> Embargo Act (1807)

Embargo Act (1807) A law promoted by President Thomas Jefferson prohibiting American ships from leaving for foreign ports, in order to safeguard them from British and French attacks. This ban on American exports proved disastrous to the U.S. economy.

Anti-Jefferson sentiment
This 1807 Federalist cartoon compares Washington (left, flanked by a British lion and American eagle) and Jefferson (right, with a snake and a lizard). Below Jefferson are volumes of French philosophy while Washington's volumes simply read: *Law*, *Order*, and *Religion*.

trade with foreign nations in an effort to avoid war by exerting "peaceable coercion" against Britain and France. New England Federalists, eager to renew trade with Europe, now used the argument that their states' rights were being violated by the national government.

The outrage over "Jefferson's embargo" demoralized the president and other Republicans and helped revive the Federalist party in New England, which charged that the president was trying to help the French by shutting off American trade with London. At the same time, farmers and planters in the South and West also suffered; they needed to sell their surplus grain, cotton, and tobacco. A gloomy Jefferson finally accepted failure and repealed the ill-conceived embargo in 1809, shortly before he ended the "splendid misery" of his presidency and retired "to my family, my books, and my farms" in Virginia. No one, he said, could be more relieved "on shaking off the shackles of power."

President Jefferson learned a hard lesson that many of his successors would also confront: a second term is rarely as successful as the first. As Jefferson admitted, "No man will ever carry out of that office [the presidency] the reputation which carried him into it." In the election of 1808, the presidency passed to another prominent Virginian, Jefferson's close friend and fellow Republican, Secretary of State James Madison. The Federalists, backing Charles C. Pinckney of South Carolina and Rufus King of New York, won only 47 electoral votes to Madison's 122.

James Madison and the Drift to War

In his inaugural address, President Madison observed that he inherited a situation "full of difficulties." He soon made them worse. Although he may have been a talented legislator and the "Father of the Constitution," he proved to be a poor chief executive. When members of Congress questioned several of his cabinet appointments, the president backed down and ended up naming second-rate men to key positions. In fact, Madison's sparkling wife, Dolley, was the only truly excellent member of his inner circle. Seventeen years younger than the president and twice his size, she was a superb First Lady who excelled at using the White House to entertain political leaders and foreign dignitaries. Journalists called her the "Queen of Washington City."

From the beginning, Madison's presidency was entangled in foreign affairs and crippled by his lack of executive experience. Madison and his advisers repeatedly overestimated the young republic's diplomatic leverage and military strength in shaping foreign policy. The result was humiliation.

Like Jefferson, Madison insisted on upholding the principle of freedom of the seas for the United States and other neutral nations, but he was unwilling to create a navy strong enough to enforce it. He continued the policy of "peaceable coercion," which was just as ineffective for Madison as it had been for Jefferson. In place of the ill-conceived embargo, Madison convinced Congress to pass the Non-Intercourse Act (1809), which reopened trade with all countries *except* France and Great Britain and their colonies. It also authorized the president to reopen trade with France or Great Britain if either stopped violating American rights.

Non-Intercourse Act (1809)

Madison's restrictions on American trade sparked an economic recession and brought no change in the British navy's misbehavior on the high seas. By 1811, the United States was again on the verge of war, with Americans seriously divided again about whether Britain or France was more responsible for violating American shipping rights. When the British refused to give in, Madison reluctantly asked Congress to declare war on June 1, 1812. If the United States did not defend its rights as a neutral nation, the president explained, then Americans were "not independent people, but colonists and vassals."

On June 5, the House of Representatives voted for war 79–49. Two weeks later, the Senate concurred by a narrower vote, 19–13. Every Federalist in Congress resisted what they called "Mr. Madison's War"; 80 percent of Republicans supported it. The southern and western states wanted war; the northeastern states, fearful of losing their essential maritime trade, opposed it. By declaring war, Republicans hoped to unite the nation, discredit the Federalists, and put an end to British-led Indian attacks along the Great Lakes and in the Ohio Valley. To generate popular support, Jefferson advised Madison that he needed, above all, "to stop Indian barbarities. The conquest of Canada will do this." Jefferson and others lusting for war presumed that the French Canadians were eager to rise up against their British rulers. With their help, the Republicans assumed, American invaders would easily conquer Britain's northern colony. It did not work out that way.

America declares war on Great Britain (1812)

CORE **OBJECTIVE**

3. Explain the primary causes of the American decision to declare war on Great Britain in 1812.

The War of 1812

In the **War of 1812** the United States found itself in yet another conflict with Great Britain, barely thirty years after the Revolutionary War had ended. It was the first time in American history that Congress formally used its war-making powers detailed in the Constitution. Great Britain did not want the war; it was preoccupied with defeating Napoléon in Europe. In fact, on June 16, 1812, the British government sought to avert war by deciding to quit interfering with American shipping. But President Madison and the Republicans were not satisfied; they said the war would proceed in order to put an end to the British practice of impressment as well as British-inspired Indian attacks. Why the United States chose to declare the war remains a puzzle still debated among historians.

American Shipping Rights and Honor

British impressment of U.S. sailors and invasion of shipping rights

The main cause of the war—the repeated British violations of American shipping rights and the practice of "impressing" sailors off American ships dominated President Madison's war message. Most of the votes for war came from congressmen representing rural regions from Pennsylvania southward and westward, where farmers and planters grew surpluses for export to Europe. They had real economic interests that were being hurt by the raids on American merchant ships. However, the representatives from the New England states, which bore the brunt of British attacks on U.S. shipping, voted *against* the declaration of war, 20–12. As a New England minister roared, let the "southern *Heroes* fight their own battles."

One explanation for this seeming inconsistency is that many Americans in the South and West, especially Tennessee and Kentucky, voted for war because they believed America's national honor was at stake. A proud Tennessean, Andrew Jackson, declared that he was eager to fight "for the re-establishment of our national character." When asked what the United States would "lose by maintaining the peace," Kentucky Congressman Henry Clay, the new Speaker of the House, answered forcefully: "Commerce, character, a nation's best treasure, honor!" In the popular phrase of the time, the war was needed to protect "Free Trade and Sailors' Rights!"

Native American Conflicts

War of 1812 (1812–1815)
Conflict fought in North America and at sea between Great Britain and the United States over American shipping rights and British-inspired Indian attacks on American settlements. Canadians and Native Americans also fought in the war on each side.

Another factor leading to war was the growing number of British-allied Indian attacks in the Ohio Valley. During the early nineteenth century, land-hungry settlers and speculators kept moving into Indian lands. The constant pressure on Native Americans to sell land repeatedly forced or persuaded Indians to sign treaties they did not always understand. It was an old story, dating from the Jamestown settlement, but one that took a new turn with the rise of two brilliant Shawnee leaders, Tecumseh and his brother, Tenskwatawa.

Tecumseh (Shooting Star) knew that the fate of the native peoples in America depended on their being unified. His hope was to create a single Indian nation powerful enough, with British assistance, to fend off further American expansion. His half brother Tenskwatawa (the "Open Door"), a one-eyed recovering alcoholic with a fierce temper who was known as "the Prophet" and claimed to have been visited by the Great Spirit, gained a large following among Native Americans for his repeated prediction that the white Americans ("children of the devil") were on the verge of collapse. He demanded that the indigenous peoples abandon all things European: clothing, customs, Christianity, and especially liquor. If they did so, the Great Spirit would reward them by turning the whites' gunpowder to sand.

From his large village called Prophetstown on the Tippecanoe River in northern Indiana, Tecumseh, inspired by his brother's spiritual message, traveled in 1811 from Canada to the Gulf of Mexico to form alliances with other Native American nations (Shawnee and Creek; Cherokee and Mohegan; Miami, Delaware, and Kickapoo; Choctaw and Chickasaw; Chippewa and Ottawa) to defend their hunting grounds. "The whites have driven us from the sea to the lakes," he declared. "We can go no further." Tecumseh disavowed the many treaties whereby indigenous peoples had "sold" ancient Indian lands. "No tribe," he declared, "has the right to sell [land], even to each other, much less to strangers. . . . Sell a country!? Why not sell the air, the great sea, as well as the earth? Didn't the Great Spirit make them all for the use of his children?" No land transfer to whites was valid without the consent of all the Indian peoples, he insisted, since they held the land in common.

William Henry Harrison, governor of the Indiana Territory, learned of Tecumseh's bold plans, met with him twice, and described him as "one of those uncommon geniuses who spring up occasionally to produce revolutions and overturn the established order of things." Yet Harrison vowed to eliminate Tecumseh and his dream of a unified Indian nation. In the fall of 1811, he gathered 1,000 troops and advanced on Tecumseh's capital, Prophetstown, while the Indian leader was away. His brother Tenskwatawa was lured into making a foolish attack on Harrison's encampment. The **Battle of Tippecanoe** was a disastrous defeat for the Native Americans. Harrison's troops burned the village and destroyed its supplies. **Tecumseh's Indian Confederacy** went up in smoke, and he fled to Canada.

The Lust for Canada and Florida

Some Americans wanted war with Great Britain because they wanted to acquire Canada, not only as a means of expanding American territory and eliminating the British presence there, but also as a way to gain a monopoly over the lucrative fur trade with the indigenous peoples ("First Nations") in Canada. That there were nearly 8 million Americans in 1812 and only 300,000 Canadians led many pro-war Americans to believe that the

Tecumseh Shawnee leader who tried to unite Indian tribes in defense of their lands, later killed in 1813 at the Battle of the Thames.

The British-allied Indian attacks in Ohio Valley

Battle of Tippecanoe (1811) Battle in northern Indiana between U.S. troops and Native American warriors led by prophet Tenskwatawa, the brother of Tecumseh.

Tecumseh's Indian Confederacy A group of Native American nations under leadership of Shawnee leader Tecumseh and Tenskwatawa; its mission of fighting off American expansion was thwarted in the Battle of Tippecanoe (1811), when the confederacy fell apart.

conquest of sparsely populated Canada would be quick and easy. Jefferson had told Madison that the American "acquisition of Canada" was simply a "matter of marching" north with a military force.

> **U.S. desire to acquire Canada and Florida**

The British were also vulnerable far to the south. East Florida, which the British had returned to Spain in 1783, posed a threat to the Americans because Spain was too weak (or simply unwilling) to prevent Indian attacks across the border with Georgia. In the absence of effective Spanish control of the border, British agents and traders remained in East Florida, smuggling goods and conspiring with Indians along the coast of the Gulf of Mexico. Spanish Florida had also long been a haven for runaway slaves from Georgia and South Carolina. Many Americans living along the Florida-Georgia border hoped that the war against Great Britain would enable them to oust the British and Spain from Florida and make it an American territory.

War Fever

> **Defending America's "national honor"**

Such concerns helped generate excited support for a war against Great Britain. In the Congress that assembled in late 1811, young new representatives from southern and western districts shouted for war in defense of "national honor" and to rid the Northwest of the "Indian problem." Among the "war hawks" were Henry Clay of Kentucky and John C. Calhoun of South Carolina. After they entered the House, John Randolph of Virginia said, "We have heard but one word . . . one eternal monotonous tone— Canada! Canada! Canada!" Clay, the new Speaker of the House, was a tall, rawboned man who yearned for war. He was all "for resistance by the *sword*," and boasted that the Kentucky militia alone could conquer British Canada.

Clay's bravado inspired others. "I don't like Henry Clay," Calhoun said. "He is a bad man, an imposter, a creator of wicked schemes. I wouldn't speak to him, but, by God, I love him" for wanting war. When Calhoun heard about Madison's decision for war, he threw his arms around Clay's neck and led his war-hawk colleagues in an Indian war dance. Virginian James Monroe was also delighted by the onset of a "manly war."

In New England and much of New York, however, there was little enthusiasm for the war. Another conflict with Great Britain threatened to cripple the region's dominant industry, shipping, since Great Britain remained the region's largest trading partner. Federalists not only criticized President Madison for declaring war; a few of them, both men and women, were charged with being British spies ("the blackest treason"—but technically not yet a crime for civilians to do so) while others were caught smuggling goods to the British. Other Americans who opposed the war discouraged men from enlisting in the military and making loans to the government. In 1814 the Massachusetts governor secretly asked the British what they would do if New England seceded from the United States. Republicans dismissed the anti-war Federalists as traitors. Former president Jefferson claimed that the "Republicans are the nation," implying that the Federalists were British loyalists.

War Preparations

As it turned out, the war hawks would get neither Canada nor Florida because the United States was unprepared for war, both financially and militarily. The emphasis of Republican presidents Jefferson and Madison on small federal budgets and military cutbacks proved to be an ineffective way to win a war, and Madison, a small, soft-spoken man, lacked the military qualities needed to inspire national confidence and resolve. He was no George Washington.

Moreover, the national economy was weak. In 1811, despite pleas from the Treasury secretary, Congress had let the charter of the Bank of the United States expire. In addition, once war began, the mighty British navy blockaded American ports and cut off imports, a major source of national revenue. By March 1813, Albert Gallatin warned Madison that the U.S. Treasury had "hardly enough money to last till the end of the month." Furthermore, the demise of the Bank of the United States brought confusion to the nation's financial system. Loans were needed to cover the war's costs, and northeastern opponents of the war were reluctant to lend money to the federal government.

The military situation was almost as bad. When the War of 1812 began, the U.S. Army numbered only 3,287 ill-trained and poorly equipped men, led by mostly incompetent officers with little combat experience. In January 1812, Congress authorized an army of 35,000 men, but a year later, just 18,500 had been recruited, many of them poor Irish immigrants who hated the English—and then only by enticing them with promises of land and cash bounties. President Madison refused to allow free blacks or slaves to serve in the army, so he was forced to plead with the state governors to provide militiamen, only to see the Federalist governors in anti-war New England refuse. The British, on the other hand, had thousands of soldiers stationed in Canada and the West Indies. And, as was true during the Revolutionary War, the British, offering food, guns, and ammunition, recruited more Native American allies than did the Americans in 1812. In all, more than two dozen Indian nations participated in the war.

The U.S. Navy was in better shape than the army, with able officers and well-trained seamen, but there were only sixteen warships, compared to Britain's 600. In the first year of the war, the navy produced the only U.S.

U.S. Naval victories John Bull (the personification of England) "stung to agony" by *Wasp* and *Hornet*, two American ships that clinched early victories in the War of 1812.

victories, in isolated duels with British vessels. But courageous American seamen could not stop the British from blockading the U.S. coast, except for New England, where the British hoped to strengthen anti-war sentiment. The lopsided military strength of the British led President Madison to mutter that the United States was in "an embarrassing situation."

A Continental War

The War of 1812 was really three wars fought on three separate fronts. One theatre of conflict was the Chesapeake Bay along the coast of Maryland and Virginia, including Washington, D.C. The second was in the South, in Alabama, Mississippi, and West and East Florida, culminating in the Battle of New Orleans in 1815. In that region, American forces led by General Andrew Jackson invaded lands owned by the Creeks and the Spanish. The third war might be more accurately called the Canadian-American War. It began in what is now northern Indiana and Ohio, southeastern Michigan, and regions around Lakes Huron and Michigan. There the fighting raged back and forth along the ill-defined border between the United States and British Canada.

The War in the North

The only place where the United States could attack the British on land was Canada. There the war would essentially become a civil war, very much like the American Revolution. One side—Canadians, many of whom were former American Loyalists who had fled north in 1783—remained loyal to the British Empire, while the Americans and a few French Canadians sought to push Britain out of North America. Indians armed with British-supplied weapons dominated the heavily wooded area around the Great Lakes. Michigan's governor recognized that the British and their Indian allies were dependent on each other: "The British cannot hold Upper Canada without the assistance of the Indians," but the "Indians cannot conduct a war without the assistance of a civilized nation [Great Britain]."

For the American assault on British Canada, President James Madison approved a three-pronged plan. It called for one U.S. army to move north through upstate New York, along Lake Champlain, to take Montreal, while another was to advance into Upper Canada by crossing the Niagara River between Lakes Ontario and Erie. The third attack would come from the west, with an American force moving east into Upper Canada from Detroit, Michigan. The plan was to have all three attacks begin at the same time in order to force the British troops in Canada to split up. Like so many complex war plans, this one was a disaster, in large part because the Americans could barely field one army, not three, and communications among the various commanders was spotty at best.

In July 1812, General William Hull, a Revolutionary War veteran and governor of the Michigan Territory, marched his disorganized and poorly supplied army across the Detroit River into Canada, announcing to the Canadians, most of them French, that he was there to free them from "tyranny and oppression." But the Americans were soon pushed back to Detroit by a smaller number of British troops and their Indian allies. Sickly and distracted by too much whiskey, the timid Hull was tricked by the opposing British commander's threats to unleash thousands of Indian warriors led by Tecumseh. Fearing a massacre by "savages," Hull suddenly surrendered his entire force to the British bluff. His capitulation, giving up 2,500 troops and loads of weapons and munitions that the Americans could not afford to lose, shocked the nation and opened the Old Northwest region to raids by British troops and their Indian allies. Madison and the Republicans felt humiliated; the American soldiers appeared to be cowards. In Kentucky, a Republican said General Hull must be a "traitor" or "nearly an idiot" or "part of both." Hull was eventually put on trial and sentenced to death, only to be pardoned by President Madison and dismissed from the army.

The second prong of the American invasion plan, the assault on Montreal, never got off the ground. The third American attack began at dawn on October 13, 1812. U.S. troops led by General Stephen Van Rensselaer, New York's wealthiest landowner, rowed across the Niagara River from Lewiston, New York, to invade at the Canadian village of Queenston, but suffered a

MAJOR NORTHERN CAMPAIGNS OF THE WAR OF 1812

- American forces
- British forces
- Battle site

■ How did the War of 1812 begin?
■ What was the American strategy in regard to Canada?
■ Describe the battle that is the subject of "The Star-Spangled Banner."

crushing defeat in the Battle of Queenston Heights. Some 925 American soldiers surrendered, and Van Rensselaer resigned his command in shame. Many Americans lost hope that they could win the war. In early 1813, a Kentuckian warned that any more military disasters would result in "disunion," and the "cause of Republicanism will be lost."

Thereafter, in the northern borderland between the United States and Canada, a powerful alliance of British troops, Canadian militiamen, and Indians repeatedly repelled U.S. invasion attempts. The bruised Americans then sought to gain naval control of the Great Lakes and other inland waterways along the Canadian border. If the Americans could break the British naval supply line and secure Lake Erie, they could divide the British and their Indian allies. In 1813 at Presque Isle, Pennsylvania, (near Erie), twenty-eight-year-old Oliver Hazard Perry supervised the construction of warships from timber cut in nearby forests. By the end of the summer, Commodore Perry set out in search of the British, finally finding them at Lake Erie's Put-in-Bay on September 10. After completing preparations for battle, Perry told his aide, "This is the most important day of my life."

Two British warships used their superior weapons to pound the *Lawrence*, Perry's flagship. After four hours of intense shelling, none of the *Lawrence*'s guns were working, and most of the crew were dead or wounded. But Perry refused to quit. He switched to another vessel, kept fighting, and, miraculously, ended up forcing the surrender of the entire British squadron. Hatless and bloodied, Perry reported that "we have met the enemy and they are ours."

American naval control of Lake Erie forced the British to evacuate Upper Canada. They gave up Detroit and were then defeated at the Battle of the Thames in southern Canada on October 5, 1813. During the battle, the British fled, leaving Tecumseh and 500 warriors to face the wrath of the Americans. When Tecumseh was killed, the remaining Indians retreated. Perry's victory on Lake Erie and the army's defeat of Tecumseh and the British force enabled the Americans to recover control of Michigan and seize the Western District of Upper Canada. At last, the war on the western front had turned in favor of the Americans. Thereafter, the war in the north lapsed into a military stalemate along the Canadian border punctuated by occasional plunder and looting, with neither side able to dislodge the other.

The Creek War

In the South, too, the war flared up in 1813. The Creeks in Georgia and Alabama had split into two factions: the Upper Creeks (or Red Sticks), who opposed American expansion into their lands and sided with the British and Spanish during the War of 1812, and the Lower Creeks, who wanted to remain on good terms with the Americans. On August 30, Red Sticks, allied with the British, attacked Fort Mims, on the Alabama River thirty miles above the Gulf coast town of Mobile, killing 553 men, women, and children, butchering and scalping half of them.

The massacre outraged Americans, especially those eager to remove the Native Americans from the Mississippi Territory (which then included Alabama). Thirsting for revenge, Andrew Jackson, commanding general of the Army of West Tennessee, recruited about 2,500 volunteers and headed south. Jackson was a natural warrior and a gifted commander. From a young age, he had embraced violence, gloried in it, and prospered by it. He had a volcanic temper and a ferocious will that inspired obedience and loyalty. He told all "brave Tennesseans" that their "frontier [was] threatened with invasion by the savage foe" and that the Indians were advancing "with scalping knives unsheathed, to butcher your wives, your children, and your helpless babes. Time is not to be lost."

Jackson's volunteers crushed the Red Sticks in Alabama. The decisive battle occurred on March 27, 1814, at Horseshoe Bend on the Tallapoosa River. Jackson's soldiers and their Cherokee and Creek allies surrounded a Red Stick fort, set fire to it, and shot the Indians as they tried to escape.

MAJOR SOUTHERN CAMPAIGNS OF THE WAR OF 1812

Legend:
→ American forces
→ British forces
✳ Battle site

- Why did Jackson march into Florida on his way to New Orleans?
- Why did he have the advantage in the Battle of New Orleans?
- Why was the Battle of New Orleans important to the Treaty of Ghent?

Nine hundred of them were killed, including 300 who drowned in a desperate effort to cross the river. Jackson reported to his wife that the *carnage was dreadful.* His men had "regained all the scalps taken from Fort Mims." Fewer than fifty of Jackson's soldiers were killed.

The Battle of Horseshoe Bend was the worst defeat ever inflicted upon Native Americans. With the Treaty of Fort Jackson, signed in August 1814, the devastated Red Stick Creeks were forced at gunpoint to give up two-thirds of their land—some 23 million acres—including southwest Georgia and much of Alabama. Red Eagle, chief of the Red Sticks, told Jackson: "I am in your power. . . . My people are all gone. I can do no more but weep over the misfortunes of my nation." For his part, Jackson declared that "the power of the Creeks is I think forever broken." President Madison rewarded Jackson by naming him a major general in the regular army of the United States.

Soon after the Battle of Horseshoe Bend, events in Europe took a dramatic turn when the British, Spanish, and Portuguese armies repelled

French emperor Napoléon's effort to conquer Spain and Portugal. Now free to deal with the United States, the British in the summer of 1814 sent 16,000 veteran soldiers from Europe to try again to invade America from Canada. The British navy extended their blockade to include the New England ports, and they bombarded coastal towns from Delaware to Florida. The final piece of the British plan was to seize New Orleans and sever American access to the Mississippi River, lifeline of the western states.

Thomas Macdonough's Naval Victory

The main British military effort in the War of 1812 focused on launching a massive invasion of the United States from Canada. But the outnumbered American defenders at Plattsburgh, New York, along Lake Champlain, were saved by the superb ability of Commodore Thomas Macdonough, commander of the U.S. naval squadron. On September 11, 1814, the British soldiers attacked the Americans at Plattsburgh while their warships engaged Macdonough's navy in a battle that surprisingly ended with the entire British fleet either destroyed or captured. The Battle of Lake Champlain (also called the Battle of Plattsburgh) forced the British to abandon the northern campaign. The British forces retreated back into Canada. When the British officers came aboard the American flagship to surrender, Macdonough said, "Gentlemen, return your swords to your scabbards; you are worthy of them."

Fighting in the Chesapeake

The American naval victory at Lake Champlain could not have been more timely. Just weeks before, U.S. forces had suffered the most humiliating experience of the war as British troops captured and burned Washington, D.C. In August 1814, 4,000 British soldiers landed at Benedict, Maryland, and headed briskly for the American capital, thirty-five miles away. Thousands of frightened Americans fled the city. President Madison frantically called out the poorly led and untrained militia, then courageously left the White House (Madison was the first president to call it that) to encourage the soldiers confronting the British army. But their feeble defense disintegrated in the face of the British attack.

On August 24 the British marched unopposed into the American capital. British officers ate a meal in the White House that had been prepared for Madison and his wife, Dolley, who had fled the grounds just in time, after first saving a copy of the Declaration of Independence and George Washington's portrait. The vengeful British, aware that American troops had earlier burned the Canadian capital at York (Toronto), then torched the White House, the Capitol, the Library of Congress, and most other government buildings. A tornado the next day compounded the damage, but a violent thunderstorm dampened both the fires and the enthusiasm of the British forces, who headed north to assault Baltimore.

The destruction of Washington, D.C., infuriated Americans. A Baltimore newspaper reported that the "spirit of the nation is roused." That spirit of determination showed itself when fifty British warships sailed into Baltimore Harbor on September 13 while the British army assaulted the city on land. About a thousand Americans held Fort McHenry on an island in the harbor. The British fleet unleashed a nightlong bombardment of the fort. Yet the Americans refused to surrender. Francis Scott Key, a Washington, D.C., lawyer and occasional poet, watched the siege from a British ship, having been sent to negotiate the release of a captured American. The sight of the American flag still flying over Fort McHenry at dawn meant that the city had survived the British onslaught. The scene inspired Key to scribble the verses of what came to be called "The Star-Spangled Banner," which began, "Oh, say can you see by the dawn's early light?" Later revised and set to the tune of an English drinking song, it eventually became America's national anthem. The inability of the British to conquer Fort McHenry led them to abandon the attack on Baltimore.

The Burning of the Capitol This 1817 etching of the burnt Capitol shows shackled slaves (bottom right) and angels overhead. It appeared in a book arguing that the destruction of "the temple of freedom" was a sign that God disapproved of slavery.

The war in the Chesapeake, despite the destruction of Washington, D.C., was ultimately a British failure, since the invading army was forced to withdraw to its ships and leave the region. Still, the British raids into Maryland and Virginia were terribly unsettling to Americans, especially slaveholders, because the presence of British troops encouraged thousands of slaves to run away and join the invaders. As had happened during the Revolutionary War, the British promised freedom to slaves who aided or fought with them, and almost 3,000 ran away to join British units before eventually being taken to Canada. One of them, Jeremiah West, wrote his former owner in Virginia in 1818: "Thank God I can enjoy all comforts under the flag of England and here I shall remain." Another liberated slave from Virginia declared that "we have as much right to fight for our liberty as any men."

The Aftermath of the War

While the fighting raged in the United States, American diplomats had begun meetings in Ghent, near Brussels in present-day Belgium, to discuss ending the war. The negotiations were at a standstill when news arrived of the American victory at the Battle of Lake Champlain and the failure of the British invasion of Baltimore. The British grew more flexible, but negotiations dragged on throughout the fall. Finally, on Christmas Eve, 1814, the diplomats reached an agreement to stop the fighting.

CORE **OBJECTIVE**
4. Analyze the most significant outcomes of the War of 1812 on the United States.

The Treaty of Ghent (1814)

The Treaty of Ghent

The war-weary British decided to end the war in part because of military setbacks but also because London merchants were eager to renew the profitable trade with America. The British government had also concluded that the war was not worth the cost (the prime minister said he had come to recognize the "inconvenience of the continuation of the war"). By the **Treaty of Ghent**, signed on December 24, 1814, the two sides agreed to end the war, return the prisoners, and restore the previous boundaries. The British also pledged to stop spurring Indian attacks along the Great Lakes. What had begun as an American effort to protect its honor, end impressment, and invade and conquer Canada had turned into a second war of independence against the world's greatest empire. Although the Americans lost the war for Canada and saw their national capital captured and burned, they won the southern war to defeat the Indians and take their lands. More important, the treaty saved the fragile and splintered republic from possible civil war and financial ruin.

The Battle of New Orleans

Because it took six weeks for news of the Treaty of Ghent to reach the United States, fighting continued in America. Along the Gulf coast during December 1814, forty-seven-year-old General Andrew Jackson had, without authorization, invaded the Panhandle region of Spanish Florida and taken Pensacola, putting an end to British efforts to organize Indian attacks on American settlements. In mid-December he was back in Louisiana, where he supervised efforts to defend New Orleans. A British fleet, with some 8,000 seasoned soldiers fresh from victory over Napoléon Bonaparte in Europe, took up positions just south of New Orleans, the second busiest port in the United States (after New York City). The British hoped to capture New Orleans and thereby control the entire Mississippi Valley. New England Federalists, fed up with "Mr. Madison's War," predicted that New Orleans would be lost; some called for Madison's impeachment.

British general Sir Edward Pakenham's painfully careful approach—he waited weeks until he had cannons in place to support his soldiers—gave Jackson time to organize hundreds of slaves "loaned" by planters to erect American defenses around New Orleans. The Americans built up an almost invulnerable position, but Pakenham rashly ordered a frontal assault at dawn on January 8, 1815. His brave but blundering redcoats, including all-black units from the Caribbean islands, ran into a murderous hail of artillery shells and rifle fire. Before the British withdrew, nearly 2,000 had been wounded or killed, including Pakenham and two other generals. American casualties were minimal. A British naval officer wrote that there "never was a more complete failure." When the British finally boarded their ships to leave America, several hundred runaway slaves joined them.

Treaty of Ghent (1814) Agreement between Great Britain and the United States that ended the War of 1812.

Jackson's army defends New Orleans Andrew Jackson's defeat of the British at New Orleans, January 1815.

Although the **Battle of New Orleans** occurred after the Treaty of Ghent had already been signed in Europe, it was still a vitally important psychological victory, as the treaty had yet to be officially ratified by either the United States or Great Britain. Had the British won at New Orleans, they might have tried to revise the treaty in their favor. Jackson's lopsided victory ensured that both governments would act quickly to officially approve the treaty. The unexpected American triumph at New Orleans also generated a wave of patriotic nationalism that would later help transform Jackson into a dynamic president eager to move the nation into an era in which the "common man" would be celebrated. The rough-hewn Jackson, wrote a southerner in April 1815, "is everywhere hailed as the savior of the country. . . . He has been feasted, caressed, & I may say idolised."

Battle of New Orleans (1815)

The Hartford Convention

Weeks before the Battle of New Orleans, many New Englanders, fed up with the war and the loss of revenue caused by the stoppage of trade, tried to take matters into their own hands at a meeting in Hartford, Connecticut. The **Hartford Convention** was the climax of New England's disgust with "Mr. Madison's War." The region, dominated by Federalists, had managed to remain detached from the war politically while still profiting from smuggling. Both Massachusetts and Connecticut had refused to contribute soldiers to the war effort, and merchants had continued to sell supplies to British troops in Canada. In 1814, however, the British navy extended its blockade to New England, occupied Maine, and raided several coastal towns. Even Boston seemed threatened. Instead of rallying to the American flag, however, Federalists in the Massachusetts legislature voted in October 1814 to hold a convention of New England states to protest the war.

On December 15, 1814, the Hartford Convention assembled with delegates from Massachusetts, Rhode Island, Connecticut, Vermont, and New Hampshire. The convention proposed seven constitutional amendments designed to limit Republican (and southern) influence: abolishing the

Battle of New Orleans (1815) Final major battle in the War of 1812, in which the Americans under General Andrew Jackson unexpectedly and decisively countered the British attempt to seize the port of New Orleans, Louisiana.

Hartford Convention (1815) A series of secret meetings in December 1814 and January 1815 at which New England Federalists protested American involvement in the War of 1812 and discussed several constitutional amendments, including limiting each president to one term, designed to weaken the dominant Republican party.

counting of slaves in determining a state's representation in Congress, requiring a two-thirds supermajority rather than a simple majority vote to declare war or admit new states, prohibiting trade embargoes lasting more than sixty days, excluding foreign-born people from holding federal office, limiting the president to one term, and barring successive presidents from the same state (a provision clearly directed at Virginia).

Their call for a later convention in Boston carried the unmistakable threat of secession—the possibility of New England leaving the United States—if these demands were dismissed. Yet the threat quickly evaporated. In February 1815, when messengers from Hartford reached Washington, D.C., they found the battered capital celebrating the good news from New Orleans. "Their position," according to a French diplomat, was "awkward, embarrassing, and lent itself to cruel ridicule." Ignored by Congress and the president, the Hartford delegates swiftly withdrew their recommendations. The incident proved fatal to the Federalist party, which never recovered from the shame of disloyalty stamped on it by the Hartford Convention. News of the victory at New Orleans and the arrival of the peace treaty from Europe transformed the national mood. Almost overnight, President Madison had gone from being denounced to being hailed a national hero.

The War's Legacies

There was no clear victor in the War of 1812, nor much clarification about the issues that ignited the war. The Treaty of Ghent ended the fighting but failed to address the reasons why President Madison had declared war in the first place: the disputes about maritime rights and the British practice of impressment.

> "Second war of independence"

But that did not mean that the war was without consequences. For all the clumsiness with which it was fought, the war generated an intense patriotism across much of the nation and reaffirmed American independence. The young republic was at last secure from British or European threats. "By the war," said Secretary of State James Monroe, "we have acquired a character and a rank among the other nations, which we did not enjoy before." The nation grew more confident and more powerful by surviving a "second war of independence" against the greatest power on earth. America emerged from the fighting with new symbols of nationhood and a new gallery of heroes. The people, observed Treasury secretary Albert Gallatin, "are more American; they feel and act more as a nation; and I hope that the permanency of the Union is thereby better secured."

> Economic independence

The war also propelled the United States toward economic independence, as the wartime interruption of trade with Europe encouraged the growth of American manufactures. The British blockade of the American coast during the war created a shortage of cotton cloth in the United States, leading to the creation of the nation's first cotton-manufacturing industry, in Waltham, Massachusetts. By the end of the war, there were over a hundred cotton mills in New England and sixty-four more in Pennsylvania. "Our people have 'cotton mill fever,' as it is called," said Moses Brown of Rhode Island. "Every place [is] almost occupied with cotton mills." Even Thomas Jefferson admitted in 1815 that his beloved agricultural republic had been transformed: "We must now place the manufacturer by the agriculturalist." After nearly forty years of independence, the new American republic was emerging as an agricultural, commercial, and industrial world power. "Never did a country occupy more lofty ground," said U.S. Supreme Court Justice Joseph Story in 1815. "We have stood the contest, single-handed, against the conqueror of Europe; and we are at peace, with all our blushing victories thick crowding on us."

> Emergence as a world power

One of the strangest results of the War of 1812 and its aftermath was a reversal of attitudes toward government policy by the Republicans and the Federalists. The wartime experience taught James Madison and the Republicans some lessons in nationalism. First, the British invasion of Washington, D.C., impressed upon Madison the necessity of a strong army and navy. Second, the lack of a national bank had greatly complicated the financing of the war; state banks were so unstable and in such turmoil that it was difficult for states and the federal government to raise the funds needed to support the war effort. In 1816, Madison, who had been formerly opposed to a national bank, changed his mind and created the Second Bank of the United States. Third, the rise of new industries during the war prompted business owners to call for increased tariffs on imports to protect the new American companies from unfair foreign competition. Madison went along, despite his criticism of tariffs in the 1790s.

While Madison reversed himself by embracing nationalism and a broader interpretation of the Constitution, the Federalists similarly reversed themselves and took up Madison's and Jefferson's original emphasis on states' rights and strict construction of the Constitution as they tried to defend the special interests of their regional stronghold, New England. It was the first great reversal of partisan political roles in constitutional interpretation. It would not be the last.

> Reversal of political roles for Republicans and Federalists

While no borders changed because of the War of 1812, the end of the fighting proved devastating to all of the eastern Indian nations, most of which had fought with the British. By agreeing to the Treaty of Ghent, the British essentially abandoned their Indian allies. None of their former lands were returned to them, and the British vacated their frontier forts that had long served as supply centers for the Indians. The Lakota chief Little Crow expressed the betrayal felt by all of the British-allied Native Americans when he rejected the consolation gifts from the British commander: "After we have fought for you, endured many hardships, lost some of our people, and awakened the vengeance of our powerful neighbors, you make peace for yourselves.... You no longer need our service; you offer us these goods to pay us for [your] having deserted us. But no, we will not take them; we hold them and yourselves in equal contempt." In the years after the war, the United

Managing Foreign Policy in the Early Republic

In his farewell address as president, George Washington warned Americans to avoid entanglements with Europe. During the administrations of Jefferson and Madison, however, avoiding such entanglements became increasingly difficult. Below are four events in which America became involved beyond its borders.

Event	Causes	Reactions	Outcomes
War with the Barbary pirates (1801–1804)	Barbary pirates demand increased payments in exchange for ceasing attacks on U.S. ships in Mediterranean Sea.	Jefferson sends U.S. Navy to blockade Tripoli, on the north African coast.	After demanding $300,000, the pasha of Tripoli settles for $60,000 as "tribute" to free captured Americans.
Louisiana Purchase (1803)	After the devastation of the French army in Haiti, Napoléon seeks funds to finance France's war against Great Britain. Americans desire free navigation of the Mississippi River and access to New Orleans.	Napoléon sells the French Louisiana Territory to the United States for about $15 million.	Louisiana Purchase nearly doubles U.S. territory. The Lewis and Clark expedition (1804) maps the West and establishes U.S. claims on Oregon Country.
Embargo Act (1807)	As part of their war against each other, British and French navies interfere with U.S. shipping. British navy increases impressment of American sailors. United States wishes to avoid foreign entanglements and trade freely with all European nations.	Congress and Jefferson pass the Embargo Act (1807), forbidding American ships from traveling to foreign ports.	U.S. exports plummet, devastating the U.S. economy. Jefferson declines to seek a third term as president. President Madison reopens U.S. trade with all nations, except Britain and France.

States negotiated over 200 treaties with native peoples that transferred Indian lands to America and created reservations west of the Mississippi River where the Indians were relocated.

Westward expansion

As the Indians were pushed out, tens of thousands of Americans moved west into the Great Lakes region and southwest into Georgia, Alabama, and Mississippi after the war, occupying more territory in a single generation than had been settled in the 150 years of colonial history. With nearly an

(CONTINUED)

Event	Causes	Reactions	Outcomes
War of 1812 (1812–1815)	British navy continues to interfere with U.S. shipping in Great Britain's war with France. Americans are land-hungry for British Canada and seek end to British influence over Native Americans.	United States declares war on Great Britain. United States fails to capture Canada. British troops burn Washington, D.C. United States forces defeat British forces and their Native American allies in the Battles of Lake Champlain (1814) and New Orleans (1815), and the West.	United States and Great Britain end the war with the Treaty of Ghent. United States experiences surge in patriotism and economic independence. The Hartford Convention weakens the Federalist Party. The Republican Party seeks to increase federal government's economic and military power.

QUESTIONS FOR ANALYSIS

1. What interests shaped American foreign affairs?

2. What were the common causes of U.S. foreign involvement?

3. How did foreign events affect U.S. domestic affairs and politics?

entire continent to explore and exploit, Americans streamed westward. Between 1800 and 1820, the trans-Appalachian population rose from 300,000 to 2 million. By 1840, more than 40 percent of Americans lived west of the Appalachians in eight new states. At the same time, the growing significance of slavery and its controversial extension into new western territories set in motion an explosive national debate that would test again the grand American experiment in republican government.

■ **Jefferson's Administration** The Jeffersonian Republicans did not dismantle much of Hamilton's Federalist economic program, but they did repeal the whiskey tax, cut back on government expenditures, and promoted what was called *republican simplicity* whereby they championed the virtues of smaller government and plain living. While Republicans idealized the agricultural world that had existed prior to 1800, the first decades of the 1800s were a period of explosive economic and population growth in the United States, transforming the nation. Large-scale commercial agriculture and exports to Europe flourished; Americans moved west in huge numbers. The *Louisiana Purchase,* which resulted from negotiations with French emperor Napoléon Bonaparte following French setbacks in Haiti, their colony in the Caribbean, dramatically expanded the boundaries of the United States. Jefferson's *Lewis and Clark Expedition* explored the new region and published reports that excited interest in the Far West. In *Marbury v. Madison* (1803), the Federalist chief justice of the Supreme Court, John Marshall, declared a federal act unconstitutional for the first time. With that decision, the Court assumed the right of judicial review over acts of Congress and established the constitutional supremacy of the federal government over state governments.

■ **War in Europe** Thomas Jefferson sent warships to subdue the *Barbary pirates* and negotiated with the Spanish and French to ensure that the Mississippi River remained open to American commerce. Renewal of war between Britain and France in 1803 complicated matters for American commerce with Europe. Neither country wanted its enemy to purchase U.S. goods, so both declared blockades of each other's ports. In retaliation, Jefferson convinced Congress at the end of 1807 to pass the *Embargo Act,* which prohibited all foreign trade.

■ **War of 1812** Renewal of the European war in 1803 created conflicts with Britain and France. Neither country wanted its enemy to purchase U.S. goods, so both declared blockades. In retaliation, Jefferson had Congress pass the Embargo Act, which prohibited all foreign trade. James Madison ultimately declared war over the issue of neutral shipping rights and the fear that the British were inciting Native Americans to attack frontier settlements.

■ **Aftermath of the War of 1812** The *Treaty of Ghent* (1814) ended the war by essentially declaring it a draw. A smashing American victory in January of 1815 at the *Battle of New Orleans* occurred before news of the peace treaty had reached the continent, but the lopsided American triumph helped to ensure that the treaty would be ratified and enforced. One effect of the conflict over neutral shipping rights was to establish the economic independence of the United States, as goods previously purchased from Great Britain were now manufactured at home. During and after the war, Federalists and Republicans seemed to exchange roles: delegates from the waning Federalist party met at the *Hartford Convention* (1815) to defend states' rights and threaten secession, while Republicans now promoted nationalism and a broad interpretation of the Constitution.

KEY TERMS

CHRONOLOGY

1800	U.S. population reaches over 5,000,000
1801	Thomas Jefferson inaugurated as president in Washington, D.C.
	Barbary pirates harass U.S. shipping and capture American sailors; the pasha of Tripoli declares war on the United States
1803	Supreme Court issues *Marbury v. Madison* decision
	Louisiana Purchase
1804–1806	Lewis and Clark expedition
1804	Jefferson overwhelmingly reelected
1807	British interference with U.S. shipping increases
1808	International slave trade ended in the United States
1811	Defeat of Tecumseh's Indian Confederacy at the Battle of Tippecanoe
1812	Congress declares war on Britain
	U.S. invasion of Canada
1813–1814	Creek War
1814	British capture and burn Washington, D.C.
	Hartford Convention
1815	Battle of New Orleans
	News of the Treaty of Ghent reaches the United States

INQUIZITIVE

Go to InQuizitive to see what you've learned—and learn what you've missed—with personalized feedback along the way.

DEBATING Thomas Jefferson and Slavery

One of the more difficult tasks that historians face is assessing the beliefs and actions of historical figures within an ethical framework. Should individuals be assessed by the standards of their time or by those of today? Should we hold celebrated historical figures to a higher ethical standard? For Part II, *Building a Nation*, the complex relationship of Thomas Jefferson to slavery demonstrates how historians can disagree when they evaluate historic individuals from an ethical perspective.

This exercise involves two tasks:

PART 1: Compare the two secondary sources on Thomas Jefferson and slavery.

PART 2: Using primary sources, evaluate the arguments of the two secondary sources.

PART I Comparing and Contrasting Secondary Sources

Below are secondary sources from two scholars who have written on the question of Jefferson and his relationship with slavery. The first is from Douglas L. Wilson, Professor Emeritus of English and Co-Director of the Lincoln Studies Center at Knox College; the second is written by Paul Finkelman, Professor of Law and Public Policy at the Albany Law School. In these selections, Wilson and Finkelman explore one of the great contradictions in early American history: that Thomas Jefferson, an outspoken critic of slavery and writer of perhaps the most famous phrase in American history, "All men are created equal," was himself a slave owner. Further complicating the matter was Jefferson's relationship with Sally Heming, a slave with whom he likely had several children. Both passages grapple with the issue of *presentism,* the application of present day ideas and beliefs onto the past.

Compare the views of these two scholars by answering the following questions. Be sure to find specific examples in the selections to support your answers.

■ How does each author address the issue of presentism?

■ What ethical standards do each of the authors use to evaluate Jefferson?

■ What type of evidence do they offer when evaluating Jefferson?

■ How does each author think Jefferson meets or fails to meet the ethical standard the author established?

■ What ethical standard would you use?

Secondary Source 1

Douglas L. Wilson, "Thomas Jefferson and the Character Issue" (1992)

How could the man who wrote that "All men are created equal" own slaves? This, in essence, is the question most persistently asked of those who write about Thomas Jefferson, and by all indications it is the thing that contemporary Americans find most vexing about him . . . The question carries a silent assumption that because he practiced slave holding, Jefferson must have somehow believed in it, and must therefore have been a hypocrite. My belief is that this way of asking the question . . . reflects the pervasive presentism of our time. Consider, for example, how different the question appears when inverted and framed in more historical terms: How did a man who was born into a slave holding society, whose family and admired friends owned slaves, who inherited a fortune that was dependent on slaves and slave labor, decide at an early age that slavery was morally wrong and forcefully declare that it ought to be abolished?

But when the question is explained in this way, another invariably follows: If Jefferson came to believe that holding slaves was wrong, why did he continue to hold them?... Obstacles to emancipation in Jefferson's Virginia were formidable, and the risk was demonstrably great that emancipated slaves would enjoy little, if any, real freedom and would, unless they could pass as white, be more likely to come to grief in a hostile environment. In short, the master whose concern extended beyond his own morality to the well-being of his slaves was caught on the horns of a dilemma. Thus the question of why Jefferson didn't free his slaves only serves to illustrate how presentism involves us in mistaken assumptions about historical conditions — in this case that an eighteenth-century slave holder wanting to get out from under the moral stigma of slavery and improve the lot of his slaves had only to set them free.

Although we may find Jefferson guilty of failing to make adequate allowance for the conditions in which blacks were forced to live, Jefferson did not take the next step of concluding that blacks were fit only for slavery. This rationalization of slavery was indeed the common coin of slave holders and other whites who condoned or tolerated the "peculiar" institution, but it formed no part of Jefferson's thinking. In fact, he took the opposite position: that having imposed the depredations of slavery on blacks, white Americans should not only emancipate them but also educate and train them to be self-sufficient, provide them with necessary materials, and establish a colony in which they could live as free and independent people.

Source: Wilson, Douglas L. "Thomas Jefferson and the Character Issue." *The Atlantic Monthly* 270, no. 5 (November 1992), pp. 57–74.

Secondary Source 2

Paul Finkelman, "Jefferson and Slavery" (1993)

An understanding of Jefferson's relationship to slavery requires analysis of his statements on and beliefs about the institution and an account of his actions as a public leader and a private individual. Scrutinizing the contradictions between Jefferson's professions and his actions does not impose twentieth-century values on an eighteenth-century man. Because he was the author of the Declaration of Independence and a leader of the American Enlightenment, the test of Jefferson's position on slavery is not whether he was better than the worst of his generation, but whether he was the leader of the best; not whether he responded as a southerner and a planter, but whether he was able to transcend his economic interests and his sectional background to implement the ideals he articulated. Jefferson fails the test. When Jefferson wrote the Declaration, he owned over 175 slaves. While many of his contemporaries freed their slaves during and after the Revolution, Jefferson did not.

In the fifty years from 1776 until his death in 1826, a period of extraordinary public service, he did little to end slavery or to dissociate himself from his role as the master of Monticello. To the contrary, as he accumulated more slaves he worked assiduously to increase the productivity and the property values of his labor force. Nor did he encourage his countrymen to liberate their slaves, even when they sought his blessing. Even at his death Jefferson failed to fulfill the promise of his rhetoric. In his will he emancipated only five bondsmen, condemning nearly two hundred others to the auction block...

... He knew slavery was wrong. It could not have been otherwise for an eighteenth-century natural law theorist. Many of his closest European and American friends and colleagues were leaders of the new abolition societies. Jefferson was part of a cosmopolitan "republic of letters" that was overwhelmingly hostile to slavery. But, for the most part, he suppressed his doubts, while doing virtually nothing to challenge the institution. On this issue Jefferson's genius failed him. As David Brion Davis observes, "Jefferson had only a theoretical interest in promoting the cause of abolition."

Jefferson could not live without slaves. They built his house, cooked his meals, and tilled his fields. In contrast to George Washington, Jefferson failed to carefully manage his lands and finances and lived beyond his means. Washington refused to traffic in slaves. Chronically in debt, Jefferson overcame his professed "scruples about selling negroes but for delinquency or on their own request," selling scores of slaves in order to make ends meet. Jefferson could not maintain his extravagant life style without his slaves and, to judge from his lifelong behavior, his grand style was far more important than the natural rights of his slaves.... Throughout his life, as he condemned slavery, Jefferson almost always implied that, however bad it was for slaves, the institution was somehow worse for whites. His concerns about the institution had more to do with its effect on whites and white society than on its true victims.... Jefferson's concerns were solely with the "morals and manners" of the master class. He was concerned that slavery leads to despotism by the masters; but he never expressed regret for the mistreatment of the slave. Similarly, throughout his life Jefferson expressed his fears of miscegenation and a weakening of white society through contact with blacks. He favored some form of colonization that would put blacks "beyond the reach of mixture."

Source: Finkelman, Paul. "Jefferson and Slavery: 'Treason Against the Hopes of the World.'" In *Jeffersonian Legacies*, ed. Peter S. Onuf. Charlottesville, Va.: The University Press of Virginia, 1993, pp. 181–221.

Using Primary Sources to Evaluate Secondary Sources

When historians are faced with competing interpretations of the past, they often look at primary source material as part of the process of evaluating the different arguments. Below are a selection of primary source materials relating to Thomas Jefferson's relationship with slavery. The first document is an excerpt from a draft of the Declaration of Independence largely written by Thomas Jefferson. This excerpt was removed from the final version of the declaration. The second document is a selection from Jefferson's 1785 book on the state of Virginia, relating to slaves and slavery. The third document is a letter Jefferson wrote while serving in Paris as the U.S. minister (ambassador) to France in 1788, while the fourth is a letter from April 1820 expressing his feelings regarding the Missouri compromise which admitted Missouri as a slave state and created a northern boundary for slavery in the western territories.

Carefully read each of the following primary sources and answer the following questions. Decide which of the primary source documents support or refute Wilson's and Finkelman's arguments about Jefferson. You may find that some documents do both, but for different parts of each historian's interpretation. Be sure to identify which specific components of each historian's argument the documents support or refute.

■ Which of the two historians' *arguments* is best supported by the *primary source* documents? Or, if you find that both arguments are well supported by the evidence, why do you think the two historians had such different interpretations about Jefferson?

■ Based on the ethical standard you choose in part I and these documents, how would *you* assess Jefferson's relationship with slavery? You may consider how Jefferson's views change over time.

■ What has using primary sources to evaluate the Wilson and Finkelman arguments taught you about making ethical assessments of historical figures?

Primary Source 1

Thomas Jefferson, a draft section omitted from the Declaration of Independence (1776)

He [King George III] has waged cruel war against human nature itself, violating its most sacred rights of life & liberty in the persons of a distant people [Africans] who never offended him, captivating & carrying them into slavery in another hemisphere, or to incur miserable death in their transportation thither. This piratical warfare, the opprobrium of infidel powers, is the warfare of the Christian king of Great Britain. Determined to keep open a market where men should be bought & sold, he has prostituted his negative for suppressing every legislative attempt to prohibit or to restrain this execrable (disgusting) commerce: and that this assemblage of horrors might want no fact of distinguished die, he is now exciting those very people to rise in arms among us, and to purchase that liberty of which he has deprived them, & murdering the people upon whom he also obtruded them; thus paying off former crimes committed against the liberties of one people, with crimes which he urges them to commit against the lives of another.

Source: Jefferson, Thomas. "Thomas Jefferson, June 1776, Rough Draft of the Declaration of Independence," 1776. *The Thomas Jefferson Papers Series 1. General Correspondence. 1651–1827.* American Memory, Library of Congress, Washington, D. C.

Primary Source 2

Thomas Jefferson, *Notes on the State of Virginia* (1787)

It will probably be asked, Why not retain and incorporate the Blacks into the State [after emancipation], and thus save the expense of supplying, by importation of white settlers, the vacancies they will leave? Deep-rooted prejudices entertained by the Whites; ten thousand recollections by the Blacks, of the injuries they have sustained; new provocations; the real distinctions which nature has made; and many other circumstances, will divide us into parties, and produce convulsions, which will probably never end but in the extermination of the one or the other race. To these objections, which are political, may be added others, which are physical and moral . . . . Comparing them by their faculties of memory, reason, and imagination, it appears to me, that in memory they are equal to the Whites; in reason much inferior, . . . and that in imagination they are dull, tasteless and anomalous . . . .

To our reproach it must be said, that though for a century and a half we have had under our eyes the races of Black and of Red men, they have never yet been viewed by us as subjects of natural history. I advance it therefore as a suspicion only, that the Blacks, whether originally a distinct race, or made distinct by time and circumstances, are inferior to the Whites in the endowments both of body and mind. It is not against experience to suppose, that different species of the same genus, or varieties of the same species, may possess different qualifications. Will not a lover of natural history then, one who views the gradations in all the races of animals with the eye of philosophy, excuse an effort to keep those in the department of man as distinct as nature has formed them? This unfortunate difference of colour, and perhaps of faculty, is a powerful obstacle to the emancipation of these people. Many of their advocates, while they wish to vindicate the liberty of human nature, are anxious also to preserve its dignity and beauty. Some of these, embarrassed by the question 'What further is to be done with them?' join themselves in opposition with those who are actuated by sordid avarice (greed) only. Among the Romans emancipation required but one effort. The slave, when made free, might mix with, without staining the blood of his master. But with us a second is necessary, unknown to history. When freed, he is to be removed beyond the reach of mixture . . . . There must, doubtless, be an unhappy influence on the manners of our people, produced by the existence of slavery among us. The whole commerce between master and slave is a perpetual exercise of the most boisterous passions, the most unremitting despotism on the one part, and degrading . . . . For if a slave can have a country in this world, it must be any other in preference to that in which he is born to live and labor for another.

Source: Jefferson, Thomas. "Laws, Query XIV." In *Notes on the State of Virginia*. London: Printed for John Stockdale, Opposite Burlington-House, Piccadilly, 1787, pp. 229–271.

Primary Source 3

Thomas Jefferson, Letter to M. Warville (February 11, 1788)

Sir,

I am very sensible of the honor you propose to me, of becoming a member of the society for the abolition of the slave-trade. You know that nobody wishes more ardently, to see an abolition, not only of the trade, but of the condition of slavery: and certainly nobody will be more willing to encounter every sacrifice for that object. But the influence and information of the friends to this proposition in France will be far above the need of my association. I am here as a public servant, and those whom I serve, having never yet been able to give their voice against the practice, it is decent for me to avoid too public a demonstration of my wishes to see it abolished. Without serving the cause here, it might render me less able to serve it beyond the water. I trust you will be sensible of the prudence of those motives, therefore, which govern my conduct on this occasion, and be assured of my wishes for the success of your undertaking, and the sentiments of esteem and respect, with which I have the honor to be, Sir, your most obedient, humble servant,

Th: Jefferson.

Source: Jefferson, Thomas. "Jean Plumard Brissot de Warville to Thomas Jefferson, February 11, 1788," 1788. *The Thomas Jefferson Papers Series 1. General Correspondence. 1651–1827.* American Memory, Library of Congress, Washington, D. C.

Primary Source 4

Thomas Jefferson, Letter to John Holmes (April 22, 1820)

I thank you, dear Sir, for the copy you have been so kind as to send me of the letter to your constituents on the Missouri question [the admission of Missouri as slave state] . . . The cession of that kind of property[slaves] (for so it is misnamed) . . . would not cost me a second thought, if, in that way, a general emancipation and expatriation could be effected: and, gradually, and with due sacrifices, I think it might be. But as it is, we have the wolf by the ears, and we can neither hold him, nor safely let him go. Justice is in one scale, and self-preservation in the other. Of one thing I am certain, that as the passage of slaves from one State to another, would not make a slave of a single human being who would not be so without it, so their diffusion over a greater surface would make them individually happier, and proportionally facilitate the accomplishment of their emancipation . . . .

Th: Jefferson.

Source: Jefferson, Thomas. "Thomas Jefferson to John Holmes, April 22, 1820," 1820. *The Thomas Jefferson Papers Series 1. General Correspondence. 1651–1827.* American Memory, Library of Congress, Washington, D. C.

A CARD.

BLOUNT & DAWSON,

NERAL BROKERS

the Purchase and Sale of Negroes and Other
PROPERTY.

AVANNAH,   GEORGIA.

ken the Office and New Jail completed by Wm. Wright, Esq., we are
rd secure and good accommodations for all negroes left with us for Sale
ping, would respectfully solicit a share of public patronage.

Two Doors East of J. Bryan & Co., opposite
the State Bank.

LOUNT.   W. C. DAWSON.

leased the above gentlemen my office and jail, would take pleasure in
ding them to my patrons and the public generally.

WM. WRIGHT.

An Expanding Nation

During the nineteenth century, the United States experienced a wrenching change from being a predominantly agrarian society to having a more diverse economy, with factories and cities emerging alongside farms and towns. The pace of life quickened, and American ambitions mushroomed. Between 1790 and 1820, the nation grew rapidly; its boundaries expanded and its population—both white and black—soared while the number of Native Americans continued its long decline. By the early 1820s, the total number of enslaved Americans was more than two and a half times greater than in 1790, and the number of free blacks doubled. The white population of the United States grew just as rapidly.

Accompanying the industrialization of the economy was the relentless expansion of the United States westward. Until the nineteenth century, most of the population was clustered near the seacoast and along rivers flowing into the Atlantic Ocean. The great theme of early-nineteenth-century American history was the migration of millions of people westward across the Allegheny and Appalachian Mountains into the Middle West. Waves of adventurous Americans then crossed the Mississippi River and spread out across the Great Plains. By the 1840s, Americans had reached the Pacific Ocean, transported there by horses, wagons, canals, flatboats, steamboats, and eventually railroads and steamships.

While the feverish expansion into the West brought more conflict with Native Americans, Mexicans, the British, and the Spanish, most Americans believed it was their God-given destiny to spread across the continent—at whatever cost and at whomever's expense. These developments—the emergence of a market economy and the growth of the nation—made the second quarter of the nineteenth century a time of restless optimism. Americans were nothing if not brash and self-assured. In 1845, an editorial in the *United States Journal* claimed that "we, the American people, are the most independent, intelligent, moral, and happy people on the face of the earth." The republic governed by highly educated "natural aristocrats" such as Thomas Jefferson, James Madison, James Monroe, and John Quincy Adams gave way to the frontier democracy promoted by Andrew Jackson. Americans began to demand government of, by, and for the people.

During the first half of the nineteenth century, two very different societies—North and South—developed in the United States. The North was the more dynamic and faster-growing region. It embraced the Industrial Revolution, large cities, foreign immigrants, and the ideal of "free labor." By contrast, the South remained rural, agricultural, and increasingly committed to enslaved labor as the backbone of its economy. Two great underlying fears worried southerners: the daily threat of slave uprisings and the growing possibility that a northern-controlled Congress might abolish slavery. The planter elite's aggressive efforts to preserve and expand slavery stifled reform impulses in the South and ignited a prolonged political controversy with the North that would eventually lead to civil war.

The so-called Jacksonian Era during the first half of the nineteenth century celebrated individual freedom and self-expression. Religious life, for example, experienced another wave of energetic revival centered on the

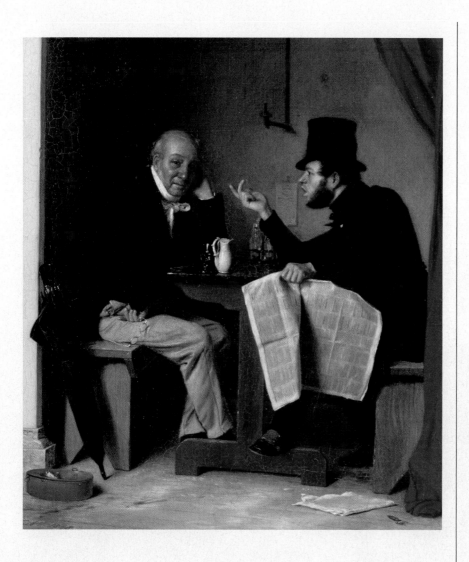

power of individuals to embrace Christ and attain salvation on their own. Such an emphasis on individualism and freedom of expression shaped cultural life in general.

The Romantic movement, originating in Europe and then spreading to America, applied democratic ideals to philosophy, religion, literature, and the fine arts. In New England, Ralph Waldo Emerson and Henry David Thoreau joined other "transcendentalists" in promoting a radical individualism. At the same time, activists of all types fanned out to reform and even "perfect" American society by creating public schools accessible to all children, working to abolish slavery, combating the consumption of alcohol, and striving to improve living conditions for the disabled, the insane, the poor, and the imprisoned.

***LACKAWANNA VALLEY* (1855)** Often hailed the father of American landscape painting, George Inness was commissioned by a railroad company to capture its trains coursing through the lush Lackawanna River Valley in northeastern Pennsylvania. New inventions and great technological growth would continue to change the American landscape.

The Emergence of a Market Economy

1815–1850

Amid the postwar celebrations in 1815, Americans set about transforming their victorious young nation. Within a year or so after war's end, prosperity returned as British and European markets again welcomed American ships and commerce. During the war, the cutting off of trade with Britain and Europe had forced the United States to develop more factories and mills of its own, spurring the development of the more diverse economy that Alexander Hamilton had championed in the 1790s. Between 1815 and 1850, the United States became a transcontinental power, expanding all the way to the Pacific coast. Hundreds of thousands of land-hungry people streamed westward toward the Mississippi River and beyond. In just six years following the end of the war in 1815, six new states were added to the Union (Alabama, Illinois, Indiana, Mississippi, Missouri, and Maine).

The lure of cheap land and plentiful jobs, as well as the promise of political and religious freedom, attracted millions of European immigrants in the first half of the nineteenth century. They were not always welcomed. Ethnic prejudices, religious persecution, and language barriers made it difficult for many new immigrants, mostly from Ireland and Germany, to adapt to American culture.

In the Midwest and West, large-scale commercial agriculture emerged as big farms grew corn, wheat, pigs, and cattle to be sold in distant markets. In the South, cotton became so profitable and widespread that it increasingly

CORE
OBJECTIVES INQUIZITIVE

1. Describe how changes in transportation and communications altered the economic landscape during the first half of the nineteenth century.

2. Explain the impact of the Industrial Revolution on the way people worked and lived.

3. Analyze how immigration altered the nation's population and shaped its politics.

4. Evaluate the impact of the expanding capitalist "market economy" on workers, professionals, and women.

dominated the region's economy, luring farmers and planters (wealthy farmers with hundreds or even thousands of acres worked by large numbers of slaves) into the new states of Alabama, Mississippi, Louisiana, and Arkansas. Cotton cloth was the first great consumer product of the Industrial Age. As the cotton culture expanded into new southern territories and states, it required growing numbers of enslaved workers, many of whom were sold and relocated from Virginia and the Carolinas. Meanwhile, the Northeast experienced an industrial revolution that reshaped the region's economy as mills and factories began to dot the landscape and transform the nature of work; most of the early mill workers were young farm women. In the North and Midwest, an urban middle class emerged as Americans left farms and moved to towns and cities, drawn primarily by jobs in new mills, factories, and banks.

By 1850, the United States had become one of the world's major commercial and manufacturing nations—and the fastest growing. The dynamic economy also generated changes in most other areas, from politics to the legal system, from the family to social values. These social and economic developments in turn helped expand prosperity and freedom for whites and free blacks. These changes also prompted vigorous political debates over economic policies, transportation improvements, and the extension of slavery into the new territories. The economy was being transformed into a national marketplace enabled by dramatic improvements in communication and transportation. In the process, the nation began to divide into three powerful regional political blocs—North, South, and West—whose shifting alliances would shape political life until the Civil War.

CORE **OBJECTIVE**

1. Describe how changes in transportation and communications altered the economic landscape during the first half of the nineteenth century.

market economy Large-scale manufacturing and commercial agriculture that emerged in America during the first half of the nineteenth century, displacing much of the pre-market subsistence and barter-based economy and producing boom-and-bust cycles while raising the American standard of living.

The Market Revolution

During the first half of the nineteenth century, a market revolution transformed the young American economy. In the eighteenth century, most Americans were part of what was called a local "household economy." That is, they produced enough food, livestock, and clothing for their own family's needs and perhaps a little more to barter (exchange) with their neighbors. During the nineteenth century, however, more and more farmers began producing surplus crops and livestock to sell, for cash, in more distant regional markets reached by rivers, canals, and roads. Such large-scale commercial agriculture, often called a **market economy**, produced boom-and-bust cycles, but overall the standard of living rose and Americans experienced unprecedented opportunities for economic gain and geographic mobility. The transition from a traditional household economy to a modern market economy was neither easy nor simple; it involved massive changes in the way people lived, worked, traveled, and voted.

Transportation

Speed is the defining aspect of modern life. The most important break-throughs in creating the national market economy were dramatic improvements in transportation. Until the nineteenth century, travel in America had been slow, tedious, and expensive. It took a stagecoach four days to travel from New York City to Boston. Because of long travel times, many farm products could only be sold locally before they spoiled. That changed during the first half of the nineteenth century. An array of innovations in transportation—larger horse-drawn wagons, called *Conestogas*; new roads; canals; steamboats; and railroads—knit together the expanding national market for goods and services and greatly accelerated the pace of life. During the first quarter of the nineteenth century, stagecoaches increased their speed as the quality of roads improved. In addition, stagecoach lines began using continual relays, or "stages," of fresh horses made available every 40 miles or so. This made travel faster, less expensive, and more accessible to more people.

> A revolution in transportation

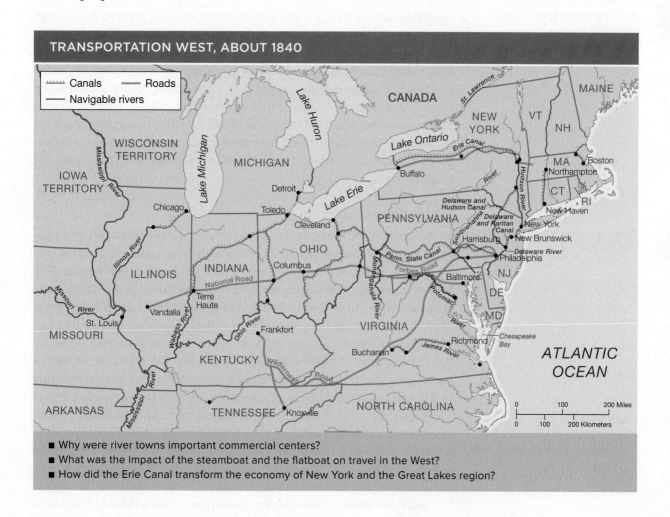

TRANSPORTATION WEST, ABOUT 1840

- Why were river towns important commercial centers?
- What was the impact of the steamboat and the flatboat on travel in the West?
- How did the Erie Canal transform the economy of New York and the Great Lakes region?

Traveling the western waters
Steamboats at the levee at St. Paul, Minnesota, in 1859.

New Roads

Road transportation: Building turnpikes

As settlers moved west, people demanded better roads. In 1795 the Wilderness Road, along the trail first blazed by Daniel Boone twenty years earlier, was opened to wagon and stagecoach traffic, thereby easing the over-the-mountains route from North Carolina into Kentucky and Tennessee. To the northeast, a movement for graded and paved roads (using packed-down crushed stones) gathered momentum after the Philadelphia-Lancaster Turnpike was completed in 1794 (the term *turnpike* derives from a pole, or pike, at the tollgate, which was turned to admit the traffic in exchange for a small fee). By 1821, some 4,000 miles of turnpikes had been built, and stagecoach and freight companies emerged to move more people and cargo at lower rates.

Water Transportation

Water transportation: Steamboats

By the early 1820s, the turnpike boom was giving way to dramatic advances in water transportation. River steamboats, flatboats, and canal barges carried people and goods far more cheaply than did horse-drawn wagons. The first steamboat appeared when Robert Fulton and Robert R. Livingston sent the *Clermont* north up the Hudson River from New York City in 1807. Thereafter, the use of wood-fired **steamboats** spread rapidly to other eastern rivers and to the sprawling Ohio and Mississippi river systems, opening nearly half the continent to water traffic. By bringing two-way traffic to the Mississippi Valley (the third-largest drainage system in the world, surpassed only by the Amazon and the Congo), steamboats created a transcontinental market and an agricultural empire that produced much of the nation's timber, wheat, corn, cattle, and hogs. By 1836, there were 750 steamboats operating on American rivers, more than twice the number in Europe. Steamboats transformed St. Louis, Missouri, from a sleepy frontier village into a booming river port. New Orleans developed even faster. By 1840, it was the wealthiest and third largest American city, having developed a thriving trade with

steamboats Ships and boats powered by wood-fired steam engines that made two-way traffic possible in eastern river systems, creating a transcontinental market and an agricultural empire.

the Caribbean islands and the new Latin American republics that had overthrown Spanish rule.

Canals also sped the market revolution. The historic **Erie Canal** in New York spurred the creation of a national economy. After it opened in 1825, having taken eight years to build, the new canal drew eastward much of the midwestern trade that earlier had been forced to make the long journey down the Ohio and Mississippi Rivers to the Gulf of Mexico. The Erie Canal had enormous economic and political consequences, tying together the regional economies of the Midwest and the East while further isolating the Deep South.

The remarkable Erie Canal, forty feet wide and four feet deep, extended 364 miles across New York from Albany to Buffalo. Additional branches soon put most of the state within its reach. The canal, built by tens of thousands of manual laborers, mostly Irish immigrants, brought a "river of gold" to New York City in the form of an unending stream of goods going to and from the Midwest. The Erie Canal reduced travel time from New York City to Buffalo from twenty days to six, and the cost of moving a ton of freight plummeted from $100 to $5. Such dramatic improvements enabled New York City to rush past Boston, New Orleans, and Baltimore and become the nation's busiest port. The success of the New York canal system inspired the construction of more canals in other states. By 1837, there were 3,000 miles of canal waterways across the nation.

> Water transportation: Canal systems

Railroads

But the canal era was short-lived. During the second quarter of the nineteenth century, a more versatile and powerful form of transportation emerged: the railroad. In 1825, the year the Erie Canal was completed, the world's first steam-powered railway began operating in England. Soon thereafter, a railroad-building craze struck the United States. In 1830 the nation had only 23 miles of railroad track. Over the next twenty years, railroad coverage grew to 30,626 miles.

> Railroads connect the continent

The railroad surpassed other forms of transportation because of its speed, carrying capacity, and reliability. **Railroads** could carry more people and freight faster, farther, and cheaper. The early trains averaged ten miles per hour, more than twice the speed of stagecoaches and four times that of boats and barges. The ability of railroads to operate year-round also gave them a huge advantage over canals that froze over in winter and dirt roads that became rivers of mud during rainstorms.

In addition, railroads provided indirect benefits by encouraging new western settlement and the expansion of commercial agriculture. Building railroads stimulated the national economy not only by improving transportation but by creating a huge demand for iron, wooden crossties, bridges, locomotives, freight cars, and equipment of various kinds needed to operate railroads. Perhaps most important, railroads enabled towns and cities not served by canals or turnpikes to compete economically. In other words, the

Erie Canal (1817) Most important and profitable of the many barge canals built in the early nineteenth century, connecting the Great Lakes to the Hudson River, and conveying so much cargo that it made New York City the nation's largest port.

railroads Steam-powered vehicles that improved passenger transportation, quickened western settlement, and enabled commercial agriculture in the nineteenth century.

THE GROWTH OF RAILROADS, 1850 AND 1860

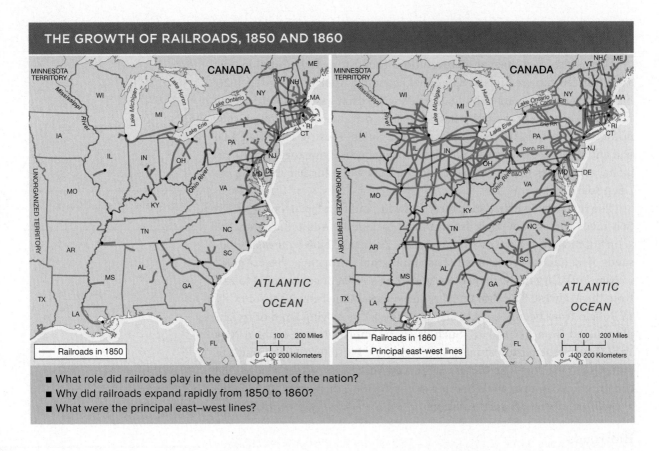

Railroads in 1850

Railroads in 1860
Principal east-west lines

- What role did railroads play in the development of the nation?
- Why did railroads expand rapidly from 1850 to 1860?
- What were the principal east–west lines?

railroads eventually changed what in the eighteenth century had been a cluster of mostly local markets into an interconnected national marketplace for goods and services. Railroads thereby expanded the geography of American capitalism, making possible larger industrial and commercial enterprises.

Ocean Transportation

Ocean transportation: Clipper ships enable high-speed ocean travel

The year 1845 brought a great innovation in ocean transport with the launching of the first clipper ship, the *Rainbow*. Built for speed, the sleek **clipper ships** were the nineteenth-century equivalent of the supersonic jetliner. They were twice as fast as the older merchant ships. Long and lean, with taller masts and more sails, they cut dashing figures during their brief but colorful career, which lasted less than two decades. It was the American thirst for Chinese tea that prompted the clipper boom. Asian tea leaves had to reach the market quickly after harvest, and the fast clipper ships made this possible. Even more important, the discovery of gold in California in 1848 lured thousands of prospectors and entrepreneurs from the Atlantic seaboard. The massive wave of would-be miners generated an urgent demand for goods on the West Coast, and the clippers met it. In 1854 the *Flying Cloud* took eighty-nine days and eight hours to travel from

clipper ships Tall, slender ships favored over older merchant ships for their speed; ultimately gave way to steamships because clipper ships lacked cargo space.

Building a clipper ship This 1833 oil painting captures the Messrs. Smith & Co. Ship Yard in Manhattan, where shipbuilders are busy shaping timbers to construct a clipper ship.

New York to San Francisco, less than half as long as the trip would have taken in a conventional ship. But clippers, while fast, lacked ample space for cargo or passengers. After the Civil War, the clipper ship would give way to the steamship.

Communications

Innovations in transportation also helped spark amazing improvements in communications, which knit the nation closer together. At the beginning of the nineteenth century, traveling any distance was slow and difficult. It took days—often weeks—for news to travel along the Atlantic seaboard. For example, after George Washington died in 1798 in Virginia, the news of his death did not appear in New York City newspapers until a week later. By 1829, it was possible to deliver President Andrew Jackson's inaugural address from Washington, D.C., to New York City by relay horse riders in less than twenty hours. Mail deliveries also improved. The number of U.S. post offices soared from 75 in 1790 to 28,498 in 1860. In addition, the mass production of newspapers enabled by new steam-powered printing presses reduced their cost from six cents to a penny each, enabling virtually everyone to benefit from the news contained in the "penny press."

But the century's most important advance in communications occurred with the development of a national electromagnetic **telegraph system**,

telegraph system System of electronic communication invented by Samuel F. B. Morse that could transmit messages instantaneously across great distances.

invented by Samuel F. B. Morse, a portrait painter turned inventor. In May 1844, Morse sent the first intercity telegraph message from Washington, D.C. to Baltimore, Maryland. It read: "What Hath God Wrought?" By the end of the decade, most major cities were connected by telegraph lines. By enabling people to communicate faster and more easily across long distances, the electrical telegraph system triggered many changes, not the least of which was helping railroad operators to schedule trains more precisely and thus avoid collisions. A New Orleans newspaper claimed that with the invention of the telegraph "scarcely anything now will appear to be impossible."

The Role of Government

Taken together, the communications and transportation improvements of the first half of the nineteenth century reshaped the contours of economic, social, and political life. Steamboats, canals, and railroads helped connect the western areas of the country with the East, boost trade, open up the Far West for settlement, and spark dramatic growth in cities such as Buffalo, Cleveland, and Chicago. Between 1800 and 1860, an undeveloped nation of scattered farms, primitive roads, and modest local markets was transformed into an engine of capitalist expansion, urban energy, and global reach.

Government financing for internal improvements

The dramatic transportation improvements were financed by both state governments and private investors. Unlike in Europe, virtually all of the railroads in the United States were built by private companies and investors rather than by the national government. But the federal government helped, too, despite intense political debates over whether it was constitutional to use federal funds or assets like government-owned land to finance such "internal improvements." The national government bought stock in turnpike and canal companies and, after the success of the Erie Canal, awarded land grants to several western states in order to support canal and railroad projects. By 1860, Congress had given railroad companies more than 20 million acres of federal lands. The national government also sent federal cavalry troops to "pacify" the Indians along the route of the railroads.

CORE **OBJECTIVE**

2. Explain the impact of the Industrial Revolution on the way people worked and lived.

The Industrial Revolution

The concentration of population in cities, coupled with the transportation and communication revolutions, greatly increased the number of potential customers for a given product. This in turn gave rise to *mass production*, whereby companies used new technologies (machine tools) to produce much greater quantities of products which could be sold at lower prices while generating higher profits. The application of water-powered mills and coal-powered steam engines, as well as the application of new technologies to make manufacturing more efficient, sparked an industrial revolution in Europe and America from the mid-eighteenth century to the late nineteenth century. The **Industrial Revolution**, centered on the invention of the steam engine, was the most important development in human history since the advent of agriculture. Prior to 1800, most products were made by hand by skilled artisans. That changed quickly with the development, first, of textile machinery, soon followed by a dazzling array of machinery invented to manufacture almost everything. Factories, mills, and industrial plants emerged during the first half of the nineteenth century to replace many artisans and craftsmen making clothing, shoes, clocks and watches, furniture, firearms, and an array of other items.

American Technology

During the nineteenth century, Americans became known around the world for their "practical" inventiveness. Between 1790 and 1811, the U.S. Patent Office approved an annual average of seventy-seven new patents certifying new inventions; by the 1850s, the Patent Office was approving more than 28,000 new inventions each year. Many of those new inventions generated dramatic changes. In 1844, for example, Charles Goodyear patented a process for "vulcanizing" rubber, which made the product stronger, more elastic, waterproof, and winter-proof. Vulcanized rubber was soon being used for a variety of products, from shoes and boots to seals, gaskets, and hoses and, eventually, tires. In 1846 Elias Howe patented his design of the sewing machine, soon improved upon by Isaac Merritt Singer, who founded the Singer Sewing Machine Company, which first produced only industrial sewing machines for use in textile mills but eventually offered machines for home use. The availability of sewing machines helped revolutionize "women's work." Sewing machines dramatically reduced the time for making clothes at home, thus freeing up more leisure time for many women.

Technological advances helped improve living conditions; houses could be larger, better heated, and better illuminated. The first sewer systems helped clean up cities by ridding their streets of human and animal waste. Mechanization of factories meant that more goods could be produced faster with less labor, and machines also enabled industries to produce "standardized parts" that could be assembled by unskilled workers. Machine-made clothes using standardized forms fit better and were cheaper than those sewn by hand; machine-made newspapers and magazines were more abundant and affordable, as were clocks, watches, guns, and plows.

Another such invention would launch an economic revolution. In 1792 Eli Whitney, a recent Yale graduate from New England, visited Mulberry Grove plantation in coastal Georgia, where he "heard much said of the difficulty of ginning cotton"—that is, separating the fibers from the seeds. The person who invented a "machine" to gin cotton, it was said, would become wealthy overnight. A few days later, Whitney devised a simple mechanism (he called it "an absurdly simple contrivance"), using nails attached to a roller, to remove the seeds from cotton bolls. Whitney's **cotton gin** (short for *engine*) proved to be fifty times more productive than a hand laborer.

American inventiveness: The sewing machine (1846)

Industrial Revolution Major shift in the nineteenth century from hand-made manufacturing to mass production in mills and factories using water-, coal-, and steam-powered machinery.

cotton gin Hand-operated machine invented by Eli Whitney that quickly removed seeds from cotton bolls, enabling the mass production of cotton in nineteenth-century America.

Almost overnight, the cotton gin made cotton America's most profitable cash crop, and in the process transformed southern agriculture and northern industry.

Cotton

During the first half of the nineteenth century, southern-grown **cotton** became the dominant force driving the national economy and the controversial efforts to expand slavery into the western territories. Cotton became so profitable that it was called "white gold"; it brought enormous wealth to southern planters and merchants as well as New England textile mill owners and New York shipowners. Until the nineteenth century, most clothing had been made of wool, linen, or silk. Cotton was a more comfortable fabric, but until the cotton "gin" was invented, it was much more expensive to produce. By 1812, because of the widespread use of cotton gins, the cost of producing cotton yarn had plunged by 90 percent. The spread of textile mills in Britain and Europe during the late eighteenth century created a rapidly growing global market for cotton. By the mid-nineteenth century, people worldwide were wearing more-comfortable and easier-to-clean cotton clothing. When British textile manufacturers chose the less brittle American cotton over the varieties grown in the Caribbean, Brazil, and India, the demand for southern cotton skyrocketed, as did its price. During the first half of the nineteenth century, cotton became America's largest export. By 1860, British textile mills were processing a billion pounds of cotton a year, 92 percent of which came from the American South. The commercial growing of cotton for world markets spread plantation slavery across the South, spurred the development of textile mills in New England, and expanded the shipping fleets of New York City.

Cotton first engulfed the Piedmont region of the Carolinas and Georgia, between the coast and the mountains. After the War of 1812, it migrated into the contested Indian lands to the west—Tennessee, Alabama, Florida, Mississippi, Louisiana, Arkansas, and Texas. New Orleans became a bustling port—and active slave market—because of the cotton being grown throughout the region and shipped down the Mississippi River. From the mid-1830s to 1860, cotton accounted for more than half of American exports. The South harvested raw cotton, and northern buyers and shipowners carried it to New England, Great Britain, and France, where textile mills spun the fiber into thread and fabric.

The Expansion of Slavery

Cotton is a labor-intensive crop, requiring 70 percent more labor than corn. While a person could pick as much as fifty pounds of cotton in a day, that same person working all day could separate barely one pound of fiber from seeds. With the invention of the cotton gin, the demand for cotton increased and southerners solved the labor problem by using lots of slaves to plant the fields and pick the cotton. As a result, the price of slaves soared with the price of cotton. As farmland in Maryland and Virginia lost its fertility after

cotton White fibers harvested from plants that made comfortable, easy-to-clean products, especially clothing; the most valuable cash crop driving the economy in nineteenth-century United States and Great Britain.

years of relentless tobacco planting, which strips soil of its nutrients, many whites shifted to growing corn and wheat (the climate in Maryland and Virginia was too cold for cotton). Many Virginia and Maryland planters sold their surplus slaves to work in the new cotton-growing areas in Alabama and Mississippi. Between 1790 and 1860, some 835,000 slaves were "sold south." In 1790, planters in Virginia and Maryland had owned 56 percent of all the slaves in the United States; by 1860, they owned only 15 percent. A new cotton farmer in Mississippi urged a friend in Kentucky to sell his farm and join him: "If you could reconcile it to yourself to bring your negroes to the Mississippi Territory, they would certainly make you a handsome fortune in ten years by the cultivation of Cotton." Slaves became so valuable that stealing slaves became a common problem in the southern states, especially Alabama and Mississippi.

> Cotton production expands slavery

Farming the West

The westward flow of planters and slaves to Alabama and Mississippi mirrored another migration through the Ohio Valley and the Great Lakes region, where Native Americans had been forcibly pushed westward. By 1860, more than half the nation's population lived west of the Appalachian Mountains. The fertile farmlands in the Midwest—Ohio, Michigan, Indiana, Illinois, and Iowa—drew farmers from the rocky hillsides of New England and the exhausted soils of Virginia. A new national land law of 1820 reduced the price of federal land. Even that was not enough for westerners, however. They demanded "preemption," the right of squatters (people who simply built a cabin and started farming without actually purchasing government land) to purchase land at the minimum price, and "graduation," the progressive reduction of the price of land that did not sell immediately.

Congress eventually responded to the land mania with two bills. Under the Preemption Act of 1830, squatters could get 160 acres at the minimum price of $1.25 per acre. Under the Graduation Act of 1854, prices of unsold lands were to be lowered in stages over thirty years.

Technology also enabled greater agricultural productivity. The development of effective iron plows (rather than wooden plows) greatly eased the backbreaking job of tilling the soil. In 1819, Jethro Wood of New York introduced an iron plow with separate parts that could be easily replaced when worn out or broken. Further improvements would follow, including Vermonter John Deere's steel plow (1837), whose sharp edges could cut through the tough prairie grass in the Midwest and the Great Plains. By 1845, Massachusetts alone had seventy-three plants making more than 60,000 plows per year. Most were sold to western farmers, illustrating the emergence of a national marketplace for goods and services made possible by the transportation revolution.

> Growth of commercial agriculture: Steel plows (1837) and mechanical reapers (1831)

Other technological improvements quickened the growth of commercial agriculture, whereby huge farms produced surplus for national and world markets. By the 1840s, new mechanical seeders had replaced the process of

McCormick's Reaping Machine This illustration appeared in the catalog of the Great Exhibition, held at the Crystal Palace in London in 1851. The plow eased the transformation of rough plains into fertile farmland, and the reaping machine accelerated farm production.

sowing seed by hand. Even more important, in 1831 twenty-two-year-old Virginian Cyrus Hall McCormick (1809–1884) invented a mechanical reaper pulled by horses to harvest wheat, a development as significant to the agricultural economy of the Midwest, Old Northwest, and Great Plains as the cotton gin was to the South. McCormick tinkered with his reaping machine for almost a decade. In 1847 the **McCormick reaper** began selling so fast that he moved to Chicago and built a manufacturing plant. Within a few years he had sold thousands of the giant farm machines, transforming the scale of commercial agriculture. Using a handheld sickle, a farmer could harvest a half acre of wheat a day; with a McCormick reaper, two people could work twelve acres a day. By reducing the number of workers needed, such new agricultural machines helped send displaced laborers to work on railroads and in textile mills, iron foundries, shoe factories, coal mines, oil fields, and other new industries in towns and cities.

Early Textile Manufacturers

Rise of the factory system: Steam-powered mills

While technological breakthroughs such as the cotton gin, mechanical harvester, and railroads had quickened agricultural development and created a national economy, other technology altered the economic landscape even more profoundly by giving rise to the factory system. Mills and factories were initially powered by water wheels and then by coal-fired steam engines that dramatically increased productivity. The shift from water power to steam as a source of energy is what enabled the growth of the textile industry (and industries of all types), initiating an industrial revolution destined to end Britain's domination of the world economy.

McCormick reaper Mechanical reaper invented by Cyrus Hall McCormick in 1831 that dramatically increased the production of wheat.

In 1800, the output of America's factories amounted to only one-sixth of Great Britain's production. The growth of American textile production was slow and faltering until Thomas Jefferson's embargo in 1807 stimulated the production of cloth made in America. By 1815, hundreds of textile mills in New England, New York, and Pennsylvania were producing thread, cloth, and clothing. By 1860, the output of America's factories would be a third and by 1880 two-thirds that of the British industrial economy.

After the War of 1812, British textile companies flooded American markets with cheap cotton cloth. Such "dumping" nearly killed the infant American textile industry by lowering the prices of thread and cloth. A delegation of New England mill owners traveled to Washington, D.C., to demand a federal tariff (tax) on imported cloth to deter the British from selling their cloth in the United States for less than the prices charged by American manufacturers. The efforts of the American mill owners to gain political assistance created a culture of industrial lobbying for Congressional tariff protection that continues to this day.

What the mill owners neglected to admit was that import tariffs hurt American consumers by forcing them to pay higher prices. Over time, as the Scotsman Adam Smith explained in his book on capitalism, *The Wealth of Nations* (1776), consumers not only pay higher prices for foreign goods as a result of tariffs, but they also pay higher prices for domestic goods, since businesses invariably take advantage of opportunities to raise the prices charged for their products. Tariffs helped "protect" American industries from foreign competition, but competition is the engine of innovation and efficiency in a capitalist economy. New England shipping companies opposed higher tariffs because they would reduce the amount of goods being sent across the Atlantic from Britain and Europe. Many southerners also opposed tariffs because of fears that Britain and France would retaliate with tariffs on American cotton and tobacco shipped to their ports. In the end, the New England mill owners won the political debate. Congress passed the Tariff of 1816, which placed a tax on imported cloth. Such tariffs were a major factor in the industrialization of America during the nineteenth century. By impeding foreign competition, they enabled American manufacturers to dominate the national marketplace.

> Import tariffs

The Lowell System

The factory system sprang full-blown upon the American scene at Waltham, Massachusetts, in 1813, when a group known as the Boston Associates constructed the first textile mill in which the processes of spinning yarn and weaving cloth by machinery (copied from English mills) were brought together under one roof. In 1822, the Boston Associates, led by Francis Cabot Lowell, developed another cotton mill at a village along the Merrimack River twenty-eight miles north of Boston, which they renamed Lowell. It soon became the model for mill towns throughout New England, often referred to as the **Lowell system**.

Lowell system Model New England factory communities that provided employees, mostly young women, with meals, a boardinghouse, moral discipline, and educational opportunities.

Technological Innovation and a National Marketplace

In the first half of the nineteenth century, technological innovations or improvements dramatically changed the economic landscape. They transformed the way Americans traveled, transported goods, farmed, and manufactured products. Indeed, by the 1830s what had once been a series of local markets loosely connected to each other had become a national market economy: farmers, manufacturers, financiers, publishers, and others could envision a single extensive, nationwide market through which to sell their products and increase their profits. But the rise of a national market economy did not create economic or social uniformity across the nation. Regional differences among the North, West, and South, already present, continued to grow. To examine this development, review the two charts below.

TECHNOLOGICAL INNOVATIONS AND IMPROVEMENTS

Transportation	Agriculture	Manufacturing
More extensive graded and paved roads (the Wilderness Road)	Mass production of cotton gins that mechanically separate seed from fiber	New and improved machinery to mass-produce standardized parts
More extensive canals (Erie Canal)	Mass production of steel plows that open up more land to cultivation	Use of coal-burning steam engines to power factories
Steamboats (powered by steam engines)	Mass production of mechanical reapers to harvest wheat	Vulcanization, a process that made rubber more durable
Railroads (powered by steam engines)		
Clipper ships that shorten the time of transoceanic travel and transportation		

REGIONAL ECONOMIC DEVELOPMENTS

North	West	South
Northeastern states underwent an industrial revolution. Factories, using new and improved machinery and steam engines, began mass producing textiles, shoes, iron, clocks, and guns for national consumption.	Western states' agriculture greatly expanded due to improvements in transportation. Steel plows opened up more land for production, and mechanical reapers vastly increased the productivity of individual farmers.	Southern states saw a vast expansion of the cotton plantation economy. The use of slaves to cultivate cotton, and the cotton gin to process the cotton, vastly increased the amount available for export.

QUESTIONS FOR ANALYSIS

1. How did technological innovations bring Americans together?

2. How did technological innovations create different regional patterns of economic development?

3. How did the emergence of a national market reinforce these different regional patterns?

The founders of the Lowell system had a much larger vision than just Lowell system improved industrial efficiency; they also sought to develop model industrial communities. To avoid the crowded, wretched life of the English textile-mill villages, they located their four- and five-story brick-built mills along rivers in the countryside. Factory workers at Waltham and Lowell were mostly young women aged 15 to 30 from farm families. Mill owners preferred to hire women because of their skill in operating machines and their willingness to stomach the mind-numbing boredom of operating spinning machines and looms for wages lower than those paid to men (even though their wages, $2–5 per week, were the highest in the world for women). Moreover, by the 1820s there was a surplus of women in New England because so many men had migrated westward in search of cheap land and new economic opportunities. In the early 1820s, a steady stream of single women began flocking toward Lowell to work in the mills. To reassure worried parents, the mill owners promised to provide the "Lowell girls" with tolerable work, prepared meals, comfortable boardinghouses (four girls to a room), moral discipline, and educational and cultural opportunities.

Initially the "Lowell idea" worked pretty much according to plan. The "Lowell girls" lived in dormitories staffed by housemothers who enforced church attendance and evening curfews. Despite thirteen-hour work days and five-and-a-half day workweeks (longer hours than those imposed upon prison inmates), some of the women found the time and energy to form study groups, publish a literary magazine, and attend lectures. The mill managers required bedtime curfews, church attendance, and only limited contact with men.

Mill girls Massachusetts mill workers of the mid-nineteenth century, photographed holding shuttles.

But Lowell soon lost its innocence as it grew—and as the owners accumulated "unbelievable profits." Greed led mill owners to produce too much cloth, which depressed prices. Wages were cut, and the pace of work was quickened. By 1834, the Lowell women began going on strike to protest the deteriorating working and living conditions. The mill owners were not pleased. They labeled the 1,500 striking women "ungrateful" and "unfeminine"—and tried to get rid of the strike's leaders. One mill manager reported that "we have paid off several of these Amazons & presume that they will leave town on Monday."

The economic success of the New England textile mills raises an obvious question: why didn't the South build its own mills close to the cotton fields to keep its profits in the region? A few mills did appear, but they struggled to find workers because white farmers resisted factory work, and planters refused to allow slaves to leave the fields. African Americans, it was assumed, could not work efficiently indoors, and cotton planters considered textile mills an inefficient use of their labor resources. Agricultural slavery had made them rich. Why should they change?

Industrialization, Cities, and the Environment

Rapid growth of cities

The rapid growth of commerce and industry spurred the growth of cities. Lowell's population in 1820 was 200. By 1830, it was 6,500 and ten years later had soared to 21,000. By 1840, there were thirty-two mills and factories in operation, and the once rural town of Lowell had become an industrial city—busy, grimy, and bleak. Other similar factory centers sprouted up across New England, displacing forests, farms, and villages while filling the air with smoke, noise, and stench. In addition, the profusion of dams—built to harness water to turn the mill wheels—flooded pastures and decimated fish populations, spawned urban growth that in turn polluted the rivers, and aroused intense local resentment. In 1859, farmers far upstream of the big Massachusetts textile factories tried to destroy a massive dam in Lake Village, New Hampshire, but their axes and crowbars caused little damage. By then, the Industrial Revolution could not be stopped. The textile system was not only transforming lives and property—it was reshaping nature as well.

Between 1820 and 1840, the number of Americans engaged in manufacturing increased 800 percent, and the number of city dwellers more than doubled. As Thomas Jefferson and other agrarians feared, the United States was rapidly becoming a global industrial power, second only to Great Britain, producing its own clothing and shoes, iron and engines. Between 1790 and 1860, the proportion of urban to rural populations grew from 3 percent to 16 percent. Because of their strategic locations along rivers flowing into the ocean, the Atlantic seaports of New York City, Philadelphia, Baltimore, and Boston remained the largest cities. New Orleans became the nation's fifth-largest city

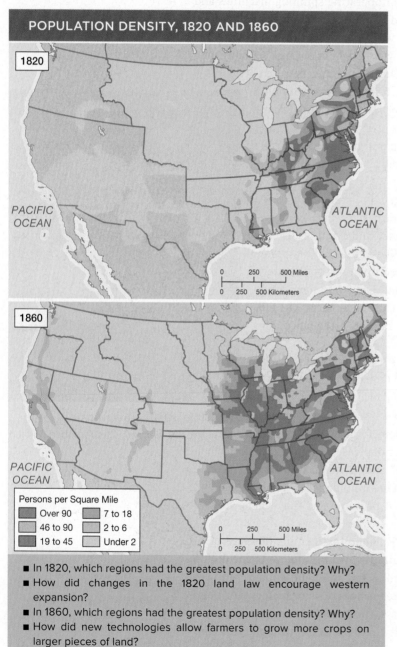

POPULATION DENSITY, 1820 AND 1860

1820

PACIFIC OCEAN

ATLANTIC OCEAN

0   250   500 Miles
0   250   500 Kilometers

1860

PACIFIC OCEAN

ATLANTIC OCEAN

Persons per Square Mile

Over 90 | 7 to 18
46 to 90 | 2 to 6
19 to 45 | Under 2

0   250   500 Miles
0   250   500 Kilometers

- In 1820, which regions had the greatest population density? Why?
- How did changes in the 1820 land law encourage western expansion?
- In 1860, which regions had the greatest population density? Why?
- How did new technologies allow farmers to grow more crops on larger pieces of land?

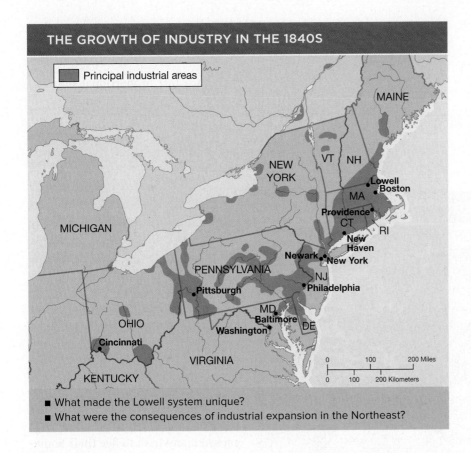

THE GROWTH OF INDUSTRY IN THE 1840S

Principal industrial areas

MAINE

VT NH

NEW YORK

MA

Lowell
Boston

Providence
CT

RI

MICHIGAN

New Haven

Newark
New York

PENNSYLVANIA

NJ

Pittsburgh

Philadelphia

MD

Baltimore

Washington

DE

OHIO

Cincinnati

VIRGINIA

0   100   200 Miles
0   100   200 Kilometers

KENTUCKY

- What made the Lowell system unique?
- What were the consequences of industrial expansion in the Northeast?

because of its role in shipping goods that were floated down the Mississippi River to the East Coast and to Europe. New York outpaced all its competitors in growth. By 1860, it was the first city to reach a population of more than 1 million, largely because of its superior harbor and its access to the commerce floating down the Hudson River from the Erie Canal.

Immigration

During the forty years from the outbreak of the Revolution to the end of the War of 1812, immigration had slowed to a trickle. The French Revolution and the Napoleonic Wars restricted travel to and from Europe until 1815. Thereafter, however, the number of immigrants to America rose steadily, and throughout the nineteenth century the United States remained a magnet for immigrants. People on ships packed with humanity arrived from all over the world, eager to experience the American Dream—the shimmering, seductive promise that in the United States everyone had a chance to become something else, something better. After 1837, a worldwide financial panic and economic slump accelerated the tempo of immigration to the

> CORE **OBJECTIVE**
> **3.** Analyze how immigration altered the nation's population and shaped its politics.

United States. American employers began aggressively recruiting foreigners, in large part because they were often willing to work for lower wages than Americans.

Massive increase in immigration

The years from 1845 to 1854 saw the greatest proportional influx of immigrants in U.S. history, 2.4 million, or about 14.5 percent of the total population in 1845. In 1860, America's population was 31 million, with more than one of every eight residents foreign born. British immigrants continued to arrive in the United States in large numbers during the first half of the nineteenth century. By the 1850s, the rapid development of California was also attracting the Chinese, and Scandinavians and Norwegians began immigrating and settling mostly in Wisconsin and Minnesota, where the climate and woodlands reminded them of home. But by far, the largest number of immigrants between 1840 and 1860 came from Ireland and Germany.

The Irish

A prolonged agricultural crisis that brought immense social hardships caused many Irish to flee their homeland in the mid-nineteenth century for North America. Irish farmers primarily grew potatoes; in fact, fully a third of the people were dependent on the potato harvest for survival. In 1845, an epidemic of potato fungus triggered what came to be called the Irish potato famine. The average adult male in Ireland ate five pounds of potatoes a day. So when the fungus destroyed the potato crop, more than a million people died, and almost two million more left Ireland, whose total population was eight million. Most of them traveled to Canada and the United States. As one group of exiles explained, "All we want to do is get out of Ireland; we must be better anywhere but here." America, they knew, had plenty of paying jobs and "plenty to eat."

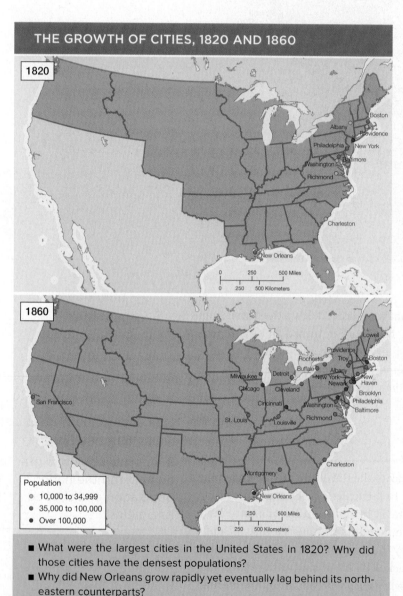

THE GROWTH OF CITIES, 1820 AND 1860

1820

1860

Population
- 10,000 to 34,999
- 35,000 to 100,000
- Over 100,000

- What were the largest cities in the United States in 1820? Why did those cities have the densest populations?
- Why did New Orleans grow rapidly yet eventually lag behind its northeastern counterparts?
- Why did Chicago, Pittsburgh, Cincinnati, and St. Louis become major urban centers in the mid-nineteenth century?

The Crow Quadrilles This sheet-music cover, printed in 1837, shows eight vignettes caricaturing African Americans. Minstrel shows enjoyed nationwide popularity while reinforcing racial stereotypes.

By the 1850s, the Irish made up more than half the population of Boston and New York City and were almost as dominant in Philadelphia. Most of them were crowded into filthy, poorly ventilated tenements (low-income urban apartment buildings) that were plagued by high crime rates, deadly diseases, prostitution, and alcoholism. The archbishop of New York described the Irish as "the poorest and most wretched population that can be found in the world." One Irishman lamented that he worked like "a slave for the Americans."

Irish immigrants confronted humiliating stereotypes and intense anti-Catholic prejudice. Many employers posted signs reading "No Irish Need Apply." Irish Americans, however, could be equally mean-spirited toward other groups, such as free African Americans, who competed with them for low-wage jobs. In 1850, the *New York Tribune* expressed concern that the Irish, having escaped from "a galling, degrading bondage" in their homeland, voted against proposals for equal rights for blacks and frequently arrived at the polls shouting, "Down with the Nagurs! Let them go back to Africa, where they belong." For their part, many African Americans viewed the Irish with equal contempt. In 1850, a slave expressed a common sentiment: "My Master is a great tyrant, he treats me badly as if I were a common Irishman."

But many enterprising Irish immigrants forged remarkable careers. Twenty years after arriving in New York, Alexander T. Stewart became the owner of the nation's largest department store and thereafter accumulated vast real estate holdings in Manhattan. Michael Cudahy, who began working at age fourteen in a Milwaukee meatpacking business, became head of the Cudahy Packing Company and developed a process for the curing of meats under refrigeration. Dublin-born Victor Herbert emerged as one of America's most revered composers, and Irish dancers and playwrights came to dominate the stage. Irishmen were equally successful in the boxing arena and on the baseball diamond. And it was Irish manual laborers who built much of nineteenth-century America, including the Erie Canal, much of the national railway network, and most of the relentless construction in the nation's rapidly expanding cities.

> **Irish immigration: Unskilled labor and the growth of Roman Catholicism**

Perhaps the greatest collective achievement of the Irish immigrants was stimulating the growth of the Roman Catholic Church in the United States. Years of persecution had instilled in Irish Catholics a fierce loyalty to the doctrines of the church as "the supreme authority over all the affairs of the world." Such passion for Catholicism generated both unity among Irish Americans and fear among American Protestants. By 1860, Roman Catholicism had become the largest denomination in the United States.

The Germans

> **German immigration: Skilled and diverse workers**

A new wave of German immigration peaked in 1854, just a few years after the crest of Irish arrivals, when 215,000 Germans arrived in U.S. ports. These immigrants included a large number of learned, cultured, professional people—doctors, lawyers, teachers, engineers—some of whom were refugees from the failed German revolution of 1848. In addition to an array of political opinions, the Germans brought with them a variety of religious preferences. Most of them were Protestants (usually Lutherans), a third were Roman Catholics, and a significant number were Jews. Among the German immigrants who prospered in the New World were Heinrich Steinweg, a piano maker who in America changed his name to Steinway and became famous for the quality of his instruments, and Levi Strauss, a Jewish tailor who followed the gold rush to California and began making work pants, later dubbed "Levi's."

Unlike the Irish, Germans settled more often in rural areas than in cities. Many were independent farmers, skilled workers, and shopkeepers who were able to establish themselves immediately. More so than the Irish, they migrated in families and groups. This clannish quality helped them better sustain elements of their language and culture in the New World. More of them also tended to return to their native country. About 14 percent of the Germans eventually went back to their homeland, compared with just 9 percent of the Irish.

Nativism

> **Nativism: Anti-Catholic violence**

Not all Americans welcomed the flood of immigrants. Many "nativists," people born in the United States, resented the newcomers, with their strange languages and customs, and sought to restrict or stop immigration altogether. The flood of Irish and German Catholics aroused Protestant hostility. There were also fears that German immigrants were bringing to America dangerous political ideas such as socialism and communism, and that the Irish were voting solely for the Democratic party. In 1844, armed clashes between Protestants and Catholics in Philadelphia caused widespread injuries and deaths.

Nativists pursued organized efforts to stop the tide of immigrants. The Order of the Star-Spangled Banner, founded in New York City in 1849, grew into a powerful new political organization known officially as the American party. Members pledged never to vote for any foreign-born or Catholic candidates. When asked about the secretive organization, they were told to say, "I know nothing," a phrase which gave rise to the informal name for the American party: the **Know-Nothing party**. For a while, the Know-Nothings appeared to be on the brink of major-party status. In the state and local campaigns of 1854, they carried one election after another. They swept the Massachusetts legislature, winning all but two seats in the lower house, and that fall they elected more than forty congressmen.

The Know-Nothings demanded that immigrants and Roman Catholics be excluded from public office and that the waiting period for naturalization (earning citizenship) be extended from five to twenty-one years, but the party never developed enough strength to enact such legislation. Nor did Congress restrict immigration in any way during that period. For a while, the Know-Nothings threatened to control New England, New York, and Maryland and showed strength elsewhere, but the anti-Catholic movement subsided when slavery became the focal issue of the 1850s.

> Nativism: The Know-Nothings

Organized Labor and New Professions

> CORE **OBJECTIVE**
> **4.** Evaluate the impact of the expanding "market economy" on workers, professionals, and women.

While most Americans continued to work as farmers during the nineteenth century, a growing number found employment in new or expanding enterprises: textile mills, shoe factories, banks, railroads, publishing, retail stores, teaching, preaching, medicine, law, construction, and engineering. Technological innovations (steam power, power tools, and new modes of transportation) and their social applications (mass communication, turnpikes, the postal service, banks, and corporations) fostered an array of new industries and businesses that transformed the nature of work for many Americans, both men and women.

Early Unions

Proud apprentices, journeymen, and master craftsmen, who controlled their labor and invested their work with an emphasis on quality rather than quantity, resented the spread of mills and factories populated by masses of "half-trained" workers, often young women as in the Lowell textile mills, dependent upon an hourly wage and subject to the sharp fluctuations of the larger economy. Skilled workers in American cities before and after the Revolution were called artisans, craftsmen, or mechanics. They made or

Nativists Native-born Americans who viewed immigrants as a threat to their job opportunities and way of life.

Know-Nothing party Nativist, anti-Catholic third party organized in 1854 in reaction to large-scale German and Irish immigration.

The shoe factory When Philadelphia shoemakers went on strike in 1806, a court found them guilty of a "conspiracy to raise wages." Here, shoemakers work in the bottoming room at a Massachusetts shoe factory.

repaired shoes, hats, saddles, silverware, jewelry, glass, ropes, furniture, and a broad array of other products. During the 1820s and 1830s, artisans who emphasized quality and craftsmanship found it hard to compete with the low prices made possible by the new factories and mass-production workshops.

In the early nineteenth century, a growing fear that they were losing status led artisans in the major cities to become involved in politics and unions. At first, these workers organized themselves into interest groups representing their individual skills or trades. Such "trade associations" were the first type of labor unions. They pressured politicians for tariffs to protect their industries from foreign imports, provided insurance benefits, and drafted regulations to improve working conditions. In addition, they sought to control the number of tradesmen in their profession so as to maintain wage levels.

Creation of National Trades' Union (1834)

Early labor unions faced major legal obstacles—in fact, they were prosecuted as unlawful conspiracies. In 1806, for instance, Philadelphia shoemakers were found guilty of conspiring "to raise their wages." The court's decision broke the union. In 1842, though, the Massachusetts Supreme Court issued a landmark ruling in *Commonwealth v. Hunt* declaring that forming a trade union was not in itself illegal, nor was a demand that employers hire only members of the union. The court also said that union workers could strike if an employer hired laborers who refused to join the union.

Until the 1820s, labor organizations took the form of local trade unions, each confined to one city and one craft or skill. From 1827 to 1837, however, organization on a larger scale began to take hold. In 1834 the **National Trades' Union** was formed to organize all of the citywide trade unions into a stronger national association. At the same time, shoemakers, printers, carpenters, and weavers established national craft unions. But all the national groups and most of the local ones vanished during the terrible economic depression in the late 1830s.

The Rise of the Professions

The dramatic social changes of the first half of the nineteenth century opened up an array of new **professions**. Bustling new towns required new services—retail stores, printing shops, post offices, newspapers, schools, banks, law firms, medical practices, and others—that created more high-status professions than had existed before. By definition, professional workers are those who have specialized knowledge and training. In 1849, Henry Day delivered a lecture on "The Professions" at the Western Reserve School of Medicine. He declared that the most important social functions in modern life were the professional skills. In fact, Day claimed, American society had become utterly dependent upon "professional services."

Teaching

Teaching was one of the fastest-growing vocations in the first half of the nineteenth century. Horace Mann of Massachusetts was instrumental in promoting the idea of free public education for all children as the best way to transform youths into disciplined, judicious republican citizens. Many states, especially in the North, agreed, and the number of schools exploded during the second quarter of the nineteenth century. New schools required teachers, and Horace Mann helped create "normal schools" around the nation to train young people to be teachers. Public schools initially preferred men as teachers, usually hiring them at age seventeen or eighteen. The pay was so low that few stayed in the profession their entire career, but for many educated, restless young adults, teaching offered independence and social status, as well as an alternative to the rural isolation of farming. Church groups and civic leaders started private academies, or seminaries, for girls.

Law, Medicine, and Engineering

Teaching was a common stepping-stone for men who became lawyers. In the decades after the Revolution, growing numbers of young men would teach for a year or two before joining an experienced attorney as an apprentice (what today would be called an *intern*). They would learn the practice of law in exchange for their labors. (There were no law schools in the first half of the nineteenth century.) The absence of formal standards for legal training helps explain why there were so many attorneys in the pre–Civil War period.

National Trades' Union Formed in 1834 to organize all local trade unions into a stronger national association; dissolved amid the economic depression in the late 1830s.

professions Occupations requiring specialized knowledge of a particular field; the Industrial Revolution and its new organization of labor created an array of professions in the nineteenth century.

Like attorneys, physicians in the early nineteenth century often had little formal academic training. Healers of every stripe assumed the title of *doctor* and established medical practices without regulation. Most were self-taught or had learned their profession by assisting a physician for several years, occasionally supplementing their internships with a few classes at the handful of medical schools. By 1860, there were 60,000 self-styled physicians, many of whom were "quacks" or frauds. As a result, the medical profession lost the public's confidence.

> **New professions for men: Lawyers, doctors, engineers**

The industrial expansion of the United States also spurred the profession of engineering, a field that would eventually become the nation's largest professional occupation for men. Specialized expertise was required for the design and construction of canals and railroads, the development of machine tools and steam engines, and the building of roads, bridges, and factories. By the outbreak of the Civil War, engineering had become one of the largest professions in the nation.

"Women's Work"

> **New professions for women: Teachers and nurses**

During the first half of the nineteenth century, despite the influx of young women into New England textile mills, most women still worked primarily in the home or on a farm. The only professions readily available to them were nursing (often midwifery, the delivery of babies) and school teaching. Many middle-class women spent their time outside the home doing religious and social-service work. Then as now, women were the backbone of most churches.

A few women, however, courageously pursued careers in male-dominated professions. Elizabeth Blackwell of Ohio managed to gain admission to Geneva Medical College (now Hobart and William Smith College) in western New York despite the disapproval of the faculty. When she arrived at her first class, a hush fell upon the students "as if each member had been struck with paralysis." Blackwell had the last laugh when she finished first in her class in 1849, but thereafter the medical school refused to admit any more women. The first American woman to earn a medical degree, Blackwell went on to start the New York Infirmary for Women and Children and later had a long career as a professor of gynecology at the London School of Medicine for Women.

Equal Opportunities

The dynamic market economy that emerged during the first half of the nineteenth century helped spread the idea that individuals should have an equal opportunity to better themselves in the workplace through their abilities and hard work. Equality of opportunity, however, did not assume equal outcomes. Americans wanted an equal chance to earn unequal amounts of wealth. In America, observed a journalist in 1844, "one has as good a chance as another according to his talents, prudence, and personal exertions." The same ideals that prompted so many white immigrants to risk everything to come to the United States, however, were equally appealing to those groups that still did not enjoy equal opportunities to pursue their American dream: African Americans and women. By the 1830s, they, too, began to demand their right to "life, liberty, and the pursuit of happiness." Such desires of "common people" to pursue economic opportunities would quickly spill over into the political arena. The great theme of political life in the first half of the nineteenth century would be the continuing democratization of opportunities for white men, regardless of income or background, to vote and hold office.

Reviewing the
CORE OBJECTIVES | INQUIZITIVE

■ **Transportation and Communication Revolutions** Canals and other improvements in transportation such as the *steamboat* that could be used on the nation's rivers and lakes allowed goods to reach markets more quickly and cheaply, helping to create a national *market economy* in which people bought and sold goods at larger distances. *Clipper ships* shortened the amount of time to transport goods across the oceans. The *railroads* (which expanded rapidly during the 1850s) and the *telegraph system* diminished the isolation of the West and united the country economically and socially. The *Erie Canal (1817)* contributed to New York City's emerging status as the nation's economic center even as it spurred the growth of Chicago and other midwestern cities. Improvements in transportation and communication linked rural communities to a worldwide marketplace.

■ **The Industrial Revolution** Inventions in machine tools and technology spurred an *Industrial Revolution* during the nineteenth century. The *cotton gin* dramatically increased cotton production, and a rapidly spreading *cotton* culture boomed in the South, with a resultant increase in slavery. Other inventions, such as John Deere's steel plow and the mechanized *McCormick reaper,* helped Americans, especially westerners, farm their land more efficiently and more profitably. In the North, mills and factories, at first water powered and eventually powered by coal-fired steam engines, spread rapidly. They initially produced textiles for clothing and bedding from southern cotton, as well as iron, shoes, and other products. The federal government's tariff policy encouraged the growth of domestic manufacturing, especially cotton textiles, by reducing imports of British cloth. Between 1820 and 1840, the number of Americans engaged in manufacturing increased 800 percent. Many mill workers, such as the women employed in the *Lowell system* of New England textile factory communities, worked long hours for low wages in unhealthy conditions. Industrialization, along with increased commerce, helped spur the growth of cities. By 1860, 16 percent of the population lived in urban areas.

■ **Immigration** The promise of cheap land and good wages drew millions of immigrants to America. By 1844, 14.5 percent of the population was foreign born. Many of those who arrived in the 1840s came not just from the Protestant regions of Northern Europe that had supplied most of America's previous immigrants. The devastating potato famine led to an influx of poor Irish Catholic families. By the 1850s, they represented a significant portion of the urban population in the United States, constituting a majority in New York and Boston. German migrants, many of them Catholics and Jews, migrated to the country at the same time. Not all native-born Americans welcomed the immigrants. *Nativists* became a powerful political force in the 1850s, with the *Know-Nothing party* nearly achieving major-party status with its message of excluding immigrants and Catholics from the nation's political community.

■ **Workers, Professionals, and Women** Skilled workers (artisans) in American cities had long formed trade associations to protect their members and to lobby for their interests. As the *Industrial Revolution* spread, some workers expanded these organizations nationally, forming the *National Trades' Union.* The growth of the *market economy* also expanded opportunities for those with formal education to serve in new or expanding *professions.* The number of physicians, teachers, engineers, and lawyers grew rapidly. By the mid-nineteenth century, women, African Americans, and immigrants began to agitate for equal social, economic, and political opportunities.

KEY TERMS

CHRONOLOGY

1793	Eli Whitney invents the cotton gin
1794	Philadelphia-Lancaster Turnpike is completed
1795	Wilderness Road opens
1807	Robert Fulton and Robert Livingston launch steamship transportation on the Hudson River in New York
1825	Erie Canal opens in upstate New York
1831	Cyrus McCormick invents a mechanical reaper
1834	National Trades' Union is organized
1837	John Deere invents the steel plow
1842	Massachusetts Supreme Judicial Court issues *Commonwealth v. Hunt* decision
1845	The *Rainbow*, the first clipper ship, is launched
1845	Irish Potato Famine
1846	Elias Howe invents the sewing machine
1848	California gold rush begins
1855	Know-Nothing party (American party) formed

INQUIZITIVE

Go to InQuizitive to see what you've learned—and learn what you've missed—with personalized feedback along the way.

PARADE OF THE VICTUALLERS (1821) On a beautiful day in March 1821, Philadelphia butcher William White organized a parade celebrating America's own high-quality meats. Many townspeople watched from their windows and balconies, while the spectators below could also enjoy the foods of various street vendors, such as the African American oyster peddler (bottom left). This watercolor by John Lewis Krimmel captures the new, vibrant nationalism that emerged in America after the War of 1812.

Nationalism and Sectionalism

1815–1828

After the War of 1812, the British navy stopped interfering with American shipping, and Americans were freed from British restrictions on their economic activities. The United States could now grow new industries and exploit new markets around the globe. It was not simply Alexander Hamilton's financial initiatives and the capitalistic energies of wealthy investors and speculators that sparked America's dramatic economic growth in the early nineteenth century. It was also the strenuous efforts of ordinary men and women who were willing to take risks, uproot families, use unstable paper money issued by unregulated local banks, purchase factory-made goods, and tinker with new machines and tools. In short, by 1828 the agrarian republic nestled along the Atlantic seaboard was poised to become a sprawling commercial nation connected by networks of roads and canals as well as regional economic relationships—all energized by a restless spirit of enterprise, experimentation, and expansion.

But for all of the energy and optimism exhibited by Americans after the war, the fundamental tension between *nationalism* and *sectionalism* remained: how to balance the particular issues and purely sectional concerns of the nation's three regions—North, South, and West—with the national interest? Each region (that is, each section) had different economic interests and political goals. Complicating the tensions between nationalists and sectionalists, some of whom changed their perspective over time, with sectionalists becoming nationalists and vice versa,

CORE
OBJECTIVES INQUIZITIVE

1. Analyze how the new spirit of nationalism that emerged after the War of 1812 affected economic policies and judicial decisions.

2. Summarize the issues and ideas that promoted sectional conflict during this era.

3. Explain the emergence of the "Era of Good Feelings" and the factors that led to its demise.

4. Identify the federal government's diplomatic accomplishments during this era, and analyze their impact.

5. Evaluate the influence of Andrew Jackson on national politics in the 1820s and the developments that enabled him to become president.

was the ongoing debate over the meaning of the U.S. Constitution and whether its language should be interpreted loosely or strictly. Some sectionalists were single-mindedly focused on promoting their region's priorities: shipping and commerce in the Northeast, slave-based agriculture in the South, low land prices and transportation improvements in the West. Nationalists, on the other hand, tried to find policies and offer proposals that would serve the interests of the nation as a whole. This required each region to compromise, to recognize that no single section could get all it wanted without threatening the survival of the nation. Of all the issues dividing the young American republic, the passions aroused by slavery proved to be the most difficult to resolve.

CORE **OBJECTIVE**

1. Analyze how the new spirit of nationalism that emerged after the War of 1812 affected economic policies and judicial decisions.

A New Nationalism

Postwar Nationalism and Economic Policy

After the War of 1812, Americans experienced a wave of patriotic excitement. They had won their independence from Britain for a second time. A surge of prosperity fed a widespread sense of optimism about the young nation's future. In his first message to Congress in late 1815, President James Madison revealed how much the challenges of the war, especially the weaknesses of the armed forces and the national economy, had changed his attitudes toward the role of the federal government. Now, he and other leading Republicans such as South Carolina's John C. Calhoun reversed themselves and acted like nationalists rather than states' rights sectionalists. They abandoned many of Thomas Jefferson's presidential policies (reducing the armed forces and opposing a national bank, for example) in favor of *economic* nationalism developed earlier by Federalists Alexander Hamilton and George Washington as a means of preserving political unity. Many Republicans such as Jefferson and Madison, once they were in charge of actually running the government, discovered that many of the Federalist policies, such as a strong national bank, were in fact wise. Madison, for example, now supported a larger army and navy, a national bank, and tariffs to protect American manufacturers from foreign competitors. "The Republicans have out-Federalized Federalism," one New Englander remarked after Madison's speech.

The Bank of the United States

After President Madison and congressional Republicans allowed the charter for the First Bank of the United States to expire, in 1811, the nation's finances fell into a muddle. States began chartering new local banks with little or no regulation, and their banknotes (paper money) flooded the economy with different currencies of uncertain value. Imagine trying to do business on a national basis when each state-chartered bank had its own currency, which often was not accepted by other banks or in other states.

In response to the growing financial turmoil and the financial problems that emerged during the war, Madison and most of the younger generation of Republicans swallowed their longstanding reservations about a powerful national bank. In 1816, Madison urged Congress to establish a **Second Bank of the United States** (B.U.S.). The B.U.S., which could establish branches throughout the states, was intended primarily to create a stable national currency that would promote economic growth. With the help of Clay and Calhoun, Congress created the new B.U.S., which, like its predecessor, was based in Philadelphia and was designated to hold and disburse all federal government funds.

Economic nationalism: New national bank and currency

A Protective Tariff

The long controversy with Great Britain over shipping rights convinced most Americans of the need to develop their own manufacturing sector in order to end their dependence on British goods. Efforts to develop American iron and textile industries, begun in New York and New England during the Embargo of 1807, which ended American trade with other nations, had accelerated during the War of 1812, since the war cut off American access to European goods. After the war ended, however, the British flooded American markets with their less-expensive products. Northern business leaders urged Congress to create federal tariffs to protect their infant industries from what they called "unfair" British competition. Congress responded by passing the **Tariff of 1816**, which placed a 20–25 percent tax on a long list of imported goods. Like so many government policies, tariffs benefited some regions (the Northeast) more than others (the South), thus worsening sectional tensions and grievances.

Economic nationalism: Tariff of 1816 and federal financing for "internal improvements"

Internal Improvements

The third major element of economic nationalism in the first half of the nineteenth century involved federal financing of **internal improvements**, which meant the construction of roads, canals, and harbors intended to benefit the flow of goods and people. During the War of 1812, American military leaders had also grown frustrated by the difficulty of moving troops through the western region. In 1803, when Ohio became a state, Congress had ordered that 5 percent of the money from land sales in the state would go toward building a National Road from the Atlantic coast into Ohio and westward. Construction finally began in 1811. The road was cleared eighty feet wide with a twenty-foot-wide, stone-paved strip down the middle. Originally called the Cumberland Road, it was the first interstate roadway financed by the federal government. By 1818 the road was open from Cumberland, Maryland, westward to Wheeling, Virginia (now West Virginia), where it crossed the Ohio River. By 1838 the road extended 600 miles farther westward to Vandalia, Illinois. By reducing transportation costs and opening up new markets, the National Road helped accelerate

Second Bank of the United States Established in 1816 after the first national bank's charter expired; it stabilized the economy by creating a sound national currency, by making loans to farmers, small manufacturers, and entrepreneurs, and by regulating the ability of state banks to issue their own paper currency.

Tariff of 1816 Taxes on various imported items, to protect America's emerging iron and textile industries from British competition.

internal improvements Construction of infrastructural projects intended to facilitate the flow of goods and people.

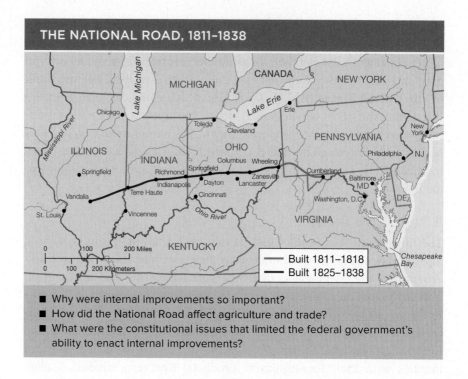

THE NATIONAL ROAD, 1811–1838

Built 1811–1818
Built 1825–1838

■ Why were internal improvements so important?
■ How did the National Road affect agriculture and trade?
■ What were the constitutional issues that limited the federal government's ability to enact internal improvements?

John Marshall A pillar of judicial nationalism, Marshall was appointed chief justice of the U.S. Supreme Court at the young age of forty-six, ruling on *Marbury v. Madison* just two years later.

the settlement of the West and the emergence of a truly national market economy, with the commercialization of agriculture, whereby farmers increasingly sold their produce and livestock to distant rather than merely local markets. But using federal money to finance such "internal improvements" remained controversial. Critics concerned about the expansion of federal power argued that the U.S. Constitution did not allow for such activities; only the local and state governments, or private investors, should fund road, canal, and harbor projects.

Postwar Nationalism and the Supreme Court

The postwar emphasis on nationalism also flourished in the Supreme Court, where Chief Justice John Marshall strengthened the constitutional powers of the federal government at the expense of states' rights. Marshall was a consistent nationalist. He viewed his cousin Thomas Jefferson and his Republican followers as a dangerous threat to the nation because they preferred states' rights over federal authority. During Marshall's early years on the Court (he served thirty-four years altogether), his judicial nationalism affirmed that the Supreme Court had the authority (and responsibility) to judge the constitutionality of state and federal legislative actions (oversight called *judicial review*). In *Marbury v. Madison* (1803) the Court had, for the first time, struck down a federal law as unconstitutional. In the cases of *Martin v. Hunter's Lessee* (1816) and *Cohens v. Virginia* (1821), the Court ruled

Sectional Conflict and Economic Policies

After the War of 1812, Congress created many policies that would arouse fierce debate over several decades. Policies regarding the monetary system, tariffs, and internal improvements ignited sectional conflict as people viewed specific policies as damaging to their varied regional interests.

Federal Initiative	Northeast Region Economy (manufacturing, shipping, investment, some commercial farming)	Southern Region Economy (plantation-based agriculture, esp. cotton cultivation)	Western Region Economy (commercial farming)	Congressional Action
Protective Tariff	Opposed by shippers Supported by manufacturers	Opposed	Supported	Tariff of 1816 passed
National Bank	Generally supported	Generally opposed	Intensely opposed, due to Western shortage of hard currency	Second Bank of the United States created
Internal Improvements	Opposed	Opposed	Supported	National Road is built

QUESTIONS FOR ANALYSIS

1. How were the regions diverging economically?

2. How did the different economies in each section shape their support or opposition to the tariff, the Bank of the United States, and federally financed internal improvements?

3. How did sectional conflict affect politics at the national level?

4. Which policies did Congress enact and sustain? Which proved more difficult to pursue?

that the U.S. Constitution, as well as the laws and treaties of the United States, could remain the supreme law of the land only if the Court could review the decisions of state courts.

Protecting Contract Rights

Judicial nationalism: *Dartmouth College v. Woodward* (1819)

In the fateful year of 1819, the Supreme Court made two more major decisions that limited the powers of states and strengthened the power of the federal government. One of them, ***Dartmouth College v. Woodward***, involved an attempt by the New Hampshire legislature to alter a provision in Dartmouth College's charter under which the college's trustees elected their own successors. In 1816 the state's Republican legislature, offended by the Federalist majority on the college's board, placed Dartmouth under a new board of trustees named by the governor. The college's original group of trustees sued to block the move. They lost in the state courts but won on appeal to the Supreme Court. The college's original charter, wrote John Marshall in drafting the Court's opinion, was a valid contract that the state legislature had violated, an act forbidden by the Constitution. This decision implied a new and enlarged definition of *contract* that seemed to put corporations beyond the reach of the states that had chartered them. Thereafter, states commonly wrote into the charters incorporating businesses and other organizations provisions making them subject to state oversight. Such provisions were then part of the "contract."

Protecting A National Currency

Judicial nationalism: *McCulloch v. Maryland* (1819)

The second major Supreme Court case of 1819 was Marshall's single most important interpretation of the constitutional system: ***McCulloch v. Maryland***. James McCulloch, a clerk in the Baltimore branch of the federal Bank of the United States, had refused to apply state taxes to B.U.S. currency, as required by a Maryland law. Indicted by the state, McCulloch, acting for the bank, appealed to the Supreme Court, which handed down a unanimous judgment upholding the power of Congress to charter the B.U.S. and denying the state's right to tax it. In a lengthy opinion, Chief Justice Marshall said that Maryland's effort to tax the national bank conflicted with the supreme law of the land. One great principle that "entirely pervades the Constitution," Marshall wrote, is "that the Constitution and the laws made in pursuance thereof are supreme: . . . They control the Constitution and laws of the respective states, and cannot be controlled by them." The effort by a state to tax a federal bank therefore was unconstitutional, for the "power to tax involves the power to destroy"—which was precisely what the legislatures of Maryland and several other states had in mind with respect to the national bank. The Marshall court ruled that Congress had the right (that is, one of its "implied powers") to take any action not forbidden by the Constitution as long as the purpose of such laws was within the "scope of the Constitution."

***Dartmouth College v. Woodward* (1819)** Supreme Court ruling that enlarged the definition of *contract* to put corporations beyond the reach of the states that chartered them.

***McCulloch v. Maryland* (1819)** Supreme Court ruling that declared it unconstitutional for states to tax the Bank of the United States.

***Gibbons v. Ogden* (1824)** Supreme Court case that gave the federal government the power to regulate interstate commerce.

***Steamboat Travel on the Hudson River* (1811)** This watercolor of an early steamboat was painted by a Russian diplomat, Pavel Petrovich Svinin, who was fascinated by early techological innovations and the unique culture of America.

Regulating Interstate Commerce

John Marshall's last great judicial decision, ***Gibbons v. Ogden*** (1824), established the federal government's supremacy in regulating interstate commerce. In 1808, the New York legislature granted Robert Fulton and Robert R. Livingston the exclusive right to operate steamboats on the state's rivers and lakes. Fulton and Livingston then gave Aaron Ogden the exclusive right to ferry people and goods up the Hudson River between New York and New Jersey. Thomas Gibbons, however, operated ships under a federal license that competed with Ogden. On behalf of a unanimous Court, Marshall ruled that the monopoly granted by the state to Ogden conflicted with the federal license issued to Gibbons.

Thomas Jefferson detested John Marshall's judicial nationalism. The Court's ruling in the *Gibbons* case, said the eighty-two-year-old former president, revealed how "the Federal branch of our Government is advancing towards the usurpation of all the rights reserved to the States, and the consolidation in itself of all powers, foreign and domestic."

> Judicial nationalism: *Gibbons v. Ogden* (1824)

Debates over the American System

The major economic initiatives debated by Congress after the War of 1812— the national bank, federal tariffs, and federally-financed roads and canals— were interrelated pieces of a comprehensive economic plan to strengthen

> CORE **OBJECTIVE**
> **2.** Summarize the issues and ideas that promoted sectional conflict during this era.

and unify the nation called the **American System**. The term was coined by Republican Henry Clay, the powerful Congressional leader from Kentucky who would serve three terms as Speaker of the House before becoming a U.S. senator Clay was a leading *nationalist*. He insisted that "I know of no South, no North, no East, no West to which I owe my allegiance. The Union is my country." Clay saw in the American System a way for the United States to become independent of the British economically while tying together the diverse regions of the nation politically.

In promoting the American System, Clay sought to give each region or section of the country its top economic priority. He argued that high tariffs on imports were needed to block the sale of British products in the United States in order to protect fragile new American industries from unfair foreign competition. To convince the skeptical western states to support the tariffs wanted by New England manufacturers, Clay called for the federal government to use tariff revenues to build much-needed infrastructure in the frontier West: roads, canals, and other "internal improvements" were desperately needed to enable speedier travel and the shipment of goods. Second, Clay's American System would raise prices for the purchase of federal lands and "distribute" the additional revenue to the states to help finance more roads, bridges, and canals. Third, Clay endorsed a strong national bank to create a single national currency and to regulate the often unstable state and local banks.

Clay was the era's supreme political deal-maker and economic nationalist. In many respects, he assumed responsibility for sustaining Alexander Hamilton's vision of a strong federal government nurturing a diversified national economy that combined agriculture, industry, and commerce. The debates over the merits of the American System would continue throughout the first half of the nineteenth century. The success of Clay's program depended on each section's willingness to compromise in order to maintain national unity. For a while, it worked.

The much-discussed American System aroused both widespread support and intense opposition. Critics argued that higher prices for federal lands would discourage western migration and that tariffs benefited the northern manufacturing sector at the expense of southern and western farmers and the "common" people, who had to pay higher prices for the goods produced by tariff-protected industries. Many westerners and southerners also feared that the Philadelphia-based Second Bank of the United States would become so powerful that it could dictate the nation's economic future at the expense of states' rights and the needs of particular sections of the nation. Missouri senator Thomas Hart Benton predicted that cash-strapped western towns would now be at the mercy of a powerful national bank in Philadelphia. The West, he feared, would be "devoured" by the East and its national banking system. Westerners, Benton worried, "are in the jaws of the monster! A lump of butter in the mouth of a dog! One gulp, one swallow, and all is gone!"

Regional differences over the American System

American System Economic plan championed by Henry Clay of Kentucky that called for federal tariffs on imports, a strong national bank, and federally-financed internal improvements—roads, bridges, canals—all intended to strengthen the national economy and end American dependence on Great Britain.

The bitter debate over the B.U.S. helped set the pattern of deepening sectional disputes among the North, South, and West on the economic issues associated with Henry Clay's American System. Support for federal spending on internal improvements came largely from the West, which badly needed good roads, bridges, canals, and port facilities to connect its economy to the other regions. Many New Englanders and southerners opposed the use of federal money to finance transportation projects in the West, arguing that such projects should be paid for by the states. On his last day in office, in 1817, President Madison vetoed a bill that would have funded more internal improvements because he could not find a provision in the Constitution authorizing such federal expenditures. Nor was he willing to claim that such funding was an "implied power" within the Constitution. As a result, internal improvements remained, with few exceptions, the responsibility of the states for another hundred years. The federal government did not enter the field again on a large scale until passage of the Federal Highways Act of 1916.

In championing his American System, Henry Clay was forced to resolve explosive sectional conflicts over slavery in the western territories and states. Many of the Americans pouring across the Appalachian Mountains took with them a commitment to cotton production and the slave system that supported it. The possibility of new western states becoming "slave states" created the greatest political controversy of the nineteenth century. Former president Thomas Jefferson admitted that the issue scared him "like a firebell in the night." It "awakened and filled me with terror. I considered it at once as the knell of the Union." Jefferson realized that the United States, which he and others had worked so hard to create and nurture, was increasingly at risk of disintegrating over the future of slavery, the explosive issue that no longer could be avoided. And like Thomas Jefferson, Henry Clay lived with the daily contradiction of being a slave owner opposed to the expansion of slavery.

> Conflict over extending slavery into the western states

"Era of Good Feelings"

James Monroe

As James Madison approached the end of his presidency, he, as Thomas Jefferson had done before him, turned to a fellow Virginian, another secretary of state, to be his successor. For Madison that man was James Monroe, who went on to win the Republican nomination. In the 1816 election, Monroe overwhelmed his Federalist opponent, Rufus King of New York, with 183 to 34 votes in the Electoral College. The "Virginia dynasty" of presidents continued.

Like George Washington, Thomas Jefferson, and James Madison, Monroe was a slaveholding Virginia planter. At the outbreak of the Revolutionary War, he was beginning his studies at the College of William and Mary. He

> CORE **OBJECTIVE**
> **3.** Explain the emergence of the "Era of Good Feelings" and the factors that led to its demise.

James Monroe Portrayed as he began his presidency in 1817.

joined the army at the age of sixteen, served under George Washington during the Revolution, and later studied law with Jefferson. Washington called him a "brave, active, and sensible army officer."

Tall, blue-eyed James Monroe was eminently qualified to be president. He had served as a representative in the Virginia assembly, as governor of the state, as a representative in the Confederation Congress, as a U.S. senator, and as U.S. minister (ambassador) to Paris, London, and Madrid. Under President Madison, he served as secretary of state and doubled as secretary of war. South Carolina's John C. Calhoun, who would serve as Monroe's secretary of war, said that the new president was "among the wisest and most cautious men I have ever known." Thomas Jefferson was even more lavish with his praise. He noted that Monroe was "a man whose soul might be turned wrong side outwards without discovering a blemish to the world."

Monroe's administration began with the nation at peace and its economy flourishing. A Boston newspaper said the new president's arrival in office coincided with an "Era of Good Feelings" and the label became a popular catchphrase for the strong economy and political good will during Monroe's administration. In 1820 Monroe would be re-elected without opposition; by then, the Federalists were so weak that they did not even put up a candidate. The Republican party was dominant.

The nationalist priorities during the so-called Era of Good Feelings did not last long, however, for sectional loyalties continued to battle with national perspectives. Two crucial events signaled the end of the Era of Good Feelings and warned of stormy times ahead: the financial Panic of 1819 and the political conflict over statehood for Missouri.

The Panic of 1819

End of Era of Good Feelings: Collapse of cotton prices

The financial **Panic of 1819** was caused by the sudden collapse of cotton prices after British textile mills quit buying high-priced American cotton—the nation's leading export—in favor of cheaper cotton from other parts of the world, especially Egypt and India. The collapse of cotton prices was especially devastating for southern planters, but it also reduced the world demand for other American goods. New American factory owners struggled to find markets for their goods and to fend off more-experienced foreign competitors. The financial panic thus renewed sectional tensions between northern and southern economic interests.

Other factors caused the financial panic to become a prolonged economic recession. Business owners, farmers, and land speculators had recklessly borrowed money to fuel their business ventures. In many cases, land speculators had purchased large tracts of government land, paying only a fourth of the full cost, and then sold the parcels to settlers with the understanding that they would pay the remaining installments. With the collapse of crop prices and the decline of land values during and after 1819, both speculators and settlers saw their income plummet.

Panic of 1819 A financial panic that began a three-year economic crisis triggered by reduced demand in Europe for American cotton, declining land values, and reckless practices by local and state banks.

The equally reckless lending practices of the numerous new state banks compounded the economic confusion. To generate more loans, the banks issued more paper money. Even the Second Bank of the United States, which was supposed to bring financial stability to the nation, was caught up in the easy-credit mania. In 1819 newspapers revealed a case of extensive fraud and embezzlement in the Baltimore branch of the Bank of the United States. The disclosure prompted the appointment of Langdon Cheves, a former congressman from South Carolina, as the new president of the B.U.S. Cheves rescued the bank from near ruin, but only by putting pressure on state banks to keep more gold coins in their vaults to back up the loans they were making. State banks in turn put pressure on their debtors, who found it harder to renew old loans or to get new ones. The economic depression lasted about three years, and many people blamed the B.U.S. After the panic passed, resentment of the national bank lingered, especially in the South and the West.

End of the Era of Good Feelings: Financial Panic of 1819

The Missouri Compromise

As the financial panic deepened into a depression, another cloud appeared on the horizon: the onset of a fierce sectional controversy between North and South over expanding slavery into the new western territories. By 1819 the United States had an equal number of slave and free states—eleven of each. The Northwest Ordinance (1787) had banned slavery north of the Ohio River, and the Southwest Ordinance (1790) had authorized slavery south of the Ohio. In the vast region west of the Mississippi River, however, no move had been made to extend the dividing line across the vast Louisiana Territory, where slavery had existed since the days when France and Spain first colonized the area. At the time, the Missouri Territory encompassed all of the Louisiana Purchase except the state of Louisiana and the Arkansas Territory. The old French town of St. Louis became the funnel through which settlers, largely southerners who brought their slaves with them, rushed westward beyond the Mississippi River.

In 1819, residents in the Missouri Territory asked the House of Representatives, where members from free states outnumbered those from slave states, to approve legislation enabling them to draft a constitution and apply for statehood, its population having passed the minimum of 60,000 white settlers. At that point, Representative James Tallmadge Jr., a New York Republican, stunned Congress by proposing a resolution banning the transport of any more slaves into Missouri. Tallmadge's resolution enraged southern slave owners, many of whom had developed a profitable trade selling slaves to be taken out west. Any effort to restrict slavery in the western territories, southern congressmen threatened, could lead to "disunion" and civil war. In addition, southerners worried that the addition of Missouri as a free state would tip the balance in the Senate against the slave states. After fiery debates, the House, with its northern majority, passed

End of the Era of Good Feelings: Tallmadge Amendment

THE MISSOURI COMPROMISE, 1820

- Free states
- Slave states
- States and territories covered by the compromise

- What caused the sectional controversy over slavery in 1819?
- What were the terms of the Missouri Compromise?
- What was Henry Clay's solution to the Missouri constitution's ban on free blacks in that state?

End of the Era of Good Feelings: Missouri Compromise

the Tallmadge Amendment on an almost strictly sectional vote. The Senate, however, rejected it—similarly along sectional lines.

At about the same time, Maine, which had been part of Massachusetts, applied for statehood. The Senate decided to link Maine's request for statehood with Missouri's, voting to admit Maine as a free state and Missouri as a slave state, thus maintaining the key political balance between free and slave states. Illinois senator Jesse Thomas further extended the so-called **Missouri Compromise** by introducing an amendment to exclude slavery in the rest of the Louisiana Purchase north of latitude 36°30′, Missouri's southern border. Slavery thus would continue in the Arkansas Territory and in the new state of Missouri but would be excluded from the remainder of the sprawling area west of the Mississippi River. By a close vote, the Thomas Amendment passed the House on March 2, 1820.

Then another problem arose. The pro-slavery faction that dominated Missouri's constitutional convention inserted in the proposed state constitution a ban on free blacks and mulattoes (mixed-race people) from residing in the state. This clearly violated the U.S. Constitution. Free blacks were already citizens of many states, including the slave states of North Carolina and Tennessee.

Missouri Compromise (1820) Legislative decision to admit Missouri as a slave state while prohibiting slavery in the area west of the Mississippi River and north of the parallel 36°30′.

The renewed controversy threatened to unravel the deal to admit Missouri as a state until Speaker of the House Henry Clay formulated a "second" Missouri Compromise whereby Missouri's admission as a state would depend upon assurances from its legislature that it would never deny free blacks their constitutional rights. The Missouri legislature approved Clay's suggestion but denied that it had any power to bind the people of the state to the pledge. On August 10, 1821, Missouri became the twenty-fourth state, and the twelfth where slavery was allowed.

Nationalists praised the Missouri Compromise for resolving difficult issues that threatened the stability of the Union. But the ferocity of the debate over the extension of slavery revealed that the compromise had settled little. Sectionalism erupted even within the president's cabinet. President Monroe, a Virginian, insisted that any effort to restrict the spread of slavery violated the spirit if not the language of the Constitution. His secretary of state, the future president John Quincy Adams of Massachusetts, disliked the Missouri Compromise for the opposite reason: because it sustained the Constitution's immoral "bargain between freedom and slavery." A great divide was widening between the nation's two sections: the North dominated by shipping, commerce, manufacturing, and small farms, the South becoming more and more dependent on cotton and slavery.

Henry Clay of Kentucky Clay entered the Senate at twenty-eight, despite the requirement that senators be at least thirty years old. Here, Clay is pictured on a fifty-dollar bill issued in the 1860s.

Nationalist Diplomacy

The efforts of Henry Clay to promote economic nationalism and John Marshall to affirm *judicial* nationalism were reinforced by efforts to practice *diplomatic* nationalism. John Quincy Adams, the secretary of state in the Monroe administration and the son of former president John Adams, aggressively exercised America's growing power abroad so as to clarify and expand the nation's boundaries. He also wanted to establish the nation's dominance in the Western Hemisphere. He thus supported the efforts of Spain's remaining colonies to declare their independence and form their own republics modeled after the American example.

Relations with Britain

The Treaty of Ghent had ended the War of 1812, but it left unsettled several remaining disputes between the United States and Great Britain. American statesmen were eager to resolve those disputes in ways that would reinforce economic nationalism. During James Monroe's presidency, John Quincy Adams oversaw the negotiations of two important treaties, the Rush-Bagot Agreement of 1817 (named after the diplomats who arranged it) and the Convention of 1818, both of which eased tensions with Great Britain. In the Rush-Bagot Agreement, the two nations agreed to limit the number of warships on the Great Lakes between Canada and the United States. The Convention of

> CORE **OBJECTIVE**
> **4.** Identify the federal government's diplomatic accomplishments during this era, and analyze their impact.

> The Rush-Bagot Agreement of 1817 and the Convention of 1818

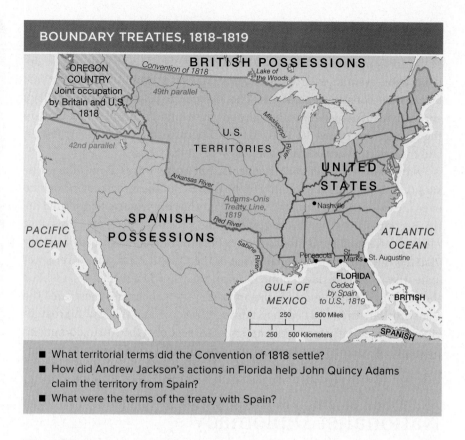

BOUNDARY TREATIES, 1818–1819

- What territorial terms did the Convention of 1818 settle?
- How did Andrew Jackson's actions in Florida help John Quincy Adams claim the territory from Spain?
- What were the terms of the treaty with Spain?

1818 finally settled the disputed northern limit of the Louisiana Purchase by extending America's northern boundary along the 49th parallel westward from what would become Minnesota to the crest of the Rocky Mountains. West of that point, the Oregon Country would be jointly occupied by the British and the Americans, though the boundary remained unsettled.

The Extension of Boundaries

The heightened sense of American nationalism after the War of 1812 revealed itself in continuing efforts to expand the nation's boundaries. Spanish control over Florida during the early nineteenth century was more a technicality than an actuality. Spain, once dominant in the Americas and the world, was now a declining power, unable to enforce its obligations under Pinckney's Treaty of 1795 to keep Indians in the region from raids into American territory. In 1816, U.S. soldiers clashed with a group of escaped slaves who had taken over a British fort (renamed Negro Fort) on the Apalachicola River in West Florida, in the present-day Florida Panhandle. At the same time, Seminole Indians were fighting white settlers in the area. In 1817, Americans burned a Seminole village on the border, killed five Indians, and dispersed the rest.

At that point, Secretary of War John C. Calhoun ordered federal troops to crush the Seminoles. To do so, he summoned General Andrew Jackson from

Massacre of the Whites by Indians and Blacks in Florida (1836) Published in a southerner's account of the Seminole War, this is one of the earliest known depictions of African Americans and Native Americans fighting as allies.

Nashville, Tennessee, to lead an army into Florida. Jackson's orders allowed him to pursue Indians into Spanish territory but not to attack any Spanish forts. A frustrated Jackson pledged to President Monroe that if the United States wanted Spanish Florida, he could conquer it in sixty days.

When it came to Spaniards or Indians, few white Tennesseans—and certainly not Jackson, the hero of the Battle of New Orleans—bothered with legal technicalities. In early 1818, without presidential approval, General Jackson ordered his force of 2,000 federal soldiers, volunteer Tennessee militiamen, and Indian allies among the Creeks to cross into Spanish Florida from their encampment in south Georgia. In April, the Americans assaulted a Spanish fort at St. Marks and destroyed several Seminole villages along the Suwannee River. They also captured and court-martialed British traders accused of provoking Indian attacks. When told that a military trial of the British citizens was illegal, Jackson gruffly replied that the laws of war did not "apply to conflicts with savages." Jackson ordered the immediate execution of the British traders, an illegal action that angered the British government and alarmed Monroe's cabinet. But the Tennessee general kept moving. In May, he captured Pensacola, the Spanish capital of West Florida, and established a provisional American government.

While Jackson's military exploits in what came to be called the Seminole War excited American expansionists, they aroused resentment in Spain and concern in Washington, D.C. Spain demanded that its territory be returned and that Jackson be punished. Monroe's cabinet was at first prepared to disavow Jackson's illegal acts, especially his direct attack on Spanish posts. Privately, Secretary of War Calhoun criticized Jackson for disobeying orders—a stand that would later cause bad blood between these two proud men. But Jackson was highly popular with the public. He also had an important friend, Secretary of State John Quincy Adams. Adams realized that Jackson's conquest of Florida had strengthened his own hand

Andrew Jackson
The controversial general was painted by Anna Claypoole Peale in 1819, the year of his military exploits in Florida. The niece of famed portraitist Charles Willson Peale, she captures the confident demeanor that made Jackson so popular with the public.

in negotiating with the Spanish minister to purchase the territory. American forces withdrew from Florida, but negotiations resumed with the knowledge that the U.S. Army could retake Florida at any time.

With the fate of Florida a foregone conclusion, Adams turned his eye to a larger goal: a precise definition of the western boundary of the Louisiana Purchase and—his boldest stroke—extension of its boundary all the way to the Pacific coast. In lengthy negotiations with Spain, Adams gradually gave ground on American claims to Texas, then a province of New Spain. But in the final version of the deal, he stuck to his demand that the boundary of the Louisiana Purchase extend all the way to the Pacific Ocean. In 1819, Adams convinced the Spanish to sign the **Transcontinental Treaty** (also called the Adams-Onís Treaty), which gave all of Florida to the United States in return for the U.S. government paying $5 million to settle claims of American citizens against the Spanish government. Florida thus became a U.S. territory. In 1845, it would become a state. The treaty also clarified the western boundary separating the Louisiana Territory from New Spain, explaining that it would run from the Gulf of Mexico north along the Sabine River separating Louisiana from Texas and then in stair-step fashion up to the Red River, along the Red, and up to the Arkansas River. From the source of the Arkansas it would go north to the forty-second parallel and then west to the Pacific coast.

The Monroe Doctrine

Perhaps the most important diplomatic policy crafted by President James Monroe and Secretary of State John Quincy Adams was a determined effort to end all European colonialism in the Western Hemisphere. The Spanish, British, French, Portuguese, Dutch, and Russians still controlled one or more colonies. One consequence of the Napoleonic Wars raging across Europe and the French occupation of Spain and Portugal was a series of independence movements among the Spanish colonies. Within little more than a decade after the flag of rebellion was first raised in 1809 in Ecuador, Spain had lost almost its entire empire in the Americas: La Plata (later Argentina), Bolivia, Chile, Ecuador, Peru, Colombia, Mexico, Paraguay, Uruguay, and Venezuela had all proclaimed their independence, as had Portuguese Brazil, and the United States was the first nation in the world to recognize them as new nations. The only areas still under Spanish control were the islands of Cuba and Puerto Rico and the colony of Santo Domingo on the island of Hispaniola.

In 1823, rumors circulated that the monarchs of Europe were planning to help Spain recover its Latin American colonies by military force. The British foreign minister, George Canning, told the United States that the two countries should jointly oppose any new incursions by Spain, France, and Russia in the Western Hemisphere. Monroe initially agreed with the British proposal—if the London government would agree to recognize the independence of the new nations of Latin America. Adams, however, urged the president to go it

Transcontinental Treaty (1819)
Treaty between Spain and the United States that clarified the boundaries of the Louisiana Purchase and arranged for the transfer of Florida to the United States in exchange for cash.

alone in prohibiting European involvement in the hemisphere. Adams knew that, as a practical matter, the British navy would stop any aggressive action by European powers in Latin America. The British, moreover, wanted the United States to agree not to acquire any more Spanish territory, including Cuba. Adams preferred to avoid any such commitment.

Monroe incorporated the substance of Adams's views into his annual message to Congress in December 1823. The **Monroe Doctrine**, as it was named a generation later, contained four major points: (1) that "the American continents . . . are henceforth not to be considered as subjects for future colonization by any European powers"; (2) that the political system of the European monarchies was different from that of the United States, which would "consider any attempt on their part to extend their system to any portion of this hemisphere as dangerous to our peace and safety"; (3) that the United States would not interfere with existing European-controlled colonies; and (4) that the United States would keep out of the internal affairs of European nations and their wars.

Monroe Doctrine (1823)

Although the Monroe Doctrine was a dramatic assertion of American nationalism and became one of the cherished principles of American foreign policy, it had no standing in international law; it was merely a bold statement sent by an American president to Congress. Certainly, none of the European nations recognized the legitimacy of the Monroe Doctrine. The Russian ruler, czar Alexander I, viewed it with "profound contempt." The Russians then controlled Alaska and claimed to own the Oregon Territory as well. Symbolically, however, the Monroe Doctrine was an important statement of American intentions to prevent European involvement in the Western Hemisphere and an example of the young nation's determination to take its place among the world's great powers.

The Rise of Andrew Jackson

America had become a one-party political system after the War of 1812. The refusal of the Federalists to support the war effort against Great Britain had virtually killed the party. In 1820 Monroe was reelected without opposition; the Federalists were so weak they did not even nominate a candidate. While the Republican party was dominant for the moment, however, it was about to follow the Federalists into oblivion. If Monroe's first term was the Era of Good Feelings, his second term became the Era of Bad Feelings, as sectional controversies among the North, South, and West erupted into disputes so violent that they gave birth to a new political party: the Democrats.

One-Party Politics

Almost from the start of James Monroe's second term, in 1821, leading Republicans began positioning themselves to be the next president. Three members of the president's cabinet became active candidates: Secretary of

CORE **OBJECTIVE**

5. Evaluate the influence of Andrew Jackson on national politics in the 1820s and the developments that enabled him to become president.

Monroe Doctrine (1823) U.S. foreign policy that barred further colonization in the Western Hemisphere by European powers and pledged that there would be no American interference with any existing European colonies.

War John C. Calhoun, Secretary of the Treasury William H. Crawford, and Secretary of State John Quincy Adams. Speaker of the House Henry Clay also hungered for the presidency. And a new force appeared in former general Andrew Jackson, a celebrated military hero and the hated enemy of the British, Spanish, Red Stick Creeks, and Seminoles. Jackson had only recently entered the national political scene, having been elected to the U.S. Senate from Tennessee in 1823. The emergence of four strong Republican candidates revealed how fractured the party had become.

Presidential Nominations

In 1822, the Tennessee legislature named Jackson as its choice to succeed President Monroe. Two years later, a mass meeting of Pennsylvanians also endorsed Jackson for president and John C. Calhoun for vice president. Meanwhile, the Kentucky legislature had nominated its favorite son, Henry Clay, in 1822. The Massachusetts legislature nominated John Quincy Adams in 1824. That same year, a group of Republican congressmen nominated William Crawford of Georgia.

Crawford's friends emphasized his devotion to states' rights and strict construction (interpretation) of the Constitution. For his part, Henry Clay continued to champion the economic nationalism of his "American System." Adams shared Clay's belief that the national government should finance internal improvements to stimulate economic development, but he was less strongly committed to tariffs. And meanwhile, Jackson tried to capitalize on his own popularity as a military hero. Thomas Jefferson remained skeptical, believing that Jackson lacked the education and polish to be president: "He is one of the most unfit men I know."

As a self-made military hero, Jackson was an attractive candidate, especially to voters of Irish and Scots-Irish backgrounds. In Jackson, the Irish immigrants found a hero. The son of poor Scots-Irish colonists, he was beloved for having defeated the hated English in the Battle of New Orleans. In addition, the Irish immigrants' distaste for aristocracy, which they associated with centuries of English rule, attracted them to a politician who claimed to represent "the common man."

The "Corrupt Bargain"

The results of the 1824 election were inconclusive. In the Electoral College, Jackson had 99 votes, Adams 84, Crawford 41, and Clay 37. But Jackson did not have the necessary majority of the total votes. In such a circumstance, as in the 1800 election, the Constitution specified that the House of Representatives would make the final decision from among the top three candidates. By the time the House could convene, however, Crawford had suffered a stroke and was ruled out. Whatever else might have been said about the outcome between Jackson and Adams, one thing seemed apparent—the election revealed how deeply divided the nation had become. Sectionalism had defeated nationalism as the Republicans split into warring regional factions. The election was a particularly humiliating defeat for Henry Clay and his American System; voters in New England and New York opposed his call for federal funding of internal improvements, and the South rejected his promotion of the protective tariff.

Now that the deadlocked election had been thrown into the House of Representatives, however, Clay's influence, as Speaker, would be decisive. He scorned the other candidates, but he had little trouble choosing from among them, since he regarded Jackson, his western rival, as a "military chieftain" unfit for the office. Clay disliked Adams, and vice versa, but Adams supported most of what Clay wanted, particularly high tariffs, internal transportation improvements, and a strong national bank. Clay also expected Adams to name him secretary of state, the office that usually led to the White House. A deal between Clay and Adams broke the election deadlock. Clay endorsed Adams, and the House of Representatives elected Adams with 13 state delegation votes to Jackson's 7 and Crawford's 4.

The victory proved costly for Adams, however, as it united his foes and crippled his administration before it even began. Jackson dismissed Clay as a "scoundrel," the "Judas of the West," who had entered into a **"corrupt bargain"** with Adams. Clay would never live down Jackson's claim that he had sold his vote to make Adams president. Almost immediately after the 1824 decision, Jackson's supporters launched a campaign to elect him president in 1828. Crawford's supporters soon moved into the Jackson camp. So, too, did the new vice president, John C. Calhoun of South Carolina, who had run on the ticket with both Adams and Jackson but favored Jackson. (Until the political parties created presidential nominating conventions in 1832, state legislatures could nominate candidates, thus at times creating several nominees from each party).

> Corrupt bargain (1824)

John Quincy Adams

John Quincy Adams was one of the ablest men, hardest workers, and finest intellects ever to enter the White House. Yet he also was one of the most ineffective presidents, undercut from the start of his administration by the controversy surrounding his deal with Henry Clay to make him president. In his inaugural address, Adams admitted to voters that he was "less possessed of your confidence . . . than any of my predecessors." Like his father, the stiff and formal Adams lacked the common touch and the politician's gift for compromise. A stubborn, snobbish man, Adams saw two brothers and two sons die from alcoholism. Adams himself suffered from chronic bouts of depression that reinforced his grim self-righteousness and tendency toward self-pity, qualities that did not endear him to fellow politicians or the public. He acknowledged the "defects" in his character, but confessed that he could not change his ways.

Adams's first message to Congress included a grand blueprint for national development, set forth in such a blunt way that it became a disaster for

"corrupt bargain" Scandal in which presidential candidate and Speaker of the House, Henry Clay, secured John Quincy Adams's victory over Andrew Jackson in the 1824 election, supposedly in exchange for naming Clay secretary of state.

him politically. In the boldness and magnitude of its conception, his vision of an expanded federal government outdid the plans of Alexander Hamilton, James Monroe, and Henry Clay. The federal government, Adams stressed, should finance internal improvements (roads, canals, harbors, and bridges), create a national university, support scientific explorations, build astronomical observatories, and establish a department of the interior to manage the vast federal lands. To refrain from using broad federal powers, Adams insisted, "would be treachery to the most sacred of trusts."

Adams's explicit support for increasing the powers of the federal government was so controversial that it led to the death of the Republican party and sparked the emergence of a new party system. Those who agreed with the economic nationalism of Adams and Clay began calling themselves National Republicans. The opposition—the growing party of those supporting Andrew Jackson and states' rights—began calling themselves Democratic Republicans; they would eventually drop the name Republican and become simply Democrats.

President Adams's outspoken efforts to expand the scope of the federal government and his refusal to play backroom politics with Congress condemned his administration to utter frustration from the start. Congress largely ignored his ambitious domestic proposals, and in foreign affairs the triumphs he had scored as secretary of state had no sequels during his presidency.

John Quincy Adams A brilliant man but an ineffective leader, he appears here in his study in 1843. He was the first U.S. president to be photographed.

The Election of Andrew Jackson

Thus the stage was set for the savage **election of 1828**. Both sides engaged in vicious partisan attacks, including false claims that Jackson was the son of a prostitute whose husband was a slave. Adams's supporters denounced Jackson as a hot-tempered, ignorant barbarian, a gambler and slave trader who had participated in numerous duels and frontier brawls, a man whose fame rested upon his reputation as a killer. In addition, his enemies dredged up the story that Jackson had lived in adultery with his wife, Rachel, before they were legally married. (In fact, they had lived together for two years in the mistaken belief that her divorce from her first husband had been approved. As soon as the divorce was official, Andrew and Rachel had remarried.) A furious Jackson blamed Henry Clay for the slurs against his wife. He called Clay "the basest, meanest scoundrel that ever disgraced the image of his god."

election of 1828 Bitter presidential contest between Democrat Andrew Jackson and National-Republican John Quincy Adams (running for re-election), resulting in Jackson's victory.

The Jacksonians, for their part, were equally vicious, condemning Adams as an aristocrat and monarchist, a professional politician who had never had a real job, had been corrupted by foreigners in the courts of Europe, and had allegedly delivered up an American girl to serve the lust of Czar Alexander I while serving as ambassador to Russia. They stressed that Adams despised the common people and that he had gained the presidency in 1824 by a "corrupt bargain" with Clay.

In the 1828 campaign, Jackson held most of the advantages. As a military hero and a fabled Indian fighter, he was beloved in the western and southern states, and as a plantation owner, lawyer, and slaveholder, he had the trust of the southern elite. Debtors and small bankers who hated the national bank also embraced Jackson, and he benefited from a growing spirit of democracy in which many voters viewed Adams as an elitist. When Adams's supporters began referring to Jackson as a "jackass," Jackson embraced the name, using the animal as a symbol for his "tough" campaign. The jackass eventually became the enduring symbol of the Democratic party.

The Rise of the "Common Man" in Politics

Jackson's campaign explicitly appealed to the "common" voters, many of whom were able to vote in a presidential election for the first time. After the Revolution, and especially after 1800, more and more white men had gained the right to vote. In 1776 Pennsylvania had given voting rights to all adult males (black or white) who paid taxes. Vermont, immediately upon its admission to statehood in 1791, became the first state to allow all men to vote, whether they owned property or not. Kentucky, admitted to the Union in 1792, became the second. Tennessee, admitted as a state in 1796, had only a modest property-owning qualification for voting. New Jersey in 1807 and Maryland and South Carolina in 1810 abolished property and taxpaying requirements for voting, and after 1815 the new western states entered the Union with either suffrage for all white men or a low taxpaying requirement. Connecticut in 1818, Massachusetts in 1821, and New York in 1821 abolished property requirements for voting.

Jackson Forever Proclaiming Jackson a "man of the people," this 1828 poster identifies him with the democratic impulse of the time.

The "democratization" of politics, in which more and more men were allowed to vote, also affected many free black males in northern states, half of which allowed blacks to vote alongside whites. Rufus King, a member of the New York delegation to the Constitutional Convention in 1787, declared that in New York, "a citizen of color was entitled to all the privileges of a citizen . . . [and] entitled to vote."

The extension of voting rights to people with little or no wealth led to the election of politicians sprung from the people rather than the social elite. Jackson, a frontiersman of humble origin who had scrambled up the political ladder by will and tenacity, fit this more democratic ideal. "Adams can write," went one of the campaign slogans, "but Jackson can fight." The former general could write, too, though he once said that he had no respect for a man who could think of only one way to spell a word.

Democratization of voting

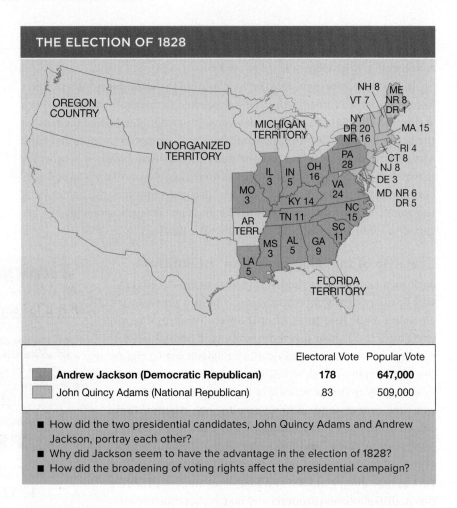

THE ELECTION OF 1828

	Electoral Vote	Popular Vote
Andrew Jackson (Democratic Republican)	178	647,000
John Quincy Adams (National Republican)	83	509,000

- How did the two presidential candidates, John Quincy Adams and Andrew Jackson, portray each other?
- Why did Jackson seem to have the advantage in the election of 1828?
- How did the broadening of voting rights affect the presidential campaign?

Labor Politics

Political participation by labor unions and reformers

With the widespread removal of property qualifications for voting, the working class became an important political force in the form of the Workingmen's parties, first formed in Philadelphia in 1828, and followed soon thereafter by parties in New York City and Boston. The Workingmen's parties were reformist groups in the nation's largest cities devoted to promoting the interests of laborers, including shorter working hours, public schools, allowing all males to vote regardless of the amount of property owned. The Workingmen's parties faded quickly, however. The inexperience of labor politicians left these reformist groups prey to manipulation by political professionals. In addition, major national parties, especially the Democrats, co-opted some of their issues. Labor parties also proved vulnerable to charges of social radicalism, and the courts typically sided with business owners, not workers. Yet while the working-class parties elected few candidates, they did succeed in drawing notice to their demands, many of which attracted the support of middle-class reformers. Above all, they promoted free public education for all children and sought to end the practice of imprisoning people for not paying their debts, causes that won widespread popular support. The labor parties and unions also called for a ten-hour workday to prevent employers from abusing workers. In large part because of his background as a "common man," union members loved Andrew Jackson.

President Jackson

When the 1828 election returns came in, Jackson had won by a comfortable margin. The electoral vote was 178 to 83, and the popular vote was about 647,000 to 509,000 (the figures vary). Adams had won New Jersey, Delaware, all of New England (except 1 of Maine's 9 electoral votes), 16 of the 36 electoral votes from New York, and 6 of the 11 from Maryland. The rest belonged to Jackson. The new president, the first to come from a western state, entered office still seething with resentment at the way his opponents had smeared the reputation of his wife, who had died a few days after learning of the political attacks on her and her "tarnished" marriage. President-elect Jackson wept at her funeral while reading the inscription on her gravestone: "A being so gentle, so virtuous, slander might wound but could not dishonor." Now, he relished the chance to take revenge on those whose attacks had caused Rachel's heart attack and death. More important, Jackson wanted to launch a new "democratic" era in American political development that would silence his critics, restore government to "the people," and take power away from the Eastern "elite."

Reviewing the
CORE OBJECTIVES | INQUIZITIVE

■ **Nationalism** After the War of 1812, the federal government pursued many policies to strengthen the national economy. The *Tariff of 1816* protected American manufacturing from foreign competition, and the *Second Bank of the United States* provided a stronger currency. Madison, Monroe, and Adams all promoted an active economic role for the federal government, including a national bank, a protective tariff, and federally-funded *internal improvements*, such as roads and canals. Led by John Marshall, the Supreme Court limited the powers of states and strengthened the power of the federal government in *Dartmouth College v. Woodward (1819)* and *McCulloch v. Maryland (1819)*. The Marshall court interpreted the Constitution as giving Congress the right to take any action not forbidden by the Constitution as long as the purpose of such laws was within the "scope of the Constitution." In *Gibbons v. Ogden (1824)*, the Marshall court protected contract rights against state action and established the federal government's supremacy over interstate commerce, thereby promoting growth of the national economy.

■ **Sectionalism** Henry Clay's American System supported economic nationalism by endorsing a national bank, a protective tariff, and federally-funded internal improvements, such as roads and canals. Many Americans, however, remained more tied to the needs of their particular sections of the country. People in the different regions—North, South, and West—disagreed about which economic policies best served their interests. As settlers streamed west, the extension of slavery into the new territories became the predominant political concern, eventually requiring both sides to compromise repeatedly to avoid civil war.

■ **Era of Good Feelings** James Monroe's term in office was initially labeled the Era of Good Feelings because it began with peace and prosperity. Two major events spelled the end of the Era of Good

Feelings: the financial *Panic of 1819* and the controversial *Missouri Compromise (1820)*. The explosive growth of the cotton culture transformed life in the South, in part by encouraging the expansion of slavery, which moved west with southern planters. But in 1819 the sudden collapse of world cotton prices devastated the southern economy and soon affected the national economy as well. The Missouri Compromise, a short-term solution to the issue of allowing slavery in the western territories, exposed the emotions and turmoil that the tragic system generated.

■ **National Diplomacy** The main diplomatic achievements of the period between the end of the War of 1812 and the coming civil war concerned the extension of America's contested boundaries and the resumption of trade with its old enemy, Great Britain. To the north, U.S. diplomatic achievements established northern borders with Great Britain. To the south, the *Transcontinental Treaty (1819)* with Spain extended the boundaries of the United States. The *Monroe Doctrine (1823)* declared that the Americas were no longer open to colonization and proclaimed American neutrality in European affairs.

■ **The Election of 1828** The demise of the Federalists ended the first party system in America, leaving the Republicans as the only political party in the nation. The seeming unity of the Republicans was shattered by the election of 1824, which Andrew Jackson lost as a result of what he believed was a *"corrupt bargain"* between John Quincy Adams and Henry Clay. Andrew Jackson won the presidency in the *election of 1828* by rallying southern and western voters with his appeal to the common man. His election opened a new era in national politics that reflected the democratization of voting in most states (at least for white men) and the development of political organizations that rallied voters to particular personalities and issues.

KEY TERMS

CHRONOLOGY

1811	Construction of the National Road begins
1816	Second Bank of the United States is established
	First "protective" tariff goes into effect
1817	Rush-Bagot Agreement between the United States and Great Britain creates an unfortified border between the United States and Canada
1818	The Convention of 1818 establishes the northern border of the Louisiana Purchase at the 49th parallel and the joint occupation of Oregon by the United States and Great Britain
1819	Supreme Court issues *McCulloch v. Maryland* decision
	United States and Spain agree to the Transcontinental Treaty
	Tallmadge Amendment
1820	Congress accepts the Missouri Compromise
1821	Florida, Maine, and Missouri become states
1823	President Monroe enunciates the principles of the Monroe Doctrine
1824	Supreme Court issues *Gibbons v. Ogden* decision
	John Quincy Adams wins the presidential election by what some critics claim is a "corrupt bargain" with Henry Clay
1828	Andrew Jackson wins presidential contest

INQUIZITIVE

Go to InQuizitive to see what you've learned—and learn what you've missed—with personalized feedback along the way.

317

HARD TIMES IN THE JACKSONIAN ERA Although Andrew Jackson championed the "poor and humble," his economic policies contributed to the Panic of 1837, a financial crisis that hit the working class the hardest. This cartoon illustrates New York City during the seven-year depression: a frantic mob storms a bank, while in the foreground, a widow begs on the street with her child, surrounded by a banker or landlord and a barefoot sailor. At left, there is a drunken member of the Bowery Toughs gang and a down-on-his-luck militiaman. The cartoonist places the blame on Jackson, whose hat, glasses, and pipe overlook the scene. The white flag at left wryly states: "July 4, 1827, 61st Anniversary of Our Independence."

The Jacksonian Era

1828–1840

A ndrew Jackson was the first president from a western state (Tennessee), the first to have been born in a log cabin, the first not to have come from a prominent colonial family, and the last to have participated in the Revolutionary War. Born in 1767 along the border between the two Carolinas, he grew up in a struggling single-parent household. Jackson's father was killed in a farm accident three weeks before Andrew was born, forcing his widowed mother Elizabeth to scratch out a living as a housekeeper.

During the Revolution, the Jackson boys joined in the fighting against the British, and one of Andrew's brothers died in battle. In 1781, fourteen-year-old Andrew was captured and imprisoned. When he refused to shine a British officer's boots, the officer slashed him with a sword, leaving ugly scars on his head and arm. Soon after her son was released, Elizabeth Jackson, who had helped nurse injured American soldiers, died of cholera. The orphaned Andrew Jackson thereafter despised the British, blaming them for the deaths of his brother and mother.

Andrew Jackson loved a good fight. During one duel in 1806 with a man who had insulted his wife, Jackson let his opponent fire first. For his gallantry, the future president received a bullet that wedged itself next to his heart and nearly killed him. He nevertheless straightened himself, patiently took aim, and killed his foe. "I should have hit him," Jackson claimed, "if he had shot me through the brain."

CORE
OBJECTIVES INQUIZITIVE

1. Describe Andrew Jackson's major beliefs regarding the common man, the presidency, and the proper role of government in the nation's economy.

2. Evaluate Jackson's response to the nullification crisis.

3. Analyze Andrew Jackson's legacy regarding the status of Indians in American society.

4. Explain the causes of the economic depression of the late 1830s and the emergence of the Whig party.

5. Assess the strengths and weaknesses of Jackson's transformational presidency.

After the Revolution, the self-taught Jackson became a frontier attorney in backwoods Tennessee, where he dealt mostly with disputes over land claims. He moved to Nashville in 1788, where he fell in love with Rachel Donelson Robards, a woman he lived with before she was legally divorced from her first husband. The Jacksons developed a happy marriage, but gossip about the origins of their relationship dogged them until Rachel's heart attack and death in December 1828.

In 1796, when Tennessee became a state, voters elected Jackson to the U.S. House and then to the Senate, where he served only a year before returning to Tennessee and becoming a judge. The ambitious Jackson made a lot of money, first as an attorney, then as a buyer and seller of horses, land, and slaves. Jackson eventually owned a hundred slaves on his large cotton plantation, called the Hermitage, near Nashville. Like most of his neighbors, he had no moral reservations about slavery and at times could be a cruel master. After one of his slaves escaped, Jackson offered a large reward for his recapture, and promised "ten dollars extra for every hundred lashes a person will give [him] to the amount of three hundred." When not farming or raising racehorses, Jackson served as the iron-willed commander of the Tennessee militia.

Many American political leaders cringed at the thought of the rough-hewn, short-tempered Jackson, who had run roughshod over international law in his war against the British and Seminoles in Florida, presiding over the nation. "His passions are terrible," said elderly Thomas Jefferson. John Quincy Adams scorned Jackson "as a barbarian and savage who could scarcely spell his name." Jackson dismissed such criticism as an example of the "Eastern elite" trying to control American politics.

Concerns about Jackson's fitness for the presidency were heightened by the riotous scene at the White House after his inauguration ceremony in March 1829. In a symbolic effort to reach out to the "common" people, Jackson opened the party to anyone. To his surprise, the huge crowd of jubilant Democrats quickly turned into a drunken mob. Dishes and glasses were smashed and furniture broken. Revelers in the presidential mansion stood in muddy boots on chairs, ripped down drapery, and trampled on rugs. Supreme Court Justice Joseph Story said he had never seen such "a mixture" of people in the White House. "The reign of KING MOB seemed triumphant," he wrote. The partying crowd was finally lured out of the White House when the liquor barrels were carried out onto the lawn.

Jackson was a quite different kind of president from George Washington, Thomas Jefferson, and James Madison. He smoked a corncob pipe and chewed tobacco. Tall and lean—over six feet tall but only 140 pounds—with penetrating eyes, a long nose, jutting chin, and iron-gray hair that intensified his steely personality, *Old Hickory* (a nickname given to Jackson by his soldiers because he was as tough as the hard wood of a hickory tree) loved the rough-and-tumble combat of political life. "I was born for a storm," he once boasted. "A calm [life] does not suit me."

In his extraordinary novel *Moby-Dick* (1851), Herman Melville observed that it was the "great democratic God" who picked "up Andrew Jackson from the pebbles; who didst hurl him upon a warhorse; who didst thunder him higher than a throne!" General Jackson did indeed take the nation by storm. No political figure was so widely loved or more deeply hated. As a self-made soldier, politician, and planter, Jackson craved wealth and fame, and he won both. He symbolized the emergence of the "market revolution" in the economy and the "common man" in politics (he meant white men only) and stamped his name and, more important, his ideas, personality, and values on an entire era of American history.

Jacksonian Democracy

CORE **OBJECTIVE**

1. Describe Andrew Jackson's major beliefs regarding the common man, the presidency, and the proper role of government in the nation's economy.

Promoting the "common man"

Expanded presidential authority

During the 1820s and 1830s, American political life was transformed as more and more working men were allowed to vote and hold office. Most of the new western states admitted to the Union reduced property-owning requirements for voting and allowed virtually any white male to run for elected office. "The principle of universal suffrage," announced the *U.S. Magazine and Democratic Review*, "meant that white males of age constituted the political nation." Jacksonian Democrats expanded economic opportunity and political participation for the "common man" (white factory workers, craftsmen and mechanics, small farmers, and land-hungry frontiersmen). Andrew Jackson promised to protect "the poor and humble" from the "tyranny of wealth and power." His goal was to elevate the "laboring classes" of white men who "love liberty and desire nothing but equal rights and equal laws." Jackson's concept of greater democracy, however, did not include women, African Americans, or Native Americans.

Jackson was the first president to view himself as a representative of "the people." As such, he expected to exercise expanded executive powers at the expense of the legislative and judicial branches. The ruling political and economic elite must be removed, he said, for "the people" are "the government, the sovereign power" in the United States, and they had elected him president. In general, Jackson and the Democrats believed that "the world is governed too much." The nation's seventh president wanted to reduce federal spending, pay off the federal debt (a "national curse"), destroy the Second Bank of the United States, and remove the "ill-fated race" of Indians from the East so that they could retain their way of life while white Americans exploited their ancestral lands. In pursuing these ambitious goals, he exercised presidential authority more boldly than any of his predecessors.

Jackson's heroic stature and combative personality attracted enthusiastic supporters among westerners as well as workingmen in the East. Jackson was also an openly partisan president. He actively lobbied Congress and benefited from a national Democratic party "machine" run by his trusted

All Creation Going to the White House In this depiction of Jackson's inauguration party, satirist Robert Cruikshank draws a visual parallel to Noah's Ark, suggesting that people of all walks of life were now welcome to the White House.

secretary of state (later his vice-president) Martin Van Buren, a New York lawyer with a shrewd political sense whose investments had made him rich.

The Spoils System and Presidential Conventions

The spoils system

To dislodge the eastern political elite, Jackson replaced many federal officials with his own supporters. Government jobs, he argued, belonged to the people, not to career bureaucrats. During his two presidential terms, Jackson replaced about a fifth of the federal officeholders with his own friends and supporters, not all of whom were qualified for their new positions. Such partisan behavior came to be called "the spoils system," since, as a prominent Democrat declared, "to the victor goes the spoils."

Birth of presidential nominating conventions

Jackson also sought to "democratize" the way that presidential candidates were selected. Since the presidency of George Washington, most nominees had been chosen by party "caucuses" of prominent congressmen and senators. Jackson hated the idea of legislators nominating presidents. Their doing so had led to the "corrupt bargain" between Henry Clay and John Quincy Adams that had denied him the presidency and instead elected Adams to succeed James Monroe in 1824. In 1832, he would convince the Democrats to stage their first presidential nominating convention as a means of involving more people in the process of selecting a candidate. The innovation of presidential nominating conventions reinforced Jackson's image as a man of the people fighting against entrenched special interests.

The Eaton Affair

From the outset, Andrew Jackson's administration was divided between supporters of Secretary of State Martin Van Buren and those of Vice President John C. Calhoun of South Carolina, both of whom wanted to succeed Jackson as president. Jackson turned mostly to Van Buren for advice. But

Calhoun, a Yale graduate of towering intellect and fiery determination, could not be taken lightly. Although earlier a nationalist, he now was determined to defend southern interests, especially the preservation of the slave-based cotton economy that had made him a rich planter.

In his rivalry with Calhoun, Van Buren had luck on his side in the form of a social scandal known as the Peggy Eaton affair. John Eaton, a former Tennessee senator, was a close friend of Jackson who had managed his 1824 presidential campaign. Three months before Eaton became Jackson's secretary of war, he had married his mistress, Peggy O'Neale Timberlake, whose husband, a naval officer, had reportedly committed suicide upon learning of her affair with Eaton. Eaton's enemies criticized the "unseemly haste" of the marriage, and Peggy Eaton, the lively, flirtatious daughter of an Irish tavern owner, was not a virtuous woman in the eyes of the proper ladies of Washington. Floride Calhoun, the vice president's wife, especially objected to Mrs. Eaton's lowly origins and unsavory past. She pointedly snubbed her, and the other cabinet wives followed suit.

> The politics of social scandal

Mrs. Eaton's plight reminded Jackson of the mean-spirited gossip that had plagued his own wife, Rachel. He strenuously defended Mrs. Eaton, insisting that she was as pure "as a virgin." His cabinet members, however, were unable to cure their wives of what the unmarried Van Buren dubbed "the Eaton Malaria." Mrs. Eaton finally withdrew from the social scene in Washington, and her husband resigned from the cabinet. The outraged Jackson linked the social abuse heaped on Peggy Eaton to his arch-enemy, John C. Calhoun. Secretary of War Eaton was the only cabinet member who did not support Calhoun's plan to be the next president. In a vengeful rage, Jackson concluded that Vice President Calhoun was one of the "most dangerous men living—a man devoid of principle" who "would sacrifice his friend, his country, and forsake his god, for selfish personal ambition."

Jackson decided that the only way to restore harmony in his warring cabinet was to disband it and start over. On April 4, 1829, the president accepted John Eaton's resignation. Four days later, Martin Van Buren resigned. The rest of the cabinet members left in following weeks, enabling Jackson to appoint a new group of senior officers. "A revolution has taken place in the Capitol of the United States," announced the newspaper headlines. Thereafter, Jackson relied more upon the advice of his so-called "kitchen cabinet," an informal group of close friends and supporters. Critics claimed that Jackson did not have the skill to lead the nation. One newspaper announced that the ship of state "is sinking and the rats are flying! The hull is too leaky to mend, and the hero of two wars and a half has not the skill to keep it afloat."

> Jackson's "kitchen cabinet"

Internal Improvements

Concerns that Jackson was not in control of things quickly disappeared, however, for he decisively used his executive authority to limit the role of the federal government—while at the same time delivering additional blows to John C. Calhoun and to Henry Clay, the man Jackson blamed for

> Jackson vetoes the Maysville Road Bill

King Andrew the First
Opponents considered Jackson's veto of the Maysville Road Bill an abuse of power. This cartoon shows "King Andrew" trampling on the Constitution, internal improvements, and the Bank of the United States.

Second Bank of the United States National bank established in 1816 when the charter for the First Bank of the United States expired.

The Bank War Political struggle in the early 1830s between President Jackson and financier Nicholas Biddle over the renewing of the Second Bank's charter.

having "stolen" the 1824 election from him. In 1830, Congress passed a bill supported by Calhoun and Clay that authorized the use of federal monies to build a sixty-mile-long road from Maysville, Kentucky, to Lexington, Kentucky, Clay's hometown. President Jackson, urged on by Martin Van Buren, vetoed the bill on the grounds that the proposed road was a "purely local matter," being solely in the state of Kentucky, and thus outside the domain of Congress; funding such local projects would require a constitutional amendment. Clay was stunned. "We are all shocked and mortified by the rejection of the Maysville road," he wrote a friend. But he had no luck convincing Congress to override the presidential veto.

The Bank War

Jackson showed the same principled stubbornness in dealing with the national bank as he did in vetoing the Maysville Road Bill. The charter for the First Bank of the United States (B.U.S.) had expired in 1811 and had been renewed in 1816 as the **Second Bank of the United States**, which soon became the largest corporation in the nation and the only truly national business enterprise. The second B.U.S. held all federal funds (mostly from land sales) and also issued paper money (backed by gold and silver) as the national currency. With twenty-nine branches around the nation, the B.U.S. had helped accelerate business expansion. It had also supplied a stable currency by forcing the 464 state banks to keep enough gold coins in their vaults to back their own paper currency, which they loaned to people and businesses. With federal revenues soaring from land sales during the early 1830s, the B.U.S., led by the brilliant but arrogant Nicholas Biddle, had accumulated massive amounts of money—and economic power.

Even though the national bank was beneficial to the infant American economy, it had been controversial from the start. Local banks and state governments, especially in the South and West, feared the growing power of the "monopolistic" national bank. Southerners and westerners claimed that the small group of B.U.S. directors, most of whom lived in the Northeast, were preventing the state banks from lending as much as they wanted and impeding businesses from borrowing as much as they wanted.

Throughout his life Andrew Jackson had hated banks and bankers, whom he called "vipers and thieves." He admitted that he had "always been afraid of banks"—especially the national bank—because they exercised too much power over the economy and the people. Jackson spoke for many Americans who felt that banks favored the "rich and powerful" men in the East. Jackson also distrusted paper money because banks printed too much of it, causing prices to rise (inflation). He wanted only coins to be used for economic transactions. "I think it right to be perfectly frank with you," Jackson told Nicholas Biddle in 1829. "I do not dislike your Bank any more than [I dislike] all banks."

Early on, the president resolved to destroy the B.U.S., pledging "to put his foot upon the head of the monster and crush him to the dust." The national bank may have become too powerful, but **The Bank War** between Jackson and Biddle revealed that the president never truly understood the bank's

Rechartering the Bank
Jackson's effort to defeat the recharter of the B.U.S. is likened to fighting a hydra, a many-headed serpent from Greek mythology. Just as the hydra would sprout two heads when one was severed, for every one B.U.S. supporter that Jackson subdued, even more B.U.S. supporters would emerge to take his place.

role or policies. The national bank had provided a stable currency for the expanding economy, as well as a mechanism for controlling the pace of economic growth by regulating the ability of branch banks and state banks to issue paper currency.

The Recharter Effort

Although the second B.U.S. charter would run through 1836, Nicholas Biddle could not afford to wait until then for its renewal. Leaders of the National Republican party, especially Henry Clay and Daniel Webster (who was legal counsel to the B.U.S. as well as a senator), told Biddle that he needed to get the charter renewed before the 1836 presidential election. They assured Biddle that the Congress would renew the charter. And Biddle himself grew overconfident about his bank's future. "This worthy President thinks because he has scalped Indians . . . he is to have his way with the Bank." Biddle thought otherwise. "I have been for years in the daily exercise of more personal authority than any President habitually enjoys." But Biddle and his political allies failed to grasp both Jackson's tenacity and the depth of public resentment toward the national bank. Jackson's disgust for the B.U.S. reflected the concerns of many voters. In the end, Biddle, Clay, and the National Republicans unintentionally handed Jackson a popular issue on the eve of the election.

Early in the summer of 1832, both houses of Congress passed the Bank Recharter Bill. On July 10, 1832, however, Jackson vetoed the bill, sending it back to Congress with a blistering criticism of the bank's monopoly powers. Jackson claimed that the B.U.S. was both unconstitutional (although the

Jackson vetoes renewal of B.U.S. charter

Supreme Court disagreed) and "dangerous to our liberties." The B.U.S. made "the rich richer and the potent more powerful" while discriminating against "the humble members of society—the farmers, mechanics, and laborers" who were justified in their complaints about the "injustice" of the national bank. Daniel Webster accused Jackson of using the bank issue "to stir up the poor against the rich." But Webster could not convince the Senate to override the veto, thus setting the stage for a nationwide financial crisis and a dramatic presidential campaign. The overriding issue in the 1832 election was the future of the Bank of the United States.

CORE **OBJECTIVE**

2. Evaluate Jackson's response to the nullification crisis.

Nullification

The vetoes of the Maysville Road bill and the B.U.S. recharter illustrated Jackson's forceful personality. He eventually would veto twelve congressional bills, more than all of the previous presidents combined. Critics claimed that his behavior was "monarchical" in its frequent defiance of the will of Congress. Jackson, however, remained determined to strengthen the executive branch in order to strengthen the Union. His commitment to nationalism over sectionalism was nowhere more evident than in his handling of the nullification crisis in South Carolina.

Calhoun and the Tariff

Vice President John C. Calhoun became Andrew Jackson's fiercest critic. In part because of his personal feud with the president, the brilliant but brittle South Carolinian had abandoned his earlier stance as an economic nationalist and had become the leading states' rights advocate for the South. Conditions in his home state led him to change his political position. The financial panic of 1819 had sparked a nationwide depression, and throughout the 1820s, South Carolina had suffered from a collapse in cotton prices. The state lost almost 70,000 residents who moved west during the 1820s; it would lose nearly twice that number in the 1830s, with many moving to Texas.

Most South Carolinians blamed their economic woes on the Tariff of 1828, which aroused such hatred it was referred to as the **"Tariff of Abominations."** By taxing British textiles coming into U.S. markets, the 1828 tariff on imported cloth hurt southern cotton growers by reducing British demand for raw cotton from America. It also hurt southerners by raising the prices they had to pay for imports.

The tariff debate revealed how the North and South had developed into quite different regions, with different economic interests and different ways of protecting those interests. Massachusetts was prospering while South Carolina was struggling. But the tariff was not the only factor explaining South Carolina's problems. Thousands of acres of farmland across the state were exhausted from constant overplanting. In addition, South Carolina

"Tariff of Abominations" (1828) Tax on imported goods, including British cloth and clothing, that strengthened New England textile companies but hurt southern consumers, who experienced a decrease in British demand for raw cotton grown in the South.

cotton planters now faced competition from the new cotton-growing states in the Old Southwest: Alabama, Mississippi, Louisiana, and Arkansas.

In a lengthy pamphlet called the *South Carolina Exposition and Protest* (1828), written in secret by John C. Calhoun, the South Carolinian claimed that the Tariff of 1828 favored the interests of New England textile manufacturing over southern agriculture. Under such circumstances, he argued, a state could "nullify," or veto, a federal law it deemed unconstitutional. **Nullification** was the ultimate weapon for those determined to protect states' rights against federal authority. As President Jackson and others pointed out, however, allowing states to pick and choose which federal laws they would follow would have created national confusion.

> Calhoun's theory of nullification

The Webster-Hayne Debate

The controversy over the Tariff of 1828 simmered until 1830, when the great Webster-Hayne debate in Congress sharpened the lines between the respective proponents of states' rights and national authority. In a fiery speech, Senator Robert Y. Hayne of South Carolina, a rising star among southern defenders of states' rights, argued that the Union was created by the states, and the states therefore had the right to nullify federal laws.

> Webster-Hayne debate: States' rights vs. national unity

Senator Daniel Webster of Massachusetts then rose to defend the North—and the Union. Blessed with a thunderous voice and a theatrical

nullification Right claimed by some states to veto a federal law deemed unconstitutional.

***Webster Replying to Senator Hayne* (1848)** The eloquent Massachusetts senator challenges the argument for nullification in the Webster-Hayne debate.

flair, Webster presented a nationalistic view of the Constitution, arguing that if a single state could nullify a federal law, then the Union would be a "rope of sand." How could there ever be a "nation" in which the individual states could pick and choose which federal laws to follow? For America to remain a nation, Webster said, a state could neither nullify a federal law nor secede from the Union. South Carolina's defiance of federal authority, he charged, "is nothing more than resistance by *force*—it is disunion by *force*—it is secession by *force*—it is Civil War."

Webster's closing statement was printed in virtually every newspaper in the nation: "Liberty and Union, now and forever, one and inseparable." Abraham Lincoln later called it "the very best speech ever delivered." In the end, Webster had the better argument. The Union and majority rule meant more to westerners, including President Jackson, than the abstractions of states' rights and nullification. And most political leaders agreed with Webster that the states could not act separately from the national government. As Jackson said, the Constitution and its laws were "supreme."

The Split with Calhoun

Jackson: The preservation of the Union

Like Calhoun, Jackson was a cotton-planting southern slaveholder, so many southerners expected him to support their resistance to the federal tariff. Jackson was sympathetic—until Calhoun and South Carolina threatened to "nullify" federal laws they did not like. He then turned on Calhoun and South Carolina with the same angry force he had directed toward the advancing British army at New Orleans in 1815. On April 13, 1830, the Democratic party hosted the first annual Jefferson Day dinner to honor the birthday of the former president. When it was Jackson's turn to propose a toast to Jefferson's memory, he raised his glass, glared at Calhoun, and announced: "Our Union—It must be preserved!" Calhoun then stood and countered with a toast to "the Union, next to our liberty most dear! May we all remember that it can only be preserved by respecting the rights of the States and distributing equally the benefit and the burden of the Union!" Jackson's toast had set off a bombshell that exploded the plans of Calhoun and the nullifiers. The rift between the two proud men prompted Jackson to take a dramatic step: he removed all of Calhoun's supporters from his cabinet. Five of eight cabinet members were forced to resign.

The South Carolina Nullification Ordinance

In the fall of 1831, Jackson announced his willingness to serve a second term as president. He also tried to defuse the confrontation with South Carolina by calling on Congress to reduce the tariff. Congress responded with the Tariff of 1832, which lowered duties on many imported items, although tariffs on cloth and iron remained high.

The new tariff, however, was not enough to satisfy Calhoun and others in his home state. South Carolina seethed with resentment toward Jackson and the federal government. One hotheaded South Carolina congressman called the Union a "foul monster." He and other white South Carolinians, living in the only state where enslaved Africans were a majority of the population, feared that if the northern representatives in Congress were powerful enough to create such discriminatory tariffs, they might eventually vote to end slavery. Calhoun declared that the "peculiar domestic institutions of the southern states" (by which he meant slavery) were at stake in the debate over tariff policy.

In November 1832, a South Carolina state convention overwhelmingly adopted a Nullification Ordinance that repudiated the "unconstitutional" federal tariff acts of 1828 and 1832 (declaring them "null, void, and no law"). If federal authorities tried to use force to collect the tariffs, South Carolina would secede from the Union, they vowed. The reassembled state legislature then chose Senator Robert Hayne as governor and elected Calhoun to succeed him as senator. Calhoun resigned as vice president so that he could defend the nullification policy in the Senate.

South Carolina Nullification Ordinance

Jackson's Firm Response

In the nullification crisis, South Carolina, "feisty as a gamecock," found itself standing alone. Other southern states expressed sympathy, but none endorsed nullification. President Jackson's public response was moderate. He promised to use "firmness and forbearance" with South Carolina but stressed that nullification "means insurrection and war; and the other states have a right to put it down."

In private, however, Jackson was furious. He threatened to hang Calhoun, Hayne, and other "nullifiers" if there was any bloodshed. "Surely the president is exaggerating," Governor Hayne of South Carolina remarked to Senator Thomas Hart Benton of Missouri. Benton, who years before had been in a fistfight with Jackson, replied: "I have known General Jackson a great many years, and when he speaks of hanging it is time to look for a rope."

In his annual message to the nation, delivered December 4, 1832, Jackson appealed to the people of South Carolina not to follow false leaders such as Calhoun: "The laws of the United States must be executed. . . . Those who told you that you might peaceably prevent their execution, deceived you. . . . Their object is disunion. . . . Disunion by armed force is treason."

Clay's Compromise

President Jackson then sent federal soldiers and a warship to Charleston to uphold national authority. Governor Hayne responded by mobilizing the state militia, and the two sides verged on civil war. In early 1833, the president requested from Congress the **"Force Bill"** authorizing him to use the U.S. Army to "force" compliance with federal law in South Carolina. At that point, the nullifiers backed down; the South Carolina legislature postponed the actual enforcement of the nullification ordinances in hopes that a

The "Force Bill" (1833)
Legislation, sparked by the nullification crisis in South Carolina, that authorized the president's use of the army to compel states to comply with federal law.

compromise might be reached. Passage of the compromise bill in Congress depended upon the support of Senator Henry Clay, himself a slaveholding planter, who finally yielded to those urging him to save the day for the Union. A fellow senator told Clay that these "South Carolinians are good fellows, and it would be a pity to see Jackson hang them." Clay agreed. On February 12, 1833, he circulated a plan to reduce the federal tariff gradually. It was less than South Carolina preferred, but it got the nullifiers out of the dilemma they had created. Calhoun supported the compromise: "He who loves the Union must desire to see this agitating question [the tariff] brought to a termination."

On March 1, 1833, Congress passed the compromise tariff and the Force Bill, and the next day Jackson signed both. Calhoun rushed home to convince the rebels in his state to back down. The South Carolina convention then met and rescinded its nullification of the tariff acts. In a face-saving gesture, the delegates nullified the Force Bill, which Jackson no longer needed. Both sides were able to claim victory. Jackson had upheld the supremacy of the Union, and South Carolina had secured a reduction of the federal tariff. But there was still the fundamental issue of southern slaveholders feeling increasingly threatened by growing anti-slavery sentiment in the North. "The struggle, so far from being over," a defiant Calhoun wrote, "is not more than fairly commenced."

Jackson's Indian Policy

CORE OBJECTIVE

3. Analyze Andrew Jackson's legacy regarding the status of Indians in American society.

If President Jackson's firm stance against nullification constituted his finest hour, his forcible removal of Indians from their ancestral lands was one of his lowest moments. Like most white frontiersmen, Jackson viewed Indians as barbarians without rights, who should be treated as "subjects," not "nations." After his election in 1828, he recommended that the Eastern Indians be moved to the Great American Desert west of the Mississippi River, in what became Oklahoma. State laws in Alabama, Georgia, and Mississippi had already abolished tribal units and stripped them of their powers, rejected ancestral Indian land claims, and denied Indians the right to vote or testify in court. Jackson claimed that relocating the Eastern Indians was a pragmatic act of mercy, a "wise and humane policy" that would save the Indians from "utter annihilation" if they tried to hold on to their lands.

Indian Removal

Indian Removal Act (1830) Law permitting the forced relocation of Indians to federal lands west of the Mississippi River in exchange for the land they occupied in the East and South.

In response to a request from Jackson, Congress in 1830 debated the **Indian Removal Act**, which authorized the president to disavow earlier treaty commitments and force the 74,000 Indians remaining in the East and South to move to federal lands west of the Mississippi River. Relocating the Native Americans was President Jackson's top priority. But it provoked opposition, not only among the Indian peoples but also among

American reformers, who deluged Congress with petitions that criticized the removal policy and warned that the policy would bring "enduring shame" on the nation. Even David "Davy" Crockett of Tennessee, a frontiersman like President Jackson, opposed the forced removal of the Indian nations. But to no avail. In late May 1830, Congress narrowly passed and Jackson eagerly signed the Indian Removal Act.

By 1835, some 46,000 Indians had been relocated across the Mississippi River at government expense. The policy was enacted with remarkable speed, but not fast enough to satisfy whites in the South and Southwest. Unlike in the Ohio Valley and the Great Lakes region, where the flow of white settlers had constantly *pushed* the Indians westward, settlers in the Old Southwest moved across Kentucky, Tennessee, and Georgia into Florida, Alabama, and Mississippi, *surrounding* the so-called Five Civilized Tribes: the Cherokee, Choctaw, Chickasaw, Creek, and Seminoles—the Indian peoples who had taken on many features of white society, abandoning traditional hunting practices to develop farms, build roads, schools, and churches, and create trading posts and newspapers. Many Cherokees, Creeks, and Choctaws had married whites, adopted their clothing and food, and converted to Christianity.

Most of the northern Indians were too weak to resist being relocated. But in Illinois and the Wisconsin Territory, the Black Hawk War erupted in 1832. The Illinois militia mobilized to expel the Sauk and Fox peoples, chased them into the Wisconsin Territory, ignored the Indians' effort to surrender under a white flag, and massacred women and children as they tried to escape across the Mississippi River. Six weeks later, their leader, Black Hawk, was captured and imprisoned. After eight months, President Jackson ordered that he be brought to Washington, D.C. by carriage, steamboat, and railroad, to impress upon the Indian leader the greatness and power of the United States before releasing him.

> Resistance: Black Hawk War (1832)

In the South, the Seminoles, led by Osceola (called by U.S. soldiers "the still unconquered red man") resisted the federal removal policy from 1835 to 1842 by fighting a guerrilla war in the swamps of the Florida Everglades—the longest, most expensive, and deadliest war ever fought by Native Americans. But the Seminoles' heroic resistance waned after 1837, when Osceola, the most famous Native American of the time, was captured, imprisoned, and left to die at Fort Moultrie near Charleston, South Carolina. After 1842, only a few hundred Seminoles remained, hiding out in the swamps. It was not until 1934 that the few surviving Seminoles in Florida became the last Native American tribe to end their war with the United States.

> Resistance: Seminole guerrilla war

The Trail of Tears

The Cherokee Nation occupied northwest Georgia and the mountainous areas of Alabama, Tennessee, and North Carolina. In 1827, the Cherokees, relying upon their established treaty rights, adopted a constitution as an

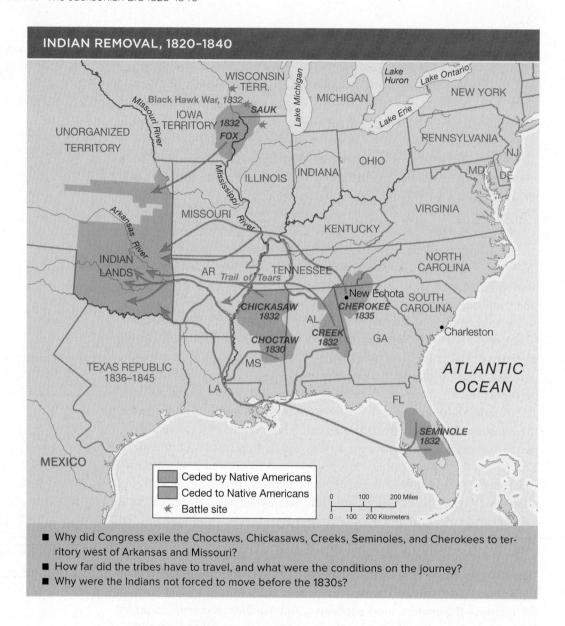

INDIAN REMOVAL, 1820–1840

Legend:
- Ceded by Native Americans
- Ceded to Native Americans
- ★ Battle site

- Why did Congress exile the Choctaws, Chickasaws, Creeks, Seminoles, and Cherokees to territory west of Arkansas and Missouri?
- How far did the tribes have to travel, and what were the conditions on the journey?
- Why were the Indians not forced to move before the 1830s?

independent nation in which they declared that they were not subject to the laws or control of any state or the federal government. In 1828, shortly after Jackson's election, Georgia announced that after June 1, 1830, the authority of state law would extend to the Cherokees living within the boundaries of the state. According to the Georgia state government, the Cherokees would no longer be a "nation within a nation."

Of all the so-called Civilized Tribes, the Cherokees had come closest to adopting the customs of white America. But the discovery of gold in north Georgia in 1829 fed whites' appetite for Cherokee land and attracted trespassing prospectors. The Cherokees sought relief in the Supreme Court. In

Cherokee Nation v. Georgia (1831) and *Worcester v. Georgia* (1832)

Cherokee Nation v. Georgia (1831), Chief Justice John Marshall ruled that the Cherokees were a "domestic dependent nation" rather than a foreign state. He added, however, that the Cherokees had "an unquestionable right" to their lands "until title should be extinguished by voluntary cession to the United States." The following year, the Supreme Court ruled in *Worcester v. Georgia* (1832) that the Cherokee Nation was "a distinct political community" within which Georgia law had no force. Both of these Supreme Court decisions had the effect of favoring the Cherokee argument that their ancestral lands could not be taken from them.

President Jackson, however, refused to enforce the Court's "wicked" decisions, claiming that he had no constitutional authority to intervene in Georgia. Jackson's rejection of the Court's ruling reflected his many contradictions. When dealing with Indians in Georgia, he refused to interfere with the state's refusal to abide by U.S. Supreme Court rulings. By contrast, in the nullification crisis with South Carolina, he used military force to deny the right of a state to defy the federal government.

Meanwhile, the Indians were forced out. There was nothing for the Cherokees (who had fought with Jackson as allies against the Creeks) to do but sign a treaty, which they did in 1835. They gave up their land in the Southeast (about 100 million acres) in exchange for 32 million acres in the "Indian Territory" to the west of Arkansas—part of present-day Oklahoma. By 1838, 17,000 Cherokees had been evicted and moved west on the **Trail of Tears**, an eight-hundred-mile forced journey mostly on foot. Four thousand of the refugees died along the way. A few held out in the mountains and acquired title to federal land in North Carolina; they became known as the "Eastern Band" of Cherokees.

Cherokees divided While many Cherokee elite fought against Jackson's policies, Elias Boudinot, editor of the first Native American newspaper, *Cherokee Phoenix*, signed the Indian Removal Treaty in 1835. He was subsequently murdered.

Trail of Tears (1838–1839) The Cherokees' eight-hundred-mile journey from the southern Appalachians to Indian Territory.

Trail of Tears Thousands of Cherokees died on a nightmarish forced march from Georgia to Oklahoma after being forced from their native lands.

CORE **OBJECTIVE**

4. Explain the causes of the economic depression of the late 1830s and the emergence of the Whig party.

Political Battles

Jackson's controversial policies regarding the Indians, nullification, and the B.U.S. aroused so much opposition that new political parties were formed to oppose him. Some congressional opponents talked of impeaching him. Jackson received so many death threats that he decided his political opponents were trying to kill him. In January 1835, the threat became real. After attending the funeral service for a member of Congress, Jackson was leaving the Capitol when an unemployed English-born housepainter named Richard Lawrence emerged from the shadows and pointed a pistol at the president's heart—only a few feet away. When he pulled the trigger, however, the gun misfired. Jackson lifted his walking stick and charged at Lawrence, who pulled out another pistol, but it, too, miraculously misfired, and he was arrested. Jackson charged that his political foes, including John C. Calhoun, had planned the attack. A jury, however, decided that Lawrence, the first person to try to kill a U.S. president, was insane and ordered him confined in an asylum.

A Third Party

In 1832, for the first time in a presidential election, a third party entered the field. The Anti-Masonic party grew out of popular hostility toward the Masonic fraternal order, a large, all-male social organization that originated in Great Britain early in the eighteenth century. By 1830, there were some 2,000 Masonic "lodges" scattered across the United States with about 100,000 members, including Andrew Jackson and Henry Clay.

The Anti-Masonic party

Suspicions of the Masonic order as a secret elite organization intent on undermining democracy gave rise to the grassroots movement known as the Anti-Masonic party. More than 100 Anti-Masonic newspapers emerged across the nation. Their common purpose was to stamp out an organization that was contaminating the "heart of the republic." Former president John Quincy Adams said that disbanding the "Masonic institution" was the most important issue facing "us and our posterity."

Opposition to a fraternal organization was hardly the foundation upon which to build a lasting political party, but the Anti-Masonic party had three important firsts to its credit: in addition to being the first third party, it was the first party to hold a national convention to nominate a presidential candidate and the first to announce a platform of specific policy goals.

The 1832 Election

The Democrats and the National Republicans followed the example of the Anti-Masonic party by holding presidential nominating conventions of their own. In December 1831, the National Republicans assembled in Baltimore to nominate Henry Clay. Eager to demonstrate popular support for his own party's candidates, Jackson endorsed the idea of a nominating convention for the Democratic party as well.

The Democratic convention, also meeting in Baltimore, first adopted the two-thirds rule for nomination (which prevailed until 1936, when the requirement became a simple majority), then named Martin Van Buren as Jackson's running mate. The Democrats, unlike the other two parties, adopted no formal platform and relied to a substantial degree upon the popularity of the president to carry their cause.

The outcome was an overwhelming endorsement of Jackson in the Electoral College, with 219 votes to 49 for Clay, and a solid victory in the popular vote, 688,000 to 530,000. William Wirt carried only Vermont, winning seven electoral votes. Wayward South Carolina, unable to stomach either Jackson or Clay, delivered its 11 votes to Governor John Floyd of Virginia.

The Removal of Government Deposits

Jackson interpreted his lopsided reelection as a "decision of the people against the bank." Jackson ordered the Treasury Department to transfer federal monies from the national bank to twenty-three state banks—called "pet banks" because many were in the western states and were run by friends and allies of Jackson. Transferring the government's deposits from the B.U.S. to the pet banks was probably illegal, and the Senate, led by Henry Clay, voted on March 28, 1834, to censure Jackson for it, the only time an American president has been reprimanded in this way as opposed to actual impeachment. Jackson was so angry about being censured that he wanted to challenge Clay to a duel to "bring the rascal to a dear account."

Meanwhile, Nicholas Biddle refused to surrender. He ordered the B.U.S. to quit making loans and demanded that state banks exchange their paper currency for gold or silver coins as quickly as possible. Through such deflationary policies that reduced the amount of money circulating in the economy, the desperate Biddle was trying to create a depression, and thus reveal the importance of maintaining the national bank. An infuriated Jackson said the B.U.S. under Biddle was "trying to kill me, but I will kill it!"

> Jackson's war on the B.U.S.

Jackson prevailed. The B.U.S. would shut down by 1841. With the restraining effects of Biddle's national bank removed, hundreds of new state banks sprouted like mushrooms, each printing its own paper currency to lend to land speculators and new businesses. Sales of federal- or state-owned lands rose from 4 million acres in 1834 to 20 million in 1836. At the same time, the states plunged themselves heavily into debt to finance the building of roads and canals. By 1837, total state indebtedness had soared. The irony of Jackson's war on the national bank was that it sparked the dangerous misbehavior among small state banks that he most feared. As Senator Thomas Hart Benton, one of Jackson's most loyal supporters, said in 1837, he had not helped kill the B.U.S. to create a "wilderness of local banks. I did not join in putting down the paper currency of a national bank to put up a national paper currency of a thousand local banks."

The Money Question

The Distribution Act (1836)

The surge of unstable paper money being issued by state banks peaked in 1836, when events combined suddenly to destroy the value of the bank notes. Two key developments, the **Distribution Act** and the Specie Circular, would combine to devastate the nation's financial system and throw the surging economy into a sudden tailspin. During the 1830s, the federal government was acquiring huge amounts of cash from the sale of government-owned lands. For a time, the annual surpluses from land sales were used to pay off the federal debt. The debt, reduced to $7 million by 1832, was completely paid off by 1835, the first time that any nation had done so.

And the federal surplus continued to mount. In June 1836, Congress decided that the money from land sales should be "distributed" to the states in proportion to each state's representation in Congress. The distribution of the surplus resulted in the withdrawal of federal funds from the state banks. In turn, the state banks had to require many borrowers to repay their loans immediately so that the banks could replace the lost federal funds. This situation caused even greater disarray in the already unstable banking sector.

Specie Circular (1836)

A month after the Distribution Act was signed into law, Andrew Jackson signed the Specie Circular, which announced that the federal government would accept only gold or silver coins in payment for land. The requirement that only "specie" (coins) be accepted for federal land purchases put an added strain on the nation's already-tight supplies of gold and silver. Eastern banks had to transfer much of their gold and silver reserves to western banks, where most federal lands were being sold. As banks reduced their reserves of gold and silver, they had to reduce their lending. Soon, the once-bustling economy began to slow into a recession.

The Whig Coalition

Whigs vs. "King Andrew I"

Jackson had removed the Indians from the eastern United States and had slain the dual monsters of nullification in South Carolina and the national bank in Philadelphia, and many loved him for it. But in 1834, a new anti-Jackson coalition emerged, united chiefly by their hostility to the president's authoritarian style. Jackson's domineering manner had given rise to the nickname "King Andrew I." His Democratic followers were deemed Tories, supporters of the "tyrannical" king, and his opponents became known as the **Whig party**, a name that linked them to the Patriots of the American Revolution (as well as the parliamentary opponents of the Tories in Britain).

The Whigs grew out of the National Republican party of John Quincy Adams, Henry Clay, and Daniel Webster. They also attracted members of the Anti-Masonic and Democratic parties, who for one reason or another were irritated by Jackson's stand on the national bank, states' rights, and his disregard of the Supreme Court, among other grievances. Of the forty-one Democrats in Congress who had voted against Jackson on rechartering the national bank, twenty-eight had joined the Whigs by 1836, including David

Distribution Act (1836) Law requiring distribution of the federal budget surplus to the states, creating chaos among unregulated state banks dependent on such federal funds.

Whig party Political party founded in 1834 in opposition to the Jacksonian Democrats; supported federal funding for internal improvements, a national bank, and high tariffs on imports.

Crockett, the famous frontiersman and storyteller now representing Tennessee in the House of Representatives. For the next twenty years, the Whigs and the Democrats would be the two major political parties, and so for a second time a **two-party system** emerged.

Most Whigs supported Clay and his "American System" of economic nationalism. They favored federal support for internal improvements—roads, bridges, canals—to foster economic growth. They also supported a national bank and high tariffs. In the South, the Whigs tended to be bankers and merchants. In the West, the Whigs were farmers who valued government-funded internal improvements. Unlike the Democrats, who attracted Catholic voters from Germany and Ireland, Whigs tended to be native-born Protestants—Congregationalists, Presbyterians, Methodists, and Baptists—who promoted social reforms such as the abolition of slavery and legislation to prohibit the sale of alcoholic beverages.

> Whigs support Clay's "American System"

The Election of 1836

In 1835, eighteen months before the presidential election, the Democrats nominated Jackson's handpicked successor, Vice President Martin Van Buren. The Whig coalition, united chiefly in its opposition to Jackson, adopted a strategy of multiple candidacies, hoping to throw the election into the House of Representatives. The Whigs put up three favorite sons: Daniel Webster, nominated by the Massachusetts legislature; Hugh Lawson White, chosen by anti-Jackson Democrats in the Tennessee legislature; and William Henry Harrison of Indiana, nominated by a predominantly Anti-Masonic convention in Harrisburg, Pennsylvania. In the South, the Whigs made heavy inroads by arguing that only a southerner—that is, Hugh White—could be trusted as president. But their complicated multi-candidate strategy failed. In the popular vote of 1836, though, Van Buren outdistanced the entire Whig field, with 765,000 votes to 740,000 for the three Whigs. Van Buren won 170 electoral votes; Harrison, 73; White, 26; and Webster, 14.

Martin Van Buren Van Buren earned the nickname the "Little Magician," for not only his short stature but also his "magical" ability to exploit his political and social connections.

The Eighth President

Martin Van Buren was the first president of Dutch ancestry. Although trained as an attorney, he had spent most of his adult life as a skillful politician whose ability to organize and manipulate the New York political "machine" earned him the nickname the "Little Magician." Elected governor of New York in 1828, he had resigned to join Andrew Jackson's cabinet and became vice president in 1833. He had been Jackson's closest adviser and ally.

The Panic of 1837

Fortunately for Jackson, the financial **Panic of 1837** did not erupt until he was out of the White House. His successor got the blame. The financial panic President Van Buren inherited mushroomed into an economic depression lasting seven years. During the mid-1830s, the already-precarious economy was tipped over by a depression in Great Britain, America's largest trading

two-party system Domination of national politics by two major political parties, such as the Whigs and Democrats during the 1830s and 1840s.

Panic of 1837 A financial calamity in the United States brought on by a dramatic slowdown in the British economy and falling cotton prices, failed crops, high inflation, and reckless state banks.

partner, which resulted in a sharp drop in demand for American cotton and caused English capitalists to cut back on their investments in the U.S. economy. On top of everything else, in 1836 there had been a failure of the wheat crop, the export of which in good years had helped offset the drain of gold payments abroad. In April 1837, some 250 businesses failed in New York City alone.

As a newspaper editorial complained in December 1836, the nation's economy "has been put into confusion and dismay by a well-meant, but *extremely mistaken*" pair of decisions by Congress and President Jackson: the destruction of the B.U.S. and the Distribution Act. Adding to the stresses on the economy was the Specie Circular. Its requirement that all federal land purchases be transacted in gold or silver caused government land sales to plummet, thus pinching the federal budget. American banks were forced to borrow gold from European banks, but they could not get enough to prevent a financial panic and a deepening depression.

In April 1836, *Niles' Weekly Register*, the nation's leading business journal, reported that the economy was "approaching a momentous crisis." The government was lucky to sell land for $3 an acre that had been going for $10 an acre. States had to cancel plans to build roads, bridges, railroads, canals, and ports. Forty percent of the state banks shut their doors. Even the federal government itself, having put most of its gold and silver in state banks, was verging on bankruptcy. The *National Intelligencer* newspaper reported in May that the federal treasury "has not a dollar of gold or silver in the world!"

The poor, as always, were particularly hard hit during the economic slump. By the fall of 1837, a third of the nation's workers were jobless, and those still fortunate enough to have jobs had their wages slashed. At the same time, prices for food and clothing soared. As the winter of 1837 approached, a New York City journalist reported that 200,000 people were "in utter and hopeless distress with no means of surviving the winter but those provided by charity." The nation had a "poverty-struck feeling." Every part of the country was "a scene of suffering, of anguish, and distress."

The unprecedented economic calamity sent shock waves through the political system. Critics called the president "Martin Van Ruin" because he did not believe that he or the government had any responsibility to rescue hard-pressed farmers, bankers, or businessmen, or to provide relief for the jobless and homeless. He did call a special session of Congress in 1837, which canceled the distribution of the federal surplus to the states because there was no longer any surplus to distribute.

An Independent Treasury

Independent Treasury Act (1840) System created by Van Buren that moved federal funds from favored state banks to the U.S. Treasury, whose financial transactions could only be in gold or silver.

Van Buren believed that the federal government should stop risking its deposits in shaky state banks. Instead, he wanted to establish an independent treasury system whereby the government would keep its funds in its own bank vaults and do business entirely in gold or silver, not paper currency. At his urging, Congress passed the **Independent Treasury Act** on July 4, 1840.

Although it lasted little more than a year (the Whigs repealed it in 1841), it would be restored in 1846.

The "Log Cabin and Hard Cider" Campaign

By 1840, an election year, the Van Buren administration had become the target of growing discontent. The president won re-nomination easily enough but could not get the Democratic convention to agree on his vice-presidential choice, which was left up to the Democratic electors.

Because of the economic depression, the Whigs were confident they would win the 1840 presidential election. At their nominating convention, they passed over Henry Clay, the Kentucky legislator who had been Jackson's consistent foe, in favor of William Henry Harrison, whose credentials were impressive: victor at the Battle of Tippecanoe against Tecumseh's Shawnees in 1811, former governor of the Indiana Territory, and former congressman and senator from Ohio. To rally their states'-rights wing, the Whigs chose for vice president John Tyler of Virginia.

The Whigs had no platform, since they believed that the economic depression was enough to ensure their victory. But they hit upon a catchy campaign slogan: "Tippecanoe and Tyler Too." And they soon had a rousing campaign theme, which the *Baltimore Republican*, a Democratic newspaper, unwittingly supplied when it declared that General Harrison, at 67 the oldest candidate yet to seek the presidency, was the kind of man who would spend his retirement "in a log cabin [sipping apple cider] on the banks of the Ohio [River]." The Whigs seized upon the cider and log cabin symbols to depict Harrison as a simple man sprung from the people, in contrast to President

UNCLE SAM'S PET PUPS! Or, Mother BANK'S last refuge.

Uncle Sam's Pet Pups!
A woodcut showing William Henry Harrison luring "Mother Bank," Andrew Jackson, and Martin Van Buren into a barrel of hard (alcoholic) cider. While Jackson and Van Buren sought to destroy the Bank of the United States, Harrison promised to reestablish it, hence his providing "Mother Bank" a refuge in this scene.

Creating a Two-Party System: Democrats vs. Whigs

While controversial, Andrew Jackson had a broad appeal to the voters in his time and left an enduring mark on the presidency of the United States. A man of strong convictions, Jackson championed the common man against the wealthy and privileged, but his economic policies led the nation into financial depression. His often contradictory policies and positions brought about intense opposition that eventually coalesced into the Whig party, a rival to his Democratic political organization. By 1840, there were two nationally competitive political parties in the United States. Each party competed at the national level, and each party had to create coalitions of voters, many of whom had differing views on major issues. However, no politician would prove as popular as Andrew Jackson or would win two successive terms to the presidency until Abraham Lincoln did so nearly thirty years after him.

Jackson's Positions and Policies	Democrats on Jackson's Policies	Whigs on Jackson's Policies	Regions on Jackson's Policies
Equality of Opportunity Jackson believed that all white men should rise and fall according to their own talents. He hated elitism and social deference.	**Support**	**Support**	**Strong support** in Northeast (especially factory workers) and West (especially frontiersmen)
Internal Improvements Jackson opposed government spending on internal improvements, which he felt favored certain regions.	**Opposition** to federally funded internal improvements	**Support** for federally funded internal improvements	**Strong support** in West (farmers needed internal improvements to help transport agricultural products to national markets)
Second Bank of the United States Jackson distrusted bankers and viewed the national bank as a government-sanctioned monopoly favoring the rich and privileged, as well as the Northeast, where the first B.U.S. was located.	**Opposition** to rechartering the Second Bank of the United States	**Support** for rechartering the Second Bank of the United States	**Support** in Northeast **Strong opposition** in West

Van Buren's wealthy, aristocratic lifestyle. (Harrison was actually from one of Virginia's wealthiest families).

As expected, Van Buren lost by the thumping margin of 234 votes to 60 in the Electoral College. The Whigs had promised a return to prosperity

Jackson's Positions and Policies	Democrats on Jackson's Policies	Whigs on Jackson's Policies	Regions on Jackson's Policies
Tariffs Jackson believed in lowering taxes but had no strong position on tariffs, until Southern opposition to tariffs convinced him to support lowering them.	**Support** for lowering tariffs	**Opposition** to lowering tariffs	**Support** in Northeast **Strong opposition** in South
Nullification A strong supporter of the Union, Jackson stood down South Carolina when it declared the Tariffs of 1828 and 1832 unconstitutional and not applicable in its borders.	**Opposition** to nullification	N/A (did not yet exist as a party)	**Support** in South (especially South Carolina) **Opposition** in West and North
Indian Policy Jackson did not believe that Native Americans should be part of America's economic, political, and social fabric. Congress approved his forcible removal of Native Americans to the West.	**Support** for forced removal of Native Americans	**Opposition** to forced removal of Native Americans	**Support** in South and Southwest by whites (especially settlers moving into areas surrounding the Cherokee, Choctaw, Chickasaw, Creek, and Seminoles)

QUESTIONS FOR ANALYSIS

1. Who could vote during the 1830s, and how did Jackson's views appeal to voters?

2. How did Jackson's policies lead to a second two-party system, this time made up of Democrats and Whigs? In what particular regions was Jackson's message most popular? In what regions were the Whigs the most popular?

3. Why did Jackson generate support across the country among voters from a variety of occupations and a variety of incomes?

without explaining how such prosperity was to be generated. It was simply time for a change. What was most remarkable about the election of 1840 was the turnout. Over 80 percent of white American men voted, many for the first time—the highest turnout before or since.

Assessing the Jacksonian Era

The nation Andrew Jackson governed as president was vastly different from that led by George Washington and Thomas Jefferson. In 1828 the United States boasted twenty-four states and nearly 13 million people, many of them recent arrivals from Germany and Ireland. The national population was growing at a phenomenal rate, doubling every twenty-three years. During the Jacksonian Era, the nation witnessed booming industrialization, rapidly growing cities, rising tensions between the North and South over slavery, accelerating westward expansion, and the emergence of the second two-party system, featuring Democrats and Whigs. A surge in foreign demand for southern cotton and other American goods, along with substantial British investment in an array of new American enterprises, helped generate an economic boom and a transportation revolution. That President-elect Jackson rode to his inauguration in a horse-drawn carriage and left Washington, D.C., eight years later on a train symbolized the dramatic changes occurring in American life.

A New Political Landscape

The Whigs may have captured the presidency in 1840, but the Jacksonian Democrats had permanently altered American politics. A transformational figure in a transformational era, Andrew Jackson initiated a new era in American politics. He enabled the "common man" to play a greater role in the political arena at the same time that working men were forming labor unions to increase their economic power. He helped establish the modern Democratic party and attracted to it the working poor from eastern cities as well as farmers from the South and East. He saved the Union by suppressing the nullification crisis through a nimble combination of force and compromise. And, in 1835, he paid off the national debt.

White men's democracy

In Jackson's 1837 farewell address, he looked back over eight controversial years in the White House and stressed that he had worked on behalf of "the farmer, the mechanic, and the laboring classes of society—the bone and sinew of the country—men who love liberty and desire nothing but equal rights and equal laws." But his concept of "the people" was limited to a "white men's democracy," as it had been for all earlier presidents, and the phenomenon of Andrew Jackson, the heroic symbol of the times, continues to spark historical debate.

A Controversial Presidency

President Jackson's repeated charges that the "rich and powerful" too often controlled the government for their own "selfish purposes" obscured the fact that in practice Andrew Jackson, along with his advisers and supporters, proved to be as opportunistic and manipulative as the Eastern political and economic elite they displaced. The Jacksonians were largely men "on the make" who promoted greater democracy for the nation while pursuing greater wealth for themselves. Accordingly, Jackson's opponents challenged the sincerity of his commitment to "the people." As Henry Clay charged in 1833, Jackson often seemed to be seeking "the concentration of all power in the hands of one man." But in Jackson's view, the president was the only government official chosen by *all* the people, unlike senators and representatives, and this gave the chief executive the responsibility—and expanded powers—to serve the good of all the people.

Jackson's forceful use of that presidential power was not always wise, however. His controversial decision to eliminate the national bank led to a prolonged depression. One of Jackson's opponents once wrote a letter to the president brutally outlining his faults: "Your besetting sins are ambition and the love of money. . . . You are naturally and constitutionally irritable, overbearing and tyrannical. . . . When you become the enemy of any man you will put him down if you can, no matter by what means, fair or foul. . . . You are miserably deficient in principle, and have seldom or never had power without abusing it."

> A controversial presidency

Limited Equality

While a typical white American was better off than the average European in 1840, the supreme irony of the so-called age of the common man—that is, of Jacksonian democracy—is that it was actually an era of growing economic and social *in*equality. Jacksonian Democrats championed political equality for white males, giving everyone, regardless of wealth, the right to vote and hold office. They also promoted equality of opportunity, not equality of outcomes, and certainly not equality of wealth. "Distinctions in society will always exist under every just government," Jackson observed. "Equality of talents, or education, or of wealth cannot be produced by human institutions." Jacksonian Democrats wanted every white man to have an equal chance to compete in the political arena and to grow rich, but they never promoted equality of results.

> Jacksonian equality of opportunity

During the years before the Civil War, the notion of young men rising from rags to riches was a popular myth. Speaking to the Senate in 1832, Henry Clay claimed that almost all the successful factory owners he knew were "enterprising, self-made men, who have whatever wealth they possess by patient and diligent labor." In fact, however, those who started out poor and uneducated seldom made it to the top. In 1828, the top 1 percent of New York's families (those worth $34,000 or more) held 40 percent of the wealth, and the top 4 percent held 76 percent of the wealth. Similar circumstances prevailed in Philadelphia, Boston, and other cities. But Jackson and others who celebrated the "common man" and talked frequently of "equality" never expected people to be equal in wealth. "True republicanism," one commentator explained, "requires that every man shall have an equal chance—that every man shall be free to become as *unequal* as he can." That is what Jackson believed as well.

> Jacksonian economic and social inequality

■ **Jackson's Views and Policies** The Jacksonians sought to democratize the political process and expand economic opportunity for the "common man" (that is, "poor and humble" white men). As the representative of "the people," he expanded the role of the president in economic matters, reducing federal government spending and eliminating the powerful *Second Bank of the United States*. His *Bank War* painted the national bank as full of "vipers and thieves" and was hugely popular, but Jackson did not understand its long-term economic consequences. In addition, his views on limited government were not always reflected in his policies. He left the high taxes on imports from the *"Tariff of Abominations" (1828)* in place until opposition in the South created a national crisis.

■ **Nullification Controversy** The concept of *nullification*, developed by South Carolina's John C. Calhoun, enabled a state to disavow a federal law. When a South Carolina convention nullified the Tariffs of 1828 and 1832, Jackson requested that Congress pass a *"Force Bill" (1833)* authorizing the U.S. Army to compel compliance with the tariffs. After South Carolina, under the threat of federal military force, accepted a compromise tariff put forth by Henry Clay, the state convention nullified the force bill. The crisis was over, with both sides claiming victory.

■ **Indian Removal Act of 1830** The *Indian Removal Act of 1830* authorized the relocation of eastern Indians to federal lands west of the Mississippi River. The Cherokees used the federal court system in *Cherokee Nation v. Georgia* and *Worcester v. Georgia* to try to block this relocation. Despite the Supreme Court's decisions in their favor, President Jackson forced them to move; the event and the route they took came to be known as the *Trail of Tears (1838–1839)*. By 1840 only a few Seminoles and Cherokees remained in remote areas of the Southeast.

■ **Democrats and Whigs** Jackson's arrogant behavior, especially his use of the veto, led many to regard him as "King Andrew I." Groups who opposed him organized a new party, known as the *Whig party*, thus producing the country's *two-party system*. Two acts—the *Distribution Act (1836)* and the *Specie Circular*—ultimately destabilized the nation's economy. Andrew Jackson's ally and vice president, Martin Van Buren, succeeded him as president, but Jacksonian bank policies led to the financial *Panic of 1837* and an economic depression. Van Buren responded by establishing the *Independent Treasury Act (1840)* to safeguard the nation's economy but offered no help for individuals in distress. The economic calamity ensured a Whig victory in the election of 1840.

■ **The Jackson Years** Andrew Jackson's America was very different from the America of 1776. Most white men had gained the vote when states removed property qualifications for voting, but political equality did not mean economic equality. Democrats wanted every American to have an equal chance to compete in the marketplace and in the political arena, but they never promoted equality of results. Inequality between rich and poor widened during the Jackson Era.

KEY TERMS

CHRONOLOGY

1828	Andrew Jackson wins presidential election
	"Tariff of Abominations" goes into effect
1830	Congress passes the Indian Removal Act
	Andrew Jackson vetoes the Maysville Road Bill
	The Eaton affair divides Andrew Jackson's warring cabinet
1831	Supreme Court issues *Cherokee Nation v. Georgia* decision
1832	Supreme Court issues *Worcester v. Georgia* decision
	South Carolina passes Nullification Ordinance
	Andrew Jackson vetoes the Bank Recharter Bill
1833	Congress passes the Force Bill, authorizing military force in South Carolina
	Congress passes Henry Clay's compromise tariff with Jackson's support
1836	Democratic candidate Martin Van Buren is elected president
1837	Financial panic deflates the economy
1838–1839	Eastern Indians are forced west on the Trail of Tears
1840	Independent Treasury Act established
1840	Whig candidate William Henry Harrison is elected president

INQUIZITIVE

Go to InQuizitive to see what you've learned—and learn what you've missed—with personalized feedback along the way.

THE OLD SOUTH One of the enduring myths of the South is captured in this late nineteenth-century painting of a plantation on the Mississippi River: strong slaves tending the lush cotton fields, a paddle steamer easing down the wide river, and the planter's family retiring in the cool of their white-columned mansion. Novels and films like *Gone with the Wind* (1939) would perpetuate the notion of the Old South as a stable, paternalistic agrarian society led by white planters who were the "natural" aristocracy of virtue and talent within their communities.

The South and Slavery

1800–1860

Of all the regions of the United States during the first half of the nineteenth century, the Old South (that is, the pre–Civil War South) was the most distinctive. The southern states remained rural and agricultural long after the rest of the nation had embraced urban-industrial development. By the 1840s, the North and South had developed different economies and political goals. The North wanted high tariffs on imported manufactured goods to "protect" its new mills and factories from foreign competition. Southerners, on the other hand, favored "free trade"—no tariffs—because they wanted to buy British goods in exchange for the raw cotton they sold to British textile mills.

The rapid settlement of the western territories during the first half of the nineteenth century set in motion a ferocious competition between North and South for political influence in the West. Would the new western territories and states be "slave" or "free"? Much was riding on that issue, since congressional representatives and senators from the newly admitted western states would tip the delicate political balance in Washington, D.C., one way or the other, slave or free.

The efforts of southerners to expand slavery in the face of growing criticism from the North ignited

CORE OBJECTIVES INQUIZITIVE

1. Explain the various factors that made the South distinct from the rest of the United States during the early nineteenth century.

2. Discuss the role that cotton production and slavery played in the South's economic and social development.

3. Distinguish among the major groups within southern white society and explain why each group was committed to the continuation and expansion of slavery.

4. Describe the impact of slavery on African Americans, both free and enslaved, throughout the South.

5. Analyze how enslaved peoples responded to the inhumanity of their situation.

a prolonged political controversy that would end in civil war. Many southerners, then and since, despised being told what to do by others—especially outsiders. And white southerners especially resented northern demands for the abolition of slavery. A prickly defensiveness came to define southern attitudes and actions. The nineteenth-century white South became famous for its defiant pride, its violence-prone sense of honor, and its spirited independence, all rooted in the region's commitment to cotton and race-based slavery.

CORE **OBJECTIVE**

1. Explain the various factors that made the South distinct from the rest of the United States during the early nineteenth century.

Climate, geography, and the plantation system

The Distinctiveness of the Old South

Explanations of what set the Old South apart from the rest of the nation generally focus on the impact of the region's climate and geography in shaping its culture and economy, and on the effects of human decisions and actions over many years. The South's warm, humid climate was ideal for the cultivation of profitable commercial crops such as tobacco, cotton, rice, indigo, and sugar cane. Those cash crops led to the plantation system of large commercial agriculture and its dependence upon enslaved labor. Unlike the North, the South had few large cities, few banks, few railroads, and few factories. Most of the commerce in the South was related to the storage, distribution, and sale of agricultural products, especially cotton. With the cotton economy booming, there was little reason to create robust financial and industrial sectors.

A Triracial Culture

While geography and climate were key factors in shaping the South's economy and culture, what made the region most distinctive was the diminishing presence of Native Americans and the expanding institution of race-based slavery. During the early decades of the nineteenth century, all three groups—blacks, whites, and Indians—regularly intermingled and adopted aspects of each other's cultures. By 1840, however, few Native Americans remained in the South; most had been forced onto lands in the West.

The South's "peculiar institution"

As the number of Native Americans declined in the South, the number of enslaved African Americans increased. Most southern whites did not own slaves (also called bondpeople), but they supported what was often called the South's **"peculiar institution"** because slavery was so central to the society's way of life. The phrase enabled southerners to avoid using the charged word *slavery*, while the adjective *peculiar* implied that slavery was *unique* to the South. What virtually all white southerners shared during the first half of the nineteenth century was an often brutal racial prejudice against both Native Americans and African Americans.

"peculiar institution" Phrase used by whites in the antebellum South to refer to slavery without using the word slavery.

Assumptions of White Superiority

The profitability and convenience of owning slaves—as well as the psychological appeal of racial superiority among those who did not own slaves—created a sense of racial unity that bridged class differences among whites. Poor whites who owned no slaves could still claim racial superiority to enslaved blacks. Because of race-based slavery, explained Georgia attorney Thomas R. Cobb, every white "feels that he belongs to an elevated class. It matters not that he is no slaveholder; he is not of the inferior race; he is a free-born citizen." In reality, only a very few southerners owned great plantations, but many southern whites dreamed of acquiring large land-holdings and becoming members of a "natural" aristocracy within their communities.

> Belief in racial superiority

The Old South differed from other sections of the country, too, in its high proportion of native-born Americans, both whites and blacks. The South attracted few overseas immigrants after the Revolution. One reason for the lack of foreign migrants was that the main shipping lines connected Europe to northern ports such as Boston, New York City, and Philadelphia. Most immigrants were penniless; they could not afford to travel to the South. Moreover, European immigrants, most of whom were manual laborers, could not compete with slave labor and the poor whites already living in the South.

Conflicting Myths

Southerners, a North Carolina editor wrote, are "a mythological people, created half out of dream and half out of slander, who live in a still-legendary land." He was referring to the conflicting visions of the South that emerged before the Civil War and have since defined the region. A powerful belief among white southerners—that the South was both different *and* better than the North—was central to the self-image of white southerners, then and since. The white South's increasing defensiveness about slavery reflected the economic and political elite's proud sense of its region's distinctiveness and superiority. The dominance of farming remained a vital regional characteristic, whether pictured as the Jeffersonian small farmer living by his manual labor or the lordly planter overseeing his slaves. "We want no manufactures; we desire no trading, no mechanical or manufacturing classes," an Alabama politician told an English visitor. The agrarian ideal and the penchant in the South for fighting, guns, horsemanship, and the military painted a picture of the Old South as full of honest small farmers and aristocratic gentlemen, young belles and beautiful ladies, who led leisurely lives of well-mannered graciousness, honor, and courage, all the while sipping mint juleps in a world of white-columned mansions.

> Myth of the Old South: Agrarian "aristocracy"

In defending the South and slavery from northern abolitionists, southerners claimed that their region was morally superior to the North. Kind planters supposedly provided happy slaves with food, clothing, shelter, and security—in contrast to a North populated with greedy bankers and heartless factory owners who treated their wage laborers worse than slaves. John C. Calhoun insisted that in the northern states where slavery had been banned, "the condition of the African, instead of being improved, has become worse," while in the South, the Africans "have improved greatly in every respect."

In this mythic version of the Old South, slavery is a positive good benefiting both slaves and owners rather than a necessary evil that must one day disappear, as Thomas Jefferson and George Washington had insisted at the end of the eighteenth century. In *Aunt Phillis's Cabin; or, Southern Life As It Is* (1852), novelist Mary Henderson Eastman stresses "the necessity of the existence of slavery at present in our Southern States, and that, as a general thing, the slaves are comfortable and contented, and their owners humane and kind."

The contrasting myth of the Old South was a much darker one developed by northern abolitionists who pictured the region as being caught in the grip of an outdated economic system that led whites to exploit blacks and Native Americans. In this version, the theme of violence runs deep. The white planters were rarely "natural aristocrats" like Thomas Jefferson. More often, they were ambitious self-made men, humble in origins, who had seized opportunities to become rich by planting and selling cotton—and trading in slaves. Many of these farmers-turned-planters were portrayed by abolitionists such as Harriet Beecher Stowe as crude capitalists who raped enslaved women, brutalized slaves, and lorded over their local communities with arrogant disdain. They treated slaves like cattle, broke up slave families, and sold slaves "down the river" to toil in the Louisiana sugar mills and rice plantations.

Like all myths, both of these warring images of the Old South contained elements of truth and distortion. Yet myths often shape human perceptions and actions more than reality. Certainly that has been true in the American South, which itself is a fabric made of many different threads. The mythic image of slavery as a beneficial system for blacks, however, fails the test of credibility. As a bondwoman who escaped to freedom in Canada recalled, "I look upon slavery as the worst evil that ever was. My life has been taken from me in a measure by it. If any are disposed to apologize for slavery, it would be well for them to try it awhile."

A Variety of Souths

For all the common threads tying the Old South together, it in fact included three distinct subregions with different economic interests and diverging degrees of commitment to slavery. Throughout the first half of the nineteenth century, the seven states of the Lower South (South Carolina, Georgia, Florida, Alabama, Mississippi, Louisiana, and parts of Texas) grew increasingly dependent upon labor-intensive cotton production—and the large-scale cultivation of cotton was utterly dependent on slave labor. A traveler in Mississippi observed in 1835 that all of the ambitious whites wanted "to sell cotton in order to buy negroes—to make more cotton to buy negroes"—forever. By 1860, slaves represented nearly half the population of the Lower South.

The states of the Upper South (Virginia, North Carolina, Tennessee, and Arkansas) had more diversified agricultural economies—a mixture of large commercial plantations and small family farms, or "yeoman" farms, where crops were grown mostly for local or personal use rather than for sale in national or international markets. Many southern states also had large areas without slavery, especially in the mountains of Virginia, the western Carolinas, eastern Tennessee, and northern Georgia.

In the Border South (Delaware, Maryland, Kentucky, and Missouri), slavery was disappearing both because cotton could not thrive in those states and because of widespread—and growing—abolitionist sentiment. By 1860, 90 percent of Delaware's black population and half of Maryland's were already free.

> Distinctive southern economies in Upper, Border, and Lower states

What the three subregions shared was opposition to the immediate abolition of slavery. White slave owners in the Border South, who held far fewer slaves than their counterparts in the Lower South, often adopted an attitude of paternalism toward slaves by incorporating them into their households and, to a degree, treating them as if they were family members. A few prominent slave owners actually worked to end slavery by stopping the African slave trade, which officially ended in 1807. Others supported "colonization" efforts to ship slaves and freed blacks to Africa or encouraged owners upon their deaths to free their slaves, as did George Washington.

Slave owners in the Lower South, however, had a disproportionately large investment in slavery. They increasingly believed that only constant supervision, intimidation, and punishment would keep the fast-growing population of bondpeople under control, in part because the working and living conditions for the enslaved were so brutal. "I'd rather be dead," said a white overseer in Louisiana, "than a nigger in one of those big [sugar cane] plantations."

The greatest fear of whites in the Lower South was an organized slave revolt as had occurred in 1791 in French-controlled Saint-Domingue—a decade later to become the independent Republic of Haiti—where plantations and factories were burned, and whites, who were outnumbered by the slaves ten to one, were slaughtered. "For our declaration of independence," one of the rebel leaders announced, "we should have the skin of a white man for parchment, his skull for an inkwell, his blood for ink, and a bayonet for a pen!" At the same time, as the dollar value of slaves soared, thanks to the dramatically increasing demand for cotton, white planters from the Lower South led efforts to transplant slavery into the new western territories.

The Cotton Kingdom

Tobacco, Rice, Sugar, and Livestock

During the first half of the nineteenth century, cotton became the most profitable cash crop in the South. But other crops were grown as well. Tobacco, the region's first main cash crop, had been the economic mainstay of Virginia and Maryland during the colonial era and was also common in North Carolina. After the Revolution, as the tobacco fields in the Chesapeake lost their fertility, the tobacco economy spread into Kentucky and as far west as Missouri. Since rice was the most expensive crop to produce, requiring floodgates, irrigation ditches, and machinery, it was limited to large plantations in the coastal areas ("low country") of the Carolinas and Georgia, where fields could easily be flooded and drained by tidal rivers flowing into the ocean. Sugar cane, like rice, was also an expensive crop to produce, and it required expensive machinery to grind the cane to release the sugar syrup. In addition to such staple crops, the South led the nation in the production of livestock: hogs, horses, mules, and cattle.

The Lower South

Massive migration to Lower South / Old Southwest

Cotton, however, eventually outpaced all the other crops, thanks largely to the invention of the cotton gin that so dramatically increased productivity. In 1805, a visiting Frenchman reported that "the great profits derived from cotton" were enticing an "immense number" of people to the Lower South. At the end of the War of 1812, annual cotton production in the United States was less than 150,000 bales (a bale is a bundle of cotton weighing between 400 and 500 pounds). In 1860, production was 4 *million* bales. As the oldest southern states—Virginia and the Carolinas—experienced soil

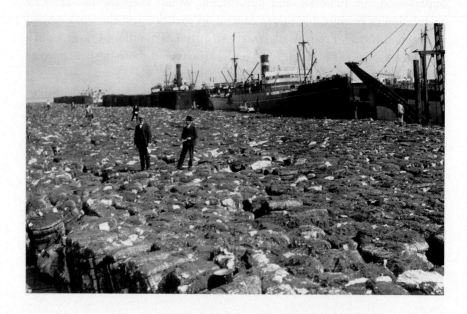

Atop the cotton kingdom This photograph offers a glimpse of the staggering rates of cotton production. These cotton bales are so densely packed and plentiful that men are walking upon them at this Galveston, Texas port.

exhaustion from the overplanting of tobacco and cotton, farmers and planters moved to inexpensive cotton lands in the region called **The Old Southwest**—western Georgia, Alabama, Mississippi, Louisiana, Arkansas, and, eventually, Texas.

The Old Southwest region's low land prices and fertile soil served as a powerful magnet, luring hundreds of thousands of settlers when the seaboard economy faltered during the 1820s and 1830s. Where an acre of land in South Carolina produced only 300 pounds of cotton, an acre in Alabama could generate 800 pounds. A planter who moved to the Mississippi Territory urged a friend back in Kentucky to join him: "If you could . . . bring your negroes to the Miss. Terr., they would certainly make you a handsome fortune in ten years by the cultivation of Cotton." An Alabaman wrote to his father than he had "never seen such a Migration in my life" as huge numbers of Americans picked up and moved to the Old Southwest. A North Carolinian reported that the *"Alabama Fever* . . . has *carried off* vast numbers of our citizens." Between 1810 and 1840, the combined population of Georgia, Alabama, and Mississippi increased from about 300,000 (252,000 of whom were in Georgia) to 1,657,799. More than 40 percent of the new residents were enslaved blacks, many of whom had been moved in chained gangs (called "coffles") from plantations and slave markets in the Carolinas, Virginia, and New Orleans, a "city of bustle and business."

The Spreading Cotton Kingdom

By 1860, the center of the "**cotton kingdom**" stretched from eastern North Carolina, South Carolina, and Georgia through the fertile Alabama-Mississippi "black belt" (so called for the color of the fertile soil), through Louisiana, on to Texas, and up the Mississippi Valley as far as southern Illinois. As cotton prices soared, farmers began shifting away from growing other crops, in part because cotton could be grown on small farms, unlike sugar cane and rice. Many tobacco farmers in Virginia and Maryland pulled up stakes and moved west and south into the "cotton belt." In addition, the emergence of steamboats enabled the Mississippi River to become the cotton

COTTON PRODUCTION, 1821

Each dot represents 1,000 bales of cotton.

- Why was cotton an appealing staple crop?
- What regions produced the most cotton in 1821?
- Keeping in mind what you read about cotton in Chapter 11, what innovations would you suppose allowed farmers to move inland and produce cotton more efficiently?

The Old Southwest Region covering western Georgia, Alabama, Mississippi, Louisiana, Arkansas, and Texas, where low land prices and fertile soil attracted droves of settlers after the American Revolution.

cotton kingdom Cotton-producing region, relying predominantly on slave labor, that spanned from North Carolina west to Louisiana and reached as far north as southern Illinois.

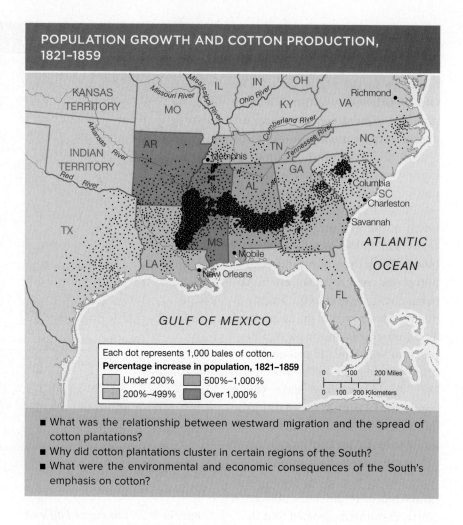

POPULATION GROWTH AND COTTON PRODUCTION, 1821–1859

Each dot represents 1,000 bales of cotton.
Percentage increase in population, 1821–1859
- Under 200%
- 200%–499%
- 500%–1,000%
- Over 1,000%

■ What was the relationship between westward migration and the spread of cotton plantations?
■ Why did cotton plantations cluster in certain regions of the South?
■ What were the environmental and economic consequences of the South's emphasis on cotton?

highway. Millions of bales were sent downriver to New Orleans, where merchant ships took the cotton to New York, New England, Great Britain, and France.

Cotton boom expands slavery

By 1860, Alabama, Mississippi, and Louisiana were the three top-producing cotton states in the nation. At the same time, more millionaires per capita lived in Natchez, Mississippi, along the great river, than anywhere else in the world. The rapid expansion of the cotton belt throughout the South ensured that the region became more, rather than less, dependent on enslaved black workers. More than half of the slaves in the South worked in cotton production.

Slavery became such a powerful engine of economic development in the South that it resisted any criticism and helps explain why southerners became so defiantly defensive about preserving slavery. By 1860, the dollar value of enslaved blacks outstripped the value of *all* American banks, railroads, and factories combined. The South led the nation in exports because of King Cotton. The result was staggering wealth for a few; the twelve richest counties in the United States in 1860 were all in the South. A land surveyor described the economic boom drawing hordes of people to Louisiana: "Money, Negroes, Sugar, Cotton, and Land seem to engross all their time and attention."

The soaring profitability of cotton made some southerners brashly overconfident. In a speech to the U.S. Senate in 1858, South Carolina's former governor, James Henry Hammond, a Democrat who owned a huge cotton plantation worked by slaves, warned the North: "You dare not make war on cotton. No power on earth dares make war upon it. Cotton is King."

What Hammond failed to acknowledge was that the southern economy had grown dangerously dependent on European (largely British and French) demand for raw cotton. By 1860, Britain was importing more than 80 percent of its cotton from the South. Hammond and other southern leaders failed to anticipate what they could least afford: a sudden collapse in world demand for southern cotton that began in 1860. The expansion of the British textile industry peaked in 1860, but by then the Lower South was locked into large-scale cotton production for generations to come.

Increased southern dependence on Britain

White Social Groups in the South

White Planters

Although there were only a few giant plantations in each southern state, their owners exercised disproportionate influence in economic, political, and social life. As a western Virginian observed in the mid-1830s, "the old slaveholding families exerted a great deal of control . . . and they affected the manner and prejudices of the slaveholding part of the state." The large planters in each state behaved like an aristocracy, controlling political, economic, and social life. "The planters here are essentially what the nobility are in other countries," claimed a self-serving James Henry Hammond. "They stand at the head of society and politics. . . . Slavery does indeed create an aristocracy—an aristocracy of talents, of virtue, or generosity, and courage." The largest planters were determined to retain their control over southern society. To do so, they frequently defended their right to rule their neighbors. "Inequality is the fundamental law of the universe," declared one planter.

What distinguished a plantation from a farm, in addition to its size, was the use of a large number of slaves supervised by overseers. A clear-cut distinction between management and labor set the planter apart from the small slaveholder, who often worked side by side with slaves. If, as historians have agreed, one had to own at least twenty slaves to be called a **planter**, only one out of every thirty whites in the South in 1860 was a planter. The 1860 U.S. Census listed eleven planters with 500 slaves and one with as many as 1,000. The planters, making up less than 4 percent of the white men in the South, held more than half the slaves, and the number of slaveholders was only

CORE OBJECTIVE
3. Distinguish among the major groups within southern white society and explain why each group was committed to the continuation and expansion of slavery.

planters Owners of large farms in the South that were worked by twenty or more slaves and supervised by overseers.

Cotton and the Transformation of the South

Between 1800 and 1860, the production of cotton transformed the southern region of the United States. The following chart explores the growth of cotton production and slavery, as well as where slavery and cotton production was concentrated in the region by 1860.

FACT 1
Increased Cotton Production

In 1815, the South produced 150,000 bales of cotton. By 1860, it produced 4 million bales. Cotton was the nation's leading export.

FACT 2
Increased Number of Slaves

In 1790, there were 700,000 slaves in the United States. In 1830, there were 2 million. By 1860, there were 4 million.

FACT 3
Concentration of Slaves

By 1860, more than half of all slaves worked on cotton plantations.

FACT 4
Concentration of Cotton Production

Cotton production was concentrated in the fertile "black belt" regions of The Old Southwest, eventually stretching westward from the Carolinas and Georgia all the way to Texas. In 1860, Louisiana, Mississippi, and Alabama were the top-producing cotton states.

FACT 5
Concentration of Slave Ownership

In 1860, whites who owned twenty or more slaves were considered planters. They constituted only 4 percent of the white population. Only roughly 25 percent of white families owned slaves, most owning fewer than twenty.

FACT 6
Value of Slaves

By 1860, the dollar value of slaves outstripped the value of all American banks, railroads, and factories combined.

FACT 7
Value of Cotton

Southern cotton fueled the growth of the modern textile industry, particularly in Europe. By 1860, Great Britain imported 80 percent of its raw cotton from the American South. Southern planters, dependent on slavery, grew overconfident that their economic and social system was indestructible.

QUESTIONS FOR ANALYSIS

1. Why did southerners invest so much in cotton production?

2. Where was cotton production concentrated?

3. How did increased cotton production affect slavery?

4. How did increased cotton production affect the distribution of wealth in the South?

383,637 out of a total white population of 8 million. But assuming that each family numbered five people, then almost two million people, or roughly a fourth of the South's white population, had a direct interest in slavery.

Few planters were wealthy enough not to work. Most of them were full-time commercial farmers who spent their days, including weekends, carefully managing their agricultural business. Most planters had begun their careers as land traders, investors, cotton merchants (called "factors"), and farmers. Over time, they made enough money to acquire a plantation worked by slaves. Frederick Stanton, a cotton broker near Natchez, Mississippi, became a planter with 444 slaves working 15,000 acres of cotton.

Success as a cotton planter required careful monitoring of the world markets for cotton, land, and slaves as well as careful management of the workers and production. When not working, planters enjoyed hunting, horse racing, and cards. As a plantation slave recalled, his master on Sundays liked to "gamble, run horses, or fight game-cocks, discuss politics, and drink whisky, and brandy and water all day long."

> The planter elite

From colonial times, most southern white men, but especially the planter and political elite, embraced a social code centered on an easily offended sense of personal honor in which a man was expected to defend his reputation—with words, fists, or guns. Duels to the death were the ultimate expression of personal honor and manly courage. Although not confined to the South, dueling was much more common there than in the rest of the nation, a fact that gave rise to the observation that southerners would be polite until they were angry enough to kill you. Many of the most prominent southern leaders—congressmen, senators, governors, editors, and planters—engaged in duels, although dueling was technically illegal in many states. The roster of participants included President Andrew Jackson of Tennessee and Senator Henry Clay of Kentucky.

> Honor and violence: Dueling

The Plantation Mistress

The **plantation mistress**, like the master, seldom led a life of idle leisure, nor was she a frail, helpless creature focused solely on planning parties and balls. Although the mistress of the plantation had slaves to wait on her and attend to her needs, she also supervised the domestic household in the same way as the planter took care of the cotton business, overseeing the supply and preparation of food and linens, the housecleaning and care of the sick, and many other details, including the birthing of babies. A plantation slave reported that her mistress "was with all the slave women every time a baby was born. Or, when a plague of misery hit the folks, she knew what to do and what kind of medicine to chase off the aches and pains." The son of a Tennessee slaveholder remembered that his mother and grandmother were "the busiest women I ever saw." Mary Boykin Chesnut, a plantation mistress in South Carolina, complained that "there is no slave, after all, like a wife." She admitted that she herself had few rights in the household, since her husband was the "master of the house." Planters ruled their wives and children as well

Mary Boykin Chesnut Her diary describing the Civil War was republished in 1981 and won the Pulitzer Prize.

plantation mistress Matriarch of a planter's household, responsible for supervising the domestic aspects of the estate.

as their slaves, and southern white women were even more confined to the "domestic arena" than their counterparts in the North. Virginian George Fitzhugh, a celebrated Virginia attorney and writer, spoke for most southern men when he explained that a "man loves his children because they are weak, helpless, and dependent. He loves his wife for similar reasons."

White women living in a slaveholding culture confronted a double standard in terms of moral and sexual behavior. They were expected to be examples of Christian morality and sexual purity, and to "obey" their fathers and husbands, even as their husbands, brothers, and sons often followed an unwritten rule of self-indulgent hedonism. "God forgive us," Mary Chesnut wrote in her diary, "but ours is a monstrous system. Like the patriarchs of old, our men live all in one house with their wives and their [enslaved] concubines [lovers]; and the mulattoes [people of mixed races] one sees in every family partly resemble the white children. Any lady is ready to tell you who is the father of all the mulatto children in everybody's household but her own. Those, she seems to think, drop from the clouds." Such a double standard reinforced the arrogant authoritarianism displayed by many white planters. Yet for all their private complaints and daily burdens, few plantation mistresses spoke out against the male-dominated social order and racist climate.

Overseers and Drivers

White overseers

The whites who worked on the large plantations were usually *overseers* who managed the slaves to ensure that they worked hard and efficiently. They generally came from the middle class of white farmers or skilled workers, or were younger sons of planters. Most hoped to become slaveholders themselves. They moved often, seeking better wages and cheaper land. A Mississippi planter described white overseers as "a worthless set of vagabonds." Usually, the highest managerial position a slave could hope for on a plantation was that of *driver*, a man whose job was to oversee a small group ("gang") of slaves. There were, however, a few black overseers. Francis Frederic, a slave in Kentucky, remembered that his grandmother's white master was a "hard one." He appointed her son, a slave, as the plantation's overseer. After the planter discovered that Frederic's grandmother had committed the crime of attending a prayer meeting, he ordered her son to give her "forty lashes with a thong of a raw cow's-hide, her master standing over her the whole time blaspheming and threatening what he would do if her son did not lay it on."

"Plain White Folk"

"plain white folk" Yeoman farmers who lived and worked on their own small farms, growing food and cash crops to trade for necessities.

The most numerous white southerners were the small farmers—the **"plain white folk"** who were usually uneducated and often illiterate, eking out hardscrabble lives of bare self-sufficiency separate from the market revolution. These small farmers ("yeomen") lived with their families in simple two-room cabins, raised a few hogs and chickens, grew some corn and cotton, and traded with neighbors more than they bought from stores. Women on these farms worked in the fields during harvest time but spent most of their days doing household chores. Some of these "middling" farmers owned a handful of slaves with whom they worked alongside, but most had none. In the backcountry and mountainous regions of the South, small farmers dominated the social structure; there were few plantations in western North Carolina and Virginia, upcountry South Carolina, eastern Tennessee, northern Georgia, and northern Alabama.

Southern farmers tended to be fiercely independent and suspicious of government authority, and they overwhelmingly identified with the Democratic party of Andrew Jackson and the spiritual energies of the evangelical Protestant denominations such as Baptists and Methodists. Although only a minority of the small farm owners held slaves, most supported the slave system for both economic and racial reasons. They feared that the slaves, if freed, would compete with them for land and jobs, and they enjoyed the privileged status that race-based slavery afforded them. As a white farmer told a northern traveler, "Now suppose they [slaves] was free. You see they'd all think themselves as good as we." James Henry Hammond and other wealthy white planters frequently reminded their poorer white neighbors who owned no slaves that "in a slave country, every freeman is an aristocrat" because blacks are beneath them in the social order. Such racist sentiments pervaded the Lower South—and much of the rest of the nation—throughout the nineteenth century.

"Poor Whites"

Visitors to the Old South often had trouble telling small farmers apart from the "poor whites," a category of desperately poor people relegated to the least desirable land, living on the fringes of polite society, often in the upland areas or in the Appalachian Mountains. The "poor whites," often derided as "crackers," or "hillbillies," were often day laborers or squatters who owned neither land nor slaves. Some 40 percent of white southerners worked as "tenants," renting land from others, or as farm laborers, toiling for others. And what land they owned was often the least desirable for farming. They were often forced to take refuge in the pine barrens, the mountain hollows, and the swamps after having been pushed aside by the more enterprising and the more successful. They usually lived in log cabins or shacks and often made their own clothing, barely managing each year to keep their families clothed, warm, dry, and fed. The "poor whites" were regularly satirized and caricatured. In 1860, D. R. Hundley wrote in *Social Relations in Our Southern States* that the poor white southerner was descended from criminals deported to America from Great Britain. "He is bony and lank, with a sallow complexion, awkward manners, and a natural stupidity or dullness of intellect that almost surpasses belief."

CORE **OBJECTIVE**

4. Describe the impact of slavery on African Americans, both free and enslaved, throughout the South.

Slave codes

Black Society in the South

However immoral and degrading, slavery was one of the fastest-growing elements of national life during the first half of the nineteenth century. Owning, working, and selling slaves was the quickest way to wealth and social status in the nineteenth-century South. In 1790, the United States had fewer than 700,000 black slaves. By 1830 it had more than 2 million, and by 1860 almost 4 million. As the enslaved population grew, slave owners felt the need to develop a complex system of rules, regulations, and restrictions to govern the slaves' daily lives. Throughout the seventeenth and well into the eighteenth century, slavery had largely been an uncodified system of forced labor. Slaves were initially treated like indentured servants, who worked for a designated number of years and then, at some point after they had fulfilled their service, would be freed.

After the American Revolution, however, slavery became a highly regulated institution centered on lifelong service. Slaves were treated like property rather than people; babies became slaves at birth; slaves could be moved, sold, rented, whipped, or raped, as their master saw fit. Formal **slave codes** in each state governed the treatment of slaves in order to deter runaways or rebellions. Some state codes, for example, prohibited slaves from gathering in groups of more than three. Slaves could not leave their owner's land or household without permission or stay out after dark (curfew) without an identification pass. "No slave dare leave the plantation to which he belongs," said Charles Ball, a bondman who lived in several states, explained, not for a "single mile" or a "single hour, by night . . . practice to leave their owners' property without a pass from the overseer, or master."

Some codes made it a crime for slaves to learn how to read and write, for fear that they might use notes to plan a revolt. A former Kentucky slave, John W. Fields, remembered that the white slaveholders "were very harsh if we were caught trying to learn or write. . . . Our ignorance was the greatest hold the South had on us." If a white was caught teaching a slave to read, they were subject to a fine and imprisonment. Fields also explained that the slaves in his rural community were never allowed to go to town for fear that they might hatch an escape. Slaves in most states could not testify in court, legally marry, own firearms, or hit a white man, even in self-defense. Yet despite such restrictions and brutalities, the enslaved managed to create their own community and culture within the confines of the slave system.

"Free Persons of Color"

In the South, free persons of color tended to live in cities. In fact they were anything but free; they occupied an uncertain social status between slavery and freedom. In South Carolina, for example, free blacks had to pay

slave codes Codes governing the treatment of slaves in each state in order to deter runaways and rebellions.

an annual tax and were not allowed to leave the state. After 1823, they were required to have a white "guardian." Blacks became "free" in a number of ways. Over the years, some slaves were able to purchase their freedom, and others were freed ("manumitted") by their owners. By 1860, there were approximately 250,000 free blacks in the slave states, most of whom lived in coastal cities such as Baltimore, Charleston, Mobile, and New Orleans. Some were tailors or shoemakers or carpenters; others worked as painters, bricklayers, butchers, blacksmiths, or barbers. Still others worked on the docks or on steamships. Free black women usually worked as seamstresses, laundresses, or house servants. Free blacks had more rights than slaves. They could enter into contracts, marry, own property (including slaves of their own), and pass on their property to their children.

Among the free black population were a large number of **mulattoes**, people of mixed racial ancestry. The census of 1860 reported 412,000 mulattoes in the United States, or about 10 percent of the black population—probably a drastic undercount. In cities such as Charleston, South Carolina, and especially New Orleans, Louisiana, "colored" society occupied a status somewhere between that of blacks and that of whites. Some mulattoes built substantial fortunes and even became slaveholders themselves. In Louisiana, a mulatto, Cyprien Ricard, paid $250,000 for an estate that had ninety-one slaves. In Natchez, Mississippi, William Johnson, son of a white father and a mulatto mother, operated three barbershops, owned 1,500 acres of land, and held several slaves. Black slaveholders were few in number, however. The 1830 census reported that 3,775 free blacks, about 2 percent of the total free black population, owned 12,760 slaves. Most often, black slaveholders were free blacks who bought their own family members with the express purpose of freeing them.

Yarrow Mamout As an enslaved African Muslim, Mamout purchased his freedom, acquired property, and settled in present-day Washington, D.C. Charles Willson Peale executed this portrait in 1819 when Mamout was over 100 years old.

The Trade in Slaves

The rapid increase in the slave population mainly occurred naturally, through slave births, especially after Congress and President Thomas Jefferson outlawed American involvement with the African slave trade in 1808. But banning the importation of slaves from Africa also had the effect of increasing the cash value of slaves in the United States. This in turn convinced some owners to treat their slaves better. As one planter remarked in 1849, "The time has been that the farmer would kill up and wear out one Negro to buy another, but it is not so now."

The dramatic rise in the dollar value of enslaved workers prompted better treatment for many. "Massa was purty good," one ex-slave recalled. "He treated us jus' 'bout like you would a good mule." Another said his master "fed us reg'lar on good, 'stantial food, jus' like you'd tend to you hoss [horse], if you had a real good one." A slave born in 1850 had a life expectancy of 36 years; the life expectancy of whites was 40 years. Some slaveholders hired white wage laborers, often Irish immigrants, for dangerous work rather than risk the lives of the more valuable slaves.

mulattoes Mixed-race people who constituted most of the South's free black population.

Domestic slave trade

Once the African slave trade was outlawed, the slave-trading network *within* the United States became even more important. Selling slaves for profit became big business, and slave markets and auction houses sprang up in every southern city. Most often, slaves along the Atlantic coast were sold and moved from the worn-out lands of Virginia and the Carolinas into the booming Old Southwest. Perhaps the worst aspect of the domestic slave trade was the separation of children from parents and husbands from wives. "Them days was hell," a former slave woman named Delia Garlic remembered. "Babies were snatched from their mother's breast and sold to speculators. Chilrens was separated from sisters and brothers and never saw each other again. Course they cried. You think they not cry when they was sold like cattle?" Only Louisiana and Alabama (from 1852) prohibited separating a child younger than ten from his or her mother, and no state prevented the separation of a slave husband from his wife.

The business of slavery This advertisement for the Blount & Dawson guarantees its clients "secure and good accommodations for all negroes left with us for Sale or Safe-Keeping" in its newly acquired jail, opposite the state bank.

Almost a million captive blacks were "sold South" and taken to the Old Southwest during the first half of the nineteenth century. A third of the transplanted slaves were transported with their owners. The other two-thirds were sold at auctions where slaves were stripped to show their physique and often told to jump and dance to display their agility. White owners—as well as Indians who purchased enslaved blacks—worked the slaves especially hard in the "howling wilderness" of the Old Southwest, cutting down vast forests, operating sawmills, draining swamps, clearing land, building roads, and planting cotton. A white Virginian noted in 1807 that "there is a great aversion amongst our Negroes to be carried to distant parts, and particularly to our new countries [in the Old Southwest]."

Rural and Urban Slavery

Plantation field hands

The vast majority of slaves across the South were **field hands**, both men and women, including children, organized into work gangs, usually supervised by a black "driver" or white overseer. Plantation slaves were usually housed in one- or two-room wooden shacks or log cabins with dirt floors. The wealthiest planters built slave cabins out of brick. A set of clothes was distributed twice a year, but shoes were generally provided only in winter; slaves went barefoot most of the year. About half of all slave babies died in their first year, a rate more than twice that of whites. The food provided slaves was cheap and monotonous: cornmeal, pork, molasses, and chicken.

field hands Slaves who toiled in the cotton or cane fields in organized work gangs.

Solomon Northup, a free-born African American from New York with a wife and three children, was kidnapped in 1845 by slave traders, taken first to Washington, D.C., and then to New Orleans, and eventually sold to a

THE SLAVE POPULATION, 1820 AND 1860

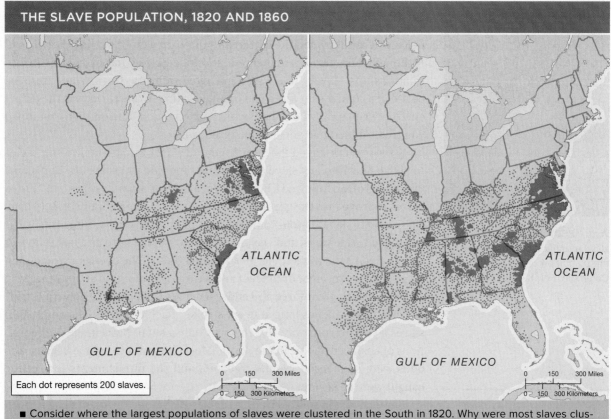

Each dot represents 200 slaves.

- Consider where the largest populations of slaves were clustered in the South in 1820. Why were most slaves clustered in these regions and not in others?
- Compare this map with the map of cotton production on page 354. What patterns do you see?
- Why did slavery spread west? Why did many slaves resist migrating west?

"repulsive and coarse" Louisiana cotton planter. More than a decade later, he was able to gain his freedom. In *Twelve Years a Slave* (1853), he wrote about his living and working conditions as a slave. His bed "was a plank twelve inches wide and ten feet long. My pillow was a stick of wood. The bedding was a coarse blanket." The log cabin where he and others slept had a dirt floor and no windows. Each day, "an hour before daylight, the horn is blown. Then the slaves arouse, prepare their breakfast . . . and hurry to the field." If found in their "quarters after daybreak," or if they failed to harvest enough cotton, he added, slaves were flogged. "It was rarely that a day passed by without one or more whippings. . . . The crack of the lash, and the shrieking of the slaves, can be heard from dark till bed time, on Epps' plantation, any day almost during the entire period of the cotton-picking season."

Field hands worked from sunrise to sunset, six days a week. Amanda McDaniel, enslaved in Georgia, remembered that her parents "had to get

Brutal force and rural slaves

***Jack* (1850)** Daguerreotype of a slave identified only as Jack, on the plantation of B. F. Taylor in Columbia, South Carolina.

up at four o'clock every morning and feed the stock [cattle, pigs, horses, and mules] first. By the time it was light enough to see they had to be in the fields where they hoed the cotton and the corn as well as the other crops." Although some owners and slaves developed close and even affectionate relationships, slavery was a system rooted in brutal force. The difference between a good owner and a bad one, according to one slave, was the difference between one "who did not whip you too much" and one who "whipped you till he'd bloodied you and blistered you."

Slave owners staged the punishment of slaves into theatrical spectacles to strike fear into any slave considering rebellion or escape. In Louisiana, whippings often followed a horrific procedure, as a visitor reported: "Three stakes is drove into the ground in a triangular manner, about six feet apart. The culprit [slave] is told to lie down . . . flat on his belly. The arms is extended out, side ways, and each hand tied to a stake hard and fast. The feet is both tied to the third stake, all stretched tight." The overseer would then step back "seven, eight or ten feet and with a rawhide whip about 7 feet long . . . lays on with great force and address across the Buttocks," cutting strips of flesh "7 or 8 inches long at every stroke." Such cruelties led over 50,000 slaves a year to run away. But this was only a small percentage of the millions of enslaved people in the South. Most chose not to escape because the odds were so stacked against freedom, and the punishments for getting caught were so severe.

Greater mobility for city slaves

Slaves living in southern cities such as Richmond or Atlanta had a much different experience from those on farms and plantations. City life meant that slaves interacted not only with their white owners but also with the extended interracial community—shopkeepers and police, neighbors and strangers. Some slaves in cities were "hired out" on the condition that they paid a percentage of their earned wages to their owners. Generally speaking, slaves in cities enjoyed greater mobility and freedom than their counterparts in rural areas living on isolated farms or plantations.

Slave Women

Although enslaved men and women often performed similar chores, they did not experience slavery in the same way. "Slavery is terrible for men," the former North Carolina slave Harriet Jacobs stressed in her autobiography, *Incidents in the Life of a Slave Girl*, "but it is far more terrible for women. Superadded to the burden common to all, they have wrongs, and sufferings, and mortifications peculiarly their own."

Female slaves and reproduction

Once slaveholders realized how profitable a fertile female slave could be over time by giving birth to babies that could later be sold, they "encouraged" female slaves to have as many children as possible. A South Carolina planter named William Johnson explained in 1815 that the "interest of the owner is to obtain from his slaves labor *and increase* [in their numbers]." Some owners rewarded pregnant slaves by giving them less work and more food, and rewarded new mothers with dresses and silver dollars.

But if motherhood provided enslaved women with greater stature and benefits, it also was exhausting. Within days after childbirth, the mothers were put to work spinning, weaving, or sewing. A few weeks thereafter, they were sent back to the fields; breast-feeding mothers were often forced to take their babies with them, strapped to their backs. Enslaved women were expected to do "man's work": cut trees, haul logs, spread fertilizer, plow fields, dig ditches, slaughter animals, hoe corn, and pick cotton. As an escaped slave reported, "Women who do outdoor work are used as bad as men."

Once women passed their childbearing years, around the age of forty, their workload increased. Slaveholders put middle-aged women to work full-time in the fields or performing other outdoor labor. On large plantations, elderly women, called *grannies*, kept the children during the day while their mothers worked outside. Slave women worked as cooks and seamstresses, midwives and nurses, healers and folk doctors.

Enslaved girls, women, and some men were often sexually abused by their owners, both men and women. James Henry Hammond, the prominent South Carolina planter and political leader who confessed that he only succeeded "when everything is under my control," had a long affair with one of his female slaves, Sally Johnson, who bore several of his children, and then began another affair with one of her daughters, twelve-year-old Louisa. (A lusty man with voracious sexual appetites, Hammond also had scandalous affairs with four teen-aged nieces and two daughters of his sister-in-law). Sometimes a white master or overseer would rape a woman in the fields or cabins. Sometimes a woman would be locked in a cabin with a male slave whose task was to impregnate her. Enslaved women responded to sexual assaults in different ways. Some seduced their owner away from his wife. Others fiercely resisted the sexual advances—and were usually whipped or even killed for their disobedience. Some women aborted or killed their babies rather than see them grow up in slavery.

> Female slaves and sexual abuse

Slave family in a Georgia cotton field The invention of the cotton gin sent cotton production soaring, deepening the South's dependence on slavery.

Celia

A single historical example helps illustrate the exploitation, deprivation, and vulnerability of enslaved people. The tragic story of a teenager named Celia reveals the complexity of slavery and the limited options available to the enslaved. As Celia discovered, slaves often could improve their circumstances only by making horrible choices that offered no guarantee of success.

In 1850, fourteen-year-old Celia was purchased by Robert Newsom, a Missouri farmer who told his daughters that he had bought the girl to be their servant. In fact, however, the recently widowed Newsom wanted a sexual slave. After purchasing Celia, he raped her, and for the next five years, he treated her as his mistress, even building her a brick cabin fifty yards from his house. During that time, she gave birth to two children, presumably his offspring.

On June 23, 1855, the sixty-five-year-old Newsom entered Celia's cabin, ignored her frantic appeals, and kept assaulting her until she struck and killed him with a large stick. Celia was not allowed to testify at her murder trial because she was a slave. The judge and jury, all white men, pronounced her guilty, and on December 21, 1855, she was hanged. The grim story of Celia's abusive owner and brief life illustrates the lopsided power structure in southern society at the time. Celia bore a double burden, that of a slave and of a woman living in a male-dominated society rife with racism and sexism.

CORE **OBJECTIVE**

5. Analyze how enslaved peoples responded to the inhumanity of their situation.

Forging a Slave Community

To generalize about slavery is to miss the diversity of its experiences. Enslaved African Americans were victims of terrible injustice and abuse, but such an obvious truth neglects important evidence of their endurance, resilience, and achievement. The Africans who were brought to America represented a variety of ethnic, linguistic, and tribal origins. Wherever they could, they forged their own sense of community, asserted their individuality, and devised ingenious ways of resisting their confinement. African American folklore invented stories of resistance such as "Brer [Brother] Rabbit," where the smart little rabbit eludes the animals stalking it by hiding in a patch of prickly briars. Many **spirituals**, sacred folk songs, expressed a longing to be free. Although most slaves were prohibited from marrying, the law did not prevent them from choosing partners and forging a family life within the rigid constraints of the slave system.

The Slave Family

spirituals Songs with religious messages sung by slaves to help ease the strain of field labor and to voice their suffering at the hands of their masters and overseers.

Slave marriages had no legal status, but many slaveholders accepted unofficial marriages as a stabilizing influence on the plantation. Sometimes they performed the marriages themselves or had a minister officiate. Whatever the formalities, the norm for the slave community, as for the white, was the nuclear family, with the father regarded as the head of the household. Most slave children were socialized by means of the nuclear family, which afforded some degree of independence from white influence. Childhood was short for slaves. At five or six years of age, children were put to work; they collected trash and firewood, picked cotton, scared away crows from planted fields, weeded gardens and fields, and ran errands. By age ten they were full-time field hands. The frequent buying and selling of slaves meant that children were often separated from their parents and sold to new masters. In Missouri, one enslaved woman saw six of her seven children, aged one to eleven, sold to six different owners. Given the fragility of the family, enslaved African Americans often extended the fellowship of family to those who worked together, with older slave women being addressed as "granny," or co-workers as "sis" or "brother." Such efforts to create a sense of extended family resembled similar kinship practices in Africa. One white teacher visiting a slave community observed that they "all belonged to one immense family."

African American Religion

Among the most important elements of African American culture was its dynamic religion, a unique mixture of African, Caribbean, and Christian elements often practiced in secret because many slaveholders feared enslaved workers might use group religious services as a means of organizing rebellions. Slaves found in religion both relief for the soul and release for their emotions. Most Africans brought with them to the Americas belief in a Creator, or Supreme God, whom they could recognize in the Christian God, and whom they might identify with Christ, the Holy Ghost, and the saints. But they also maintained beliefs in spirits, magic, and conjuring. Most slave owners tried to erase African religion and spirituality from the slave experience.

***Plantation Burial* (1860)** The slaves of Mississippi governor Tilghman Tucker gather together in the woods to bury and mourn for one of their own. The painter of this scene, Englishman John Antrobus, would serve in the Confederate Army during the Civil War.

By 1860, about 20 percent of adult slaves had joined Christian denominations. Many others displayed aspects of the Christian faith in their forms of worship but were not considered Christians. As a white minister observed, "Their notions of the Supreme Being; of the character and offices of Christ and of the Holy Ghost; of a future state; and of what constitutes the holiness of life are indefinite and confused." Some slaves had "heard of Jesus Christ, but who he is and what he has done for a ruined world, they cannot tell."

> African American religion and spirituals

Slaves found the Bible inspiring in its support for the poor and oppressed, and they embraced its promise of salvation through the sacrifice of Jesus. Likewise, the lyrics of religious spirituals helped slaves endure the strain of field labor. The abolitionist Frederick Douglass, himself a former slave, stressed that "slaves sing most when they are most unhappy." Spirituals offered them deliverance from their worldly woes. One popular spiritual, "Go Down, Moses," derived from the plight of the ancient Israelites held captive in Egypt, says: "We need not always weep and moan, / Let my people go. / And wear these slavery chains forlorn, / Let my people go."

Slave Rebellions

Southern whites feared slave uprisings more than anything. As a prominent Virginian explained, a slave revolt would "deluge the southern country with blood." Any sign of resistance or rebellion therefore risked a brutal response. In 1811, for example, two of Thomas Jefferson's nephews, Lilburn and Isham Lewis, tied a seventeen-year-old slave named George to the floor of their Kentucky cabin and killed him with an axe in front of seven other slaves, all because George had run away several times. They then handed the axe to one of the slaves and forced him to dismember the body and put the pieces in the fireplace. The Lewises, who had been drinking heavily, wanted "to set an example for any other uppity slaves."

> Slave rebellions

The overwhelming authority and firepower of southern whites made organized resistance by slaves very risky. The nineteenth-century South witnessed only four major slave insurrections. In 1800, a slave named Gabriel Prosser, who worked as a blacksmith on a plantation near Richmond, Virginia, hatched a revolt involving perhaps a thousand other slaves. They planned to seize key points in the city, capture the governor, James Monroe, and overthrow the white elite. Gabriel expected the "poor white people" to join their effort. But someone alerted whites to the scheme. Gabriel and twenty-six of his fellow "soldiers" were captured, tried, and hanged. Before his execution, Gabriel explained that he was only imitating George Washington: "I have ventured my life in endeavoring to obtain the liberty of my countrymen." A white Virginian who observed the hangings noted that the rebels on the gallows displayed a "sense of their [natural] rights, [and] a contempt for danger."

In early 1811, the largest slave revolt in American history occurred just north of New Orleans in the Louisiana Territory, where wealthy sugarcane planters had acquired one of the largest populations of slaves in North America, five times as many as the whites who owned them. Many of those slaves were ripe for revolt. Sugarcane was known as a "killer crop" because the working conditions were so harsh that many slaves died from exhaustion in the heat and humidity of Louisiana.

Late on January 8, a group of slaves broke into their owner's plantation house along the east bank of the Mississippi River. The planter was able to escape, but his son was hacked to death. The leader of the assault was Charles Deslondes, a trusted slave overseer. Deslondes and his fellow rebels seized weapons, horses, and militia uniforms from the plantation. Reinforced by more slaves and emboldened by liquor, the rebels headed toward New Orleans, burning houses and killing whites along the way. Over the next two days, the ranks of the rebels swelled to over 200. But their success was short-lived. Angry whites—as well as several free blacks who were later praised for their "tireless zeal and dauntless courage"—suppressed the insurrection. U.S. Army units and militia joined the effort. Dozens of slaves were killed or wounded; most who fled were captured over the next week. "We made considerable slaughter," reported one white planter. Deslondes had his hands severed and thighs broken before he was shot and his body burned. As many as 100 slaves were tortured, killed, and beheaded. Their severed heads were placed on poles along the Mississippi River in order to strike fear into enslaved workers. A month after the rebellion was put down, a white resident noted that "all the negro difficulties have subsided and gentle peace prevails."

Denmark Vesey Revolt

The Denmark Vesey plot in Charleston, South Carolina, discovered in 1822, involved a similar effort to assault the white population. Vesey, born in 1767 on the Caribbean island of St. Thomas, was purchased by a slave trader based in Charleston. In 1799 he purchased a lottery ticket and won $1,500, which he used to buy his freedom, joining 3,600 other free blacks in Charleston. He thereafter opened a carpentry shop and organized a Bible study class in the African Methodist Episcopal (AME) Church.

In 1822, Vesey and several slaves developed a plan for a massive slave revolt. They would first capture the city's arsenal and distribute its hundreds of rifles to free and enslaved blacks. All whites in the city would then be killed, along with any blacks who refused to join the rebellion. Vesey then planned to burn the city, seize ships in the harbor, and head for the black republic of Haiti, where slaves in the former French sugar colony, then called Saint-Domingue, had staged a successful revolt in 1791.

The Vesey plot never got off the ground, however. As Vesey and others secretly tried to recruit slaves, one of them told his master what was going on. Soon Vesey and a hundred other supposed slave rebels were captured and tried. The court found Vesey guilty of plotting a slave uprising intended to "trample on all laws, human and divine; to riot in blood, outrage, rapine . . . and conflagration, and to introduce anarchy and confusion in their most horrid forms." Vesey and thirty-four others were executed; three dozen more were transported to Spanish Cuba and sold. The AME church in Charleston where Vesey hatched his plan was closed and demolished. When told that he would be hanged, Vesey replied that "the work of insurrection will go on."

Denmark Vesey's planned rebellion led officials in South Carolina to place even more restrictions on the mobility of free blacks and black religious gatherings. It also influenced John C. Calhoun to abandon the nationalism of his early political career and become the South's most forceful spokesman for states' rights.

Nat Turner Rebellion

The Nat Turner insurrection of August 1831, in a rural area of Virginia where enslaved blacks greatly outnumbered free whites, again panicked whites throughout the South. Turner, a trusted black overseer, was also a preacher who believed God had instructed him to lead a slave rebellion. The revolt began when a small group of slaves joined Turner in methodically killing his owner's family. They then repeated the process at other farmhouses, where other slaves joined in. Before the revolt ended, fifty-seven whites had been killed, most of them women and children. Turner later explained that he had also killed the "man who was to me a kind master." Federal troops, Virginia militiamen, and volunteers, driven by anger and fear, indiscriminately killed hundreds of slaves in the process of putting down the rebels. A Virginia newspaper said the behavior of the white vigilantes was comparable in "barbarity to the atrocities of the insurgents." Seventeen slaves were hanged; several were decapitated, with their severed heads placed on poles along the highway. Turner, called the "blood-stained monster," avoided capture for six weeks. He then was tried, found guilty, and hanged. His dead body was dismembered, with body parts given to the victims' families.

Nat Turner's Rebellion (1831) Insurrection in rural Virginia led by black overseer Nat Turner, who murdered slave owners and their families; in turn, federal troops indiscriminately killed hundreds of slaves in the process of putting down Turner and his rebels.

More than any other slave uprising, **Nat Turner's Rebellion** terrified white southerners by making real the lurking fear that enslaved blacks might revolt. The Virginia legislature responded by restricting the ability of slaves to learn to read and write and gather for religious meetings. "We were no more than dogs," an enslaved woman recalled. "If they caught us with a piece of paper in our pockets, they'd whip us. They was afraid we'd learn to read and write, but I never got the chance." Throughout the South after Nat Turner's Rebellion, states created vigilante groups of whites, slave owners as well as non-owners, who would patrol their communities looking for runaways. A former slave highlighted the "thousand obstacles thrown in the way of the flying slave. Every white man's hand is raised against him—the patrollers are watching for him—the hounds are ready to follow on his track, and the nature of the country is such as renders it impossible to pass through it with any safety."

The Lure of Freedom

But slaves kept running away—a powerful example of the enduring lure of freedom and the extraordinary courage of those who yearn for it. Frederick Douglass decided that risking death was better than staying in bondage: "I had as well be killed running as die standing." As Douglass implied, the odds were stacked against escape, in part because most slaves could not read, had no maps, and could not use public transportation such as stagecoaches, steamboats, and railroads. Blacks, whether free or enslaved, had to have an identity pass or official emancipation papers to go anywhere on their own. Most runaways were tracked down by bloodhounds or bounty hunters. Even in the 1850s—the height of efforts by many northerners to help runaways through the "underground railroad," a secret network of safe houses and abolitionists—only about 1,000 slaves each year made it to safety.

But slaves who did not escape resisted in other ways. They often faked illness, engaged in sabotage, stole or broke tools, or destroyed crops or livestock. Yet there were constraints on such behavior, for laborers would likely eat better on a prosperous plantation than on a struggling one. And the shrewdest slaveholders knew that offering rewards was more profitable than inflicting pain.

> Runaways: The "underground railroad"

> Everyday forms of resistance

The South—a Region Apart

The recurring theme of southern politics and culture from the 1830s to the outbreak of civil war in 1861 was the region's determination to remain a society dominated by whites who lorded over people of color. Slavery increasingly became the paramount issue controlling all else in the South. A South Carolinian asserted that "slavery with us is no abstraction—but a great and vital fact. Without it, our every comfort would be taken from us."

Protecting the right of southerners to own, transport, and sell slaves in the new western territories became the overriding focus of southern political leaders during the 1830s and after. As a Mississippi governor insisted in 1850, slavery "is entwined with our political system and cannot be separated from it." It was race-based slavery that provided the South's prosperity as well as its growing sense of separateness from the rest of the nation.

Throughout the 1830s, southern state legislatures were "one and indivisible" in their efforts to preserve race-based slavery. They shouted defiance against northern abolitionists who called for an end to the immorality of slavery. Virginia's General Assembly, for example, declared that only the southern states had the right to control slavery and that such control must be "maintained at all hazards." The Georgia legislature agreed, announcing that "upon this point there can be no discussion—no compromise—no doubt." The increasingly militant efforts of northerners to restrict or abolish slavery helped reinforce the sense of southern unity while provoking an emotional defensiveness that would result in secession and war—and the unexpected end of slavery.

■ **The Southern Distinctiveness** The South remained rural and agricultural in the first half of the nineteenth century as the rest of the nation embraced urban industrial development. The region's climate favored the growth of cash crops such as tobacco, rice, indigo, and, increasingly, cotton. These crops led to the spread of the plantation system of large commercial agriculture dependent on enslaved labor. The Southern planter elite sought not only to preserve slavery in the nineteenth century but also to expand it, despite growing criticism of this *"peculiar institution"* outside the region.

■ **A Cotton Economy** Throughout the pre–Civil War era the South became increasingly committed to a cotton economy. Despite efforts to diversify the economy, the wealth and status associated with cotton, as well as soil exhaustion and falling prices from Virginia to Georgia, prompted the westward expansion of the plantation culture to *The Old Southwest.* Moreover, sons of southern planters wanted to take advantage of cheap land on the frontier in order to make their own fortunes. Slaves were worked harshly as they prepared the terrain for cotton cultivation and experienced the breakup of their families. By 1860, the *cotton kingdom* stretched from the Carolinas and Georgia through eastern Texas and up the Mississippi River to Illinois. More than half of all slaves worked on cotton plantations.

■ **Southern White Culture** White society was divided between the planter elite, or those who owned at least twenty slaves or more, and all the rest. *Planters* made up around 4 percent of the white population and exercised a disproportionately powerful political and social influence. Other whites owned a few slaves, but most owned none. A majority of whites were *"plain white folk"*— simple farmers who raised corn, cotton, hogs, and chickens. Southern white women spent most of their time on household chores. The *plantation mistress* supervised her home and household slaves. Most whites were fiercely loyal to the institution of slavery. Even those who owned no slaves feared the competition they believed they would face if slaves were freed, and they enjoyed the privileged status that race-based slavery gave them.

■ **Southern Black Culture** As slavery spread and the southern economy became more dependent on slave labor, the enslaved faced more regulations and restrictions on their behavior. The vast majority of Southern blacks were slaves who served as *field hands.* They had few rights and could be bought and sold and moved at any time. Their movements were severely limited and they had no ability to defend themselves. Any violation of these restrictions could result in severe punishments. Most Southern blacks were slaves, but a small percentage were free. Many of the free blacks were *mulattoes,* having mixed-race parentage. Free blacks often worked for wages in towns and cities.

■ **African American Resistance and Resilience** Originally, slaves were treated more as indentured servants, eligible for freedom after a specified number of years, but during the eighteenth century *slave codes* codified practices of treating slaves as property rather than people. The enslaved responded to their oppression in a variety of ways. Although many slaves attempted to run away, only a few openly rebelled because the consequences were so harsh. Organized revolts such as *Nat Turner's Rebellion (1831)* in Virginia were rare. Most slaves survived their hardships by relying on their own communities, family ties, and Christian faith, and by developing their own culture, such as the singing of *spirituals* to express frustration, sorrow, and hope for their eventual deliverance.

KEY TERMS

CHRONOLOGY

1790	Enslaved population of the United States nearly reaches 700,000
1791	Slave revolt in Saint-Domingue (Haiti)
1800	Gabriel conspiracy in Richmond, Virginia
1808	U.S. participation in the international slave trade is outlawed
1811	Charles Deslondes revolt in Louisiana
1814	Annual cotton production in the United States is 150,000 bales
1822	Denmark Vesey conspiracy is discovered in Charleston, South Carolina
1830	U.S. slave population exceeds 2 million
1831	Nat Turner leads slave insurrection in Virginia
1840	Population in the Old Southwest tops 1.5 million
1852	Harriet Beecher Stowe's *Uncle Tom's Cabin* is published
1860	Annual cotton production in the United States reaches 4 million bales
	Slave population in the United States reaches 4 million

INQUIZITIVE

Go to InQuizitive to see what you've learned—and learn what you've missed—with personalized feedback along the way.

THE VOYAGE OF LIFE: CHILDHOOD (1839–1840) In his *Voyage of Life* series, Thomas Cole draws upon both the religious revivalism and Romantic ideals of the period to depict the four stages of a man's life: childhood (shown above), youth, manhood, and old age. In this painting, an infant drifts along the River of Life with his guardian angel into the fertile landscape from the dark cave, meant to be "emblematic of our earthly origin, and the mysterious Past."

Religion, Romanticism, and Reform

1800–1860

D uring the first half of the nineteenth century, the world's largest—and youngest—republic was a nation of contrasts. Europeans traveling in America marveled at its restless energy and expansive optimism, its commitment to democratic ideals, and its remarkable capitalist spirit. However, visitors also noticed that the dynamic young republic was experiencing growing pains as the market revolution continued to excite a lust for profits and to widen economic inequality. At the same time, sectional tensions over economic policies, and increasingly heated debates over the morality and future of slavery, made for a combative political environment whose conflicts were mirrored in social and cultural life.

Unlike nations of the Old World, which had long been steeped in history and romance, the United States in the early nineteenth century was a young nation whose founding leaders had embraced the rational ideas of the Enlightenment. Those "reasonable" ideas about government and the pursuit of happiness, most vividly set forth in Thomas Jefferson's Declaration of Independence, influenced religion, literature, and the arts, as well as various social reform movements. Politics was not the only contested battleground during the first half of the nineteenth century; religious and cultural life also experienced intense conflicts and radical new outlooks.

CORE OBJECTIVES InQuizitive

1. Describe the major changes in the practice of religion in America in the early nineteenth century, and analyze their impact.

2. Examine the emergence of transcendentalism in American culture in the early nineteenth century.

3. Explain the origins of the major social reform movements in the early nineteenth century, and analyze their influence on American society and politics.

4. Analyze the impact on American society and politics of the emergence of the anti-slavery movement.

After the Revolution, many Americans were as interested in religious salvation as political engagement. Christian evangelists democratized the path to salvation at the same time that Jacksonian Democrats democratized the political process. So-called free-will ministers assured people that they could *choose* to be saved by embracing Jesus's promise of salvation just as more men who owned no property were allowed to *choose* their elected officials.

Christian activists assumed that the United States had a God-mandated mission to provide a shining example of representative government, much as Puritan New England had once stood as an example of an ideal Christian community. The concept of America having a special *mission* to create an ideal society still carried strong spiritual overtones. This ideal also contained an element of perfectionism—and an element of impatience when reality fell short of expectations. The combination of widespread religious energy and intense social activism brought major reforms and advances in human rights during the first half of the nineteenth century. It also brought disappointments that at times triggered cynicism and disillusionment.

CORE **OBJECTIVE**

1. Describe the major changes in the practice of religion in America in the early nineteenth century, and analyze their impact.

Religion

The contrasting currents of the rational Enlightenment and the spiritual Great Awakening, now mingling, now parting, flowed from the colonial period on into the nineteenth century. In different ways they eroded the old Calvinist view that people were innately sinful and that God had chosen only a select few for heavenly salvation ("predestination"). As time passed, many believers embraced a more optimistic religious outlook. Just as Enlightenment rationalism stressed humanity's natural goodness rather than its sinfulness and encouraged a belief in progress through social reforms and individual improvement, Protestant churches in the early nineteenth century stressed that people were capable of perfection through the guiding light of Christ.

Rational Religion

Deistical societies

Enlightenment ideas during the eighteenth century, including the religious concept of *Deism*, inspired prominent leaders such as Thomas Jefferson and Benjamin Franklin. Deists believed in a rational God—creator of the rational universe—and that all people were created as equals. They prized science and reason over traditional religion and blind faith. Interest in Deism increased after the American Revolution. In every major city, Deist societies emerged, and college students in particular took delight in criticizing conventional religion. Through the use of reason and scientific research, Deists believed, people might grasp the natural laws governing the universe. Deists rejected the belief that every statement in the Bible was literally true. They were skeptical of miracles and questioned the divinity of Jesus. Deists also defended free speech and opposed religious coercion.

Unitarianism and Universalism

Most Christians could hardly distinguish Deism from atheism, but the same ideals of Enlightenment rationalism that excited Deists soon began to make deep inroads into American Protestantism as well. The old Puritan churches in and around Boston proved especially vulnerable to the appeal of religious liberalism. Boston's progress—or, some would say, its degeneration—from Puritanism to prosperity had persuaded many wealthy families that they were anything but sinners at the mercy of an angry God. By the end of the eighteenth century, many well-educated New Englanders were embracing Unitarianism, a belief system that emphasizes the oneness ("unity") and compassion of a loving God, the natural goodness of humankind, and the superiority of calm reason over emotional forms of worship. **Unitarians** believe that Jesus was a saintly man but was not divine. People are not inherently sinful, Unitarians stress; people are capable of doing tremendous good by following the teachings of Jesus, and *all* people are eligible for the gift of salvation from a God of boundless love. Boston became the center of the Unitarian movement, which flourished chiefly within Congregational churches. During the early nineteenth century, "liberal" churches adopted the name *Unitarian*. Although Unitarianism never attracted large numbers of followers, many of its believers were among the best-educated and wealthiest New Englanders.

A parallel religious movement, Universalism, attracted a different—and much larger—social group: the working poor. In 1779, John Murray, a British clergyman and former Methodist, founded the first Universalist church, in Gloucester, Massachusetts. **Universalists** stressed that salvation was available to everyone; it was "universal," not for just a predestined few. God, it teaches, is too merciful to condemn anyone to eternal punishment. "Thus, the Unitarians and Universalists were in fundamental agreement," wrote one historian, "the Universalists holding that God was too good to damn man; the Unitarians insisting that man was too good to be damned." Although both sects remained relatively small, they exercised a powerful influence over intellectual life, especially in New England.

The Second Great Awakening

During the first Great Awakening in the early 1700s, traveling evangelists had stirred up religious life by challenging the established denominations, particularly Anglicanism, and promoting a more intense and personal relationship with God. In addition, Anglicanism suffered from being aligned historically with the Church of England and lost its status as the official religion in most states after the American Revolution. To help erase their pro-British image, Virginia Anglicans renamed themselves *Episcopalians*. But even the new name did not prevent the denomination from losing its leadership position in the South. Newer denominations, especially Baptists and Methodists, 20 percent of whom were African Americans, emerged and

Unitarians

Universalists

Unitarians Members of the liberal New England Congregationalist offshoot, who profess the oneness of God and the goodness of rational man, often well-educated and wealthy.

Universalists Members of a New England religious movement, who believed in a merciful God and universal salvation, often from the working class.

attracted masses of followers. These new Christian sects were organized in accord with more democratic principles, allowing individual congregations to exercise more power on their own than did the elaborate governance structures of the Anglican Church.

Second Great Awakening

Around 1800, the United States experienced a much larger wave of religious revivals called the **Second Great Awakening**, the first having swept across the American colonies in the first half of the eighteenth century. On and off over the next forty years, the flames of revivalism raced across the country in response to the dramatic economic growth and social changes transforming American life. The nation's rampant materialism furnished evangelical ministers with plenty of ammunition, as did soaring crime rates. Without religion, revivalists warned, the American republic would give way to "unbridled appetites and lust."

Statistics reveal the impact of the evangelical revivals. In 1780, there were only fifty Methodist churches in America; by 1860, there were 20,000, far more than any other denomination. The percentage of Americans who joined Protestant churches increased sixfold between 1800 and 1860. Thus, one of the major effects of the Second Great Awakening was that more Americans than ever were joining and supporting churches.

The Second Great Awakening involved two different centers of activity. One developed among the elite New England colleges that were founded as religious centers of learning, then spread westward like a wildfire across New York into Pennsylvania and Ohio, Indiana, and Illinois. The other emerged in the backwoods of Tennessee and Kentucky and spread across rural America. Both the urban and rural phases of Protestant revivalism shared a simple message: salvation is available not just to a select few, as the Calvinists had claimed, but to *anyone* who repents and embraces Christ.

Frontier Revivals

Traveling evangelists

In its frontier phase, the Second Great Awakening, like the first, generated tremendous excitement and dramatic behavior. It gave birth, moreover, to two religious phenomena—the traveling backwoods evangelist and the camp meeting—that helped keep the fires of revivalism and spiritual intensity burning. People found the supernatural inside as well as outside of churches; they readily believed in magic, dreams, visions, miraculous healing, and speaking in tongues. Evangelists and "exhorters" with colorful nicknames such as Jumpin' Jesus or Crazy Dow or Mad Isaac found ready audiences among lonely frontier folk hungry for spiritual intensity and a sense of community. Revivals in the backwoods were family-oriented, community-building events; they truly represented social democracy, bridging social, economic, political, and even racial divisions. Women, especially, flocked to the rural revivals, readily gave their souls to Jesus, and served as the backbone of religious life on the frontier.

Second Great Awakening
Religious revival movement that arose in reaction to the growth of secularism and rationalist religion; spurred the growth of the Baptist and Methodist churches.

At the end of the eighteenth century, ministers visiting the new western territories reported that there were few frontier churches and few people attending them. To remedy the situation, evangelists began to stoke the fires of religious fervor. The first camp meeting occurred in 1801 on a Kentucky hillside called Cane Ridge. Some 10,000 people came from miles around, camping in tents under the stars. White and black ministers from many denominations preached day and night, often chanting their sermons in ways that prompted listeners to cry: "Amen!" "Hallelujah!" "Lord, have mercy!"

Like the revivals of the earlier Great Awakening, the **frontier revivals** generated intense emotions. One participant observed that "some of the people were singing, others praying, some crying for mercy." He added that "shrieks and shouts" punctuated every sermon. Soon, camp

Religious revivalism Frontier revivals and prayer meetings ignited religious fervor within both minister and participant. In this 1830s camp meeting, the women are so intensely moved by the sermon that they shed their bonnets and fall to their knees.

meeting revivals were occurring in every state. But not all were swept up in the religious emotionalism. Frances Trollope, a distinguished British woman writer who toured the United States in 1827, attended a frontier revival and thought the participants behaved like raving lunatics. She fled the roiling scene in panic.

Baptists and Methodists

The frontier revivals included many Presbyterians but were dominated by Baptists and Methodists. The Baptist theology was grounded in biblical fundamentalism—a certainty that every word and story in the Bible are literally true. Unlike the earlier Puritans, however, the Baptists believed that everyone could gain salvation in heaven by choosing (via "free will") to receive God's grace and by being baptized as adults. The Baptists also stressed the social equality of all before God, regardless of wealth, status, or education.

The Methodists, who shared with Baptists the belief that everyone could gain salvation by an act of "free will," developed the most effective evangelical method of all: the "circuit rider," a traveling evangelist on horseback, who sought out converts in remote frontier settlements. The system began with Francis Asbury, a tireless British-born revivalist who scoured the Ohio Valley for lost souls, traveling across fifteen states and preaching thousands of sermons. Asbury established a mobile evangelism perfectly suited to the frontier environment and the new democratic age.

After Asbury, Peter Cartwright emerged as the most successful circuit rider and became famous for his highly charged sermons. Cartwright had

> Growth of Baptist and Methodist denominations

frontier revivals Religious revival movement within the Second Great Awakening, that took place in frontier churches in western territories and states in the early nineteenth century.

grown up in one of the most violent and lawless regions of frontier Kentucky. His brother was hanged as a murderer and his sister was said to be a prostitute. At age sixteen, he converted to Methodism, and the following year became an "exhorter," preaching the faith even though he was not yet an ordained minister. By age eighteen, Cartwright began roaming across Kentucky, Tennessee, Ohio, and Indiana, and for more than twenty years preached a sermon a day. His message was simple: salvation is free for all to embrace.

Revivalism and African Americans

Equal participation for African Americans

African Americans were especially attracted to the emotional energies of the Methodist and Baptist churches. Richard Allen, who would later help found the African Methodist Episcopal (AME) Church, said in 1787 that "there was no religious sect or denomination that would suit the capacity of the colored people as well as the Methodist." He decided that the "plain and simple gospel suits best for any people; for the unlearned can understand [it]." Even more important, the Methodists actively recruited blacks. They were "the first people," Allen noted, "that brought glad tidings to the colored people." The Baptists did as well. As African Americans joined white Baptist or Methodist churches, they infused the congregations with exuberant energy and the emotional songs called *spirituals*.

During the early nineteenth century, the energies of the Great Revival, as the Second Great Awakening was called, spread through the western states and into more settled regions back East, and Americans were building a thousand new churches each year. The fastest growth was along the frontier, where the camp meetings

Black Methodists Holding a Prayer Meeting **(1811)** This caricature of an African American Methodist meeting in Philadelphia shows a preacher in the church doorway, while his congregation engages in exuberant prayer.

were an expression of the frontier's democratic spirit; they welcomed "all sorts and conditions" of people. Revivals were typically held in late summer or fall, when farm work eased. People came from far and wide, camping in wagons, tents, or crude shacks. African Americans, whether enslaved or free, were encouraged to attend.

Camp Meetings and Women

The largest meetings tended to be ecumenical affairs, with Baptist, Methodist, and Presbyterian ministers working as a team. Crowds often numbered in the thousands, and the unrestrained atmosphere at times got out of hand.

Mass excitement swept up even the most skeptical onlookers, and infusions of the spirit sparked strange behavior. Some went into trances; others contracted the "jerks," laughed "the holy laugh," babbled in unknown tongues, or got down on all fours and barked like dogs to "tree the devil," as a hound might tree a raccoon.

But dwelling on the bizarre aspects of the camp meetings gives a distorted view of an activity that offered a welcome social outlet to isolated rural folk. This was especially true for women, for whom the camp meetings provided a communal alternative to the rigors and loneliness of farm life. Women, in fact, played the predominant role at camp meetings, as they had in earlier revivals. Evangelical ministers repeatedly applauded the spiritual energies of women and affirmed their right to give public witness to their faith.

Camp meetings provided opportunities for women to participate as social equals to men, both as preachers and parishioners. Jarena Lee, a free black who lived in the Philadelphia area, was the first African American woman to be allowed to preach in the African Methodist Episcopal Church (AME). As she wrote, "If the man may preach, because the Saviour died for him, why not the woman? Seeing [as] he died for her also. Is he not a whole Saviour, instead of a half one, as those who hold it wrong for a woman to preach, would seem to make it appear?" Lee became a tireless revivalist during the 1830s, walking as many as twelve miles a day. According to her own records, she "traveled 2,325 miles and preached 178 sermons."

| Religious leadership for women |

The organizational needs of large revivals offered ample opportunities for women to exercise leadership roles outside the home, including service as traveling evangelists themselves. Phoebe Worrall Palmer, for example, hosted prayer meetings in her New York City home that included men as well as women, a controversial innovation for the time. She then traveled across the United States as a camp meeting "exhorter," assuring listeners that they could gain a life without sin, what then was called "perfectionism" or "holiness."

Women like Phoebe Palmer found public roles within evangelical religion because of its emphasis on individual religious experiences rather than conventional male-dominated church structures. Palmer claimed a woman's right to preach by citing the biblical emphasis on obeying God rather than man. "It is always right to obey the Holy Spirit's command," she stressed, "and if that is laid upon a woman to preach the Gospel, then it is right for her to do so; it is a duty she cannot neglect without falling into condemnation."

Such opportunities to assume traditional male religious roles reinforced women's self-confidence and expanded their horizons. Their religious enthusiasm often inspired them to pursue social reforms, including expanded educational opportunities for women and the right to vote. So in many ways and on many levels, the energies of the revivals helped spread a more democratic faith among people living on the frontier.

Religion and Reform

Regions swept up by revival fever were compared to forests devastated by fire. Western New York, in fact, experienced such intense levels of evangelical activity that it was labeled the *burned-over district* because it was so often fired by the flames of the Holy Spirit. One reason the area was such a hotbed of evangelical activity was that it was being transformed by the Erie Canal, which opened in 1825. Both the construction of and traffic on the canal turned many "canal towns" into rollicking scenes of lawlessness: gambling, prostitution, public drunkenness, and crime. Such widespread sinfulness made the region ripe for revivalism.

Finney and the "burned-over" district

The most successful evangelist in the burned-over district was a Presbyterian minister named Charles Grandison Finney. In the winter of 1830–1831, he preached with "a clear, shrill voice" for six months in Rochester, then a canal boomtown in upstate New York. In the process, he generated some 100,000 conversions and became the most celebrated minister in the country. Finney claimed that he was enabling "the greatest revival of religion . . . since the world began." While rural camp meeting revivals attracted farm families and other working-class groups, Finney's audiences in the Northeast attracted more prosperous seekers. "The Lord," Finney declared, "was aiming at the conversion of the highest classes of society." In 1836, he built a huge church in New York City to accommodate his rapidly growing congregation.

Finney focused on the question that had preoccupied Protestantism for centuries: what role can the individual play in earning salvation? The Puritans and other Calvinists had argued that people could neither earn nor choose salvation. They believed in "predestination": that salvation was a gift of God to a select few. In contrast, Finney and other "free will" evangelists wanted to democratize the opportunity for salvation by insisting that everyone, rich or poor, black or white, could *choose* to be "saved" simply by embracing the promise of Jesus.

Finney's democratic gospel combined faith and good works: revival led to efforts at social reform. "The great business of the church," Finney insisted, is "to reform the world." By embracing Christ, a convert could thereafter be free of sin, but Christians also had an obligation to improve society. Christians should "aim to be holy and not rest satisfied until they are as perfect as God." Finney helped found an array of groups designed to reform various social ills: alcoholism, prostitution, war, and slavery. The revivals thus provided much of the energy behind the sweeping reform impulse that characterized the age.

The Mormons

Joseph Smith and *The Book of Mormon*

The spiritual stirrings of the Second Great Awakening also helped produce new religious groups. The burned-over district in western New York gave rise to several religious movements, the most important of which was Mormonism. Its extraordinary founder, Joseph Smith Jr., the child of intensely religious Vermont farm folk who settled in the village of Palmyra in western New York, was born and raised amid the excitement of the Second Great Awakening. In 1823, the eighteen-year-old Smith reported that an angel named Moroni had led him to a hillside near his father's farm, where he had unearthed golden tablets on which was etched a lost "gospel" of the Bible that describes a group of ancient Israelites ("Nephites") who crossed the Atlantic on barges and settled America 2,000 years before Columbus. Smith, who could barely read, set about translating and dictating to others the "reformed Egyptian" inscriptions on the plates (which no one else ever saw before he returned them to Moroni). Smith convinced a friend to mortgage his farm to pay for the publication of the first 5,000 copies of the 500-page text he called *The Book of Mormon: An Account Written by the Hand of Mormon upon Plates Taken from the Plates of Nephi.*

With this remarkable book as his gospel, young Smith began telling the story of his "marvilous [sic] experience" and gathering converts ("saints") who shared his desire to live together in accordance with the teachings of Jesus. Eventually, convinced that his religious authority came directly from God, Smith formed what he called the Church of Jesus Christ of Latter-day Saints, more popularly known as **Mormons**. God "is a man like one of you," Smith told his followers. His was a democratic faith run by plain people and intended for all people.

In his self-appointed role as Prophet, Smith criticized the sins of the rich, preached universal salvation, dismissed all Christian denominations (Protestant and Catholic) as frauds, denied that there was a hell, urged his followers to avoid liquor, tobacco, and hot drinks, and promised that the Second Coming of Christ was looming. Within a few years, the charismatic Smith, whom the Mormons simply called Joseph, had gathered thousands of converts, most of them poor New England farmers who, like Smith's family, had migrated to western New York. "The people fairly adored him," said a Mormon woman.

From the outset, the Mormon "saints" upset both their neighbors and the civil authorities. Mormons stood out with their secret rituals, their refusal to abide by local laws and conventions, and their clannishness: they worshipped together, voted together, and traveled together. Smith denied the legitimacy of civil governments and the U.S. Constitution. As a result, no community wanted to host him and his "peculiar people." In their search for a refuge from persecution and for the "promised land," the ever-growing contingent of Mormons moved from western New York to Ohio, then to Missouri, and finally, in 1839, to the half-built town of Commerce, Illinois, on swampy land along the west bank of the Mississippi River. They renamed the town Nauvoo (a crude transliteration of a Hebrew word meaning "beautiful land").

Within a few years, thanks to Smith's organizing genius and absolute authority, Nauvoo had become a bustling, well-planned community of 12,000, with an impressive, neo-classical temple overlooking the river. The community was run according to strict Mormon principles. There were no saloons or brothels. A New York newspaper reported that the Mormons at

Mormons Members of the Church of Jesus Christ of Latter-day Saints, which dismissed other Christian denominations, emphasizing universal salvation and a modest lifestyle; often persecuted for their secrecy and clannishness.

Nauvoo were "organizing a religious empire in the far west that will astonish the world." Joseph Smith, "the Prophet," became the community's religious dictator: he was Nauvoo's leading planner, businessman, and political czar. He owned the hotel and general store, published the newspaper and sold real estate, served as mayor, chief justice, and commander of the city's 2,000-strong army (the Nauvoo Legion), and was the trustee of the church. Smith's lust for power grew as well. He began excommunicating dissidents, and in 1844 he announced his intention to become America's president. He proclaimed that the United States should peacefully acquire not only Texas and Oregon but all of Mexico and Canada, and that slavery should be ended.

Smith also caused controversy by practicing "plural marriage" (polygamy); he accumulated over two dozen wives and encouraged other Mormon leaders to do the same. In 1844, a crisis arose when Mormon dissenters, including Smith's first wife, Emma, denounced his polygamy. The result was not only a split in the church but also an attack on Nauvoo by non-Mormons from neighboring counties. When Smith ordered Mormons to destroy an opposition newspaper, he and his brother Hyrum were arrested and charged with treason. On June 27, 1844, a mob stormed the jail in the nearby town of Carthage and killed the Smith brothers. Joseph Smith, the thirty-eight-year-old prophet, had become a martyr. A New York newspaper predicted that his death would kill Mormonism: "They cannot get another Joe Smith. The holy city must tumble into ruins."

But in Brigham Young, the Mormons found a new and, in many ways, better leader. Strong-minded, intelligent, authoritarian, and a compelling speaker (as well as husband eventually to dozens of wives, who bore fifty-six children), Young was a Vermont-born carpenter who in 1813 moved with his family to western New York, where he became an early convert to Mormonism. In 1844, he was elected to succeed Smith.

Nauvoo continued to arouse the suspicions of non-Mormons, leading Young to look for another home for his flock. Their new destination was 1,300 miles away in the isolated, barren valley near the Great Salt Lake in Utah, a vast, sparsely populated area that was part of Mexico. In early 1846, in wagons and on foot, 12,000 Mormons started their grueling exodus across Nebraska and Wyoming to their new Zion, the "promised land" of Utah. On a good day they traveled only about ten miles. The first to arrive at the Great Salt Lake in July 1847 found "a broad and barren plain hemmed in by the mountains . . . the paradise of the lizard, the cricket and the rattlesnake." But Brigham Young declared that "this is the place" for the Mormons to settle. It was "a good place to make saints."

By the end of 1848, the Mormons had developed an efficient irrigation system for their farms, and over the next decade they brought about a spectacular greening of the desert. At first they organized their own state, named Deseret (meaning "Land of the Honeybee"), and elected Young governor. But their independence was short-lived. In 1848, Mexico signed the Treaty of Guadalupe Hidalgo, transferring to the United States what is now

Brigham Young Young was the president of the Mormons for thirty years.

MORMON TREK, 1830–1851

- ☥ Mormon settlements
- → The Mormon Trail, 1830–1851
- ▢ Proposed state of Deseret

■ Where were Mormon settlements established between 1830 and 1851?
■ Why did Joseph Smith initially lead his congregation west?
■ Why was the Utah Territory an ideal place for the Mormons to settle, at least initially?

California, Nevada, Utah, Texas, and parts of Arizona, New Mexico, Colorado, and Wyoming. Two years later, Congress incorporated the Utah Territory, including the Mormons' Salt Lake settlement, into the United States. Nevertheless, when Brigham Young was named the territorial governor, the new arrangement gave the Mormons virtual independence. For more than twenty years, Young ruled the territory with an iron hand, allowing no dissent and defying federal authority. Not until 1896, after the Mormons disavowed the practice of polygamy, was Utah admitted as a state.

Romanticism in America

The revival of religious life during the early 1800s was one of many efforts throughout the United States and Europe to unleash the stirrings of the spirit. Another great cultural shift from the scientific rationalism of the Enlightenment was the Romantic movement in thought, literature, and the arts. It began in Europe, as young people rebelled against the well-ordered

CORE OBJECTIVE

2. Examine the emergence of transcendentalism in American culture in the early nineteenth century.

rational world promoted by the eighteenth-century Enlightenment. Were there not, after all, more things in the world than reason, science, and logic could box up and explain: spontaneous moods, impressions, and feelings; mysterious, unknown, and half-seen things? In areas in which science could neither prove nor disprove concepts, the Romantics believed that people were justified in having faith. They preferred the stirrings of the heart over the calculations of the head, nonconformity over traditional behavior, and the mystical over the rational. Americans also embraced the Romantics' emphasis on individualism, idealizing the virtues of common people.

Transcendentalism

Transcendentalism

The most intense advocates of Romantic ideals in the United States were the transcendentalists of New England, America's first group of rebellious intellectuals committed to reshaping the nation's cultural life. What **transcendentalism** actually entailed is hard to define. The name derived from its emphasis on thoughts and things that *transcend* (or rise above) the limits of reason and logic. Transcendentalism, said one of its champions, meant an interest in areas "a little beyond" the scope of reason. Transcendentalism thus at times seemed irrational, rejecting both religious orthodoxy and the "corpse-cold" rationalism of Unitarianism. The transcendentalists believed that reality was not simply what you can touch and see; reality also included the unexplored realms of the mind, such as intuition. Above all, the transcendentalists believed in "self-reliance" and embraced a pure form of personal spirituality uncorrupted by organized religion. Transcendentalists wanted individuals to look *within* themselves, not follow the guidance of

transcendentalism Philosophy of New England writers and thinkers who advocated personal spirituality, self-reliance, social reform, and harmony with nature.

***The Indian's Vespers* (1847)** Asher B. Durand's painting of a Native American saluting the sun captures the Romantic ideals of personal spirituality and the uncorrupted natural world that swept America in the wake of the Enlightenment.

ministers, for spiritual insights. They also wanted to unleash a romantic spirituality in harmony with nature. All people, they believed, had the capacity for self-realization, enabling them to tap the divine potential ("spark") present in all of God's creatures and creations. By the 1830s, New England transcendentalism had become the most influential force in American culture.

In 1836, an informal discussion group known as the Transcendental Club began to meet in Boston and nearby Concord to discuss philosophy, literature, and religion. They teasingly called themselves the "club of the like-minded," quipped a Boston preacher, "because no two . . . thought alike." The club included liberal clergymen, militant reformers, writers such as Theodore Parker, George Ripley, Henry David Thoreau, Nathaniel Hawthorne, and brilliant women such as Elizabeth Peabody, her sister Sophia (who married Hawthorne in 1842), and Margaret Fuller. Fluent in six languages, Fuller organized a transcendentalist discussion group and edited its magazine, the *Dial* (1840–1844), for two years before the duty fell to Ralph Waldo Emerson, the high priest of transcendentalism.

Ralph Waldo Emerson

More than anyone else, Ralph Waldo Emerson embodied the transcendentalist gospel promoting individual freedom and "self-culture." Tall and slender, with bright blue eyes, he became the most popular speaker in the United States during the second quarter of the nineteenth century, in part because Emerson led the crusade to end America's dependence on European literary and artistic traditions. Emerson strove to help "extract the tapeworm of Europe from America's body," to "cast out the passion for Europe," and replace it with "the passion for America," exhorting the young republic to shed its cultural inferiority complex and create its own distinctive literature and art.

Descended from a line of New England Calvinist ministers and the son of a Unitarian preacher, Emerson graduated from Harvard College in 1821 and became a Unitarian parson in 1829, but he quit the "cold and cheerless" denomination three years later and turned away from all organized religions because they stifled free thinking. "In the Bible," he explained, "you are not directed to be a Unitarian or a Calvinist or an Episcopalian." Such group identities disgusted him. After traveling in Europe, where he met England's greatest Romantic writers, Emerson settled in Concord to take up the life of an essayist, poet, and lecturer ("preacher to the world") promoting radical individualism. He now found God in nature and came to believe in human perfectibility. Emerson celebrated the virtues of optimism, self-reliance, and the individual's unlimited potential. In 1836 he published the pathbreaking book *Nature*, which helped launch the Transcendental movement. In it, he stressed that sensitive people could "transcend" the material world and discover the "spirit" animating the universe. Individuals, in other words, could exercise godlike powers.

The spirit of self-reliant individualism in Emerson's lectures and writings provided the energetic core of the transcendentalist outlook. "The

Emerson and cultural nationalism

American Scholar," a speech he delivered at Harvard in 1837, urged young Americans to put aside their reverence for European culture and explore the beauties and freedoms of their own new world. The speech was "our intellectual Declaration of Independence," said one observer.

Emerson's essay "Self-Reliance" (1841) is crammed with crisply formulated assertions that express the distinctive transcendentalist outlook:

"Self-Reliance" (1841)

> Whoso would be a man, must be a nonconformist. . . . Nothing is at last sacred but the integrity of your own mind. . . . It is easy in the world to live after the world's opinion; it is easy in solitude to live after our own; but the great man is he who in the midst of a crowd keeps with perfect sweetness the independence of solitude. . . . A foolish consistency is the hobgoblin of little minds, adored by little statesmen and philosophers and divines. . . . Speak what you think now in hard words and tomorrow speak what tomorrow thinks in hard words again, though it contradict everything you said today. . . . To be great is to be misunderstood.

Emerson's democratic belief that every man and woman possessed godlike virtues inspired generations. He was a down-to-earth transcendentalist who championed a self-reliant individualism that reinforced the democratic energies inspiring Jacksonian America.

Henry David Thoreau

Emerson's philosophical young friend and neighbor, Henry David Thoreau, practiced the thoughtful self-reliance that Emerson preached. "I like people who can do things," Emerson stressed, and Thoreau, fourteen years his junior, could do many things: carpentry, masonry, painting, surveying, sailing, gardening. The son of a man who was a pencil maker and a woman who was a domineering reformer, Thoreau displayed a powerful sense of uncompromising integrity and prickly individuality. "If a man does not keep pace with his companions," Thoreau wrote, "perhaps it is because he hears a different drummer."

Thoreau marched to a different drummer all his life. He once described himself as "a mystic, a transcendentalist, and a natural philosopher." Born in 1817, he attended Harvard, where he exhausted the library's resources before graduating. After a brief stint as a teacher, during which he got in trouble for refusing to cane his students, Thoreau worked with his father making pencils. But like Emerson, he made frequent escapes to admire the beauties of nature. Thoreau viewed "the indescribable innocence" of nature as a living bible; the earth to him was a form of poetry, full of hidden meanings and life-giving energies. Walks in the woods inspired him more than attending church. He also showed no interest in the scramble for wealth, for it too often corrupted the pursuit of happiness. "The mass of men," he wrote, "lead lives of quiet desperation" because they were preoccupied with making money rather than pursuing happiness. Thoreau became famous for his

Henry David Thoreau Thoreau was a lifelong abolitionist.

strong opinions and frankness. Most of what his neighbors deemed good, he believed "in his soul to be bad."

A born rebel, Thoreau yearned to experience the "extremities" of life and not be bound by stuffy traditions, unjust laws, "good behavior," or the opinions of his elders. "I have lived thirty years on this planet," he wrote, "and I have yet to hear the first syllable of valuable advice from my seniors. They have told me nothing, and probably cannot tell me anything." He committed himself to leading what Emerson called a simple life centered on "plain living and high thinking." He loved to be alone, wrapped in his own thoughts and free to think for himself.

Thoreau rented a room at the Emersons' home for a time, tending the family garden and taking long walks with his host. "I delight much in my young friend," Emerson wrote, "who seems to have as free and erect a mind as any I have ever met." In 1844, when Emerson bought fourteen acres along Walden Pond, Thoreau decided to embark upon an unusual experiment in self-reliance. On July 4, 1845, at age twenty-seven, he took to the woods to live in a tiny, one-room cabin he had built for $28 on Emerson's land at Walden Pond, just a few miles outside of Concord. Having decided that a "man is rich in proportion to the number of things he can do without," Thoreau wanted to free himself from the constraints of conventional life and devote his time to gardening, studying nature, swimming in the pond, and recording his thoughts and observations in his journal. "I went to the woods because I wished to live deliberately," he wrote in *Walden, or Life in the Woods* (1854), ". . . and not, when I came to die, discover that I had not lived."

> Thoreau's *Walden* (1854)

During Thoreau's two years at Walden Pond, the United States declared war against Mexico, largely in order to acquire Texas, then part of Mexico. He felt it was an unjust war pushed by southern cotton planters eager to add more slave territory. His disgust for the war led him to refuse to pay taxes, for which he was put in jail (for only one night; an aunt paid the tax). This incident inspired him to write his now-classic essay, "Civil Disobedience" (1849), which would later influence Martin Luther King Jr. in shaping the civil rights movement in the 1950s and '60s. "If the law is of such a nature that it requires you to be an agent of injustice to another," Thoreau wrote, "then, I say, break the law." Until his death in 1862, Thoreau continued to attack slavery and applaud those who worked to undermine it. "The law will never make men free," he insisted. "It is men who have got to make the law free." The continuing influence of Thoreau's creed of taking individual action against injustice shows the impact that a thoughtful person can have on the world of action.

> "Civil Disobedience" (1849)

An American Literature

Thoreau and Emerson portrayed the transcendentalist movement as an expression of moral idealism; critics dismissed it as outrageous self-centeredness. Though the transcendentalists attracted only a small following in their own time, they inspired a generation of writers that produced the first great age of American literature. The half decade of 1850 to 1855 witnessed an outpouring of extraordinary writing in the United States, a nation that had long suffered an inferiority complex about the quality of its arts. Those five years saw the writing of *Representative Men* by Emerson, *Walden* by Thoreau, *The Scarlet Letter* and *The House of the Seven Gables* by Nathaniel Hawthorne, *Moby-Dick* by Herman Melville, *Leaves of Grass* by Walt Whitman, and hundreds of unpublished poems by Emily Dickinson.

Literary Giants

Emily Dickinson, the most strikingly original of the New England poets, spent much of her life in her second-story bedroom in Amherst, Massachusetts, writing poetry that few people saw during her lifetime. Only a handful of her almost 1,800 poems were published (anonymously) before her death, in 1886. As she once prophetically wrote, "Success is counted sweetest / By those who ne'er succeed." Neither she nor her sister married, and they lived out their lives in their parents' home. Perhaps it was Dickinson's severe eye trouble during the 1860s that caused her solitary withdrawal from the larger society; perhaps it was the aching despair generated by her love for a married minister. Whatever the reason, her intense isolation and lifelong religious doubts led her to probe her own shifting psychological state. Her often-abstract themes were elemental: life, death, fear, loneliness, nature, and above all, God, a "Force illegible," "a distant, stately lover."

Emily Dickinson Dickinson offered the world of New England literature a fresh female voice.

The most provocative writer during the nineteenth century was New Yorker Walt Whitman. The swaggering Whitman was a startling figure, with his frank sexuality and homoerotic overtones. There was something elemental in Whitman's overflowing character, something bountiful and generous and compelling—even his faults and inconsistencies were ample. Born on a Long Island farm, he moved with his family to Brooklyn, where he worked as a teacher, journalist, a Democratic party activist, and an editor of the *Brooklyn Eagle*. Whitman frequently took the ferry across the East River to bustling Manhattan. The city's restless energies fascinated him, and he gorged himself on the urban spectacle: the vibrant vistas of shipyards, crowds, factories, and shop windows.

When Whitman first met Ralph Waldo Emerson, he had been "simmering, simmering," but Emerson "brought him to a boil" with his emphasis on defying tradition and celebrating the commonplaces of life, all of which found their way into his controversial first book of poems, *Leaves of Grass* (1855), which often dispensed with stanzas and rhymes. Whitman introduced his new book by declaring that "I celebrate myself, and sing myself." He wanted to leave the past behind. He was a pioneer on behalf of "a new mightier world, a varied world," a "world of labor" and "common people." Although *Leaves of Grass* was banned in Boston, Emerson found it "the most extraordinary piece of wit and wisdom that America has yet contributed," but more-conventional critics shuddered at the shocking frankness of Whitman's sexual references. Thoreau, however, loved the earthy poetry. He described Whitman as "the greatest democrat the world has seen."

Walt Whitman This engraving of a thirty-seven-year-old Walt Whitman appeared in his acclaimed poetry collection, *Leaves of Grass.*

The Reform Impulse

CORE **OBJECTIVE**

3. Explain the origins of the major social reform movements in the early nineteenth century, and analyze their influence on American society and politics.

In 1842, the monthly *Gazette* reported that the "spirit of reform is in every place" across America. The United States in the first half of the nineteenth century was awash in reform movements led by dreamers and activists who saw injustice and fought to correct it. Lyman Beecher, a champion of evangelical Christian revivalism (as well as the father of writer Harriet Beecher Stowe), stressed that the Second Great Awakening was not focused simply on promoting individual conversions; it was also intended to "reform human society." Evangelical societies fanned out across America to organize Sunday schools to spread the gospel and distribute Bibles to the children of the working poor. Other reformers tackled urgent social issues such as dreadful conditions in prisons and workplaces, care of the disabled, reducing the consumption of alcoholic beverages (temperance), women's rights, and the abolition of slavery. Some reformers proposed legislative remedies for social ills; others stressed personal conversion or private philanthropy. Whatever the method or approach, earnest social reformers mobilized in great numbers during the second quarter of the nineteenth century. That they often met resistance, persecution, violence, and even death testified to the sincerity of their convictions and the power of their example.

***Politics in an Oyster House* (1848)**
Commissioned by social activist John H. B. Latrobe, this painting captures the public debates that were fueled by newspapers and other print periodicals.

While an impulse to "perfect" people and society helped excite the reform movements, social and economic changes helped spur many reformers themselves, most of whom were women. The rise of an urban middle class offered growing numbers of women more time to devote to societal concerns. Prosperity enabled them to hire cooks and maids, often Irish immigrants, who in turn freed them from household chores. As had been true for two centuries, many women used their free time to join churches and charitable organizations, most of which were led by men.

Temperance

The **temperance** crusade to reduce alcohol consumption was perhaps the most widespread of the reform movements. The census of 1810 reported some 14,000 distilleries producing 25 million gallons of alcoholic spirits each year. William Cobbett, an English reformer who traveled in the United States, noted in 1819 that one could "go into hardly any man's house without being asked to drink wine or spirits, even *in the morning*." In 1826, a group of ministers in Boston organized the American Society for the Promotion of Temperance, which sponsored lectures, press campaigns, and the formation of local and state societies. A favorite device was to ask each person who took the pledge to put by his or her signature a T for "total abstinence." With that a new word entered the language: *teetotaler*.

temperance A widespread reform movement led by militant Christians that focused on reducing the use of alcoholic beverages.

The American Temperance
Union

In 1833, the society organized a national convention in Philadelphia, where the American Temperance Union was formed. Like nearly every reform movement of the day, temperance had a wing of absolutists. They would accept no compromise with Demon Rum and carried the day with a resolution that liquor was evil and ought to be prohibited by law. The Temperance Union, at its spring convention in 1836, called for abstinence from all alcoholic beverages—which caused moderates to abstain from the temperance movement instead.

Prisons and Asylums

Prison and asylum reform

The Romantic impulse often included the liberal belief that people are innately good and capable of improvement. Such an optimistic view brought about major changes in the treatment of prisoners, the disabled, and dependent children. Public institutions (often called asylums) arose that were dedicated to the treatment of social ills. If removed from society, the theory went, the needy and the deviant could be made whole again. Unhappily, however, the asylums had a way of becoming breeding grounds for brutality and neglect.

Gradually, the idea of the penitentiary developed as a new approach to reforming criminals. It would be a place where the guilty paid for their crimes but also underwent rehabilitation. An early model of the new system, widely copied, was the Auburn Penitentiary, which opened in New York in 1816. The prisoners at Auburn had separate cells and gathered only for meals and group labor. Discipline was severe. The men were marched out in lockstep and never put face-to-face or allowed to talk. But they were reasonably secure from abuse by their fellow prisoners. The system, its advocates argued, had a beneficial effect on the prisoners and saved money, since the workshops supplied prison needs and produced goods for sale at a profit. By 1840, there were twelve Auburn-type penitentiaries scattered across the nation.

The Romantic reform impulse also found an outlet in the care of the insane. Before 1800, few hospitals provided care for the mentally ill. The insane were usually confined at home with hired keepers, or in jails or almshouses, where homeless debtors were housed. In the years after 1815, however, asylums that separated the disturbed from the criminal began to appear.

Dorothea Dix reforms care for
the mentally ill

The most important figure in heightening awareness of the plight of the mentally ill was Dorothea Lynde Dix. A pious Boston schoolteacher, she was asked to instruct a Sunday-school class at the East Cambridge House of Correction in 1841. There she found a roomful of insane people who had been completely neglected. She was so disturbed by the scene that she began a two-year investigation of jails and almshouses in Massachusetts. In a report to the state legislature in 1843, she revealed that insane people were confined "in *cages, closets, cellars, stalls, pens! Chained, naked, beaten with rods,* and *lashed* into obedience." Those managing asylums dismissed her charges as "slanderous lies," but she won the support of leading reformers. From Massachusetts she carried her campaign throughout the country and abroad. By 1860 she had persuaded twenty states to heed her advice, thereby helping to transform social attitudes toward mental illness.

Women's Rights

Dorothea Dix was but one sterling example of the countless middle-class women who devoted themselves to improving the quality of life in America. Others argued that women should first focus on enhancing home life. In 1841, Harriet Beecher Stowe's sister, Catharine Beecher, a leader in the public education movement and founder of women's schools in Connecticut and Ohio, published *A Treatise on Domestic Economy*, which became the leading handbook promoting the **cult of domesticity**, a powerful ideology that called upon women to celebrate their role as manager of the household and the children. While Beecher upheld high standards in women's education, she accepted the prevailing view that the "woman's sphere" was inside the home. She, and many other prominent women, argued that young women should be trained not for the workplace but in the domestic arts—managing a kitchen, running a household, and nurturing the children. Women, explained a Philadelphia doctor, were crucial to the future of the Republic because they instructed their children "in the principles of liberty and government." This *cult of domesticity* was especially strong among Mormons. From its inception, the Mormon Church was patriarchal, ruled by men. Women were limited to running the household and raising the children.

The official status of women during the first half of the nineteenth century remained much as it had been in the colonial era. They were barred from the ministry and most other professions. Higher education was hardly an option. Women could not serve on juries, nor could they vote. A wife often had no control over her property or even her children. She could not make a will, sign a contract, or bring suit in court without her husband's permission. Her subordinate legal status was similar to that of a minor or a free black.

Gradually, however, women began to protest, and men began to listen. The organized movement for women's rights emerged in 1840, when the anti-slavery movement split over the question of women's right to participate. Women decided then that they needed to organize on behalf of their own emancipation.

In 1848, two prominent advocates of women's rights, Lucretia Mott, a Philadelphia Quaker, and Elizabeth Cady Stanton, a graduate of New York's Troy Female Seminary who refused to be merely "a household drudge," called a convention to discuss "the social, civil, and religious condition and rights of women." On July 19, 1848, the **Seneca Falls Convention** issued a clever paraphrase of the Declaration of Independence. Called the **Declaration of Sentiments**, it proclaimed that "all men and women

Cult of domesticity

cult of domesticity Pervasive nineteenth-century ideology urging women to celebrate their role as manager of the household and nurturer of the children.

Seneca Falls Convention (1848) Convention organized by feminists Lucretia Mott and Elizabeth Cady Stanton to promote women's rights and issue the pathbreaking Declaration of Sentiments.

Declaration of Sentiments (1848) Document based on the Declaration of Independence that called for gender equality, written primarily by Elizabeth Cady Stanton and signed by Seneca Falls Convention delegates.

Elizabeth Cady Stanton and Susan B. Anthony Stanton (left, in 1856) was a young mother who called the Seneca Falls Convention, while Anthony (right, in 1848) started as an anti-slavery and temperance activist in her twenties. The two would meet in 1851 and form a lifelong partnership in the fight for women's suffrage.

are created equal." All laws that placed women "in a position inferior to that of men, are contrary to the great precept of nature, and therefore of no force or authority." Such language was too strong, too radical, for most of the 1,000 delegates, and only about a third of them signed the document. Nevertheless, the Seneca Falls gathering represented an important first step in the evolving campaign for women's rights.

From 1850 until the Civil War, leaders of the women's rights movement held annual conventions, delivered lectures, and circulated petitions. The movement struggled in the face of meager funds and widespread anti-feminist sentiment. A mother and housewife criticized the women reformers for "aping mannish manners" and wearing "absurd and barbarous attire." The typical feminist, she claimed, "struts and strides, and thinks that she proves herself superior to the rest of her sex." The movement's eventual success resulted from the work of a few undaunted women who refused to be stopped by the odds against them.

Susan B. Anthony, already active in temperance and anti-slavery groups, joined the crusade in the 1850s. Unlike Stanton and Mott, she was unmarried and therefore able to devote most of her attention to the women's crusade. As one observer put it, Stanton "forged the thunderbolts and Miss Anthony hurled them." Both were young when the movement started, and both lived into the twentieth century, focusing after the Civil War on demands for women's suffrage (the right to vote).

Women's suffrage

The fruits of the women's rights movement ripened slowly. Women did not gain the vote in national elections in the nineteenth century, but they did make legal gains. In 1839, Mississippi became the first state to grant married women control over their property; by the 1860s, eleven more states had done so. Still, the only jobs open to educated women in any number were nursing and teaching. Both professions brought relatively lower status and pay than "man's work," despite the skills, training, and responsibilities involved.

Early Public Schools

Early America, like most rural societies, offered few educational opportunities for the masses. That changed in the first half of the nineteenth century as reformers lobbied for **public schools** serving all children, rich or poor. The working poor wanted free schools to give their children an equal chance to pursue the American dream. In 1830, the Workingmen's party of Philadelphia called for "a system of education that shall embrace equally all the children of the state, of every rank and condition." Education, it was argued, would improve manners and at the same time reduce crime and poverty.

A well-informed citizenry equipped with knowledge not only for gaining employment but also for good citizenship was another of the basic premises of a republic. If political power resided with the people, as the Constitution asserted, then the citizenry needed to be well-educated. Literacy in Jacksonian America was surprisingly widespread. In 1840, according to census data, some 78 percent of the total population and 91 percent of the white population could read and write. Ever since the colonial period, in fact, Americans had had a higher literacy rate than that in Europe. Most children were taught to read at home, in church (Sunday school), or in private schools. By 1830, however, no state had a public school system in the modern sense.

Horace Mann of Massachusetts, a state legislator and attorney, led the early drive for statewide, tax-supported school systems open to everyone, regardless of class, race, or ethnicity, including immigrant children. He sponsored the creation of a state board of education, and then served as its leader. Mann went on to promote many reforms in Massachusetts, including the first state-supported "normal school" for the training of teachers, a state association of teachers, and a minimum school year of six months. He saw the public school system as a way not only to ensure that everyone had a basic level of knowledge and skills but also to reinforce values such as hard work and clean living. "If we do not prepare children to become good citizens, if we do not enrich their minds with knowledge," Mann warned, "then our republic must go down to destruction." Such a holistic education, Mann argued, would enhance social stability and equal opportunity, as well as give women opportunities for rewarding work outside the home, as teachers. Mann said they could become "mothers away from home" for the children they taught. In 1846, Catharine Beecher organized a Board of National Popular Education, which recruited unmarried women to serve as public school teachers in the Midwest.

> Highest literacy rates in the world

> Horace Mann's "normal school"

public schools Elementary and secondary schools funded by the state and free of tuition.

By the 1840s, most states in the North and Midwest, but not the South, had joined the public school movement. The initial conditions for public education, however, were seldom ideal. Funds for buildings, books, and equipment were limited; teachers were poorly paid and often poorly prepared. Most students going beyond the elementary grades attended private academies, often organized by churches. Such schools, begun in colonial days, multiplied until in 1850 there were more than 6,000 of them.

In 1821, the Boston English High School opened as the nation's first free public secondary school, set up mainly for students not going on to college. By a law of 1827, Massachusetts required every town of five hundred or more residents to have a high school; in towns of four thousand or more, the school had to offer Latin, Greek, rhetoric, and other college-preparatory courses. Public high schools became well established only after the Civil War. In 1860 there were barely three hundred in the whole nation.

By 1850, half of the white children between ages 5 and 19 were enrolled in schools, the highest percentage in the world. But very few of those students were southerners. The South had very few public schools until after the Civil War. In most states, enslaved children were prohibited from learning to read and write or attend school. A former slave recalled that his owner "didn't teach 'em nuthin' but work." The South had some 500,000 illiterate whites, more than half the total in the country. In the South, North Carolina led the way in state-supported education, enrolling more than two-thirds of its white school-age population by 1860. But the school year was only four months long because of the rural state's need for children to do farm work. The prolonged disparities between North and South in the number and

The George Barrell Emerson School, Boston (ca. 1850) Although higher education for women initially met with some resistance, seminaries, like this one, started in the 1820s and 1830s, taught women mathematics, physics, and history, as well as music, art, and social graces.

quality of educational opportunities help explain the growing economic and cultural differences between the two regions. Then, as now, undereducated people were more likely to remain economically deprived, less healthy, and less engaged in political life.

Utopian Communities

Amid the pervasive climate of reform during the early nineteenth century, the quest for utopia—communities with innovative social and economic relationships—flourished. Plans for ideal communities had long been an American passion, at least since the Puritans set out to build a wilderness Zion in New England. More than 100 **utopian communities** sprang up between 1800 and 1900. Many of them were *communitarian* experiments in that they emphasized the welfare of the entire community rather than individual freedom. Some experimented with "free love," socialism, and special diets.

Those communities founded by the Shakers (officially the United Society of Believers in Christ's Second Appearing) proved to be long lasting. Ann Lee (known as Mother Ann Lee) arrived in New York from England with eight followers in 1774. Believing religious fervor to be a sign of inspiration from the Holy Ghost, Mother Ann and her followers had strange fits in which they saw visions and issued prophecies (predictions about the future). These manifestations later evolved into a ritual dance—hence the name "Shakers." Shaker doctrine held God to be a dual personality. In Christ, the masculine side was revealed; in Mother Ann, the feminine element. Mother Ann preached celibacy to prepare Shakers for the perfection that was promised them in heaven.

> Shakers

Mother Ann died in 1784, but the group found new leaders, and the movement spread from New York into New England, Ohio, and Kentucky. By 1830 about twenty groups were flourishing. In these Shaker communities all property was held in common. Shaker farms were among the nation's leading sources of garden seed and medicinal herbs, and many of their products, including clothing, household items, and especially furniture, were prized for their simple beauty.

John Humphrey Noyes, founder of the Oneida Community, had a very different vision of the ideal community. The son of a Vermont congressman, Noyes attended Dartmouth College and Yale Divinity School. But in 1834 he was expelled from Yale and his license to preach was revoked after he announced that he was "perfect" and free of all sin. In 1836 Noyes gathered a group of "Perfectionists" around his home in Putney, Vermont. Ten years later, he announced a new doctrine, "complex marriage," which meant that every man in the community was married to every woman, and vice versa. "In a holy community," he claimed, "there is no more reason why sexual intercourse should be restrained by law, than why eating and drinking should be." Authorities thought otherwise, and Noyes was charged with adultery for practicing his theology of "free love" (he coined the term). He fled to New York and

> The Oneida Community

utopian communities Ideal communities that offered innovative social and economic relationships to those who were interested in achieving salvation.

in 1848 established the Oneida Community, which had more than 200 members by 1851 and became famous for its production of fine silverware.

Brook Farm

Brook Farm in Massachusetts was the most celebrated utopian community because it grew out of the transcendental movement. George Ripley, a Unitarian minister and transcendentalist, conceived of Brook Farm as a kind of early-day think tank, combining high philosophy and plain living. In 1841 he and several dozen like-minded utopians moved to the 175-acre farm nine miles southwest of Boston. Brook Farm became America's first secular utopian community. One of its members, novelist Nathaniel Hawthorne, called it "our beautiful scheme of a noble and unselfish life." Its residents shared the tasks of maintaining the buildings, tending the fields, and preparing the meals. They also organized picnics, dances, lectures, and discussions. The place survived, however, mainly because of an excellent school that drew tuition-paying students from outside. In 1846, Brook Farm's main building burned down, and the community spirit died in the ashes.

Utopian communities, with few exceptions, quickly ran out of steam. The communal social experiments had little impact on the outside world, where reformers wrestled with the sins of the multitudes. Among all the targets of the reformers' zeal, one great evil would take precedence over the others: human bondage. Transcendentalist reformer Theodore Parker declared that slavery was "the blight of this nation, the curse of the North and the curse of the South." The paradox of American freedom being coupled with American slavery, of what novelist Herman Melville called "the world's fairest hope linked with man's foulest crime," would inspire the climactic crusade of the age, abolitionism, one that would ultimately sweep the nation into an epic civil war.

CORE **OBJECTIVE**
4. Analyze the impact on American society and politics of the emergence of the anti-slavery movement.

The Anti-Slavery Movement

The men who drafted the U.S. Constitution in 1787 hoped to keep the new nation from splitting apart over the question of the slavery. They negotiated compromises that avoided dealing with the issue. But most of them knew that there eventually would be a day of reckoning. That day approached as the nineteenth century unfolded.

Early Opposition to Slavery

Efforts to weaken or abolish slavery increased after 1800. The first organized emancipation movement appeared in 1816 with the formation of the **American Colonization Society**, whose mission was to raise funds to "repatriate" free blacks back to Africa. Its supporters included such prominent figures as James Madison, James Monroe, Henry Clay, John Marshall, and Daniel Webster. Some supported the colonization movement because of

American Colonization Society Established in 1816, an organization whose mission was to return freed slaves to Africa.

their opposition to slavery; others saw it as a way to get rid of potentially troublesome free blacks. "We must save the Negro," as one missionary explained, "or the Negro will ruin us." Leaders of the free black community denounced the colonization idea from the start. The United States of America, they stressed, was their native land. Nevertheless, in 1821, agents of the American Colonization Society acquired land in West Africa that became the nucleus of a new nation. In 1822, African Americans were transported to what became the Republic of Liberia. But the African colonization movement received only meager support. In all, only about 15,000 American blacks went to Africa, a tiny figure compared with the number of slave births each year in the United States.

From Gradualism to Abolitionism

In the early 1830s, blacks in Boston and whites in the anti-slavery movement adopted an aggressive new strategy. Its initial efforts to promote a *gradual* end to slavery by prohibiting it in the western territories and encouraging owners to free their slaves gave way to demands for *immediate* **abolition** everywhere. A zealous white Massachusetts activist named William Lloyd Garrison illustrated the change in outlook.

In 1831, free blacks in Boston helped convince Garrison to launch a new anti-slavery newspaper, *The Liberator*, which became the voice of the first civil rights movement. In the newspaper's first issue, he renounced "the popular but pernicious doctrine of gradual emancipation." He would promote immediate abolition because slavery was a crime against humanity and a sin before God. The crusading Garrison dreamed of true racial equality in all spheres of American life. In pursuing that dream he vowed to be "as harsh as truth, and as uncompromising as justice. . . . I am in earnest—I will not equivocate—I will not excuse—I will *not retreat a* single inch—AND I WILL BE HEARD."

William Lloyd Garrison A vocal abolitionist and an advocate of immediate emancipation.

Garrison's fierce courage in denouncing slavery outraged slave owners in the South as well as some whites in the North. In 1835, a mob of angry whites dragged him through the streets of Boston at the end of a rope. The Georgia state legislature promised a $5,000 reward to anyone who kidnapped Garrison and brought him south for trial. A southern slaveholder warned Garrison "to desist your infamous endeavors to instill into the minds of the negroes the idea that 'men must be free.'" Garrison reminded his critics that, however violent his language, he was opposed to the use of force. "We do not preach rebellion," he stressed. The prospect "of a bloody insurrection in the South fills us with dismay," but "if any people were ever justified in throwing off the yoke of their tyrants, the slaves are the people."

During the 1830s, Garrison became the nation's most unyielding foe of slavery. Two prominent New York City evangelical merchants, Arthur and Lewis Tappan, provided financial support for *The Liberator*. In 1833, they

abolitionism Movement that called for an immediate end to slavery throughout the United States.

joined with Garrison and a group of Quaker reformers, free blacks, and evangelicals to organize the American Anti-Slavery Society. That same year, Parliament ended slavery throughout the British Empire by passing the Emancipation Act, whereby slaveholders were paid to give up their "human property." In 1835, the Tappans hired the famous revivalist Charles G. Finney to head the anti-slavery faculty at Oberlin, a new college in northern Ohio that would be the first to admit black students.

The American Anti-Slavery Society, financed by the Tappans, created a national network of newspapers, offices, and chapters, almost all of which were affiliated with a local Christian church. By 1840, some 160,000 people belonged to the American Anti-Slavery Society, which stressed that "slaveholding is a heinous crime in the sight of God, and that the duty, safety, and best interests of all concerned, require its *immediate abandonment*." The society even argued that blacks should have complete social and civil rights. In 1835, the group began flooding the South with anti-slavery pamphlets and newspapers. Infuriated southern slaveholders called for state and federal laws to prevent the distribution of the literature, and post offices began destroying what was called "anti-slavery propaganda."

> **The American Anti-Slavery Society (1833)**

The most radical figure among the mostly white Garrisonians was David Walker, a free black man who owned a clothing store in Boston. In 1829, he published *Walker's Appeal*, a pamphlet which denounced the hypocrisy of Christians in the South for defending slavery and urged slaves to revolt. "Are we men?" he asked. "I ask you, O my brethren, are we MEN? Did our Creator make us to be slaves to dust and ashes like ourselves?" Walker shocked whites by encouraging rebellious slaves to use the "crushing arm of power" to gain their freedom. "Woe, woe will be to you if we have to obtain our freedom by fighting."

> **Walker's Appeal (1829)**

A Split in the Movement

As the abolitionist movement spread, debates over tactics intensified. The Garrisonians felt that slavery had corrupted virtually every aspect of American life: politics, the economy, and social and religious life. Garrison himself came to embrace every important reform movement of the day: abolition, temperance, pacifism, and women's rights. He also championed equal social and legal rights for African Americans. His unconventional religious ideas led him to break with the established Protestant churches, which to his mind were in league with slavery. The federal government was all the more so. The U.S. Constitution, he said, was "a covenant with death and an agreement with hell." Garrison refused to vote and encouraged others to do the same, arguing that the American republic could not continue to proclaim the ideal of liberty while tolerating the reality of slavery. He fiercely believed that the South could simply be shamed into ending slavery.

Other reformers were more practical. They saw American society as fundamentally sound and they concentrated on purging it of slavery. Garrison struck them as an unrealistic fanatic. A showdown came in 1840 on the issue of women's rights. Women had joined the abolition movement from the start, but largely in groups without men. At that time, women were rarely allowed to speak to organizations that included men. Then the activities of the Grimké sisters brought women's rights to center stage.

Women's rights and abolition

Sarah and Angelina Grimké, daughters of a wealthy South Carolina family, were raised in luxury and served by many slaves. In 1821, soon after her father's death, Sarah moved from Charleston to Philadelphia, joined the Society of Friends (Quakers), and renounced slavery as a sin. Angelina soon left home and joined her. In 1835 the two sisters joined the abolitionist movement, speaking to women's groups in what were called "parlor meetings." By 1835 they had joined the circle of female abolitionist leaders. After they appealed to southern Christian women to put an end to slavery, the mayor of Charleston told their mother that her daughters would be jailed if they ever returned home.

The energetic Grimké sisters traveled throughout the northern states, speaking first to audiences of women and eventually to both women and men. Their unconventional behavior in speaking to mixed-gender audiences prompted criticism from male reformers. The chairman of the Connecticut Anti-Slavery Society declared, "No woman shall speak or vote where I am a moderator." Catharine Beecher reminded the Grimké sisters that women occupy "a subordinate relation in society to the other sex" and that they should limit their activities to the "domestic and social circle" rather than public organizations. Angelina Grimké stoutly rejected such arguments. "It is a woman's right," she insisted, "to have a voice in all laws and regulations by which she is to be governed, whether in church or in state." Soon, she and her sister began linking their efforts to free the slaves with their desire to free women. "Men and women are CREATED EQUAL!" Sarah Grimké insisted. "Whatever is right for man to do is right for woman." The Grimké sisters joined others in claiming that women were being kept in "domestic slavery" by male traditionalists.

The debate over the role of women in the anti-slavery movement finally exploded at the Anti-Slavery Society's meeting in 1840, where the Garrisonians convinced a majority of delegates that women should participate equally in the organization. The Tappans and their supporters walked out of the convention and formed the American and Foreign Anti-Slavery Society.

A third faction of the American Anti-Slavery Society also broke with Garrison. Its members had grown skeptical that the nonviolent "moral suasion" promoted by Garrison would ever lead to abolition. In 1840, they formed the Liberty Party in an effort to elect an American president who would abolish slavery. Their nominee, James Gillespie Birney, executive secretary of the American Anti-Slavery Society, was a former slaveholder turned abolitionist. In the 1840 election, he polled only 7,000 votes, but in 1844 he won 60,000. From that time forward an anti-slavery party contested

The Liberty Party (1840)

every national election until the Thirteenth Amendment officially ended slavery in 1865.

Black Anti-Slavery Activity

Although many whites worked courageously to end slavery, most of them, unlike Garrison, adopted the racist attitudes common at the time, insisting that blacks were socially inferior to whites. Freedom for slaves, in other words, did not mean social equality for blacks. Many white abolitionists, for example, expected free blacks to take a backseat in the movement to end slavery. Yet despite such discrimination, many free African Americans such as David Walker, Sarah Parker Redmond, and Sarah Mapps Douglass, among others, were active in white anti-slavery societies. Former slaves such as Henry Bibb and William Wells Brown, both escapees from Kentucky, and Frederick Douglass, who had escaped from Maryland, were the most effective critics of the South's "peculiar institution."

Brown was just twenty years old and illiterate when he escaped from his owner, a steamboat pilot on the Ohio River. An Ohio Quaker named Wells Brown helped him escape, and Brown adopted his name in the process of forging a new identity as a free man. Brown settled in Cleveland, Ohio, married, had three children, and helped numerous runaway slaves escape to Canada. By 1842 he had learned to read and write and began to publish columns in abolitionist newspapers. In 1847 Brown moved to Boston, where the Massachusetts Anti-Slavery Society hired him as a traveling lecturer. That same year, the organization published his autobiography, *Narrative of William W. Brown, A Former Slave, Written by Himself,* which became a best-seller. Brown gave thousands of speeches in America and Europe calling for an end to slavery and equality for both blacks and women. He repeatedly stressed that the African American "is endowed with those intellectual and amiable qualities which adorn and dignify human nature."

Narrative of the Life of Frederick Douglass (1845)

Through his writings and dazzling speeches, Douglass became the best-known black man in America. "I appear before the immense assembly this evening as a thief and a robber," he told a Massachusetts group in 1842. "I stole this head, these limbs, this body from my master, and ran off with them." Fearful of capture after publishing his *Narrative of the Life of Frederick Douglass, An American Slave, Written by Himself* (1845), he left for an extended lecture tour of the British Isles, returning two years later with enough money to purchase his freedom. He then started an abolitionist newspaper for blacks, the *North Star,* in Rochester, New York. He named the newspaper after the star that runaway slaves used to guide them at night toward freedom.

The female counterpart to Frederick Douglass was Sojourner Truth. Born to slaves in the Dutch farming culture of upstate New York in 1797, Sojourner Truth was given the name Isabella "Bell" Hardenbergh but

Frederick Douglas and Sojourner Truth Both Douglass and Truth were leading abolitionists and captivating orators.

renamed herself in 1843 after experiencing a conversation with God, who told her "to travel up and down the land" preaching against slavery. Having been a slave until she was freed by a New York law in 1827, Sojourner Truth was able to speak with conviction and knowledge about the evils of the "peculiar institution" and the inequality of women. She traveled throughout the North during the 1840s and 1850s, urging audiences to support women's rights and the immediate abolition of slavery. As she told the Ohio Women's Rights Convention in 1851, "I have plowed, and planted, and gathered into barns, and no man could head me—and ar'n't I a woman? I have borne thirteen children, and seen 'em mos' all sold off into slavery, and when I cried out with a mother's grief, none but Jesus heard—and ar'n't I a woman?"

Through such compelling testimony, Sojourner Truth demonstrated the powerful intersection of abolitionism and feminism. In the process, she tapped the distinctive energies that women brought to reformist causes. "If the first woman God ever made was strong enough to turn the world upside down all alone," she concluded in her address to the Ohio gathering, "these women together ought to be able to turn it back, and get it right side up again!"

> Black abolitionists and women's rights

Underground Railroad

While runaways often made it out of slavery on their own, many were aided by the **Underground Railroad**, a vast national network of secret routes and "safe houses," where free blacks and white abolitionists called "conductors" concealed runaway slaves in basements, attics, barns, and wagons before helping the fleeing "passengers" to the next "station" and eventually to freedom, often over the Canadian border.

Underground Railroad
A secret system of routes and safe houses through which runaway slaves were led to freedom in the North.

The Underground Railroad

In many northern cities, blacks and whites organized "vigilance committees" to protect from and thwart the slave catchers. In February 1851, Shadrach Minkins, a "stout, copper-colored man" who worked as a waiter at a Boston coffee house, was seized by U.S. marshals claiming that he was a runaway slave from Virginia. During a court hearing, a group of black and white members of the anti-slavery Boston Vigilance and Safety Committee active in the Underground Railroad startled the judge and observers by rushing in, overcoming armed guards, and snatching "the trembling prey of the slave hunters." Abolitionists hid him for days in Boston before taking him to safety in Canada, where he married an Irish woman and had four children. An outraged President Millard Fillmore issued a proclamation demanding that citizens obey the law and that those responsible for "kidnapping" Minkins be prosecuted. None of the Bostonians charged in the case were convicted.

Between 1810 and 1850, tens of thousands of other southern slaves ran away and fled north. Escaped slaves would make their way, usually at night, from one station to the next. The conductors included free-born blacks, white abolitionists, former slaves, and Native Americans. Many of them were motivated by religious concerns. Quakers, Presbyterians, Methodists, and Baptists participated. A few courageous runaway slaves returned to the South to organize more escapes. Harriet Tubman, the most celebrated runaway, was born a slave in Maryland in 1820 but escaped to Philadelphia in 1849. During the 1850s she risked everything to venture back to the South nineteen times to help some 300 slaves, including her parents, escape over several years. She "never lost a passenger."

Reactions to Abolitionism

Even in the North, abolitionists confronted hostile white crowds who disliked blacks or found anti-slavery agitation bad for business. In 1837, a mob in Illinois killed Elijah P. Lovejoy, editor of an anti-slavery newspaper, giving the movement a martyr to the causes of both abolition and freedom of the press.

Mob violence

Lovejoy had begun his career as a Presbyterian minister in New England. He moved to St. Louis, in slaveholding Missouri, where his newspaper repeatedly denounced alcohol, Catholicism, and slavery. When a proslavery mob destroyed his printing office, he moved across the Mississippi River to a warehouse in Alton, Illinois, where he tried to start an antislavery society. There mobs twice more destroyed his printing press. When a new press arrived, Lovejoy and several supporters armed themselves and took up defensive positions. On November 7, 1837, thugs began hurling stones and firing shots into the building. One of Lovejoy's allies fired back, killing one of the rioters. The mob then set fire to the warehouse, shouting, "Kill every damned abolitionist as he leaves." A shotgun blast killed Lovejoy. His murder aroused a frenzy of indignation. Former president John Quincy

Adams said that Lovejoy's death sent "a shock as of an earthquake throughout the continent." At one of the hundreds of memorial services across the North, a grizzled John Brown rose, raised his right hand, and declared, "Here, before God, in the presence of these witnesses, from this time, I consecrate my life to the destruction of slavery!" Brown and other militants decided that only violence would dislodge the sin of slavery.

The Defense of Slavery

The growing strength and visibility of the abolitionist movement prompted southerners to launch an equally aggressive defense of slavery. During the 1830s and after, pro-slavery leaders worked out an elaborate rationale for what they considered the benefits of slavery. The Bible was cited; had not the patriarchs of the Hebrew Bible held people in bondage? Had not Saint Paul advised servants to obey their masters and told a runaway servant to return to his master? And had not Jesus remained silent on the subject?

Soon even bolder arguments emerged to defend the South's "peculiar institution." In February 1837, South Carolina's John C. Calhoun, the most prominent southern political leader, told the Senate that slavery was not evil. Instead, it was "good—a great good," rooted in the Bible. He brazenly asserted that the "savage" Africans brought to America "had never existed in so comfortable, so respectable, or so civilized a condition, as that which is now enjoyed in the Southern states." If slavery were abolished, Calhoun warned, the principle of white racial supremacy would be compromised: "the next step would be to raise the negroes to a social and political equality with the whites." What is more, Calhoun and other defenders of slavery claimed, blacks could not be expected to work under conditions of freedom. They were too shiftless, the argument went, and if freed, they would be a danger to themselves and to others. White workers, on the other hand, feared the competition for jobs if slaves were freed. Calhoun's strident defense of slavery as a "positive good" led Henry Clay of Kentucky, himself a slave owner, to describe Calhoun as "a rigid, fanatic, ambitious, selfishly partisan and sectional turncoat with too much genius and too little common sense, who will either die a traitor or a madman."

Southern white resistance

The increasingly heated debate over slavery drove a wedge deeply between North and South. In 1831, William Lloyd Garrison noted that the "bond of our Union is becoming more and more brittle." He predicted—correctly—that an eventual "separation between the free and slave States" was "unavoidable." By mid-century, a large number of Americans, mostly Whigs, had decided that southern slavery was an abomination that should not be allowed to expand into the new western territories. The militant reformers who were determined to prevent slavery from expanding outside the South came to be called "free soilers," and their crusade to improve American life would reach a fiery climax in the Civil War.

Abolitionism

Revolutions in transportation and communication allowed more Americans to share ideas, explore new ways of thinking, and connect with other like-minded individuals. But this often caused rifts in American society as many groups and individuals increasingly challenged social norms and institutions. Nothing divided Americans and generated more debate than abolitionism. Abolitionists not only called for an immediate end to slavery, but also demanded full social and political equality for African Americans. Though appealing to many reformers, particularly Christian evangelicals, it drew an equally passionate yet hostile response from its opponents. Furthermore, abolitionism propelled discussion of the place of all men and women in American society, questions that often divided abolitionists themselves.

Reactions to Abolitionism	North	South	African Americans	Women
General Position	**Pro-Abolition** Inspired by the Second Great Awakening, northern supporters considered slavery a sin.	**Pro-Slavery** Most southerners viewed abolition as a threat to the cotton economy and the social fabric of white supremacy.	**Pro-Abolition** Plantation economy and southern culture split slave families and legalized brutality toward African Americans.	**Pro-Abolition** Many women viewed abolition as part of broader reform movements advocating universal suffrage and gender equality.
Main Goals and Issues	Immediate emancipation, full political and social equality for African Americans Disagreed over tactics and relationship to other reform movements	Slavery improved "the condition of the African" by bringing Christianity and civilization to a "savage," inferior race	Immediate emancipation, full political and social equality, access to education Some called for a violent overthrow of slavery (such as *Walker's Appeal*)	Immediate emancipation, full political and social equality, access to education
Major Figures	■ William Lloyd Garrison ■ Arthur and Lewis Tappan ■ Charles G. Finney ■ James Birney ■ John Brown	■ Senator John C. Calhoun	■ Frederick Douglass ■ Sojourner Truth ■ Harriet Tubman	■ Angelina and Sarah Grimké ■ Sojourner Truth ■ Harriet Tubman ■ Lucretia Mott ■ Elizabeth Cady Stanton ■ Susan B. Anthony

(CONTINUED)

Reactions to Abolitionism	North	South	African Americans	Women
Key Events	■ 1831 – Garrison publishes *The Liberator*, first anti-slavery newspaper ■ 1833 – American Anti-Slavery Society is formed ■ 1837 – Abolitionist editor Elijah Lovejoy murdered by pro-slavery mob ■ 1840 – Liberty Party is formed	■ 1831 – Nat Turner's Rebellion ■ 1830s – Stricter slave codes adopted ■ 1835 – "Anti-slavery propaganda" made illegal in South after abolitionists distribute pro-abolition literature	■ 1816 – First African American church founded in Philadelphia ■ 1845 – *Narrative of the Life of Frederick Douglass* published ■ 1850s – Underground Railroad reaches its height; "vigilance committees" established	■ 1830s – Anti-Slavery Society splits over participation of women ■ 1840 – Emergence of women's rights movement ■ 1851 – Sojourner Truth delivers "Ar'n't I a Woman" speech
Outcomes by 1860	■ Many northerners continued to oppose abolition ■ Many northern politicians refused discussion of slavery issue	■ Slave codes further strengthened ■ Southern Baptist and Methodist denominations dissociated themselves from northern counterparts over slavery issue	■ Underground Railroad brings more than 300,000 to freedom in 1850s–1860s ■ Join forces with women's rights movement ■ National leaders and platforms for abolitionism emerge	■ Association of women's rights and abolitionist movements caused southern women to also oppose women's rights

QUESTIONS FOR ANALYSIS

1. How did residents of northern and other free states respond to abolitionists?

2. How did southerners respond?

3. How did abolitionism affect many African Americans and women?

4. How did abolitionism change American attitudes towards slavery and social reform?

■ **Religious Developments** Starting in the late eighteenth century, *Unitarians* and *Universalists* in New England challenged the notion of predestination and advocated that all humans are capable of good deeds and could receive salvation, not just a select few. Echoing these ideas with their conception of salvation by free will, the preachers of the *Second Great Awakening* generated widespread interest among Protestants in *frontier revivals*. The more democratic sects, such as Baptists and Methodists, gained huge numbers of converts, especially among women and African Americans. Religion went hand in hand with reform in the "burned-over district" in western New York, which was also the birthplace of several religious movements, including the Church of Jesus Christ of Latter-day Saints (the *Mormons*).

■ **Transcendentalists** embraced a moral and spiritual idealism (Romanticism) in reaction to scientific rationalism and Christian orthodoxy. In their writings, they sought to "transcend" reason and the material world and encourage more independent thought and reflection. At the same time, *transcendentalism* influenced the works of novelists, essayists, and poets, who created a uniquely American literature. A cultural nationalism emerged with political ideals for a more moral American society.

■ **Social Reform Movements** The *cult of domesticity* celebrated a "woman's sphere" in the home and argued that young women should be trained not for the workplace but in the domestic arts—managing a kitchen, running a household, and nurturing the children. However, the rise of an urban middle class offered growing numbers of women more time to devote to societal concerns. Social reformers—many of them women—sought to improve society and eradicate social evils. The most widespread movement was for *temperance*, the elimination of excessive drinking. Many were also active in reforming prisons and asylums. At the *Seneca Falls Convention of 1848,* social reformers launched the women's rights movement with the *Declaration of Sentiments (1848)*. In many parts of the country, social reformers called for greater access to education through *public schools* for the nation's young, which would also offer women an occupation outside the home. One educational reformer, Horace Mann, said that teaching was a way for women to become "mothers away from home" for the students. Amid the pervasive climate of reform during the early nineteenth century, more than 100 *utopian communities* were established, including the Shakers, Brook Farm, and the Oneida Community.

■ **Anti-Slavery Movement** Northern opponents of slavery promoted several solutions, including the *American Colonization Society's* call for gradual emancipation and the deportation of African Americans to colonies in Africa. *Abolitionism* emerged in the 1830s, demanding an immediate end of slavery. Some abolitionists went even further, calling for full social and political equality among the races, although they disagreed over tactics. Abolitionist efforts in the North provoked a strong reaction among southern whites, stirring fears for their safety and resentment of interference. Yet many northerners shared the belief in the racial inferiority of Africans and were hostile to the tactics and message of the abolitionists. African Americans in the North joined with abolitionists to create an *Underground Railroad*, a network of safe havens to help slaves escape their bondage in the South.

KEY TERMS

CHRONOLOGY

1779	Universalist Church founded in Massachusetts
1816	Auburn Penitentiary opens in New York
1826	Ministers organize the American Society for the Promotion of Temperance
1830–1831	Charles G. Finney begins preaching in upstate New York
1830	Percentage of American churchgoers has doubled since 1800
	Joseph Smith reveals *The Book of Mormon*
1831	William Lloyd Garrison begins publishing *The Liberator*
1833	American Anti-Slavery Society is founded
1836	Transcendental Club holds its first meeting
1837	Abolitionist editor Elijah P. Lovejoy is murdered
1840	Abolitionists form the Liberty Party
1840s	Methodists have become largest Protestant denomination in America
1845	*Narrative of the Life of Frederick Douglass* is published
1846	Mormons, led by Brigham Young, make the difficult trek to Utah
1848	At the Seneca Falls Convention, feminists issue the Declaration of Sentiments
	John Humphrey Noyes establishes the Oneida Community
1851	Sojourner Truth delivers her famous speech "Ar'n't I a Woman?"
1854	Henry David Thoreau's *Walden, or Life in the Woods* is published

INQUIZITIVE

Go to InQuizitive to see what you've learned—and learn what you've missed—with personalized feedback along the way.

DEBATING Separate Spheres

Politics and present-day events often influence *historiography*, the study of how interpretations of history change over time. In the 1960s, *social* history gained popularity. Drawing on methodologies from the social sciences, historians emphasized the importance of processes and structures in societies and applied them to groups that had been ignored by previous generations of historians. Three concepts of great importance to social historians are *race, class*, and *gender*. For Part 3, *An Expansive Nation*, we will see how historians use these concepts to debate the importance of the "separate spheres" ideology. This ideology emerged during a period where rapid industrialization spurred the growth of the middle class. In the first half of the nineteenth century, before the Civil War, the "separate spheres" ideology promoted separate and distinct roles for women and men. The female sphere was within the home and focused on domesticity, while the male sphere was outside the home and was centered on economic and political competition.

For this exercise you have two tasks:

PART 1: Compare the two secondary sources on women and separate spheres.

PART 2: Using primary sources, evaluate the arguments of the two secondary sources.

PART I **Comparing Secondary Sources**

Below are secondary sources from two social historians who have written on the separate spheres ideology in American life before the Civil War. The first is from Catherine Clinton of Queens University in Belfast, Ireland; the second from Nancy Hewitt of Rutgers, the State University of New Jersey. Both Clinton and Hewitt use race, class, and gender analysis to look at how separate spheres impacted American women and how women responded to that ideology.

Compare the views of these two scholars by answering the following questions. Be sure to find specific examples in the selections to support your answers.

- What is the subject of each article?

- What classes of women does each author focus on?

- According to each author, how did the ideology of separate spheres impact American women?

- In what ways does each author use race, class, and gender in constructing her argument?

Secondary Source 1

Catherine Clinton, "The Ties that Bind" (1984)

The nineteenth century ushered in a social as well as an economic revolution for American women. The refinement of middle-class ideology profoundly affected females during the antebellum [pre-Civil War] era. . . . The creation of the cult of domesticity, the redefinition of the home as women's domain, was a delicate process designed to channel women's contributions into a proper course. . . .

[I]nstead of liberty and equality, subordination and restriction were drummed into women, a refrain inherited from the colonial era. Women's only reward was lavish exaltation of their vital and unmatchable contributions to the civic state as mothers. This rejuvenated ethic was accompanied by a confinement to the domestic sphere.

Once segregated from men by the confines of a new ideological order, women set about turning their liabilities into assets. Forbidden traditional pathways to success, post-Revolutionary women pursued other means of achieving esteem and influence within their society. These alternatives were pioneered by women who were in search of new influence but who refrained from invading the male domain—not for the sake of modesty, but rather as a strategy. . . .

Woman's domain was, despite confinement, expansive. She was charged with the moral, spiritual, and physical well-being of her entire family. . . . She was supervisor of the education of her children, tender of the heath, and the symbol of the home. These indispensable functions, although primarily carried out within the home, were not restricted to it. Women perceived that they might extend female jurisdiction into the public and hitherto exclusively male realm by using their "domestic" role as a lever—wedging themselves into positions of power, however limited, through exploitation of their domesticity. In the early decades of the century, creative women took their rather circumscribed nooks and crannies, within the culture, and turned them into springboards. Women's talents and contributions were soon apparent within the larger social arena.

Source: Clinton, Catherine. "The Ties that Bind." *The Other Civil War, American Women in the Nineteenth Century.* New York: Hill and Wang, first published in 1984; revised edition, 1999, 40-42.

Secondary Source 2

Nancy A. Hewitt, "Beyond the Search for Sisterhood: American Women's History in the 1980s" (1985)

The bonds that encircled past generations of women were initially perceived as restrictive, arising from female victimization at the hands of patriarchs in such institutions as medicine, education, the church, the state, and the family. Historians soon concluded, however, that oppression was a double-edged sword; the counterpart of subordination in or exclusion from male-dominated domains was inclusion in an all-female enclave. The concept of womanhood, it soon appeared, "bound women together even as it bound them down." The formative works in American women's history have focused on the formation of these separate sexual spheres, particularly among the emerging urban bourgeoisie in the first half of the nineteenth century. Reified in prescriptive literature, realized in daily life, and ritualized in female collectivities, this 'woman's sphere' came to be seen as the foundation of women's culture and community in antebellum [pre-Civil War] America. . . . The community that has become the cornerstone of North American women's history was discovered within the Victorian middle class. . . . Yet evidence from the lives of slaves, mill operatives, miners' wives, immigrants, and southern industrial workers as well as from "true women" indicates that there was no single woman's culture or sphere. There was a culturally dominant definition of sexual spheres promulgated by an economically, politically, and socially dominant group. That definition was firmly grounded in the sexual division of labor appropriate to that class, just as other definitions developed based on the sexual division of labor in other class and racial groups. All of these divisions were characterized by sufficient sex-stereotyping to assure the formation of distinct female circles of labor and distinct rituals and values rooted in that laboring experience. To date historians have focused on the parallels in the establishment of women's spheres across classes, races, and ethnic groups and have asserted certain commonalities among them, assuming their common origin in the modernization of society during the nineteenth century. A closer examination now reveals that no such universal sisterhood existed, and in fact that the development of a sense of community among various classes of women served as a barrier to an all-embracing bond of womanhood. Finally, it is now clear that privileged women were willing to wield their sex-specific influence in ways that, intentionally or unintentionally, exploited other women in the name of "true-womanhood."

Source: Hewitt, Nancy A. "Beyond the Search for Sisterhood: American Women's History in the 1980s." *Social History* 10 (1985), pp. 299-321.

PART II Using Primary Sources to Evaluate Secondary Sources

When historians are faced with conflicting interpretations of the past, they often look at primary source material as part of the process of evaluating the different arguments. Below are three excerpts from political statements by three remarkable but very different women. The first is from Lucretia Mott, a middle class and highly educated woman who became a Quaker speaker, leading abolitionist, and co-organizer of the first women's rights conventions, the Seneca Falls Convention. The second excerpt is from Sojourner Truth, a former slave and leading abolitionist. The final excerpt is from Harriett Robinson, who at the age of ten began work in the textile mills of Lowell, Massachusetts. Robinson went on to write her autobiography, and was involved in the women's suffrage movement. While not all of these documents directly engage with the term "separate spheres," each address women's place in American society.

Carefully read each of the following primary sources and answer the following questions. Decide which of the primary source documents support or refute Clinton and Hewitt's arguments about women's separate sphere. You may find that some documents do both but for different parts of each historian's interpretation. Be sure to identify which specific components of each historian's argument the documents support or refute.

■ How did the ideology of separate spheres impact the lives of these three women?

■ What can we learn about separate spheres from those primary sources that do not directly discuss the concept?

■ Which of the primary sources do you think Clinton and Hewitt would find most useful, and how might they use them to support their argument?

■ Which of the secondary sources do you think is best supported by the primary source evidence?

■ What have these primary sources taught you about using race, class, and gender in historical analysis?

Primary Source 1

Lucretia Mott, *Discourse on Women* (1849)

This age is notable for its works of mercy and benevolence—for the efforts that are made to reform the inebriate and the degraded, to relieve the oppressed and the suffering. Women as well as men are interested in these works of justice and mercy. They are efficient co-workers, their talents are called into profitable exercise, their labors are effective in each department of reform. The blessing to the merciful, to the peacemaker is equal to man and to woman. It is greatly to be deplored, now that she is increasingly qualified for usefulness, that any view should be presented, calculated to retard her labors of love.

Why should not woman seek to be a reformer? . . . [I]f she is to fear to exercise her reason, and her noblest powers, lest she should be thought to "attempt to act the man," and not "acknowledge his supremacy"; if she is to be satisfied with the narrow sphere assigned her by man, nor aspire to a higher, lest she should transcend the bounds of female delicacy; truly it is a mournful prospect for woman. We would admit all the difference, that our great and beneficent Creator has made, in the relation of man and woman, nor would we seek to disturb this relation; but we deny that the present position of woman, is her true sphere of usefulness: nor will she attain to this sphere, until the disabilities and disadvantages, religious, civil, and social, which impede her progress, are removed out of her way. These restrictions have enervated her mind and paralyzed her powers. . . . So far from her "ambition leading her to attempt to act the man," she needs all the encouragement she can receive, by the removal of obstacles from her path, in order that she may become a "true woman." As it is desirable that man should act a manly and generous part, not "mannish," so let woman be urged to exercise a dignified and womanly bearing, not womanish. Let her cultivate all the graces and proper accomplishments of her sex, but let not these degenerate into a kind of effeminacy, in which she is satisfied to be the mere plaything or toy of society, content with her outward adorning's, and with the tone of flattery and fulsome adulation too often addressed to her. True, nature has made a difference in her configuration, her physical strength, her voice, etc.—and we ask no change, we are satisfied with nature. But how has neglect and mismanagement increased this difference! It is our duty to develop these natural powers, by suitable exercise, so that they may be strengthened "by reason of use."

Source: Mott, Lucretia. *Discourse on Women*. Philadelphia, Penn.: T.B. Peterson, 1850.

Primary Source 2

Sojourner Truth, "And Ar'n't I a Woman?" (1851)

And ar'n't I a woman? Look at me! Look at my arm! (*And she bared her right arm to the shoulder, showing her tremendous muscular power.*) I have plowed, and planted, and gathered into barns, and no man could head me—and ar'n't I a woman? I could work as much and eat as much as a man when I could get it and bear de lash as well—and ar'n't I a woman ? I have borne thirteen children, and seen 'em mos' all sold off to slavery, and when I cried out with my mother's grief, none but Jesus heard me—and ar'n't I a woman? . . . If my cup won't hold but a pint, and your'n holds a quart, wouldn't ye be mean not to let me have my little half-measure full? . . . He say women can't have as much rights as men, 'cause Christ wan't a woman! Whar did your Christ come from? . . . From God and a woman! Man had nothin' to do with Him.

Source: Truth, Sojourner. "And Ar'n't I a Woman?" (Speech at the Ohio Women's Rights Convention, 1851, Akron, Ohio). *History of Woman Suffrage*, Vol 1.1848-1861. Ed. Elizabeth Cady Stanton, Susan B. Anthony, and Matilda Joslyn Gage. Rochester, New York: Susan B. Anthony, 1887.

Primary Source 3

Harriett H. Robinson, *Loom and Spindle or Life among the Early Mill Girls* **(1898)**

One of the first strikes of cotton-factory operatives that ever took place in this country was that in Lowell, in October, 1836. When it was announced that the wages were to be cut down, great indignation was felt, and it was decided to strike, en masse. This was done. The mills were shut down, and the girls went in procession from their several corporations to the "grove" on Chapel Hill, and listened to "incendiary" speeches from early labor reformers. One of the girls stood on a pump, and gave vent to the feelings of her companions in a neat speech, declaring that it was their duty to resist all attempts at cutting down the wages. This was the first time a woman had spoken in public in Lowell, and the event caused surprise and consternation among her audience. . . . It was estimated that as many as twelve or fifteen hundred girls turned out, and walked in procession through the streets. They had neither flags nor music, but sang songs, a favorite (but rather inappropriate) one being a parody on "I won't be a nun."

"Oh ! isn't it a pity, such a pretty girl as I—

Should be sent to the factory to pine away and die?

Oh ! I cannot be a slave,

I will not be a slave,

For I'm so fond of liberty

That I cannot be a slave."

Source: Robinson, Harriett H. *Loom and Spindle or Life among the Early Mill Girls*. New York and Boston: Thomas Y. Crowell and Company, 1898.

FOR SALE HERE

AN EDITION FOR THE MILLION, COMPLETE IN 1 Vol., PRICE 37 1-2 CENT
"   "   IN GERMAN, IN 1 Vol., PRICE 50 CENTS.
"   "   IN 2 Vols., CLOTH, 6 PLATES, PRICE $1.50.
SUPERB ILLUSTRATED EDITION. IN 1 Vol., WITH 153 ENGRAVINGS,
PRICES FROM $2.50 TO $5.00.

A House Divided and Rebuilt

During the first half of the nineteenth century, Americans, restless and energetic, were mostly optimistic about the future as their young nation matured into a global power. The United States had already become the world's largest republic. Its population continued to grow rapidly, economic conditions were improving, and tensions with Great Britain had eased. Above all, Americans continued to move westward, where vast expanses of cheap government-owned land lured farmers, ranchers, and miners. By the end of the 1840s, the United States—yet again—had dramatically expanded its territory, from Texas west to California and the Pacific Northwest. In the process of dislodging Native Americans and Mexicans, it assembled a continental empire from the Atlantic to the Pacific.

This extraordinary surge of territorial expansion was not an unmixed blessing, however. How to deal with the new western territories became the nation's flashpoint issue as the differences between America's three distinctive regions—North, South, and West—became more divisive. During the first half of the nineteenth century, a series of political compromises had glossed over the fundamental issue of slavery, but growing numbers of anti-slavery activists opposed efforts to extend slavery into the new western territories. Moreover, the 1850s brought a new generation of national politicians who were less willing to compromise. The continuing debate over allowing slavery into new territories eventually led more and more Americans to decide that the nation could not survive half-slave and half-free. Something had to give.

In a last-ditch effort to preserve the institution of slavery, eleven southern states seceded from the Union and declared themselves a separate Confederate nation. That, in turn, prompted northerners, led by President Abraham Lincoln, to support a civil war to restore the Union. No one realized in 1861 how costly that war would become: more than 700,000 soldiers and sailors would die in four years of fighting. Nor did anyone envision how sweeping the war's effects would be upon the nation's future. The northern victory in 1865 restored the Union and helped accelerate America's trans-

formation into a modern nation-state. A national consciousness began to replace the sectional divisions of the prewar era, and a Republican-led Congress passed a wave of federal legislation to promote industrial and commercial development and western expansion. In the process the United States began to leave behind the Jeffersonian dream of America as a decentralized agrarian republic.

Although the Civil War also ended slavery, the status of the freed African Americans remained uncertain and even life-threatening. Former slaves found themselves legally free, but few had property, homes, education, or training. Although the Fourteenth Amendment (1868) guaranteed the civil rights of African Americans and the Fifteenth Amendment (1870) declared that black men could vote, southern officials often ignored the new laws, and African Americans continued to suffer social abuse and physical harm.

The restoration of the former Confederate states to the Union did not come easily. Bitterness and resistance grew among the defeated southerners. Although former Confederate leaders were initially stripped of the right to vote and hold office, they continued to exercise considerable authority in political and economic matters. In 1877, when the last federal troops were removed from the occupied South, former Confederates declared themselves "redeemed" from the stain of Northern military occupation. By the end of the nineteenth century, most states of the former Confederacy had developed a system of legal discrimination against blacks that re-created many aspects of slavery.

EMIGRANTS CROSSING THE PLAINS, OR THE OREGON TRAIL (1869) German American painter
Albert Bierstadt captures the majestic sights of the frontier, though the transcontinental trek was
also grueling and bleak for many pioneers.

Western Expansion and Southern Secession

1830–1861

During the 1840s and after, wave after wave of Americans moved west. "If hell lay to the west," one pioneer declared, "Americans would cross heaven to get there." By 1860, some 4.3 million Americans had crossed the mile-wide Mississippi River and spread out across the Great Plains. Westward expansion was especially important to southerners, many of whom wanted new lands to plant cotton using slave labor. In addition, southerners had long enjoyed disproportionate political power because of the provision in the U.S. Constitution that counted slaves as part of the population in determining the number of Congressional seats for each state. Thirteen of the first sixteen presidents were from the South, and most Congressional leadership positions were held by southerners. But southern political influence began to wane as the industrializing Midwest and Northeast grew more rapidly, increasing those regions' representation in Congress. Southerners wanted new western states to boost pro-southern representation in Congress as a means of ensuring that slavery would never be threatened by northern abolitionists. As a Mississippi senator

CORE
OBJECTIVES INQUIZITIVE

1. Explain how, why, and where Americans moved west of the Mississippi River during the 1830s and 1840s.

2. Examine the impact of the Mexican-American War on national politics.

3. Describe how the federal government tried to resolve the issue of slavery in the western territories during the 1850s.

4. Analyze what appealed to northern voters about the Republican party and how that led to Abraham Lincoln's victory in the 1860 presidential contest.

5. Explain why seven southern states seceded from the Union shortly after Lincoln's election in 1860.

explained, "I would spread the blessings of slavery . . . to the uttermost ends of the earth." Such motives made the addition of new western territory controversial. Would the territory be slave or free?

Emigrants moved west largely for economic reasons. "To make money was their chief object," said a pioneer woman in Texas, "all things else were subsidiary to it." Trappers and farmers, miners and merchants, hunters, ranchers, teachers, servants, and prostitutes, among others, headed west to seek their fortune. Others—such as the Mormons and Christian missionary organizations—sought religious freedom and the chance to win converts to their faith. The Indians and Hispanics who had long inhabited the region were swept aside by the onslaught of Americans, all enabled by presidents and congressmen eager to complete the nation's expansion to the Pacific coast.

CORE **OBJECTIVE**

1. Explain how, why, and where Americans moved west of the Mississippi River during the 1830s and 1840s.

Moving West

In 1845, a New York newspaper editor and Democratic-party propagandist named John L. O'Sullivan gave a catchy name to America's aggressive spirit of westward expansion. "Our manifest destiny," he wrote, "is to overspread the continent allotted by Providence for the free development of our yearly multiplying millions." The phrase "**manifest destiny**" assumed that the United States had a God-given right to extend its rapidly growing Christian republic and capitalist civilization across the continent from the Atlantic to the Pacific—and beyond. This widely embraced notion of manifest destiny offered a powerful religious justification for territorial expansion, even at the expense of the prior claims of Native Americans and Hispanics, Spaniards and the British, on western lands.

The Western Frontier

Western migration: Population growth, land, and Overland Trails

Most of the western pioneers during the second quarter of the nineteenth century were American-born whites from the Upper South and the Midwest. Only a few free African Americans joined in the migration. What spurred the massive migration westward was the continuing population explosion in the United States and the desire for land.

Although some people traveled by sea to California, most went overland. Between 1841 and 1867, some 350,000 men, women, and children made the difficult trek to California or Oregon, while hundreds of thousands of others settled along the way in areas such as Colorado, Texas, and Arkansas. Most of the pioneers who made their way westward on the **Overland Trails** traveled in family groups. Oregon-bound wagon trains usually left Missouri in late spring and completed the grueling 2,000-mile trek in six months. By 1845, some 5,000 people were making the journey annually. The discovery of gold in California in 1848 brought some 30,000 pioneers along the Oregon Trail in 1849. By 1850, the peak year of travel along the trail, the annual count had risen to 55,000.

manifest destiny The widespread belief that America was "destined" by God to expand westward across the continent into lands claimed by Native Americans as well as European nations.

Overland Trails Trail routes followed by wagon trains bearing settlers and trade goods from Missouri to the Oregon Country, California, and New Mexico, beginning in the 1840s.

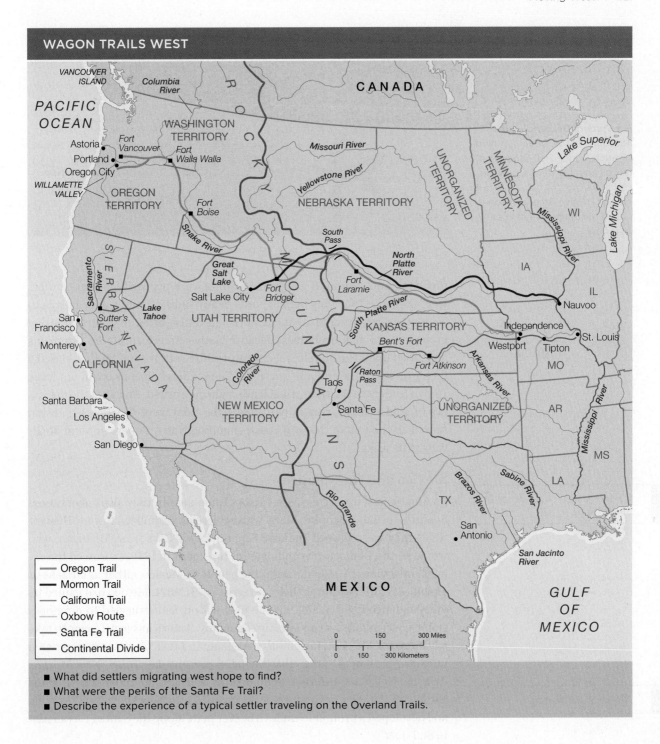

WAGON TRAILS WEST

Legend:
- Oregon Trail
- Mormon Trail
- California Trail
- Oxbow Route
- Santa Fe Trail
- Continental Divide

- What did settlers migrating west hope to find?
- What were the perils of the Santa Fe Trail?
- Describe the experience of a typical settler traveling on the Overland Trails.

Plains Indians

More than 325,000 Indians inhabited the Southwest, the Great Plains, California, and the Pacific Northwest in 1840, when the great migration of American settlers into the region began. The Native Americans were divided into more than 200 nations, each with its own language, religion, cultural

Conflicts over Indian lands

Fur Traders Descending the Missouri (1845) Originally titled "French-Trader, Half-Breed Son," this oil painting depicts a white settler sailing down the river with his half–Native American son—not an uncommon sight in early America.

practices, and system of governance. Some were primarily farmers; others were nomadic, following buffalo herds; many Indian nations were hostile to each other, resulting in frequent wars and raids—often to control hunting grounds or to acquire horses. Because Native American life on the plains depended upon the buffalo, the influx of white settlers and hunters posed a direct threat to the Indians' survival. When federal officials could not force Indian leaders to sell their tribal lands, fighting ensued. And after the discovery of gold in California in early 1848, the tidal wave of white expansion flowed all the way to the west coast, engulfing Native Americans and Mexicans in its wake.

Mexico and the Spanish West

Mexico gains independence from Spain (1821)

As American settlers trespassed across Indian lands, they also encountered Spanish-speaking peoples. Many whites were as prejudiced toward Hispanics as they were toward Indians. Senator Lewis Cass from Michigan, who would be the Democratic candidate for president in 1848, expressed the expansionist view: "We do not want the people of Mexico, either as citizens or as subjects. All we want is their . . . territory." In 1821, Mexico had gained its independence from Spain, but the new nation had struggled to develop a stable government and an effective economy. Americans were eager to take advantage of Mexico's instability, especially in Mexico's sparsely populated northern provinces—areas that included present-day Texas, New Mexico, Arizona, Nevada, California, and portions of Colorado, Oklahoma, Kansas,

American fur traders

and Wyoming. American fur traders streamed into New Mexico and Arizona and developed a profitable trade in beaver pelts along the Santa Fe Trail east to St. Louis.

The Rocky Mountains and Oregon Country

British-American joint occupation of the Oregon Country

During the early nineteenth century, the Far Northwest consisted of the Nebraska, Washington, and Oregon Territories. The Oregon Country included what became the states of Oregon, Idaho, and Washington, as well as parts of Montana, Wyoming, and the Canadian province of British Columbia. It was an unsettled region claimed by both Great Britain and the United States. By the Convention of 1818, the two nations had agreed to "joint occupation" of the Oregon Country.

Word of Oregon's fertile soil, plentiful rainfall, and magnificent forests gradually spread eastward. By the late 1830s, a trickle of emigrants—farmers, missionaries, fur traders, and shopkeepers—was flowing along the Oregon Trail, a 2,000-mile footpath connecting the Missouri River near St. Louis with Oregon. Soon, however, **Oregon Fever** swept the nation. In 1841 and 1842, the first sizable wagon trains made the trip, and in 1843 the movement became a mass migration. One pioneer remembered that the wagon trains were like mobile communities. "Everybody was supposed to rise at daylight, and while the women were preparing breakfast, the men rounded up the cattle, took down the tents, yoked the oxen to the wagons, and made everything ready to start" once breakfast was over. They found Oregon in a "primitive state" requiring backbreaking work to create self-sustaining homesteads. Women worked as hard as men, day and night. "I am a very old woman," reported twenty-nine-year-old Sarah Everett. "My face is thin, sunken, and wrinkled, my hands bony, withered, and hard." Another Oregon pioneer warned that a "woman that cannot endure almost as much as a horse has no business here." By 1845 there were about 5,000 settlers in Oregon's Willamette Valley.

The Settlement of California

California was also a powerful magnet for new settlers and adventurers. By the nineteenth century, Spanish Catholic missionaries, aided by Spanish soldiers, had control over most of the coastal Indians. The friars (priests) lured the local Indians into "missions" by offering gifts or impressing them with their "magical" religious rituals. Once inside the missions, the Indians were baptized as Catholics, taught Spanish, and stripped of their native heritage. Soldiers living in the missions enforced the will of the friars, and rebellious Indians were whipped or imprisoned. Mission Indians died at an alarming rate; the Native American population along the California coast declined from 72,000 in 1769 to 18,000 by 1821. Saving souls cost many lives.

For all of its rich natural resources, California remained thinly populated well into the nineteenth century. Californians took comfort that Mexico City, the Mexican capital, was too far away to exercise effective control over them. Between 1821, when Mexico gained its independence, and 1841, Californians, including many recent American arrivals, staged ten revolts against Mexican governors.

Yet the shift from Spanish to Mexican rule did produce one dramatic change in California. In 1824, Mexico passed a colonization act that granted hundreds of huge *ranchos* (estates) to prominent Mexicans. Yet the *rancheros* (largest landowners) wanted more, especially the vast estates controlled by the Catholic missions, which were usually on the most fertile and valuable land. In 1833–1834, they persuaded the Mexican government to pass the "secularization act" which allowed the government to take the missions,

Oregon Fever

Oregon Fever The lure of fertile land and economic opportunities in the Oregon Country that drew thousands of settlers westward, beginning in the late 1830s.

release the Indians from church control, and transfer the missions' vast farmlands to *rancheros*. Within a few years, some 700 new *rancho* grants of 4,500 to 50,000 acres were issued along the California coast. These sprawling ranches resembled southern plantations—but the death rate among brutalized Indian workers was twice as high as that among enslaved blacks in the Lower South.

Among the most ambitious white immigrants in California in the mid-nineteenth century was John A. Sutter, a Swiss settler who had founded a colony of European emigrants. At the junction of the Sacramento and American Rivers (later the site of the city of Sacramento), Sutter built an enormous fort to protect the settlers and their shops. New Helvetia (Americans called it Sutter's Fort), completed in 1843, stood at the end of what became the most traveled western route through the Sierra Nevada mountains, the California Trail, which forked southward off the Oregon Trail and led through the mountains. By the start of 1846, there were perhaps 800 Americans in California, along with approximately 10,000 *Californios* (settlers of Hispanic descent).

American Settlements in Texas

The American passion for new western land focused on the closest of all the northern Mexican borderlands, Texas. During the 1820s, the United States had twice offered to buy Texas, but the Mexican government refused to sell. Mexicans were frightened and infuriated by the idea of America acquiring their "sacred soil." But that is what happened anyway. The leading promoter of American settlement in Texas was Stephen Fuller Austin, a visionary land developer (*empresario*) who convinced Mexican leaders that he could recruit energetic American families to settle in Texas and thereby create a "buffer" on the northern frontier between the feared Comanche Indians and the Mexican settlements to the south. Thousands of hardy souls settled in Austin's Anglo-Texas "colony." They were mostly ranchers or farmers drawn to the fertile lands in the river valleys that sold for only a few cents an acre—much less than the price of federal land in the United States. A few of the settlers were wealthy planters who brought large numbers of slaves with them at a time when Mexico prohibited the importation of slaves. By 1830, the coastal region of Texas had far more Americans living there than Hispanics—about 20,000 white settlers (Anglo-Texans, or "Texians"), and 1,000 enslaved blacks, brought to grow and harvest cotton.

Huge *ranchos* dominate Mexican-owned California

California: Sutter's Fort

"Texians" settle lands in northern Mexico

American pioneers This 1850 photograph captures only a few of the thousands of pioneers who headed west for brighter futures.

In 1828, José María Sánchez, a Mexican official, visited Austin's settlement in Texas and warned that the effort to take Texas from Mexico "will start from this colony" because the Mexican government was not taking "vigorous measures to prevent it."

The Texas War for Independence

Mexican officials were so worried about the cultural tensions created by too many non-Catholic and slave-owning Americans living in Texas that in April 1830 they abruptly outlawed immigration from the United States and built forts to enforce the new law. But Americans, who viewed the Mexicans and their army with contempt, kept coming. By 1835, the Texians and their enslaved blacks outnumbered the *Tejanos* (Hispanic Texans) ten to one.

Changing political circumstances in Mexico aggravated the growing tensions. In 1834, General Antonio López de Santa Anna, the Mexican president, suspended the national congress and became a dictator, calling himself the "Napoleon of the West." Texians feared that Santa Anna planned to free "our slaves and to make slaves of us." When Santa Anna imprisoned Stephen Austin in 1834, Texians decided that they must gain their independence from Mexican control. After Austin was released from jail eighteen months later, he called for Texians to revolt: "War is our only resource. There is no other remedy. We must defend our rights, ourselves, and our country by force of arms." He urged that Texas become fully American, promote slavery, and join the United States. In the fall of 1835, wary Texians followed Austin's lead and rebelled against Santa Anna's "despotism." A furious Santa Anna ordered all Americans expelled, all Texians disarmed, and all rebels arrested and executed. As sporadic fighting erupted, hundreds of armed volunteers from southern states rushed to assist the 30,000 Texians in the **Texas Revolution** against a Mexican nation of 7 million people. "The sword is drawn!" Austin proclaimed.

The Alamo and Goliad

At San Antonio, in southern Texas, General Santa Anna's army assaulted a small group of fewer than 200 Texians, Tejanos, and American volunteers holed up in an abandoned Catholic mission called the Alamo. The rebels were led by William B. Travis, a hot-tempered, twenty-six-year-old Alabama lawyer and teacher who had recently been named a lieutenant colonel in the newly formed Texian Army. Travis ignored orders to retreat from the Alamo, insisting that "death was preferable to disgrace." Among the other Americans at the Alamo, the most celebrated was David Crockett, the Tennessee frontiersman, bear hunter, and sharpshooter who had fought Indians under Andrew Jackson and served as an anti-Jackson Whig congressman. He told his fellow defenders that he had come "to aid you all that I can in your noble cause."

In February 1836, Santa Anna demanded that the Americans in the Alamo surrender. Travis answered with cannon fire. He then sent urgent

Texas Revolution (1835–1836)

The Alamo

Texas Revolution (1835–1836) Conflict between Texas colonists and the Mexican government that resulted in the creation of the separate Republic of Texas in 1836.

The Alamo David Crockett, pictured fighting with his rifle over his head, joined the legendary battle to defend the Alamo against the Mexican army.

appeals for help, while promising that *"I shall never surrender or retreat. . . .* VICTORY OR DEATH!" But help did not come, and Santa Anna launched a series of assaults against the outnumbered defenders. For eleven days, the Mexicans were thrown back and suffered heavy losses. Then, on March 6, the defenders of the Alamo were awakened by the sound of Mexican bugles playing the dreaded "Degüello" ("No Mercy to the Defenders"). Colonel Travis shouted: "The Mexicans are upon us—give 'em Hell!" Wave after wave of Santa Anna's men attacked from every side. They were twice forced back, but on the third try they broke through the battered north wall. Out of bullets, the rebels fought with tomahawks, knives, and rifle butts, but in the end, virtually all were killed or wounded.

A handful of Alamo defenders, perhaps including Crockett, survived and were captured. General Santa Anna ordered them hacked to death with swords. A Mexican officer wrote that the captives "died without complaining and without humiliating themselves before their torturers." The only survivors of the Alamo were a handful of women, children, and slaves. It was a complete victory for the Mexicans, but a costly one, for the Battle of the Alamo claimed more than 600 Mexican lives and provided a rallying cry for angry Texians thereafter. While Santa Anna proclaimed a "glorious victory," his aide wrote ominously in his diary, "One more such 'glorious victory' and we are finished."

The furious fighting at the Alamo turned the rebellion into a war for Texas independence. On March 2, 1836, during the siege of the Alamo, delegates from all fifty-nine Texas towns met at the village of Washington-on-the-Brazos, 150 miles northeast of San Antonio. There they signed a declaration of independence. Over the next seventeen days, the delegates drafted a constitution for the new Republic of Texas and established a government. Two weeks later, at the Battle of Coleto, a Mexican force again defeated a smaller Texian army, many of them recently arrived volunteers from southern states. The Mexicans marched the 465 captured Texians to a fort in the nearby town of Goliad. Despite pleas from his own men to show mercy, Santa Anna ordered the captives killed as "pirates and outlaws." On Palm Sunday, March 27, 1836, 303 Texians were marched out of Goliad and then killed. The massacres at the Alamo and Goliad fueled a burning desire for revenge among the Texians.

The Battle of San Jacinto

The commander in chief of the Texian Army was the remarkable Sam Houston, a hard-drinking frontiersman born in Virginia to Scots-Irish immigrants. At age fourteen, after his father died, Houston had moved with his mother and siblings to eastern Tennessee, where he lived among the Cherokees for a time. Like David Crockett, he had served under General Andrew Jackson during the War of 1812 before becoming an attorney, a U.S. congressman, and governor of Tennessee. He resigned the governorship two years later because his aristocratic young wife had left him, claiming she had discovered that he had sustained a "dreadful injury" in the Creek War that had left him impotent (a falsehood). In 1829, Houston joined the Cherokee migration westward to the Arkansas Territory, where he married a Cherokee woman and was formally "adopted" by the Cherokee Nation. In December 1832, he moved to Texas and immediately joined the rebellion against Mexico.

A giant of a man said to drink "a barrel of whiskey a day," Houston was fearless, a quality sorely needed by the Texians as they struggled against the much larger Mexican army. After learning of the massacre at the Alamo, Houston's outnumbered troops retreated, hoping that Santa Anna's pursuing army would make a mistake. On April 21, 1836, the cocky Mexican general walked into a trap, when Houston's army surprised the Mexicans near the San Jacinto River, about twenty-five miles southeast of the modern city of Houston. The Texians and Tejanos charged, yelling "Remember the Alamo." They overwhelmed the panic-stricken Mexicans, most of whom had been caught napping during the afternoon *siesta*.

The battle lasted only eighteen minutes; Houston's troops then spent the next two hours slaughtering fleeing Mexican soldiers. It was, said a Texian, a "frightful sight to behold." Some 630 Mexicans were killed and 700 captured. The Texians lost only nine men. Santa Anna escaped in his underwear but was captured the next day. He bought his freedom by signing a treaty recognizing the independence of the Republic of Texas, with the Rio Grande as its southern boundary with Mexico. The Texas Revolution had been accomplished in seven weeks.

The Battle of San Jacinto (1836)

The Lone Star Republic

The Republic of Texas (1836)

In 1836, the Lone Star Republic, as Texians nicknamed their new nation, drafted a constitution for Texas that legalized slavery and banned free blacks, elected Sam Houston its first president, and voted overwhelmingly for annexation by the United States. No one expected the huge Republic of Texas, with only 40,000 people, to remain independent for long.

The American president at the time was Houston's friend and former commander, Andrew Jackson, who eagerly wanted Texas to join the Union. But Jackson decided it was better to wait a few years. He knew that adding Texas as a slave state would ignite an explosive sectional quarrel between North and South that would fracture the Democratic party and endanger the election of New Yorker Martin Van Buren, Jackson's handpicked successor. Worse, any effort to add Texas to the Union would likely mean a war with Mexico, which refused to recognize Texan independence. So Jackson delayed official recognition of the Republic of Texas until his last day in office, early in 1837. Van Buren, Jackson's successor, did as predicted: he avoided all talk of Texas annexation during his single term as president.

The Tyler Presidency and Texas

When William Henry Harrison became president in 1841, he was the oldest man (sixty-eight) and the first Whig to win the office. The Whigs had first emerged in opposition to Andrew Jackson and continued to promote strong federal government support for industrial development and economic growth: high tariffs to deter imports and funding for internal improvements. Yet Harrison was elected primarily on the strength of his military record and because he had avoided taking public stances on controversial issues. In the end, it mattered little, for Harrison served the shortest term of any president.

Tyler assumes the presidency after Harrison's death (1841)

On April 4, 1841, exactly one month after his inauguration, he died of pneumonia, and John Tyler of Virginia became president. When the Whigs had chosen Tyler as their vice-presidential nominee in 1840, no one expected him to become president. The powerful anti-Jackson Whig, Senator Henry Clay, had wanted a southerner to balance the Whig ticket but expected that he would dominate the Harrison presidency.

Tyler, however, was not so easily dominated. At fifty-one, the tall, thin, slave-owning Virginian was the youngest president to date, but he had lots of political experience, having served as a state legislator, governor, congressman, and senator. Originally a Democrat, Tyler had broken with the party over President Andrew Jackson's "condemnation" of South Carolina's attempt to nullify federal laws. Tyler believed that South Carolina had a constitutional right to secede from the nation.

Now, as president, Tyler was stubbornly opposed to everything associated with the Whig party's "American System," Clay's celebrated program of economic nationalism that called for the federal government to support industrial development. Like Thomas Jefferson, Tyler also endorsed territorial expansion, and soon after becoming president in 1841, he began working to make Texas the twenty-eighth American state.

When Congress met in a special session in 1841, Henry Clay introduced a series of controversial resolutions. He called for the repeal of the Independent Treasury Act and the creation of another Bank of the United States, proposed to revive the distribution program whereby the money raised from federal land sales was given to the states, and urged that tariffs be raised on imported goods. The "haughty and imperious" Clay then set about pushing his program through Congress. "Tyler dares not resist. I will drive him before me," he said. With more tact Clay might have avoided a series of nasty disputes with Tyler over financial issues. But for once, driven by his inextinguishable quest to be president, Clay, the Great Compromiser, lost his instinct for compromise.

Although Tyler agreed to the repeal of the Independent Treasury Act and signed a higher tariff bill, the president vetoed Clay's pet project: a new national bank. Clay responded by attacking the president in Congress, calling him a traitor to his party. He also convinced Tyler's entire cabinet to resign, with the exception of Secretary of State Daniel Webster. Tyler replaced the defectors with anti-Jackson Democrats who, like him, had become Whigs. The Whigs then expelled Tyler from the party. By 1842, Tyler had become a president without a party, shunned by both Whigs and Democrats, but loved by those promoting territorial expansion.

> Tyler vetos national bank bill

The political turmoil coincided with the continuing economic depression. Bank failures mounted, and unemployment soared. People rioted in the streets of Philadelphia, and an armed rebellion flared up in Rhode Island over the failure of the state to allow non-landowners to vote. The self-assured Tyler, however, refused to let either the sputtering economy or an international crisis with Great Britain deflect him from his determination to annex more territory into the United States.

Tensions with Britain

In late 1841, slaves being transported from Virginia to Louisiana on the American ship *Creole* revolted and took charge of the ship after killing a slave trader. They sailed into Nassau, in the Bahamas, where British authorities set 128 of them free (Great Britain had abolished slavery throughout its empire in 1834). It was the most successful slave revolt in American history. Southerners were furious, and the incident mushroomed into an international crisis with Great Britain. Secretary of State Daniel Webster demanded that the slaves be returned as American property, but the British refused. (The dispute was not settled until 1853, when Britain paid $110,000 to the owners of the freed slaves.)

At this point, the British government decided to send Alexander Baring, Lord Ashburton, to meet with Webster. The meetings concluded with the signing of the Webster-Ashburton Treaty (1842), which provided for joint

> Webster-Ashburton Treaty (1842)

naval patrols off the coast of Africa to police the outlawed slave trade. The treaty also resolved a long-standing dispute over the northeastern U.S. boundary with British Canada.

Efforts to Annex Texas

Texas annexation treaty defeated

In April 1843, South Carolinian John C. Calhoun, then secretary of state, sent to the Senate for ratification a treaty annexing Texas. But there it died by a vote of 35–16. Northern senators, many of whom were abolitionists, refused to add another slave state. Others were concerned that annexing Texas would trigger a war with Mexico.

Texan leaders were frustrated that their new independence had not led to annexation. Houston threatened to expand the Republic of Texas to the Pacific. But with little money in the treasury, a rising government debt, and continuing tensions with Mexico, which insisted that it remained at war with Texas, this was mostly talk. The Lone Star Republic also had no infrastructure—no banks, no schools, no industries. It remained largely a frontier community of scattered log cabins. Houston decided that Texas had only two choices: annexation to the United States or closer economic ties to Great Britain, which extended formal diplomatic recognition to the republic and began buying cotton from Texas planters. Meanwhile, thousands more Americans poured into Texas. The population more than tripled between 1836 and 1845, from 40,000 to 150,000, and the enslaved black population grew even faster than the white population.

The Election of 1844

James K. Polk elected president (1844)

Leaders in both political parties hoped to keep the divisive Texas issue out of the 1844 presidential campaign. Whig Henry Clay (of Kentucky) and Democrat Martin Van Buren (of New York), the leading candidates for each party's nomination, agreed that adding Texas to the Union would be a mistake. Van Buren's southern supporters, including Andrew Jackson, abandoned him because he opposed annexation. At the Democratic Convention, annexationists, including Jackson, nominated James Knox Polk, former Speaker of the House and former governor of Tennessee. Like Tyler, Polk was an aggressive expansionist who wanted to make the United States a transcontinental global power. On the ninth ballot, he became the first "dark horse" (unexpected) candidate to win a major-party nomination. The Democrats' platform called for the annexation of both the Oregon Country and Texas.

The 1844 presidential election proved to be one of the most significant in American history. By promoting southern and western expansionism, the Democrats offered a winning strategy, one so popular that it forced Whig candidate Henry Clay to alter his position on Texas at the last minute; he now claimed that he had "no personal objection to the annexation" if it could be achieved "without dishonor, without war, with the common consent of the Union, and upon just and fair terms."

Clay's change of heart on Texas shifted more anti-slavery votes to the new Liberty party (the anti-slavery party formed in 1840), which increased its count in the presidential election from about 7,000 in 1840 (the year it was founded) to more than 62,000 in 1844. In the western counties of New York, the Liberty party drew enough votes from Clay and the Whigs to give the state to Polk and the Democrats. Had he carried New York, Clay would have won the national election by seven electoral votes. Instead, Polk won a narrow national plurality of 38,000 popular votes (the first president since John Quincy Adams to win without a majority) but a clear majority of the Electoral College, 170–105. Clay had lost his third and last effort to win the presidency. Clay could not understand how he could have lost to Polk, a "third-rate" politician lacking natural leadership abilities.

Polk wins 1844 election

Yet Polk had been surprising people his whole career. Born near Charlotte, North Carolina, he graduated first in his class at the University of North Carolina, then moved to Tennessee, where he became a successful lawyer and planter, entered politics, and served fourteen years in Congress (four as Speaker of the House) and two years as governor. At age forty-nine, often called "Young Hickory" because of his admiration for Andrew Jackson, Polk was America's youngest president up to that time. Yet he worked so hard during his four years in the White House that his health failed, and he died in 1849, at fifty-three, just three months after leaving office.

The State of Texas

Texas, the political hot potato, had been added to the Union just before Polk became president. In his final months in office, President John Tyler had asked Congress to annex Texas by joint resolution, which required only a simple majority in each house rather than the two-thirds Senate vote needed to ratify a *treaty*. The resolution narrowly passed, with most Whigs opposed. On March 1, 1845, in his final presidential action, President Tyler signed the resolution admitting Texas to the Union as the twenty-eighth state, and fifteenth slave state, on December 29, 1845. By 1850, the population—both white and black—had soared by almost 50 percent. (The census then did not include Native Americans.) By 1860, Texas was home to 600,000 people, most of them southerners intent on growing cotton.

Texas becomes a state (1845)

Polk's Goals

Like Andrew Jackson, the slave-owning Polk sought to avoid any public discussion of the merits or future of slavery while focusing on four major objectives, all of which he accomplished: 1) reduce tariffs on imports; 2) re-establish the Independent Treasury ("We need no national banks!"); 3) settle the Oregon boundary dispute with Britain; and 4) acquire California from Mexico. Polk's top priority was territorial expansion. He wanted to add Oregon, California, and New Mexico to the Union. In keeping with longstanding Democratic beliefs, Polk wanted lower tariffs to allow more foreign goods to compete in the American marketplace, and thereby help drive consumer prices down. Congress agreed by approving the Walker Tariff of 1846, named after Robert J. Walker, the secretary of the Treasury.

In the same year, Polk persuaded Congress to restore the Independent Treasury Act that President Martin Van Buren had signed into law in 1840 and the Whig-dominated Congress had repealed the next year. The act established independent treasury deposit offices separate from private or state banks to receive all federal government funds. The system was intended to replace the Second Bank of the United States, which Jackson had "killed," so as to offset the rapid growth of unregulated state banks, whose reckless lending practices had helped cause the depression of the late 1830s. The new Independent Treasury established by Polk entrusted the federal government, rather than favored state banks, with the exclusive management of government funds and required that all disbursements be made in gold or silver, or paper currency backed by gold or silver. Polk also sought to reverse Whig policy on the federal funding of roads and harbors. Twice he vetoed Whig-passed bills for federally funded infrastructure projects. His blows to Whig economic policies satisfied the slaveholding South but angered northerners who wanted higher tariffs to protect their industries from British competition and westerners who wanted federally financed roads and harbors for their bustling new economies.

Tariff of 1846 This political cartoon illustrates the public outcry—represented by a Quaker woman brandishing switches, ready to whip Polk—against the Tariff of 1846, one of the lowest in the nation's history.

Oregon

Meanwhile, the dispute with Great Britain over the Oregon Country boundary heated up as expansionists insisted that Polk take the whole region rather than split it with the British. In his inaugural address, Polk said that the American claim to the enormous Oregon Country was "clear and unquestionable," and he was willing to go to the brink of war to achieve his goals. "If we do have war," Polk said, "it will not be our fault."

Fortunately for the reckless Polk, the British were not willing to risk war over a remote wilderness territory. In 1846, they suggested extending the border between the United States and British Canada westward to the Pacific coast along the 49th parallel. On June 15, James Buchanan, Polk's secretary of state, signed what was called the Buchanan-Pakenham Treaty, which did just that.

Buchanan-Pakenham Treaty (1846): Oregon becomes American territory

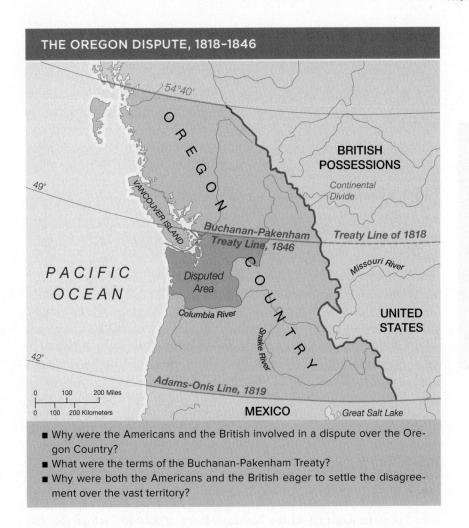

THE OREGON DISPUTE, 1818–1846

■ Why were the Americans and the British involved in a dispute over the Oregon Country?
■ What were the terms of the Buchanan-Pakenham Treaty?
■ Why were both the Americans and the British eager to settle the disagreement over the vast territory?

The Mexican-American War

CORE **OBJECTIVE**
2. Examine the impact of the Mexican-American War on national politics.

The Outbreak of War

On March 6, 1845, two days after James K. Polk took office, the Mexican government broke off relations with the United States to protest the annexation of Texas. The president was willing to wage war against Mexico to acquire California, but he did not want Americans to fire the first shot. So Polk ordered several thousand U.S. troops under General Zachary Taylor to advance some 150 miles south of the Texas frontier and take up positions around Corpus Christi, near the Rio Grande. The U.S. troops were knowingly in disputed territory; Mexico recognized neither the American annexation of Texas nor the Rio Grande boundary.

Westward expansionism and war fever

On the evening of May 9, 1845, Polk learned that Mexican troops had attacked U.S. soldiers north of the Rio Grande. Eleven Americans were killed. Polk's scheme to provoke an attack had worked. In his war message to Congress, the president claimed that war was the only response to

Mexican aggression. Mexico, he reported, "has invaded our territory, and shed American blood upon the American soil." Congress quickly passed the war resolution and authorized the recruitment of 50,000 soldiers. The outbreak of fighting thrilled many Americans. "LET US GO TO WAR," screamed a New York newspaper. In the South, where expansion fever ran high, the war with Mexico was immensely popular. So many men rushed to volunteer that thousands had to be turned back. Eventually, 112,000 whites served in the war (blacks were banned).

Opposition to the War

In New England, however, there was much less enthusiasm for "Mr. Polk's War." Congressman John Quincy Adams, who voted against the war resolution, called it "a most unrighteous war" designed to extend slavery into new territories. Many other New Englanders involved with the growing abolitionist movement denounced the war as the work of pro-slavery southerners. The fiery Boston abolitionist William Lloyd Garrison charged that the war against Mexico was one "of aggression, of invasion, of conquest." A few miles away, in Concord, Henry David Thoreau spent a night in jail rather than pay taxes that might help fund the war. Most Whigs across the North, including a young Illinois congressman named Abraham Lincoln, opposed the war, stressing that President Polk had maneuvered the Mexicans to attack. The United States, they argued, had no reason for placing its army in the disputed border region between Texas and Mexico.

Preparing for Battle

Regardless of the conflict's legitimacy, the United States was again ill prepared for a major war. At the outset, the regular army numbered barely over 7,000, in contrast to the Mexican force of 32,000. Before the war ended, the U.S. military had grown to almost 79,000 troops, many of whom were frontier toughs lacking uniforms, equipment, and discipline. Repeatedly, some of these soldiers engaged in plunder, rape, and murder. Yet the American troops outfought the larger Mexican forces, which had their own problems with training, discipline, morale, supplies, and munitions. The Mexican-American War would last two years, from March 1846 to April 1848, and would be fought on four fronts: southern Texas, central Mexico, New Mexico, and California. Early in the fighting, General Zachary Taylor's army scored two victories over Mexican forces north of the Rio Grande, at Palo Alto (May 8) and Resaca de la Palma (May 9). On May 18, Taylor's army crossed the Rio Grande and occupied Matamoros. These quick victories brought General Taylor, a Whig, instant popularity, and Polk agreed to public demands that Taylor be made overall commander.

The Annexation of California

Along the Pacific coast, the conquest of Mexican territory was under way before news of the start of the Mexican-American War had arrived. Near the end of 1845, John C. Frémont, an army officer and ardent expansionist

Zachary Taylor Like Andrew Jackson, Taylor was a popular war hero whose public support paved the way to presidency.

California becomes an American territory (1846)

known as "the Pathfinder" for having helped map the eastern half of the Oregon Trail, recruited a band of sixty frontiersmen and headed into California's Sacramento Valley, where they encouraged Americans to declare their independence from Mexico. They captured Sonoma on June 14, 1846, proclaimed the Republic of California, and hoisted a flag featuring a grizzly bear and star, a version of which would later become the state flag. But the Bear Flag Republic lasted only a month. In July, the commodore of the U.S. Pacific Fleet, having heard of the outbreak of hostilities, sent troops ashore to raise the American flag and claim California as part of the United States.

Before the end of July, another navy officer, Robert F. Stockton, led the American occupation of Santa Barbara and Los Angeles, on the southern California coast. By mid-August 1846, Mexican resistance had evaporated. On August 17, Stockton declared himself governor, with Frémont as military governor in the north. At the same time, another American military expedition headed for New Mexico. On August 18, General Stephen Kearny and a small army entered Santa Fe. Kearny then led 300 men westward toward southern California, where they joined Stockton's forces at San Diego. They took control of Los Angeles on January 10, 1847, and the remaining Mexican forces surrendered.

> U.S. Army takes New Mexico (1846)

War in Northern Mexico

Both California and New Mexico had been taken from Mexican control before General Zachary Taylor fought his first major battle in northern Mexico. In September 1846, Taylor's army assaulted the fortified city of Monterrey, which surrendered after a five-day siege. Then the old dictator General Antonio López de Santa Anna, forced out of power in 1845, got word to Polk from his exile in Cuba that he would end the war if he were allowed to return. Polk assured the Mexican leader that the U.S. government would pay well for any territory taken from Mexico. In August 1846, on Polk's orders, Santa Anna was permitted to return to Mexico. But the crafty Santa Anna had lied. Soon he was again president of Mexico and in command of the Mexican army. As it turned out, however, he was much more talented at raising armies than leading them in battle. In October 1846, Santa Anna prepared to attack. When the Mexican general invited the outnumbered Americans to surrender, Zachary Taylor responded, "Tell him to go to hell." That launched the hard-fought Battle of Buena Vista (February 22–23, 1847), in northern Mexico. Both sides claimed victory, but the Mexicans lost five times as many killed and wounded as the Americans. However, one of the U.S. soldiers killed was Henry Clay Jr., "the pride and hope" of his famous father who had lost to Polk in the 1844 presidential campaign. The elder Clay, devastated by his son's death, condemned Polk's "unnecessary" war of "offensive aggression" and opposed any effort to use the war as a means of acquiring Mexican territory "for the purpose of introducing slavery into it."

> The Battle of Buena Vista (1847)

Meanwhile, the long-planned American assault on Mexico City had begun on March 9, 1847, when General Winfield Scott's army landed on the beaches south of Veracruz and began marching toward the Mexican capital. After a series of battles in which they overwhelmed the Mexican defenses, U.S. forces entered Mexico City on September 13. News of the victory thrilled American expansionists. The editor John O'Sullivan, who had coined the phrase "manifest destiny," shouted, "More, More, More! Why not take all of Mexico?"

The Treaty of Guadalupe Hidalgo

Treaty of Guadalupe Hidalgo (1848)

After the fall of Mexico City, Santa Anna resigned and fled the country. Peace talks began on January 2, 1848. By the **Treaty of Guadalupe Hidalgo**, signed on February 2, Mexico gave up all claims to Texas north of the Rio Grande and transferred control of California and New Mexico to the United States. In return for half a million square miles of territory—more than half of Mexico—the United States agreed to pay $15 million. The Senate ratified the treaty on March 10, 1848. By the end of July, the last remaining U.S. soldiers had left Mexico.

The War's Legacies

An expanded United States

The United States lost 1,733 soldiers from combat in the Mexican-American War. Another 4,152 were wounded, and far more—11,550—died of disease. The war remains the deadliest in American history in terms of the percentage of soldiers killed. Out of every 1,000 U.S. soldiers in Mexico, some 110 died. The next highest death rate would be in the Civil War, with 65 dead out of every 1,000 participants. As a result of the conflict, the United States acquired the future states of California, Nevada, and Utah and parts of New Mexico, Arizona, Colorado, and Wyoming. Except for a small addition made by the Gadsden Purchase of 1853, these annexations rounded out the continental United States and nearly doubled its size.

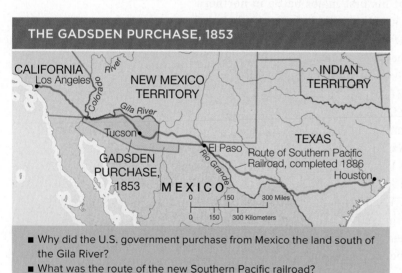

THE GADSDEN PURCHASE, 1853

- Why did the U.S. government purchase from Mexico the land south of the Gila River?
- What was the route of the new Southern Pacific railroad?
- How did the debate over the national railroad open up sectional conflicts?

The victory in Mexico also helped end the long economic depression. As the years passed, however, the Mexican-American War was increasingly seen as a shameful war of conquest and imperialistic plunder directed by a president bent on territorial expansion for the sake of slavery. Ulysses S. Grant, who fought in the war, later called it "one of the most unjust wars ever waged by a stronger against a weaker nation."

Treaty of Guadalupe Hidalgo (1848) Treaty between United States and Mexico that ended the Mexican-American War.

Slavery in the Territories

President Polk acquired more new territory for the United States than any president before or since. Yet he naively assumed that expanding the nation to the Pacific would strengthen "the bonds of Union." He was wrong. No sooner was Texas annexed and gold discovered in California than a violent debate erupted over the extension of slavery into the new territories. That debate, spurred by growing southern fears that a larger, richer, and more powerful North would eventually abolish slavery, culminated in a controversial war that nearly destroyed the Union.

CORE **OBJECTIVE**

3. Describe how the federal government tried to resolve the issue of slavery in the territories during the 1850s.

The Wilmot Proviso

The Mexican-American War was less than three months old when a new political conflict erupted over slavery. On August 8, 1846, a Democratic congressman from Pennsylvania, David Wilmot, delivered a speech to the House of Representatives in which he endorsed the earlier annexation of Texas as a slave state. But slavery had come to an end in the rest of Mexico, he noted, and if any *new* Mexican territory should be acquired as a result of the war, he declared, "God forbid that we should be the means of planting this institution [slavery] upon it." If any additional land should be acquired from Mexico, Wilmot proposed, slavery would be banned there, in part because he and other northerners were "jealous of the power of the South" and did not want any new states joining the slave-state alliance.

The proposed **Wilmot Proviso** re-ignited the debate over the westward extension of slavery. The issue had been lurking for a generation, ever since the Missouri controversy of 1819–1821. The Missouri Compromise had provided a temporary solution by protecting slavery in states where it already existed but not allowing it in newly acquired territories north of the 36th parallel. Now, with the addition of the territories taken from Mexico, the stage was set for an even more explosive debate.

Wilmot Proviso (1846)

In 1846, the House of Representatives adopted the Wilmot Proviso, but the Senate balked. When Congress reconvened in December 1846, President Polk dismissed the proviso as "mischievous and foolish." He convinced Wilmot to withhold his amendment from any bill dealing with the annexation of Mexican territory. By then, however, others were ready to take up the cause. In one form or another, Wilmot's idea of restricting the expansion of slavery would continue to crop up in Congress. Abraham Lincoln later recalled that during his one term as a congressman, in 1847–1849, he voted for it "as good as forty times."

Senator John C. Calhoun of South Carolina, meanwhile, countered Wilmot's proviso with his own plan, which he presented to the Senate on February 19, 1847. Calhoun insisted that Wilmot's effort to exclude slaves from territories acquired from Mexico would violate the Fifth Amendment, which forbids Congress to deprive any person of life, liberty, or property

Wilmot Proviso (1846) Proposal by Congressman David Wilmot, a Pennsylvania Democrat, to prohibit slavery in any land acquired in the Mexican-American War.

without due process of law. Slaves, he argued, were *property*. By this clever stroke of logic, Calhoun turned the Bill of Rights into a guarantee of slavery. Senator Thomas Hart Benton of Missouri, himself a slaveholder but also a nationalist eager to calm sectional tensions, found in Calhoun's stance a set of dangerous abstractions "leading to no result." Wilmot and Calhoun between them, he said, had fashioned a pair of scissors. Neither blade alone would cut very well, but joined together they could sever the nation in two.

Popular Sovereignty

The "popular sovereignty" plan

Benton and others tried to deflect the brewing conflict over slavery. President Polk was among the first to suggest simply extending the Missouri Compromise, dividing free and slave territory at the latitude of 36°30′, all the way to the Pacific Ocean. Senator Lewis Cass of Michigan suggested that the citizens of a territory "regulate their own internal concerns in their own way," like the citizens of a state. Such an approach would take the issue of slavery in new territories out of Congress and put it in the hands of those directly affected. "**Popular sovereignty**," as Cass's idea was called, appealed to many Americans.

Polk had promised to serve only one term, and having accomplished his major goals, he refused to run again in 1848. Cass won the Democrats' presidential nomination, but the party refused to endorse his "popular sovereignty" plan. Instead, it simply denied the power of Congress to interfere with slavery in the states and criticized all efforts by anti-slavery activists to bring the question before Congress. The Whigs devised an even more ingenious strategy in the process of selecting a presidential candidate. Once again, as in 1840, they passed over their party leader, Henry Clay, in favor of General Zachary Taylor, whose fame had grown since the Battle of Buena Vista. Taylor, born in Virginia and raised in Kentucky, was a Louisiana resident who owned more than 100 slaves. But he was an unusual slaveholder in that he vigorously opposed the extension of slavery into new western territories.

The Free-Soil Coalition

The Free-Soil party

As it had done in the 1840 election, the Whig party in 1848 adopted no platform in an effort to avoid the divisive issue of slavery. But the anti-slavery crusade was not easily silenced. Americans who worried about slavery but shied away from calling for outright abolition could readily endorse the exclusion of slavery from the western territories. The Northwest Ordinance and the Missouri Compromise supplied honored precedents for doing so. As a result, "free soil" in the new territories became the rallying cry for a new political party: the Free-Soil coalition, which focused on preventing the spread of slavery into the western territories.

The **Free-Soil party** attracted three major groups: northern Democrats opposed to slavery, anti-slavery northern Whigs, and members of the abolitionist Liberty party, created in 1840. In 1848, at a convention in Buffalo,

popular sovereignty Legal concept by which the white male settlers in a new U.S. territory would vote to decide whether to permit slavery.

Free-Soil party A political coalition created in 1848 that opposed the expansion of slavery into the new western territories.

The Wilmot Proviso Taylor would refuse to veto the proviso as president, even though he was a slave owner. This political cartoon, "Old Zack at Home," points out his seeming hypocrisy.

New York, Free-Soilers nominated former Democratic president Martin Van Buren as their candidate. The party's platform stressed that slavery would not be allowed in the western territories. The new anti-slavery party infuriated John C. Calhoun and other southern Democrats. Calhoun called Van Buren a "bold, unscrupulous, and vindictive demagogue." The impact of the Free-Soil party on the election was mixed. The Free-Soilers split the Democratic vote enough to throw New York to the Whig Zachary Taylor, and they split the Whig vote enough to give Ohio to the Democrat Lewis Cass. But Van Buren's 291,000 third-party votes lagged well behind the totals of 1,361,000 for Taylor and 1,222,000 for Cass. Taylor won with 163–127 electoral votes.

The California Gold Rush

Meanwhile, a new issue had emerged to complicate the debate over the western territories. On January 24, 1848, on the property of John A. Sutter along the south fork of the American River (Sutter's Fort), gold was discovered in the Mexican province of California, which nine days later would be transferred to the United States through the treaty ending the Mexican-American War. Word of the gold strike spread quickly. In 1849 nearly 100,000 Americans, mostly men, set off for California, eager to find riches; by 1854, the number would top 300,000. So many men left New England as part of the **California Gold Rush** that it would be years before the region's gender ratio evened out again.

The gold rush was the greatest mass migration in American history— and one of the most significant events in the first half of the nineteenth century. Between 1851 and 1855, California produced almost half of the

California Gold Rush (1849) A massive migration of gold hunters, mostly men, who transformed the economy of California after gold was discovered in northern California.

world's output of gold. The infusion of California gold into the U.S. economy triggered a surge of prosperity that eventually helped finance the Union military effort in the Civil War. The gold rush also transformed the sleepy coastal village of San Francisco into the nation's largest city west of Chicago. In addition, it shifted the nation's center of gravity westward, spurred the construction of railroads and telegraph lines, and excited dreams of an American empire based in the Pacific.

Gold miners Chinese immigrants and white settlers mine for gold in the Auburn Ravine of California in 1856.

California Statehood

New president Zachary Taylor opposed the expansion of slavery into new territories and states. In 1849, he decided to use California's request for statehood to end the stalemate in Congress over slavery. Why not make California and New Mexico free states immediately, he reasoned, and bypass the issue of slavery? But Californians, in desperate need of organized government, were ahead of him. By December 1849, without consulting Congress, they had put a free-state (no-slavery) government into operation. New Mexico responded more slowly, but by 1850 Americans there had also adopted a free-state constitution.

The Compromise of 1850

In his annual message on December 4, 1849, President Taylor endorsed immediate statehood for California and urged Congress to avoid injecting slavery into the issue. The new Congress, however, was in no mood for simple solutions. By 1850, tensions over slavery were boiling over. Irate southerners threatened to leave the Union if Taylor brought California and New Mexico in as free states. "I avow before this House and country, and in the presence of the living God," shouted Robert Toombs, a Georgia congressman, "that if by your legislation you seek to drive us [slaveholders] from the territories of California and New Mexico . . . and to abolish slavery in this District [of Columbia] . . . I am for disunion."

The spotlight fell on the Senate, where an all-star cast—Henry Clay, John C. Calhoun, and Daniel Webster (all of whom would die within two years), with William H. Seward, Stephen A. Douglas, and Jefferson Davis in supporting roles—staged one of the great dramas of American politics: the **Compromise of 1850**, a series of resolutions intended to reduce the tensions between North and South.

Compromise of 1850

Compromise of 1850 A package of five bills presented to the Congress by Henry Clay intended to avoid secession or civil war by reducing tensions between North and South over the status of slavery.

The Great Debate

With southerners threatening secession, Congressional leaders in early 1850 again turned to Clay, now 72, who, as Abraham Lincoln said, was "regarded by all, as *the* man for the crisis." Unless some compromise could be found, Clay warned, a "furious" civil war would fracture the Union. On January 29, 1850, having gained support from Webster, Clay presented to Congress eight resolutions meant to settle the "controversy between the free and slave states, growing out of the subject of slavery." He proposed (1) to admit California as a free state; (2) to organize the territories of New Mexico and Utah without restrictions on slavery, allowing the residents to decide the issue for themselves; (3) to deny Texas its extreme claim to much of New Mexico; (4) to compensate Texas by having the federal government pay the pre-annexation Texas debts; (5) to retain slavery in the District of Columbia, but (6) to abolish the sale of slaves in the nation's capital; (7) to adopt a more effective federal fugitive slave law; and, (8) to deny congressional authority to interfere with the interstate slave trade. His complex cluster of proposals became in substance the Compromise of 1850, but only after seven months of negotiations punctuated by the greatest debates in Congressional history.

On March 4, a grim John C. Calhoun, the uncompromising defender of slavery, left his sickbed to sit in the Senate chamber and listen to a colleague read his defiant speech, in which he blamed the North for inciting civil war by opposing slavery in the territories. Clay's compromise should be rejected, Calhoun urged. The South simply needed Congress to protect the rights of slave owners to take their "property" into the new territories. Otherwise, Calhoun warned, the "cords which bind" the Union would be severed. The southern states would leave the Union (secede) and form their own national government.

Three days later, Calhoun, who would die in just three weeks, returned to the Senate to hear Daniel Webster speak. "I wish to speak today," Webster began, "not as a Massachusetts man, not as a Northern man, but as an American. . . . I speak today for the preservation of the Union." The geographic extent of slavery had already been determined, Webster insisted, by the Northwest Ordinance in 1787 and by the Missouri Compromise in 1820. He criticized extremists on both sides and suggested that some new territories should become slave states and others free states.

Webster's evenhanded speech was savaged by northerners for betraying the region's anti-slavery ideals. On March 11, William Seward, the Whig senator from New York, declared that *any* compromise with slavery was "radically wrong and essentially vicious." There was, he said, "a *higher law* than the Constitution," and it demanded the abolition of slavery.

Compromise Efforts

On July 4, 1850, supporters of the Union staged a grand rally at the base of the unfinished Washington Monument in Washington, D.C. President Zachary Taylor went to hear the speeches and lingered in the heat and humidity. Five days later, he died of a violent stomach disorder, likely caused by tainted food or water.

Taylor's sudden death strengthened the chances of a compromise in Congress. His successor, Vice President Millard Fillmore, supported Clay's

THE COMPROMISE OF 1850

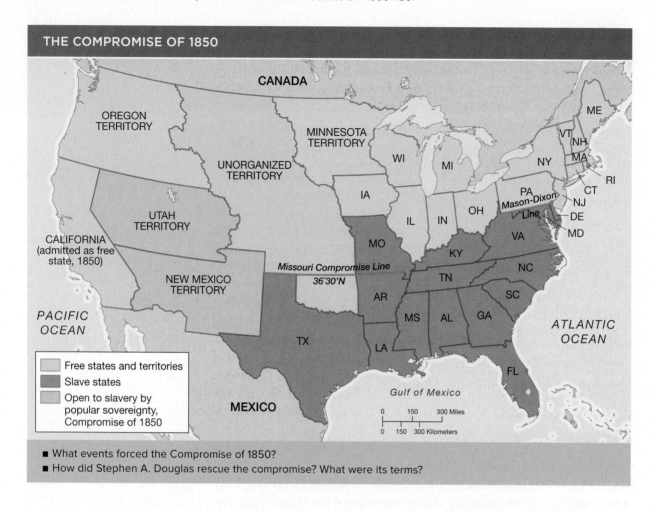

Free states and territories

Slave states

Open to slavery by popular sovereignty, Compromise of 1850

- What events forced the Compromise of 1850?
- How did Stephen A. Douglas rescue the compromise? What were its terms?

proposals. It was a strange switch: Taylor, the Louisiana slaveholder, had been ready to make war on his native South; Fillmore, who southerners thought opposed slavery, was ready to make peace.

At this point, young senator Stephen A. Douglas of Illinois, a rising star in the Democratic party who was friendly to the South, rescued Clay's faltering plan. Short and stocky, brash and brilliant, Douglas suggested that the best way to approve Clay's "comprehensive scheme" was to break it up into separate proposals and vote on each of them, one at a time. The plan worked. By September 20, President Fillmore had signed the last of the measures into law, claiming that they represented a "final" solution to sectional tensions over slavery. True, the Compromise of 1850 had defused an explosive situation and settled each of the major points at issue, but it only postponed secession and civil war for ten years.

In its final version, the Compromise of 1850 included the following elements: (1) California entered the Union as a free state, ending forever the old balance of free and slave states; (2) the Texas–New Mexico Act made New Mexico a territory and set the Texas state boundary at its present location. In return for giving up its claims, Texas was paid $10 million, which secured payment of the state's debt; (3) the Utah Act set up the Utah Territory and gave the territorial legislature authority over "all rightful subjects of legislation" (including slavery); (4) a Fugitive Slave Act required the federal government and northern states to help capture and return runaway slaves to the South; and, (5) as a gesture to anti-slavery groups, the public sale of slaves, but not slavery itself, was abolished in the District of Columbia.

The Fugitive Slave Act

The **Fugitive Slave Act** was the most controversial element of the Compromise of 1850. It did more than strengthen the hand of slave catchers; it provided a strong temptation to kidnap free blacks in northern "free" states, claiming that they were runaway slaves. The law denied fugitives a jury trial. In addition, federal marshals could require citizens to help locate and capture runaways: violators could be imprisoned for up to six months and fined $1,000. Abolitionists fumed. "This filthy enactment was made in the nineteenth century, by people who could read and write," Ralph Waldo Emerson marveled in his diary. He advised neighbors to break the new law "on the earliest occasion." The occasion soon arose in Detroit, Michigan, where only military force stopped the rescue of a fugitive slave by an outraged group in October 1850. There were relatively few such incidents, however. In the first six years of the Fugitive Slave Act, only three runaways were forcibly rescued from slave catchers. On the other hand, probably fewer than two hundred were returned to bondage during those years. The Fugitive Slave Act was a powerful emotional and symbolic force deepening the anti-slavery impulses in the North.

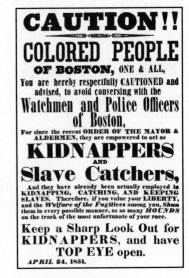

Threats to free blacks This 1851 notice warned free blacks about police and others who could easily, under the new Fugitive Slave Act, kidnap and sell them back into slavery.

Uncle Tom's Cabin

During the 1850s, anti-slavery forces found their most persuasive new weapon not in the Fugitive Slave Act but in the fictional drama of Harriet Beecher Stowe's best-selling novel, *Uncle Tom's Cabin* (1852). Stowe, whose father, husband, and five brothers were Congregationalist ministers, epitomized the powerful religious underpinnings of the abolitionist movement. While living in Cincinnati, Ohio, during the 1830s and 1840s, she helped runaway slaves who had crossed the Ohio River from Kentucky. Stowe was disgusted with the Fugitive Slave Act of 1850. In the spring of 1850, having moved to Maine, she began writing *Uncle Tom's Cabin*, urged on by her anti-slavery family. "The time has come," she wrote, "when even a woman or a child who can speak a word for freedom and humanity is bound to speak."

Uncle Tom's Cabin was a smashing commercial success. The first printing sold out within two days, and by the end of its first year in print, the book had sold 300,000 copies in the United States and over a million in Great Britain. Soon it was translated in thirty-seven different languages. By 1855 *Uncle Tom's Cabin* had become "the most popular novel of our day." The novel revealed how the brutal realities of slavery harmed everyone associated with it. The abolitionist leader Frederick Douglass, a former slave himself, said that *Uncle Tom's Cabin* was like "a flash" that lit "a million

Fugitive Slave Act (1850) Part of the Compromise of 1850, a provision that authorized federal officials to help capture and then return escaped slaves to their owners without trials.

135,000 SETS, 270,000 VOLUMES SOLD.

UNCLE TOM'S CABIN

FOR SALE HERE.

AN EDITION FOR THE MILLION, COMPLETE IN 1 Vol. PRICE 37 1-2 CENTS.
" " IN GERMAN, IN 1 Vol., PRICE 50 CENTS.
" " IN 2 Vols., CLOTH, 6 PLATES, PRICE $1.50.
SUPERB ILLUSTRATED EDITION, IN 1 Vol. WITH 153 ENGRAVINGS,
PRICES FROM $2.50 TO $5.00.

The Greatest Book of the Age.

"The Greatest Book of the Age"
Uncle Tom's Cabin, as this
advertisement indicated, was
an influential best seller.

camp fires in front of the embattled host of slavery." Slaveholders were incensed by the book, calling Stowe that "wretch in petticoats." One of them mailed her a parcel containing the severed ear of a disobedient slave.

The Election of 1852

In 1852, the Democrats chose boyishly handsome Franklin Pierce of New Hampshire as their presidential candidate; their platform endorsed the Compromise of 1850. For their part, the Whigs repudiated the lackluster Millard Fillmore, who had faithfully supported the Compromise of 1850, and chose General Winfield Scott, a hero of the Mexican-American War and a Virginia native. Scott, however, was an inept politician and carried only Tennessee, Kentucky, Massachusetts, and Vermont. Pierce overwhelmed him in the Electoral College, 254–42, although the popular vote was fairly close: 1.6 million–1.4 million. The third-party Free-Soilers mustered only 156,000 votes for John P. Hale, in contrast to the 291,000 they had tallied for Van Buren in 1848.

The forty-eight-year-old Pierce had fought in the Mexican-American War and was, like James Polk, touted as another Andrew Jackson despite his undistinguished record as a congressman and senator. He eagerly promoted western expansion, even if it meant adding more slave states to the Union, but he also acknowledged that the nation had recently survived a "perilous crisis" that was defused by the Compromise of 1850. He urged both North and South to avoid aggravating the other. But as a Georgia editor noted, the feud between the two regions might be "smothered, but never overcome." Pierce, the youngest president to date, was timid and indecisive, unable to unite the warring factions of his own party. By the end of his first year in office, Democratic leaders had decided he was a failure. By trying to be all things to all people, Pierce was labeled a "doughface": a "Northern man with Southern principles."

The Kansas-Nebraska Crisis

Kansas-Nebraska Act (1854)

During the mid-nineteenth century, Americans discovered the vast markets of Asia. As the amount of trade with China and Japan grew, merchants and manufacturers called for a transcontinental railroad line connecting the eastern seaboard with the Pacific coast to facilitate both the flow of commerce with Asia and the settlement of the western territories. Those promoting the building of a railroad linking the far-flung regions of the new United States did not realize that the issue would renew sectional rivalries and reignite the debate over the westward extension of slavery. In 1852 and 1853, Congress debated several proposals for a transcontinental rail line. Secretary of War Jefferson Davis of Mississippi favored a southern route across the territories acquired from Mexico. Senator Stephen A. Douglas of Illinois insisted that Chicago be the transcontinental railroad's Midwest hub. To promote that idea, he urged Congress in 1854 to pass the **Kansas-Nebraska Act** so that the vast territory west of Missouri and Iowa could be settled.

Kansas-Nebraska Act (1854)
Controversial legislation that created two new territories taken from Native Americans, Kansas and Nebraska, where residents would vote to decide whether slavery would be allowed (popular sovereignty).

New western territories, however, raised again the worrisome question of whether slavery would be allowed in them. To win the support of southern legislators, Douglas championed the principle of "popular sovereignty," whereby voters in each new territory could decide themselves whether to allow slavery. It was a clever way to get around the 1820 Missouri Compromise, which excluded slaves north of the 36th parallel, where Kansas and Nebraska were located. Southerners demanded even more, so Douglas, even though he knew it would "raise a hell of a storm," supported the formal repeal of the Missouri Compromise and the creation of *two* new territorial governments rather than one: Kansas, west of Missouri, and Nebraska, which then included the Dakotas, west of Iowa and Minnesota. In Congress, Douglas masterfully assembled the votes for his Kansas-Nebraska Act. President Pierce helped get several reluctant Democrats to vote for the measure (though about half the northern Democrats refused to yield), and in 1854 it passed by a vote of 37–14 in the Senate and 113–100 in the House. The anti-slavery faction in the Congress, mostly Whigs, had been crushed.

But Douglas's passion for the new rail line backfired. However honest his motives in promoting the Kansas-Nebraska Act, he had blundered politically, damaging his presidential chances and setting the country on the road to civil war by pushing the slavery issue back to the forefront of national concerns. In abandoning the long-standing Missouri Compromise boundary line and allowing territorial voters to decide the issue of slavery, Douglas unwittingly inflamed the tensions between North and South.

The Emergence of the Republican Party

The dispute over the Kansas-Nebraska Act destroyed the already weakened Whig party. Northern Whigs now gravitated toward two new parties. One was the American ("Know-Nothing") party, which had emerged in response to the surge of mostly Catholic immigrants from Ireland and Germany. The anti-Catholic "Know-Nothings" embraced nativism (opposition to foreign immigrants) and proposed that citizenship be denied to newcomers. In the early 1850s, Know-Nothings won several local elections in Massachusetts and New York.

The other new party, the Republicans, attracted even more northern Whigs. The party was formed in 1854 when the anti-slavery "conscience Whigs" split from the southern pro-slavery "cotton Whigs" and joined with independent Democrats and Free-Soilers to form a new Republican party whose members initially stood for only one principle: the exclusion of slavery from the western territories. A young Illinois congressman named Abraham Lincoln made the transition from being a Whig to a Republican. He said that the passage of Douglas's Kansas-Nebraska Act angered him "as he had

CORE **OBJECTIVE**

4. Analyze the appeal of the Republican party to northern voters and how it led to Abraham Lincoln's victory in the 1860 presidential contest.

Anti-Catholic "Know-Nothings"

New Republican party (1854)

never been before" and transformed his views on slavery. Unless the North mobilized to stop the efforts of pro-slavery southerners, Lincoln believed, the future of the Union was endangered. From that moment on, Lincoln focused his career on reversing the Kansas-Nebraska Act and preventing the extension of slavery into any new territories.

"Bleeding Kansas"

After the passage of the Kansas-Nebraska Act in 1854, attention turned to the plains of Kansas, where opposing elements gathered to stage a rehearsal for civil war. While Nebraska would become a free state, Kansas was up for grabs. According to the Kansas-Nebraska Act, the people living in the Kansas Territory were "perfectly free to form and regulate their domestic institutions [including slavery] in their own way, subject only to the Constitution." This is what was meant by "popular sovereignty." But the law said nothing about *when* Kansans would decide about slavery, so each side tried to gain political control of the fifty-million-acre territory.

Rival groups for and against slavery in the North and South recruited emigrants to move to the new territory. "Every slaveholding state," said an observer, "is furnishing men and money to fasten slavery upon this glorious land, by means no matter how foul." When Kansas's first federal governor arrived in 1854, he scheduled an election for a territorial legislature in 1855. On election day, several thousand hard-fisted "border ruffians" from Missouri crossed into Kansas, illegally elected pro-slavery legislators, and vowed to kill every "God-damned abolitionist in the Territory." The governor denounced the fraudulent vote but did nothing to alter the results, for fear of being killed himself. The territorial legislature expelled its few anti-slavery members and declared that the territory would be open to slavery.

"Bleeding Kansas" (1856)

Outraged free-state advocates in Kansas rejected this "bogus" government and elected their own delegates to a constitutional convention which met in Topeka in 1855, drafted a state constitution excluding slavery, and applied for statehood. By 1856, a free-state "governor" and "legislature" were functioning in Topeka; thus there were two illegal governments in the Kansas Territory. And soon there was a civil war in Kansas, which journalists called "**Bleeding Kansas**."

In May 1856, a pro-slavery mob of Missourians and Alabamans decided to invade the free-state town of Lawrence, Kansas. David Atchison, a former U.S. senator from Missouri, urged the southern raiders not "to slacken or stop until every spark of free-state, free-speech, free-niggers, or free in any shape is quenched out of Kansas." As they prepared to teach the "damned abolitionists a southern lesson," Atchison yelled: "Boys, this is the happiest day of my life!" The mob then rampaged through the town, destroying the newspaper, burning the governor's house, and demolishing the Free-State Hotel.

Bleeding Kansas (1856)
A series of violent conflicts in the Kansas Territory between anti-slavery and pro-slavery factions over the status of slavery.

The "Sack of Lawrence" resulted in just one casualty, but the excitement aroused a passionate white abolitionist named John Brown. He believed that slavery was the most wicked of sins and that blacks deserved both

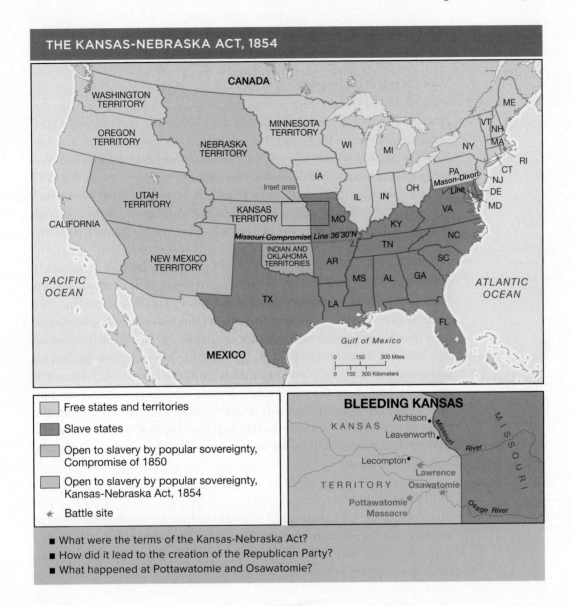

THE KANSAS-NEBRASKA ACT, 1854

Legend:
- Free states and territories
- Slave states
- Open to slavery by popular sovereignty, Compromise of 1850
- Open to slavery by popular sovereignty, Kansas-Nebraska Act, 1854
- ✳ Battle site

BLEEDING KANSAS

- What were the terms of the Kansas-Nebraska Act?
- How did it lead to the creation of the Republican Party?
- What happened at Pottawatomie and Osawatomie?

liberty and full social equality in the United States. A newspaper reporter said that the selfless Brown was a "strange" and "iron-willed" old man with a "fiery nature and a cold temper, and a cool head—a volcano beneath a covering of snow." Two days after the attack on Lawrence, Brown set out with four of his sons for Pottawatomie, Kansas, a pro-slavery settlement near the Missouri border. There they dragged five men from their houses and hacked them to death with swords. One of the murdered men had had his fingers and arms cut off. "God is my judge," Brown told one of his sons upon their return from the raid. "We were justified under the circumstances." Without "the shedding of blood," he added, "there is no remission of sins."

The Pottawatomie Massacre (May 24–25, 1856) set off a guerrilla war in the Kansas Territory. On August 30, Missouri ruffians raided the free-state settlement at Osawatomie, Kansas. They looted and burned the houses and shot Frederick Brown, John's son, through the heart. By the end of 1856, about 200 settlers on both sides had been killed in "Bleeding Kansas."

Violence in the Senate

The violence in Kansas spilled over into Congress. On May 22, 1856, the day after the burning of Lawrence and two days before the Pottawatomie Massacre, an incident on the Senate floor electrified the whole country. Just two days earlier, Republican Senator Charles Sumner of Massachusetts, a passionate foe of slavery, had delivered a fiery speech in which he insulted slave owners, including Andrew Pickens Butler, an elderly senator from South Carolina. Butler, Sumner charged, had "chosen a mistress . . . who . . . though polluted in the sight of the world, is chaste [pure] in his sight—I mean the harlot [prostitute], Slavery."

> **"Bleeding Sumner" (1856)**

Sumner's speech enraged Butler's young cousin Preston S. Brooks, a South Carolina congressman with a hair-trigger temper. On May 22, Brooks confronted Sumner at his Senate desk and began beating him about the head with a gold-headed cane. While stunned colleagues looked on, Brooks beat Sumner until his cane broke and others finally intervened. The helpless Sumner nearly died. In satisfying his rage, though, Brooks had created a martyr—"Bleeding Sumner"—for the anti-slavery cause. For two and a half years, Sumner's empty Senate seat was a solemn reminder of the violence done to him. His brutal beating also had an unintended political effect: it drove more northerners into the new Republican party. In the South, by contrast, Butler was celebrated as a hero. Dozens of people sent him new canes.

Sectional Politics

> **Republican party opposed to expanding slavery**

The violence during the spring of 1856 set the tone for another presidential election—one in which the major parties could no longer evade the slavery issue. At its first national convention, the Republican party fastened on an

"Bully" Brooks attacks Charles Sumner This outbreak of violence in Congress worsened the strains on the Union.

eccentric military hero, John C. Frémont, "the Pathfinder," who had led the conquest of Mexican-controlled California. The Republican platform also owed much to the Whigs. It favored federal funding for a transcontinental railroad and, in general, more government-financed internal improvements. It condemned the repeal of the Missouri Compromise, the Democratic party's policy of territorial expansion, and the "barbarism" of slavery. For the first time, a major-party platform had taken a stand against slavery.

In picking a presidential candidate, the Democrats dumped the widely unpopular Franklin Pierce. The president had become the most hated person in the nation by 1856, and he remains the only elected president to be denied re-nomination by his own party. Instead, the Democrats nominated James Buchanan of Pennsylvania, a former senator and secretary of state who had long sought the nomination. The Democratic platform endorsed the Kansas-Nebraska Act, called for vigorous enforcement of the fugitive slave law, and stressed that Congress should not interfere with slavery in states or territories. In the campaign of 1856, the Republicans had very few southern supporters and only a handful in the border slave states of Delaware, Maryland, Kentucky, and Missouri, where fear of disunion held many Whigs in line. Buchanan thus went into the campaign as the candidate of the only remaining national party. Frémont swept the northernmost states with 114 electoral votes, but Buchanan added five free states—Pennsylvania, New Jersey, Illinois, Indiana, and California—to his southern majority for a total of 174.

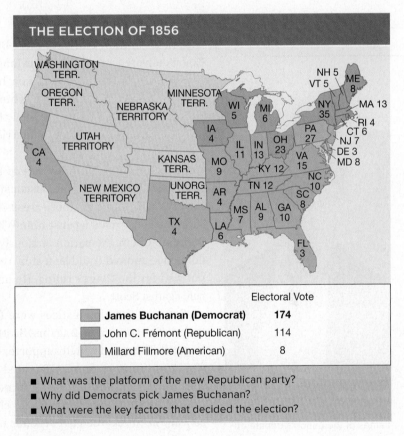

THE ELECTION OF 1856

	Electoral Vote
James Buchanan (Democrat)	**174**
John C. Frémont (Republican)	114
Millard Fillmore (American)	8

- What was the platform of the new Republican party?
- Why did Democrats pick James Buchanan?
- What were the key factors that decided the election?

President Buchanan

The sixty-five-year-old Buchanan, America's first unmarried president, tall and solid, his head topped with a mane of white hair, had built his impressive political career on his commitment to states' rights and his aggressive promotion of territorial expansion. He believed that saving the Union depended upon the nation making concessions to the South. Republicans charged that he lacked the backbone to stand up to the southern slaveholders who dominated the Democratic majorities in Congress. His choice of four slave-state men and only three free-state men for his cabinet seemed another bad sign. It was.

During James Buchanan's first six months in office in 1857, two major events brought about his undoing: (1) the Supreme Court decision in the *Dred Scott* case, and (2) new troubles in strife-torn Kansas. For all of Buchanan's experience as a legislator and diplomat, he failed to handle either of those issues with confidence or strength. The Financial Panic of 1857 only made a bad situation worse for both the new president and the nation as a whole. By 1857, the American economy was growing too fast. Too many railroads and factories were being built even as European demand for American corn and wheat was slackening. The result was a financial panic triggered by the failure of the Ohio Life Insurance and Trust Company on August 24, 1857.

The Dred Scott Case

The *Dred Scott* case (1857)

On March 6, 1857, two days after Buchanan's inauguration, the Supreme Court delivered a decision in the long-pending case of ***Dred Scott v. Sandford***. Scott, born a slave in Virginia, had been taken to St. Louis in 1830 and sold to an army surgeon, who took him to Illinois, then to the Wisconsin Territory (later Minnesota), and finally back to St. Louis in 1842. While in the Wisconsin Territory, Scott had married Harriet Robinson, and they eventually had two daughters.

In 1846, Dred Scott filed suit in the Missouri courts, claiming that his residence in Illinois and the Wisconsin Territory had made him free because slavery was outlawed in those areas. A jury decided in his favor, but the state supreme court ruled against him. When the case rose on appeal to the U.S. Supreme Court, the nation anxiously awaited its opinion on whether freedom once granted could be lost by returning to a slave state. Buchanan did not wait for the Court's ruling. He privately pressured one of the judges to rule against Scott.

Seven of the nine justices were Democrats, five of whom were southerners. The vote was 7–2 against Scott. Seventy-nine-year-old Chief Justice Roger B. Taney, a devoted supporter of the South and of slavery, wrote the Court's majority opinion. He ruled that Scott lacked legal standing because, like all former slaves, he was not an American citizen. At the time the Constitution was adopted, Taney claimed, blacks "had for more than a century been regarded as . . . so far inferior, that they had no rights which the white man was bound to respect." On the issue of Scott's residency, Taney argued that the Missouri Compromise of 1820 had deprived citizens of property by prohibiting slavery in selected states, an action "not warranted by the Constitution."

The upshot was that the Supreme Court had declared an act of Congress unconstitutional for the first time since *Marbury v. Madison* (1803). Congress had repealed the Missouri Compromise in the Kansas-Nebraska Act three years earlier, but the *Dred Scott* decision now challenged the concept of "popular sovereignty." If Congress itself could not exclude slavery from a territory, as Taney argued, then neither could a territorial government created by an act of Congress.

Dred Scott Scott's lawsuit over his family's freedom fanned the flames of the nation's debate on slavery.

***Dred Scott v. Sandford* (1857)** U.S. Supreme Court ruling that slaves were not U.S. citizens and therefore could not sue for their freedom and that Congress could not prohibit slavery in the western territories.

Yet instead of settling the issue of slavery in the territories, Taney's ruling fanned the flames. Pro-slavery advocates greeted the Court's opinion as binding, and President Buchanan approved. Republicans, on the other hand, were outraged by the *Dred Scott* decision because it nullified their anti-slavery program. They threatened to remove the justices and reverse the decision if they secured control of the federal government.

The Lecompton Constitution

Meanwhile, in the Kansas Territory, the struggle over slavery continued with both sides resorting to voting trickery and violence. Just before Buchanan's inauguration, in early 1857, the pro-slavery territorial legislature called for a constitutional convention. The governor vetoed the measure, but the legislature overrode his veto. The governor resigned in protest, and President Buchanan replaced him with Robert J. Walker. With Buchanan's approval, Walker pledged to the free-state Kansans (who made up an overwhelming majority of the residents) that the new constitution would be submitted to a fair vote. But when the pro-slavery constitutional convention, meeting at Lecompton, drafted a constitution under which Kansas would become a slave state, those opposed to slavery boycotted the vote on the new constitution.

Lecompton Constitution (1858)

At that point, President Buchanan took a fateful step. Influenced by southern advisers and politically dependent upon powerful southern congressmen, he endorsed the pro-slavery Lecompton convention, sparking a new wave of outrage across the northern states. Stephen A. Douglas, the most prominent Midwestern Democrat, broke with the president over the issue, siding with anti-slavery Republicans because the people of Kansas had been denied the right to decide the issue. Douglas told a newspaper reporter that "I made Mr. James Buchanan, and by God, sir, I will unmake him." The rigged election in Kansas went as predicted: 6,226 for the constitution with slavery, 569 for the constitution without slavery.

Meanwhile, a new acting governor had convened the anti-slavery legislature, which called for another election to vote the Lecompton Constitution up or down. Most of the pro-slavery settlers boycotted this election. The result, on January 4, 1858, was overwhelming: 10,226 voted against the Lecompton Constitution, while only 138 voted for it. In April 1858, the U.S. Congress ordered that Kansans vote again on the Lecompton Constitution. On August 2, 1858, voters rejected the Lecompton Constitution, 11,300 to 1,788. With that vote, Kansas cleared the way for its eventual admission as a free state in 1861.

Douglas versus Lincoln

The controversy over slavery in Kansas put severe strains on the Democratic party. To many, Stephen A. Douglas, one of the few remaining Democrats with support in both the North and the South, seemed the best hope for national unity and union. The year 1860 would give him a chance for the presidency, but first he had to secure his home base in Illinois, where in 1858 he faced re-election to the Senate.

To oppose him, Illinois Republicans selected a rustic lawyer from Springfield, Abraham Lincoln, the former Whig legislator. Lincoln had served in the Illinois legislature and in 1846 had won a seat in the U.S. Congress. After a single unremarkable term in Washington, D.C., he returned to Springfield. In 1854, however, the Kansas-Nebraska Act drew Lincoln back into the political arena. Lincoln hated slavery but was no abolitionist. He did not believe that the nation should force the South to end slavery, but he did insist that slavery not be expanded into new western territories. In 1856, Lincoln joined the rapidly growing Republican party, and two years later he emerged as the obvious choice to oppose Douglas for the Senate seat. Because he was the underdog, Lincoln sought to raise his profile by challenging Douglas to a series of debates across the state.

The **Lincoln-Douglas debates** took place from August 21 to October 15, 1858. They attracted tens of thousands of spectators and transformed the contest for an Illinois Senate seat into a battle for the future of the Republic. The two men differed as much physically as they did politically. Douglas was barely five feet tall, stocky with a big head. Lincoln was tall and thin, well over six feet tall. The basic political difference between the two men, Lincoln argued, lay in Douglas's indifference to the immorality of slavery. Douglas, he said, did not care whether slavery in the territories was "voted up, or voted down." Douglas was preoccupied only with process ("popular sovereignty"); Lincoln claimed to be focused on principle. He insisted that the American government could not "endure, permanently half *slave* and half *free*. . . . It will become *all* one thing, or *all* the other." If Lincoln had the better of the argument in the long view, Douglas had the better of a close election, but, while a losing cause, Lincoln's energetic campaign had elevated him to being a national figure.

An Outnumbered South

By the late 1850s, national politics was undergoing profound changes. In May 1858, the free state of Minnesota entered the Union; in February 1859, another non-slave territory, Oregon, gained statehood. The slave states of the South were quickly becoming a minority, and their political insecurity deepened into paranoia. At the same time, political tensions over slavery were becoming more violent. In 1858, members of Congress engaged in the largest brawl ever staged on the floor of the House of Representatives, with more than fifty legislators shoving, punching, and wrestling one another.

Like the scuffling congressmen, more and more Americans began to feel that slavery could be ended or defended only with violence. The editor of a pro-slavery Kansas newspaper wanted to kill abolitionists: "If I can't kill a man, I'll kill a woman; and if I can't kill a woman, I'll kill a child." Some southerners were already talking of secession. In 1858, former Alabama congressman William L. Yancey, a member of a group of hot-tempered southern secessionists called "fire-eaters," threatened that it would be easy "to precipitate the Cotton States into a revolution."

Abraham Lincoln A lanky and rawboned small-town lawyer, Lincoln challenged Douglas to debate him in 1858.

Lincoln-Douglas debates (1858) In the Illinois race between Republican Abraham Lincoln and Democrat Stephen A. Douglas for a seat in the U.S. Senate, a series of seven dramatic debates focusing on the issue of slavery in the territories.

John Brown's Raid

Such violent threats to maintain slavery drove John Brown into a desperate act. On the cool, rainy night of October 16, 1859, iron-willed Brown launched his supreme effort to end slavery. From a Maryland farm, he crossed the Potomac River with about twenty men, mostly unmarried and in their twenties, including three of Brown's sons and five African Americans. Under cover of darkness, they approached the federal rifle arsenal in Harpers Ferry, Virginia (now West Virginia), a factory town some sixty miles northwest of Washington, D.C. Brown's mad scheme was to give the arsenal's muskets to thousands of slaves in the area, in the hope of triggering mass uprisings across the South. "I want to free all the negroes in this state," Brown said. "If the citizens interfere with me, I must burn the town and have blood."

Raid on Harpers Ferry (1859)

Brown and his comrades took the town by surprise, cut the telegraph lines, and occupied the arsenal. He then sent a handful of men to kidnap several prominent slave owners and spread the word for local slaves to rise up and join the rebellion. But only a few slaves heeded the call. By dawn, enraged townsmen had surrounded the raiders. Brown and a dozen of his men, along with eleven white hostages (including George Washington's great-grandnephew, the area's most prominent resident) and two of their slaves, remained holed up for thirty-two hours. Meanwhile, hundreds of armed men poured into Harpers Ferry to capture Brown and his raiders. Lieutenant Colonel Robert E. Lee arrived with a force of U.S. Marines, having been dispatched from Washington, D.C., by President Buchanan. On the morning of October 18, the marines broke down the arsenal's barricaded doors and rushed in. The siege was over. Altogether, Brown's men had killed four townspeople and wounded another dozen. Of their own group, ten were killed (including two of Brown's sons) and five were captured; another five escaped.

John Brown On his way to the gallows, Brown predicted that slavery would end only "after much bloodshed."

Brown and his accomplices were quickly convicted of treason, murder, and "conspiring with Negroes to produce insurrection." At his sentencing, Brown delivered one of America's classic speeches: "Now, if it is deemed necessary that I should forfeit my life for the furtherance of the ends of justice, and mingle my blood further with the blood of my children and with the blood of millions in this slave country whose rights are disregarded by wicked, cruel, and unjust enactments, I say, let it be done." For weeks, as Brown waited in his cell to be executed, he continued to crusade against slavery by mailing a stream of letters, many of which were printed in anti-slavery newspapers.

Brown was hanged on December 2, 1859. (Among the crowd watching the execution was a popular young stage actor named John Wilkes Booth, who would later assassinate Abraham Lincoln.) If Brown had failed to ignite a massive slave rebellion, he had achieved two things: he had become a martyr for the anti-slavery cause, and he had set off a panic throughout the slaveholding South. "John Brown may be a lunatic," said a Boston newspaper, but if so, "one-fourth of the people of Massachusetts are madmen." The transcendentalist leader Ralph Waldo Emerson called Brown a "saint" who had made "the gallows glorious like a cross." The leading black abolitionist, former slave Frederick Douglass, called Brown "our noblest American hero" whose commitment to ending slavery "was far greater than mine."

Outlawing anti-slavery activity

John Brown's daring but hopeless attack on Harper's Ferry stirred the South's worst nightmare: that armed slaves would revolt. Caught up in a frenzy of fear, southerners equated Brown's violent abolitionism with the Republican party. Throughout the fall and winter of 1859–1860, wild rumors of abolitionist conspiracies and slave insurrections swept through the southern states, leading many to outlaw any anti-slavery activity. Some 300 abolitionists were murdered or forced out of the region. "We regard every man in our midst an enemy to the institutions of the South," said the *Atlanta Confederacy*, "who does not boldly declare that he believes African slavery to be a social, moral, and political blessing."

The Democrats Divide

Amid such emotional hysteria the nation mobilized for another presidential election, destined to be the most fateful in its history. In April 1860 the squabbling Democrats gathered for what would become a disastrous presidential nominating convention in Charleston, South Carolina, a pro-slavery hotbed where Northern delegates in their hotel rooms could hear the sound of drums beating each evening, a warning to free blacks that they must be off the streets after sunset. Stephen A. Douglas's northern supporters tried to straddle the divisive issue of slavery by promising southerners to defend the "peculiar institution" in their region while assuring northerners that slavery would not spread to new states. Southern firebrands, however, demanded federal protection for slavery in the territories as well as the states. When the pro-slavery advocates lost the platform fight, delegates from eight southern states walked out of the convention. "We say, go your way," exclaimed a Mississippi delegate to Douglas's supporters, "and we will go ours."

The Democratic convention then dissolved into factions. Douglas's supporters reassembled in Baltimore on June 18 and nominated him for president. Southern Democrats met first in Richmond and then in Baltimore, where they adopted the pro-slavery platform defeated in Charleston and named John C. Breckinridge, vice president under Buchanan, as their candidate. Thus another cord of union had snapped: the last remaining national party had split into northern and southern factions. The fracturing of the Democratic party made a Republican victory in 1860 almost certain.

Lincoln's Election

The Republican nominating convention was held in May in the fast-growing city of Chicago, where everything suddenly came together for Abraham Lincoln, the uncommon common man who won the presidential nomination over New York senator William H. Seward. The resulting cheer, wrote one journalist, was "like the rush of a great wind." Inside the convention building, the "wildest excitement and enthusiasm" swelled to a "perfect roar." The convention reaffirmed the party's opposition to the extension of slavery and, in an effort to gain broader support, endorsed a series of traditional Whig policies promoting national economic expansion: a higher protective tariff, free farms on federal lands out west, and federally financed internal improvements, including a transcontinental railroad.

The rival Democratic and Republican presidential nominating conventions revealed that opinions about the future of slavery were becoming more radical in the Northeast and the Lower South. Attitude followed latitude. In the border states of Maryland, Delaware, Kentucky, and Missouri, the prevailing sense of moderation aroused former Whigs to make one more try at reconciliation. Meeting in Baltimore a week before the Republicans met in Chicago, they reorganized themselves as the Constitutional Union party and nominated John Bell of Tennessee for president. Their platform centered on a vague statement promoting "the Constitution of the Country, the Union of the States, and the Enforcement of the Laws."

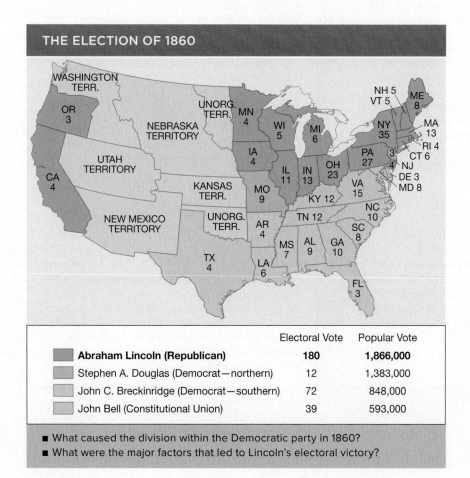

THE ELECTION OF 1860

	Electoral Vote	Popular Vote
Abraham Lincoln (Republican)	**180**	**1,866,000**
Stephen A. Douglas (Democrat—northern)	12	1,383,000
John C. Breckinridge (Democrat—southern)	72	848,000
John Bell (Constitutional Union)	39	593,000

■ What caused the division within the Democratic party in 1860?
■ What were the major factors that led to Lincoln's electoral victory?

Slavery, Territorial Expansion, and Secession

In 1840, Whigs and Democrats dominated national and state politics. They each drew significant support from voters in free and slave states, North and South, East and West. They each avoided discussing the issue of slavery and instead debated the merits of an active federal government and its involvement in the economy and ordinary people's lives. By 1860, the Whig party had disappeared, the Democrats had split between supporters from free and slave states, and a new party—the Republican party dedicated to stopping the expansion of slavery into American territories—had gained the majority of support among voters in the free states. The election of Abraham Lincoln that year provoked the secession crisis in which eleven slave states eventually revoked their membership in the federal union.

Texas

In the waning days of the Tyler administration, Congress annexed Texas and in 1845 it was admitted to the Union as a slave state. Settlers from southern states had begun moving into this northern Mexican province in the 1820s, bringing their slaves with them to grow cotton, even though the Mexican government discouraged the use of African slave labor in the province. Ultimately, the "Texian" settlers revolted and in 1836 established an independent Republic of Texas that they hoped the United States would soon annex. However, Presidents Jackson and Van Buren postponed any discussion of annexation in an effort to avoid a national controversy over the expansion of slavery within the United States.

The Oregon Country

Until 1846, the entire Oregon Country—Oregon, Washington, Idaho, and parts of Wyoming, Montana, and British Columbia—was jointly claimed by both the United States and Great Britain. The Buchanan-Pakenham Treaty divided the region between them with the United States controlling the land below the 49th parallel. Oregon's status as a free-soil territory caused little dispute.

California and New Mexico

In the Treaty of Guadalupe Hidalgo (1848), the federal government purchased from Mexico the territories of California and New Mexico (which included the current states of Utah, Nevada, Arizona, New Mexico, and part of Colorado). Even before the war officially ended, many anti-slavery politicians attempted to ban the expansion of slavery into this vast new territory. After the election of the Whig candidate Zachary Taylor, the discovery of gold in California, and the ensuing rapid migration of settlers into that region starting in 1849, Congress had to address the issue head-on when California applied for statehood in 1850 as a free state.

The Compromise of 1850

Congress ultimately agreed to California's status as a free state, but left the issue of slavery up to the settlers themselves, a compromise known as "popular sovereignty," thus leaving the possibility of future slave states joining the Union. Congress also pleased opponents of slavery by ending the slave trade in the District of Columbia, but at the same time, as part of the Compromise, Congress also passed the controversial Fugitive Slave Act, which enhanced the ability of slave owners to recapture slaves who had escaped to free states, demonstrating the federal government's support for the rights of slave owners.

The Kansas-Nebraska Act

In 1854, Senator Stephen Douglas of Illinois persuaded Congress to renounce the Missouri Compromise of 1820 and allow some of the territory from the Louisiana Purchase to be opened up to the expansion of the slave system. The Kansas-Nebraska Act allowed for the organization of a Kansas Territory in which the issue of slavery would be determined through a vote by the settlers, called "popular sovereignty." The new Republican party was founded in opposition to the Kansas-Nebraska Act, attracting politicians from the Democratic, Whig, and Free-Soil parties into a broad coalition that opposed any further efforts to expand slavery into the territories.

Bleeding Kansas

Anti- and pro-slavery settlers rushed to the newly organized Kansas territory in 1855. Disputes, often violent, flared between each side. Eventually each faction created a territorial constitution supporting their position. President James Buchanan, a northern Democrat, sided with the pro-slavery faction. Nevertheless, anti-slavery settlers ultimately prevailed, and by 1858 Kansas was on its way to becoming a free state.

The *Dred Scott* Decision

In its 1857 *Dred Scott* decision, the U.S. Supreme Court weighed in on the issue of the expansion of slavery into the western territories. Enslaved Dred Scott had sued his owner on the basis that he and his owner had lived for a substantial amount of time in territory where slavery was prohibited by the Missouri Compromise. The Court ruled against him, dismissing his standing as a U.S. citizen because of his race and deciding further that the Constitution did not allow Congress to prohibit slavery from any territory. Thus, the *Dred Scott* decision ruled that the 1820 Missouri Compromise was unconstitutional.

The Lower South secedes

In 1860, Abraham Lincoln, the Republican nominee for president, won a small plurality of the vote by carrying every free state (but none of the slave states). Southerners, especially those in the cotton states, feared that the anti-slavery views of Lincoln and the Republicans would incite slave insurrections and the destruction of the cotton economy. Before Lincoln was inaugurated in March 1861, seven southern states passed secession ordinances and formed the Confederate States of America.

QUESTIONS FOR ANALYSIS

1. How did American expansion intensify the national debate over slavery in the territories? What was the political significance of whether territories were "free" or "slave"?

2. How did the slavery controversy make the annexation of new states so controversial and lead to the Compromise of 1850?

3. Why did violence over slavery escalate after the passage of the Kansas-Nebraska Act? What role did Bleeding Kansas and the Kansas-Nebraska Act play in national politics?

4. Why did the *Dred Scott* decision by the Supreme Court make compromise more difficult?

5. What role did territorial expansion play in the secession of the states of the Lower South in 1860?

The bitterly contested presidential campaign in 1860 thus became a choice between Lincoln and Douglas in the North (Lincoln was not even on the ballot in the South), and between Breckinridge and Bell in the South. Douglas, the only candidate to mount a nationwide campaign, promised that he would "make war boldly against" extremists in both regions: "Northern abolitionists and Southern disunionists." But his effort to preserve the Union by preserving slavery did no good.

By midnight on November 6, Lincoln's victory was clear. In the final count he had 39 percent of the total popular vote, the smallest plurality ever, but he won a clear majority (180 votes) in the Electoral College. He carried *all* eighteen free states and *none* of the slave states.

Abraham Lincoln elected president (1860)

The Response in the South

CORE OBJECTIVE
5. Explain why seven southern states seceded from the Union soon after Lincoln's election in 1860.

Southern fears of a Lincoln presidency

Between November 8, 1860, when Lincoln was elected, and March 4, 1861, when he was inaugurated, the United States of America disintegrated. The election of Lincoln panicked southerners who believed that the Republican party, as a Richmond, Virginia, newspaper asserted, was founded for one reason: "hatred of African slavery."

South Carolina, which had long been the state most resistant to federal authority, viewed Lincoln's election as the final signal to abandon the Union. After Lincoln's victory, South Carolina's entire delegation of U.S. congressmen and senators resigned. Federal district judge Andrew McGrath in Charleston also resigned, dramatically ripping off his federal robe. The South Carolina legislature then appointed a convention to decide whether the state should secede from the Union. Among the convention delegates were former governors, four former U.S. senators, the presidents of Furman University and Limestone College, and a dozen ministers, all of whom assumed that Lincoln would try to abolish slavery. Nearly all of the delegates owned slaves. Twenty-seven owned a hundred or more slaves, and one delegate, former governor John Manning, owned more than 650 slaves. One of the delegates, Thomas Jefferson Withers, declared that the "true question for us all is how shall we sustain African slavery in South Carolina from a series of annoying attacks."

South Carolina's slaveholding elite pushes secession

South Carolina then was the third wealthiest state in the Union. It had a higher percentage of slaves in its population (60 percent) than any other state, and its political leadership was dominated by slave-owning hotheads. It had been a one-party state (Democratic) for decades, and it was then the only state in the Union that did not allow its citizens to vote in presidential elections; the state legislature, controlled by white planters, did the balloting.

Meeting in Charleston on December 20, 1860, the special convention, most of whose 169 delegates were wealthy slave owners, unanimously approved an Ordinance of Secession, explaining that President-elect Lincoln was a man "whose opinions and purposes are hostile to slavery."

David Jamison Rutledge, the man who presided over the secession convention, announced that "the Ordinance of Secession has been signed and ratified, and I proclaim the State of South Carolina an Independent Commonwealth." (Jamison would have four sons killed in the Civil War and see his house burned to the ground by Union soldiers.) James L. Petigru, one of the few Unionists in Charleston, claimed that those who voted for secession were lunatics. South Carolina, he quipped, "is too small to be a Republic and too large to be an insane asylum." As the news of secession spread through Charleston, church bells rang and shops closed. New flags were unfurled and cadets at The Citadel, the state's military college, fired artillery salutes. "THE UNION IS DISSOLVED!" screamed the headline of the *Charleston Mercury*, a pro-secession newspaper. One Unionist in Charleston kept a copy of the newspaper, scribbling on the bottom of it: "You'll regret the day you ever done this. I preserve this to see how it ends."

"The Union Is Dissolved!" A newspaper headline announcing South Carolina's secession from the Union.

Buchanan's Waiting Game

The nation's gravest crisis needed a bold, decisive president, but lame-duck James Buchanan was timid and hesitant. He blamed the crisis on fanatical abolitionists, but then declared that secession was illegal, only to claim that he lacked the constitutional authority to force a state to rejoin the Union. In the face of Buchanan's inaction, all the southerners in his cabinet resigned, and secessionists in the South seized federal forts. Among those federal forts was Fort Sumter, nestled on a tiny island at the mouth of Charleston Harbor, in the very jaws of the Confederacy. When South Carolina secessionists demanded that Major Robert Anderson, a Kentucky Unionist, surrender the undermanned federal fort, he refused, vowing to hold on at all costs. On January 5, 1861, President Buchanan sent an unarmed ship, the *Star of the West*, to resupply Fort Sumter. As the ship approached Charleston Harbor on January 9, Confederate cannons opened fire and drove it away. It was an act of war, but Buchanan chose to ignore the challenge and ride out the remaining weeks of his term, hoping that one of several compromise proposals would succeed in averting war.

Secession of the Lower South

By February 1, 1861, the seven states of the Lower South—South Carolina, Mississippi, Florida, Alabama, Georgia, Louisiana, and Texas—had seceded. Although the states' secession ordinances mentioned various grievances against the federal government, including tariffs on imports, they made clear that the primary reason for leaving the Union was the preservation of slavery. Texas's ordinance explained that the purpose of secession and the formation of the Confederacy was to *"secure the rights of the slave-holding*

> The formation of the Confederacy

States in their domestic institutions." The Texas convention, displaying the paternalistic racism at work in secession, called African Americans "an inferior and dependent race" for whom slavery was actually "beneficial."

On February 4, 1861, representatives of the seceding states, 90 percent of whom were slave owners, met in Montgomery, Alabama, where they adopted a constitution for the Confederate States of America. It mandated that "the institution of negro slavery, as it now exists in the Confederate States, shall be recognized and protected." Mississippi's Jefferson Davis was elected president, with Alexander H. Stephens of Georgia as vice president. The tiny, sickly Stephens left no doubt about why the Confederacy was formed. "Our new government," he declared, "is founded upon . . . the great truth that the negro is not equal to the white man; that slavery, subordination to the superior [white] race, is his natural and normal condition." In mid-February 1861, President Jefferson Davis ominously claimed that "the time for compromise is now passed."

Final Efforts at Compromise

The Crittenden Compromise fails (1861)

Amid the secession fever, several members of Congress desperately sought a compromise that would avert a civil war. On December 18, 1860, Senator John J. Crittenden of Kentucky proposed a series of resolutions that allowed for slavery in the new western territories *south* of the 1820 Missouri Compromise line (36°30′ parallel) and guaranteed the preservation of slavery where it already existed. President-elect Lincoln, however, opposed any plan that would allow for the extension of slavery westward, and the Senate defeated the Crittenden Compromise, 25–23. Several weeks later, in February 1861, twenty-one states sent delegates to a peace conference in Washington, D.C. Former president John Tyler presided, but the peace convention's proposal, substantially the same as the Crittenden Compromise, failed to win the support of either house of Congress. The only proposal that met with any success was a constitutional amendment guaranteeing slavery where it existed. Many Republicans, including Lincoln, were prepared to go that far to save the Union, but no farther.

As it happened, after passing the House, the slavery amendment, needing a two-thirds majority, passed the Senate without a vote to spare, 24–12, on the dawn of Lincoln's inauguration day, March 4, 1861. It would have become the Thirteenth Amendment, with the first use of the word *slavery* in the Constitution, but the states never ratified it. When a Thirteenth Amendment was eventually ratified, in 1865, it did not guarantee slavery—it abolished it.

Lincoln's Inauguration

In mid-February 1861, Abraham Lincoln boarded a train in Springfield, Illinois, that would carry him to Washington, D.C., for his presidential inauguration. Along the way, he told the New Jersey legislature that he was "devoted to peace" but warned that "it may be necessary to put the foot down." At the end of the weeklong journey, Lincoln reluctantly agreed that threats against his life made it too risky for him to enter the capital in daylight. Accompanied by bodyguards, he passed through Baltimore unnoticed on a night train and slipped into Washington, D.C., before daybreak on February 23, 1861.

In his March 4 inaugural address, the fifty-two-year-old Lincoln repeated his pledge not "to interfere with the institution of slavery in the states where it exists." But the immediate question facing the nation and the new president had shifted from slavery to secession. Lincoln insisted that "the Union of these States is perpetual." No state, he stressed, "can lawfully get out of the Union." He pledged to defend "federal forts in the South," such as Fort Sumter, but beyond that "there will be no invasion, no using of force against or among the people anywhere." Lincoln closed by appealing for regional harmony:

> We are not enemies, but friends. We must not be enemies. Though passion may have strained, it must not break our bonds of affection. The mystic chords of memory, stretching from every battlefield and patriot grave to every living heart and hearthstone all over this broad land, will yet swell the chorus of the Union, when again touched, as surely they will be, by the better angels of our nature.

Southerners were not impressed, however. A North Carolina newspaper warned that Lincoln's inauguration speech made civil war "inevitable." On both sides, people assumed that if fighting erupted, it would be over quickly and that their daily lives would go on as usual. The new president of the United States continued to seek a peaceful solution. But in early 1861, the possibility of compromise waned and civil war grew more likely.

The End of the Waiting Game

On March 5, 1861, his first day in office, President Lincoln learned that time was running out for the federal troops at Fort Sumter. Major Robert Anderson reported that his men had enough food for only a few weeks, and that Confederates were encircling the fort with a "ring of fire." On April 4, 1861, Lincoln ordered that ships be sent to resupply the sixty-nine soldiers at Fort Sumter. His counterpart, Jefferson Davis, president of the Confederate states, was determined to stop any effort to resupply the fort. On April 11, Confederate general Pierre G. T. Beauregard, a Louisiana native who had studied under Robert Anderson at West Point, demanded that his former professor surrender Fort Sumter. Major Anderson refused. At 4:30 on the morning of April 12, the Confederate shelling of Fort Sumter began. After some thirty-four hours, his ammunition exhausted, the outgunned Anderson lowered the "stars and stripes." The Civil War had begun.

Civil War begins (April 12, 1861)

- **Westward Migration** In the 1830s, Americans came to believe in *"manifest destiny"*—that the U.S. expansion to the Pacific coast was divinely ordained. A population explosion and the lure of cheap, fertile land prompted large numbers of Americans to endure the hardships of the *Overland Trails* to Oregon (*"Oregon Fever"*) and California. Many southerners moved to the Mexican province of Texas with their slaves to grow cotton. The Mexican government would not sanction slavery, however, and in 1830 forbade further immigration. Texians rebelled, winning their independence from Mexico in the *Texas Revolution*. But Texas would not become a state for another decade because the U.S. was determined to avoid war with Mexico and the divisive issue of adding another slave state to the Union.

- **Mexican-American War** When the United States finally annexed Texas, the Mexican government refused to recognize the loss of its northern province. President Polk sought to acquire California, New Mexico, and Texas, but negotiations failed. When Mexican troops crossed the Rio Grande and fired on U.S. soldiers, Polk urged Congress to declare war. U.S. forces prevailed, despite experiencing high casualties. By the terms of the *Treaty of Guadalupe Hidalgo* (1848), Mexico ceded California and New Mexico to the United States and gave up claims to land north of the Rio Grande.

- **Slavery in the Territories** The *Wilmot Proviso* (1846), never became law but, by declaring that slavery prohibited in the newly acquired Mexican territories, stirred anti-slavery sentiment. The new *Free-Soil party* also demanded that slavery be banned in the new territories. But the *California Gold Rush* of 1849 escalated tensions. Most Californians wanted their territory to be a free state. Southerners feared losing federal protection of their "peculiar institution" if free states outnumbered slave states. Some political leaders urged the voters in each territory to decide with *popular sovereignty*. The much celebrated *Compromise of 1850* allowed California to enter the Union as a free state, established the territories of Texas, New Mexico, and Utah without direct reference to slavery, banned the slave trade in Washington, D.C., and passed a stronger *Fugitive Slave Act*. Tensions turned violent with the passage of the *Kansas-Nebraska Act* (1854), which overturned the Missouri Compromise by allowing slavery in the territories where it had been banned in 1820.

- **The Republican Party's Appeal** Northerners were outraged by violent pro-slavery mobs as the territory of Kansas prepared to enter the Union. Yet anti-slavery zealots were equally violent, such as John Brown in *Bleeding Kansas*. The Supreme Court's pro-slavery *Dred Scott v. Sandford* (1857) decision further fueled sectional conflict. Northern voters increasingly gravitated toward the anti-slavery Republican party. Republicans also advocated for protective tariffs and the development of national infrastructure, which appealed to northern manufacturers and commercial farmers. In the 1860 presidential election, Lincoln carried every free state and won a clear electoral college victory.

- **The Secession of the Lower South** South Carolina seceded from the Union a month after Lincoln's presidential victory. Before Lincoln was even inaugurated, six other states had joined South Carolina to form the Confederate States of America, claiming a right to secede in order to ensure the preservation of slavery. South Carolinians fired at Fort Sumter in Charleston Harbor, and so the Civil War began.

KEY TERMS

CHRONOLOGY

1821	Mexico gains independence from Spain
1836	American "Texians" are defeated at the Alamo
1842	United States and Great Britain agree to the Webster-Ashburton Treaty
1845	United States annexes Texas
1846	Mexican-American War begins
1848	Treaty of Guadalupe Hidalgo ends Mexican-American War
1849	California Gold Rush begins
1854	Congress passes the Kansas-Nebraska Act
	The Republican party is founded
1856	Bleeding Kansas and Bloody Sumner
1857	*Dred Scott v. Sandford* and Lecompton Constitution
1858	Lincoln-Douglas debates
1859	John Brown's raid at Harpers Ferry, Virginia
1860–1861	Seven southern states secede from the Union
March 4, 1861	Abraham Lincoln is inaugurated president
April 1861	Fort Sumter falls to Confederate forces

INQUIZITIVE

Go to InQuizitive to see what you've learned—and learn what you've missed—with personalized feedback along the way.

***LINCOLN'S DRIVE THROUGH RICHMOND* (1866)** Shortly after the Confederate capital of Richmond, Virginia, fell to Union forces in April 1865, President Abraham Lincoln visited the war-torn city. His carriage was swarmed by enslaved blacks who were freed by the war, as well as whites whose loyalties were with the Union.

The War of the Union

1861–1865

The fall of Fort Sumter started the war of the Union and triggered a wave of patriotic bluster on both sides. A southern woman prayed that God would "give us strength to conquer them, to exterminate *them*, to lay waste every Northern city, town and village, to destroy them utterly." By contrast, the writer Nathaniel Hawthorne reported from Massachusetts that his transcendentalist friend Ralph Waldo Emerson was "breathing slaughter" as the Union army prepared for its first battle.

Many southerners, then and since, argued that the Civil War was not about slavery but about the South's effort to defend states' rights. Confederate president Jefferson Davis, for example, claimed that the war was fought on behalf of the states' right to secede from the Union and the South's need to defend itself against a "tyrannical majority," by whom he meant those who had elected President Abraham Lincoln, the anti-slavery Republican. "All we ask," he said, "is to be let alone."

For his part, Lincoln stressed repeatedly that the war's goal was simply to restore the Union. In an 1862 letter, he declared that the "paramount object in this struggle *is* to save the Union, and is *not* either to save or to destroy slavery. If I could save the Union without freeing *any* slave I would do it, and if I could save it by freeing *all* the slaves I would do it; and if I could save it by freeing some and leaving others alone I would also do that." If the southern states

CORE
OBJECTIVES INQUIZITIVE

1. Identify the respective advantages of the North and South and explain how they affected the military strategies of the Union and the Confederacy.

2. Evaluate Lincoln's decision to issue the Emancipation Proclamation and its impact on the war.

3. Analyze how the war affected social and economic life in the North and South.

4. Describe the military turning points in 1863 and 1864 that ultimately led to the Confederacy's defeat.

5. Explain how the Civil War changed the nation.

Jefferson Davis President of the Confederacy.

returned to the Union, he promised, they could retain their slaves. None of the Confederate states accepted Lincoln's offer, in large part because most white southerners were convinced that Lincoln was lying. The "Black Republican," as they called the president, was determined to end slavery, no matter what he said.

However much Jefferson Davis and other southerners argued that secession and the war were about states' rights, the states of the Lower South seceded in 1860–1861 to preserve slavery. The South Carolina Declaration on the Immediate Causes of Secession was quite clear on the matter, highlighting the "increasing hostility on the part of the non-slaveholding states to the institution of slavery." Southerners claimed their *right* to secede from the Union, but protecting slavery was the *reason* southern leaders repeatedly used to justify secession and war. In 1860, William Preston of South Carolina declared: "Cotton is not our king—slavery is our king. Slavery is our truth. Slavery is our divine right." As Lincoln noted in his second inaugural address, everyone knew that slavery "was somehow the cause of the war."

CORE **OBJECTIVE**

1. Identify the respective advantages of the North and South and explain how they affected the military strategies of the Union and the Confederacy.

Mobilizing Forces in the North and South

On April 15, three days after the Confederate attack on Fort Sumter, President Lincoln called upon the loyal states to supply 75,000 soldiers to suppress the rebellion. Volunteers on both sides flocked to military recruiting offices. The pro-slavery Senator Stephen Douglas now insisted, "There are only two sides to the question [of civil war]. Every man must be for the United States or against it. There can be no neutrals in this war, only patriots—or traitors." The Civil War would force everyone—men and women, white and black, immigrants and Native Americans, free and enslaved—to choose sides. Thousands of southerners fought for the Union; thousands of northerners fought for the Confederacy. Thousands of European volunteers fought on both sides.

Taking Sides

The first seven states that seceded were all from the Lower South—South Carolina, Mississippi, Florida, Alabama, Georgia, Louisiana, and Texas—where the cotton economy was strongest. All the states in the Upper South, especially Tennessee and Virginia, had areas (mainly in the mountains) where whites were poor, slaves were scarce, and Union support was strong. Nevertheless, the outbreak of actual fighting led four more southern slave states to join the Confederacy: Virginia, Arkansas, Tennessee, and North Carolina.

In east Tennessee, however, the mountain counties would supply more volunteers to the Union army than to the Confederate cause, and people living in western Virginia were so loyal to the Union that they split off and

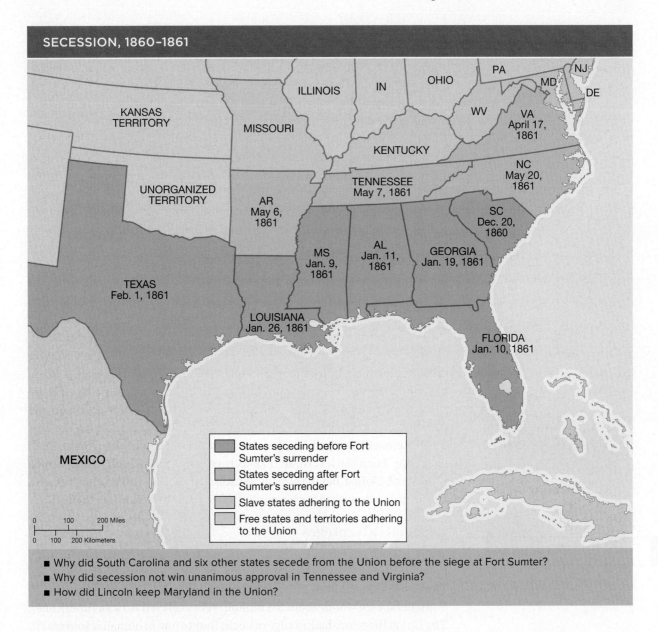

SECESSION, 1860–1861

ILLINOIS
IN
OHIO
PA
NJ
MD
DE
KANSAS TERRITORY
MISSOURI
WV
VA
April 17, 1861
KENTUCKY
UNORGANIZED TERRITORY
AR
May 6, 1861
TENNESSEE
May 7, 1861
NC
May 20, 1861
SC
Dec. 20, 1860
MS
Jan. 9, 1861
AL
Jan. 11, 1861
GEORGIA
Jan. 19, 1861
TEXAS
Feb. 1, 1861
LOUISIANA
Jan. 26, 1861
FLORIDA
Jan. 10, 1861
MEXICO

States seceding before Fort Sumter's surrender
States seceding after Fort Sumter's surrender
Slave states adhering to the Union
Free states and territories adhering to the Union

0   100   200 Miles
0   100   200 Kilometers

■ Why did South Carolina and six other states secede from the Union before the siege at Fort Sumter?
■ Why did secession not win unanimous approval in Tennessee and Virginia?
■ How did Lincoln keep Maryland in the Union?

formed the new state of West Virginia. Of the border states, Delaware remained firmly in the Union, but Maryland, Kentucky, and Missouri went through bitter struggles to decide which side to support. "I think to lose Kentucky is nearly the same as to lose the whole game," Lincoln said to a friend, explaining the situation in his home state. "Kentucky gone, we cannot hold Missouri, nor, as I think, Maryland." Kentuckian Mary Todd Lincoln, the president's wife, saw her youngest brother join the Confederate army, as did three of her half-brothers and a brother-in-law.

If Maryland had seceded, Confederates would have surrounded Washington, D.C. To keep Maryland in the Union, Lincoln had pro-Confederate leaders arrested, including Baltimore's mayor and chief of police. The fragile neutrality of Kentucky lasted till September 3, when Confederate and Union armies moved into the divided state. Kentucky voters elected a secessionist governor and a Unionist majority in the state legislature, as did Missouri, a state with many European immigrants, especially Germans. When a pro-Confederate militia gathered in St Louis, hoping to take control of the federal arsenal, it was surprised and disarmed by German immigrants "eager to teach the German-haters a never-to-be-forgotten lesson." The German militiamen then chased the pro-Confederate governor across the border to Arkansas. When news of the Civil War reached Missouri, 4,200 men volunteered to join the Union army; all but one hundred of them were German Americans.

The outbreak of war forced the men already serving in the U.S. Army to make an agonizing choice. On the eve of the Civil War, the U.S. Army had only 16,400 men, about 1,000 of whom were officers. Of these, about 25 percent, like the future Confederate general Robert E. Lee, resigned to join the Confederate army. On the other hand, many southerners made great sacrifices to remain loyal to the Union. Some left their native region once the fighting began; others remained in the South but found ways to support the Union. Some 100,000 men from the southern states fought *against* the Confederacy.

In areas of the South where Union sentiment was strong, the Civil War was brutally uncivil. In January 1863, a detachment of Confederate soldiers in mountainous Madison County, North Carolina, was escorting thirteen ragged men and boys to Knoxville, Tennessee, to be tried for desertion and treason. The prisoners never made it to Knoxville, however. Along the way, the detachment stopped, lined up five of the captives, and killed them. Then five more. Then the last three. Thirteen-year-old David Shelton was among the last to be killed, having already witnessed his father and brother's deaths. He begged to be spared for his mother's sake, but was killed like the rest.

Regional Advantages

| Union advantage: Population |

Once battle lines were finally drawn, the Union held twenty-three states, including four border slave states, while the Confederacy had eleven states. The population count was about 22 million in the Union to 9 million in the Confederacy (of whom about 3.5 million were enslaved African Americans). The Union therefore had an edge of about four to one in human resources. To help balance the odds, the Confederacy mobilized 80 percent of its military-age white men, a third of whom would die during the four-year war.

| Union advantage: Greater industrial development, railroads, and ships |

An even greater advantage for the North was its industrial development. As the southern character Rhett Butler complains in the classic movie *Gone with the Wind* (1939), "Why, all we have [in the South] is cotton and slaves and arrogance." The hated Yankees, he adds, have "the factories, the foundries, the shipyards, the iron and coal mines—all the things we haven't got." The southern states produced just 7 percent of the nation's manufactured goods on the eve of the war. The Union states produced 97 percent of the firearms and 96 percent of the railroad equipment. The North's advantage in transportation, particularly ships, also weighed heavily as the war went on. At the start of the war, the Union had ninety warships while the South at first had no navy at all. Federal gunboats and transports played a direct role in securing the Union's control of the Mississippi River and its larger tributaries, which provided easy invasion routes into the center of the Confederacy. And early on, the Union navy's blockade of the major southern ports sharply reduced the amount of cotton that could be exported to Britain and France as well as the flow of goods (including military weapons) imported from Europe. In addition, the Union had more wagons and horses than the Confederacy, and an even more impressive edge in the number of railroad locomotives.

The Confederacy, however, enjoyed a major geographic advantage: it could fight a defensive war on its own territory. In warfare, it is usually easier to defend than to attack. And in the Civil War, 90 percent of the time, armies that assaulted well-defended positions were beaten. Many Confederate leaders assumed that if their new nation could hold out long enough, perhaps the North would lose the will to continue the war.

> Confederate advantage: Waging a defensive war on its own territory

As the two sides mobilized for the first battles, the Confederate armies had more experienced military leaders and better horsemen. Many Confederates also displayed a brash sense of confidence in facing the more numerous and better equipped Union forces. After all, had not the Revolutionaries of 1776 defeated a much stronger British army? "Britain could not conquer three million [Americans]," a Louisianan declared, and "the world cannot conquer the South."

> Confederate advantage: Experienced military leaders

The War's Early Strategies

After the fall of Fort Sumter, excited civilians on both sides pressured the generals to strike quickly. "Forward to Richmond!" screamed a New York newspaper headline. In the summer of 1861, Jefferson Davis allowed the battle-hungry General Beauregard to hurry the main Confederate army to Manassas Junction, a railroad crossing in northern Virginia, about twenty-five miles southwest of Washington. Lincoln hoped that the Union army (often called *Federals*) would overrun the outnumbered Confederates (often called *Rebels*) and quickly push on to Richmond, only 107 miles to the south. "What a picnic," predicted a New York soldier, "to go down South for three months and clean up the whole business."

> Union strategy: Capture the Confederate capital

First Bull Run

When word reached Washington, D.C. that the two opposing armies were converging for battle, hundreds of congressmen and civilians packed picnic lunches and rode in carriages or on horseback to watch the romantic spectacle. It was a hot, dry day on July 21, 1861, when 37,000 untested Union recruits in colorful uniforms breezily marched to battle, some of them breaking ranks to eat blackberries or drink water from streams along the way. Many of them died with the berries still staining their lips as they engaged the Confederates dug in behind a branch of the Potomac River called Bull Run near

> Confederate advantage: Victory at First Battle of Bull Run (1861)

First Bull Run Moments before battle, a spectator in a top hat chats with Union soldiers (bottom right), while an artist sketches the passing troops heading to war (at left).

Thomas "Stonewall" Jackson The aggressive commander of a Confederate brigade at Bull Run, Jackson would later die of friendly fire in the Battle of Chancellorsville.

the vital Manassas Junction railroad station. The Union troops almost won early in the afternoon. "We fired a volley," wrote a Massachusetts private, "and saw the Rebels running. . . . The boys were saying constantly, in great glee, 'We've whipped them.' 'We'll hang Jeff Davis from a sour apple tree.' 'They're running.' 'The war is over.'" But Confederate reinforcements poured in to tip the balance. Amid the furious fighting, a South Carolina officer, soon to be killed himself, rallied his troops by pointing to the courageous example of Thomas Jackson's men: "Look! There is General Jackson with his Virginians, standing like a stone wall!" Jackson ordered his men to charge the faltering Union ranks, urging them to "yell like furies!" From that day forward, "Stonewall" became Jackson's nickname, and he would be the most celebrated—and feared—Confederate commander.

The Union army's retreat from Bull Run turned into a panicked rout (the "great skedaddle") as fleeing soldiers and terrified civilians clogged the road to Washington, D.C. But the Confederates were themselves so disorganized and exhausted that they failed to give chase. Unionists were devastated. New Yorker George Templeton Strong, a wealthy attorney and civic leader, wrote that "we are utterly and disgracefully routed, beaten, whipped by secessionists."

The First Battle of Bull Run (or First Manassas)* was a sobering experience for both sides, each of which had underrated the other's strength and tenacity. Much of the romance—the colorful uniforms, bright flags, and rousing songs—gave way to the agonizing realization that this would be a long, costly struggle. *Harper's Weekly* bluntly warned: "From the fearful day at Bull Run dates war. Not polite war, not incredulous war, but war that breaks hearts and blights homes."

---

* The Federals most often named battles for natural features; the Confederates, for nearby towns—thus Bull Run (Manassas), Antietam (Sharpsburg), Stones River (Murfreesboro), and the like.

The Union's "Anaconda" Plan

The Battle of Bull Run demonstrated that the war would not be decided with one sudden stroke. General Winfield Scott, the seasoned seventy-five-year-old commander of the Union war effort, devised a three-pronged strategy that called first for the Army of the Potomac, the main Union army, to defend Washington, D.C., and exert constant pressure on the Confederate capital at Richmond. At the same time, the Federal navy's blockade of southern ports would cut off the Confederacy's access to foreign goods and weapons. The third and final component of the plan called for other Union armies to divide the Confederacy by pushing south along the crucial inland water routes: the Mississippi, Tennessee, and Cumberland Rivers. This so-called **Anaconda Plan** was intended to slowly trap and crush the southern resistance, like an anaconda snake strangling its prey.

Union strategy: Naval blockade and control of inland rivers

Confederate Strategy

The Confederate war plan was simpler. Jefferson Davis was better prepared than Lincoln at the start of the war to guide military strategy. A graduate of the U.S. Military Academy at West Point, he had served as an officer during the Mexican War and was U.S. secretary of war from 1853 to 1857. If the Union forces could be held off and the war prolonged, as Davis and others hoped, then the British or French, desperate for southern cotton, might be persuaded to join their cause. Or, perhaps a long war would change public sentiment in the North and force Lincoln to seek a negotiated settlement. So while armies were forming in the South, Confederate diplomats were seeking military and financial assistance in London and Paris, and Confederate sympathizers in the North were urging an end to the Union's war effort.

Confederate strategy: A lengthy war to erode northern morale

The Confederate representatives in Paris won a promise from France to recognize the Confederacy as a new nation *if* Great Britain would do the same. But the British foreign minister refused to work with the Confederates, partly in response to pressure from President Lincoln and partly out of Britain's desire to maintain its trade with the United States. Confederate leaders had assumed that Britain would support the South in order to get its cotton. "The cards are in our hands!" crowed the *Mercury*, a Charleston newspaper. "And we intend to play them out to the bankruptcy of every cotton factory in Great Britain and France for the acknowledgement of our independence." As it turned out, however, the British, although eventually losing 400,000 jobs in their textile mills, were able to import enough cotton from their Asian colony, India, to maintain production of cloth. In the end, Confederate diplomacy in Europe was more successful in getting military supplies than in gaining official recognition of the Confederacy as an independent nation.

Confederate strategy: Cotton diplomacy in Europe

Forming Armies

Once the fighting began, President Lincoln called for 500,000 more men, a staggering number at the time and one that the Confederacy struggled to match. "War! And volunteers are the only topics of conversation or thought," wrote a student at Ohio's Oberlin College. "I cannot study. I cannot sleep,

Anaconda Plan Union's primary war strategy calling for a naval blockade of major southern seaports and then dividing the Confederacy by gaining control of the Tennessee, Cumberland, and Mississippi Rivers.

and I don't know as I can write." In Illinois, Ulysses S. Grant, a graduate of the U.S. Military Academy at West Point who had fought in the Mexican-American War, rejoined the army in 1861, explaining that there "are but two parties now—traitors and patriots—and I want hereafter to be ranked with the latter." Confederates were equally committed to their cause. Charleston, wrote Mary Chesnut, the literary wife of a prominent planter, was "crowded with soldiers" who feared "the war will be over before they get a sight of the fun." Tennessee's twenty-one-year-old Sam Watkins reported that everyone in his town "was eager for the war."

The basic unit of the nineteenth-century U.S. Army was the regiment, about a thousand soldiers, and during the Civil War most regiments on both sides were made up of friends, neighbors, and relatives from the same local community. Ethnic groups also formed their own regiments. A quarter of the Union troops were foreign-born. The Union army, for example, included a Scandinavian regiment (the 15th Wisconsin Infantry), a French regiment (the 55th New York Infantry), a Polish Legion (the 58th New York Infantry), and a mixed regiment of Poles, Hungarians, Germans, Spaniards, and Italians (the 39th New York Infantry). Many immigrant soldiers spoke no English. They were attracted to serve by many motives: a strong belief in the Union cause, cash bonuses, regular pay, or the need for a steady job. Whatever the reason, the high proportion of immigrants in the Union army gave it an ethnic diversity absent in the Confederate ranks. Many of the first Confederate army units chose flamboyant names: the Frontier Guards, Rough-and-Ready Grays, Game Cocks, Tigers, Cherokee Lincoln Killers, Tallapoosa Thrashers, and Raccoon Roughs.

In the Confederacy, the smaller male population than in the North forced Jefferson Davis to enact a conscription law (a mandatory military draft). On April 16, 1862, all white males aged eighteen to thirty-five were declared members of the army for three years, and those already in uniform were required to serve until the war ended. Many resented being

Union soldiers Smoking their pipes, these soldiers share a moment of rest and a bottle of whiskey.

drafted. "From this time until the end of the war," a Tennessee soldier wrote, "a soldier was simply a machine, a conscript. . . . All our pride and valor had gone, and we were sick of war and cursed the Southern Confederacy." In 1862, the upper age for military service was raised to forty-five; and in 1864, the age range was further extended to fifty. But age often did not matter, since recruiting officers frequently decided for themselves which boys "were old enough."

The Confederate conscription law included controversial loopholes, however. First, a draftee might escape service either by providing an able-bodied "substitute" who was not of draft age or by paying $500 in cash. Second, elected officials and key civilian workers, as well as planters with twenty or more slaves, were exempted from military service. Many among the planter elite argued that if they left to fight in the army, their slaves would escape or riot. Equally galling to many Confederate soldiers was the behavior of wealthy officers who brought their enslaved servants with them to army camps.

The Union took nearly another year to force men into service. In 1863, with the war going badly for the Federal armies, the government began to draft men aged twenty to forty-five. But many younger men served in the war. The Union army had over a thousand soldiers under the age of fifteen, some of whom served as regimental "drummer boys"; one of these was just nine years old. As in the South, there were ways for northerners to avoid military service. Exemptions were granted to selected federal and state officeholders and to others on medical or compassionate grounds. In the North, a draftee might pay $300 to avoid service. The fathers of Theodore and Franklin Roosevelt paid for substitutes, as did two future presidents, Chester A. Arthur and Grover Cleveland. Such exemptions led to bitter complaints on both sides about the conflict being "a rich man's war and a poor man's fight." Widespread public opposition to the draft emerged in both the North and South.

The average Civil War soldier or sailor was twenty-five years old, stood five feet eight inches, and weighed 143 pounds. A third of the southern soldiers could neither read nor write. One in nine would be killed or wounded. Half of the Union soldiers and two-thirds of the Confederates were farmers. Army camps featured their own libraries, theatrical stages, churches, and numerous "mascot" pets—and monotonous routine. A witty Pennsylvania private wrote home that "the first thing in the morning is drill. Then drill, then drill again. Then drill, drill, a little more drill, then drill, lastly drill."

Blacks in the South

As had happened during the Revolutionary War and the War of 1812, enslaved African Americans took advantage of the confusion created by the war to run away, engage in sabotage, join the Union war effort, or pursue their own interests. A plantation owner in Tennessee was disgusted by the war's effect on his slaves, as he confessed in his diary: "My Negroes all at home, but working only as they see fit, doing little." Some of them had

> Union advantage: Slaves run away from southern owners

reported that they had "rather serve the federals than work on the farm." Later, he revealed that when Union armies arrived in the area, his slaves had "stampeded" to join the Yankees: "Many of my servants have run away and most of those left had [just] as well be gone, they being totally demoralized and ungovernable." Some enslaved blacks escaped and served as spies or guides for Union forces; others later in the war escaped to join the Union army or navy.

Fighting in the West

During the Civil War, fighting spilled across the Mississippi River into the Great Plains and all the way to California. In 1862 a small Confederate army tried to conquer the New Mexico territory, which then included Arizona, but was repelled. Amid sporadic fighting, western settlement slowed but did not stop. New discoveries of gold and silver in the Sierra Nevada mountains in eastern California and in Montana and Colorado lured more prospectors and their suppliers. Dakota, Colorado, and Nevada gained territorial status in 1861, Idaho and Arizona in 1863, and Montana in 1864. Silver-rich Nevada gained statehood in 1864.

Kansas and Indian Territory

The most intense fighting west of the Mississippi occurred along the Kansas-Missouri border, where the disputes that had developed between the pro-slavery and anti-slavery settlers in the 1850s turned into brutal guerrilla warfare. The most prominent pro-Confederate leader in the area was William Quantrill. He and his followers, mostly teenagers, fought under a black flag, meaning that they would kill anyone who surrendered. In destroying Lawrence, Kansas, in 1863, Quantrill ordered his men to "kill every male and burn every house." By the end of the day, 182 boys and men had been massacred. Their opponents, the Jayhawkers, responded in kind. They tortured and hanged pro-Confederate prisoners, burned houses, and destroyed livestock.

Many Indian nations were caught up in the Civil War. Indian regiments fought on both sides, and in Oklahoma they fought against each other. Indians among the "Five Civilized Tribes" held African-American slaves and felt a bond with southern whites. Oklahoma's proximity to Texas influenced the Choctaws and Chickasaws to support the Confederacy. The Cherokees, Creeks, and Seminoles were more divided in their loyalties. For them, the Civil War fractured their unity. The Cherokees, for example, split in two, some supporting the Union and others the Confederacy.

Kentucky and Tennessee

Little happened of military significance east of the Appalachian Mountains before May 1862. On the other hand, important battles occurred in the West (from the Appalachians to the Mississippi River). In western Kentucky,

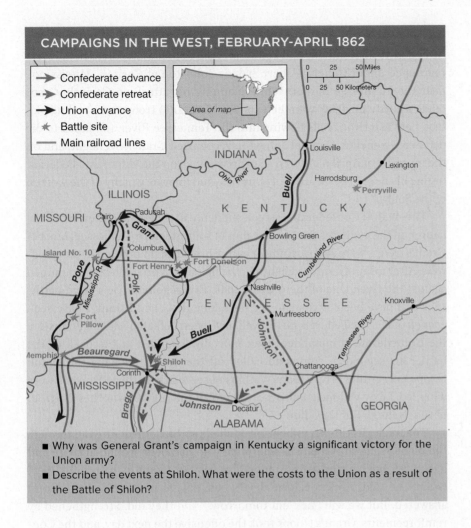

CAMPAIGNS IN THE WEST, FEBRUARY–APRIL 1862

→ Confederate advance
-→ Confederate retreat
→ Union advance
✳ Battle site
— Main railroad lines

- Why was General Grant's campaign in Kentucky a significant victory for the Union army?
- Describe the events at Shiloh. What were the costs to the Union as a result of the Battle of Shiloh?

Confederate general Albert Sidney Johnston had perhaps 40,000 men stretched over some 150 miles. Early in 1862, General Ulysses S. Grant, a superb horseman but inexperienced commander, made the first Union thrust against the weak center of Johnston's overextended lines. Moving on boats out of Cairo, Illinois, and Paducah, Kentucky, the Union army steamed up the Tennessee River and captured Fort Henry in northern Tennessee on February 6. Grant then moved quickly overland to attack nearby Fort Donelson, where, on February 16, some 12,000 Confederates surrendered.

This first major Union victory touched off wild celebrations throughout the North. President Lincoln's delight, however, was tempered by the death in the White House of his eleven-year-old son Willie, who succumbed to typhoid fever. The tragedy "overwhelmed" the president. It "showed me my weakness as I had never felt it before," Lincoln confessed to a friend. A White House staff member said she had never seen "a man so bowed down in grief."

Shiloh

After defeats in Kentucky and Tennessee, the Confederate forces in the West regrouped under General Albert Sydney Johnston at Corinth, Mississippi, near the Tennessee border. While planning his attack on Corinth, Grant made a costly mistake when he exposed his 42,000 troops on a rolling plateau between two creeks flowing into the Tennessee River and failed to dig defensive trenches. General Johnston recognized Grant's oversight, and on the morning of April 6 ordered a surprise attack on the vulnerable Federals, urging his men to be "worthy of your race and lineage; worthy of the women of the South."

The 44,000 Confederates struck suddenly at Shiloh, a whitewashed log church in the center of the Union camp in southwestern Tennessee. Most of Grant's troops were still sleeping or eating breakfast; many died in their bedrolls. After a day of confused fighting, the fleeing Union soldiers were pinned against the river. One of them wrote that "this is going to be a great battle, such as I have been anxious to see for a long time, and I think I have seen *enough* of it." The Federals might well have been defeated had not Johnston, the Confederate commander, been mortally wounded at the peak of the battle; his second in command called off the attack, allowing the Union troops to regroup. Private Sam Watkins observed that "those Yankees were whipped, fairly whipped, and according to all the rules of war they ought to have retreated. But they didn't."

That night, as Union gunboats fired shells at the Confederates all through the night, General William T. Sherman, who had been wounded twice and had three horses shot from under him, visited Grant as rain fell. "Well, Grant," he said, "we've had the devil's own day, haven't we?" "Yes," Grant answered. But we will "lick 'em tomorrow." And they did. Strengthened by reinforcements, Grant's troops took the offensive the next day, and the Confederates glumly withdrew twenty miles to Corinth. The Union army was too battered to pursue.

Shiloh, a Hebrew word meaning "Place of Peace," was the largest and costliest battle in which Americans had ever engaged up to that point. Some 100,000 men had fought each other, and a quarter of them had been killed or wounded. The 3,477 killed were more than had been killed in all of the War of 1812. Grant remembered that the battlefield was so littered with corpses that he could not walk in any direction without "stepping on dead bodies." He now realized that the only way the cruel war would end would be through "complete conquest." Like so many battles to come, Shiloh was a story of missed opportunities and lucky accidents. Throughout the Civil War, winning armies would fail to pursue their retreating foes, thus allowing the wounded opponent to slip away and fight again.

After Shiloh, Union general Henry Halleck, already jealous of Grant's success, spread a false rumor that Grant had been drinking during the battle. Some urged Lincoln to fire Grant, but the president refused: "I can't spare this man; he fights." Halleck, however, took Grant's place as field

Union victory: Battle of Shiloh

Union strategy: "Complete conquest"

commander, and as a result the Union thrust in the Mississippi Valley southward ground to a halt.

New Orleans

Union seizes New Orleans

Just three weeks after the Battle of Shiloh, the Union won a great naval victory at New Orleans, as sixty-year-old David G. Farragut's warships blasted their way past Confederate forts under cover of darkness to take control of the largest city in the Confederacy. Union general Benjamin F. Butler, a cross-eyed Massachusetts Democrat, thereafter served as the military governor of captured New Orleans. When a Confederate sympathizer ripped down a Union flag, Butler had him hanged. After a Rebel woman leaned out her window and emptied her chamber pot on the head of newly promoted Admiral Farragut, General Butler decreed that any woman who was disrespectful of Union soldiers would be treated as a "woman of the town plying her avocation" (that is, as a prostitute). Residents of the captured towns thereafter referred to General Butler as "the Beast," but they also quit harassing his soldiers. By shutting off the flow of goods, especially cotton, coming down the Mississippi River to the Gulf of Mexico, the loss of New Orleans was a devastating blow to the Confederate economy as the Union army took control of 1,500 cotton plantations and 50,000 slaves in the Mississippi Valley. The slave system was "forever destroyed and worthless" in Louisiana, reported a northern journalist. "New Orleans gone—and with it the Confederacy?" a worried Mary Chesnut wrote in Richmond.

Perryville

Union victory: Battle of Perryville (1862)

In the late summer of 1862, Confederate General Braxton Bragg's Army of Mississippi, 30,000 strong, used railroads to link up with General Edmund Kirby Smith's Army of East Tennessee. Their goal was to invade the North by taking control of the border state of Kentucky. They hoped to recruit volunteers for the Confederacy as well as push the Union army out of the state across the Ohio River. After early success, the Confederates installed a governor in Frankfort, only to cancel the inaugural ball because of the approaching Union Army of Ohio led by General Don Carlos Buell. The two forces met at the village of Perryville in central Kentucky in October 1862. In the ensuing battle, the outnumbered Confederates attacked the Union lines, pushing them back over a mile. But when Bragg learned that Union reinforcements were rushing to the battle, he, against the advice of his officers, ordered the Army of Mississippi to withdraw south toward Tennessee. After the Battle of Perryville, the Union retained control of Kentucky for the rest of the war. Jefferson Davis was so upset by Bragg's timid leadership that he ordered him to Richmond for a tongue lashing.

Fighting in the East

The fighting in the East remained fairly quiet for nine months after the Battle of Bull Run. In the wake of the Union defeat, Lincoln had appointed General George B. McClellan, Stonewall Jackson's classmate at West

Point and a former railroad president, as head of the Army of the Potomac. The thirty-four-year-old McClellan, who encouraged journalists to call him "Little Napoleon," set about building the Union's most powerful, best-trained army. Yet for all of his self-confidence and organizational ability, McClellan's cautiousness would prove crippling. Months passed while he remained in a state of perpetual preparation, building and training his massive army to meet the superior numbers of Confederates he mistakenly believed were facing him. Worried that the Union was running out of money, Lincoln finally lost his patience and ordered McClellan to attack. "[You] must strike a blow," he told his reluctant commander.

McClellan's Peninsular Campaign

In mid-March 1862, McClellan finally moved his huge army of 122,000 men on 400 ships and barges down the Potomac River and the Chesapeake Bay to the mouth of the James River at the tip of the Yorktown peninsula, southeast

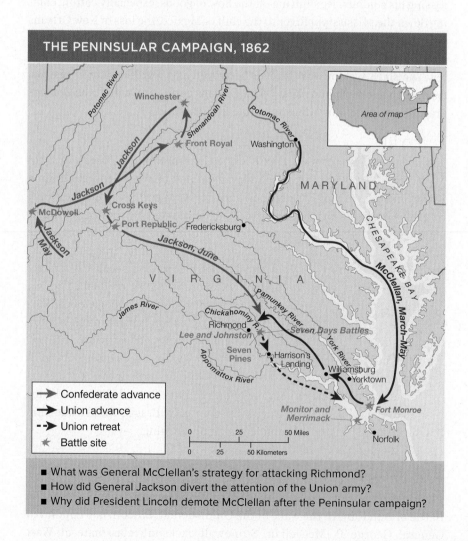

THE PENINSULAR CAMPAIGN, 1862

→ Confederate advance
→ Union advance
--→ Union retreat
⁕ Battle site

0 — 25 — 50 Miles
0 — 25 — 50 Kilometers

- What was General McClellan's strategy for attacking Richmond?
- How did General Jackson divert the attention of the Union army?
- Why did President Lincoln demote McClellan after the Peninsular campaign?

of Richmond, Virginia. McClellan's "Peninsular Campaign" boldly put the Union forces within sixty miles of the Confederate capital. Thousands of residents fled the city in panic, but McClellan waited too long to strike, over-estimating the number of Confederate defenders. As a frustrated Lincoln told McClellan, the war could be won only by *engaging* the rebel army, not by endless maneuvers and efforts to occupy Confederate territory. "Once more," Lincoln told his commanding general, "let me tell you, it is indispensable to *you* that you strike a blow."

On May 31, 1862, it was the Confederate general Joseph E. Johnston who struck the first blow at McClellan's army along the Chickahominy River, six miles east of Richmond. In the Battle of Seven Pines (Fair Oaks), only the arrival of Federal reinforcements, who somehow crossed the swol-len river, prevented a disastrous Union defeat. Both sides took heavy casual-ties, and General Johnston was severely wounded. At this point, Robert E. Lee assumed command of the Confederates' main army, the Army of North-ern Virginia, a development that changed the course of the war. Dignified yet fiery, the brilliant Lee, fluent in French and Latin, had graduated second in his class at West Point. During the Mexican War, he had impressed Gen-eral Winfield Scott as the "very best soldier I ever saw in the field." In 1857, Scott predicted that Lee would become America's greatest military leader. Now, as the commander of the Army of Northern Virginia, Lee would prove to be a daring, even reckless, strategist who was as aggressive as McClellan was timid. "He is silent, inscrutable, strong, like a God," said a Confederate officer.

On July 9, when President Lincoln visited McClellan's headquarters on the coast of Virginia, the general complained that the administration had failed to support him and lectured the president at length on military strat-egy. Such insubordination was ample reason to remove McClellan. After re-turning to Washington, Lincoln called Henry Halleck from the West to take charge as general in chief. Miffed at his demotion, McClellan angrily dis-missed Halleck as an officer "whom I know to be my inferior."

Robert E. Lee Military adviser to President Jefferson Davis and commander of the Army of Northern Virginia.

Robert E. Lee takes command of Confederate forces

Lincoln's search for a "fighting general" Abraham Lincoln and George B. McClellan confer at Antietam, October 4, 1862.

Second Bull Run

Confederate victory: Second Battle of Bull Run

Lincoln and Halleck ordered McClellan to move his troops back to Washington, D.C., and join forces with General John Pope, commander of the Union Army of Virginia, in a new assault on Richmond. Pope declared that his goal "was attack and not defense." In a letter to his wife, a jealous McClellan predicted—accurately—that "Pope will be thrashed and disposed of" by Lee's army. Lee moved northward to strike Pope's army before McClellan's troops arrived. The Confederate commander knew that his only chance was to drive a wedge between the two larger Union armies so that he could deal with them one at a time. Violating a basic rule of military strategy, Lee riskily divided his forces, sending Stonewall Jackson's "foot cavalry" around Pope's flank to attack his supply lines in the rear. At the Second Battle of Bull Run (or Manassas), fought in exhausting heat on almost the same site as the earlier battle, a confused Pope assumed that he faced only Jackson, but Lee's main army by that time had joined in. On August 30, 1862, a crushing Confederate attack drove the larger Union army from the field, giving the Confederates a sensational victory and leading one disheartened Union officer to confess from his death bed that "General Pope had been outwitted. . . . Our generals have defeated us." In contrast, a Rebel soldier from Georgia wrote home that "General Lee stands now above all generals in modern history. Our men will follow him to the end."

Emancipation

CORE **OBJECTIVE**

2. Evaluate Lincoln's decision to issue the Emancipation Proclamation and its impact on the war.

The Confederate victories in 1862 devastated northern morale and convinced Lincoln that he had to take bolder steps to win the war over an enemy fighting for and aided by enslaved labor. Now the North had to assault slavery itself. Once fighting began in 1861, the Union's need to keep the border slave states (Delaware, Kentucky, Maryland, and Missouri) in the Union had dictated caution on the volatile issue of emancipation. Beyond that, Lincoln had to contend with a deep-seated racial prejudice among most northerners, who were willing to allow slavery to continue in the South. Lincoln himself harbored doubts about his constitutional authority to emancipate slaves.

Slaves in the War

"Contrabands of war"

The expanding war forced the issue. As Federal forces pushed into the Confederacy, runaway slaves began to turn up in Union army camps, and the commanders did not know whether to declare them free. One general designated the fugitive slaves "contrabands of war," and thereafter the slaves who sought protection and freedom with Union forces were known as "**contrabands.**" Some Union officers put the contrabands to work digging trenches and building fortifications; others simply set them free.

Lincoln, meanwhile, began to edge toward emancipation. On April 16, 1862, he signed an act that abolished slavery in the District of Columbia; on

contrabands Runaway slaves who sought refuge in Union military camps or who lived in areas of the Confederacy under Union control.

Contrabands Former slaves on a farm in Cumberland Landing, Virginia, 1862.

June 19 another act excluded slavery from the western territories. Still, Lincoln insisted that the war was about restoring the Union, not ending slavery in the South. Like most northerners, he was more determined to end secession than to end slavery.

But the course of the war changed Lincoln's outlook and transformed the conflict into a struggle for human freedom. In the summer of 1862, Lincoln decided that emancipation of slaves in the Confederate states was necessary to win the war. Many of the more than 3 million enslaved laborers in the Confederacy, he knew, were being forced to aid the Rebel war effort. Further, morale in the North needed a boost, and public opinion was swinging toward emancipation. In July 1862, Lincoln confided to his cabinet that "decisive and extreme measures must be adopted." Emancipation, he said, had become "a military necessity, absolutely necessary to the preservation of the Union. We must free the slaves or be ourselves subdued." Secretary of State William H. Seward agreed, but advised Lincoln to delay the announcement until after a Union battlefield victory to avoid being viewed as desperate.

> Emancipation: Military necessity

Antietam

Robert E. Lee made his own momentous decision in the summer of 1862: he would invade Maryland and thereby force the Union army to leave northern Virginia and relieve the pressure on Richmond, the Confederate capital. He also hoped to gain official recognition of the Confederate nation from Great Britain and France, which would bring desperately needed military supplies to the Confederacy. In addition, Lee and Jefferson Davis hoped to capture

Maryland, with its many Confederate supporters, and separate it from the Union. For those reasons and others, in September 1862, Lee and his troops, many of them ragged and barefoot and all of them underfed, pushed north into western Maryland.

Battle of Antietam (1862)

On September 17, 1862, the Union and Confederate armies clashed in the furious **Battle of Antietam** (Sharpsburg). Had not Union soldiers discovered Lee's detailed battle plans, wrapped around three cigars, which one of his officers had carelessly dropped on the ground, the Confederates might have won. Instead, McClellan, if he moved quickly, could attack Lee's outnumbered forces while they were scattered and on the move. But, as always, McClellan moved slowly, enabling Lee to regroup his scattered units at Sharpsburg, along Antietam Creek. There the poorly coordinated Union army launched repeated attacks. The fighting was savage; a Union officer counted "hundreds of dead bodies lying in rows and in piles." The scene after "five hours of continuous slaughter" was "sickening, harrowing, horrible. O what a terrible sight!"

The next day, Lee braced for another Union attack, but it never came. That night, cloaked by fog and drizzling rain, the battered Confederates slipped south back across the Potomac River to the safety of Virginia. "The 'barefoot boys' have done some terrible fighting," a Georgian wrote his parents. "We are a dirty, ragged set [of soldiers], mother, but courage & heroism find many a true disciple among us."

Although the battle was technically a draw, Lee's northern invasion had failed. McClellan, never known for his modesty, claimed that he "had fought the battle splendidly." To him, the Battle of Antietam was "the most terrible battle of the age." Indeed, it was the bloodiest single day in American military history. Some 6,400 soldiers on both sides were killed, twice as many as at Shiloh, and another 17,000 were wounded. The Confederate people, said a soldier, wanted "an active [military] campaign, and General Lee has certainly given it to us."

President Lincoln was pleased that Lee's army had been forced to retreat, but he was disgusted by McClellan's failure to attack the retreating Confederates and win the war. The president sent a sarcastic message to the general: "I have just read your dispatch about sore-tongued and fatigued horses. Will you pardon me for asking what the horses of your army have done . . . that fatigues anything?" Failing to receive a satisfactory answer, Lincoln again relieved McClellan of his command of the Army of the Potomac and assigned him to recruiting duty in New Jersey. Never again would McClellan command troops, but he would challenge Lincoln for the presidency in 1864 as a Democrat.

The Battle of Antietam had several important results. It revived sagging northern morale, dashed the Confederacy's hopes of forging alliances with Great Britain and France, and convinced Abraham Lincoln to free the slaves in the Confederate states as a military necessity.

Battle of Antietam (1862) Turning-point battle near Sharpsburg, Maryland, leaving over 20,000 soldiers dead or wounded, in which Union forces halted a Confederate invasion of the North.

Emancipation Proclamation

The victory at Antietam convinced President Lincoln to take a momentous step. Using his powers as commander in chief of the armed forces, by the stroke of a pen, he changed the conflict from a war to restore the Union to a struggle to end slavery. On September 22, 1862, five days after the battle, he signed the **Emancipation Proclamation**, which announced that "as a necessary war measure" all slaves in the Rebel states were to be made "forever free" on January 1, 1863. He added that free blacks and escaped slaves would now be welcomed into the Union army and navy. The Emancipation Proclamation did not free the 500,000 enslaved blacks in the four Union border states of Delaware, Kentucky, Maryland, and Missouri, or the 300,000 slaves in Tennessee, western Virginia, coastal Carolina, and parts of Louisiana which were back under Union control. As he signed the Emancipation Proclamation, Lincoln said, "I never, in my life, felt more certain that I was doing the right thing than I do in signing this paper." Simply restoring the Union was no longer the purpose of the war; the transformation of the South was now the goal.

> Emancipation Proclamation: Civil War becomes a struggle to end slavery

Reactions to Emancipation

Although Lincoln's proclamation technically freed only the slaves where Confederates remained in control, many slaves in both the North and the South claimed their freedom anyway. As Lincoln had hoped, word of his landmark proclamation spread rapidly among the slave community in the Confederacy, arousing hopes of freedom, creating general confusion in the cities, and encouraging thousands to escape to approaching Union armies. George Washington Albright, an enslaved teen in Mississippi, recalled that white planters tried to prevent slaves from learning about the Proclamation but word of it slipped through the "grapevine." His father, in fact, was inspired by Lincoln's declaration to escape and join the Union army. The younger Albright served as a "runner" for the 4Ls ("Lincoln's Legal Loyal League"), a secret group created to spread the news about the proclamation to slaves throughout the region.

> Union armies liberate Confederate slaves

Confederate leaders were outraged by Lincoln's action, predicting it would ignite a race war in the South. By contrast, Frederick Douglass, the African American abolitionist leader, was overjoyed at Lincoln's "righteous decree" for he knew that, despite its limitations, it would inspire abolitionists in the North and set in motion the eventual end of slavery throughout the United States.

As Lincoln had hoped, the Emancipation Proclamation did indeed aid the Union war effort, not only by enlisting blacks in the army and navy but also by undermining support for the Confederacy in Europe. The conversion of the Civil War from a conflict simply to restore the Union into a crusade to end slavery gave the federal war effort greater moral legitimacy in

Emancipation Proclamation (1863) Military order issued by President Abraham Lincoln that freed slaves in areas still controlled by the Confederacy.

Union view of the Emancipation Proclamation A thoughtful Lincoln composes the proclamation with the Constitution and the Holy Bible in his lap. The Scale of Justice hangs on the wall behind him.

the eyes of Europeans. At the same time, however, many northern Democrats savagely attacked Lincoln's proclamation, calling it dictatorial, unconstitutional, and catastrophic. "We Won't Fight to Free the Nigger," proclaimed one popular banner. A Massachusetts army officer agreed. "I am a strong Union man," he said, "but I am not willing to shed one drop of blood to fight Slavery."

As the war continued and Union armies advanced into the southern states, they liberated the slaves. At Camp Saxton, a former plantation on the coast of South Carolina near Beaufort, the 1st South Carolina Volunteers, a new Union army regiment made up of former slaves, gathered on January 1, 1863, to celebrate the Emancipation Proclamation. After the proclamation was read aloud, it was "cheered to the skies." As Colonel Thomas W. Higginson, a noted white abolitionist from Massachusetts who was the new unit's commander, unfurled an American flag, the black troops spontaneously began singing "My Country 'Tis of Thee / Sweet land of liberty / Of thee I sing!" Higginson reported his emotional reaction: "I never saw anything so electric; it made all other words cheap; it seemed the choked voice of a race at last unloosed. Just think of it!—the first day they had ever had a country, the first flag they had seen which promised anything to their people."

Fredericksburg

In his search for a new general to lead the Union war effort, Lincoln now made the worst choice of all. In the fall of 1862, he turned to 38-year-old Ambrose E. Burnside, a tall, imposing figure whose distinctive facial hair gave rise to the term "sideburns." Twice before, Burnside had turned down the job because he felt unfit for so large a command. He was right, as it turned out. Burnside was an eager fighter but a poor strategist who, according to

Confederate view of the Emancipation Proclamation
Surrounded by demonic faces hidden in his furnishings, Lincoln pens the proclamation with a foot trampling on the Constitution. The devil holds the inkwell before him.

Fanny Seward, the secretary of state's daughter, had "ten times as much heart as he has head." And the Union army soon paid for his mistakes.

On December 13, 1862, Burnside foolishly sent the 122,000 men in the Army of the Potomac west across the icy Rappahannock River to assault Lee's outnumbered forces, who were well entrenched on a line of ridges and behind stone walls west of Fredericksburg, Virginia, midway between Richmond and Washington, D.C. Confederate cannons and muskets chewed up the advancing federal soldiers as they crossed half a mile of open land. The assault was, a Union general regretted, "a great slaughter-pen," more like murder than warfare. Wave after wave of blue-clad troops surged toward the well-protected Confederates. None of the Union soldiers made it. The awful scene led Lee to remark: "It is well that war is so terrible—we should grow too fond of it." After attempting fourteen assaults and taking 12,600 casualties, compared with fewer than 5,300 for the Confederates, a weeping Burnside told his men to withdraw back across the river as darkness fell. As Burnside rode past his retreating men, his aide called for three cheers for their commander. All he got was sullen silence.

The year 1862 ended with forces in the East deadlocked and the Union advance in the West stalled. Union morale plummeted: northern Democrats were victorious in the fall Congressional elections, sharply reducing the Republican majorities in the House and the Senate. Many Democrats were calling for a negotiated peace. Republicans—even Lincoln's own cabinet members—grew increasingly critical of the president's leadership. "If there is a worse place than hell," Lincoln sighed, "I am in it." Newspapers circulated rumors that Lincoln was going to resign. General Burnside, too, was under fire, with some of his own officers eager to testify publicly to his shortcomings. One of them claimed that the general was "fast losing his mind."

> Lincoln loses support over deadlocked war

CAMPAIGNS IN VIRGINIA AND MARYLAND, 1862

Legend:
→ Confederate advance
⇢ Confederate retreat
→ Union advance
⇢ Union retreat
✶ Battle site

- How did the Confederate army defeat General Pope at the Second Battle of Bull Run?
- Why was General Burnside's decision to attack at Fredericksburg a mistake?

New York City Draft Riots

Northern resistance to the war effort

Lincoln's proclamation freeing slaves in the Confederacy created anxiety and anger among many laborers in the North who feared that freed southern blacks would eventually migrate north and take their jobs. In New York City, such fears erupted into violence. In July 1863, a group of 500 wage workers, led by volunteer firemen, assaulted the army draft office, shattering its windows, then burning it down. When the city police superintendent arrived at the scene, he was beaten unconscious, and the outnumbered policemen were forced to retreat. The rioters, now swollen by thousands of working-class whites, mostly Irishmen and including women and children, ruthlessly took out their frustrations over the unfair military draft on blacks. Mobs rampaged through the streets of Manhattan, randomly assaulting African Americans, beating them, dragging them through the streets, and lynching a disabled black man while chanting "Hurrah for Jeff Davis." Thugs also burned down over fifty buildings, including the mayor's home, police stations, two Protestant churches, and the Colored Orphan Asylum, forcing 233 children to flee. The violence went on for three days, killing 105 people and injuring thousands. Only the arrival of federal soldiers put an end to the rioting. Thousands of terrified blacks thereafter moved out of the city for fear of continuing racial violence. Similar riots occurred in other northern cities, including Boston.

Blacks in the Military

In July 1862, in an effort to strengthen the Union war effort, the U.S. Congress had passed the **Militia Act**, which authorized the army to use freed slaves as laborers or soldiers (they were already eligible to serve in the navy). But Lincoln did not encourage the use of freed slaves as soldiers because he feared the reaction in the border states where slavery remained in place. It was only after issuing the Emancipation Proclamation in September that the Union army aggressively recruited blacks. On May 22, 1863, the U.S. War Department created the Bureau of Colored Troops to recruit free blacks and freed slaves. More than 180,000 blacks enlisted in the new U.S. Colored Troops. Some 80 percent of them were from southern states, and 38,000 of them gave their lives. In the navy, African Americans accounted for about a fourth of all enlistments; of these, more than 2,800 died. Initially, blacks were not allowed in combat, but the need to win the prolonged war changed that. Once in battle, they fought tenaciously. A white Union army private reported in the late spring of 1863 that the black troops "fight like the Devil."

To be sure, a still-powerful racism in the North influenced the status of African Americans in the Union military. Many people who opposed slavery did not support racial equality. Black soldiers and sailors were placed in all-black units led by white officers. They were also paid less than whites ($7 per month for black recruits versus $16 for white recruits) and were ineligible for the enlistment bonus paid to whites. Still, as Frederick Douglass declared, "this is no time for hesitation. . . . This is our chance, and woe betide us if we fail to embrace it." Service in the Union army provided former slaves a unique opportunity to grow in confidence, awareness, and maturity. A northern social worker in the South Carolina Sea Islands was "astonished" at the positive effects of "soldiering" on ex-slaves: "Some who left here a month ago to join [the army were] cringing, dumpish, slow," but now they "are ready to look you in the eye—are wide awake and active." By mid-1863, African American units were fighting in battles. Commenting on Union victories at Port Hudson and Milliken's Bend, Louisiana, Lincoln reported that "some of our commanders . . . believe that . . . the use of colored troops constitutes the heaviest blow yet dealt to the rebels."

Black Union Army Sergeant Wearing his sergeant uniform and sword, he poses with a copy of J. T. Headley's *The Great Rebellion* in his hand.

Militia Act (1862) Congressional measure that permitted freed slaves to serve as laborers or soldiers in the United States Army.

CORE **OBJECTIVE**

3. Analyze how the war affected social and economic life in the North and South.

The War behind the Lines

Feeding, clothing, and supplying the vast armies required tremendous sacrifices on the home fronts, both North and South. Farms and villages were transformed into battlefields, churches became makeshift hospitals, civilian life was disrupted, and families grieved the soldiers who would not be coming home.

Women and the War

While breaking the bonds of slavery, the Civil War also loosened traditional restraints on female activity. "No conflict in history," a journalist wrote at the time, "was such a woman's war as the Civil War." Women on both sides played prominent roles. They worked in mills and factories, sewed uniforms, composed patriotic poems and songs, and raised money and supplies. In Greenville, South Carolina, when T. G. Gower went off to fight, his wife Elizabeth took over the family business, converting their carriage factory to produce military wagons and ambulances. Three thousand northern women worked as nurses with the U.S. Sanitary Commission, a civilian agency that provided medical relief and other services for soldiers. Other women, black and white, supported the freedmen's aid movement to help impoverished freed slaves.

In the North alone, some 20,000 women served as nurses or other health-related volunteers. The most famous nurses were Dorothea Lynde Dix and Clara Barton, both untiring volunteers in service to the wounded and the dying. Barton explained that her place was "anywhere between the bullet and the battlefield." Dix declared that nurses should be "sober, earnest, self-sacrificing, and self-sustained" women between the ages of thirty-five and fifty who could "bear the presence of suffering and exercise entire self-control" and who could be "calm, gentle, quiet, active, and steadfast in duty." Barton, who later founded the American Red Cross, claimed that the war advanced by fifty years the progress of women in gaining social and economic equality.

In many southern towns and counties, the home front became a world of white women and children and African American slaves. A resident of Lexington, Virginia, reported that there were "no men left" in town by mid-1862. Women suddenly found themselves full-time farmers or plantation managers, clerks, and teachers. Hundreds of women disguised themselves as men and fought in the war, and dozens served as spies. Others traveled with the armies, cooking meals, writing letters, and assisting with amputations. New Yorker Mary Edwards Walker, a Union battlefield surgeon, was captured and imprisoned by the Confederates for spying. She was the only woman in the war (and since) to be awarded the Congressional Medal of Honor, the nation's highest military award. In 1864, President Lincoln told a soldier that all the praise of women over the centuries did not do justice "for their conduct during the war."

Clara Barton She oversaw the distribution of medicines to Union troops and would later help found the American Red Cross.

Susie King Taylor Born into slavery, she served as a nurse in Union-occupied Georgia and operated a school for freedmen.

Government during the War

While freeing the slaves was a momentous social and economic revolution, an even broader political revolution began as a result of power in Congress shifting from the South to North after secession. Before the war, southern Democratic congressmen exercised considerable influence, but once the secessionists had abandoned Congress to the Republicans, a dramatic change occurred. Several Republican economic projects that had been stalled by southern opposition were adopted before the end of 1862. Congress passed a higher tariff bill to raise government revenue and "protect" American businesses from foreign competition. For the rest of the nineteenth century, U.S. manufacturers were the most protected in the world in terms of high federal tariffs discouraging foreign imports. The Republican Congress also approved construction of a transcontinental railroad to run westward through Omaha, Nebraska, to Sacramento, California. A **Homestead Act** granted 160 acres of public land to settlers who agreed to work the land for five years. The National Banking Act followed in 1863. It created a new federal banking system that effectively eliminated paper currency issued by state banks and created a system of national banks that could issue paper money. Two other key pieces of legislation were the **Morrill Land Grant Act** (1862), which provided federal aid to state-supported colleges and universities teaching "agriculture and mechanic arts," and the Contract Labor Act (1864), which encouraged the importation of immigrant labor. Congress also created a new cabinet-level agency, the Department of Agriculture. All of these wartime measures had long-term significance for the growth of the national economy—and the expansion of the federal government.

> Expanding a national economy and federal government

Union Finances

In December 1860, as southern states announced their plans to secede, the federal treasury was virtually empty. There was not enough cash on hand to fund a massive war. To meet the war's huge expenses, Congress focused on three options: raising taxes, printing paper money, and selling government bonds to investors. The taxes came chiefly in the form of the Morrill Tariff on imports and taxes on manufactures and nearly every profession. A butcher, for example, had to pay thirty cents for every head of beef he slaughtered, ten cents for every hog, and five cents for every sheep.

In 1862, Congress created the Internal Revenue Service to implement the first income tax on citizens and corporations. The first income tax rate was 3 percent on those with annual incomes more than $800. The tax rate went up to 5 percent on incomes over $10,000. Yet very few people paid the taxes. Only 250,000 people out of a population of 39 million had income high enough to pay taxes. The concept of "progressive" taxation, in which tax rates rose with designated income levels, horrified Representative Justin S. Morrill, a Vermont Republican who had authored the Land Grant Act and the Tariff Act of 1862. He argued that the government should not tax "a man

> Financing the war: Internal Revenue Service

Homestead Act (1862)
Legislation granting "homesteads" of 160 acres of government-owned land to settlers who agreed to work the land for at least five years.

Morrill Land Grant Act (1862)
Federal statute that allowed for the creation of land-grant colleges and universities, which were founded to provide technical education in agriculture, mining, and industry.

[more] because he is richer than another. The very theory of our institutions is entire equality, that we make no distinction between the rich man and the poor man." Morrill lost the argument.

Financing the war: Legal Tender Act (1862)

The new federal tax revenues trickled in so slowly—in the end they would meet only 21 percent of wartime expenditures—that Congress in 1862 resorted to printing paper money. Beginning with the Legal Tender Act of 1862, Congress ultimately authorized $450 million in paper currency, which soon became known as *greenbacks* because of the color of the ink used to print the bills. The decision to print paper money was extremely important for the economy. Unlike previous paper currencies issued by local banks, greenbacks could not be exchanged for gold or silver. Instead, their value relied upon public trust in the government. Many bankers were outraged by the issuance of the greenbacks, but the desperate need to finance the war demanded extreme measures. The federal government also relied upon the sale of bonds to help finance the war effort. A Philadelphia banker named Jay Cooke (sometimes tagged the "Financier of the Civil War") mobilized a nationwide campaign to sell $2 billion in government bonds to private investors.

Confederate Finances

Financing the Confederate war effort: Taxation, currency troubles, soaring inflation, and social unrest

Confederate finances were a disaster by comparison. The Confederate government had to create a treasury and a revenue-collecting system from scratch. Moreover, the South's agrarian economy was land-rich but cash-poor compared to that of the North. While the Confederacy owned 30 percent of America's assets (businesses, land, slaves) in 1861, its currency in circulation was only 12 percent of that in the North. In its first year, the Confederacy created a property tax, which should have yielded a hefty amount of revenue. But the collection of the taxes was left to the states, and the result was chaos. In 1863, the desperate Confederate Congress began taxing nearly everything, but enforcement was poor and evasion easy. Altogether, taxes covered no more than 5 percent of Confederate war costs; bond issues accounted for less than 33 percent; and treasury notes (paper money), for more than 66 percent. Over the course of the war, the Confederacy issued more than $1 billion in paper money, which, along with a shortage of consumer goods, caused prices to soar. By 1864 a turkey sold in the Richmond market for $100, flour brought $425 a barrel, and bacon was $10 a pound.

Such rampant inflation (price increases) caused great distress. Poverty drove some southerners to take desperate measures. Frustrations over the burdens of war increasingly erupted into rioting, looting, military desertions, and mass protests against the Confederate government. A poor farmer in Alabama refused to serve in the Confederate army because the war was being fought to preserve the "infurnal negroes" owned by wealthy planters. David Harris, another farmer, deserted from the army because the cause was lost: "I am now going to work instead of to the war," he wrote home.

Union Politics and Civil Liberties

Within his own Republican party, Lincoln faced a radical wing composed mainly of militant abolitionists. Led by Thaddeus Stevens in the House and Charles Sumner in the Senate, the Radical Republicans wanted Union armies to seize southern plantations and give the land to the former slaves. The majority of Republicans, however, continued to back Lincoln's reluctance to confiscate private property.

The Democratic party in the North suffered the loss of its southern wing and the death of its leader, Stephen A. Douglas, in June 1861. By and large, northern Democrats favored the war only for the purpose of restoring the Union "as it was" before 1860, giving reluctant support to Lincoln's war policies but opposing Republican economic legislation. So-called War Democrats, such as Tennessee senator Andrew Johnson and Secretary of War Edwin M. Stanton, backed Lincoln's policies, while a peace wing of the party preferred an end to the fighting, even if that meant risking the Union.

An extreme fringe of the peace wing flirted with outright disloyalty. The **Copperhead Democrats** (poisonous snakes), as they were called, were strongest in states such as Ohio, Indiana, and Illinois. They openly sympathized with the Confederacy and called for an end to the war.

Such support for the enemy led Lincoln to crack down hard. Like all war-time leaders, he faced the challenge of balancing the urgent needs of winning a war with the protection of civil liberties. Early in the war, Lincoln assumed emergency powers, including the power to suspend the writ of *habeas corpus*, which guarantees arrested citizens a speedy hearing before a judge. The Constitution states that the right of *habeas corpus* may be suspended only in cases of rebellion or invasion, but Supreme Court justice Roger Taney and several congressional leaders argued that Congress alone had the authority to take such action. By the Habeas Corpus Act of 1863, Congress authorized the president to suspend the writ. Thereafter, Union soldiers and local sheriffs arrested many Confederate sympathizers in the northern states. Union general Henry Halleck arrested one Missourian for saying, "[I] wouldn't wipe my ass with the stars and stripes."

> Violation of civil liberties in the North

Confederate Politics and States' Rights

Unlike Lincoln, Jefferson Davis never had to face a presidential contest. He and his vice president, Alexander Stephens, were elected without opposition in 1861 for a six-year term. But discontent grew as the war dragged on. Poor white southerners expressed bitter resentment of the planter elite while food grew scarce and prices skyrocketed. A bread riot in Richmond on April 2, 1863, ended only when President Davis himself threatened to shoot the protesters (mostly women).

Davis's greatest challenge came from the southern politicians who had embraced secession and then criticized the powers of the Confederate government in Richmond. As a general reported, "The state of feeling between the President [Davis] and Congress is bad—could not be worse." Critics

Copperhead Democrats
Democrats in northern states who opposed the Civil War and argued for an immediate peace settlement with the Confederates; Republicans labeled them "Copperheads," likening them to poisonous snakes.

asserted states' rights against the authority of the Confederate government, just as they had against the Union. Georgia's governor Joseph Brown hated Jefferson Davis, explaining that he joined the Confederacy to "sustain the rights of the states and prevent the consolidation of the Government, and I am still a *rebel* . . . no matter who may be in power."

States' rights vs. war effort

Among other fatal flaws, the Confederacy suffered from Davis's difficult personality. Whereas Lincoln was a pragmatist, Davis, blind in one eye and suffering chronic headaches, was a brittle ideologue with a stinging temper. Once he made a decision, nothing could change his mind, and he could never admit a mistake. One southern politician said that Davis was "as stubborn as a mule." Such a personality was ill suited to the chief executive of an infant—and fractious—nation. Cabinet members resigned almost as soon as they were appointed. During the four years of the Confederacy, there were three secretaries of state and six secretaries of war. Vice President Stephens carried on a running battle against President Davis's "military despotism," claiming Davis was so "timid, petulant, peevish, and obstinate" that he eventually left Richmond in 1862 to sulk at his Georgia home.

Chancellorsville

After the Union disaster at Fredericksburg at the end of 1862, Lincoln turned to General Joseph Hooker, a hard-fighting, hard-drinking leader whose fierceness had earned him the nickname "Fighting Joe." With a force of 130,000 men, the largest Union army yet gathered, and a brilliant plan, an overconfident Hooker failed his leadership test at Chancellorsville, not a town but a solitary home, the Chancellor House, surrounded by woods in eastern Virginia, in the first week of May, 1863. "My plans are perfect. . . . May God have mercy on General Lee," Hooker boasted, "for I will have none." He spoke too soon. The always bold Robert E. Lee, with perhaps half as many troops, split his army in thirds and gave Hooker a lesson in the art of elusive mobility when Stonewall Jackson's 28,000 Confederates again surprised the Union army, smashing into its exposed right flank, and forcing it to retreat. "It was pandemonium," recalled a Union soldier. "My God, my God," moaned Lincoln when he heard the news. "What will the country say?" The Confederate victory at Chancellorsville was the peak of Lee's military career, but it would also be his last significant victory.

CORE **OBJECTIVE**

4. Describe the military turning points in 1863 and 1864 that ultimately led to the Confederacy's defeat.

The Faltering Confederacy

The Confederate strategy of fighting largely a defensive war worked well in the early years of the war. As the armies maneuvered for battle in the spring of 1863, Robert E. Lee's superior generalship boosted Confederate spirits—until Lincoln found a commanding general as capable as Lee: Ulysses S. Grant.

Vicksburg

While Lee's army held the Federals at bay in the East, Ulysses S. Grant had been inching his army down the Mississippi River toward the Confederate stronghold of Vicksburg, a busy commercial town situated on high bluffs overlooking a sharp horseshoe bend in the river. Capturing the Rebel stronghold, Grant stressed, "was of the first importance." Vicksburg was the only rail and river junction between Memphis, Tennessee, and New Orleans. President Lincoln said Vicksburg held the "key" to a Union victory in the war. If Union forces could gain control of the Mississippi River, they could split the Confederacy in two and prevent Western food and livestock from reaching the Confederate armies in the East. While the Union navy ran gunboats and transports past the Confederate cannons overlooking the river, Grant moved his army eastward on a campaign through Mississippi that Lincoln later called "one of the most brilliant in the world." Grant captured Jackson, Mississippi, before pinning the 31,000 Confederates inside Vicksburg so tightly that "not a cat could have crept out . . . without being discovered."

In the **Battle of Vicksburg**, Grant decided to wear down the encircled Confederates through constant bombardment and gradual starvation. The Rebel soldiers and the city's residents were hopelessly trapped; they could neither escape nor be reinforced nor resupplied with food and ammunition. As the weeks passed, the besieged Confederates ate their horses and mules, then dogs and cats, and, finally, rats. The Confederate commander at Vicksburg wrote Jefferson Davis that the situation was "hopeless." A group of soldiers pleaded with their commander: "If you can't feed us, you had better surrender us, horrible as that idea is."

> Battle of Vicksburg: Gaining control of the Mississippi River

Gettysburg

Vicksburg's plight led Davis to ask Robert E. Lee to send troops to break the siege. Lee, however, had a better idea. He would make another daring strike into the North in hopes of forcing the Union army surrounding Vicksburg to retreat. He also hoped that his northern offensive would persuade peace-seeking northern Copperhead Democrats to end the war on terms favorable to the Confederacy. A Confederate general said the invasion would "either destroy the Yankees or bring them to terms." Or be a disaster for Lee.

In June 1863, the fabled Army of Northern Virginia, which Lee said was made up of "invincible troops" who would "go anywhere and do anything if properly led," again moved northward across western Maryland, taking thousands of animals and wagons as well as throngs of slaves to support the army. The Confederates moved quickly. As a Rebel soldier said, he had enjoyed "breakfast in Virginia, whiskey in Maryland, and supper in Pennsylvania." A Maryland woman reported that the Confederate soldiers were "the dirtiest I ever saw, a most ragged, lean, and hungry set of wolves."

Once the Union commanders realized the Confederates were again moving north, they gave chase, but Lee lost track of the Federals because of the unexplained absence of General J. E. B. Stuart's 5,000 horse soldiers,

Battle of Vicksburg (1863)
A protracted battle in northern Mississippi in which Union forces under Ulysses Grant besieged the last major Confederate fortress on the Mississippi River, forcing the inhabitants into starvation and then submission.

"A Harvest of Death" Timothy H. O'Sullivan's grim photograph of the dead at Gettysburg.

Battle of Gettysburg: Confederate counterstrategy— a northern offensive

who were Lee's "eyes and ears." Stuart, it turned out, had decided to create a panic in the Union capital by threatening an attack on Washington, D.C. On June 28, Lee uttered in exasperation: "I cannot think what has become of Stuart. I ought to have heard from him long before now."

Neither side expected Gettysburg, a crossroads farming town of 2,400 people in southeastern Pennsylvania, a land of rocky ridges and green hillsides crisscrossed with fences, to be the site of a monumental battle. Both armies were caught by surprise when Confederate troops entered the town at dawn on June 30 and encountered Union cavalry units that had been tracking their movements. The main forces of both sides—65,000 Confederates and 85,000 Federals—then raced to the scene, and on July 1, the two armies commenced the **Battle of Gettysburg**, the most dramatic contest of the war. As they prepared to fight, a Union cavalryman who sensed the importance of the coming battle, yelled at the soldiers from New York and Pennsylvania: "You stand alone, between the Rebel army and your homes. Fight like hell!"

Initially, the Confederates pushed the Federals out of the town, but the Union troops retreated into stronger positions on high ridges to the south and west. The new Union commander, the cautious and conservative General George Meade, rushed reinforcements to his new lines along the heights overlooking the town. On July 2, wave after wave of screaming Confederates assaulted Meade's army, pushing the Federal lines back across blood-soaked wheat fields and through peach orchards, but never breaking through. A wounded Confederate officer scrawled a note before he died: "Tell my father I died with my face to the enemy." Some 16,000 were killed or wounded on both sides during the inconclusive second day of fighting. But worse was yet to come.

Battle of Gettysburg (1863) A monumental three-day battle in southern Pennsylvania, widely considered a turning point in the war, in which Union forces successfully countered a second Confederate invasion of the North.

The next day, July 3, against the advice of his senior general, James Longstreet, Robert E. Lee staked everything on one final assault on the well-defended Union lines along Cemetery Ridge. At about two o'clock on the broiling summer afternoon, three Confederate infantry divisions—about 12,500 men in all—emerged from the woods into the brilliant sunlight and prepared for a gallant but doomed attack. General George Pickett, commander of the lead division, told them to "Charge the enemy and remember Old Virginia!"

With drums pounding and bugles blaring, a gray wave began a desperate, mile-long advance up a grassy slope crisscrossed with wooden fences. Awaiting them behind a low stone wall at the top of the ridge were 120 Union cannons and thousands of rifles. It was suicide. As a Union soldier remembered, the Confederates "came on in magnificent order with the step of men who believed themselves invincible." Once the Federals were ordered to fire, the attacking Confederates were "enveloped in a dense cloud of dust. Arms, heads, blankets, guns, and knapsacks were tossed into the clear air." Only a few Rebels made it to the top of the ridge. A general climbed atop the stone wall and shouted: "Come on, boys! Give them the cold steel! Who will follow me?" Two minutes later, he was dead—as was the Confederate assault—when Union soldiers held in reserve rushed to close the gap in their lines.

Pickett's charge

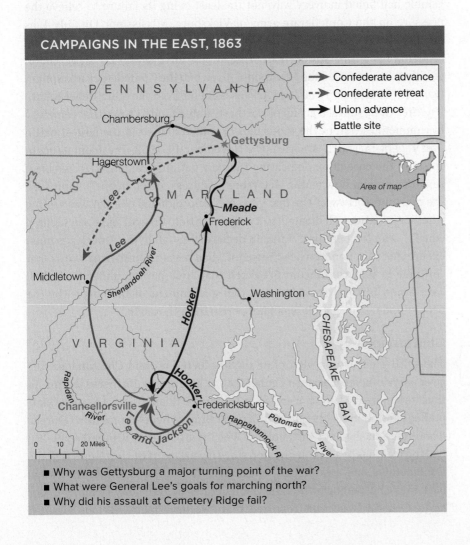

CAMPAIGNS IN THE EAST, 1863

- Why was Gettysburg a major turning point of the war?
- What were General Lee's goals for marching north?
- Why did his assault at Cemetery Ridge fail?

What General Lee had called the "grand charge" was, in the end, a grand failure. As he watched the survivors returning from the bloody field, Lee muttered, "All this has been my fault." He then ordered General Pickett to prepare his battered division for another attack, only to have Pickett tartly reply: "General Lee, I have no division now." Half of his men lay dead or wounded. Some 42,000 on both sides were killed, wounded, or missing over three days at Gettysburg. A Union soldier who witnessed the slaughter on the final day wrote home: "Great God! When will this horrid war stop?"

Again, as after Antietam, Lee's mangled army was forced to retreat back to Virginia in a driving rain—and again, the Federals failed to give chase. Had General Meade pursued Lee's army across Maryland, he might have ended the war, but yet again the winning army failed to capitalize on its victory. President Lincoln was outraged that Meade allowed the Confederates to get away: "We had them within our grasp!" he thundered to his assistant. Lee had escaped to fight again—and the war would grind on for another twenty-one months.

The last Confederate invasion of the North was over. Lee's desperate gamble had failed in every way, not the least being its failure to relieve the pressure on the Confederate army at Vicksburg, Mississippi. On July 4, as Lee's army left Pennsylvania, the Confederate commander at Vicksburg surrendered his entire 30,000-man army after a forty-seven-day siege. Union vessels now controlled the Mississippi River, and the Confederacy was split in two, with Louisiana, Texas, and Arkansas cut off from the other Rebel states.

After Gettysburg, a group of northern states funded a military cemetery in commemoration of the thousands of soldiers killed in the largest battle ever fought in North America. On November 19, 1863, President Lincoln spoke at the ceremony dedicating the new national cemetery. In his brief remarks, known now as the Gettysburg Address, he eloquently expressed the pain and sorrow of the uncivil war. The prolonged conflict was testing whether a nation "dedicated to the proposition that all men are created equal . . . can long endure." Lincoln declared that all living Americans must ensure that the "honored dead" had not "died in vain." In stirring words that continue to inspire, Lincoln predicted that "this nation, under God, shall have a new birth of freedom—and that government of the people, by the people, and for the people, shall not perish from the earth."

Chattanooga

The Battle of Chattanooga: South loses the war in the West

The third great Union victory of 1863 occurred around Chattanooga, the river port railhead of eastern Tennessee and gateway to northern Georgia. In the late summer, a Union army led by General William Rosecrans took Chattanooga and then rashly pursued General Bragg's Rebel forces into Georgia, where they clashed at Chickamauga. The intense battle (September 19–20) had the makings of a Union disaster, since it was one of the few times that the Confederates had a numerical advantage. The battered Union forces fell back into Chattanooga while the Confederates held the city virtually under siege. General Rosecrans reported that "we have met a serious disaster.

Enemy overwhelmed us, drove our right, pierced our center, and scattered troops there." Lincoln urged him to hang on: "If we can hold Chattanooga, and East Tennessee, I think [the] rebellion must dwindle and die." The Union command rushed in reinforcements, and on November 24 and 25, the Federal troops dislodged the Confederates from Lookout Mountain and Missionary Ridge, thereby gaining effective control of east Tennessee. The South had lost the war in the West.

The North Prevails

The dramatic Union victories at Vicksburg, Gettysburg, and Chattanooga turned the tide against the Confederacy. General Lee offered his resignation to Jefferson Davis, but it was refused. He told Lee he could not find a better commander. During the summer and fall of 1863, however, Lincoln's generals in the East lost the momentum that Gettysburg had provided, thereby allowing the Army of Northern Virginia to nurse its wounds and regroup. By 1864, the tenacious Lee was ready to renew the war: "in fine spirits and anxious for a fight." Still, the tone had changed. Earlier, Confederate leaders assumed they could actually win the war and secure their independence. Now, they began to worry about defeat. A Confederate officer in Richmond, writing in his diary after the defeats at Gettysburg and Vicksburg, noted that just a few months earlier the Confederacy had been on the "pinnacle of success—today absolute ruin seems to be our fortune. The Confederacy totters to its destruction." Mary Chesnut of South Carolina confessed in her diary that the war was not going well for her beloved Confederacy. On January 1, 1864, she wrote: "God help my country!"

A Wartime Election

War or no war, 1864 was still a presidential election year. Radical Republicans, upset with the lengthy Union war effort, tried to prevent Lincoln's nomination for a second term, but he consistently outmaneuvered them. Once Lincoln was assured of the party's nomination, he selected Andrew Johnson, a "war Democrat" from Tennessee, as his running mate on the "National Union" ticket, so named to promote bipartisanship during the war. At their 1864 national convention in Chicago, the Democrats called for an immediate end to the war. They nominated General George B. McClellan, the former Union commander who had sparred with Lincoln, his commander in chief, often calling him a "gorilla" and "an idiot." The Confederates hoped that if they could gain a military advantage it might help lead to Lincoln's defeat in November.

Lincoln doubted that the war-weary voters would give him a second term. To boost his reelection chances in the 1864 election, the president brought his best general, Ulysses S. Grant, to Washington, D.C., in March 1864, gave him overall command of the Union war effort, and promised him all the troops and supplies he needed. A New York newspaper reported that Lincoln's presidency was now "in the hands of General Grant, and the failure of the General will be the overthrow of the president."

Ulysses S. Grant takes command of Union forces

Ulysses S. Grant At his headquarters in City Point (now Hopewell), Virginia.

Grant's Strategy

The cigar-chewing Grant was a hard-nosed warrior. One soldier said that Grant always looked like he was "determined to drive his head through a brick wall and was about to do it." The Union commander had a simple concept of war: "Find out where your enemy is, get to him as soon as you can, and strike him as hard as you can, and keep moving on"—regardless of the number of dead and wounded.

Grant dramatically changed the Union military strategy. He planned for the three largest Union armies, one in Virginia, one in Tennessee, and one in Louisiana to launch offensives in the spring of 1864 in which the fighting would never cease. No more short battles followed by long pauses. The Union would force the outnumbered Confederates to keep fighting constantly, thereby wearing them out. Grant assigned his trusted friend and fierce fighter, General William Tecumseh Sherman, a rail-thin, red-haired Ohioan, to lead the Union army in Tennessee and apply Grant's strategy of "complete conquest" to invade Georgia and the heart of the Confederacy. Grant and Sherman would now wage total war, confiscating or destroying civilian property that might be of use to the military. It was a ruthless and costly plan, but in the end effective.

Grant's Pursuit of Lee

In May 1864, the Union's massive Army of the Potomac, numbering about 115,000 soldiers to Lee's 65,000, moved south across the Rappahannock and Rapidan Rivers in eastern Virginia. In the nightmarish Battle of the Wilderness (May 5–6), the armies fought blindly through dense woods thick with vines, thorns, and briars. It was a hellish scene; the tangled underbrush caught fire from exploding artillery shells, and many wounded men burned to death. Grant's men suffered heavier casualties than the Confederates, but the Rebels were running out of replacements. Always before, when bloodied by Lee's troops, Union forces had pulled back to rest and recover, but Grant continued to push southward, keeping the pressure on Lee. "Whatever happens," he assured Lincoln, "we will not retreat." Grant "was like a bulldog," Lincoln said. "Let him get his teeth in, and nothing can shake him loose."

In the first days of June 1864, just as Republican party leaders were gathering to renominate Lincoln as their presidential candidate for the fall election, Grant attacked Lee's well-entrenched army at Cold Harbor near the Chickahominy River, ten miles east of Richmond. In twenty minutes, almost 4,000 attacking Federals, caught in a blistering cross-fire, were killed or wounded. A Confederate commander reported that "it was not war; it was murder."

Grant later admitted that the botched attack was his greatest mistake. Critics, including Lincoln's wife Mary, called him "the Butcher" after Cold Harbor. Yet he knew that his massive army could replace its dead and wounded; the Confederates could not. While the Confederates were winning battles, they were losing more and more men who could not be replaced.

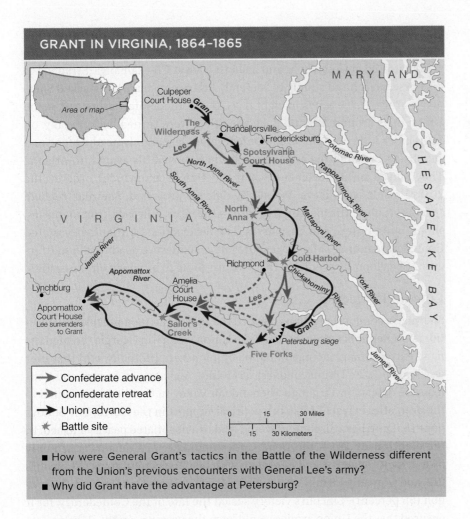

GRANT IN VIRGINIA, 1864–1865

- → Confederate advance
- --→ Confederate retreat
- → Union advance
- ✳ Battle site

0   15   30 Miles
0   15   30 Kilometers

■ How were General Grant's tactics in the Battle of the Wilderness different from the Union's previous encounters with General Lee's army?
■ Why did Grant have the advantage at Petersburg?

Grant kept the pressure on. He brilliantly maneuvered his battered forces around Lee's army and headed for Petersburg, twenty-five miles south of Richmond, where the major railroads converged. The opposing armies then dug in along long lines of trenches above and below Petersburg. Grant telegraphed Lincoln that he intended "to fight it out on this line if it takes all summer." For nine months, the two armies faced each other down. Grant's troops, twice as numerous as the Confederate army, were generously supplied by Union vessels moving up the James River, while Lee's men, hungry and cold, wasted away. Petersburg had become Lee's prison while disasters piled up for the Confederacy elsewhere.

Sherman Pushes through the South

Meanwhile, General Sherman moved his army south from Chattanooga through the Georgia mountains toward the crucial railroad hub of Atlanta. He sent a warning to the city's residents intended to frighten them: "prepare for my coming." By the middle of July, Sherman's troops had reached the outskirts of Atlanta, trapping the Confederate soldiers there. Their commander, General John Bell Hood of Texas, was a recklessly aggressive

The burning of Atlanta

fighter. A Confederate senator's wife said that "a braver man, a purer patriot, a more gallant soldier never breathed than General Hood." He had had an arm shattered at Gettysburg and had lost a leg at Chickamauga. Strapped to his horse, he refused simply to "defend" Atlanta; instead, he attacked Sherman's army. Three times in eight days, the Confederates lashed out at the Union lines around Atlanta. Each time they were turned back. Finally, on September 1 the outnumbered Confederates, desperately needing food and supplies, evacuated the city. Sherman then moved his army into Atlanta. They stayed until November, when the Union commander ordered the 20,000 residents to leave. When city officials protested, Sherman replied: "War is cruelty." His men then set fire to the city's railroads, iron foundries, shops, mills, hotels, and businesses. The destruction of Atlanta devastated Confederate morale. Mary Chesnut "felt as if all were dead within me, forever." She gloomily predicted that "we are going to be wiped off the earth."

Lincoln Reelected

Abraham Lincoln reelected (1864)

Sherman's conquest of Atlanta turned the tide of the 1864 presidential election. As a Republican senator said, the Union victory in Georgia "created the most extraordinary change in public opinion here [in the North] that ever was known." The Union conquest of Mobile, Alabama, in August, and Confederate defeats in Virginia's Shenandoah Valley in October contributed to the dramatic revival of Lincoln's political support in the North. The South's hope that northern discontent would lead to a negotiated peace vanished. In the **election of 1864**, the Democratic candidate, McClellan, carried only New Jersey, Delaware, and Kentucky, with just 21 electoral votes to Lincoln's 212, and won only 1.8 million popular votes (45 percent) to Lincoln's 2.2 million (55 percent). Lincoln's victory sealed the fate of the Confederacy, for it ensured that the Union armies would keep the pressure on the Rebels.

While Confederate forces made their last stands, Abraham Lincoln prepared for his second term as president. He was the first president since Andrew Jackson to have been reelected. The weary commander in chief had made many mistakes and weathered constant criticism during his first term, but with the war nearing its end, Lincoln now received well-deserved praise. The *Chicago Tribune* observed that the president "has slowly and steadily risen in the respect, confidence, and admiration of the people."

Sherman's "March to the Sea"

election of 1864 Abraham Lincoln's successful re-election campaign, capitalizing on Union military successes in Georgia, to defeat his Democratic opponent, former general George B. McClellan, who ran on a peace platform.

Sherman's "March to the Sea" (1864) The Union army's devastating march through Georgia from Atlanta to Savannah led by General William T. Sherman, intended to demoralize civilians and destroy the resources the Confederate army needed to fight.

In November 1864, Sherman's army began its fabled **"March to the Sea,"** advancing rapidly through Georgia, where no organized Confederate armies remained. He planned to "whip the rebels, to humble their pride, to follow them into their inmost recesses, and make them fear and dread us." Hood's Confederate army, meanwhile, went in the opposite direction, pushing northward into Tennessee, trying to lure Sherman into chasing them. But the Union commander refused to take the bait. He was determined to push southward through Georgia and into South Carolina, the seedbed of secession.

In the Battle of Franklin (November 30, 1864), near Nashville, General Hood, against the advice of his generals, sent his army across two miles of open ground defended by dug-in Union troops backed by cannons. It was another example of valiant suicide. In a few hours, Hood lost six generals and 1,750 men, more than had been killed in "Pickett's Charge" at Gettysburg. A Confederate captain, scarred by the battle's senseless butchery, wrote that the "wails and cries of the widows and orphans made at Franklin, Tennessee, will heat up the fires of the bottomless pit to burn the soul of General J. B. Hood for murdering their husbands and fathers." Finally, in the Battle of Nashville (December 15–16), the Federals scattered what was left of Hood's army. A few days later, Hood was relieved of his command. One of Hood's soldiers said that he was a "brave, good, noble, and gallant" man, "but as a general he was a failure."

Meanwhile, Sherman's 62,000 soldiers pushed southward across Georgia. His troops lived off the land, destroying plantations, farms, crops, and rail lines. Sherman said he wanted to "make Georgia howl" so as to convince the people to surrender. "We are not only fighting hostile armies," Sherman explained, "but a hostile people" who must "feel the hard hand of war." By the time Sherman's army arrived in Savannah, on the coast, after a month of plundering their way across the Georgia countryside, his troops had freed more than 40,000 slaves, burned scores of plantations, and destroyed railroads. On December 24, 1864, Sherman sent a whimsical telegram to President Lincoln offering him the city of Savannah as a Christmas present. After the war, a Confederate officer acknowledged that Sherman's march through Georgia was well conceived and well managed. "I don't think there was ever

William Tecumseh Sherman
Sherman's campaign developed into a war of maneuver, without the pitched battles of Grant's campaign, but he pushed relentlessly through Georgia.

Destroying southern railroads
Sherman's troops cut a swath of destruction across Georgia in his "March to the Sea." Here, Union troops rip up railroad tracks in Atlanta.

SHERMAN'S CAMPAIGNS, 1864–65

Legend:
→ Confederate forces
→ Union forces
✳ Battle site

- What was General Sherman's goal as he marched across Georgia?
- How much damage did Sherman do in Georgia and South Carolina?
- How did it affect the Confederate war effort?

an army in the world that would have behaved better, in a similar expedition, in an enemy country. Our army certainly wouldn't have."

After occupying Savannah, Sherman's army crossed the Savannah River into South Carolina, the "hell-hole of secession." Sherman reported that his "whole army is burning with an insatiable desire to wreak vengeance upon South Carolina. I almost tremble at her fate, but feel she deserves all that seems in store for her." The Union army burned more than a dozen South Carolina towns, including the state capital of Columbia, which was captured on February 17, 1865.

During the late winter and early spring of 1865, the shrinking Confederacy found itself besieged on all sides. Defeat was in the air. But Jefferson Davis rejected any talk of surrender. If the Confederate armies should be defeated, he wanted the soldiers to scatter and fight an unending guerrilla war. "The war came and now it must go on," he stubbornly insisted, "till the last man of this generation falls in his tracks, and his children seize his musket and fight our battle."

Appomattox

Confederate surrender at Appomattox Court House

During the spring of 1865, General Grant's army kept pushing, probing, and battering the Rebels defending Petersburg, Virginia, twenty miles south of Richmond. The badly outnumbered Confederates were slowly starving. Something had to give. On April 2, 1865, Lee's army tried to break out of

Petersburg in a desperate flight south. But the Union army was in hot pursuit. On April 7, Grant sent a note to Lee urging him to surrender. With his army virtually surrounded, Lee recognized that "there is nothing left for me to do but go and see General Grant, and I would rather die a thousand deaths."

On April 9 (Palm Sunday) the tall, dignified Lee, in his formal dress uniform, met the short, mud-spattered Grant in the village of **Appomattox Court House**. Grant displayed extraordinary generosity in keeping with Lincoln's desire for a gracious peace. At Lee's request, he let the Confederates keep their pistols, horses, and mules, and he ensured that none of them would be tried for treason, despite the demands of many Radical Republicans in Congress. Lee then confessed that his men were starving, and Grant ordered that they be provided 25,000 rations. After signing the surrender documents, Lee mounted his horse and returned to his army.

The next day, as the gaunt, hungry Confederate troops formed ranks for the last time, Joshua Chamberlain, the Union general in charge of the surrender ceremony, ordered his soldiers to salute their foes as the Rebel soldiers paraded past to give up their weapons. His Confederate counterpart signaled his men to do likewise. Chamberlain remembered that there was not a sound—no trumpets or drums, no cheers or jeers, simply an "awed stillness . . . as if it were the passing of the dead." The remaining Confederate forces surrendered in May. Jefferson Davis fled Richmond by train ahead of the advancing Federal troops, only to be captured in Georgia by Union cavalry on May 10. He was eventually imprisoned in Virginia for two years.

The brutal war was at last over. Upon learning of the Union victory, John Wilkes Booth, a popular young actor in Washington, D.C., wrote in his diary that "something decisive and great must be done" to avenge the Confederate defeat.

A Transforming War

CORE **OBJECTIVE**
5. Explain how the Civil War changed the nation.

The Civil War was the most traumatic event in American history. "We have shared the incommunicable experience of war," reflected Oliver Wendell Holmes Jr., the twice-wounded Union officer who would one day become the nation's leading jurist. "We have felt, we still feel, the passion of life to its top. . . . In our youth, our hearts were touched by fire." In Virginia, elderly Edmund Ruffin, the arch secessionist planter who had been given the honor of firing the first shots at Fort Sumter, was so distraught by the Confederate surrender that he put his rifle barrel in his mouth and blew off the top of his head.

The long war changed the nation in profound ways. A *New York Times* editorial said that the war left "nothing as it found it. . . . It leaves us a different people in everything." The war's terrible ferocity shattered countless lives and destroyed the South's economy, many of its railroads and factories, much of its livestock, and several of its cities. The former Confederacy was a

Appomattox Court House Virginia village where Confederate general Robert E. Lee surrendered to Union general Ulysses S. Grant on April 9, 1865.

Why Was the North Victorious in the Civil War?

Historians have long debated the reasons for the Union's defeat of the Confederacy in the Civil War and will continue to do so. Clearly, the North had many advantages, particularly in population and economic and financial resources.

	North	South
Population	22 million people	9 million people
Manufacturing	93% of nation's manufactured goods 97% of nation's firearms 96% of nation's railroad equipment	7% of nation's manufactured goods
Finance	**Nation's financial center** Banking reforms during the war allowed the Union to sell $2 billion in bonds to private investors and print $450 million in paper money	**Land-rich but cash-poor** Struggle to raise revenue to support the war; printing over $1 billion in paper currency without backing by revenue collection or bonds resulted in rampant inflation
Geography	Securing Union's border states gave Union troops greater access to rivers on which to launch their invasions	Much of war was fought in the South, giving Confederacy a "home-field advantage" and support from civilian population Challenge for Union to conquer large geographical area of Confederacy

landscape of ruin, wreckage, and bankruptcy. In 1860, the northern and southern economies were essentially equal in size. By 1865, the southern economy's productivity had been cut in half. Many among the southern economic and political leaders had either been killed during the war or had seen their plantations and businesses destroyed.

The Union Preserved

Expansion of federal government and power shift to the North

The war also ended the Confederacy and preserved the Union, shifted the political balance of power from South to North, in Congress the U.S. Supreme Court, and the presidency, and boosted the northern economy. The Homestead Act (1862) made more than a billion acres in the West available to the landless. The war greatly expanded the power and scope of the federal government at the expense of states' rights. In 1860, the annual federal budget was $63 million; by 1865, it was over $1 billion. In winning the war, the federal government had become the nation's largest employer.

	North	South
African Americans and Slavery	**Militia Act (1862)** Authorized African American enlistment into Union Army Some 180,000 served, over 80% in South	More than 30% of population, or 3.5 million, were slaves at the start of Civil War **Emancipation Proclamation (1863)** damaged southern economy, encouraged slaves to run away, enlist with Union, or passively resist in the South; eliminated chance of a European power (such as England or France) becoming Confederate military ally
Leadership	The pragmatic President Lincoln favored tenacious generals such as Ulysses S. Grant and William T. Sherman, over the cautious and weak Grant and Sherman developed the "total war" strategy that defeated Confederate forces in the West and eventually subdued the Confederate rebellion	Rigid and doctrinaire, President Davis was unable to maintain political support or public confidence South started with superior military leaders, but many were killed throughout war Southern governors asserted states' rights and resisted Davis's efforts to centralize power and drive war effort

QUESTIONS FOR ANALYSIS

1. What were the Union's key advantages?

2. How did President Lincoln's decision to make the Civil War a fight to end slavery affect the outcome?

3. Given critical Northern advantages, why was the Confederacy able to hold out for so long?

By the end of the war, the Union was spending $2.5 million per day on the military effort. Samuel Colt of New Haven, Connecticut, manufactured Colt pistols for the army. "Run the armory day and night with double sets of hands," he told his foreman. The war-related expenditures by the Union generated whole new industries to meet the military's needs for weapons, uniforms, food, equipment, and supplies. The massive amount of preserved food required by the Union armies, for example, helped create the canning industry and transformed Chicago into the meatpacking capital of the world. Federal contracts also accelerated the growth of new industries such as iron/steel and petroleum products, thus laying the groundwork for the postwar economic boom led by tycoons such as J. Pierpont Morgan, John D. Rockefeller, Andrew W. Mellon, and Andrew Carnegie. Ohio senator John Sherman, in a letter to his brother, General William T. Sherman, said the war had dramatically expanded the vision "of leading capitalists" who now talk of earning "millions as confidently as formerly of thousands."

> The war boosts northern industries

The First "Modern" War

Devastating human losses

In many respects, the Civil War became the first modern war. Its scope and scale were unprecedented, as it was fought across the entire continent, from Pennsylvania to New Mexico and from Florida to Kansas. One of every twelve men on both sides served in the war, and few families were unaffected. Over 730,000 soldiers and sailors (37,000 of whom were blacks fighting for the Union side) died in the conflict, 50 percent more than the number who would die in the Second World War. Of the surviving combatants, 50,000 returned home with one or more limbs amputated. Disease, however, was the greatest threat to soldiers, killing twice as many as were lost in battle. Some 50,000 civilians were also killed during the war.

Emergence of modern technologies and war reporting

Unlike previous conflicts, much of the fighting in the Civil War was "modern" in that it was distant, impersonal, and mechanical. Men were often killed at long distance, without ever knowing who had fired the shots that felled them. The opposing forces used an array of new weapons and instruments of war: cannons with "rifled," or grooved, barrels for greater accuracy; repeating rifles; ironclad ships; railroad artillery; the first military telegraph; observation balloons; and, wire entanglements. The war was also modern in that civilians could follow its activities by reading the popular newspapers that sent reporters to the front lines, or by visiting exhibitions of photographs taken at the battlefields and camps.

Social Changes Wrought by the War

The war also generated significant social changes. Women's roles were transformed. "No conflict in history," a journalist wrote at the time, "was such a woman's war as the Civil War." The requirements of war enabled women to become nurses, farm or business managers, and executives of new organizations. So many ministers left their congregations to become military chaplains that lay people, especially women, assumed even greater responsibility for religious activities in churches and synagogues. The war's awful carnage took a terrible personal toll on women. Hundreds of thousands of women were widowed by the war or saw their lives permanently transformed by the return of husbands with missing limbs or ghastly wounds.

Social changes for women and African Americans

The war also transformed the religious life of African Americans, many of whom saw the war and emancipation as a modern biblical Exodus: God's miraculous intervention on behalf of a chosen people in bondage. In those areas of the South taken over by Union armies, freed slaves were able to create their own churches for the first time.

Thirteenth Amendment

Thirteenth Amendment: Four million slaves freed

By far, however, the most important result of the war was the liberation of slaves. Lincoln had not intended to end slavery when the war began, but the course of the war changed his mind. The Emancipation Proclamation had freed only those slaves in areas still controlled by the Confederacy. As the war entered its final months, however, freedom for all slaves emerged more fully as a legal reality. Three major steps occurred in January 1865, three months before the war ended: Missouri and then Tennessee abolished slavery by state action, and, at the insistent urging of President Lincoln, the U.S. House of Representatives passed an amendment to the U.S. Constitution that banned slavery everywhere. Upon ratification by three-fourths of the reunited states, the **Thirteenth Amendment** became law eight months after the war ended, on December 18, 1865. It removed any lingering doubts about the legality of emancipation. By then, in fact, slavery remained only in the border states of Kentucky and Delaware.

The Debate Continues

In some respects, the Civil War has not yet been resolved. Historians have provided conflicting assessments of the Union victory. Some have focused on the inherent weaknesses of the Confederacy: its lack of industry and railroads, the tensions between the states and the central government in Richmond, poor political leadership, faulty political-military coordination and communication, the expense of preventing slave rebellions and runaways, and the advantages in population and resources enjoyed by the North. Still others have highlighted the erosion of Confederate morale in the face of terrible food shortages, soaring prices, and unimaginable human losses.

The debate over why the North won and the South lost will probably never end, but as in other modern wars, firepower and manpower were essential factors. Robert E. Lee's own explanation retains an enduring accuracy: "After four years of arduous service marked by unsurpassed courage and fortitude, the Army of Northern Virginia has been compelled to yield to overwhelming numbers and resources." Whatever the reasons, the North's victory resolved a key issue: no state could divorce itself from the Union. The Union, as Lincoln had insisted, was indissoluble, now and forever.

Thirteenth Amendment (1865) Amendment to the U.S. Constitution that freed all slaves in the United States.

■ **Civil War Strategies** Southerners were optimistic when the war began. The Confederates had a geographic advantage in that they were fighting a defensive war on their own territory. Confederate diplomacy also anticipated massive support from Britain and France, support that never materialized. The Union, however, held strong advantages in terms of population and industrial development. The Union quickly launched a campaign to seize the Confederate capital, Richmond, Virginia. Initial hopes for a rapid victory died at the First Battle of Bull Run. The Union then adopted the *Anaconda Plan,* which involved imposing a naval blockade on southern ports and slowly crushing resistance on all fronts.

■ **Emancipation Proclamation** Gradually, Lincoln came to see that winning the war required ending slavery. He justified the *Emancipation Proclamation* (1862) as a military necessity because it would deprive the South of its captive labor force. After the *Battle of Antietam* in September 1862, he announced his plans to free the slaves. He hoped that southern states would return to the Union before his January 1, 1863 deadline, when all slaves living in areas under Confederate control were declared free. Many slaves freed themselves by escaping to Union army camps. In July 1862, with the *Militia Act,* Congress had declared that freed slaves could join the Union army. During 1863, blacks, both free and freed, joined the Union army in large numbers, giving the Union military a further advantage over the Confederacy. Although the Emancipation Proclamation announced the war aim of abolishing slavery, it freed only those in areas still under Confederate control.

■ **Wartime Home Fronts** The Union government proved much more capable with finances than did its Confederate counterparts. Through a series of tariffs, income taxes, bond issues, and banking reforms, the Union was better able to absorb the war's soaring costs. In the absence of the southern Democrats in Congress, the Republican-controlled Congress also created a cabinet-level Department of Agriculture, approved a higher tariff, a transcontinental railroad, a *Homestead Act,* and a Contract Labor Act, all of which accelerated Union settlement of the West and the growth of a national economy. The Confederate finances, on the other hand, were pitiful in the cash-poor South. The Confederate treasury department was forced to print so much money that it created spiraling inflation of consumer prices and civil unrest. Also, most of the warfare took place in the South; thus, although the North had more casualties, the physical impact on the South was much greater.

■ **The Winning Union Strategy** The Union victories at the *Battles of Vicksburg* and *Gettysburg* in July 1863 were a major turning point of the war. With the capture of Vicksburg, Union forces cut the Confederacy in two, depriving armies in the east of western supplies and manpower. General Robert E. Lee and the Army of Northern Virginia lost a third of its troops after the defeat at Gettysburg, forcing the Confederates to adopt a defensive strategy. In 1864, Lincoln placed General Ulysses S. Grant in charge of the Union's war efforts, and he initiated a strategy to make the best use of the Union's advantages in manpower and supplies. For the next year, his forces constantly attacked Lee's in Virginia while, farther south, General William T. Sherman conquered Georgia and South Carolina. *Sherman's "March to the Sea"* across Georgia destroyed plantations, railroads, and morale. Sherman's successes helped propel Lincoln to victory in the *election of 1864.* After that, southern resistance wilted, forcing Lee to surrender his army to General Grant at *Appomattox Court House* in April 1865.

■ **The Significance of the Civil War** The Civil War involved the largest number of casualties of any American war. The Union's victory changed the course of the nation's development. Most important, the Civil War brought about the destruction of slavery. Not only did the power of the federal government increase as a result of the war, but the center of political and economic power shifted away from the South and the planter class. The Republican-controlled Congress enacted many pieces of legislation favored by northern voters that would drive the nation's economic development for the rest of the century.

KEY TERMS

CHRONOLOGY

April 1861	Virginia, North Carolina, Tennessee, and Arkansas join Confederacy; West Virginia splits from Virginia to stay with Union
July 1861	First Battle of Bull Run (Manassas)
March–July 1862	Peninsular Campaign
April–August 1862	Battles of Shiloh, Second Bull Run, and Antietam; New Orleans seized by Union forces
July 1862	Congress passes the Militia Act
September 1862	Lincoln issues Emancipation Proclamation
May–July 1863	Siege of Vicksburg, Battle of Gettysburg
November 1863	Battle of Chattanooga
March 1864	General Grant takes charge of Union military operations
September 1864	General Sherman seizes and burns Atlanta
November 1864	Lincoln is reelected
	Sherman's "March to the Sea"
April 9, 1865	General Lee surrenders at Appomattox Court House
1865	Thirteenth Amendment is ratified

INQUIZITIVE

Go to InQuizitive to see what you've learned—and learn what you've missed—with personalized feedback along the way.

***A VISIT FROM THE OLD MISTRESS* (1876)** This powerful painting by Winslow Homer depicts a plantation mistress visiting her former slaves in the postwar South. Although their living conditions are humble, these freedwomen stand firmly and eye-to-eye with the woman who kept them in bondage.

Reconstruction

1865–1877

In the spring of 1865, the Civil War was finally over. The United States was a "new nation," said an Illinois congressman, because it was now "wholly free." At a frightful cost of over 700,000 lives and the destruction of the southern economy, the Union had won the terrible war, and some 4 million enslaved Americans in the South and border states had seized their freedom. This was the most dramatic social change in the history of the nation. No longer would enslaved workers be whipped by their white owners, nor sold and separated from their families, nor prevented from learning to read and write or attending church. "I felt like a bird out of a cage," said former slave Houston Holloway from Georgia. "Amen. Amen. Amen. I could hardly ask to feel any better than I did that day."

In some places it took longer for freedom to be recognized and enforced. In 1865, Henry Adams left the Louisiana plantation where he had been enslaved "to see whether I am free by going without a pass." A group of whites confronted him on the road, asked the name of his owner, and beat him when he declared that "I now belong to no one." Some slaves rushed to give themselves new names to symbolize their new status. Other slaves left plantations and farms for cities, where, as one of them said, "freedom was free-er."

The ratification of the Thirteenth Amendment to the U.S. Constitution in December 1865 was intended to end all doubt about the status of former slaves by abolishing slavery everywhere. Now the nation faced the huge task of "reconstructing" and reuniting a ravaged South while helping to transform ex-slaves into free workers and equal citizens. It would not be easy. As

CORE
OBJECTIVES INQUIZITIVE

1. Identify the federal government's major challenges in reconstructing the South after the Civil War during the period from 1865 to 1877.

2. Describe how and why Reconstruction policies changed over time.

3. Assess the attitudes of white and black southerners toward Reconstruction.

4. Analyze the political and economic factors that helped lead to the end of Reconstruction in 1877.

5. Explain the significance of Reconstruction for the nation's future.

a South Carolina planter threatened a federal official in the fall of 1865, "The war is not over."

The postwar Reconstruction Era, from 1865 to 1877, was a period during which former slaves became citizens. In addition, political leaders of the Reconstruction Era wrestled with how best to bring the Confederate states back into the Union. Those years witnessed a complex debate about the role of the federal government in ensuring civil rights. Some northerners wanted the former Confederate states returned to the Union with little or no changes in the South's social, political, and economic life. Others wanted the former Confederate political and military leaders imprisoned or executed and the South rebuilt in the image of the rest of the nation. Still others wanted the federal government to spend less time focused on the defeated South and more time promoting northern economic growth and westward expansion. Although the Reconstruction Era lasted only twelve years, it was one of the most significant periods in U.S. history. The decisions that were made and the policies enacted are still shaping American life nearly a hundred and fifty years later.

CORE **OBJECTIVE**

1. Identify the federal government's major challenges in reconstructing the South after the Civil War during the period from 1865 to 1877.

The War's Aftermath in the South

The former Confederacy presented a sharp contrast to the victorious North. Throughout the South, people were emotionally exhausted; many lives had been shattered. In 1866, the state of Mississippi spent a fifth of its annual budget on artificial limbs for Confederate soldiers. Property values had collapsed. In the year after the war ended, eighty-one plantations in Mississippi were sold for less than a tenth of what they had been worth in 1860. Confederate money was worthless; personal savings had vanished. Confederate general Braxton Bragg returned to his "once prosperous" Alabama home to find "all, all was lost, except my debts."

Many of the largest southern cities—Richmond, Atlanta, Columbia—were in ruins; most railroads were damaged or destroyed; many southerners, white and black, were homeless and hungry. Emancipation wiped out $4 billion invested in slavery, which had enabled the explosive growth of the cotton culture. But the expansion in the cotton market was over. Not until 1879 would the cotton crop again equal the record harvest of 1860; tobacco production did not regain its prewar level until 1880; the sugar crop of Louisiana did not recover until 1893; and the old rice industry along the coast of South Carolina and Georgia never regained its prewar levels of production or profit. In 1860, just before the Civil War, the South generated 30 percent of the nation's wealth; in 1870, only ten years later, it produced but 12 percent.

The process of forming new state governments in the South first required deciding the official status of the seceded states: Were they now conquered

Deciding the status of Confederate states and freed slaves

Richmond after the Civil War Before evacuating the capital of the Confederacy, Richmond, Virginia, local mobs set fire to warehouses and factories to prevent their falling into Union hands. Pictured here is one of Richmond's burnt districts in April 1865. Women in mourning attire walk among the shambles.

territories? If so, then the Constitution assigned Congress authority to re-create their state governments. But what if, as Abraham Lincoln had argued, the Confederate states had never officially left the Union because the act of secession was itself illegal? In that circumstance, the president would be responsible for re-forming state governments. Whichever branch of government—Congress or the President—directed the reconstruction of the South, it would have to address the most complicated and controversial issue: What would be the political, social, and economic status of the freed slaves? Were they citizens? If not, what was their status as Americans?

The Battle over Political Reconstruction

> CORE **OBJECTIVE**
> **2.** Describe how and why Reconstruction policies changed over time.

The reconstruction of former Confederate states actually began during the war and went through several phases, the first of which was Presidential Reconstruction. With Union forces advancing into the South during the fighting, President Lincoln in 1862 had named army generals to serve as temporary military governors for conquered Confederate areas. By the end of 1863, he had formulated a plan for regular governments in those states liberated from Confederate rule.

Lincoln's Wartime Reconstruction Plan

Presidential Reconstruction: Lincoln's Proclamation of Amnesty and Reconstruction

In late 1863, President Lincoln issued a Proclamation of Amnesty and Reconstruction, under which any former Rebel state could form a Union government whenever a number equal to 10 percent of those who had voted in 1860 took an oath of allegiance to the Constitution and the Union and received a presidential pardon acquitting them from treason charges. Certain groups, however, were excluded from the pardon: Confederate government officials; senior officers of the Confederate army and navy; judges, congressmen, and military officers of the United States who had left their federal posts to aid the rebellion; and those who had abused captured African American soldiers.

But northern politicians disagreed over who had the authority to restore Rebel states to the Union. Many Republicans, especially the so-called Radicals, who were most committed to black civil rights, argued that Congress, not the president, should supervise Reconstruction. By contrast, a few conservative and most moderate Republicans supported Lincoln's program that immediately restored pro-Union southern governments. The **Radical Republicans**, however, favored a drastic transformation of southern society through which freed slaves would be granted full citizenship rights. Many Radical Republican leaders, motivated primarily by strongly felt religious values and moral ideals, believed that all people, regardless of race, were equal in God's eyes. They wanted no compromise with the "sin" of racism.

The Radicals also hoped to reconstruct southern society by replacing the white, Democratic planter elite with a new generation of small farmers, along with wage-earning and middle-class Republicans, both black and white, who would help replace the all-white Democratic party in the South. "The middling classes who own the soil, and work it with their own hands," explained Radical leader Thaddeus Stevens, "are the main support of every free government."

In 1864, with the war still raging, the Radical Republicans tried to take charge of Reconstruction by passing the Wade-Davis Bill, sponsored by Senator Benjamin Franklin Wade of Ohio and Representative Henry Winter Davis of Maryland. In contrast to Lincoln's 10 percent plan, the Wade-Davis Bill required that a *majority* of white male citizens declare their allegiance to the Union before a Confederate state could be re-admitted.

Lincoln vetoes Wade-Davis Bill

But the Wade-Davis Bill never became law: Lincoln vetoed it as being too harsh. In retaliation, Republicans issued the Wade-Davis Manifesto, a public statement that accused Lincoln of exceeding his constitutional authority. Unfazed by the criticism, Lincoln moved ahead with his efforts to restore the Confederate states to the Union. He also rushed to provide assistance to the freed slaves in the South.

The Freedmen's Bureau

Radical Republicans Congressmen who identified with the abolitionist cause and sought swift emancipation of the slaves, punishment of the Rebels, and tight controls over former Confederate states.

In early 1865, Congress approved the Thirteenth Amendment to the Constitution, officially abolishing slavery everywhere in the United States. The amendment, and the war that enabled it, liberated 4 million slaves, but what did freedom mean for the former slaves, most of whom had no land, no home, no food, and no education? Throughout the major northern cities, people concerned about the plight of the former slaves had formed Freedmen's Aid Societies to raise funds and recruit volunteers to help the African Americans in the South. Many churches did the same. But the needs far exceeded such grassroots efforts.

It soon fell to the federal government to take charge of coordinating efforts to address the desperate plight of the former slaves. On March 3, 1865, Congress created the **Freedmen's Bureau** (within the War Department) to assist the suffering "freedmen and their wives and children." It was the first federal experiment in providing assistance directly to people rather than to states. In May 1865, General Oliver O. Howard, commissioner of the Freedmen's Bureau, declared that freed slaves "must be free to choose their own employers, and be paid for their labor." He sent Freedmen's Bureau agents to the South to negotiate labor contracts between blacks and white landowners, many of whom resisted. The agents also provided the former slaves with medical care, food and clothing, and helped set up schools and pay teachers. By 1870, the Bureau was supervising over 4,000 new schools in the South serving almost 250,000 students, many of whose teachers were initially women volunteers from the North. The Freedmen's Bureau also helped former slaves reestablish connection with their family members. Marriages that had been prohibited during slavery were now made legal through the assistance of the Freedmen's Bureau.

Freedmen's Bureau (1865)

Freedmen's Bureau Federal Reconstruction agency established to protect the legal rights of former slaves and to assist with their education, jobs, health care, and land ownership.

Freedmen's school in Virginia Throughout the former Confederate states, the Freedmen's Bureau set up schools for former slaves, such as this one.

The Assassination of Lincoln

Abraham Lincoln offered his last view of Reconstruction in the final speech of his life. On April 11, 1865, he rejected calls by Radicals for a vengeful Reconstruction. He wanted "no persecution, no bloody work," no hangings of Confederate leaders nor any extreme efforts to restructure southern social and economic life. Three days later, on April 14, 1865, the president and his wife Mary went to see a play at Ford's Theatre in Washington, D.C. Lincoln was sitting defenseless as John Wilkes Booth slipped into the unguarded presidential box. Booth, a famous actor and a rabid Confederate, fired his small pistol point-blank at the president's head. As Lincoln slumped forward, Booth pulled out a knife, stabbed Lincoln's aide, and jumped from the box to the stage, breaking his leg in the process. He then mounted a waiting horse and fled the city. The president died nine hours later. Eleven days later, Booth was found hiding in a barn in Virginia, where he was shot and killed.

Johnson's Plan

Paying respect The only photograph of Lincoln in his coffin, displayed here in New York's City Hall rotunda.

Lincoln's murder shocked and saddened the nation and propelled into the White House Vice President Andrew Johnson of Tennessee, a combative man with a quick temper and fierce prejudices (he hated both the white southern elite and the idea of racial equality). Johnson was a pro-Union Democrat who had joined Lincoln's National Union ticket in 1864 as a gesture of wartime bipartisan unity. Like Lincoln, he was a self-made man.

Born in poverty in Raleigh, North Carolina, Johnson never attended school. At age thirteen he relocated to Greeneville, in the mountains of east Tennessee, where he became a tailor and eventually served as the mayor, a state legislator, governor, congressional representative, and U.S. senator.

Johnson's supporters were primarily the small farmers and working poor across the state. He called himself a Jacksonian Democrat "in the strictest meaning of the term. I am for putting down the [Confederate] rebellion, because it is a war [of wealthy plantation owners] against democracy." He had long disliked the planter elite, whom he dismissed as "a bloated, corrupted, damnable aristocracy." But Johnson shared the racist attitudes of most southern whites, rich and poor. "Damn the negroes," he exclaimed to a friend during the war. "I am fighting those traitorous aristocrats, their masters."

Johnson's plan to restore the Confederate states to the Union closely resembled Lincoln's lenient plan. In May 1865, the president issued a new Proclamation of Amnesty that excluded not only those ex-Confederates whom Lincoln had barred from a presidential pardon but also banned anyone with property worth more than $20,000. Johnson was determined to keep the wealthiest southerners from regaining political power in the former Confederate states. Surprisingly, however, he eventually gave pardons to most of the white "aristocrats" he claimed to despise. What brought about this change of heart? Johnson had apparently decided that he could buy the political support of prominent southerners by pardoning them, improving his own chances of reelection.

Johnson's "Restoration" Plan included the appointment of a Unionist as provisional governor in each southern state, with authority to call a convention of men elected by "loyal" (that is, not Confederate) voters. Each state convention had to ratify the Thirteenth Amendment ending slavery before it could be readmitted to the Union. Johnson also encouraged the state conventions to consider giving a few blacks voting rights, especially those with some education or with military service so as to "disarm" the "radicals who are wild upon" giving *all* African Americans the right to vote. Except for uncompromising Mississippi, each state of the former Confederacy held a convention that met Johnson's requirements but ignored his suggestion about giving voting rights to a few blacks.

Presidential Reconstruction: Johnson's "Restoration" Plan

Andrew Johnson A pro-Union Democrat from Tennessee.

The Radical Republicans

Johnson's initial assault on the southern planter elite won him the support of the Radical Republicans, but not for long. Many Radicals who wanted "Reconstruction" to provide social and political equality for blacks were frustrated by Johnson's efforts to bring the South back into the Union as quickly as possible. The leading Radical Republicans, such as Thaddeus Stevens of Pennsylvania and Charles Sumner of Massachusetts, wanted to deny former Confederates the right to vote in order to keep them from electing the old planter elite and to enable the Republican party to gain a foothold in the Democratic region. Stevens argued that the Civil War was a "*radical* revolution": the "whole fabric of southern society must be changed" in order to "revolutionize southern institutions, habits, and manners." Stevens and other Radicals wanted the federal government to confiscate the largest southern plantations, divide them into small farms, and give them to former slaves. And the Radicals claimed they had the authority to do so. The iron-willed Stevens, for example, viewed the Confederate states as "conquered provinces," subject to the absolute will of the U.S. Congress, not the president. Andrew Johnson, however, balked at such an expansion of federal authority. At base, he was committed to the states' rights to control their affairs rather than to an intrusive federal government. "White men alone must manage the South," Johnson told a visitor.

Unreconstructed Southerners

After the war most white southerners found their lives in turmoil. And it was only natural that former Confederates nursed bitter grievances against the North and the federal government. Many shared the attitude expressed by a North Carolinian in 1866 who said he felt the "bitterest hatred toward the North." He and others wanted to rebuild the new South as it had been before the war, the fabled "Old South," and they were determined to do so in their own way and under their own leadership. They saw no need for their beloved region to be "reconstructed" by outsiders.

Johnson's "Restoration" Plan Plan to require southern states to ratify the Thirteenth Amendment, disqualify wealthy ex-Confederates from voting, and appoint a Unionist governor.

So when the U.S. Congress met in December 1865, for the first time since the end of the war, the new state governments in the postwar South looked remarkably like the former Confederate governments. Southern voters had refused to extend voting rights to the newly freed slaves. Instead, they had elected as new U.S. senators and congressmen Georgia's Alexander Stephens, former vice president of the Confederacy, and four Confederate generals, eight colonels, and six Confederate cabinet members. The outraged Republicans in Congress denied seats to all such "Rebel" officials.

Then in May and July of 1866, white mobs murdered African Americans in Memphis and New Orleans. The massacres, Radical Republicans argued, resulted from Andrew Johnson's lenient policy toward white supremacists. "Witness Memphis, witness New Orleans," Massachusetts senator Charles Sumner cried. "Who can doubt that the President is the author of these tragedies?" The riots against blacks helped motivate Congress to pass the Fourteenth Amendment that year, extending federal civil rights protections to blacks.

The violence directed against southern blacks was partly sparked by black protests over restrictive laws being passed by the new all-white southern state legislatures. These "**black codes**," as a white southerner explained, were intended to make sure "the ex-slave was not a free man; he was a free Negro." A northerner visiting the South said the black codes in each state were intended to enforce a widespread insistence that "the blacks at large belong to the whites at large."

The black codes varied from state to state, but some provisions were common in many of them. While black marriages were recognized, blacks could not vote or serve on juries or testify against whites. They could own property, but they could not own farmland in Mississippi or city property in South Carolina. In Mississippi, every black male over the age of eighteen had to be apprenticed to a white, preferably a former slave owner. Any blacks not apprenticed or employed by January 1866 would be jailed as "vagrants." If they could not pay the vagrancy fine—and most of them could not—they were forced to work as convict laborers for whites. In other words, aspects of slavery were simply being restored in new ways. As a reporter observed, southern whites never agreed that "freedom for the negro means the same thing as freedom for them." The black codes infuriated Republicans. "We [Republicans] must see to it," Senator William Stewart of Nevada resolved, "that the man made free by the Constitution of the United States is a freeman indeed." And that is what they set out to do.

Johnson's Battle with Congress

Largely because of southern whites' resistance to Reconstruction, by the end of 1865, the Radical Republicans had gained a majority in Congress and were warring with Andrew Johnson over the control of Reconstruction. Johnson started the fight when he vetoed a bill renewing funding for the Freedmen's Bureau. On February 22, three days after the veto vote, Johnson criticized the Radical Republicans for promoting black civil rights. Moderate Republi-

Black codes

The Civil Rights Act (1866)

black codes Laws passed in southern states to restrict the rights of former slaves.

cans thereafter deserted the president and supported the Radicals. President Johnson had become in their eyes "an alien enemy of a foreign state," Thaddeus Stevens declared. In mid-March 1866, the Radical-led Congress passed the path-breaking Civil Rights Act, which declared that "all persons born in the United States" (except Indians) were citizens entitled to "full and equal benefit of all laws."

The new legislation enraged President Johnson. Congress, he fumed, had no authority to grant citizenship to blacks, who did not deserve it. The Civil Rights Act discriminated against the "white race." Johnson vetoed the bill, but this time, on April 9, 1866, Congress overrode the presidential veto. It was the first time in history that Congress had overturned a presidential veto of a major bill. From that point on, President Johnson, a stubborn loner unable to accept criticism or compromise, steadily lost both public and political support in the fight over Reconstruction.

Congressional Reconstruction

To remove all doubt about the legality of the new Civil Rights Act, Congress passed the **Fourteenth Amendment** to the U.S. Constitution on June 16, 1866. It went far beyond the Civil Rights Act by guaranteeing citizenship to anyone born in the United States, except Native Americans. It also prohibited any efforts to violate the civil rights of "citizens," black or white; to deprive any person "of life, liberty, or property, without due process of law"; or to "deny any person . . . the equal protection of the laws." With the Fourteenth Amendment, the federal government was assuming responsibility for protecting the civil rights of Americans.

As 1866 drew to an end, the fall congressional elections revealed the growing split between President Andrew Johnson and the Radical Republicans. To win votes for his favored candidates, Johnson went on a speaking tour of the Midwest. But his efforts backfired when several of his speeches turned into ugly shouting contests between him and his critics. In Cleveland, Ohio, Johnson described the Radical Republicans as "factious, domineering, tyrannical" men, and he exchanged hot-tempered insults with a heckler. Radical Republicans claimed that Johnson was behaving like a "drunken imbecile."

The 1866 congressional elections were a devastating defeat for Johnson and the Democrats; in each house, Radical Republican candidates won more than a two-thirds majority, the margin required to override presidential vetoes. On March 2, 1867, Congress passed, over President Johnson's

"(?) Slavery Is Dead (?)" (1867) Thomas Nast's cartoon argues that blacks were still being treated as slaves despite the passage of the Fourteenth Amendment. This detail illustrates a case in Raleigh, North Carolina: a black man was whipped for a crime despite federal orders specifically prohibiting such forms of punishment.

> Passage of the Fourteenth Amendment (1866)

Fourteenth Amendment (1866) Amendment to the U.S. Constitution guaranteeing equal protection under the law to all U.S. citizens, including former slaves.

Congressional Reconstruction:
The Military Reconstruction,
Command of Army, and Tenure
of Office Acts (1867)

vetoes, three crucial laws creating what came to be called **Congressional Reconstruction**: the Military Reconstruction Act, the Command of the Army Act, and the Tenure of Office Act.

The Military Reconstruction Act was the capstone of the Congressional Reconstruction plan. It abolished all of the new governments "in the rebel States" established under President Johnson's lenient reconstruction policies. In their place, Congress established military control over the defeated South. One state, Tennessee, was exempted because it had already ratified the Fourteenth Amendment. The other ten ex-Confederate states were divided into five military districts, each commanded by a general who acted as governor.

The Military Reconstruction Act required each state to create a new constitution that guaranteed the right of African American males to vote. (Women—black or white—did not yet have the vote and were not included in the discussions. The Radical Republicans were not so radical when it came to promoting the equality of women.) Once the new state constitution was ratified by a majority of voters in that state and accepted by Congress, a newly elected state legislature had to ratify the Fourteenth Amendment before regaining its state's representation in Congress.

The Command of the Army Act directed that all army orders from the president go through the army's commanding general, Ulysses S. Grant. The Radical Republicans feared that, to manage Reconstruction in the South, President Johnson would appoint generals who would be too lenient. So they bypassed the president and entrusted General Grant to enforce Congressional Reconstruction in the South.

The Tenure of Office Act required Senate permission for the president to remove any federal official whose appointment the Senate had confirmed. This act was intended to prevent Andrew Johnson from firing Secretary of War Edwin Stanton, the president's most outspoken critic in the cabinet. Stanton had openly criticized Johnson's lenient approach to the South and had allied himself with the Radicals.

Congressional Reconstruction thus sought to ensure that the freed slaves could participate in the creation of new state governments in the former Confederacy. As Thaddeus Stevens explained, the Congressional Reconstruction plan was designed to create a "perfect republic" based on the principle of *equal rights* for all citizens. "This is the promise of America," he insisted. "No More. No Less."

Impeaching the President

The first two years of Congressional Reconstruction saw dramatic changes in the South. One by one, a new set of southern state legislatures rewrote their constitutions and ratified the Fourteenth Amendment. Radical Republicans now seemed fully in control of Reconstruction, but one person still stood in their way—Andrew Johnson. During 1867 and early 1868, more and more Radicals decided that the defiant Democratic president must be removed from office.

Congressional Reconstruction
Phase of Reconstruction directed by Radical Republicans through the passage of three laws: the Military Reconstruction Act, the Command of the Army Act, and the Tenure of Office Act.

Johnson himself opened the door to impeachment (the formal process by which Congress charges the president with "high crimes and misdemeanors") when he tried to fire Secretary of War Edwin Stanton. The sharp-tongued Stanton had exasperated Johnson by refusing to resign from the cabinet despite his harsh criticism of the president's Reconstruction policy. Radical Republicans had passed the Tenure of Office Act in 1866 to make it illegal for Johnson to remove Stanton for championing their cause. Johnson, who considered the Tenure of Office Act an illegal restriction of presidential power, fired Stanton on August 12, 1867, appointing General Ulysses S. Grant in his place. To the Republicans, this was a declaration of war. John F. Farnsworth, an Illinois Congressman, denounced the president as an "ungrateful, despicable, besotted, traitorous man."

The Radical Republicans now saw their chance. By removing Stanton without congressional approval, Johnson had violated the law. On February 24, 1868, the Republican-dominated House passed eleven articles of impeachment (that is, specific charges against the president), most of which dealt with Stanton's firing, and all of which were flimsy. In reality, the essential grievance against the president was that he had opposed the policies of the dominant Radical Republicans. According to Secretary of the Navy Gideon Welles, Radical Republicans were so angry at Johnson that they would have tried to remove him had he been accused of stepping on a dog's tail.

Johnson's presidency in crisis

The first Senate trial of a sitting president began on March 5, 1868, and continued until May 26, with Chief Justice Salmon P. Chase presiding. It was a dramatic spectacle before a packed gallery of journalists, foreign dignitaries, corporate executives, and political leaders, all eager to watch the first effort to impeach a president. Thaddeus Stevens, the Radical leader, did not need to be convinced that Johnson should be removed. As the trial began, he warned the president: "Unfortunate, unhappy man, behold your doom!"

The five-week impeachment trial ended in May 1868 in stunning fashion, but not as the Radicals had hoped.

Trial of Andrew Johnson In this *Harper's Weekly* illustration, Johnson is seated at the center of the foreground among his defense committee. The galleries of the Senate are packed with men and women watching the proceedings.

In the end, the Senate voted 35 to 19 for conviction, only *one* vote short of the two-thirds needed for removal from office. Senator Edmund G. Ross, a young Radical from Kansas, cast the deciding vote in favor of acquittal, knowing that his vote would ruin his political career. "I almost literally looked down into my open grave," Ross explained afterwards. "Friendships, position, fortune, everything that makes life desirable . . . were about to be swept away by the breath of my mouth." Ross was thereafter shunned by the Republicans. He lost his reelection campaign and died in near poverty.

The effort by Radicals to remove Johnson was in the end a grave political mistake, for it ended up weakening public support for Congressional Reconstruction. Nevertheless, the Radical cause did gain something: to avoid being convicted, President Johnson had privately agreed to stop obstructing Congressional Reconstruction.

Republican Rule in the South

In June 1868, Congressional Republicans agreed that eight former Confederate states—all but Virginia, Mississippi, and Texas—had met the tough new conditions for readmission to the Union. Virginia, Mississippi, and Texas were readmitted in 1870, with the added requirement that they ratify the **Fifteenth Amendment**, which gave voting rights to African American men. As the prominent black leader Frederick Douglass, himself a former slave, had declared in 1865, "slavery is not abolished until the black man has the ballot."

The Fifteenth Amendment, submitted to the states in 1869 and ratified in 1870, prohibited states from denying any person the vote on grounds of "race, color, or previous condition of servitude." Susan B. Anthony and Elizabeth Cady Stanton, leaders of the movement to secure voting rights for women, demanded that the Fifteenth Amendment be revised to include women as well as black men. As Anthony stressed in a famous speech, the U.S. Constitution says: "we, the people; not we, the white male citizens; nor yet we, the male citizens; but we, the whole people, who formed the Union—women as well as men." But most men remained unreconstructed when it came to female voting rights. Radical Republicans tried to deflect the issue by declaring that it was the "Negro's hour," and women would have to wait—another fifty years, as it turned out.

> Passage of the Fifteenth Amendment (1870)

Reconstruction in Practice

When a federal official asked Garrison Frazier, a former slave in Georgia, if he and others wanted to live among whites or among themselves, he said that they preferred "to live by ourselves, for there is a prejudice against us in the South that will take years to get over." In forging new lives in freedom, Frazier and many other former slaves then set about creating their own social institutions.

The Reconstruction of Black Social Life

The northern victory in the Civil War led to a striking transformation of African American religious life in the South. Many former slaves identified their struggle for freedom with the biblical Hebrews, who were led out of

CORE OBJECTIVE

3. Assess the attitudes of white and black southerners toward Reconstruction.

Fifteenth Amendment (1870)
Amendment to the U.S. Constitution forbidding states to deny any male citizen the right to vote on grounds of "race, color or previous condition of servitude."

slavery into the "promised land." Emancipation demonstrated to them that God was on *their* side. Before the war, slaves who were allowed to attend white churches were forced to sit in the back. After the war, with the help of many northern Christian missionaries, both black and white, ex-slaves eagerly established their own African American churches.

The black churches were the first social institution the former slaves could control, and they quickly became the crossroads for African American community life. Black ministers emerged as social and political leaders as well as preachers. One could not be a real minister, one of them claimed, without looking "out for the political interests of his people."

Many African Americans became Baptists or Methodists, in part because these were already the largest denominations in the South and in part because they reached out to the working poor. In 1866 alone, the African Methodist Episcopal (AME) Church gained 50,000 members. By 1890, over 1.3 million African Americans in the South had become Baptists, nearly three times as many as had joined any other denomination.

> African American churches

African American communities in the postwar South also rushed to establish schools. Starting schools, said one former slave, was the "first proof" of freedom. Most plantation owners had denied education to blacks in part because they feared that literate slaves would read abolitionist literature and organize uprisings. After the war, the white elite worried that formal education would encourage poor whites and poor blacks to leave the South in search of better social and economic opportunities. "They didn't want us to learn nothin'," one former slave recalled. "The only thing we had to learn was how to work."

> African American schools

White opposition to education for blacks made education all the more important to African Americans. South Carolina's Mary McLeod Bethune, the fifteenth child of former slaves, rejoiced in the opportunity to gain an education: "The whole world opened to me when I learned to read." She walked five miles to school as a child, then earned a scholarship to college, and went on to become the first black woman to found a school that became a four-year college: what is today known as Bethune-Cookman University, in Daytona Beach, Florida.

African Americans in Southern Politics

Participation in the Union army or navy had given many former slaves their first opportunity to express their loyalty to the American nation. A Virginia freedman explained that the United States was "now *our* country," paid for "by the blood of our brethren" who died while serving in the Union military during the Civil War. Serving in the military enabled many former slaves to learn to read and write. Black veterans would also form the core of the first generation of African American political leaders in the postwar South.

Any African American participation in southern political life was a first. With many ex-Confederates denied voting rights, new African American voters helped elect some six hundred blacks—most of them former slaves—as Republican state legislators under Congressional Reconstruction. In

> African American vote

African American political figures of Reconstruction Blanche K. Bruce (left) and Hiram Revels (right) served in the U.S. Senate. Frederick Douglass (center) was a major figure in the abolitionist movement.

Louisiana, Pinckney Pinchback, a northern free black and former Union soldier, was elected lieutenant governor. Several other African Americans were elected lieutenant governor, state treasurer, or secretary of state. There were two black senators in Congress, Hiram Revels and Blanche K. Bruce, both Mississippi natives who had been educated in the North, as well as fourteen black members of the U.S. House of Representatives during Reconstruction.

> African American elected officials

White southern Democrats were appalled at the election of black Republican politicians. They complained that freed slaves were illiterate and had no civic experience or appreciation of political issues and processes. In this regard, of course, blacks were no different from millions of poor or immigrant white males who had been allowed to vote for years. Some freedmen frankly confessed their disadvantages. Beverly Nash, an African American delegate to the South Carolina convention of 1868, told his colleagues: "I believe, my friends and fellow-citizens, we are not prepared for this suffrage [the vote]. But we can learn. Give a man tools and let him commence to use them, and in time he will learn a trade. So it is with voting."

Land, Labor, and Disappointment

A few northerners argued that what the former slaves needed most was neither the right to vote nor the opportunity to be paid laborers on plantations but their own land, where they could gain economic self-sufficiency. "What is freedom," Ohio Congressman James A. Garfield, a former general and future president, asked in 1865. "Is it the bare privilege of not being chained? If this is all, then freedom is a bitter mockery, a cruel delusion." Freed slaves felt the same way. Freedom, explained a black minister from Georgia, meant

Freedmen Voting in New Orleans The Fifteenth Amendment, ratified in 1870, guaranteed at the federal level the right of citizens to vote regardless of "race, color, or previous condition of servitude." But former slaves had been registering to vote—and voting in large numbers—in some state elections since 1867, as in this scene.

the freedom for blacks to "reap the fruit of our own labor, and take care of ourselves."

In several southern states, former slaves had been "given" land by Union armies after they had taken control of Confederate areas during the war. But such transfers of white-owned property to former slaves were reversed during 1865 by President Andrew Johnson. In South Carolina, the Union general responsible for evicting former slaves urged them to "lay aside their bitter feelings, and become reconciled to their old masters." But the assembled freedmen shouted "No, never!" and "Can't do it!" They knew that ownership of land was the foundation of their freedom. Yes, they had no deeds or titles for the land they now worked, but it had been "earned by the sweat of *our* brows," said a group of Alabama freedmen.

President Johnson, however, was insistent that the federal government had no right to take land from former Confederates. Tens of thousands of former slaves were forced to return their farms to the white owners. In addition, it was virtually impossible for former slaves to get loans to buy farm land because there were so few banks in the postwar South, and few of these were willing to lend to blacks. The sense of betrayal among the former slaves was profound. An ex-slave in Mississippi whose farm was returned to its white owner said the former slaves were left with nothing: "no *land*, no *house*, not so much as a place to lay our head."

The intensity of racial prejudice in the South often blocked the efforts of federal troops and officials to protect the former slaves. In late June 1865, for example, Thomas Ferguson, a white plantation owner near Charleston, South Carolina, signed a contract with sixty-five of his former slaves. It called for them to "cultivate" his fields in exchange for "half of the crop raised after having deducted the seed of rice, corn, peas & potatoes." This labor system of **sharecropping**—where the landowner provided land, seed, and tools to a poor farmer in exchange for a *share* of the crop—essentially re-enslaved the workers because, as a federal army officer objected, no matter "how much they are abused, they cannot leave without permission of the owner." If they chose to leave, they would forfeit any right to a portion of the crop, and any workers who violated the terms of the contract could be evicted from the plantation, leaving them jobless and homeless—and subject to arrest. Across the former Confederacy, most white plantation owners and small farmers were determined to continue to control the lives of African Americans.

> **Sharecropping replaces slavery**

Sharecroppers A family is shown outside their Virginia home in this 1899 photograph, taken by Frances Benjamin Johnston, one of the earliest American female photojournalists.

With little money or technical training, many freed blacks preferred sharecropping over working for wages, since it freed them from day-to-day supervision by white landowners. But over time, most sharecroppers, black and white, found themselves deeper in debt to the landowner, with little choice but to remain tied to the same discouraging system of dependence that, over the years, felt much like slavery. As a former slave acknowledged, he and others had discovered that "freedom could make folks proud but it didn't make 'em rich."

"Carpetbaggers" and "Scalawags"

Most of the top positions in the new Republican southern state governments went to whites, who were dismissed as "carpetbaggers" and "scalawags" by their critics. Carpetbaggers were allegedly opportunistic northerners who rushed South with all their belongings in cheap suitcases made of carpeting ("carpetbags") to grab political power. Some northerners were indeed corrupt opportunists. However, most of the northerners in the postwar South were Union military veterans who had arrived as early as 1865 or 1866, drawn back to the South by the desire to rebuild the region's devastated economy. Others were Union soldiers who never returned home after fighting in the South. New Yorker George Spencer, for example, arrived in

sharecropping A farming system developed after the Civil War by which landless workers farmed land in exchange with the landowner for farm supplies and a share of the crop.

Alabama with the Union army during the war and decided to pursue his "chances of making a fortune" in selling cotton and building railroads. He eventually was elected to the U.S. Senate.

Many other so-called carpetbaggers were teachers, social workers, or ministers motivated by a genuine desire to help free blacks and poor whites improve the quality of their lives. Union general Adelbert Ames stayed in the South after the war because he felt a "sense of Mission with a large M" to help the former slaves develop healthy communities. He served as the military governor of Mississippi before being elected as a Republican U.S. senator in 1870. In 1873 Ames ran for governor of Mississippi in a bitter campaign against another white Republican, a "scalawag" named James Lusk Alcorn, a former Confederate general who owned the largest plantation in the Mississippi Delta and had served as Mississippi's governor from 1870 to 1871. Alcorn wrote his wife that "southerners must make the Negro their friend or the path ahead will be red with blood and damp with tears." Ames won the gubernatorial contest in 1873 and served as governor from 1874 to 1876 before resigning in the face of a resurgent white Democratic party.

Carpetbagger The cartoonist's caption to this critique of carpetbaggers reads: "The bag in front of him, filled with others' faults, he always sees. The one behind him, filled with his own faults, he never sees."

Most so-called scalawags were southerners who had opposed secession but supported the Confederacy once the war started, and then became Republicans after the war was over. Several distinguished figures became scalawags, including the former Confederate general James Longstreet, who decided after the war that the Old South must change its ways. He became a successful cotton broker in New Orleans, joined the Republican party, and supported the Congressional Reconstruction program. Another unlikely scalawag was Joseph E. Brown, the former Confederate governor of Georgia, who urged southerners to support Republicans because they were the only source of economic investment in the devastated region.

Southern Resistance and White "Redemption"

The scalawags, or southern white Republicans, were especially hated by southern Democrats, who often called them traitors. A Nashville, Tennessee, newspaper editor dismissed them as the "merest trash." Most southern whites viewed secession not as a mistake but as a noble "lost cause." At the same time, they viewed federal efforts at reconstruction as a tragedy. And they used all means possible—legal and illegal—to "redeem" their beloved South from northern control, Republican rule, and black assertiveness. An Alabama planter admitted that southern whites simply "can't learn to treat the freedmen like human beings." White southern ministers, for example, assured their congregations that God endorsed white supremacy. In an attempt to reunite the Protestant denominations of the north and south, many northern religionists became "apostles of forgiveness" for their southern

> Reconstruction's final phase: Southern white resistance and "redemption"

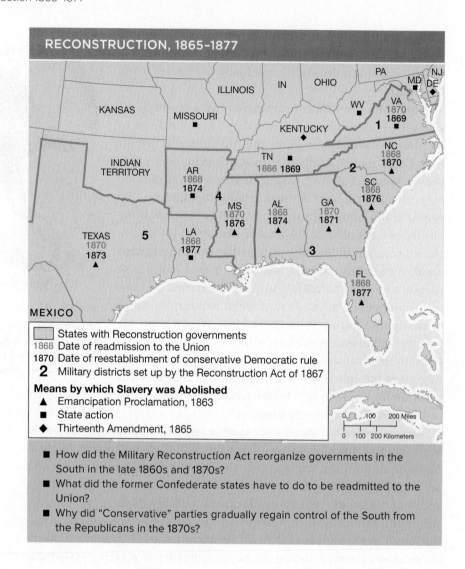

RECONSTRUCTION, 1865–1877

States with Reconstruction governments
1868 Date of readmission to the Union
1870 Date of reestablishment of conservative Democratic rule
2 Military districts set up by the Reconstruction Act of 1867
Means by which Slavery was Abolished
▲ Emancipation Proclamation, 1863
■ State action
◆ Thirteenth Amendment, 1865

- How did the Military Reconstruction Act reorganize governments in the South in the late 1860s and 1870s?
- What did the former Confederate states have to do to be readmitted to the Union?
- Why did "Conservative" parties gradually regain control of the South from the Republicans in the 1870s?

white brethren. Even abolitionists such as the Reverend Henry Ward Beecher, whose sister Harriet Beecher Stowe had written *Uncle Tom's Cabin* (1857), called for southern whites—rather than federal officials or African Americans themselves—to govern the South after the war.

The Civil War had brought freedom to enslaved African Americans, but it did not bring them protection against exploitation or abuse. The "black codes" created by white state governments in 1865 and 1866 were the first of many continuing efforts to deny equality to African Americans. With each passing year, southern whites used terror, intimidation, and violence to prevent blacks from exercising their political rights. Hundreds were killed across the South and many more injured in systematic efforts to "keep blacks in their place." In Texas a white farmer, D. B. Whitesides, told a former slave named Charles Brown that his newfound freedom would do him "damned little good . . . as I intend to shoot you"—and he did, shooting Brown in the chest as he tried to flee. Whitesides then rode his horse beside the wounded

> White violence against black political participation

Brown and asked, "I got you, did I Brown?" "Yes," a bleeding Brown replied. "You've got me good." Whitesides yelled that the wound would teach "niggers [like you] to put on airs because you are free."

Such ugly incidents revealed a harsh truth: the death of slavery did not mean the birth of true freedom for many African Americans. For a growing number of southern whites, resistance to Congressional Reconstruction and "Radical rule" became more and more violent. Several secret terrorist groups emerged to harass, intimidate, and even kill scalawags, carpetbaggers, and African Americans. The **Ku Klux Klan** (KKK), for instance, was formed in 1866 in Pulaski, Tennessee. The name *Ku Klux* was derived from the Greek word *kuklos* meaning "circle" or "band" (and *Klan* comes from the English word *clan*, or family). The Klan, and other groups like it, began initially as a social club, with costumes and secret rituals. At first a group of pranksters, its members soon turned to intimidation of blacks and white Republicans throughout the South. Their motives were varied—anger over the Confederate defeat, resentment against federal soldiers occupying the South, complaints about having to pay black workers, and an almost paranoid fear that former slaves might seek violent revenge against whites. Klansmen rode about at night in white sheets and masks spreading horrendous rumors, issuing threats, burning schools and churches. "We are going to kill all the Negroes," a white supremacist declared during one massacre.

"Worse Than Slavery" This Thomas Nast cartoon condemns the Ku Klux Klan for promoting conditions "worse than slavery" for southern blacks after the Civil War.

The Legacy of Republican Rule

Yet for all of the violent opposition directed against the Republican state governments, the new constitutions they created remained in effect for some years after the end of Radical Republican control, and later constitutions incorporated many of their most progressive features. Among the most significant innovations brought about by the Republican state governments were those intended to increase the participation of the common people in the political process: protecting black voting rights, restructuring legislatures to reflect shifting populations, and making more state offices elective to weaken the "good old boy" tradition of rewarding political supporters with state government jobs. In South Carolina, former Confederate leaders opposed the Republican state legislature not simply because of its black members but because poor whites were also enjoying political clout for the first time, thereby threatening the traditional power of wealthy white plantation owners and merchants.

Given the hostile circumstances under which the Republican state governments operated in the South, their achievements were remarkable. They constructed an extensive railroad network and established public, though racially segregated, school systems—schools funded by state governments

> Radical Republican achievements

Ku Klux Klan A secret terrorist organization founded in Pulaski, Tennessee, in 1866 targeting former slaves who voted and held political offices, as well as people the KKK labeled as carpetbaggers and scalawags.

and open to all children. Some six hundred thousand black pupils were enrolled in southern schools by 1877. State governments under the Radicals also gave more attention to the poor and to orphanages, asylums, and institutions for the deaf and the blind of both races. Public roads, bridges, and buildings were repaired or rebuilt. African Americans achieved rights and opportunities that would repeatedly be violated in coming decades but never completely taken away, at least in principle: equality before the law and the rights to own property, attend schools, learn to read and write, enter professions, and carry on business.

Yet several of the Republican state governments also engaged in corrupt practices. Bribes and kickbacks, whereby companies were awarded government contracts and then secretly rewarded officials with cash or stock, were commonplace. In Louisiana, the twenty-six-year-old Illinois carpetbagger, Henry Clay Warmoth, a Union war veteran and attorney, somehow turned an annual salary of $8,000 into a million-dollar fortune over four years serving as governor (he was impeached and removed from office). "I don't pretend to be honest," he admitted. "I only pretend to be as honest as anybody in politics." As was true in the North and the Midwest at the time, southern state governments awarded money to corporations, notably railroads, under conditions that invited shady dealings. In fact, some railroads were funded but never built at all. Republican state legislators doubled and even tripled their salaries. Bribery was rampant. Such corruption was not invented by the Radical Republican regimes, nor did it die with them. Governor Warmoth recognized as much: "Corruption is the fashion" in Louisiana, he explained.

CORE **OBJECTIVE**

4. Analyze the political and economic factors that helped lead to the end of Reconstruction in 1877.

The Grant Years and Northern Disillusionment

Democrat Andrew Johnson's crippled presidency created an opportunity for Republicans to elect one of their own in 1868. Both parties wooed Ulysses S. Grant, the "Lion of Vicksburg" credited by most Americans with the Union victory in the Civil War. His falling-out with President Johnson, however, had pushed him toward the Republicans.

The Election of 1868

The Republican party platform of 1868 endorsed Congressional Reconstruction. More important than the party platform, however, were the public expectations driving the election of Ulysses S. Grant, a heroic soldier whose campaign slogan was "Let us have peace."

African American votes help elect President Grant (1868)

The Democrats, not surprisingly, charged the Republican Congress with subjecting the South "to military despotism and Negro supremacy." They nominated Horatio Seymour, the wartime governor of New York and a passionate critic of Congressional Reconstruction. His vice-presidential running mate, Francis P. Blair Jr., a former Union general from Missouri who had served in Congress, appealed directly to white bigotry when he denounced Republicans for promoting equality for "a semi-barbarous race" of black men who sought to "subject the white women to their unbridled lust." A Democrat later said that Blair's egregiously "stupid and indefensible" remarks cost Seymour a close election. Grant swept the Electoral College, 214 to 80, but his popular majority was only 307,000 out of a total of almost 6 million votes. More than 500,000 African American voters accounted for Grant's margin of victory. The efforts of Radical Republicans to ensure that southern blacks had voting rights had paid off. When Grant was inaugurated in March 1869, a sullen Andrew Johnson refused to attend.

Grant had proved himself a great military leader, but as the youngest president ever (forty-six years old at the time of his inauguration), he was not nearly as bold a politician as he had been a general. He passively followed the lead of Congress and was often blind to the political forces and self-serving influence peddlers around him. A failure as a storekeeper before the Civil War, he was awestruck by men of wealth who lavished gifts on him, including houses. He also showed poor judgment in his selection of cabinet members. During Grant's two terms in office, his seven cabinet officers changed a total of twenty-four times. Some of them were out-and-out crooks who betrayed his trust and engaged in criminal behavior. His former comrade-in-arms, General William T. Sherman, said he felt sorry for his former commander because so many supposedly "loyal" Republicans used him for their own selfish gains.

Scandals

President Grant's new administration soon fell into a cesspool of scandal. In the summer of 1869, two unprincipled financial schemers, Jay Gould and James Fisk Jr. (known as "Jubilee Jim"), infamous for their bribing of politicians and judges, plotted with the president's brother-in-law to create a public craze for gold by purchasing massive quantities of the precious yellow metal to drive up its value. The only danger to the scheme lay in the possibility that the federal Treasury would burst the bubble by selling large amounts of its gold supply, which would deflate the value of gold by putting more in circulation. When President Grant was seen in public with Gould and Fisk, people assumed that he supported their gold scheme. As the rumor spread in New York City's financial district that the president endorsed the run-up in gold, its value soared.

On September 24, 1869—soon to be remembered as "Black Friday"—the scheme of Gould and Fisk to drive up the price of gold worked to perfection. Starting at a price of $150 an ounce, the bidding on Wall Street in New York City started rising, first to $160, then $165, leading more and more investors across the nation and around the world to join the stampede. Then, around noon, President Grant and his Treasury secretary realized what was happening and began selling huge amounts of government gold. Within fifteen minutes, the bubble created by Fisk and Gould burst, and the price of gold plummeted to $138. People who had bought gold in large amounts lost fortunes.

> Corruption in the Grant administration

Their agony, said a New Yorker, "made one feel as if the Battle of Gettysburg had been lost and the Rebels were marching down Broadway." Soon, the turmoil spread to the entire stock market, claiming thousands of victims. As Fisk noted, "It was each man drag out his own corpse." For weeks after the gold bubble collapsed, the financial markets were paralyzed and business confidence was rudely shaken. Congressman James Garfield wrote privately to a friend that President Grant had compromised his presidential integrity by his "indiscreet acceptance" of gifts from Fisk and Gould and that any investigation of "Black Friday" would lead "into the parlor of the President."

The plot to corner the gold market was only the first of several scandals that rocked the Grant administration. More disclosures of corruption followed, some involving members of the president's cabinet. The secretary of war, it turned out, had accepted bribes from merchants who traded with Indians at army posts in the West. In St. Louis, whiskey distillers—dubbed the "whiskey ring" in the press—bribed federal agents to avoid taxes, bilking the government out of millions of dollars in revenue. Grant's personal secretary was enmeshed in that scheme, taking large sums of money and other valuables in return for inside information.

There is no evidence that Grant himself was ever involved in any of the frauds, but his poor choice of associates earned him widespread criticism. Democrats scolded Republicans for their "monstrous corruption and extravagance" and launched thirty-six investigations into supposedly corrupt acts during Grant's administration.

The Money Supply

Greenbacks vs. gold coins

Complex financial issues—especially monetary policy—dominated Grant's presidency. Prior to the Civil War, the economy operated on a gold standard. That is, state banks issued paper money which could be exchanged for an equal value of gold coins. So both gold coins and state bank notes circulated as the nation's currency. **Greenbacks** (because of the dye color used on the printed dollars) were issued during the Civil War to help pay for the war.

When a nation's supply of money grows faster than the economy itself, prices for goods and services increase (inflation). This is what happened during the Civil War when the greenbacks were issued. After the Civil War, the U.S. Treasury assumed that the greenbacks issued during the conflict would be recalled from circulation so that consumer prices would decline and the nation could return to a "hard-money" currency—gold, silver, and copper coins—which had always been viewed as more reliable in value than paper currency. The most vocal supporters of a return to "hard money" were eastern creditors (mostly bankers and merchants to whom others owed money) who did not want their debtors to pay them in paper currency. Critics of the gold standard tended to be farmers and other debtors. These so-called soft-money advocates opposed taking greenbacks out of circulation because shrinking the supply of money would bring lower prices (deflation) for their crops and livestock, thereby reducing their income and making it harder for

greenbacks Paper money, issued during the Civil War, that sparked currency debates after the war.

them to pay their long-term debts. In 1868 congressional supporters of such a "soft-money" policy—mostly Democrats—had forced the Treasury to stop the withdrawal of greenbacks from circulation.

President Grant sided with the "hard-money" camp. On March 18, 1869, he signed the Public Credit Act, which said that the investors who purchased government bonds to help finance the war effort must be paid back in gold coins rather than paper currency. It was the first act of Congress that Grant signed, and it soon generated a decline in consumer prices (deflation) that hurt debtors, helped creditors, and in the process ignited a ferocious political debate over the merits of "hard" and "soft" money that would last throughout the nineteenth century—and beyond.

> Public Credit Act (1869)

Financial Panic

Grant's effort to withdraw the greenbacks from circulation unintentionally helped cause a major economic collapse. During 1873, some twenty-five railroads stopped paying their bills, leading Jay Cooke and Company, the nation's leading business lender, to go bankrupt on September 18, 1873. The resulting financial **Panic of 1873** triggered a deep economic depression. Thousands of businesses closed, and three million people lost their jobs. Those with jobs saw their wages slashed. In the major cities, unemployed, homeless Americans roamed the streets and formed long lines at charity soup kitchens.

> Panic of 1873

The terrible contraction of the economy led the U.S. Treasury to reverse course and begin printing more greenbacks. For a time, the supporters of paper money celebrated, but in 1874, President Grant vetoed a bill to issue even more greenbacks. His efforts to remove paper money from circulation pleased his supporters but only prolonged what was then the nation's worst economic depression in its history.

Liberal Republicans

The sudden collapse of the nation's economy in 1873 also contributed to northerners' losing interest in Reconstruction. Liberal Republicans, a new faction in the Republican party, called for ending federal Reconstruction efforts in the South and promoted "civil service reforms" designed to end the "patronage system" whereby new presidents rewarded political supporters with federal government jobs. In 1872 the Liberal Republicans held their own national convention, at which they accused the Grant administration of corruption, incompetence, and "despotism." They nominated an unlikely presidential candidate: Horace Greeley, the prominent editor of the *New York Tribune* and a longtime champion of a variety of causes: abolitionism, socialism, vegetarianism, and spiritualism. His image as an eccentric was complemented by his record of hostility to the Democrats, whose support the Liberal Republicans needed if they were going to win the election. The Democrats nevertheless gave their nomination to Greeley as the only hope of beating Grant.

> Reconstruction loses support

Panic of 1873 Financial collapse triggered by President Grant's efforts to withdraw greenbacks from circulation and transition the economy back to hard currency.

The result was predictable. Greeley, the shared candidate of the Liberal Republicans and Democrats, carried only six southern states and none in the North. Grant won thirty-one states and carried the national election by 3,598,235 votes to Greeley's 2,834,761. An exhausted Greeley confessed that he was "the worst beaten man who ever ran for high office." He died three weeks later.

White Terror

Violence against blacks escalates

President Grant initially fought hard to enforce federal efforts to reconstruct the postwar South. But southern resistance to "Radical rule" increased and turned brutally violent. In Grayson County, Texas, a white man and two friends murdered three former slaves because they wanted to "thin the niggers out and drive them to their holes."

Klansmen focused their terror on prominent Republicans, black and white. In Mississippi they killed a black Republican leader in front of his family. Three white "scalawag" Republicans were murdered in Georgia in 1870. That same year an armed mob of whites assaulted a Republican political rally in Alabama, killing four blacks and wounding fifty-four. In South Carolina white supremacists were especially active—and violent. In 1871, some five hundred masked men laid siege to South Carolina's Union County jail and eventually lynched eight black prisoners. In March 1871, the Klan killed thirty African Americans in Meridian, Mississippi.

Enforcement Acts (1870–1871)

At the urging of President Grant, Republicans in Congress struck back at such racial violence with three Enforcement Acts (1870–1871). The first of these measures imposed penalties on anyone who interfered with any citizen's right to vote. A second measure dispatched federal election supervisors and marshals to monitor elections in southern districts where political terrorism flourished. The third, called the Ku Klux Klan Act, outlawed the main activities of the KKK—forming conspiracies, wearing disguises, resisting officers, and intimidating officials. In 1871, the federal government singled out nine counties in upcountry South Carolina as a center of Klan-instigated violence and jailed several hundred people. In general, however, the Enforcement Acts were not consistently applied. As a result, the efforts of southern whites to use violence to thwart Reconstruction escalated in the 1870s. On Easter Sunday in 1873 in Colfax, Louisiana, a mob of white vigilantes disappointed by local election results attacked a group of black Republicans, slaughtering eighty-one. It was the bloodiest racial incident during the Reconstruction period.

Southern "Redeemers"

The Ku Klux Klan's impact on southern politics varied from state to state. In the Upper South, it played only a modest role in helping Democrats win local elections. But in the Lower South, Klan violence and intimidation had more serious effects. In overwhelmingly black Yazoo County, Mississippi, vengeful whites used terrorism to reverse the political balance of power. In the 1873 elections, for example, the Republicans cast 2,449 votes and the Democrats 638; two years later the Democrats polled 4,049 votes, the Republicans 7. Throughout the South, the activities of the Klan and other white supremacists disheartened black and white Republicans alike. "We are helpless and unable to organize," wrote a Mississippi scalawag. We "dare not attempt to canvass [campaign for candidates], or make public speeches." At the same time, during the 1870s northerners displayed a growing weariness with efforts to use federal troops to reconstruct the South and protect civil rights. "The plain truth is," noted the *New York Herald*, "the North has got tired of the Negro."

The erosion of northern interest in civil rights resulted from more than weariness, however. Western expansion, Indian wars, and political controversy over economic issues distracted attention from southern resistance to Republican rule and black rights. Given the violent intensity of diehard former Confederates' efforts to resist Reconstruction, it would have required far more patience, conviction, and resources for the federal government to protect the civil rights of blacks in the South. Republican political control in the South gradually loosened as all-white "Conservative" parties mobilized the anti-Reconstruction vote. White Democrats—the so-called **redeemers** who supposedly "saved" the South from Republican control and "black rule"—emotionalized the race issue to excite the white electorate and intimidate black voters. Where persuasion failed to work, Democrats were willing to use trickery. As one enthusiastic Democrat boasted, "The white and black Republicans may outvote us, but we can outcount them."

> Resurgence of the southern white elite

Republican political control collapsed in Virginia and Tennessee as early as 1869; in Georgia and North Carolina it ended in 1870, although North Carolina had a Republican governor until 1876. Reconstruction lasted longest in the Deep South states with the largest black population; there, whites abandoned Klan masks for barefaced intimidation in paramilitary groups such as the Mississippi Rifle Club and the South Carolina Red Shirts. By 1876, Radical Republican regimes survived only in Louisiana, South Carolina, and Florida, and those collapsed after the elections of that year.

The return to power of the old white political elite in the South undermined the country's commitment to Congressional Reconstruction. The collapse of the economy and the much-publicized political scandals hurt Republicans in the 1874 congressional elections, in which the Democrats won control of the House of Representatives and gained seats in the Senate.

> Democrats win control of Congress (1874)

The Compromise of 1877

President Grant, despite the controversies swirling around him, wanted to run again in 1876, but many Republicans had lost confidence in his leadership and opposed the idea of his becoming the nation's first three-term president. In the summer of 1875, Grant acknowledged defeat and announced his retirement, admitting that he had entered the White House

redeemers Postwar white Democratic leaders in the South who supposedly saved the region from political, economic, and social domination by northerners and blacks.

with "no political training" and had made "errors in judgment." James Gillespie Blaine of Maine, former Speaker of the House, emerged as the Republican front-runner to succeed Grant, but he, too, bore the taint of scandal when it was revealed that he had promised political favors to railroad executives in exchange for shares of stock in the company.

The scandal led the Republican Convention to pass over Blaine in favor of Ohio's favorite son, Rutherford B. Hayes. Elected governor of Ohio three times, most recently as a "hard money" advocate of gold rather than greenbacks, Hayes had also made a name for himself as a civil service reformer by trying to reduce the number of government jobs subject to political appointment. But his chief virtue was that he offended neither Radicals nor reformers. As a journalist put it, he was "obnoxious to no one."

The Democratic Convention was uncharacteristically harmonious from the start. The nomination went on the second ballot to Samuel J. Tilden, a wealthy corporate lawyer and reform governor of New York.

The 1876 campaign raised no burning issues. Both candidates favored the trend toward relaxing federal authority in the South. As Hayes said privately, he did not approve of "bayonet rule" by federal troops in the South. In the absence of strong ideological differences, Democrats aired the Republicans' dirty linen. In response, Republicans waved "the bloody shirt," whereby they linked the Democratic party to secession, civil war, and the outrages committed against Republicans in the South. As Robert G. Ingersoll, the most celebrated Republican public speaker of the time, insisted: "The man that assassinated Abraham Lincoln was a Democrat. . . . Soldiers, every scar you have on your heroic bodies was given you by a Democrat!"

Disputed election of 1876

Despite the lack of major issues, the 1876 election generated the most votes of any national election in U.S. history up to that point. Early election returns pointed to a victory for the Democrat Tilden. Nationwide, he outpolled Hayes by almost 300,000 votes. By midnight following Election Day, Tilden had won 184 electoral votes—just one vote short of victory. Hayes went to bed that night convinced that he had lost. But overnight, Republican activists realized that the election hinged on nineteen disputed electoral votes from Florida, Louisiana, and South Carolina. The Democrats needed only one of the challenged votes to claim victory; the Republicans needed all nineteen. Republicans in those key states had engaged in election fraud while Democrats had used physical intimidation to keep black voters at home. But each of the three states was then governed by a Republican who appointed the election boards, each of which reported narrow victories for Hayes. The Democrats immediately challenged the results.

In all three of the disputed southern states, rival election boards sent in conflicting counts. The nation watched and wondered as the politicians bickered about the contested election. The Constitution offered no guidance in this unprecedented situation. Days, then weeks, passed with no solution. Finally, on January 29, 1877, the Congress set up a special Electoral Commission to settle the dispute. It met daily for weeks trying to verify the disputed vote counts in the three contested southern states. Finally, on March 1, 1877, the commission voted 8 to 7 along party lines in favor of Hayes. On March 2, 1877, the House of Representatives declared Hayes president by an electoral vote of 185 to 184. Tilden decided not to protest the decision. His campaign manager explained that they preferred "four years of Hayes's administration to four years of civil war."

Hayes's victory hinged on the defection of key southern Democrats, who, it turned out, had made a number of secret deals with the Republicans. On February 26, 1877, prominent Ohio Republicans (including future president James A. Garfield) and powerful southern Democrats struck a private bargain—the **Compromise of 1877**—at Wormley's Hotel in Washington, D.C. The Republicans promised that if Hayes were named president, he would remove the last federal troops from the South, letting the state Republican governments there collapse.

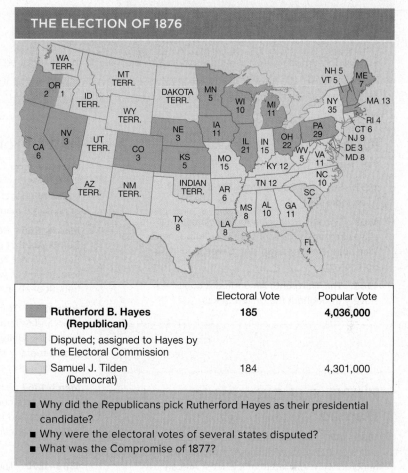

THE ELECTION OF 1876

	Electoral Vote	Popular Vote
Rutherford B. Hayes (Republican)	185	4,036,000
Disputed; assigned to Hayes by the Electoral Commission		
Samuel J. Tilden (Democrat)	184	4,301,000

■ Why did the Republicans pick Rutherford Hayes as their presidential candidate?
■ Why were the electoral votes of several states disputed?
■ What was the Compromise of 1877?

The End of Reconstruction

In 1877, newly inaugurated President Hayes fulfilled his pledge: he withdrew federal troops from Louisiana and South Carolina, whose Republican governments collapsed soon thereafter. Hayes insisted that it was not his fault. "The practical destruction of the Republican organization in the South was accomplished before my southern policy was announced." Over the next thirty years, the protection of black civil rights in the South crumbled under the pressure of restored white Democratic rule. As Henry Adams, a former Louisiana slave, observed in 1877, "The whole South—every state in the South—has got [back] into the hands of the very men that held us as slaves." New white state governments in the South rewrote their constitutions, rid their administrations of "carpetbaggers, scalawags, and blacks," and cut back spending. "The Yankees helped free us, so they

Compromise of 1877 Secret deal forged by congressional leaders to resolve disputed election of 1876; Republican Rutherford B. Hayes, who had lost the popular vote, was declared the winner in exchange for his pledge to remove federal troops from the South, marking the end of Reconstruction.

From Slave to Citizen

The following timeline highlights important developments in the legal status of African Americans during the Civil War and Reconstruction. The timeline breaks the legal status of African Americans into three phases:

PHASE I From Slaves to Freedmen

1857 Supreme Court's *Dred Scott* decision ruled that African Americans were not citizens.

1863 Lincoln's **Emancipation Proclamation** freed slaves in areas still under rebellion during the Civil War, but their citizenship status remained unresolved.

1865 The **Thirteenth Amendment** abolished slavery throughout the United States.

PHASE III Full Citizenship Denied

1866–1870 African American men in southern states participated in elections at high rates. Six hundred were elected to office. Most African American voters and office holders supported the Republican Party.

1870–1877 White terrorist organizations such as the Ku Klux Klan used violence to suppress African American voting and other forms of political participation. Over time, northern voters lost interest in the process of Reconstruction.

1877 President Hayes withdrew the last federal troops from the South. Over the next several decades, southern states severely curtailed the civil rights of African Americans, including their political participation.

PHASE II From Freedmen to Citizen

Summer 1865 As the war ended, southern states in the former Confederacy adopted a series of **black codes** to restrict the freedom of African Americans and to preserve many aspects of slavery.

March 1866 Republicans in Congress passed a **Civil Rights Act** that declared all persons born in the United States (except Native Americans) and not subject to any foreign power, were citizens entitled to full and equal benefit of all laws.

June 1866 The **Fourteenth Amendment** reaffirmed the state and federal citizenship of anyone born or naturalized in the United States (except Native Americans) and prohibited any state from allowing any citizen to be denied civil rights and equal protection of the laws.

March 1867 The **Military Reconstruction Act** called for new state constitutions in former Confederate states that had to guarantee the voting rights of African Americans (males) and to ratify the Fourteenth Amendment.

1869–1870 The **Fifteenth Amendment** to the U.S. Constitution prohibited states from denying the vote on the basis of "race, color, or previous condition of servitude."

QUESTIONS FOR ANALYSIS

1. What events and movements prompted the federal government to redefine the standing of African Americans in American society between 1857 and 1877?

2. Which of these reforms were widely accepted and which were strongly resisted?

3. How did the Thirteenth, Fourteenth, and Fifteenth Amendments to the U.S. Constitution affect the nation's politics?

4. Why did the federal government abandon its pursuit of racial equality?

say," a former North Carolina slave named Thomas Hall remembered, "but [in 1877] they let us be put back in slavery again."

Reconstruction's Significance

CORE **OBJECTIVE**
5. Explain the impact of Reconstruction on the nation's future.

After the Civil War, Congressional Reconstruction gave African Americans an opportunity to experience freedom—but not security or equality. As Thomas Hall noted in acknowledging the end of Reconstruction, African Americans were no longer slaves but they remained dependent "on the southern white man for work, food, and clothing," and most southern whites remained hostile to the notion of civil rights and social equality. The collapse of Congressional Reconstruction in 1877 had tragic consequences, for it allowed the South to renew long-standing patterns of discrimination against African Americans.

Racial discrimination continues

Yet for all of the unfulfilled promises of Congressional Reconstruction, it left an enduring legacy—the Thirteenth, Fourteenth, and Fifteenth Amendments—not dead in 1877 but dormant, waiting to be reawakened during the second reconstruction of civil rights in the 1950s and 1960s. If Reconstruction's experiment in interracial democracy did not provide true social equality or substantial economic opportunities for African Americans, it did create the essential constitutional foundation for future advances in the quest for equality and civil rights—not just for African Americans but for women and other minority groups as well. Until the pivotal Reconstruction Era, the states were responsible for protecting citizens' rights. Thereafter, thanks to the Fourteenth and Fifteenth Amendments, blacks had gained equal rights (in theory), and the federal government assumed responsibility for ensuring that states treated blacks equally in terms of their basic civil rights. Congressional Reconstruction was a half-way revolution, sighed the former governor of North Carolina Jonathan Worth, and "nobody can anticipate the action of revolutions." A hundred years later, the cause of civil rights would be embraced again by the federal government—this time permanently.

Thirteenth, Fourteenth, and Fifteenth Amendments lay groundwork for future civil rights movements

- **Reconstruction Challenges** With the defeat of the Confederacy and the passage of the Thirteenth Amendment, the federal government had to develop policies and procedures to address a number of difficult questions: What was the status of the defeated states and how would they be reintegrated into the nation's political life? What would be the political status of the former slaves and what would the federal government do to integrate them into the nation's social and economic fabric?

- **Reconstruction over Time** Abraham Lincoln and his successor, southerner Andrew Johnson, wanted a lenient and quick plan for Reconstruction. The *Freedmen's Bureau* attempted to educate and aid freed slaves, negotiate labor contracts, and reunite families. Lincoln's assassination led many northerners to favor the *Radical Republicans*, who wanted a more transformative plan designed to end the grasp of the old plantation elite on the South's society and economy. Southern whites resisted and established *black codes* to restrict the lives of blacks. *Congressional Reconstruction* responded by stipulating that to reenter the Union, former Confederate states had to ratify the *Fourteenth* and *Fifteenth Amendments* to the U.S. Constitution in order to expand and protect the rights of African Americans. Congress also passed the Military Reconstruction Act, which used federal troops to protect the voting rights and civil rights of African Americans.

- **Views of Reconstruction** Many former slaves found comfort in their families and the independent churches they established, but land ownership reverted to the old white elite, reducing newly freed black farmers to *sharecropping*. African Americans enthusiastically participated in politics, with many serving as elected officials.

Along with white southern Republicans (scalawags) and northern carpetbaggers, they worked to rebuild the southern economy. Many white southerners, however, blamed their poverty on freed slaves and Republicans, and they supported the *Ku Klux Klan's* violent intimidation of the supporters of these Reconstruction efforts and the goal of "redemption," or white Democratic control of Southern state governments.

- **Political and Economic Developments and the End of Reconstruction** Scandals during the Grant administration involved an attempt to corner the gold market and the "whiskey ring's" plan to steal millions of dollars in tax revenue. In the face of these troubles and the economic downturn caused by both the *Panic of 1873* over railroad defaults and disagreement over whether to continue the use of *greenbacks* or return to the gold standard, northern support for Reconstruction eroded. Southern white *redeemers* were elected in 1874, successfully reversing the political progress of Republicans and blacks. In the *Compromise of 1877*, Democrats agreed to the election of Republican Rutherford B. Hayes, who put an end to the Radical Republican administrations in the southern states.

- **The Significance of Reconstruction** Southern state governments quickly renewed long-standing patterns of discrimination against African Americans, but the Fourteenth and Fifteenth Amendments remained enshrined in the Constitution, creating the essential constitutional foundation for future advances in civil rights. These amendments give the federal government responsibility for ensuring equal treatment and political equality within the states, a role it would increasingly assume in the twentieth century.

KEY TERMS

CHRONOLOGY

INQUIZITIVE

Go to InQuizitive to see what you've learned—and learn what you've missed—with personalized feedback along the way.

DEBATING Reconstruction

Historians' interpretations of the past change over time. This happens for many reasons. Historians can revise their thinking in light of information from newly discovered *primary sources*. They can also interpret previously examined sources in new ways by applying new methodologies and theories. Finally, historians themselves are influenced by the values of their own society and times. Present-day events or particular personal interests can influence how historians think about the past. The study of how interpretations of history have changed is called *historiography*. It is the history of the field of history. For Part 4, *A House Divided*, the case study of Debating Reconstruction demonstrates how the views of historians have changed dramatically over time.

For this exercise you have two tasks:

PART 1: Compare the two secondary sources on Reconstruction.
PART 2: Using primary sources, evaluate the arguments of the two secondary sources.

PART I **Comparing and Contrasting Secondary Sources**

Two *secondary sources*, the work of prominent historians from different eras, are included below for you to review. The first selection comes from William Dunning's (1857–1922) *Reconstruction, Political and Economic, 1865–1877*, written in 1907. Dunning was born on the eve of the Civil War to a well-to-do New Jersey family and began his studies at Columbia University soon after the end of Reconstruction. He lived during a time when racial segregation and white supremacy were the unchallenged law of the land, and he wrote some of the first academic texts on Reconstruction. Dunning was such a compelling force in the first half of the twentieth century that the many historians trained and influenced by him are referred to as the "Dunning School." He was particularly hostile to political idealists, a group which, in his mind, included abolitionists and Radical Republicans. Like many historians of his day, Dunning never questioned his own objectivity. However, later academics and activists have noted that his writings reflect the political beliefs and prejudices of his generation.

Interpretations of Reconstruction have undergone many changes since Dunning's time. The second excerpt, written 101 years later, is from Eric Foner's *The Story of American Freedom*. Born in 1943, Foner is the son of civil rights activists (one of them a historian) deeply concerned with the plight of African Americans. Foner completed his Ph.D. in 1969 during the height of the civil rights movement. Widely regarded as a leading contemporary historian of Reconstruction, Foner's writing on the period brings together much of the scholarship that has revised "Dunning School" interpretations of Reconstruction, particularly as they described the role of African Americans in American society.

Before you begin reading these excerpts, it may be helpful to review Chapter 15 on the transition from President Andrew Johnson's Restoration Plan to Congressional Reconstruction.

Compare the work of these two historians by answering the following questions. Be sure to support your answers with specific examples drawn from the selections by Dunning and Foner.

■ What is the topic of each excerpt? What period of Reconstruction is the author writing about? What groups are examined in American society?

■ Generally, how does each author portray the Reconstruction process? What in each author's writing leads you to believe that this is how the author feels about Reconstruction? How do those feelings—whether positive or negative—affect each author's point of view?

■ How would you describe the similarities between these two excerpts?

■ What are the major differences in interpretation between the excerpts?

- What is the main argument each historian makes about the topic?

- How do these interpretations compare to that presented in Chapter 15?

- These two excerpts were written 101 years apart. How might this have influenced the development of their arguments?

Secondary Source 1

William Dunning, from *Reconstruction, Political and Economic, 1865–1877*

It was, indeed, no novelty for the people of the South to be subject to government by the United States army. . . . The reasoning by which the policy of Congress was justified in the North was regarded in the South as founded on falsehood and malice. So far as the "black codes" were concerned, it was pointed out that they could not be alleged as evidences of a tendency to restore slavery or introduce peonage [dependence], since the offensive acts had in many of the states been repealed by the legislatures themselves, and in all had been duly superseded by the civil rights act. The much-exploited outrages on freedmen and Unionists were declared to be exaggerated or distorted reports of incidents which any time of social tension must produce among the criminal classes. The rejection of the Fourteenth Amendment was considered as merely a dignified refusal by honorable men to be the instruments of their own humiliation and shame.

Under all these circumstances the southerners felt that the policy of Congress had no real cause save the purpose of radical politicians to prolong and extend their party power by means of negro suffrage [voting rights]. This and this alone was the purpose for which major-generals had been empowered to remodel the state governments at their will, to exercise through general orders the functions of executive, legislature, and courts, and to compel the white people to recognize the blacks as their equals wherever the stern word of military command could reach. It was as inconceivable to the southerners that rational men of the North should seriously approve of negro suffrage per se as it had been in 1860 to the northerners that rational men of the South should approve of secession per se. Hence, in the one case as in the other, a craving for political power was assumed to be the only explanation of an otherwise unintelligible proceeding.

Source: Dunning, William. *Reconstruction, Political and Economic, 1865–1877*. New York: Harper & Bros., 1907. 109–12.

Secondary Source 2

Eric Foner, from *The Story of American Freedom*

Rejecting the idea that emancipation implied civil or political equality or opportunities to acquire property or advance economically, rights northerners deemed essential to a free society, most white southerners insisted that blacks must remain a dependent plantation workforce in a laboring situation not very different from slavery. During Presidential Reconstruction—the period from 1865 to 1867 when Lincoln's successor, Andrew Johnson, gave the white South a free hand in determining the contours of Reconstruction—southern state governments enforced this view of black freedom by enacting the notorious Black Codes, which denied blacks equality before the law and political rights and imposed on them mandatory year-long labor contracts, coercive apprenticeship regulations, and criminal penalties for breach of contract. Through these laws, the South's white leadership sought to ensure that plantation agriculture survived emancipation.

Thus, the death of slavery did not automatically mean the birth of freedom. But the Black Codes so flagrantly violated free labor principles that they invoked the wrath of the Republican North. Southern reluctance to accept the reality of emancipation resulted in a monumental struggle between President Andrew Johnson and the Republican Congress over the legacy of the Civil War. The result was the enactment of laws and constitutional amendments that redrew the boundaries of citizenship and expanded the definition of freedom for all Americans. . . .

Much of the ensuing conflict over Reconstruction revolved around the problem, as Senator Lyman Trumbull of Illinois put it, of defining "what slavery is and what liberty is." . . . By 1866, a consensus had emerged within the Republican Party that civil equality was an essential attribute of freedom. The Civil War had elevated "equality" to a status in the vocabulary of freedom it had not enjoyed since the Revolution. . . . In a remarkable, if temporary, reversal of political traditions, the newly empowered national state now sought to identify and protect the rights of all Americans.

Source: Foner, Eric. *The Story of American Freedom*. New York: W. W. Norton & Company, 1998. 103–105.

PART II Using Primary Sources to Evaluate Secondary Sources

When historians are faced with competing interpretations of the past, they often look at primary source material as part of the process of evaluating the different arguments. In the following selections, you'll find *primary sources* relating to the period of Reconstruction.

Carefully read each of the following primary sources and answer the following questions. Decide how the primary source documents support or refute Dunning's and Foner's arguments about this period. You may find that some documents do both, but for different parts of each historian's interpretation. Be sure to identify which specific components of each historian's argument the documents support or refute.

■ Which of the two historian's arguments is best supported by the primary source documents? Or if you find that both arguments are well supported by the evidence, why do you think the two historians had such different interpretations about the period?

■ Based on your comparison of the two arguments and your analysis of the primary sources, how has the interpretation of Reconstruction by historians shifted over time? What can you conclude about historiography from the work of these two historians?

Primary Source 1

Union Army General Carl Schurz, from *Report on the Condition of the South*

A belief, conviction, or prejudice, or whatever you may call it, so widely spread and apparently so deeply rooted as this, that the negro will not work without physical compulsion, is certainly calculated to have a very serious influence upon the conduct of the people entertaining it. It naturally produced a desire to preserve slavery in its original form as much and as long as possible—and you may, perhaps, remember the admission made by one of the provisional governors, over two months after the close of the war, that the people of his State still indulged in a lingering hope slavery might yet be preserved—or to introduce into the new system that element of physical compulsion which would make the negro work. Efforts were, indeed, made to hold the negro in his old state of subjection, especially in such localities where our military forces had not yet penetrated, or where the country was not garrisoned in detail. Here and there planters

succeeded for a limited period to keep their former slaves in ignorance, or at least doubt, about their new rights; but the main agency employed for that purpose was force and intimidation. In many instances negroes who walked away from the plantations, or were found upon the roads, were shot or otherwise severely punished, which was calculated to produce the impression among those remaining with their masters that an attempt to escape from slavery would result in certain destruction. A large proportion of the many acts of violence committed is undoubtedly attributable to this motive.

Source: Schurz, Carl. *Report on the Condition of the South*, 1865, 39TH CONGRESS, SENATE. Ex. Doc., 1ST Session, No. 2, p. 19.

Primary Source 2

Mississippi Vagrant Law, 1865

All freedmen, free negroes and mulattoes in this State, over the age of eighteen years, found on the second Monday in January, 1866, or thereafter, with no lawful employment or business, or found unlawfully assembling themselves together, either in the day or night time, and all white persons so assembling themselves with freedmen, free negroes or mulattoes, or usually associating with freedmen, free negroes or mulattoes, on terms of equality, or living in adultery or fornication with a freed woman, free negro or mulatto, shall be deemed vagrants, and on conviction thereof shall be fined in a sum not exceeding, in the case of a freedman, free negro, or mulatto, fifty dollars, and a white man two hundred dollars, and imprisoned at the discretion of the court, the free negro not exceeding ten days, and the white man not exceeding six months.... All fines and forfeitures collected under the provisions of this act shall be paid into the county treasury for general county purposes, and in case any freedman, free negro or mulatto shall fail for five days after the imposition of any fine or forfeiture upon him or her for violation of any of the provisions of this act to pay the same, that it shall be, and is hereby, made the duty of the sheriff of the proper county to hire out said freedman, free negro or mulatto, to any person who will, for the shortest period of service, pay said fine and forfeiture and all costs....

Source: Mississippi Vagrant Law, *Laws of Mississippi, 1865*, 90 in *Documentary History of Reconstruction: Political, Military, Social, Religious, Educational & Industrial, 1865 to the Present Time.* Ed. Walter Lynwood Fleming. Cleveland, Oh.: The Arthur H. Clark Company, 1906. 283–86.

Primary Source 3

Civil Rights Act of 1866

Be it enacted, . . . That all persons born in the United States and not subject to any foreign power, excluding Indians not taxed, are hereby declared to be citizens of the United States; and such citizens, of every race and color, without regard to any previous condition of slavery or involuntary servitude, except as a punishment for crime whereof the party shall have been duly convicted, shall have the same right, in every State and Territory in the United States, to make and enforce contracts, to sue, be parties, and give evidence, to inherit, purchase, lease, sell, hold, and convey real and personal property, and to full and equal benefit of all laws and proceedings for the security of person and property, as is enjoyed by white citizens, and shall be subject to like punishment, pains and penalties, and to none other, any law, statute, ordinance, regulation, or custom, to the contrary notwithstanding.

Source: Civil Rights Act of 1866, *United States Statutes at Large*, vol. xiv, 27 [April 9, 1866].

Primary Source 4

Radical Republican Thaddeus Stevens, from "The Advantages of Negro Suffrage"

Unless the rebel States, before admission, should be made republican in spirit, and placed under the guardianship of loyal men, all our blood and treasure will have been spent in vain. . . . There is more reason why colored voters should be admitted in the rebel States than in the Territories. In the States they form the great mass of the loyal men. Possibly with their aid loyal governments may be established in most of those States. Without it all are sure to be ruled by traitors; and loyal men, black and white, will be oppressed, exiled, or murdered. . . . Have not loyal blacks quite as good a right to choose rulers and make laws as rebel whites? In the second place, it is a necessity in order to protect the loyal white men in the seceded States. The white Union men are in a great minority in each of those States. With them the blacks would act in a body; and it is believed that in each of said States, except one, the two united would form a majority, control the States, and protect themselves. Now they are the victims of daily murder. They must suffer constant persecution or be exiled. . . . Another good reason is, it would insure the ascendency of the Union party. . . . I believe . . . that on the continued ascendency of that party depends the safety of this great nation. If impartial suffrage is excluded in the rebel States, then every one of them is sure to send a solid rebel representative delegation to Congress, and cast a solid rebel electoral vote. . . . I am for negro suffrage in every rebel State. If it be just, it should not be denied; if it be necessary, it should be adopted; if it be a punishment to traitors, they deserve it.

Source: Stevens, Thaddeus. *Congressional Globe*, January 3, 1867, 252. In *Documentary History of Reconstruction: Political, Military, Social, Religious, Educational & Industrial, 1865 to the Present Time*. Ed. Walter Lynwood Fleming. Cleveland, Oh.: The Arthur H. Clark Company, 1906. 149–50.

Glossary

36°30′ According to the Missouri Compromise, any part of the Louisiana Purchase north of this line (Missouri's southern border) was to be excluded from slavery.

54th Massachusetts Regiment After President Abraham Lincoln's Emancipation Proclamation, the Union army organized all black military units, which white officers led. The 54th Massachusetts Regiment was one of the first of such units to be organized.

Abigail Adams (1744–1818) As the wife of John Adams, she endured long periods of separation from him while he served in many political roles. During these times apart, she wrote often to her husband, and their correspondence has provided a detailed portrait of life during the Revolutionary War.

abolition In the early 1830s, the anti-slavery movement shifted its goal from the gradual end of slavery to the immediate end or abolition of slavery.

abolitionism Movement that called for an immediate end to slavery throughout the United States.

John Adams (1735–1826) He was a signer of the Declaration of Independence and a delegate to the First and Second Continental Congresses. A member of the Federalist Party, he served as the first vice president and the second president of the United States. As president, he passed the Alien and Sedition Acts and endured a stormy relationship with France, which included the XYZ affair.

John Quincy Adams (1767–1848) As secretary of state, he urged President Monroe to issue the Monroe Doctrine, which incorporated his belief in an expanded use of federal powers. As the sixth president, Adams's nationalism and praise of European leaders caused a split in his party, causing some Republicans to leave and form the Democrat party.

Samuel Adams (1722–1803) A genius of revolutionary agitation, he believed that English Parliament had no right to legislate for the colonies. He organized the Sons of Liberty as well as protests in Boston against the British.

Jane Addams (1860–1935) She founded and ran of one of the best known settlement houses, the Hull House. Active in the peace and suffragist movements, she established child care for working mothers, health clinics, job training, and other social programs.

affirmative action Programs designed to give preferential treatment to women and minorities as compensation for past injustices.

Affordable Care Act (ACA) (2010) Vast health-care reform initiative signed into law and championed by President Obama, and widely criticized by Republicans, that aims to make health insurance more affordable and make health care accessible to everyone, regardless of income or prior medical conditions.

Agricultural Adjustment Act (1933) Legislation that paid farmers to produce less in order to raise crop prices for all; the AAA was later declared unconstitutional by the U.S. Supreme Court in the case of *United States v. Butler* (1936).

Emilio Aguinaldo (1869?–1964) He was a leader in the Filipino struggle for independence. During the war of 1898, Commodore George Dewey brought Aguinaldo back to the Philippines from exile to help fight the Spanish. However, after the Spanish surrendered to Americans, America annexed the Philippines and Aguinaldo fought against the American military until he was captured in 1901.

Alamo, Battle of the Siege in the Texas War for Independence of 1836, in which the San Antonio mission fell to the Mexicans. Davy Crockett and Jim Bowie were among the courageous defenders.

Albany Plan of Union A failed proposal by the seven northern colonies in anticipation of the French and Indian War, urging the unification of the colonies under one Crown-appointed president.

Alien and Sedition Acts of 1798 Four measures passed during the undeclared war with France that limited the freedoms of speech and press and restricted the liberty of non-citizens.

Allied Powers The nations fighting the Central Powers during the First World War, including France, Great Britain, and Russia; later joined by Italy and, after Russia quit the war in 1917, the United States.

American Anti-Imperialist League Coalition of anti-imperialist groups united in 1899 to protest American territorial expansion, especially in the Philippine Islands; its membership included prominent politicians, industrialists, labor leaders, and social reformers.

American Colonization Society Established in 1817, an organization whose mission was to return freed slaves to Africa.

American Federation of Labor Founded in 1881 as a national federation of trade unions made up of skilled workers.

American Indian Movement (AIM) Fed up with the poor conditions on Indian reservations and the federal government's unwillingness to help, Native Americans founded the American Indian Movement (AIM) in 1963. In 1973, AIM led 200 Sioux in the occupation of Wounded Knee. After a ten-week standoff with the federal authorities, the government agreed to reexamine Indian treaty rights and the occupation ended.

American Recovery and Reinvestment Act Hoping to restart the weak economy, President Obama signed this $787-billion economic stimulus bill in February of 2009. The bill included cash distributions to states, funds for food stamps, unemployment benefits, construction projects to renew the nation's infrastructure, funds for renewable-energy systems, and tax reductions.

American System Economic plan championed by Henry Clay of Kentucky that called for federal tariffs on imports, a strong national bank, and federally-financed internal improvements—roads, bridges, canals—all intended to strengthen the national economy and end American dependence on Great Britain.

American Tobacco Company Business founded in 1890 by North Carolina's James Buchanan Duke, who combined the major tobacco manufacturers of the time, ultimately controlling 90 percent of the country's cigarette production.

Anaconda Plan The Union's primary war strategy calling for a naval blockade of major southern seaports and then dividing the Confederacy by gaining control of the Tennessee, Cumberland, and Mississippi Rivers.

Annapolis Convention In 1786, all thirteen colonies were invited to a convention in Annapolis to discuss commercial problems, but only representatives from five states attended. However, the convention was not a complete failure because the delegates decided to have another convention in order to write the constitution.

Battle of Antietam (1862) Turning-point battle near Sharpsburg, Maryland, leaving over 20,000 soldiers dead or wounded, in which Union forces halted a Confederate invasion of the North.

anti-Federalists Opponents of the Constitution as an infringement on individual and states' rights, whose criticism led to the addition of a Bill of Rights to the document. Many anti-Federalists later joined Thomas Jefferson's Democratic-Republican party.

Anti-Masonic party This party grew out of popular hostility toward the Masonic fraternal order and entered the presidential election of 1832 as a third party. It was the first party to run as a third party in a presidential election as well as the first to hold a nomination convention and announce a party platform.

Appomattox Court House Virginia village where Confederate general Robert E. Lee surrendered to Union general Ulysses S. Grant on April 9, 1865.

Arab Awakening A wave of spontaneous democratic uprisings that spread throughout the Arab world beginning in 2011, in which long-oppressed peoples demanded basic liberties from generations-old authoritarian regimes.

Benedict Arnold (1741–1801) A traitorous American commander who planned to sell out the American garrison at West Point to the British; his plot was discovered before it could be executed and he joined the British army.

Articles of Confederation The first form of government for the United States, ratified by the original thirteen states in 1781; weak in central authority, it was replaced by the U.S. Constitution in 1789.

The Atlanta Compromise A speech by Booker T. Washington that called for the black community to strive for economic prosperity before attempting political and social equality.

Atlantic Charter (1941) Joint statement crafted by Franklin D. Roosevelt and British prime minister Winston Churchill that listed the war goals of the Allied Powers.

Aztec Empire A network of more than 300 city-states and upward of 30 provinces, established in the fourteenth century under the imperialistic Mexica, or Aztecs, in the valley of Mexico.

Crispus Attucks (1723–1770) During the Boston Massacre, he was supposedly at the head of the crowd of hecklers who baited the British troops. He was killed when the British troops fired on the crowd.

Stephen F. Austin (1793–1836) He established the first colony of Americans in Texas, which eventually attracted 2,000 people.

"Axis" alliance Military alliance formed in 1937 by the three major fascist powers: Germany, Italy, and Japan.

Aztec Empire Mesoamerican people who were conquered by the Spanish under Hernando Cortés, 1519–1528.

baby boom Markedly high birth rate in the years following World War II, leading to the biggest demographic "bubble" in U.S. history.

Bacon's Rebellion Unsuccessful 1676 revolt led by planter Nathaniel Bacon against Virginia governor William Berkeley's administration, which, Bacon charged, had failed to protect settlers from Indian raids.

Bank of the United States (1791) National bank responsible for holding and transferring federal government funds, making business loans, and issuing a national currency.

The Bank War Political struggle in the early 1830s between President Jackson and financier Nicholas Biddle over the renewing of the Second Bank's charter.

Barbary pirates North Africans who waged war (1801–1805) on the United States after President Thomas Jefferson refused to pay tribute (a bribe) to protect American ships.

Bay of Pigs Failed CIA operation that, in April 1961, deployed a band of Cuban rebels to overthrow Fidel Castro's Communist regime.

Battle of the Bulge On December 16, 1944, the German army launched a counterattack against the Allied forces, which pushed them back. However, the Allies were eventually able to recover and break through the German lines. This defeat was a great blow to the Nazi's morale and their army's strength. The battle used up the last of Hitler's reserve units and opened a route into Germany's heartland.

Bear Flag Republic On June 14, 1846, a group of Americans in California captured Sonoma from the Mexican army and declared it the Republic of California whose flag featured a grizzly bear. In July, the commodore of the U.S. Pacific Fleet landed troops on California's shores and declared it part of the United States.

Beats Group of bohemian, downtown New York writers, artists, and musicians who flouted convention in favor of liberated forms of self-expression.

beatnik A name referring to almost any young rebel who openly dissented from the middle-class life. The name itself stems from the Beats.

Berlin airlift (1948) Effort by the United States and Great Britain to deliver massive amounts of food and supplies flown to West Berlin in response to the Soviet land blockade of the city.

Berlin Wall Twenty-seven-mile-long concrete wall constructed in 1961 by East German authorities to stop the flow of East Germans fleeing to West Berlin.

Bessemer converter Apparatus that blasts air through molten iron to produce steel in very large quantities.

Nicholas Biddle (1786–1844) He was the president of the second Bank of the United States. In response to President Andrew Jackson's attacks on the bank, Biddle curtailed the bank's loans and exchanged its paper currency for gold and silver. In response, state banks began printing paper without restraint and lent it to speculators, causing a binge in speculating and an enormous increase in debt.

Bill of Rights First ten amendments to the U.S. Constitution, adopted in 1791 to guarantee individual rights and to help secure ratification of the Constitution by the states.

Osama bin Laden (1957–2011) The Saudi-born leader of al Qaeda, whose members attacked America on September 11, 2001. Years before the attack, he had declared *jihad* (holy war) on the United States, Israel, and the Saudi monarchy. In Afghanistan, the Taliban leaders gave bin Laden a safe haven in exchange for aid in fighting the Northern Alliance, who were rebels opposed to the Taliban. Following the Taliban's refusal to turn over bin Laden to the United States, America and a multinational coalition invaded Afghanistan and overthrew the Taliban. In May 2011, bin Laden was shot and killed by American special forces during a covert operation in Pakistan.

birth rate Proportion of births per 1,000 of the total population.

black codes Laws passed in southern states to restrict the rights of former slaves; to combat the codes, Congress passed the Civil Rights Act of 1866 and the Fourteenth Amendment and set up military governments in southern states that refused to ratify the amendment.

black power movement Militant form of civil rights protest focused on urban communities in the North and led by Malcolm X that grew as a response to impatience with the nonviolent tactics of Martin Luther King, Jr.

James Gillepsie Blaine (1830–1893) As a Republican congressman from Maine, he developed close ties with business leaders, which contributed to him losing the presidential election of 1884. He later opposed President Cleveland's efforts to reduce tariffs, which became a significant issue in the 1888 presidential election. Blaine served as secretary of state under President Benjamin Harrison.

Bleeding Kansas (1856) A series of violent conflicts in the Kansas territory between anti-slavery and pro-slavery factions over the status of slavery.

blitzkrieg (1940) The German "lightning war" strategy characterized by swift, well-organized attacks using infantry, tanks, and warplanes.

Bolsheviks Under the leadership of Vladimir Lenin, this Marxist party led the November 1917 revolution against the newly formed provisional government in Russia. After seizing control, the Bolsheviks negotiated a peace treaty with Germany, the Treaty of Brest-Litovsk, and ended their participation in World War I.

Bonus Expeditionary Force (1932) Protest march in Washington, D.C. by thousands of World War I veterans and their families, calling for immediate payment of their service bonuses certificates; violence ensued when President Herbert Hoover ordered their tent villages cleared.

boomtown Town, often in the West, that developed rapidly due to the sudden influx of wealth and work opportunities; often male-dominated with a substantial immigrant population.

Daniel Boone (1734–1820) He found and expanded a trail into Kentucky, which pioneers used to reach and settle the area.

John Wilkes Booth (1838?–1865) He assassinated President Abraham Lincoln at the Ford's Theater on April 14, 1865. He was pursued and killed.

Boston Massacre Violent confrontation between British soldiers and a Boston mob on March 5, 1770, in which five colonists were killed.

Boston Tea Party Demonstration against the Tea Act of 1773 in which the Sons of Liberty, dressed as Indians, dumped hundreds of chests of British-owned tea into Boston Harbor.

Bourbons In post–Civil War southern politics, the opponents of the Redeemers were called Bourbons. They were known for having forgotten nothing and learned nothing from the ordeal of the Civil War.

***bracero* program (1942)** System created in 1942 that permitted seasonal farm workers from Mexico to work in the United States on year-long contracts.

Joseph Brant (1742?–1807) Mohawk leader who led the Iroquois against the Americans in the Revolutionary War.

brinksmanship Secretary of State John Foster Dulles believed that communism could be contained by bringing America to the brink of war with an aggressive Communist nation. He believed that the aggressor would back down when confronted with the prospect of receiving a mass retaliation from a country with nuclear weapons.

John Brown (1800–1859) In response to a pro-slavery mob's sacking of the free-state town of Lawrence, Kansas, Brown went to the pro-slavery settlement of Pottawatomie, Kansas, which led to a guerrilla war in the Kansas territory. In 1859, he attempted to raid the federal arsenal at Harpers Ferry, hoping to use the stolen weapons to arm slaves, but he was captured and executed.

***Brown v. Board of Education* (1952)** Landmark Supreme Court case that struck down racial segregation in public schools and declared "separate-but-equal" unconstitutional.

William Jennings Bryan (1860–1925) He delivered the pro-silver "cross of gold" speech at the 1896 Democratic Convention and won his party's nomination for president. Disappointed pro-gold Democrats chose to walk out of the convention and nominate their own candidate, which split the Democratic party and cost them the White House. Bryan's loss also crippled the Populist movement that had endorsed him.

"Bull Moose" Progressive party *See* Progressive party

Bull Run, Battles of (First and Second Manassas) First land engagement of the Civil War took place on July 21, 1861, at Manassas Junction, Virginia, at which surprised Union troops quickly retreated; one year later, on August 29–30, Confederates captured the federal supply depot and forced Union troops back to Washington.

Martin Van Buren (1782–1862) During President Jackson's first term, he served as secretary of state and minister to London. In 1836, Van Buren was elected president, and he inherited a financial crisis. He believed that the government should not continue to keep its deposits in state banks and set up an independent Treasury, which was approved by Congress after several years of political maneuvering.

General John Burgoyne (1722–1792) He was the commander of Britain's northern forces during the Revolutionary War. He and most of his troops surrendered to the Americans at the Battle of Saratoga.

burial mounds A funeral tradition, practiced in the Mississippi and Ohio Valleys by the Adena-Hopewell cultures, of erecting massive mounds of earth over graves, often in the designs of serpents and other animals.

burned-over district Area of western New York strongly influenced by the revivalist fervor of the Second Great Awakening; Disciples of Christ and Mormons are among the many sects that trace their roots to the phenomenon.

Aaron Burr (1756–1836) Even though he was Thomas Jefferson's vice president, he lost favor with Jefferson's Republican supporters. He sought to work with the Federalists and run as their candidate for the governor of New York. Alexander Hamilton opposed Burr's candidacy and his stinging remarks on the subject led to Burr challenging him to duel in which Hamilton was killed.

George H. W. Bush (1924–) He served as vice president during the Reagan administration and then won the presidential election of 1988. His presidency was marked by raised taxes in the face of the federal deficit, the creation of the Office of National Drug Control Policy, and military activity abroad, including the invasion of Panama and Operation Desert Storm in Kuwait. He lost the 1992 presidential election to Bill Clinton.

George W. Bush (1946–) In the 2000 presidential election, Texas governor George W. Bush won as the Republican nominee against Democratic nominee Vice President Al Gore. After the September 11 terrorist attacks, he launched his "war on terrorism." President Bush adopted the Bush Doctrine, and United States invaded Afghanistan and Iraq with unclear outcomes leaving the countries divided. In September 2008, the nation's economy nose-dived as a credit crunch spiraled into a global economic meltdown. Bush signed into law the bank bailout fund called Troubled Asset Relief Program (TARP), but the economy did not improve.

Bush v. Gore (2000) The close 2000 presidential election came down to Florida's decisive twenty-five electoral votes. The final tally in Florida gave Bush a slight lead, but it was so small that a recount was required by state law. While the votes were being recounted, a legal battle was being waged to stop the recount. Finally, the case, *Bush v. Gore*, was presented to the Supreme Court who ruled 5–4 to stop the recount and Bush was declared the winner.

Bush Doctrine National security policy launched in 2002 by which the Bush administration claimed the right to launch preemptive military attacks against perceived enemies, particularly outlaw nations or terrorist organizations believed to possess weapons of mass destruction.

buying (stock) on margin The investment practice of making a small down payment (the "margin") on a stock and borrowing the rest of the money needed for the purchase from a broker who held the stock as security against a down market. If the stock's value declined and the buyer failed to meet a margin call for more funds, the broker could sell the stock to cover his loan.

Cahokia The largest chiefdom and city of the Mississippian Indian culture located in present-day Illinois, and the site of a sophisticated farming settlement that supported up to 15,000 inhabitants.

John C. Calhoun (1782–1850) He served in both the House of Representatives and the Senate for South Carolina before becoming secretary of war under President Monroe and then John Quincy Adams's vice president. Though he started his political career as an advocate of a strong national government, he eventually believed that states' rights, limited central government, and the power of nullification were necessary to preserve the Union.

California Gold Rush (1849) A massive migration of gold hunters, mostly men, who transformed the economy of California after gold was discovered in the foothills of northern California.

Camp David Accords (1978) Peace agreement between Prime Minister Menachem Begin of Israel and President Anwar Sadat of Egypt, the first Arab head of state to officially recognize the state of Israel.

"Scarface" Al Capone (1899–1947) The most successful gangster of the Prohibition era whose Chicago-based criminal empire included bootlegging, prostitution, and gambling.

Andrew Carnegie (1835–1919) A steel magnate who believed that the general public benefited from big business even if these companies employed harsh business practices. This philosophy became deeply ingrained in the conventional wisdom of some Americans. After retiring, he devoted himself to philanthropy in hopes of promoting social welfare and world peace.

Carnegie Steel Company Corporation under the leadership of Andrew Carnegie that came to dominate the American steel industry.

Carolina colonies English proprietary colonies comprised of North and South Carolina, whose semitropical climate made them profitable centers of rice, timber, and tar production.

carpetbaggers Northern emigrants who participated in the Republican governments of the reconstructed South.

Jimmy Carter (1924–) Elected president in 1976, Jimmy Carter was an outsider to Washington. He created the departments of Energy and Education and signed into law several environmental initiatives. In 1978, he successfully brokered a peace agreement between Israel and Egypt called the Camp David Accords. However, his unwillingness to make deals with legislators caused other bills to be either gutted or stalled in Congress. His administration was plagued with a series of crises: a recession and increased inflation, a fuel shortage, the Soviet invasion of Afghanistan, and the overthrow of the Shah of Iran, leading to the Iran Hostage Crisis. Carter struggled to get the hostages released and was unable to do so until after he lost the 1980 election to Ronald Reagan. He was awarded the Nobel Peace Prize in 2002 for his efforts to further peace and democratic elections around the world.

Jacques Cartier (1491–1557) He led the first French effort to colonize North America and explored the Gulf of St. Lawrence, reaching as far as present day Montreal on the St. Lawrence River.

Fidel Castro (1926–) In 1959, his Communist regime came to power in Cuba after two years of guerrilla warfare against the dictator Fulgenico Batista. He enacted land redistribution programs and nationalized all foreign-owned property. The latter action as well as his political trials and summary executions damaged relations between Cuba and America. Castro was turned down when he asked for loans from the United States. However, he did receive aid from the Soviet Union.

Central Intelligence Agency (CIA) Intelligence-gathering government agency founded in 1947; under President Eisenhower's orders, secretly undermined elected governments deemed susceptible to communism.

Central Powers One of the two sides during the First World War, including Germany, Austria-Hungary, the Ottoman Empire (Turkey), and Bulgaria.

Carrie Chapman Catt (1859–1947) She was a leader of a new generation of activists in the women's suffrage movement who carried on the work started by Elizabeth Cady Stanton and Susan B. Anthony.

Cesar Chavez (1927–1993) He founded the United Farm Workers (UFW) in 1962 and worked to organize migrant farm workers. In 1965, the UFW joined Filipino farm workers striking against corporate grape farmers in California's San Joaquin Valley. In 1970, the strike and a consumer boycott on grapes compelled the farmers to formally recognize the UFW. As the result of Chavez's efforts, wages and working conditions improved for migrant workers. In 1975, the California state legislature passed a bill that required growers to bargain collectively with representatives of the farm workers.

child labor The practice of sending children to work in mines, mills, and factories, often in unsafe conditions; widespread among poor families in the late nineteenth century.

Chinese Exclusion Act (1882) Federal law that barred Chinese laborers from immigrating to America.

Church of Jesus Christ of Latter-day Saints / Mormons Founded in 1830 by Joseph Smith, the sect was a product of the intense revivalism of the burned-over district of New York; Smith's successor Brigham Young led 15,000 followers to Utah in 1847 to escape persecution.

Winston Churchill (1874–1965) The British prime minister who led the country during the Second World War. Along with Roosevelt and Stalin, he helped shape the post-war world at the Yalta Conference. He also coined the term "iron curtain," which he used in his famous "The Sinews of Peace" speech.

citizen-soldiers Part-time non-professional soldiers, mostly poor farmers or recent immigrants who had been indentured servants, who played an important role in the Revolutionary War.

"city machines" Local political party officials used these organizations to dispense patronage and favoritism amongst voters and businesses to ensure their loyal support to the political party.

Civil Rights Act of 1957 First federal civil rights law since Reconstruction; established the Civil Rights Commission and the Civil Rights Division of the Department of Justice.

Civil Rights Act of 1964 Legislation that outlawed discrimination in public accommodations and employment, passed at the urging of President Lyndon B. Johnson.

civil service reform An extended effort led by political reformers to end the patronage system; led to the Pendleton Act (1883), which called for government positions to be awarded based on merit rather than party loyalty.

Henry Clay (1777–1852) In the first half of the nineteenth century, he was the foremost spokesman for the American system. As Speaker of the House in the 1820s, he promoted economic nationalism, "market revolution," and the rapid development of western states and territories. A broker of compromise, he formulated the "second" Missouri Compromise and the Compromise of 1850. In 1824, Clay supported John Quincy Adams, who won the presidency and appointed Clay to secretary of state. Andrew Jackson claimed that Clay had entered into a "corrupt bargain" with Adams for his own selfish gains.

Clayton Anti-Trust Act (1914) Legislation that served to enhance the Sherman Anti-Trust Act (1890) by clarifying what constituted "monopolistic" activities and declaring that labor unions were not to be viewed as "monopolies in restraint of trade."

Bill Clinton (1946–) The governor of Arkansas won the 1992 presidential election against President George H. W. Bush. In his first term, he pushed through Congress a tax increase, an economic stimulus package, the adoption of the North America Free Trade Agreement, welfare reform, a raise in the minimum wage, and improved public access to health insurance. His administration also negotiated the Oslo Accord and the Dayton Accords. After his re-election in 1996, he was involved in two high-profile scandals: his investment in the fraudulent Whitewater Development Corporation (but no evidence was found of him being involved in any wrongdoing) and his sexual affair with a White House intern. His attempt to cover up the affair led to a vote in Congress on whether or not to begin an impeachment inquiry. The House of Representatives voted to impeach Clinton, but the Senate found him not guilty.

Hillary Rodham Clinton (1947–) In the 2008 presidential election, Senator Hillary Clinton, the spouse of former President Bill Clinton, initially was the front-runner for the Democratic nomination, which made her the first woman with a serious chance to win the presidency. However, Senator Barack Obama's Internet-based and grassroots-orientated campaign garnered him enough delegates to win the nomination. After Obama became president, she was appointed secretary of state.

clipper ships Tall, slender, mid-nineteenth-century sailing ships that were favored over older merchant ships for their speed, but ultimately gave way to steamships because they lacked cargo space.

Coercive Acts Four parliamentary measures of 1774 that required the colonies to pay for the Boston Tea Party's damages, imposed a military government, disallowed colonial trials of British soldiers, and forced the quartering of troops in private homes.

coffin ships Irish immigrants fleeing the potato famine had to endure a six-week journey across the Atlantic to reach America. During these voyages, thousands of passengers died of disease and starvation, which led to the ships being called "coffin ships."

Columbian Exchange The transfer of biological and social elements, such as plants, animals, people, diseases, and cultural practices, among Europe, the Americas, and Africa in the wake of Christopher Columbus's voyages to the "New World."

Christopher Columbus (1451–1506) The Italian sailor who persuaded King Ferdinad and Queen Isabella of Spain to fund his expedition across the Atlantic to discover a new trade route to Asia. Instead of arriving at China or Japan, he reached the Bahamas in 1492.

Committee of Correspondence Group organized by Samuel Adams in retaliation for the *Gaspée* incident to address American grievances, assert American rights, and form a network of rebellion.

Committee on Public Information During the First World War, this committee produced war propaganda that conveyed the Allies' war aims to Americans as well as attempted to weaken the enemy's morale.

Committee to Re-elect the President (CREEP) During Nixon's presidency, his administration engaged in a number of immoral acts, such as attempting to steal information and falsely accusing political appointments of sexual improprieties. These acts were funded by money illegally collected through CREEP.

Common Sense Popular pamphlet written by Thomas Paine attacking British principles of hereditary rule and monarchical government, and advocating a declaration of American independence.

Compromise of 1850 A package of five bills presented to the Congress by Henry Clay intended to avoid secession or civil war by reducing tensions between North and South over the status of slavery.

Compromise of 1877 Deal made by a special congressional commission on March 2, 1877, to resolve the disputed presidential election of 1876; Republican Rutherford B. Hayes, who had lost the popular vote, was declared the winner in exchange for the withdrawal of federal troops from the South, marking the end of Reconstruction.

Comstock Lode Mine in eastern Nevada acquired by Canadian fur trapper Henry Comstock that between 1860 and 1880 yielded almost $1 billion worth of gold and silver.

Conestoga wagons These large horse-drawn wagons were used to carry people or heavy freight long distances, including from the East to the western frontier settlements.

conquistadores Spanish term for "conquerors," applied to Spanish and Portuguese soldiers who conquered lands held by indigenous peoples in central and southern America as well as the current states of Texas, New Mexico, Arizona, and California.

consumer culture A society in which mass production and consumption of nationally advertised products comes to dictate much of social life and status.

containment U.S. cold war strategy that sought to prevent global Soviet expansion and influence through political, economic, and, if necessary, military pressure as a means of combating the spread of communism.

Continental army Army authorized by the Continental Congress, 1775–1784, to fight the British; commanded by General George Washington.

Contract with America (1994) A list of conservative promises in response to the supposed liberalism of the Clinton administration, that was drafted by Speaker of the House Newt Gingrich and other congressional Republicans as the GOP platform for the 1994 midterm elections. More a campaign tactic than a practical program, few of its proposed items ever became law.

contrabands Slaves who sought refuge in Union military camps or who lived in areas of the Confederacy under Union control.

Contras The Reagan administration ordered the CIA to train and supply guerrilla bands of anti-Communist Nicaraguans called Contras. They were fighting the Sandinista government that had recently come to power in Nicaragua. The State Department believed that the Sandinista government was supplying the leftist Salvadoran rebels with Soviet and Cuban arms. A cease-fire agreement between the Contras and Sandinistas was signed in 1988.

Calvin Coolidge (1872–1933) After President Harding's death, his vice president, Calvin Coolidge, assumed the presidency. Coolidge believed that the nation's welfare was tied to the success of Big Business, and he worked to end government regulation of business and industry as well as reduce taxes. In particular, he focused on the nation's industrial development.

Copperhead Democrats Democrats in northern states who opposed the Civil War and argued for an immediate peace settlement with the Confederates; Republicans labeled them "Copperheads," likening them to venomous snakes.

Hernán Cortés (1485–1547) The Spanish conquistador who conquered the Aztec Empire and set the precedent for other plundering conquistadores.

General Charles Cornwallis (1738–1805) He was in charge of British troops in the South during the Revolutionary War. His surrender to George Washington at the Battle of Yorktown ended the Revolutionary War.

Corps of Discovery Meriwether Lewis and William Clark led this group of men on an expedition of the newly purchased Louisiana territory, which took them from Missouri to Oregon. As they traveled, they kept detailed journals and drew maps of the previously unexplored territory. Their reports attracted traders and trappers to the region and gave the United States a claim to the Oregon country by right of discovery and exploration.

"corrupt bargain" Scandal in which presidential candidate and Speaker of the House Henry Clay secured John Quincy Adams's victory over Andrew Jackson in the 1824 election, supposedly in exchange for Clay being named secretary of state.

cotton gin Hand-operated machine invented by Eli Whitney in the late eighteenth century that quickly removed seeds from cotton bolls, enabling the mass production of cotton in nineteenth-century America.

cotton kingdom Cotton-producing region, relying predominantly on slave labor, that spanned from North Carolina west to Louisiana and reached as far north as southern Illinois.

cotton White fibers harvested from cotton plants, spun into yarn, and woven into textiles that made comfortable, easy-to-clean products, especially clothing; the most valuable cash crop driving the economy in the United States and Great Britain during the nineteenth century.

the counterculture "Hippie" youth culture of the 1960s, which rejected the values of the dominant culture in favor of illicit drugs, communes, free sex, and rock music.

counterculture Unorganized youth rebellion against mainstream institutions, values, and behavior that more often focused on cultural rather than political activism.

court-packing plan President Franklin D. Roosevelt's failed 1937 attempt to increase the number of U.S. Supreme Court justices from nine to fifteen in order to save his Second New Deal programs from constitutional challenges.

covenant theory A Puritan concept that believed true Christians could enter a voluntary union for the common worship of God. Taking the idea one step further, the union could also be used for the purposes of establishing governments.

crop-lien system Credit system used by sharecroppers and share tenants who pledged a portion ("share") of their future crop to local merchants or land owners in exchange for farming supplies and food.

"Cross of Gold" Speech In the 1896 election, the Democratic Party split over the issue of whether to use gold or silver to back American currency. Significant to this division was the pro-silver "Cross of Gold" speech that William Jennings Bryan delivered at the Democratic convention, which was so well received that Bryan won the nomination to be their presidential candidate. Disappointed pro-gold Democrats chose to walk out of the convention and nominate their own candidate.

Cuban missile crisis Thirteen-day U.S.-Soviet standoff in October 1962, sparked by the discovery of Soviet missile sites in Cuba; the crisis was the closest the world has come to nuclear war since 1945.

cult of domesticity A pervasive nineteenth-century ideology that urged women to celebrate their role as manager of the household and nurturer of the children.

George A. Custer (1839–1876) He was a reckless and glory-seeking Lieutenant Colonel of the U.S. Army who fought the Sioux Indians in the Great Sioux War. In 1876, he and his detachment of soldiers were entirely wiped out in the Battle of Little Bighorn.

***Dartmouth College v. Woodward* (1819)** Supreme Court ruling that enlarged the definition of *contract* to put corporations beyond the reach of the states that chartered them.

Daughters of Liberty Colonial women who protested the British government's tax policies by boycotting British products, such as clothing, and who wove their own fabric, or "homespun."

Dawes Severalty Act of 1887 Federal legislation that divided ancestral Native American lands among the heads of each Indian family in an attempt to "Americanize" Indians by forcing them to become farmers working individual plots of land.

D-day June 6, 1944, when an Allied amphibious assault landed on the Normandy coast and established a foothold in Europe from which Hitler's defenses could not recover.

Jefferson Davis (1808–1889) He was the president of the Confederacy during the Civil War. When the Confederacy's defeat seemed invitable in early 1865, he refused to surrender. Union forces captured him in May of that year.

Bartolomé de Las Casas (1484–1566) A Catholic missionary who renounced the Spanish practice of coercively converting Indians and advocated their better treatment. In 1552, he wrote *A Brief Relation of the Destruction of the Indies*, which described the Spanish's cruel treatment of the Indians.

death rate Proportion of deaths per 1,000 of the total population; also called *mortality rate*.

Eugene V. Debs (1855–1926) Founder of the American Railway Union, which he organized against the Pullman Palace Car Company during the Pullman strike. Later he organized the Social Democratic party, which eventually became the Socialist Party of America. In the 1912 presidential election, he ran as the Socialist party's candidate and received more than 900,000 votes.

Declaration of Independence Formal statement, principally drafted by Thomas Jefferson and adopted by the Second Continental Congress on July 4, 1776, that officially announced the thirteen colonies' break with Great Britain.

Declaration of Sentiments Document based on the Declaration of Independence that called for gender equality, written primarily by Elizabeth Cady Stanton and signed by Seneca Falls Convention delegates in 1848.

Declaratory Act Following the repeal of the Stamp Act in 1766, Parliament passed this act which asserted Parliament's full power to make laws binding the colonies "in all cases whatsoever."

Deism Enlightenment thought applied to religion, emphasizing reason, morality, and natural law rather than scriptural authority or an ever-present God intervening in human life.

détente Period of improving relations between the United States and Communist nations, particularly China and the Soviet Union, during the Nixon administration.

George Dewey (1837–1917) On April 30, 1898, Commodore George Dewey's small U.S. naval squadron defeated the Spanish warships in Manila Bay in the Philippines. This quick victory aroused expansionist fever in the United States.

John Dewey (1859–1952) He is an important philosopher of pragmatism. However, he preferred to use the term *instrumentalism*, because he saw ideas as instruments of action.

Ngo Dinh Diem (1901–1963) Following the Geneva Accords, the French, with the support of America, forced the Vietnamese emperor to accept Dinh Diem as the new premier of South Vietnam. President Eisenhower sent advisors to train Diem's police and army. In return, the United States expected Diem to enact democratic reforms and distribute land to the peasants. Instead, he suppressed his political opponents, did little or no land distribution, and let corruption grow. In 1956, he refused to participate in elections to reunify Vietnam. Eventually, he ousted the emperor and declared himself president.

Distribution Act (1836) Law requiring the distribution of the federal budget surplus to the states, creating chaos among state banks that had become dependent on such federal funds.

Dorothea Lynde Dix (1802–1887) She was an important figure in increasing the public's awareness of the plight of the mentally ill. After a two-year investigation of the treatment of the mentally ill in Massachusetts, she presented her findings and won the support of leading reformers. She eventually convinced twenty states to reform their treatment of the mentally ill.

Dixiecrats Breakaway faction of southern Democrats who defected from the national Democratic party in 1948 to protest the party's increased support for civil rights and to nominate their own segregationist candidates for elective office.

"dollar diplomacy" practice advocated by President Theodore Roosevelt in which the U.S. government fostered American investments in less developed nations and then used U.S. military force to protect those investments

Donner party Forty-seven surviving members of a group of migrants to California were forced to resort to cannibalism to survive a brutal winter trapped in the Sierra Nevadas, 1846–1847; highest death toll of any group traveling the Overland Trail.

Stephen A. Douglas (1812–1861) As a senator from Illinois, he authored the Kansas-Nebraska Act. Running for senatorial reelection in 1858, he engaged Abraham Lincoln in a series of public debates about slavery in the territories. Even though Douglas won the election, the debates gave Lincoln a national reputation.

Frederick Douglass (1818–1895) He escaped from slavery and become an eloquent speaker and writer against the institution. In 1845, he published his autobiography entitled *Narrative of the Life of Frederick Douglass* and two years later he founded an abolitionist newspaper for blacks called the *North Star*.

dot-coms In the late 1990s, the stock market soared to new heights and defied the predictions of experts that the economy could not sustain such a performance. Much of the economic success was based on dot-com enterprises, which were firms specializing in computers, software, telecommunications, and the internet. However, many of the companies' stock market values were driven higher and higher by speculation instead of financial success. Eventually the stock market bubble burst.

***Dred Scott v. Sandford* (1857)** U.S. Supreme Court ruling that slaves were not U.S. citizens and therefore could not sue for their freedom and that Congress could not prohibit slavery in the western territories.

W. E. B. Du Bois (1868–1963) He criticized Booker T. Washington's views on civil rights as being accommodationist. He advocated "ceaseless agitation" for civil rights and the immediate end to segregation and an enforcement of laws to protect civil rights and equality. He promoted an education for African Americans that would nurture bold leaders who were willing to challenge discrimination in politics.

John Foster Dulles (1888–1959) As President Eisenhower's secretary of state, he institutionalized the policy of containment and introduced the strategy of deterrence. He believed in using brinkmanship to halt the spread of communism. He attempted to employ it in Indochina, which led to the United States' involvement in Vietnam.

Dust Bowl Vast area of the Midwest where windstorms blew away millions of tons of topsoil from parched farmland after a long drought in the 1930s, causing great social distress and a massive migration of farm families.

Eastern Woodlands Peoples Various Native American peoples, particularly the Algonquian, Iroquoian, and Muskogean regional groups, who once dominated the Atlantic seaboard from Maine to Louisiana.

Peggy Eaton (1796–1879) The wife of John Eaton, President Jackson's secretary of war, was the daughter of a tavern owner with an unsavory past. Supposedly her first husband had committed suicide after learning that she was having an affair with John Eaton. The wives of members of Jackson's cabinet snubbed her because of her lowly origins and past, resulting in a scandal known as the Eaton Affair.

Economic Opportunity Act Key legislation in President Johnson's "War on Poverty" which created the Office of Economic Opportunity and programs like Head Start and work-study.

Jonathan Edwards (1703–1758) New England Congregationalist minister who began a religious revival in his Northampton church and was an important figure in the Great Awakening.

election of 1800 Presidential election between Thomas Jefferson and John Adams; resulted in the first Democratic-Republican victory after the Federalist administrations of George Washington and John Adams.

1864 Election Abraham Lincoln's successful re-election campaign, capitalizing on Union military successes in Georgia, to defeat Democratic opponent, former general George B. McClellan, who ran on a peace platform.

election of 1912 The presidential election of 1912 featured four candidates: Wilson, Taft, Roosevelt, and Debs. Each candidate believed in the basic assumptions of progressive politics, but each had a different view on how progressive ideals should be implemented through policy. In the end, Taft and Roosevelt split the Republican party votes and Wilson emerged as the winner.

Queen Elizabeth I of England (1533–1603) The protestant daughter of Henry VIII, she was Queen of England from 1558–1603 and played a major role in the Protestant Reformation. During her long reign, the doctrines and services of the Church of England were defined and the Spanish Armada was defeated.

General Dwight D. Eisenhower (1890–1969) During the Second World War, he commanded the Allied Forces landing in Africa and was the supreme Allied commander as well as planner for Operation Overlord. In 1952, he was elected president on his popularity as a war hero and his promises to clean up Washington. His administration sought to cut the nation's domestic programs and budget, ended the fighting in Korea, and institutionalized the policies of containment and deterrence. He established the Eisenhower doctrine, which promised to aid any nation against aggression by a Communist nation.

Ellis Island Reception center in New York Harbor through which most European immigrants to America were processed from 1892 to 1954.

Emancipation Proclamation (1863) Military order issued by President Abraham Lincoln that freed slaves in areas still controlled by the Confederacy

Embargo Act (1807) A law promoted by President Thomas Jefferson prohibiting American ships from leaving for foreign ports, in order to safeguard them from British and French attacks. This ban on American exports proved disastrous to the U.S. economy.

Ralph Waldo Emerson (1803–1882) As a leader of the transcendentalist movement, he wrote poems, essays, and speeches that discussed the sacredness of nature, optimism, self-reliance, and the unlimited potential of the individual. He wanted to transcend the limitations of inherited conventions and rationalism to reach the inner recesses of the self.

encomienda A land-grant system under which Spanish army officers (*conquistadores*) were awarded large parcels of land taken from Native Americans.

Enlightenment A revolution in thought begun in Europe in the seventeenth century that emphasized reason and science over the authority and myths of traditional religion.

enumerated goods According to the Navigation Act, these particular goods, like tobacco or cotton, could only be shipped to England or other English colonies.

Environmental Protection Agency (EPA) (1970) Federal environmental agency created by Nixon to appease the demands of congressional Democrats for a federal environmental watchdog agency.

Erie Canal Most important and profitable of the barge canals of the 1820s and 1830s; stretched from Buffalo to Albany, New York, connecting the Great Lakes to the East Coast and making New York City the nation's largest port.

ethnic cleansing The systematic removal of an ethnic group from a territory through violence or intimidation in order to create a homogenous society; the term was popularized by the Yugoslav policy brutally targeting Albanian Muslims in Kosovo.

exodusters African Americans who migrated west from the South in search of a haven from racism and poverty after the collapse of Radical Republican rule.

The Fair Deal (1949) President Truman's proposals to build upon the New Deal with national health insurance, the repeal of the Taft-Hartley Act, new civil rights legislation, and other initiatives; most were rejected by the Republican-controlled Congress.

Fair Employment Practices Commission Created in 1941 by executive order, the FEPC sought to eliminate racial discrimination in jobs; it possessed little power but represented a step toward civil rights for African Americans.

falling domino theory Theory that if one country fell to communism, its neighboring countries would follow suit.

Farmers' Alliances Like the Granger Movement, these organizations sought to address the issues of small farming communities; however Alliances emphasized more political action and called for the creation of a Third Party to advocate their concerns.

fascism A radical form of totalitarian government that emerged in Italy and Germany in the 1920s in which a dictator uses propaganda and brute force to seize control of all aspects of national life.

field hands Slaves who toiled in the cotton or cane fields in organized work gangs.

Federal-Aid Highway Act (1956) Largest federal project in U.S. history that created a national network of interstate highways and was the largest federal project in history.

Federal Deposit Insurance Corporation (1933) Independent government agency, established to prevent bank panics, that guarantees the safety of deposits in citizens' savings accounts.

Federal Reserve Act (1913) Legislation passed by Congress to create a new national banking system in order to regulate the nation's currency supply and ensure the stability and integrity of member banks who made up the Federal Reserve System across the nation.

Federal Trade Commission (1914) Independent agency created by the Wilson administration that replaced the Bureau of Corporations as an even more powerful tool to combat unfair trade practices and monopolies.

Federal Writers' Project During the Great Depression, this project provided writers, such as Ralph Ellison, Richard Wright, and Saul Bellow, with work, which gave them employment and a chance to develop as artists.

federalism Concept of dividing governmental authority between the national government and the states.

The Federalist Papers Collection of eighty-five essays, published widely in newspapers in 1787 and 1788, written by Alexander Hamilton, James Madison, and John Jay in support of adopting the proposed U.S. Constitution.

Federalists Proponents of a centralized federal system and the ratification of the Constitution. Most Federalists were relatively young, educated men who supported a broad interpretation of the Constitution whenever national interest dictated such flexibility. Notable Federalists included Alexander Hamilton and John Jay.

Geraldine Ferraro (1935–) In the 1984 presidential election, Democratic nominee, Walter Mondale, chose her as his running mate. As a member of the U.S. House of Representatives from New York, she was the first woman to be a vice-presidential nominee for a major political party. However, she was placed on the defensive because of her husband's complicated business dealings.

Fifteenth Amendment This amendment forbids states to deny any person the right to vote on grounds of "race, color or pervious condition of servitude." Former Confederate states were required to ratify this amendment before they could be readmitted to the Union.

"final solution" The Nazi party's systematic murder of some 6 million Jews along with more than a million other people including, but not limited to, gypsies, homosexuals, and handicap individuals.

First New Deal (1933–1935) Franklin D. Roosevelt's ambitious first-term cluster of economic and social programs designed to combat the Great Depression.

First Red Scare Outbreak of anti-Communist hysteria that included the arrest without warrants of thousands of suspected radicals, most of whom (mainly Russian immigrants) were deported.

flappers Young women of the 1920s whose rebellion against prewar standards of femininity included wearing shorter dresses, bobbing their hair, dancing to jazz music, driving cars, smoking cigarettes, and indulging in illegal drinking and gambling.

Food Administration After America's entry into World War I, the economy of the home front needed to be reorganized to provide the most efficient means of conducting the war. The Food Administration was a part of this effort. Under the leadership of Herbert Hoover, the organization sought to increase agricultural production while reducing civilian consumption of foodstuffs.

The "Force Bill" (1833) Legislation, sparked by the Nullification Crisis in South Carolina, that authorized the president's use of the army to compel states to comply with federal law.

Gerald Ford (1913–2006) He was appointed to the vice presidency under President Nixon after the resignation of Spiro Agnew, and assumed the presidency after President Nixon's resignation. He resisted congressional pressure to both reduce taxes and increase federal spending, which sent the American economy into the deepest recession since the Great Depression. Ford retained Kissinger as his secretary of state and continued Nixon's foreign policy goals. He was heavily criticized following the collapse of South Vietnam.

Fort Laramie Treaty (1851) Restricted the Plains Indians from using the Overland Trail and permitted the building of government forts.

Fort Necessity After attacking a group of French soldiers, George Washington constructed and took shelter in this fort from vengeful French troops. Washington eventually surrendered to them after a day-long battle. This conflict was a significant event in igniting the French and Indian War.

Fort Sumter First battle of the Civil War, in which the federal fort in Charleston (South Carolina) Harbor was captured by the Confederates on April 14, 1861, after two days of shelling.

"forty-niners" Speculators who went to northern California following the discovery of gold in 1848; the first of several years of large-scale migration was 1849.

Fourteen Points President Woodrow Wilson's proposed plan for the peace agreement after the First World War that included the creation of a "league of nations" intended to keep the peace.

Fourteenth Amendment (1868) Guaranteed rights of citizenship to former slaves, in words similar to those of the Civil Rights Act of 1866.

alliance with France Critical diplomatic, military, and economic alliance between France and the newly independent United States, codified by the Treaty of Amity and Commerce and the Treaty of Alliance (1778).

Franciscan Missions In 1769, Franciscan missioners accompanied Spanish soldiers to California and over the next fifty years established a chain of missions from San Diego to San Francisco. At these missions, friars sought to convert Indians to Catholicism and make them members of the Spanish empire. The friars stripped the Indians of their native heritage and used soldiers to enforce their will.

Benjamin Franklin (1706–1790) A Boston-born American, who epitomized the Enlightenment for many Americans and Europeans, Franklin's wide range of interests led him to become a publisher, inventor, and statesman. As the latter, he contributed to the writing of the Declaration of Independence, served as the minister to France during the Revolutionary War, and was a delegate to the Constitutional Convention.

Free-Soil Party A political coalition created in 1848 that opposed the expansion of slavery into the new western territories.

Freedmen's Bureau Reconstruction agency established in 1865 to protect the legal rights of former slaves and to assist with their education, jobs, health care, and landowning.

Freedom Riders Activists who, beginning in 1961, traveled by bus through the South to test federal court rulings that banned segregation on buses and trains.

John C. Frémont "the Pathfinder" (1813–1890) He was an explorer and surveyor who helped inspire Americans living in California to rebel against the Mexican government and declare independence.

French and Indian War (Seven Years' War) The last—and most important—of four colonial wars fought between England and France for control of North America east of the Mississippi River.

French Revolution Revolutionary movement beginning in 1789 that overthrew the monarchy and transformed France into an unstable republic before Napoleon Bonaparte assumed power in 1799.

Sigmund Freud (1865–1939) He was the founder of psychoanalysis, which suggested that human behavior was motivated by unconscious and irrational forces. By the 1920s, his ideas were being discussed more openly in America.

frontier revivals Religious revival movement within the Second Great Awakening, that took place in frontier churches in western territories and states in the early nineteenth century.

Fugitive Slave Act (1850) Part of the Compromise of 1850, a provision that authorized federal officials to help capture and then return escaped slaves to their owners without trials.

fundamentalism Anti-modernist Protestant movement started in the early twentieth century that proclaimed the literal truth of the Bible; the name came from *The Fundamentals*, published by conservative leaders.

William Lloyd Garrison (1805–1879) In 1831, he started the anti-slavery newspaper *Liberator* and helped start the New England Anti-Slavery Society. Two years later, he assisted Arthur and Lewis Tappan in the founding of the American Anti-Slavery Society. He and his followers believed that America had been thoroughly corrupted and needed a wide range of reforms, embracing abolition, temperance, pacifism, and women's rights.

Marcus Garvey (1887–1940) He was the leading spokesman for Negro Nationalism, which exalted blackness, black cultural expression, and black exclusiveness. He called upon African Americans to liberate themselves from the surrounding white culture and create their own businesses, cultural centers, and newspapers. He was also the founder of the Universal Negro Improvement Association.

Citizen Genet (1763–1834) As the ambassador to the United States from the new French Republic, he engaged American privateers to attack British ships and conspired with frontiersmen and land speculators to organize an attack on Spanish Florida and Louisiana. His actions and the French radicals excessive actions against their enemies in the new French Republic caused the French Revolution to lose support among Americans.

Geneva Accords In 1954, the Geneva Accords were signed, which ended French colonial rule in Indochina. The agreement created the independent nations of Laos and Cambodia and divided Vietnam along the 17th parallel until an election in 1956 would reunify the country.

Battle of Gettysburg (1863) A monumental three-day battle in southern Pennsylvania, widely considered a turning point in the war, in which Union forces successfully countered a second Confederate invasion of the North.

Ghost Dance movement A spiritual and political movement among Native Americans whose followers performed a ceremonial "ghost dance" intended to connect the living with the dead and make the Indians bulletproof in battles to restore their homelands.

GI Bill of Rights (1944) Provided unemployment, education, and financial benefits for World War II veterans to ease their transition back to the civilian world.

***Gibbons v. Ogden* (1824)** Supreme Court case that gave the federal government the power to regulate interstate commerce.

Newt Gingrich (1943–) He led the Republican insurgency in Congress in the mid 1990s through mobilizing religious and social conservatives. Along with other Republican congressmen, he created the Contract with America, which was a ten-point anti-big government program. However, the program fizzled out after many of its bills were not passed by Congress.

Gilded Age (1860–1896): An era of dramatic industrial and urban growth characterized by widespread political corruption and loose government oversight of corporations.

The Gilded Age Mark Twain and Charles Dudley Warner's 1873 novel, the title of which became the popular name for the period from the end of the Civil War to the turn of the century.

glasnost Russian term for "openness"; applied to the loosening of censorship in the Soviet Union under Mikhail Gorbachev.

globalization An important, and controversial, transformation of the world economy whereby the Internet helped revolutionize global commerce by creating an international marketplace for goods and services. Led by the growing number of multinational companies and the Americanization of many foreign consumer cultures, with companies like McDonald's and Starbucks appearing in all of the major cities of the world.

Glorious Revolution Successful 1688 coup, instigated by a group of English aristocrats, which overthrew King James II and instated William of Orange and Mary, his English wife, to the British throne.

Barry Goldwater (1909–1998) A leader of the Republican right whose book, *The Conscience of a Conservative*, was highly influential to that segment of the party. He proposed eliminating the income tax and overhauling Social Security. In 1964, he ran as the Republican presidential candidate and lost to President Johnson. He campaigned against Johnson's war on poverty, the tradition of New Deal, the nuclear test ban and the Civil Rights Act of 1964 and advocated the wholesale bombing of North Vietnam.

Samuel Gompers (1850–1924) He served as the president of the American Federation of Labor from its inception until his death. He focused on achieving concrete economic gains such as higher wages, shorter hours, and better working conditions.

"good neighbor" policy Proclaimed by President Franklin D. Roosevelt in his first inaugural address in 1933, it sought improved diplomatic relations between the United States and its Latin American neighbors.

Mikhail Gorbachev (1931–) In the late 1980s, Soviet leader Mikhail Gorbachev attempted to reform the Soviet Union through his programs of *perestroika* and *glasnost* and pursued a renewal of détente with America, signing new arms-control agreements with President Reagan. Gorbachev allowed the velvet revolutions of Eastern Europe to occur without outside interference. Eventually the political, social, and economic upheaval he had unleashed would lead to the break-up of the Soviet Union.

Albert Gore Jr. (1948–) He served as a senator of Tennessee and then as President Clinton's vice president. In the 2000 presidential election, he was the Democratic candidate against Governor George W. Bush. The close election came down to Florida's electoral votes. While the votes were being recounted as required by state law, a legal battle was being waged to stop the recount. Finally, the case, *Bush v. Gore*, was presented to the Supreme Court who ruled 5–4 to stop the recount and Bush was declared the winner.

Jay Gould (1836–1892) As one of the biggest railroad robber barons, he was infamous for buying rundown railroads, making cosmetic improvements and then reselling them for a profit. He used corporate funds for personal investments and to bribe politicians and judges.

gradualism This strategy for ending slavery involved promoting the banning of slavery in the new western territories and encouraging the release of slaves from slavery. Supporters of this method believed that it would bring about the gradual end of slavery.

Granger Movement Began by offering social and educational activities for isolated farmers and their families and later started to promote "cooperatives" where farmers could join together to buy, store, and sell their crops to avoid the high fees charged by brokers and other middle-men.

Ulysses S. Grant (1822–1885) After distinguishing himself in the western theater of the Civil War, he was appointed general in chief of the Union army in 1864. Afterward, he defeated General Robert E. Lee through a policy of aggressive attrition. Lee surrendered to Grant on April 9th, 1865 at the Appomattox Court House. His presidential tenure suffered from scandals and fiscal problems, including the debate on whether or not greenbacks, paper money, should be removed from circulation.

Great Awakening Fervent religious revival movement that swept the thirteen colonies from the 1720s through the 1740s.

Great Compromise (Connecticut Compromise) Mediated the differences between the New Jersey and Virginia delegations to the Constitutional Convention by providing for a bicameral legislature, the upper house of which would have equal representation and the lower house of which would be apportioned by population.

Great Depression (1929–1941) Worst economic downturn in American history; it was spurred by the stock market crash in the fall of 1929 and lasted until the Second World War.

Great Migration Mass exodus of African Americans from the rural South to the Northeast and Midwest during and after the First World War.

Great Railroad Strike of 1877 A series of demonstrations, some violent, held nationwide in support of striking railroad workers in Martinsburg, West Virginia, who refused to work due to wage cuts.

Great Recession (2007–2009) Massive, prolonged economic downturn sparked by the collapse of the housing market and the financial institutions holding unpaid mortgages; it lasted from December 2007 to January 2009 and resulted in 9 million Americans losing their jobs.

Great Sioux War Conflict between Sioux and Cheyenne Indians and federal troops over lands in the Dakotas in the mid-1870s.

Great Society Term coined by President Lyndon B. Johnson in his 1965 State of the Union address, in which he proposed legislation to address problems of voting rights, poverty, diseases, education, immigration, and the environment.

Horace Greeley (1811–1872) In reaction to Radical Reconstruction and corruption in President Ulysses S. Grant's administration, a group of Republicans broke from the party to form the Liberal Republicans. In 1872, the Liberal Republicans chose Horace Greeley as their presidential candidate who ran on a platform of favoring civil service reform and condemning the Republican's Reconstruction policy.

greenbacks Paper money issued during the Civil War. After the war ended, a debate emerged on whether or not to remove the paper currency from circulation and revert back to hard-money currency (gold coins). Opponents of hard-money feared that eliminating the greenbacks would shrink the money supply, which would lower crop prices and make it more difficult to repay long-term debts. President Ulysses S. Grant, as well as hard-currency advocates, believed that gold coins were morally preferable to paper currency.

Greenback party Formed in 1876 in reaction to economic depression, the party favored issuance of unsecured paper money to help farmers repay debts; the movement for free coinage of silver took the place of the greenback movement by the 1880s.

General Nathanael Greene (1742–1786) He was appointed by Congress to command the American army fighting in the South during the Revolutionary War. Using his patience and his skills of managing men, saving supplies, and avoiding needless risks, he waged a successful war of attrition against the British.

Sarah Grimké (1792–1873) and **Angelina Grimké (1805–1879)** These two sisters gave anti-slavery speeches to crowds of mixed gender that caused some people to condemn them for engaging in unfeminine activities. In 1840, William Lloyd Garrison convinced the Anti-Slavery Society to allow women equal participation in the organization.

Half-Way Covenant Allowed baptized children of church members to be admitted to a "halfway" membership in the church and secure baptism for their own children in turn, but allowed them neither a vote in the church, nor communion.

Alexander Hamilton (1755–1804) His belief in a strong federal government led him to become a leader of the Federalists. As the first secretary of the Treasury, he laid the foundation for American capitalism through his creation of a federal budget, funded debt, a federal tax system, a national bank, a customs service, and a coast guard. His "Reports on Public Credit" and "Reports on Manufactures" outlined his vision for economic development and government finances. He died in a duel against Aaron Burr.

Alexander Hamilton's economic reforms Various measures designed to strengthen the nation's economy and generate federal revenue through the promotion of new industries, the adoption of new tax policies, the payment of war debts, and the establishment of a national bank.

Warren G. Harding (1865–1923) In the 1920 presidential election, he was the Republican nominee who promised Americans a "return to normalcy." Once in office, Harding's administration dismantled many of the social and economic components of progressivism and pursued a pro-business agenda. Harding appointed four pro-business Supreme Court Justices, cut taxes, increased tariffs, and promoted a lenient attitude towards regulation of corporations. However, he did speak out against racism and ended the exclusion of African Americans from federal positions.

Harlem Renaissance The nation's first self-conscious black literary and artistic movement; it was centered in New York City's Harlem district, which had a largely black population in the wake of the Great Migration from the South.

Hartford Convention A series of secret meetings in December 1814 and January 1815 at which New England Federalists protested American involvement in the War of 1812 and discussed several constitutional amendments, including limiting each president to one term, designed to weaken the dominant Republican Party.

Haymarket Riot (1886) Violent uprising in Haymarket Square, Chicago, where police clashed with labor demonstrators in the aftermath of a bombing.

headright A land-grant policy that promised fifty acres to any colonist who could afford passage to Virginia, as well as fifty more for any accompanying servants. The headright policy was eventually expanded to include any colonists—and was also adopted in other colonies.

Patrick Henry (1736–1799) He inspired the Virginia Resolves, which declared that Englishmen could only be taxed by their elected representatives. In March of 1775, he met with other colonial leaders to discuss the goals of the upcoming

Continental Congress and famously declared "Give me liberty or give me death." During the ratification process of the U.S. Constitution, he became one of the leaders of the anti-federalists.

Hiroshima (1945) Japanese port city that was the first target of the newly developed atomic bomb on August 6, 1945. Most of the city was destroyed.

Alger Hiss (1904–1996) During the second Red Scare he had served in several government departments and was accused of being a spy for the Soviet Union and was convicted of lying about espionage. The case was politically damaging to the Truman administration because the president called the charges against Hiss a "red herring."

Adolph Hitler (1889–1945) The leader of the Nazis who advocated a violent anti-Semitic, anti-Marxist, pan-German ideology. He started World War II in Europe and orchestrated the systematic murder of some 6 million Jews along with more than a million others.

HIV/AIDS Human immunodeficiency virus (HIV) transmitted via the bodily fluids of infected persons to cause acquired immunodeficiency syndrome (AIDS), an often-fatal disease of the immune system when it appeared in the 1980s.

holding company A corporation established to own and manage other companies' stock rather than to produce goods and services itself.

Holocaust Systematic racist attempt by the Nazis to exterminate the Jews of Europe, resulting in the murder of over 6 million Jews and more than a million other "undesirables."

Homestead Act (1862) Legislation granting "homesteads" of 160 acres of government-owned land to settlers who agreed to work the land for at least five years.

Homestead steel strike (1892) Labor conflict at the Homestead steel mill near Pittsburgh, Pennsylvania, culminating in a battle between strikers and private security agents hired by the factory's management.

Herbert Hoover (1874–1964) Prior to becoming president, Hoover served as the secretary of commerce in both the Harding and Coolidge administrations. As president during the Great Depression, he believed that the nation's business structure was sound and sought to revive the economy through boosting the nation's confidence. He also tried to restart the economy with government constructions projects, lower taxes and new federal loan programs, but nothing worked.

horizontal integration The process by which a corporation acquires or merges with its competitors.

horse A tall, four-legged mammal (*Equus caballus*), domesticated and bred since prehistoric times for carrying riders and pulling heavy loads. The Spanish introduced horses to the Americas, eventually transforming many Native American cultures.

House Committee on Un-American Activities (HUAC) Committee of the U.S. House of Representatives formed in 1938; it was originally tasked with investigating Nazi subversion during the Second World War and later shifted its focus to rooting out Communists in the government and the motion-picture industry.

Sam Houston (1793–1863) During Texas's fight for independence from Mexico, Sam Houston was the commander in chief of the Texas forces, and he led the attack that captured General Antonio López de Santa Anna. After Texas gained its independence, he was named its first president.

Jacob Riis' *How the Other Half Lives* Jacob Riis was an early muckraking journalist who exposed the slum conditions in New York City in his book *How the Other Half Lives*.

General William Howe (1729–1814) As the commander of the British army in the Revolutionary War, he seized New York City from Washington's army, but failed to capture it. He missed several more opportunities to quickly end the rebellion, and he resigned his command after the British defeat at Saratoga.

Saddam Hussein (1937–2006) The former dictator of Iraq who became the head of state in 1979. In 1980, he invaded Iran and started the eight-year-long Iran-Iraq War. In 1990, he invaded Kuwait, which caused the Gulf War of 1991. In 2003, he was overthrown and captured when the United States invaded. He was sentenced to death by hanging in 2006.

Anne Hutchinson (1591–1643) The articulate, strong-willed, and intelligent wife of a prominent Boston merchant, who espoused her belief in direct divine revelation. She quarreled with Puritan leaders over her beliefs; and they banished her from the colony.

Immigration Act of 1924 Federal legislation intended to favor northern and western European immigrants over those from southern and eastern Europe by restricting the number of immigrants from any one European country to 2 percent of the total number of immigrants per year, with an overall limit of slightly over 150,000 new arrivals per year.

Immigration and Nationality Services Act of 1965 Legislation that abolished discriminatory quotas based upon immigrants' national origin and treated all nationalities and races equally.

imperialism The use of diplomatic or military force to extend a nation's power and enhance its economic interests, often by acquiring territory or colonies and justifying such behavior with assumptions of racial superiority.

impressment The British navy used press-gangs to kidnap men in British and colonial ports who were then forced to serve in the British navy.

indentured servitude A defined period of labor (often four to seven years) which settlers consented to in exchange for having their passage to the New World paid by their "master."

Independent Treasury Act (1840) System created by President Martin Van Buren and approved by Congress in 1840 whereby the federal government moved its funds from favored state banks to the U.S. Treasury, whose financial transactions could only be in gold or silver coins of paper currency backed by gold or silver.

"Indian New Deal" This phrase refers to the reforms implemented for Native Americans during the New Deal era. John Collier, the commissioner of the Bureau of Indian Affairs (BIA), increased the access Native Americans had to relief programs and employed more Native Americans at the BIA. He worked to pass the Indian Reorganization Act. However, the version of the act passed by Congress was a much-diluted version of Collier's original proposal and did not greatly improve the lives of Native Americans.

Indian Removal Act (1830) Law permitting the forced relocation of Indians to federal lands west of the Mississippi River in exchange for the land they occupied in the East and South.

Indian wars Bloody conflicts between U.S. soldiers and Native Americans that raged in the West from the early 1860s to the late 1870s, sparked by American settlers moving into ancestral Indian lands.

Indochina This area of Southeast Asia consists of Laos, Cambodia, and Vietnam and was once controlled by France as a colony. After the Viet Minh defeated the French, the Geneva Accords were signed, which ended French colonial rule. The agreement created the independent nations of Laos and Cambodia and divided Vietnam along the 17th parallel until an election would reunify the country. Fearing a Communist take over, the United States government began intervening in the region during the Truman administration, which led to President Johnson's full-scale military involvement in Vietnam.

Industrial Revolution Major shift in the nineteenth century from hand-made manufacturing to mass production in mills and factories using water-, coal-, and steam-powered machinery.

industrial war A new concept of war enabled by industrialization that developed from the early 1800s through the Atomic Age. New technologies, including automatic weaponry, forms of transportation like the railroad and airplane, and communication technologies such as the telegraph and telephone, enabled nations to equip large, mass-conscripted armies with chemical and automatic weapons to decimate opposing armies in a "total war."

Industrial Workers of the World (IWW) A radical union organized in Chicago in 1905, nicknamed the Wobblies; its opposition to World War I led to its destruction by the federal government under the Espionage Act.

infectious diseases Also called contagious diseases, illnesses that can pass from one person to another by way of invasive biological organisms able to reproduce in the bodily tissues of their hosts. Europeans unwittingly brought many such diseases to the Americas, devastating the Native American peoples.

Intermediate-Range Nuclear Forces (INF) Treaty (1987) Agreement signed by U.S. president Ronald Reagan and Soviet premier Mikhail Gorbachev to eliminate the deployment of intermediate-range missiles with nuclear warheads.

internal improvements Construction of roads, bridges, canals, harbors, and other infrastructural projects intended to facilitate the flow of goods and people.

internationalists Prior to the United States' entry in World War II, internationalists believed that America's national security depended on aiding Britain in its struggle against Germany.

Interstate Commerce Commission An independent federal agency established in 1887 to oversee businesses engaged in interstate trade, especially railroads, but whose regulatory power was limited when tested in the courts.

interstate highway system In the late 1950s, construction began on a national network of interstate superhighways for the purpose of commerce and defense. The interstate highways would enable the rapid movement of military convoys and the evacuation of cities after a nuclear attack.

Iran-Contra affair (1987) Reagan administration scandal over the secret, unlawful U.S. sale of arms to Iran in partial exchange for the release of hostages in Lebanon; the arms money in turn was used illegally to aid Nicaraguan right-wing insurgents, the Contras.

Iranian hostage crisis (1979) Storming of the U.S. embassy in Tehran by Iranian revolutionaries, who held fifty-two Americans hostage for 444 days, despite President Carter's appeals for their release as well as a botched rescue attempt.

Irish Potato Famine In 1845, an epidemic of potato rot brought a famine to rural Ireland that killed over 1 million peasants and instigated a huge increase in the number of Irish immigrating to America. By 1850, the Irish made up 43 percent of the foreign-born population in the United States; and in the 1850s, they made up over half the population of New York City and Boston.

iron curtain Term coined by Winston Churchill to describe the cold war divide between western Europe and the Soviet Union's Eastern European satellites.

Iroquois League An alliance of the Iroquois tribes, originally formed sometime between 1450 and 1600, that used their combined strength to pressure Europeans to work with them in the fur trade and to wage war across what is today eastern North America.

Andrew Jackson (1767–1837) As a major general in the Tennessee militia, he had a number of military successes. As president, he worked to enable the "common man" to play a greater role in the political arena. He vetoed the re-chartering of the Second National Bank and reduced federal spending. When South Carolina nullified the Tariffs of 1828 and 1832, Jackson requested that Congress pass a "force bill" that would authorize him to use the army to compel the state to comply with the tariffs. He forced eastern Indians to move west of the Mississippi River so their lands could be used by white settlers. Groups of those who opposed Jackson come together to form a new political party called the Whigs.

Thomas "Stonewall" Jackson (1824–1863) A Confederate general who was known for his fearlessness in leading rapid marches, bold flanking movements, and furious assaults. He earned his nickname at the Battle of the First Bull Run for standing courageously against Union fire. During the battle of Chancellorsville, his own men accidentally mortally wounded him.

William James (1842–1910) He was the founder of Pragmatism and one of the fathers of modern psychology. He believed that ideas gained their validity not from their inherent truth, but from their social consequences and practical application.

Jay's Treaty (1794) Agreement between Britain and the United States, negotiated by Chief Justice John Jay, that settled disputes over trade, prewar debts owed to British merchants, British-occupied forts in American territory, and the seizure of American ships and cargo.

Jazz Age Term coined by writer F. Scott Fitzgerald to characterize the spirit of rebellion and spontaneity among young Americans in the 1920s, a spirit epitomized by the hugely popular jazz music of the era.

Thomas Jefferson (1743–1826) He was a plantation owner, author, the drafter of the Declaration Independence, ambassador to France, leader of the Republican party, secretary of state, and the third president of the United States. As president, he purchased the Louisiana territory from France, withheld appointments made by President Adams leading to *Marybury v. Madison,* outlawed foreign slave trade, and was committed to a "wise and frugal" government.

Jeffersonian Republicans Political party founded by Thomas Jefferson in opposition to the Federalist Party led by Alexander Hamilton and John Adams; also known as the Democratic-Republican Party.

Jesuits A religious order founded in 1540 by Ignatius Loyola. They sought to counter the spread of Protestantism during the Protestant Reformation and spread the Catholic faith through work as missionaries. Roughly 3,500 served in New Spain and New France.

"Jim Crow" laws In the New South, these laws mandated the separation of races in various public places that served as a way for the ruling whites to impose their will on all areas of black life.

Andrew Johnson (1808–1875) He was elevated to the presidency after Abraham Lincoln's assassination. In order to restore the Union after the Civil War, he issued an amnesty proclamation and required former Confederate states to ratify the Thirteenth Amendment. After disagreements over the power to restore states rights, the Radical Republicans attempted to impeach Johnson but fell short on the required number of votes needed to remove him from office.

Lyndon B. Johnson (1908–1973) Former member of the House of Representatives and the former Majority Leader of the Senate, Vice President Lyndon B. Johnson assumed the presidency after President Kennedy's assassination. During his presidency, he passed the Civil Rights Act of 1964, declared a "war on poverty" promoting his own social program called the Great Society, and signed the Immigration and Nationality Service Act of 1965. Johnson greatly increased America's role in Vietnam.

joint-stock companies Businesses owned by investors, who purchase shares of companies' stocks and share all the profits and losses.

Kansas-Nebraska Act (1854) Controversial legislation that created two new territories taken from Native Americans, Kansas and Nebraska, where residents would vote to decide whether slavery would be allowed (popular sovereignty).

Florence Kelley (1859–1932) As the head of the National Consumer's League, she led the crusade to promote state laws to regulate the number of working hours imposed on women who were wives and mothers.

George F. Kennan (1904–2005) While working as an American diplomat, he devised the strategy of containment, which called for the halting of Soviet expansion. It became America's choice strategy throughout the cold war.

John F. Kennedy (1917–1963) He was elected president in 1960. Despite the difficulties he had in getting his legislation through Congress, he established the Alliance for Progress programs to help Latin America, the Peace Corps, the Trade Expansion Act of 1962, and funding for urban renewal projects and the space program. His foreign political involvement included the failed Bay of Pigs invasion and the missile crisis in Cuba, as well as support of local governments in Indochina. In 1963, he was assassinated by Lee Harvey Oswald in Dallas, Texas.

Kent State During the spring of 1970, students on college campuses across the country protested the expansion of the Vietnam War into Cambodia. At Kent State University, the National Guard attempted to quell the rioting students. The guardsmen panicked and shot at rock-throwing demonstrators. Four student bystanders were killed.

Kentucky and Virginia Resolutions (1798–1799) Passed in response to the Alien and Sedition Acts, the resolutions advanced the state-compact theory that held states could nullify an act of Congress if they deemed it unconstitutional.

Francis Scott Key (1779–1843) During the War of 1812, he watched British forces bombard Fort McHenry, but fail to take it. Seeing the American flag still flying over the fort at dawn inspired him to write "The Star-Spangled Banner," which became the American national anthem.

Martin Luther King, Jr. (1929–1968) A central leader of the civil rights movement, he urged people to use nonviolent civil disobedience to demand their rights and bring about change. He successfully led the Montgomery Bus Boycott. While in jail for his role in demonstrations, he wrote his famous "Letter from Birmingham City Jail," in which he defended his strategy of nonviolent protest. In 1963, he delivered his famous "I Have a Dream Speech" from the steps of the Lincoln Memorial as a part of the March on Washington. A year later, he was awarded the Nobel Peace Prize. In 1968, he was assassinated.

King Philip's War A bloody, three-year war in New England (1675–1678), resulting from the escalation of tensions between Indians and English settlers; the defeat of the Indians led to broadened freedoms for the settlers and their dispossessing the region's Indians of most of their land.

King William's War (War of the League of Augsburg) First (1689–1697) of four colonial wars between England and France.

Henry Kissinger (1923–) He served as the secretary of state and national security advisor in the Nixon administration. He negotiated with North Vietnam for an end to the Vietnam War, but the cease-fire did not last; South Vietnam fell to North Vietnam. He helped organize Nixon's historic trips to China and the Soviet Union. In the Middle East, he negotiated a cease-fire between Israel and its neighbors following the Yom Kippur War and solidified Israel's promise to return to Egypt most of the land it had taken during the 1967 war.

Knights of Labor A national labor organization with a broad reform platform; reached peak membership in the 1880s.

Know-Nothing party Nativist, anti-Catholic third party organized in 1854 in reaction to large-scale German and Irish immigration.

Ku Klux Klan Organized in Pulaski, Tennessee, in 1866 to terrorize former slaves who voted and held political offices during Reconstruction; a revived organization in the 1910s and 1920s stressed white, Anglo-Saxon, fundamentalist Protestant supremacy; the Klan revived a third time to fight the civil rights movement of the 1950s and 1960s in the South.

Marquis de Lafayette (1757–1834) A wealthy French idealist excited by the American cause, he offered to serve in Washington's army for free in exchange for being named a major general. He overcame Washington's initial skepticism to become one of his most trusted aides.

laissez-faire An economic doctrine holding that businesses and individuals should be able to pursue their economic interests without government interference.

Land Ordinance of 1785 Directed surveying of the Northwest Territory into townships of thirty-six sections (square miles) each, the sale of the sixteenth section of which was to be used to finance public education.

League of Nations Organization of nations formed in the aftermath of the First World War to mediate disputes and maintain international peace; despite President Wilson's intense lobbying for the League of Nations, Congress did not ratify the treaty and the United States failed to join.

Mary Elizabeth Lease (1850–1933) She was a leader of the farm protest movement who advocated violence if change could not be obtained at the ballot box. She believed that the urban-industrial East was the enemy of the working class.

Robert E. Lee (1807–1870) Even though he had served in the United States Army for thirty years, he chose to fight on the side of the Confederacy. Lee was excellent at using his field commanders and his soldiers respected him. However, General Ulysses S. Grant eventually wore down his army, and Lee surrendered to Grant at the Appomattox Court House on April 9, 1865.

Lend-Lease Bill (1941) Legislation that allowed the president to lend or lease military equipment to any country whose own defense was deemed vital to the defense of the United States.

Levittown First low-cost, mass-produced development of suburban tract housing built by William Levitt on Long Island, New York, in 1947.

Lewis and Clark Expedition (1804) Led by Meriwether Lewis and William Clark, a mission to the Pacific coast commissioned for the purposes of scientific and geographical exploration

Lexington and Concord, Battle of The first shots fired in the Revolutionary War, on April 19, 1775, near Boston; approximately 100 Minutemen and 250 British soldiers were killed.

Liberator William Lloyd Garrison started this anti-slavery newspaper in 1831 in which he renounced gradualism and called for abolition.

Queen Liliuokalani (1838–1917) In 1891, she ascended to the throne of the Hawaiian royal family and tried to eliminate white control of the Hawaiian government. Two years later, Hawaii's white population revolted and seized power with the support of American Marines.

Abraham Lincoln (1809–1865) Shortly after he was elected president in 1860, southern states began seceding from the Union, and in April of 1861 he declared war on the seceding states. On January 1, 1863, Lincoln signed the Emancipation Proclamation. At the end of the war, he favored a reconstruction strategy for the former Confederate states that did not radically alter southern social and economic life. He was assassinated by John Wilkes Booth at Ford's Theater on April 14, 1865.

Lincoln-Douglas Debates (1858) In the Illinois race between Republican Abraham Lincoln and Democrat Stephen A. Douglas for a seat in the U.S. Senate, a series of seven dramatic debates focusing on the issue of slavery in the territories.

John Locke (1632–1704) An English philosopher whose ideas were influential during the Enlightenment. He argued in his *Essay on Human Understanding* (1690) that humanity is largely the product of the environment, the mind being a blank tablet, *tabula rasa*, on which experience is written.

Henry Cabot Lodge (1850–1924) He was the chairman of the Senate Foreign Relations Committee who favored limiting America's involvement in the League of Nations' covenant and sought to amend the Treaty of Versailles.

de Lôme letter Private correspondence written in 1898 by the Spanish ambassador to the U.S., Depuy de Lôme, that described President McKinley as "weak"; the letter was stolen by Cuban revolutionaries and published in the *New York Journal*, deepening American resentment of Spain and moving the two countries closer to war in Cuba.

Lone Star Republic After winning independence from Mexico, Texas became its own nation that was called the Lone Star Republic. In 1836, Texans drafted a constitution, legalized slavery, banned free blacks, named Sam Houston president, and voted for the annexation to the United States. However, quarrels over adding a slave state and fears of instigating a war with Mexico delayed Texas's entrance into the Union until December 29, 1845.

Huey P. Long (1893–1935) He began his political career in Louisiana where he developed a reputation for being an unscrupulous reformer. As a U.S. senator, he became a critic of President Roosevelt's New Deal Plan and offered his alternative called the Share-the-Wealth program. He was assassinated in 1935.

Louisiana Purchase (1803) President Thomas Jefferson's purchase of the Louisiana Territory from France for $15 million, doubling the size of U.S. territory.

The Lowell system Model New England factory communities that during the first half of the nineteenth century provided employees, mostly young women, with meals, a boardinghouse, and moral discipline, as well as educational and cultural opportunities.

Loyalists Colonists who remained loyal to Great Britain before and during the Revolutionary War.

Lusitania British ocean liner torpedoed and sunk by a German U-boat; the deaths of nearly 1,200 of its civilian passengers, including many Americans, caused international outrage.

Martin Luther (1483–1546) A German monk who founded the Lutheran church. He protested abuses in the Catholic Church by posting his Ninety-five Theses, which began the Protestant Reformation.

General Douglas MacArthur (1880–1964) During World War II, he and Admiral Chester Nimitz dislodged the Japanese military from the Pacific Islands they had occupied. Following the war, he was in charge of the occupation of Japan. After North Korea invaded South Korea, Truman sent the U.S. military to defend South Korea under the command of MacArthur. Later in the war, Truman expressed his willingness to negotiate the restoration of prewar boundaries which MacArthur attempted to undermine. Truman fired MacArthur for his open insubordination.

James Madison (1751–1836) He participated in the Constitutional Convention during which he proposed the Virginia Plan. He believed in a strong federal government and was a leader of the Federalists. However, he also presented to Congress the Bill of Rights and drafted the Virginia Resolutions. As secretary of state, he withheld a commission for William Marbury, which led to the landmark *Marbury v. Madison* decision. During his presidency, he declared war on Britain in response to violations of American shipping rights, which started the War of 1812.

Alfred Thayer Mahan, *The Influence of Sea Power upon History, 1660–1783* **(1890)** Historical work in which Rear Admiral Alfred Thayer Mahan argues that a nation's greatness and prosperity comes from the power of its navy; the book helped bolster imperialist sentiment in the United States in the late nineteenth century.

U.S. battleship *Maine* American warship that exploded in the Cuban port of Havana on January 25, 1898; though later discovered to be the result of an accident, the destruction of the *Maine* was attributed by war-hungry Americans to Spain, contributing to the onset of the War of 1812.

maize (corn) The primary grain crop in Mesoamerica yielding small kernels often ground into cornmeal. Easy to grow in a broad range of conditions, it enabled a global population explosion after being brought to Europe, Africa, and Asia.

Malcolm X (1925–1964) The most articulate spokesman for black power. Originally the chief disciple of Elijah Muhammad, the black Muslim leader in the United States, Malcolm X broke away and founded his own organization committed to establishing relations between African Americans and the nonwhite peoples of the world. Near the end of his life, he began to preach a biracial message of social change. In 1964, he was assassinated by members of a rival group of black Muslims.

Manchuria incident The northeast region of Manchuria was an area contested between China and Russia. In 1931, the Japanese claimed that they needed to protect their extensive investments in the area and moved their army into Manchuria. They quickly conquered the region and set up their own puppet empire. China asked both the United States and the League of Nations for help and neither responded.

Manifest Destiny The widespread belief that America was "destined" by God to expand westward across the continent into lands claimed by Native Americans as well as European nations.

Horace Mann (1796–1859) He believed the public school system was the best way to achieve social stability and equal opportunity. As a reformer of education, he sponsored a state board of education, the first state-supported "normal" school for training teachers, a state association for teachers, the minimum school year of six months, and led the drive for a statewide school system.

Marbury v. Madison **(1803)** First Supreme Court decision to declare a federal law—the Judiciary Act of 1801—unconstitutional.

March on Washington Civil rights demonstration on August 28, 1963, on the National Mall, where Martin Luther King, Jr. gave his famous "I Have a Dream" speech.

market economy Large-scale manufacturing and commercial agriculture that emerged in America during the first half of the nineteenth century, displacing much of the pre-market subsistence and barter-based economy and producing boom-and-bust cycles while raising the American standard of living.

George C. Marshall (1880–1959) As the chairman of the Joint Chiefs of Staff, he orchestrated the Allied victories over Germany and Japan in the Second World War. In 1947, he became President Truman's secretary of state and proposed the massive reconstruction program for western Europe called the Marshall Plan.

Chief Justice John Marshall (1755–1835) During his long tenure as chief justice of the supreme court (1801–1835), he established the foundations for American jurisprudence, the authority of the Supreme Court, and the constitutional supremacy of the national government over states.

Marshall Plan (1948) Secretary of State George C. Marshall's post–World War II program providing massive U.S. financial and technical assistance to war-torn European countries.

Massachusetts Bay Colony English colony founded by English Puritans in 1630 as a haven for persecuted Congregationalists.

massive resistance White rallying cry disrupting federal efforts to enforce racial integration in the South.

massive retaliation Strategy that used the threat of nuclear warfare as a means of combating the global spread of communism.

Mayflower Compact A formal agreement signed by the Separatist colonists aboard the *Mayflower* in 1620 to abide by laws made by leaders of their own choosing.

Senator Joseph R. McCarthy (1908–1957) In 1950, this senator became the shrewdest and most ruthless exploiter of America's anxiety of communism. He claimed that the United States government was full of Communists and led a witch hunt to find them, but he was never able to uncover a single communist agent.

McCarthyism Anti-Communist hysteria led by Senator Joseph McCarthy's "witch hunts" attacking the loyalty of politicians, federal employees, and public figures, despite a lack of evidence.

George B. McClellan (1826–1885) In 1861, President Abraham Lincoln appointed him head of the Army of the Potomac and, later, general in chief of the U.S. Army. He built his army into well trained and powerful force. After failing to achieve a decisive victory against the Confederacy, he was removed from command in 1862.

Cyrus Hall McCormick (1809–1884) In 1831, he invented a mechanical reaper to harvest wheat, which transformed the scale of agriculture. By hand a farmer could only harvest a half an acre a day, while the McCormick reaper allowed two people to harvest twelve acres of wheat a day.

McCormick reaper Mechanical reaper invented by Cyrus Hall McCormick in 1831 that dramatically increased the production of wheat.

William McKinley (1843–1901) As a congressman, he was responsible for the McKinley Tariff of 1890, which raised the duties on manufactured products to their highest level ever. Voters disliked the tariff and McKinley, as well as other Republicans, lost his seat in Congress the next election. However, he won the presidential election of 1896 and raised the tariffs again. In 1898, he annexed Hawaii and declared war on Spain. The war concluded with the Treaty of Paris, which gave America control over Puerto Rico, Guam, and the Philippines. Soon America was fighting Filipinos, who were seeking independence for their country. In 1901, McKinley was assassinated.

Robert McNamara (1916–) He was the secretary of defense for both President Kennedy and President Johnson and a supporter of America's involvement in Vietnam.

Medicare and Medicaid Health-care programs designed to aid the elderly and disadvantaged, respectively, as part of President Johnson's Great Society initiative.

Andrew W. Mellon (1855–1937) As President Harding's secretary of the Treasury, he sought to generate economic growth through reducing government spending and lowering taxes. However, he insisted that the tax reductions mainly go to the rich because he believed the wealthy would reinvest their money. In order to bring greater efficiency and nonpartisanship to the government's budget process, he persuaded Congress to created a new Bureau of the Budget and a General Accounting Office.

mercantilism Policy of Great Britain and other imperial powers of regulating the economies of colonies to benefit the mother country.

James Meredith (1933–) In 1962, the governor of Mississippi defied a Supreme Court ruling and refused to allow James Meredith, an African American, to enroll at the University of Mississippi. Federal marshals were sent to enforce the law which led to clashes between a white mob and the marshals. Federal troops intervened and two people were killed and many others were injured. A few days later, Meredith was able to register at the university.

Merrimack* (ship renamed the *Virginia*) and the *Monitor First engagement between ironclad ships; fought at Hampton Roads, Virginia, on March 9, 1862.

Metacomet (?–1676) or King Philip The chief of the Wampanoages, who the colonists called King Philip. He resented English efforts to convert Indians to Christianity and waged a war against the English colonists in which he was killed.

Mexica Otherwise known as "Aztecs," a Mesoamerican people of northern Mexico who founded the vast Aztec Empire in the fourteenth century, later conquered by the Spanish under Hernán Cortés in 1521.

microprocessor An electronic circuit printed on a small silicon chip; a major technological breakthrough in 1971, it paved the way for the development of the personal computer.

Middle Passage The hellish and often deadly middle leg of the transatlantic "Triangular Trade" in which European ships carried manufactured goods to Africa, then transported enslaved Africans to the Americas and the Caribbean, and finally conveyed American agricultural products back to Europe; from the late sixteenth to the early nineteenth centuries, some 12 million Africans were transported via the Middle Passage, unknown millions more dying en route.

militant nonviolence After the success of the Montgomery bus boycott, people were inspired by Martin Luther King, Jr.'s use of this nonviolent form of protest. Throughout the civil rights movement, demonstrators used this method of protest to challenge racial segregation in the South.

Militia Act (1862) Congressional measure that permitted freed slaves to serve as laborers or soldiers in the United States Army.

Ho Chi Minh (1890–1969) He was the Vietnamese communist resistance leader who drove the French and the United States out of Vietnam. After the Geneva Accords divided the region into four countries, he controlled North Vietnam, and ultimately became the leader of all of Vietnam at the conclusion of the Vietnam War.

minstrelsy A form of entertainment that was popular from the 1830s to the 1870s. The performances featured white performers who were made up as African Americans or blackface. They performed banjo and fiddle music, "shuffle" dances and lowbrow humor that reinforced racial stereotypes.

Minutemen Special units organized by the militia to be ready for quick mobilization.

***Miranda v. Arizona* (1966)** U.S. Supreme Court decision required police to advise persons in custody of their rights to legal counsel and against self-incrimination.

The Mississippi Plan Series of state constitutional amendments in 1890 which sought to severely disenfranchise black voters and were quickly adopted by other southern states.

Missouri Compromise (1820) Legislative decision to admit Missouri as a slave state and abolish slavery in the area west of the Mississippi River and north of the parallel 36°30′.

Model T Ford Henry Ford developed this model of car so that it was affordable for everyone. Its success led to an increase in the production of automobiles which stimulated other related industries such steel, oil, and rubber. The mass use of automobiles increased the speed goods could be transported, encouraged urban sprawl, and sparked real estate booms in California and Florida.

moderate Republicanism Promise to curb federal government and restore state and local government authority, spearheaded by President Eisenhower.

modernism An early-twentieth-century intellectual and artistic movement that rejected traditional notions of reality and adopted radical new forms of artistic expression.

monopoly A corporation so large that it effectively controls the entire market for its products or services.

the "money question" Late-nineteenth-century national debate over the nature of U.S. currency; supporters of a fixed gold standard were generally money lenders, and thus preferred to keep the value of money high, while supporters of silver (and gold) coinage were debtors, they owed money, so they wanted to keep the value of money low by increasing the currency supply (inflation).

James Monroe (1758–1831) He served as secretary of state and war under President Madison and was elected president. As the latter, he signed the Transcontinental Treaty with Spain which gave the United States Florida and expanded the Louisiana territory's western border to the Pacific coast. In 1823, he established the Monroe Doctrine. This foreign policy proclaimed the American continents were no longer open to colonization and America would be neutral in European affairs.

Monroe Doctrine (1823) U.S. foreign policy that barred further colonization in the Western Hemisphere by European powers and pledged that there would be no American interference with any existing European colonies.

Montgomery bus boycott Boycott of bus system in Montgomery, Alabama, organized by civil rights activists after the arrest of Rosa Parks.

Moral Majority Televangelist Jerry Falwell's political lobbying organization, the name of which became synonymous with the religious right—conservative evangelical Protestants who helped ensure President Ronald Reagan's 1980 victory.

J. Pierpont Morgan (1837–1913) As a powerful investment banker, he would acquire, reorganize, and consolidate companies into giant trusts. His biggest achievement was the consolidation of the steel industry into the United States Steel Corporation, which was the first billion-dollar corporation.

J. Pierpont Morgan and Company An investment bank under the leadership of J. Pierpont Morgan that bought or merged unrelated American companies, often using capital acquired from European investors.

Mormons Members of the Church of Jesus Christ of Latter-day Saints, which dismissed other Christian denominations, emphasizing universal salvation and a modest lifestyle; Mormons were often persecuted for their secrecy and clannishness.

Morrill Land Grant Act (1862) Federal statute that allowed for the creation of land-grant colleges and universities, which were founded to provide technical education in agriculture, mining, and industry.

Samuel F. B. Morse (1791–1872) In 1832, he invented the telegraph and revolutionized the speed of communication.

mountain men Inspired by the fur trade, these men left civilization to work as trappers and reverted to a primitive existence in the wilderness. They were the first white people to find routes through the Rocky Mountains, and they pioneered trails that settlers later used to reach the Oregon country and California in the 1840s.

muckrakers Writers who exposed corruption and abuses in politics, business, consumer safety, working conditions, and more, spurring public interest in progressive reforms.

Mugwumps Reformers who bolted the Republican party in 1884 to support Democratic Grover Cleveland for president over Republican James G. Blaine, whose secret dealings on behalf of railroad companies had brought charges of corruption.

mulattoes Mixed-race people who constituted most of the South's free black population.

Benito Mussolini (1883–1945) The Italian founder of the Fascist party who came to power in Italy in 1922 and allied himself with Adolf Hitler and the Axis powers during the Second World War.

National Association for the Advancement of Colored People (NAACP) Organization founded in 1910 by black activists and white progressives that promoted education as a means of combating social problems and focused on legal action to secure the civil rights supposedly guaranteed by the Fourteenth and Fifteenth Amendments.

North American Free Trade Agreement (NAFTA) (1994) Agreement eliminating trade barriers that was signed in 1994 by the United States, Canada, and Mexico, making North America the largest free-trade zone in the world.

North Atlantic Treaty Organization (NATO) Defensive political and military alliance formed in 1949 by the United States, Canada, and ten Western European nations to deter Soviet expansion in Europe.

National Industrial Recovery Act (1933) Passed on the last of the Hundred Days; it created public-works jobs through the Federal Emergency Relief Administration and established a system of self-regulation for industry through the National Recovery Administration, which was ruled unconstitutional in 1935.

National Labor Union A federation of labor and reform leaders established in 1866 to advocate for new state and local laws to improve working conditions.

National Recovery Administration (1933) Controversial federal agency that brought together business and labor leaders to create "codes of fair competition" and "fair labor" policies, including a national minimum wage.

National Security Act Congressional legislation passed in 1947 that created the Department of Defense, the National Security Council, and the Central Intelligence Agency.

National Socialist German Workers' Party (Nazi) Founded in the 1920s, this party gained control over Germany under the leadership of Adolf Hitler in 1933 and continued in power until Germany's defeat at the end of the Second World War. It advocated a violent anti-Semitic, anti-Marxist, pan-German ideology. The Nazi party perpetrated the Holocaust.

National Trades' Unions Formed in 1834 to organize all local trade unions into a stronger national association, only to be dissolved amid the economic depression during the late 1830s.

nativism Reactionary conservative movement characterized by heightened nationalism, anti-immigrant sentiment, and the enactment of laws setting stricter regulations on immigration.

natural rights An individual's basic rights that should not be violated by any government or community.

Navigation Acts Restrictions passed by the British Parliament between 1650 and 1775 to control colonial trade and bolster the mercantile system.

Negrophobia A violent new wave of racism that spread in the late nineteenth century largely spurred by white resentment for African American financial success and growing political influence.

new conservatism The political philosophy of those who led the conservative insurgency of the early 1980s. This brand of conservatism was personified in Ronald Reagan who believed in less government, supply-side economics, and "family values."

First New Deal Franklin D. Roosevelt's campaign promise, in his speech to the Democratic National Convention of 1932, to combat the Great Depression with a "new deal for the American people;" the phrase became a catchword for his ambitious plan of economic programs.

New Democrats Centrist ("moderate") Democrats led by President Bill Clinton that emerged in the late 1980s and early 1990s to challenge the "liberal" direction of the party.

"new economy" Period of sustained economic prosperity during the nineties marked by budget surpluses, the explosion of dot.com industries, low inflation, and low unemployment.

New France The name used for the area of North America that was colonized by the French. Unlike Spanish or English colonies, New France had a small number of colonists, which forced them to initially seek good relations with the indigenous people they encountered.

New Freedom Program championed in 1912 by the Woodrow Wilson campaign that aimed to restore competition in the economy by eliminating all trusts rather than simply regulating them.

New Frontier Proposed domestic program championed by the incoming Kennedy administration in 1961 that aimed to jump-start the economy and trigger social progress.

"new immigrants" Wave of newcomers from southern and eastern Europe, including many Jews, who became a majority among immigrants to America after 1890.

New Jersey Plan The delegations to the Constitutional Convention were divided between two plans on how to structure the government: New Jersey wanted one legislative body with equal representation for each state.

New Left Term coined by the Students for a Democratic Society to distinguish their efforts at grassroots democracy from those of the 1930s Old Left, which had embraced orthodox Marxism.

New Mexico A U.S. territory and later a state in the American Southwest, originally established by the Spanish, who settled there in the sixteenth century, founded Catholic missions, and exploited the region's indigenous peoples.

New Nationalism Platform of the Progressive party and slogan of former President Theodore Roosevelt in the presidential campaign of 1912; stressed government activism, including regulation of trusts, conservation, and recall of state court decisions that had nullified progressive programs.

"New Negro" In the 1920s, a slow and steady growth of black political influence occurred in northern cities where African Americans were freer to speak and act. This political activity created a spirit of protest that expressed itself culturally in the Harlem Renaissance and politically in "new Negro" nationalism.

New Netherland Dutch colony conquered by the English in 1667 and out of which four new colonies were created—New York, New Jersey, Pennsylvania, and Delaware.

Battle of New Orleans (1815) Final major battle in the War of 1812, in which the Americans under General Andrew Jackson unexpectedly and decisively countered the British attempt to seize the port of New Orleans, Louisiana.

New South *Atlanta Constitution* editor Henry W. Grady's 1886 term for the prosperous post–Civil War South: democratic, industrial, urban, and free of nostalgia for the defeated plantation South.

William Randolph Hearst's *New York Journal* In the late 1890s, the *New York Journal* and its rival, the *New York World*, printed sensationalism on the Cuban revolution as part of their heated competition for readership. The *New York Journal* printed a negative letter from the Spanish ambassador about President McKinley and inflammatory coverage of the sinking of the *Maine* in Havana Harbor. These two events roused the American public's outcry against Spain.

Joseph Pulitzer's *New York World* In the late 1890s, the *New York World* and its rival, *New York Journal*, printed sensationalism on the Cuban revolution as part of their heated competition for readership.

Admiral Chester Nimitz (1885–1966) During the Second World War, he was the commander of central Pacific. Along with General Douglas MacArthur, he dislodged the Japanese military from the Pacific Islands they had occupied.

Nineteenth Amendment Constitutional amendment that granted women the right to vote in 1920.

Richard M. Nixon (1913–1994) He first came to national prominence as a congressman involved in the investigation of Alger Hiss, and later served as vice president during the Eisenhower administration. After being elected president in 1968, he slowed the federal enforcement of civil rights and appointed pro-Southern justices to the Supreme Court. He began a program of Vietnamization of the war. In 1973, America, North and South Vietnam, and the Viet Cong agreed to end the war and the United States withdrew. However, the cease-fire was broken, and the South Vietnam fell to North Vietnam. In 1970, Nixon declared that America was no longer the world's policeman and he would seek some partnerships with Communist countries, historically traveling to China and the Soviet Union. In 1972, he was reelected, but the Watergate scandal erupted shortly after his victory; he resigned the presidency under threat of impeachment.

No Child Left Behind President George W. Bush's education reform plan that required states to set and meet learning standards for students and make sure that all students were "proficient" in reading and writing by 2014. States had to submit annual reports of students' standardized test scores. Teachers were required to be "proficient" in their subject area. Schools who failed to show progress would face sanctions. States criticized the lack of funding for remedial programs and noted that poor school districts would find it very difficult to meet the new guidelines.

nonviolent civil disobedience Tactic of defying unjust laws through peaceful actions championed by Dr. Martin Luther King, Jr.

Lord North (1732–1792) The first minister of King George III's cabinet whose efforts to subdue the colonies only brought them closer to revolution. He helped bring about the Tea Act of 1773, which led to the Boston Tea Party. In an effort to discipline Boston, he wrote, and Parliament passed, four acts that galvanized colonial resistance.

North Atlantic Treaty Organization (NATO) Defensive alliance founded in 1949 by ten western European nations, the United States, and Canada to deter Soviet expansion in Europe.

Northwest Ordinance (1787) Land policy for new western territories in the Ohio valley that established the terms and conditions for self-government and statehood while also banning slavery from the region.

NSC-68 (1950) Top-secret policy paper approved by President Truman that outlined a militaristic approach to combating the spread of global communism.

nullification The right claimed by some states to veto a federal law deemed unconstitutional.

Nuremberg trials At the site of the annual Nazi party rallies, twenty-one major German offenders faced an international military tribunal for Nazi atrocities. After a ten-month trial, the court acquitted three and sentenced eleven to death, three to life imprisonment, and four to shorter terms.

Barack Obama (1961–) In the 2008 presidential election, Senator Barack Obama mounted an innovative Internet based and grassroots orientated campaign. As the nation's economy nose-dived in the fall of 2008, Obama linked the Republican economic philosophy with the country's dismal financial state and promoted a message of "change" and "politics of hope," which resonated with voters. He decisively won the presidency and became America's first person of color to be elected president.

Occupy Wall Street A grassroots movement protesting a capitalist system that fostered social and economic inequality. Begun in Zuccotti Park, New York City, during 2011, the movement spread rapidly across the nation, triggering a national conversation about income inequality and protests of the government's "bailouts" of the banks and corporations allegedly responsible for the Great Recession.

Sandra Day O'Connor (1930–) She was the first woman to serve on the Supreme Court of the United States and was appointed by President Reagan. Reagan's critics charged that her appointment was a token gesture and not a sign of any real commitment to gender equality.

Ohio gang In order to escape the pressures of the White House, President Harding met with a group of people, called the "Ohio gang," in a house on K Street in Washington D.C. Members of this gang were given low-level positions in the American government and they used their White House connection to "line their pockets" by granting government contracts without bidding, which led to a series of scandals, most notably the Teapot Dome Scandal.

The Old Southwest Region covering western Georgia, Alabama, Mississippi, Louisiana, Arkansas, and Texas, where low land prices and fertile soil attracted hundreds of thousands of settlers after the American Revolution.

Frederick Law Olmsted (1822–1903) In 1858, he constructed New York's Central Park, which led to a growth in the movement to create urban parks. He went on to design parks for Boston, Brooklyn, Chicago, Philadelphia, San Francisco, and many other cities.

Open Door policy Official U.S. insistence that Chinese trade would be open to all nations; Secretary of State John Hay unilaterally announced the policy in 1899 in hopes of protecting the Chinese market for U.S. exports.

open shop Business policy of not requiring union membership as a condition of employment; such a policy, where legal, has the effect of weakening unions and diminishing workers' rights.

open range Informal system of governing property on the frontier in which small ranchers could graze their cattle anywhere on unfenced lands; brought to an end by the introduction of barbed wire, a low-cost way to fence off one's land.

Operation Desert Shield After Saddam Hussein invaded Kuwait in 1990, President George H. W. Bush sent American military forces to Saudi Arabia on a strictly defensive mission. They were soon joined by a multinational coalition. When the coalition's mission changed to the retaking of Kuwait, the operation was renamed Desert Storm.

Operation Desert Storm (1991) Assault by American-led multinational forces that quickly defeated Iraqi forces under Saddam Hussein in the First Gulf War, ending the Iraqi occupation of Kuwait.

Operation Overlord The Allies' assault on Hitler's "Atlantic Wall," a seemingly impregnable series of fortifications and minefields along the French coastline that German forces had created using captive Europeans for laborers.

J. Robert Oppenheimer (1904–1967) He led the group of physicists at the laboratory in Los Alamos, New Mexico, who constructed the first atomic bomb.

Oregon Country The Convention of 1818 between Britain and the United States established the Oregon Country as being west of the crest of the Rocky Mountains and the two countries were to jointly occupy it. In 1824, the United States and Russia signed a treaty that established the line of 54°40′ as the southern boundary of Russia's territorial claim in North America. A similar agreement between Britain and Russia finally gave the Oregon Country clearly defined boarders, but it remained under joint British and American control.

"Oregon Fever" The lure of fertile land and economic opportunities in the Oregon Country that drew thousands of settlers westward, beginning in the late 1830s.

Osceola (1804?–1838) He was the leader of the Seminole nation who resisted the federal Indian removal policy through a protracted guerilla war. In 1837, he was treacherously seized under a flag of truce and imprisoned at Fort Moultrie, where he was left to die.

Overland Trails Trail routes followed by wagon trains bearing settlers and trade goods from Missouri to the Oregon Country, California, and New Mexico, beginning in the 1840s.

A. Mitchell Palmer (1872–1936) As the attorney general, he played an active role in the government's response to the Red Scare. After several bombings across America, including one at Palmer's home, he and other Americans became convinced that there was a well-organized Communist terror campaign at work. The federal government launched a campaign of raids, deportations, and collecting files on radical individuals.

Panic of 1819 A financial panic that began a three-year-long economic crisis triggered by a reduced demand of American imports, declining land values, and reckless practices by local and state banks.

Panic of 1837 A financial calamity in the United States brought on by a dramatic slowdown in the British economy and exacerbated by falling cotton prices, failed crops, high inflation, and reckless state banks.

Panic of 1893 A major collapse in the national economy after several major railroad companies declared bankruptcy, leading to a severe depression and several violent clashes between workers and management.

panning A method of mining that used a large metal pan to sift gold dust and nuggets from riverbeds during the California gold rush of 1849.

Rosa Parks (1913–2005) In 1955, she refused to give up her seat to a white man on a city bus in Montgomery, Alabama, which a local ordinance required of blacks. She was arrested for disobeying the ordinance. In response, black community leaders organized the Montgomery bus boycott.

Parliament Legislature of Great Britain, composed of the House of Commons, whose members are elected, and the House of Lords, whose members are either hereditary or appointed.

party "boss" A powerful political leader who controlled a "machine" of associates and operatives to promote both individual and party interests, often using informal tactics such as intimidation or the patronage system.

paternalism A moral position developed during the first half of the nineteenth century which claimed that slaves were deprived of liberty for their own "good." Such a rationalization was adopted by some slave owners to justify slavery.

Patriots Colonists who rebelled against British authority before and during the Revolutionary War.

patronage An informal system (sometimes called the "spoils system") used by politicians to reward their supporters with government appointments or contracts.

Alice Paul (1885–1977) She was a leader of the women's suffrage movement and head of the Congressional Committee of National Women Suffrage Association. She instructed female suffrage activists to use more militant tactics, such as picketing state legislatures, chaining themselves to public buildings, inciting police to arrest them, and undertaking hunger strikes.

Norman Vincent Peale (1898–1993) He was a champion of the upbeat and feel-good theology that was popular in the 1950s religious revival. He advocated getting rid of any depressing or negative thoughts and replacing them with "faith, enthusiasm and joy," which would make an individual popular and well liked.

Pearl Harbor (1941) Surprise Japanese attack on the U.S. fleet at Pearl Harbor on December 7, which prompted the immediate American entry into the war.

"peculiar institution" A phrase used by whites in the antebellum South to refer to slavery without using the word slavery.

Pennsylvania English colony founded by William Penn in 1681 as a Quaker commonwealth, though it welcomed people of all religions.

Pentagon Papers Informal name for the Defense Department's secret history of the Vietnam conflict; leaked to the press by former official Daniel Ellsberg and published in the *New York Times* in 1971.

People's Party (Populists) Political party largely made up of farmers from the South and West that struggled to gain political influence from the East. Populists advocated a variety of reforms, including free coinage of silver, a progressive income tax, postal savings banks, regulation of railroads, and direct election of U.S. senators.

Pequot War Massacre in 1637 and subsequent dissolution of the Pequot Nation by Puritan settlers, who seized the Indians' lands.

perestroika Russian term for "economic restructuring"; applied to Mikhail Gorbachev's series of political and economic reforms that included shifting a centrally planned Commmunist economy to a mixed economy allowing for capitalism.

Commodore Matthew Perry (1794–1858) In 1854, he negotiated the Treaty of Kanagawa, which was the first step in starting a political and commercial relationship between the United States and Japan.

John J. Pershing United States general sent by President Wilson to put down attacks on the Mexican border led by Francisco "Pancho" Villa.

Personal Responsibility and Work Opportunity Act of 1996 (PRWOA) Comprehensive welfare-reform measure, passed by a Republican Congress and signed by President Clinton, that aimed to decrease the size of the "welfare state" by limiting the amount of government aid provided the unemployed so as to encourage recipients to find jobs.

"pet banks" During President Andrew Jackson's fight with the national bank, Jackson resolved to remove all federal deposits from it. To comply with Jackson's demands, Secretary of the Treasury Taney continued to draw on government's accounts in the national bank, but deposit all new federal receipts in state banks. The state banks that received these deposits were called "pet banks."

Pilgrims Puritan Separatists who broke completely with the Church of England and sailed to the New World aboard the *Mayflower*, founding Plymouth Colony on Cape Cod in 1620.

King Philip (?–1676) or **Metacomet** The chief of the Wampanoages, who the colonists called King Philip. He resented English efforts to convert Indians to Christianity and waged a war against the English colonists in which he was killed.

Dien Bien Phu Cluster of Vietnamese villages and site of a major Vietnamese victory over the French in the First Indochina War.

Gifford Pinchot (1865–1946) As the head of the Division of Forestry, he implemented a conservation policy that entailed the scientific management of natural resources to serve the public interest. His work helped start the conservation movement.

Elizabeth Lucas Pinckney (1722? –1793) One of the most enterprising horticulturists in colonial America, she began managing her family's three plantations in South Carolina at the age of sixteen. She had tremendous success growing indigo, which led to many other plantations growing the crop as well.

Pinckney's Treaty Treaty with Spain negotiated by Thomas Pinckney in 1795; established United States boundaries at the Mississippi River and the 31st parallel and allowed open transportation on the Mississippi.

Francisco Pizarro (1478?–1541) In 1531, he lead his Spanish soldiers to Peru and conquered the Inca Empire.

"plain white folk" Yeoman farmers who lived and worked on their own small farms, growing a food and cash crops to trade for necessities.

plantation mistress Matriarch of a planter's household, responsible for supervising the domestic aspects of the estate.

planters Owners of large farms in the South that were worked by twenty or more slaves and supervised by overseers.

political "machine" A network of political activists and elected officials, usually controlled by a powerful "boss," that attempts to manipulate local politics

James Knox Polk "Young Hickory" (1795–1849) As president, his chief concern was the expansion of the United States. Shortly, after taking office, Mexico broke off relations with the United States over the annexation of Texas. Polk declared war on Mexico and sought to subvert Mexican authority in California. The United States defeated Mexico; and the two nations signed the Treaty of Guadalupe Hidalgo in which Mexico gave up any claims on Texas north of the Rio Grande River and ceded New Mexico and California to the United States.

Pontiac's Rebellion An Indian attack on British forts and settlements after France ceded to the British its territory east of the Mississippi River, as part of the Treaty of Paris in 1763, without consulting France's Indian allies.

"Popular Sovereignty" Legal concept by which the white male settlers in a new U.S. territory would vote to decide whether or not to permit slavery.

Populist/People's party Political success of Farmers' Alliance candidates encouraged the formation in 1892 of the People's party (later renamed the Populist party); active until 1912, it advocated a variety of reform issues, including free coinage of silver, income tax, postal savings, regulation of railroads, and direct election of U.S. senators.

Pottawatomie Massacre In retaliation for the "sack of Lawrence," John Brown and his abolitionist cohorts hacked five men to death in the pro-slavery settlement of Pottawatomie, Kansas, on May 24, 1856, triggering a guerrilla war in the Kansas Territory that cost 200 settler lives.

The Powhatan Confederacy An alliance of several powerful Algonquian tribes under the leadership of Chief Powhatan, organized into thirty chiefdoms along much of the Atlantic coast in the late sixteenth and early seventeenth centuries.

Chief Powhatan Wahunsonacock He was called Powhatan by the English after the name of his tribe, and was the powerful, charismatic chief of numerous Algonquian-speaking towns in eastern Virginia representing over 10,000 Indians.

pragmatism William James founded this philosophy in the early 1900s. Pragmatists believed that ideas gained their validity not from their inherent truth, but from their social consequences and practical application.

Proclamation of 1763 Proclamation drawing a boundary along the Appalachian Mountains from Canada to Georgia in order to minimize occurrences of settler–Indian violence; colonists were forbidden to go west of the line.

professions Occupations requiring specialized knowledge of some field; the Industrial Revolution and its new organization of labor created an array of professions in the nineteenth century.

Progressive party In the 1912 election, Theodore Roosevelt was unable to secure the Republican nomination for president. He left the Republican party and formed his own party of progressive Republicans, called the "Bull Moose" party (later Progressive Party). Roosevelt and Taft split the Republican vote, which allowed Democrat Woodrow Wilson to win.

Prohibition National ban on the manufacture and sale of alcohol that lasted from 1920 to 1933, though the law was widely violated and proved too difficult to enforce effectively.

proprietary colonies A colony owned by an individual, rather than a joint-stock company.

Protestant Reformation Sixteenth-century religious movement initiated by Martin Luther, a German monk whose public criticism of corruption in the Roman Catholic Church, and whose teaching that Christians can communicate directly with God, gained a wide following.

public schools Elementary and secondary schools funded by the state and free of tuition.

pueblos The Spanish term for the adobe cliff dwellings of the indigenous people of the southwestern United States.

Pullman strike (1894) A national strike by the American Railway Union, whose members shut down major railways in sympathy with striking workers in Pullman, Illinois; ended with intervention of federal troops.

Puritans English religious dissenters who sought to "purify" the Church of England of its Catholic practices.

Quakers George Fox founded the Quaker religion in 1647. They rejected the use of formal sacraments and ministry, refused to take oaths and embraced pacifism. Fleeing persecution, they settled and established the colony of Pennsylvania.

race-based slavery Institution that uses racial characteristics and myths to justify enslaving a people.

Radical Republicans Senators and congressmen who, strictly identifying the Civil War with the abolitionist cause, sought swift emancipation of the slaves, punishment of the rebels, and tight controls over the former Confederate states after the war.

railroad Steam-powered vehicles that improved passenger transportation, quickened western settlement, and enabled commercial agriculture in the nineteenth century.

Raleigh's Roanoke Island Colony English expedition of 117 settlers, including Virginia Dare, the first English child born in the New World; colony disappeared from Roanoke Island in the Outer Banks sometime between 1587 and 1590.

A. Philip Randolph (1889–1979) He was the head of the Brotherhood of Sleeping Car Porters who planned a march on Washington D.C. to demand an end to racial discrimination in the defense industries. To stop the march, the Roosevelt administration negotiated an agreement with the Randolph group. The demonstration would be called off and an executive order would be issued that forbid discrimination in defense work and training programs and set up the Fair Employment Practices Committee.

range wars In the late 1800s, conflicting claims over land and water rights triggered violent disputes between farmers and ranchers in parts of the western United States.

Ronald Reagan (1911–2004) In 1980, the former actor and governor of California was elected president. In office, he reduced social spending, cut taxes, and increased defense spending. During his presidency, the federal debt tripled, the federal deficit rose, programs such as housing and school lunches were cut, and the HIV/AIDS crisis grew to prominence in the United States. He signed an arms-control treaty with the Soviet Union in 1987, authorized covert CIA operations in Central America, and in 1986 the Iran-Contra scandal was revealed.

Reaganomics President Reagan's "supply-side" economic philosophy combining tax cuts with the goals of decreased government spending, reduced regulation of business, and a balanced budget.

Reconstruction Finance Corporation (1932) Federal program established under President Hoover to loan money to banks and other corporations to help them avoid bankruptcy.

Red Power Activism by militant Native American groups to protest living conditions on Indian reservations through demonstrations, legal action, and, at times, violence.

First Red Scare Fear among many Americans after the First World War of Communists in particular and noncitizens in general, it was a reaction to the Russian Revolution, mail bombs, strikes, and riots.

Redeemers Post–Civil War Democratic leaders who supposedly saved the South from Yankee domination and preserved the primarily rural economy.

Dr. Walter Reed (1851–1902) His work on yellow fever in Cuba led to the discovery that the fever was carried by mosquitoes. This understanding helped develop more effective controls of the worldwide disease.

Reform Darwinism A social philosophy developed by Lester Frank War that challenged the ruthlessness of Social Darwinism by asserting that humans were not passive pawns of evolutionary forces. Instead, people could actively shape the process of evolutionary social development through cooperation, innovation, and planning.

Reformation European religious movement that challenged the Catholic Church and resulted in the beginnings of Protestant Christianity. During this period, Catholics and Protestants persecuted, imprisoned, tortured, and killed each other in large numbers.

religious right Christian conservatives with a faith-based political agenda that includes prohibition of abortion and allowing prayer in public schools.

reparations As a part of the Treaty of Versailles, Germany was required to confess its responsibility for the First World War and make payments to the victors for the entire expense of the war. These two requirements created a deep bitterness among Germans.

Alexander Hamilton's Report on Manufactures First Secretary of the Treasury Alexander Hamilton's 1791 analysis that accurately foretold the future of American industry and proposed tariffs and subsidies to promote it.

Republican ideology Political belief in representative democracy in which citizens govern themselves by electing representatives, or legislators, to make key decisions on the citizens' behalf.

Republican simplicity Deliberate attitude of humility and frugality, as opposed to monarchical pomp and ceremony, adopted by Thomas Jefferson in his presidency.

Republicans First used during the early nineteenth century to describe supporters of a strict interpretation of the Constitution, which they believed would safeguard individual freedoms and states' rights from the threats posed by a strong central government. The idealist Republican vision of sustaining an agrarian-oriented union was developed largely by Thomas Jefferson.

"return to normalcy" Campaign promise of Republican presidential candidate Warren G. Harding in 1920, meant to contrast with Woodrow Wilson's progressivism and internationalism.

Paul Revere (1735–1818) On the night of April 18, 1775, British soldiers marched toward Concord to arrest American Revolutionary leaders and seize their depot of supplies. Paul Revere famously rode through the night and raised the alarm about the approaching British troops.

Roaring Twenties The 1920s, an era of social and intellectual revolution in which young people experimented with new forms of recreation and sexuality. The Eastern, urban cultural shift clashed with conservative and insular Midwestern America, which increased the tensions between the two regions.

Jackie Robinson (1919–1972) In 1947, he became the first African American to play major league baseball. He won over fans and players and stimulated the integration of other professional sports.

rock-and-roll music Alan Freed, a disc jockey, noticed white teenagers were buying rhythm and blues records that had been only purchased by African Americans and Hispanic Americans. Freed began playing these records, but called them rock-and-roll records as a way to overcome the racial barrier. As the popularity of the music genre increased, it helped bridge the gap between "white" and "black" music.

John D. Rockefeller (1839–1937) In 1870, he founded the Standard Oil Company of Ohio, which was his first step in creating his vast oil empire. He perfected the idea of a holding company.

***Roe v. Wade* (1973)** Landmark Supreme Court decision striking down state laws that banned abortions during the first trimester of pregnancy.

Roman Catholicism The Christian faith and religious practices of the Roman Catholic Church, which exerted great political, economic, and social influence on much of Western Europe and, through the Spanish and Portuguese Empires, on the Americas.

Romanticism Philosophical, literary, and artistic movement of the nineteenth century that was largely a reaction to the rationalism of the previous century; Romantics valued emotion, mysticism, and individualism.

Eleanor Roosevelt (1884–1962) She redefined the role of the presidential spouse and was the first woman to address a national political convention, write a nationally syndicated column and hold regular press conferences. She travelled throughout the nation to promote the New Deal, women's causes, organized labor, and meet with African American leaders.

Franklin Delano Roosevelt (1882–1945) Elected during the Great Depression, Roosevelt sought to help struggling Americans through his New Deal programs that created employment and social programs, such as Social Security. After the bombing of Pearl Harbor, he declared war on Japan and Germany and led the country through most of the Second World War before dying of cerebral hemorrhage.

Theodore Roosevelt (1858–1919) As the assistant secretary of the navy, he supported expansionism, American imperialism, and war with Spain. He led the Rough Riders in Cuba during the war of 1898 and used the notoriety of this military campaign for political gain. As President McKinley's vice president, he succeeded McKinley after his assassination. His forceful foreign policy became known as "big stick diplomacy." Domestically, his policies on natural resources helped start the conservation movement. Unable to win the Republican nomination for president in 1912, he formed his own party of progressive Republicans called the "Bull Moose" party.

Roosevelt Corollary President Theodore Roosevelt's 1904 revision of the Monroe Doctrine (1823) in which he argued that the United States could use military force in Central and South American nations to prevent European nations from intervening in the Western Hemisphere.

Rough Riders The First U.S. Volunteer Cavalry, led in the War of 1898 by Theodore Roosevelt; they were victorious in their only engagement, the Battle of San Juan Hill near Santiago, Cuba, and Roosevelt was celebrated as a national hero, bolstering his political career.

Nicola Sacco (1891–1927) In 1920, he and Bartolomeo Vanzetti were Italian immigrants who were arrested for stealing $16,000 and killing a paymaster and his guard. Their trial took place during a time of numerous bombings by anarchists and their judge was openly prejudicial; many liberals and radicals believe that their conviction was based on their political ideas and ethnic origin rather than the evidence against them.

Sacco and Vanzetti case 1921 trial of two Italian immigrants that occurred at the height of Italian immigration and against the backdrop of numerous terror attacks by anarchists; despite a lack of clear evidence, the two defendants, both self-professed anarchists, were convicted of murder and were executed in 1927.

saloons Bars or taverns where mostly men would gather to drink, eat, relax, play games, and, often, to discuss politics.

salutary neglect Informal British policy during the first half of the eighteenth century that allowed the American colonies considerable freedom to pursue their economic and political interests in exchange for colonial obedience.

same-sex marriage The legal right for gay and lesbian couples to marry; it became the most divisive issue in the culture wars of the early 2010s as more and more court rulings affirmed this right in states and municipalities across the United States.

Sandinista Cuban-sponsored government that came to power in Nicaragua after toppling a corrupt dictator. The State Department believed that the Sandinistas were supplying the leftist Salvadoran rebels with Cuban and Soviet arms. In response, the Reagan administration ordered the CIA to train and supply guerrilla bands of anti-Communist Nicaraguans called Contras. A cease-fire agreement between the Contras and Sandinistas was signed in 1988.

Sandlot Incident Violence occurring during the Great Railroad Strike of 1877, when mobs of frustrated working-class whites in San Francisco attacked Chinese immigrants, blaming them for economic hardship.

General Antonio López de Santa Anna (1794–1876) In 1834, he seized political power in Mexico and became a dictator. In 1835, Texans rebelled against him and he led his army to Texas to crush their rebellion. He captured the mission called the Alamo and killed all of its defenders, which inspired Texans to continue resistance and Americans to volunteer to fight for Texas. The Texans captured Santa Anna during a surprise attack and he bought his freedom by signing a treaty recognizing Texas's independence.

battles of Saratoga Decisive defeat of 5,000 British troops under General John Burgoyne in several battles near Saratoga, New York, in October 1777; the American victory helped convince France to enter the war on the side of the Patriots.

scalawags White southern Republicans—some former Unionists—who served in Reconstruction governments.

Phyllis Schlafly (1924–) A right-wing Republican activist who spearheaded the anti-feminism movement. She believed feminists were "anti-family, anti-children, and pro-abortion." She worked against the equal-rights amendment for women and civil rights protection for gays.

Scopes Trial Highly publicized 1925 trial of a high school teacher in Tennessee for violating a state law that prohibited the teaching of evolution; the trial was seen as the climax of the fundamentalist war on Darwinism.

Winfield Scott (1786–1866) During the Mexican War, he was the American general who captured Mexico City, which ended the war. Using his popularity from his military success, he ran as a Whig party candidate for President.

Sears, Roebuck and Company By the end of the nineteenth century, this company dominated the mail-order industry and helped create a truly national market. Its mail-order catalog and low prices allowed people living in rural areas and small towns to buy products that were previously too expensive or available only to city dwellers.

secession Shortly after President Abraham Lincoln was elected, southern states began dissolving their ties with the United States because they believed Lincoln and the Republican party were a threat to slavery.

Second Bank of the United States Established in 1816 after the first national bank's charter expired; it stabilized the economy by creating a sound national currency, by making loans to farmers, small manufacturers, and entrepreneurs, and by regulating the ability of state banks to issue their own paper currency.

Second Great Awakening Religious revival movement that arose in reaction to the growth of secularism and rationalist religion; spurred the growth of the Baptist and Methodist churches.

Second Industrial Revolution Beginning in the late nineteenth century, a wave of technological innovations, especially in iron and steel production, steam and electrical power, and telegraphic communications, all of which spurred industrial development and urban growth.

Second New Deal (1935–1938) Expansive cluster of legislation proposed by President Roosevelt that established new regulatory agencies, strengthened the rights of workers to organize unions, and laid the foundation of a federal social welfare system through the creation of Social Security.

Securities and Exchange Commission (1934) Federal agency established to regulate the issuance and trading of stocks and bonds in an effort to avoid financial panics and stock market "crashes."

Seneca Falls Convention (1848) Convention organized by feminists Lucretia Mott and Elizabeth Cady Stanton to promote women's rights and issue the pathbreaking Declaration of Sentiments.

"separate but equal" Principle underlying legal racial segregation, which was upheld in *Plessy v. Ferguson* (1896) and struck down in *Brown v. Board of Education* (1954).

separation of powers Strict division of the powers of government among three separate branches (executive, legislative, and judicial) which, in turn, check and balance each other.

September 11 On September 11, 2001, Islamic terrorists, who were members of the al Qaeda terrorist organization, hijacked four commercial airliners. Two were flown into the World Trade Center, a third into the Pentagon, and a fourth plane was brought down in Pennsylvania. In response, President George W. Bush launched his "war on terrorism." His administration assembled an international coalition to fight terrorism, which invaded Afghanistan after the country's government would not turn over Osama bin Laden. Bush and Congress passed the U.S.A. Patriot Act, which allowed government agencies to try suspected terrorists in secret military courts and eavesdrop on confidential conversations.

settlement houses Product of the late nineteenth-century movement to offer a broad array of social services in urban immigrant neighborhoods; Chicago's Hull House was one of hundreds of settlement houses that operated by the early twentieth century.

Seventeenth Amendment (1913) Constitutional amendment that provided for the direct election of senators rather than the traditional practice allowing state legislatures to name them.

Shakers Founded by Mother Ann Lee Stanley in England, the United Society of Believers in Christ's Second Appearing settled in Watervliet, New York, in 1774 and subsequently established eighteen additional communes in the Northeast, Indiana, and Kentucky.

share tenants Poor farmers who rented land to farm in exchange for a substantial share of the crop, though they would often have their own horse or mule, tools, and line of credit with a nearby store.

sharecroppers Poor, mostly black farmers who would work an owner's land in return for shelter, seed, fertilizer, mules, supplies, and food, as well as a substantial share of the crop produced.

Share-the-Wealth program Huey Long offered this program as an alternative to the New Deal. The program proposed to confiscate large personal fortunes, which would be used to guarantee every poor family a cash grant of $5,000 and every worker an annual income of $2,500. This program promised to provide pensions, reduce working hours, pay veterans' bonuses, and ensures a college education to every qualified student.

Shays's Rebellion Storming of the Massachusetts federal arsenal in 1787 by Daniel Shays and 1,200 armed farmers seeking debt relief from the state legislature through issuance of paper currency and lower taxes.

Sherman's "March to the Sea" The Union army's devastating march through Georgia from Atlanta to Savannah led by General William T. Sherman, intended to demoralize civilians and destroy the resources the Confederate army needed to fight.

silent majority Term popularized by President Richard Nixon to describe the great majority of American voters who did not express their political opinions publicly—"the non-demonstrators."

Sixteenth Amendment (1913) Constitutional amendment that authorized the federal income tax.

slave codes Ordinances passed by a colony or state to regulate the behavior of slaves, often including brutal punishments for infractions.

Alfred E. Smith (1873–1944) In the 1928 presidential election, he won the Democratic nomination, but failed to win the presidency. Rural voters distrusted him for being Catholic and the son of Irish immigrants as well as his anti-Prohibition stance.

Captain John Smith (1580–1631) A swashbuckling soldier of fortune with rare powers of leadership and self-promotion, he was appointed to the resident council to manage Jamestown.

Joseph Smith (1805–1844) In 1823, he claimed that the Angel Moroni showed him the location of several gold tablets on which the Book of Mormon was written. Using the Book of Mormon as his gospel, he founded the Church of Jesus Christ of Latter-day Saints, or Mormons. In 1839, they settled in Commerce, Illinois, to avoid persecution. In 1844, Joseph and his brother were arrested and jailed for ordering the destruction of a newspaper that opposed them. While in jail, an anti-Mormon mob stormed the jail and killed both of them.

Social Darwinism The application of Charles Darwin's theory of evolutionary natural selection to human society; Social Darwinists used the concept of "survival of the fittest" to justify class distinctions, explain poverty, and oppose government intervention in the economy.

social gospel Protestant movement that stressed the Christian obligation to address the mounting social problems caused by urbanization and industrialization.

social justice An important part of the Progressive's agenda, social justice sought to solve social problems through reform and regulation. Methods used to bring about social justice ranged from the founding of charities to the legislation of a ban on child labor.

Social Security Act (1935) Legislation enacted to provide federal assistance to retired workers through tax-funded pension payments and benefit payments to the unemployed and disabled.

Sons of Liberty First organized by Samuel Adams in the 1770s, groups of colonists dedicated to militant resistance against British control of the colonies.

Hernando de Soto (1500?–1542) A conquistador who explored the west coast of Florida, western North Carolina, and along the Arkansas river from 1539 till his death in 1542.

Southern Christian Leadership Conference (SCLC) Civil rights organization formed by Dr. Martin Luther King, Jr., that championed nonviolent direct action as a means of ending segregation.

"southern strategy" This strategy was a major reason for Richard Nixon's victory in the 1968 presidential election. To gain support in the South, Nixon assured southern conservatives that he would slow the federal enforcement of civil rights laws and appoint pro-southern justices to the Supreme Court. As president, Nixon fulfilled these promises.

Spanish Armada A massive Spanish fleet of 130 warships that was defeated at Plymouth in 1588 by the English navy during the reign of Queen Elizabeth I.

Spanish flu Unprecedentedly lethal influenza epidemic of 1918 that killed more than 22 million people worldwide.

Herbert Spencer (1820–1903) As the first major proponent of social Darwinism, he argued that human society and institutions are subject to the process of natural selection and that society naturally evolves for the better. He was against any form of government interference with the evolution of society, like business regulations, because it would help the "unfit" to survive.

spirituals Songs with religious messages sung by slaves to help ease the strain of field labor and to voice their suffering at the hands of their masters and overseers.

spoils system The term—meaning the filling of federal government jobs with persons loyal to the party of the president—originated in Andrew Jackson's first term; the system was replaced in the Progressive Era by civil service.

Square Deal Roosevelt's progressive agenda of the "Three C's": control of corporations, conservation of natural resources, and consumer protection.

stagflation Term coined by economists during the Nixon presidency to describe the unprecedented situation of stagnant economic growth and consumer price inflation occurring at the same time.

Joseph Stalin (1879–1953) The Bolshevik leader who succeeded Lenin as the leader of the Soviet Union in 1924 and ruled the country until his death. During his totalitarian rule of the Soviet Union, he used purges and a system of forced labor camps to maintain control over the country, and claimed vast areas of Eastern Europe for Soviet domination.

Stalwarts Conservative Republican party faction during the presidency of Rutherford B. Hayes, 1877–1881; led by Senator Roscoe B. Conkling of New York, Stalwarts opposed civil service reform and favored a third term for President Ulysses S. Grant.

Stamp Act Act of Parliament requiring that all printed materials (e.g., newspapers, bonds, and even playing cards) in the American colonies use paper with an official tax stamp in order to pay for British military protection of the colonies.

Stamp Act Congress Twenty-seven delegates from nine of the colonies met from October 7 to 25, 1765 and wrote a Declaration of the Rights and Grievances of the Colonies, a petition to the King and a petition to Parliament for the repeal of the Stamp Act.

Standard Oil Company Corporation under the leadership of John D. Rockefeller that attempted to dominate the entire oil industry through horizontal and vertical integration.

Elizabeth Cady Stanton (1815–1902) A prominent reformer and advocate for the rights of women, she helped organize the Seneca Falls Convention to discuss women's rights. The convention was the first of its kind and produced the Declaration of Sentiments, which proclaimed the equality of men and women.

staple crop A profitable market crop, such as cotton, tobacco, or rice that predominates in a given region.

state constitutions Charters that define the relationship between the state government and local governments and individuals, and also protects their rights from violation by the national government.

steamboats Ships and boats powered by wood-fired steam engines. First used in the early nineteenth century, they made two-way traffic possible in eastern river systems, creating a transcontinental market and an agricultural empire.

Thaddeus Stevens (1792–1868) As one of the leaders of the Radical Republicans, he argued that the former Confederate states should be viewed as conquered provinces, which were subject to the demands of the conquerors. He believed that all of Southern society needed to be changed, and he supported the abolition of slavery and racial equality.

Adlai E. Stevenson (1900–1965) In the 1952 and 1956 presidential elections, he was the Democratic nominee who lost to Dwight Eisenhower. He was also the U.S. Ambassador to the United Nations and is remembered for his famous speech in 1962 before the UN Security Council that unequivocally demonstrated that the Soviet Union had built nuclear missile bases in Cuba.

Stono Rebellion A 1739 slave uprising in South Carolina that was brutally quashed, leading to executions as well as a severe tightening of the slave code.

Stonewall Riots (1969) Violent clashes between police and gay patrons of New York City's Stonewall Inn, seen as the starting point of the modern gay rights movement.

Strategic Arms Limitation Treaty (SALT I) (1972) Agreement signed by President Nixon and Secretary Brezhnev prohibiting the development of missile defense systems in the United States and Soviet Union and limiting the quantity of nuclear warheads for both.

Strategic Defense Initiative (SDI) (1983) Ronald Reagan's proposed space-based antimissile defense system, dubbed "Star Wars" by the media, that aroused great controversy and escalated the arms race between the United States and the Soviet Union.

Levi Strauss (1829–1902) A Jewish tailor who followed miners to California during the gold rush and began making durable work pants that were later dubbed blue jeans or Levi's.

Student Nonviolent Coordinating Committee (SNCC) Interracial organization formed in 1960 with the goal of intensifying the effort to end racial segregation.

Students for a Democratic Society (SDS) Major organization of the New Left, founded at the University of Michigan in 1960 by Tom Hayden and Al Haber.

suburbia Communities formed from mass migration of middle-class whites from urban centers.

Suez crisis (1956) British, French, and Israeli attack on Egypt after Nasser's seizure of the Suez Canal; President Eisenhower interceded to demand the withdrawal of the British, French, and Israeli forces from the Sinai peninsula and canal.

Sunbelt The label for an arc that stretched from the Carolinas to California. During the postwar era, much of the urban population growth occurred in this area.

the "surge" In early 2007, President Bush decided he would send a "surge" of new troops to Iraq and implement a new strategy. U.S. forces would shift their focus from offensive operations to the protection of Iraqi civilians from attacks by terrorist insurgents and sectarian militias. While the "surge" reduced the violence in Iraq, Iraqi leaders were still unable to develop a self-sustaining democracy.

Taft-Hartley Labor Act (1947) Congressional legislation that banned "unfair labor practices" by labor unions, required union leaders to sign anti-Communist "loyalty oaths," and prohibited federal employees from going on strike.

Taliban A coalition of ultraconservative Islamists who rose to power in Afghanistan after the Soviets withdrew. The Taliban leaders gave Osama bin Laden a safe haven in their country in exchange for aid in fighting the Northern Alliance, who were rebels opposed to the Taliban. After they refused to turn bin Laden over to the United States, America invaded Afghanistan.

Tammany Hall The "city machine" used by "Boss" Tweed to dominate politics in New York City until his arrest in 1871.

tariff A tax on goods imported from other nations, typically used to protect home industries from foreign competitors and to generate revenue for the federal government.

Tariff of 1816 A cluster of taxes on imports passed by Congress to protect America's emerging iron and textile industries from British competition.

Tariff of 1832 This tariff act reduced the duties on many items, but the tariffs on cloth and iron remained high. South Carolina nullified it along with the tariff of 1828. President Andrew Jackson sent federal troops to the state and asked Congress to grant him the authority to enforce the tariffs. Henry Clay presented a plan of gradually reducing the tariffs until 1842, which Congress passed and ended the crisis.

"Tariff of Abominations" (1828) Tax on imported goods, including British cloth and clothing, that strengthened New England textile companies but hurt southern consumers, who experienced a decrease in British demand for raw cotton grown in the South.

tariff reform Effort led by the Democratic party to reduce taxes on imported goods, which Republicans argued were needed to protect American industries from foreign competition.

Troubled Asset Relief Program (TARP) In 2008 President George W. Bush signed into law the bank bailout fund called Troubled Asset Relief Program (TARP), which required the Treasury Department to spend $700 billion to keep banks and other financial institutions from collapsing.

Zachary Taylor (1784–1850) During the Mexican War, he scored two quick victories against Mexico, which made him very popular in America. He used his popularity from his military victories to be elected president as a member of the Whig party, but died before he could complete his term.

Taylorism Labor system based on detailed study of work tasks, championed by Frederick Winslow Taylor, intended to maximize efficiency and profits for employers.

Tea Party Right-wing populist movement, largely made up of middle-class, white male conservatives, that emerged as a response to the expansion of the federal government under the Obama administration.

Teapot Dome Harding administration scandal in which Secretary of the Interior Albert B. Fall profited from secret leasing of government oil reserves in Wyoming to private oil companies.

Tecumseh (1768–1813) He was a leader of the Shawnee tribe who tried to unite all Indians into a confederation that could defend their hunting grounds. He believed that no land cessions could be made without the consent of all the tribes since they held the land in common. His beliefs and leadership made him seem dangerous to the American government and they waged war on him and his tribe. He was killed at the Battle of the Thames.

Tecumseh's Indian Confederacy A group of Native Americans under leadership of Shawnee leader Tecumseh and his prophet brother Tenskwatawa; its mission of fighting off American expansion was thwarted in the Battle of Tippecanoe (1811), when the confederacy fell apart.

Tejanos Texas settlers of Spanish or Mexican descent.

telegraph system System of electronic communication invented by Samuel F. B. Morse that could be transmitted instantaneously across great distances (first used in the 1840s).

Teller Amendment Addition to the congressional war resolution of April 20, 1898, which marked the U.S. entry into the war with Spain; the amendment declared that the United States' goal in entering the war was to ensure Cuba's independence, not to annex Cuba as a territory.

temperance A widespread reform movement, led by militant Christians, focused on reducing the use of alcoholic beverages.

tenements Shabby, low-cost inner-city apartment buildings that housed the urban poor in cramped, unventilated apartments.

Tenochtitlán The capital city of the Aztec Empire. The city was built on marshy islands on the western side of Lake Tetzcoco, which is the site of present-day Mexico City.

Tet offensive Surprise attack by Viet Cong guerrillas and the North Vietnamese army on U.S. and South Vietnamese forces in 1968 that shocked the American public and led to widespread sentiment against the war.

The Texas Revolution (1835–1836) Conflict between Texas colonists and the Mexican government that resulted in the creation of the separate Republic of Texas in 1836.

textile industry Commercial production of thread, fabric, and clothing from raw cotton in mills in New England during the first half of the nineteenth century, and later in the South in the late nineteenth century.

Thirteenth Amendment (1865) Amendment to the U. S. Constitution that freed all slaves in the United States.

Battle of Tippecanoe (1811) Battle in northern Indiana between U.S. troops and Native American warriors led by Tenskwatawa, the brother of Tecumseh, who had organized an anti-American Indian confederacy to fight American efforts to settle on Indian lands.

tobacco A cash crop grown in the Caribbean as well as the Virginia and Maryland colonies, made increasingly profitable by the rapidly growing popularity of smoking in Europe after the voyages of Columbus.

Gulf of Tonkin incident On August 2 and 4 of 1964, North Vietnamese vessels attacked two American destroyers in the Gulf of Tonkin off the coast of North Vietnam. President Johnson described the attacks as unprovoked. In reality, the U.S. ships were monitoring South Vietnamese attacks on North Vietnamese islands that America advisors had planned. The incident spurred the Tonkin Gulf resolution.

Tonkin Gulf Resolution Congressional action that granted the president unlimited authority to defend U.S. forces abroad, passed in August 1964 after an allegedly unprovoked attack on American warships off the coast of North Vietnam.

Tories Term used by Patriots to refer to Loyalists, or colonists who supported the Crown after the Declaration of Independence.

Townshend Acts Parliamentary measures to extract more revenue from the colonies; the Revenue Act of 1767, which taxed tea, paper, and other colonial imports, was one of the most notorious of these policies.

"Trail of Tears" The Cherokees' eight-hundred mile journey (1838–1839) from the southern Appalachians to Indian Territory (in present-day Oklahoma); four thousand died people along the way.

transcendentalism Philosophy of a small group of New England writers and thinkers who advocated personal spirituality, self-reliance, social reform, and harmony with nature.

Transcontinental railroad First line across the continent from Omaha, Nebraska, to Sacramento, California, established in 1869 with the linkage of the Union Pacific and Central Pacific railroads at Promontory, Utah.

Transcontinental Treaty (1819) (Adams-Onís Treaty) Treaty between Spain and the United States that clarified the boundaries of the Louisiana Purchase and arranged the transfer of Florida to the United States in exchange for cash.

triangular trade A network of trade in which exports from one region were sold to another region, which sent its exports to a third region, which exported its own goods back to the first country or colony.

Treaty of Ghent (1814) Agreement between Great Britain and the United States that ended the War of 1812, signed on December 24, 1814.

The Treaty of Guadeloupe Hidalgo (1848) Treaty between United States and Mexico that ended the Mexican-American War.

Treaty of Paris Settlement between Great Britain and France that ended the French and Indian War.

Treaty of Versailles Peace treaty that ended the First World War, forcing Germany to dismantle its military, pay immense war reparations, and give up its colonies around the world.

trench warfare A form of prolonged combat between the entrenched positions of opposing armies, often with little tactical movement.

Harry S. Truman (1884–1972) As President Roosevelt's vice president, he succeeded him after his death near the end of the Second World War. After the war, Truman wrestled with the inflation of both prices and wages, worked with Congress to pass the National Security Act, and banned racial discrimination in the hiring of federal employees and ended racial segregation in the armed forces. In foreign affairs, he established the Truman Doctrine to contain communism, developed the Marshall Plan to rebuild Europe, and sent the U.S. military to defend South Korea after North Korea invaded.

Truman Doctrine (1947) President Truman's program of "containing" communism in Eastern Europe and providing economic and military aid to any nations at risk of Communist takeover.

trust A business arrangement that gives a person or corporation (the "trustee") the legal power to manage another person's money or another company without owning those entities outright.

Sojourner Truth (1797?–1883) She was born into slavery, but New York State freed her in 1827. She spent the 1840s and 1850s travelling across the country and speaking to audiences about her experiences as slave and asking them to support abolition and women's rights.

Harriet Tubman (1820–1913) She was born a slave, but escaped to the North. She then returned to the South nineteen times and guided 300 slaves to freedom.

Frederick Jackson Turner An influential historian who authored the "Frontier Thesis" in 1893, arguing that the existence of an alluring frontier and the experience of persistent westward expansion informed the nation's democratic politics, unfettered economy, and rugged individualism.

Nat Turner (1800–1831) He was the leader of the only slave revolt to get past the planning stages. In August of 1831, the revolt began with the slaves killing the members of Turner's master's household. Then they attacked other neighboring farmhouses and recruited more slaves until the militia crushed the revolt. At least fifty-five whites were killed during the uprising and seventeen slaves were hanged afterwards.

Nat Turner's Rebellion (1831) Insurrection in rural Virginia led by black overseer Nat Turner, who killed slave owners and their families; in turn, federal troops indiscriminately killed hundreds of slaves in the process of putting down Turner and his rebels.

Tuskegee Airmen U.S. Army Air Corps unit of African American pilots whose combat success spurred military and civilian leaders to desegregate the armed forces after the war.

Mark Twain (1835–1910) Born Samuel Langhorne Clemens in Missouri, he became a popular humorous writer and lecturer and established himself as one of the great American satirists and authors. His two greatest books, *The Adventures of Tom Sawyer* and *The Adventures of Huckleberry Finn*, drew heavily on his childhood in Missouri.

"Boss" Tweed (1823–1878) An infamous political boss in New York City, Tweed used his "city machine," the Tammany Hall ring, to rule, plunder and sometimes improve the city's government. His political domination of New York City ended with his arrest in 1871 and conviction in 1873.

Twenty-first Amendment (1933) Repealed prohibition on the manufacture, sale, and transportation of alcoholic beverages, effectively nullifying the Eighteenth Amendment.

two-party system Domination of national politics by two major political parties, such as the Whigs and Democrats during the 1830s and 1840s.

Underground Railroad A secret system of routes and safe houses through which runaway slaves were led to freedom in the North.

Unitarians Members of the liberal New England Congregationalist offshoot, often well-educated and wealthy, who profess the oneness of God and the goodness of rational man.

United Farm Workers (UFW) Organization formed in 1962 to represent the interests of Mexican American migrant workers.

United Nations Security Council A major agency within the United Nations which remains in permanent session and has the responsibility of maintaining international peace and security. Originally, it consisted of five permanent members, (United States, Soviet Union, Britain, France, and the Republic of China), and six members elected to two-year terms. After 1965, the number of rotating members was increased to ten. In 1971, the Republic of China was replaced with the People's Republic of China and the Soviet Union was replaced by the Russian Federation in 1991.

Universalists Members of a New England religious movement, often from the working class, who believed in a merciful God and universal salvation.

USA Patriot Act (2001) Wide-reaching Congressional legislation, triggered by the War on Terror, which gave government agencies the right to eavesdrop on confidential conversations between prison inmates and their lawyers and permitted suspected terrorists to be tried in secret military courts.

U-boat German military submarine (*Unterseeboot*) used during the First World War to attack enemy naval vessels as well as merchant ships of enemy and neutral nations.

utopian communities Ideal communities that offered innovative social and economic relationships to those who were interested in achieving salvation.

Valley Forge American military encampment near Philadelphia, where more than 3,500 soldiers deserted or died from cold and hunger in the winter of 1777–1778.

Cornelius Vanderbilt (1794–1877) In the 1860s, he consolidated several separate railroad companies into one vast entity, New York Central Railroad.

Bartolomeo Vanzetti (1888–1927) In 1920, he and Nicola Sacco were Italian immigrants who were arrested for stealing $16,000 and killing a paymaster and his guard. Their trial took place during a time of numerous bombings by anarchists and their judge was openly prejudicial. Many liberals and radicals believe that their conviction was based on their political ideas and ethnic origin rather than the evidence against them.

vertical integration The process by which a corporation gains control of all aspects of the resources and processes needed to produce and sell a product.

Amerigo Vespucci (1455–1512) Italian explorer who reached the New World in 1499 and was the first to suggest that South America was a new continent. Afterward, European mapmakers used a variant of his first name, America, to label the New World.

Battle of Vicksburg (1863) A protracted battle in northern Mississippi in which Union forces under Ulysses Grant besieged the last major Confederate fortress on the Mississippi River, forcing the inhabitants into starvation and then submission.

Viet Cong Communist guerrillas in Vietnam who launched attacks on the Diem government.

Vietnamization Nixon-era policy of equipping and training South Vietnamese forces to take over the burden of combat from U.S. troops.

Vikings Norse people from Scandinavia who sailed to Newfoundland about A.D. 1001.

Francisco Pancho Villa (1877–1923) While the leader of one of the competing factions in the Mexican civil war, he provoked the United States into intervening. He hoped attacking the United States would help him build a reputation as an opponent of the United States, which would increase his popularity and discredit Mexican President Carranza.

Virginia Company A joint stock enterprise that King James I chartered in 1606. The company was to spread Christianity in the New World as well as find ways to make a profit in it.

Virginia Plan The delegations to the Constitutional Convention were divided between two plans on how to structure the government: Virginia called for a strong central government and a two-house legislature apportioned by population.

Virginia Statute of Religious Freedom A Virginia law, drafted by Thomas Jefferson in 1777 and enacted in 1786, that guarantees freedom of, and from, religion.

virtual representation The idea that the American colonies, although they had no actual representative in Parliament, were "virtually" represented by all members of Parliament.

Voting Rights Act of 1965 Legislation ensuring that all Americans were able to vote; the law ended literacy tests and other means of restricting voting rights.

Wagner Act (1935) Legislation that guaranteed workers the right to organize unions, granted them direct bargaining power, and barred employers from interfering with union activities.

George Wallace (1919–1998) An outspoken defender of segregation. As the governor of Alabama, he once attempted to block African American students from enrolling at the University of Alabama. He ran as the presidential candidate for the American Independent party in 1968, appealing to voters who were concerned about rioting anti-war protestors, the welfare system, and the growth of the federal government.

war hawks In 1811, congressional members from the southern and western districts who clamored for a war to seize Canada and Florida were dubbed "war hawks."

War of 1812 Conflict fought in North America and at sea between Great Britain and the United States, 1812–1815, over American shipping rights and British efforts to spur Indian attacks on American settlements. Canadians and Native Americans also fought in the war.

war on terror Global crusade to root out anti-American, anti-Western Islamist terrorist cells launched by President George W. Bush as a response to the 9/11 attacks.

War Powers Act (1973) Legislation requiring the president to inform Congress within 48 hours of the deployment of U.S. troops abroad and to withdraw them after 60 days unless Congress approves their continued deployment.

War Production Board Federal agency created by President Roosevelt in 1942 that converted America's industrial output to war production.

"war relocation camps" Detention camps housing thousands of Japanese Americans from the West Coast who were forcibly interned from 1942 until the end of the Second World War.

Warren Court The U.S. Supreme Court under Chief Justice Earl Warren, 1953–1969, decided such landmark cases as *Brown v. Board of Education* (school desegregation), *Baker v. Carr* (legislative redistricting), and *Gideon v. Wainwright* and *Miranda v. Arizona* (rights of criminal defendants).

Booker T. Washington (1856–1915) He founded a leading college for African Americans in Tuskegee, Alabama, and become the foremost black educator in America by the 1890s. He believed that the African American community should establish an economic base for its advancement before striving for social equality. His critics charged that his philosophy sacrificed educational and civil rights for dubious social acceptance and economic opportunities.

George Washington (1732–1799) In 1775, the Continental Congress named him the commander in chief of the Continental Army which defeated the British in the American Revolution. He had previously served as an officer in the French and Indian War. In 1787, he was the presiding officer over the Constitutional Convention, but participated little in the debates. In 1789, the Electoral College chose Washington to be the nation's first president. Washington faced the nation's first foreign and domestic crises, maintaining the United States' neutrality in foreign affairs. After two terms in office, Washington chose to step down; and the power of the presidency was peacefully passed to John Adams.

Watergate (1972–1974) Scandal that exposed the criminality and corruption of the Nixon administration and ultimately led to President Nixon's resignation in 1974.

Daniel Webster (1782–1852) As a representative from New Hampshire, he led the New Federalists in opposition to the moving of the second national bank from Boston to Philadelphia. Later, he served as representative and a senator for Massachusetts and emerged as a champion of a stronger national government. He also switched from opposing to supporting tariffs because New England had built up its manufactures with the understanding tariffs would protect them from foreign competitors.

Webster-Ashburton Treaty Settlement in 1842 of U.S.–Canadian border disputes in Maine, New York, Vermont, and in the Wisconsin Territory (now northern Minnesota).

Webster-Hayne debate U.S. Senate debate of January 1830 between Daniel Webster of Massachusetts and Robert Hayne of South Carolina over nullification and states' rights.

Western Front The contested frontier between the Central and Allied Powers that ran along northern France and across Belgium.

Whig party Political party founded in 1834 in opposition to the Jacksonian Democrats; Whigs supported federal funding for internal improvements, a national bank, and high tariffs on imported goods.

Whigs Another name for revolutionary Patriots.

Whiskey Rebellion (1794) Violent protest by western Pennsylvania farmers against the federal excise tax on corn whiskey, put down by a federal army.

Eli Whitney (1765–1825) He invented the cotton gin which could separate cotton from its seeds. One machine operator could separate fifty times more cotton than worker could by hand, which led to an increase in cotton production and prices. These increases gave planters a new profitable use for slavery and a lucrative slave trade emerged from the coastal South to the Southwest.

Wilderness Road Originally an Indian path through the Cumberland Gap, it was used by over 300,000 settlers who migrated westward to Kentucky in the last quarter of the eighteenth century.

Roger Williams (1603–1683) Puritan who believed that the purity of the church required a complete separation between church and state and freedom from coercion in matters of faith. In 1636, he established the town of Providence, the first permanent settlement in Rhode Island and the first to allow religious freedom in America.

Wendell L. Willkie (1892–1944) In the 1940 presidential election, he was the Republican nominee who ran against President Roosevelt. He supported aid to the Allies and criticized the New Deal programs. Voters looked at the increasingly dangerous world situation and chose to keep President Roosevelt in office for a third term.

Wilmot Proviso (1846) Proposal by Congressman David Wilmot, a Pennsylvania Democrat, to prohibit slavery in any land acquired in the Mexican-American War.

Woodrow Wilson (1856–1924) In the 1912 presidential election, Woodrow Wilson ran under the slogan of New Freedom, which promised to improve of the banking system, lower tariffs, and break up monopolies. At the beginning of the First World War, Wilson kept America neutral, but provided the Allies with credit for purchases of supplies; however, the sinking of U.S. merchant ships and the Zimmerman telegram caused him to ask Congress to declare war on Germany. Wilson supported the entry of America into the League of Nations and the ratification of the Treaty of Versailles, but Congress would not approve the entry or ratification.

John Winthrop Puritan leader and Governor of the Massachusetts Bay Colony who resolved to use the colony as a refuge for persecuted Puritans and as an instrument of building a "wilderness Zion" in America.

woman suffrage Movement to give women the right to vote through a constitutional amendment, spearheaded by Susan B. Anthony and Elizabeth Cady Stanton's National Woman Suffrage Association.

Women Accepted for Voluntary Emergency Services (WAVES) During the Second World War, the increased demand for labor shook up old prejudices about gender roles in the workplace and in the military. Nearly 200,000 women served in the Women's Army Corps or its naval equivalent, Women Accepted for Volunteer Emergency Service (WAVES).

Women's Army Corps Women's branch of the United States Army; by the end of the Second World War nearly 150,000 women had served in the WAC.

women's movement Wave of activism sparked by Betty Friedan's *The Feminine Mystique* (1963); it argued for equal rights for women and fought against the cult of domesticity of the 1950s that limited women's roles to the home as wife, mother, and housewife.

women's work The traditional term referring to routine tasks in the house, garden, and fields performed by women. The sphere of women's occupations expanded in the colonies to include medicine, shopkeeping, upholstering, and the operation of inns and taverns.

Woodstock In 1969, roughly a half a million young people converged on a farm near Bethel, New York, for a three-day music festival that was an expression of the flower children's free spirit.

Works Progress Administration (1935) Government agency established to manage several federal job programs created under the New Deal; it became the largest employer in the nation.

Wounded Knee, Battle of Last incident of the Indians Wars took place in 1890 in the Dakota Territory, where the U.S. Cavalry killed over 200 Sioux men, women, and children who were in the process of surrender.

XYZ affair French foreign minister Tallyrand's three anonymous agents demanded payments to stop French plundering of American ships in 1797; refusal to pay the bribe led to two years of sea war with France (1798–1800).

Yalta Conference (1945) Meeting of the "Big Three" Allied leaders, Franklin D. Roosevelt, Winston Churchill, and Joseph Stalin, to discuss how to divide control of postwar Germany and eastern Europe

yellow journalism A type of news reporting, epitomized in the 1890s by the newspaper empires of William Randolph Hearst and Joseph Pulitzer, that intentionally manipulates public opinion through sensational headlines, illustrations, and articles about both real and invented events.

yeomen Small landowners (the majority of white families in the South) who farmed their own land and usually did not own slaves.

Battle of Yorktown Last major battle of the Revolutionary War; General Cornwallis along with over 7,000 British troops surrendered to George Washington at Yorktown, Virginia, on October 17, 1781.

Brigham Young (1801–1877) Following Joseph Smith's death, he became the leader of the Mormons and promised Illinois officials that the Mormons would leave the state. In 1846, he led the Mormons to Utah and settled near the Salt Lake. After the United States gained Utah as part of the Treaty of Guadalupe Hidalgo, he became the governor of the territory and kept the Mormons virtually independent of federal authority.

youth culture The youth of the 1950s had more money and free time than any previous generation which allowed a distinct youth culture to emerge. A market emerged for products and activities that were specifically for young people such as transistor radios, rock records, *Seventeen* magazine, and Pat Boone movies.

Zimmermann telegram Message sent by a German official to the Mexican government in 1917 urging an invasion of the United States; the telegram was intercepted by British intelligence agents and angered Americans, many of whom called for war against Germany.

Appendix

The Declaration of Independence (1776)

When in the Course of human events, it becomes necessary for one people to dissolve the political bands which have connected them with another, and to assume among the powers of the earth, the separate and equal station to which the Laws of Nature and of Nature's God entitle them, a decent respect to the opinions of mankind requires that they should declare the causes which impel them to the separation.

We hold these truths to be self-evident, that all men are created equal, that they are endowed by their Creator with certain unalienable Rights, that among these are Life, Liberty and the pursuit of Happiness. —That to secure these rights, Governments are instituted among Men, deriving their just powers from the consent of the governed, —That whenever any Form of Government becomes destructive of these ends, it is the Right of the People to alter or to abolish it, and to institute new Government, laying its foundation on such principles and organizing its powers in such form, as to them shall seem most likely to effect their Safety and Happiness. Prudence, indeed, will dictate that Governments long established should not be changed for light and transient causes; and accordingly all experience hath shewn, that mankind are more disposed to suffer, while evils are sufferable, than to right themselves by abolishing the forms to which they are accustomed. But when a long train of abuses and usurpations, pursuing invariably the same Object evinces a design to reduce them under absolute Despotism, it is their right, it is their duty, to throw off such Government, and to provide new Guards for their future security.— Such has been the patient sufferance of these Colonies; and such is now the necessity which constrains them to alter their former Systems of Government. The history of the present King of Great Britain is a history of repeated injuries and usurpations, all having in direct object the establishment of an absolute Tyranny over these States. To prove this, let Facts be submitted to a candid world.

He has refused his Assent to Laws, the most wholesome and necessary for the public good.

He has forbidden his Governors to pass Laws of immediate and pressing importance, unless suspended in their operation till his Assent should be obtained; and when so suspended, he has utterly neglected to attend to them.

He has refused to pass other Laws for the accommodation of large districts of people, unless those people would relinquish the right of Representation in the Legislature, a right inestimable to them and formidable to tyrants only.

He has called together legislative bodies at places unusual, uncomfortable, and distant from the depository of their public Records, for the sole purpose of fatiguing them into compliance with his measures.

He has dissolved Representative Houses repeatedly, for opposing with manly firmness his invasions on the rights of the people.

He has refused for a long time, after such dissolutions, to cause others to be elected; whereby the Legislative powers, incapable of Annihilation, have returned to the People at large for their exercise; the State remaining in the mean time exposed to all the dangers of invasion from without, and convulsions within.

He has endeavoured to prevent the population of these States; for that purpose obstructing the Laws for Naturalization of Foreigners; refusing to pass others to encourage their migrations hither, and raising the conditions of new Appropriations of Lands.

He has obstructed the Administration of Justice, by refusing his Assent to Laws for establishing Judiciary powers.

He has made Judges dependent on his Will alone, for the tenure of their offices, and the amount and payment of their salaries.

He has erected a multitude of New Offices, and sent hither swarms of Officers to harrass our people, and eat out their substance.

He has kept among us, in times of peace, Standing Armies without the Consent of our legislatures.

He has affected to render the Military independent of and superior to the Civil power.

He has combined with others to subject us to a jurisdiction foreign to our constitution, and unacknowledged by our laws; giving his Assent to their Acts of pretended Legislation:

For quartering large bodies of armed troops among us:

For protecting them, by a mock Trial, from punishment for any Murders which they should commit on the Inhabitants of these States:

For cutting off our Trade with all parts of the world:

For imposing Taxes on us without our Consent:

For depriving us in many cases, of the benefits of Trial by Jury:

For transporting us beyond Seas to be tried for pretended offences

For abolishing the free System of English Laws in a neighbouring Province, establishing therein an Arbitrary government, and enlarging its Boundaries so as to render it at once an example and fit instrument for introducing the same absolute rule into these Colonies:

For taking away our Charters, abolishing our most valuable Laws, and altering fundamentally the Forms of our Governments:

For suspending our own Legislatures, and declaring themselves invested with power to legislate for us in all cases whatsoever.

He has abdicated Government here, by declaring us out of his Protection and waging War against us.

He has plundered our seas, ravaged our Coasts, burnt our towns, and destroyed the lives of our people.

He is at this time transporting large Armies of foreign Mercenaries to compleat the works of death, desolation and tyranny, already begun with circumstances of Cruelty & perfidy scarcely paralleled in the most barbarous ages, and totally unworthy the Head of a civilized nation.

He has constrained our fellow Citizens taken Captive on the high Seas to bear Arms against their Country, to become the executioners of their friends and Brethren, or to fall themselves by their Hands.

He has excited domestic insurrections amongst us, and has endeavoured to bring on the inhabitants of our frontiers, the merciless Indian Savages, whose known rule of warfare, is an undistinguished destruction of all ages, sexes and conditions.

In every stage of these Oppressions We have Petitioned for Redress in the most humble terms: Our repeated Petitions have been answered only by repeated injury. A Prince whose character is thus marked by every act which may define a Tyrant, is unfit to be the ruler of a free people.

Nor have We been wanting in attentions to our Brittish brethren. We have warned them from time to time of attempts by their legislature to extend an unwarrantable jurisdiction over us. We have reminded them of the circumstances of our emigration and settlement here. We have appealed to their native justice and magnanimity, and we have conjured them by the ties of our common kindred to disavow these usurpations, which, would inevitably interrupt our connections and correspondence. They too have been deaf to the voice of justice and of consanguinity. We must, therefore, acquiesce in the necessity, which denounces our Separation, and hold them, as we hold the rest of mankind, Enemies in War, in Peace Friends.

We, therefore, the Representatives of the united States of America, in General Congress, Assembled, appealing to the Supreme Judge of the world for the rectitude of our intentions, do, in the Name, and by Authority of the good People of these Colonies, solemnly publish and declare, That these United Colonies are, and of Right ought to be Free and Independent States; that they are Absolved from all Allegiance to the British Crown, and that all political connection between them and the State of Great Britain, is and ought to be totally dissolved; and that as Free and Independent States, they have full Power to levy War, conclude Peace, contract Alliances, establish Commerce, and to do all other Acts and Things which Independent States may of right do. And for the support of this Declaration, with a firm reliance on the protection of divine Providence, we mutually pledge to each other our Lives, our Fortunes and our sacred Honor.

Georgia
Button Gwinnett
Lyman Hall
George Walton

North Carolina
William Hooper
Joseph Hewes
John Penn

South Carolina
Edward Rutledge
Thomas Heyward, Jr.
Thomas Lynch, Jr.
Arthur Middleton

Massachusetts
John Hancock

Maryland
Samuel Chase
William Paca
Thomas Stone
Charles Carroll
   of Carrollton

Virginia
George Wythe
Richard Henry Lee
Thomas Jefferson
Benjamin Harrison
Thomas Nelson, Jr.
Francis Lightfoot Lee
Carter Braxton

Pennsylvania
Robert Morris
Benjamin Rush
Benjamin Franklin
John Morton
George Clymer
James Smith
George Taylor
James Wilson
George Ross

Delaware
Caesar Rodney
George Read
Thomas McKean

New York
William Floyd
Philip Livingston
Francis Lewis
Lewis Morris

New Jersey
Richard Stockton
John Witherspoon
Francis Hopkinson
John Hart
Abraham Clark

New Hampshire
Josiah Bartlett
William Whipple

Massachusetts
Samuel Adams
John Adams
Robert Treat Paine
Elbridge Gerry

Rhode Island
Stephen Hopkins
William Ellery

Connecticut
Roger Sherman
Samuel Huntington
William Williams
Oliver Wolcott

New Hampshire
Matthew Thornton

Articles of Confederation (1787)

To ALL TO WHOM these Presents shall come, we the undersigned Delegates of the States affixed to our Names send greeting.

Whereas the Delegates of the United States of America in Congress assembled did on the fifteenth day of November in the Year of our Lord One Thousand Seven Hundred and Seventy-seven, and in the Second Year of the Independence of America agree to certain articles of Confederation and perpetual Union between the States of Newhampshire, Massachusetts-bay, Rhodeisland and Providence Plantations, Connecticut, New York, New Jersey, Pennsylvania, Delaware, Maryland, Virginia, North-Carolina, South-Carolina and Georgia in the Words following, viz.

Articles of Confederation and perpetual Union between the States of Newhampshire, Massachusetts-bay, Rhodeisland and Providence Plantations, Connecticut, New-York, New-Jersey, Pennsylvania, Delaware, Maryland, Virginia, North-Carolina, South-Carolina and Georgia.

ARTICLE I. The stile of this confederacy shall be "The United States of America."

ARTICLE II. Each State retains its sovereignty, freedom and independence, and every power, jurisdiction and right, which is not by this confederation expressly delegated to the United States, in Congress assembled.

ARTICLE III. The said States hereby severally enter into a firm league of friendship with each other, for their common defence, the security of their liberties, and their mutual and general welfare, binding themselves to assist each other, against all force offered to, or attacks made upon them, or any of them, on account of religion, sovereignty, trade or any other pretence whatever.

ARTICLE IV. The better to secure and perpetuate mutual friendship and intercourse among the people of the different States in this Union, the free inhabitants of each of these States, paupers, vagabonds and fugitives from justice excepted, shall be entitled to all privileges and immunities of free citizens in the several States; and the people of each State shall have free ingress and regress to and from any other State, and shall enjoy therein all the privileges of trade and commerce, subject to the same duties, impositions and restrictions as the inhabitants thereof respectively, provided that such restrictions shall not extend so far as to prevent the removal of property imported into any State, to any other State of which the owner is an inhabitant; provided also that no imposition, duties or restriction shall be laid by any State, on the property of the United States, or either of them.

If any person guilty of, or charged with treason, felony, or other high misdemeanor in any State, shall flee from justice, and be found in any of the United States, he shall upon demand of the Governor or Executive power, of the State from which he fled, be delivered up and removed to the State having jurisdiction of his offence.

Full faith and credit shall be given in each of these States to the records, acts and judicial proceedings of the courts and magistrates of every other State.

ARTICLE V. For the more convenient management of the general interests of the United States, delegates shall be annually appointed in such manner as the legislature of each State shall direct, to meet in Congress on the first Monday in November, in every year, with a power reserved to each State, to recall its delegates, or any of them, at any time within the year, and to send others in their stead, for the remainder of the year.

No State shall be represented in Congress by less than two, nor by more than seven members; and no person shall be capable of being a delegate for more than three years in any term of six years; nor shall any person, being a delegate, be capable of holding any office under the United States, for which he, or another for his benefit receives any salary, fees or emolument of any kind.

Each State shall maintain its own delegates in a meeting of the States, and while they act as members of the committee of the States.

In determining questions in the United States, in Congress assembled, each State shall have one vote.

Freedom of speech and debate in Congress shall not be impeached or questioned in any court, or place out of Congress, and the members of Congress shall be protected in their persons from arrests and imprisonments, during the time of their going to and from, and attendance on Congress, except for treason, felony, or breach of the peace.

ARTICLE VI. No State without the consent of the United States in Congress assembled, shall send any embassy to, or receive any embassy from, or enter into any conference, agreement, alliance or treaty with any king, prince or state; nor shall any person holding any office of profit or trust under the United States, or any of them, accept of any present, emolument, office or title of any kind whatever from any king, prince or foreign state; nor shall the United States in Congress assembled, or any of them, grant any title of nobility.

No two or more States shall enter into any treaty, confederation or alliance whatever between them, without the consent of the United States in Congress assembled, specifying accurately the purposes for which the same is to be entered into, and how long it shall continue.

No State shall lay any imposts or duties, which may interfere with any stipulations in treaties, entered into by the United States in Congress assembled, with any king, prince or state, in pursuance of any treaties already proposed by Congress, to the courts of France and Spain.

No vessels of war shall be kept up in time of peace by any State, except such number only, as shall be deemed necessary by the United States in Congress assembled, for the defence of such State, or its trade; nor shall any body of forces be kept up by any State, in time of peace, except such number only, as in the judgment of the United States, in Congress assembled, shall be deemed requisite to garrison the forts necessary for the defence of such State; but every State shall always keep up a well regulated and disciplined militia, sufficiently armed and accoutred, and shall provide and constantly have ready for use, in public stores, a due number of field pieces and tents, and a proper quantity of arms, ammunition and camp equipage.

No State shall engage in any war without the consent of the United States in Congress assembled, unless such State be actually invaded by enemies, or shall have received certain advice of a resolution being formed by some nation of Indians to invade such State, and the danger is so imminent as not to admit of a delay, till the United States in Congress assembled can be consulted: nor shall any State grant commissions to any ships or vessels of war, nor letters of marque or reprisal, except it be after a declaration of war by the United States in Congress assembled, and then only against the kingdom or state and the subjects thereof, against which war has been so declared, and under such regulations as shall be established by the United States in Congress assembled, unless such State be infested by pirates, in which case vessels of war may be fitted out for that occasion, and kept so long as the danger shall continue, or until the United States in Congress assembled shall determine otherwise.

ARTICLE VII. When land-forces are raised by any State of the common defence, all officers of or under the rank of colonel, shall be appointed by the Legislature of each State respectively by whom such forces shall be raised, or in such manner as such State shall direct, and all vacancies shall be filled up by the State which first made the appointment.

ARTICLE VIII. All charges of war, and all other expenses that shall be incurred for the common defence or general welfare, and allowed by the United States in Congress assembled, shall be defrayed out of a common treasury, which shall be supplied by the several States, in proportion to the value of all land within each State, granted to or surveyed for any person, as such land and the buildings and improvements thereon shall be estimated according to such mode as the United States in Congress assembled, shall from time to time direct and appoint.

The taxes for paying that proportion shall be laid and levied by the authority and direction of the Legislatures of the several States within the time agreed upon by the United States in Congress assembled.

ARTICLE IX. The United States in Congress assembled, shall have the sole and exclusive right and power of determining on peace and war, except in the cases mentioned in the sixth article—of sending and receiving ambassadors—entering into treaties and alliances, provided that no treaty of commerce shall be made whereby the legislative power of the respective States shall be restrained from imposing such imposts and duties on foreigners, as their own people are subjected to, or from prohibiting the exportation or importation of and species of goods or commodities whatsoever—of establishing rules for deciding in all cases, what captures on land or water shall be legal, and in what manner prizes taken by land or naval forces in the service of the United States shall be divided or appropriated—of granting letters of marque and reprisal in times of peace—appointing courts for the trial of piracies and felonies committed on the high seas and establishing courts for receiving and determining finally appeals in all cases of captures, provided that no member of Congress shall be appointed a judge of any of the said courts.

The United States in Congress assembled shall also be the last resort on appeal in all disputes and differences now subsisting or that hereafter may arise between two or more States concerning boundary, jurisdiction or any other cause whatever; which authority shall always be exercised in the manner following. Whenever the legislative or executive authority or lawful agent of any State in controversy with another shall present a petition to Congress, stating the matter in question and praying for a hearing, notice thereof shall be given by order of Congress to the legislative or executive authority of the other State in controversy, and a day assigned for the appearance of the parties by their lawful agents, who shall then be directed to appoint by joint consent, commissioners or judges to constitute a court for hearing and determining the matter in question: but if they cannot agree, Congress shall name three persons out of each of the United States, and from the list of such persons each party shall alternately strike out one, the petitioners beginning, until the number shall be reduced to thirteen; and from that number not less than seven, nor more than nine names as Congress shall direct, shall in the presence of Congress be drawn out by lot, and the persons whose names shall be so drawn or any five of them, shall be commissioners or judges, to hear and finally determine the controversy, so always as a major part of the judges who shall hear the cause shall agree in the determination: and if either party shall neglect to attend at the day appointed, without reasons, which Congress shall judge sufficient, or being present shall refuse to strike, the Congress shall proceed to nominate three persons out of each State, and the Secretary of Congress shall strike in behalf of such party absent or refusing; and the judgment and sentence of the court to be appointed, in the manner before prescribed, shall be final and conclusive; and if any of the parties shall refuse to submit to the authority of such court, or to appear or defend their claim or cause, the court shall nevertheless proceed to pronounce sentence, or judgment, which shall in like manner be final and decisive, the judgment or sentence and other proceedings being in either case transmitted to Congress, and lodged among the acts of Congress for the security of the parties concerned: provided that every commissioner, before he sits in judgment, shall take an oath to be administered by one of the judges of the supreme or superior court of the State where the case shall be tried, "well and truly to hear and determine the matter in question, according to the best of his judgment, without favour, affection or hope of reward:" provided also that no State shall be deprived of territory for the benefit of the United States.

All controversies concerning the private right of soil claimed under different grants of two or more States, whose jurisdiction as they may respect such lands, and the states which passed such grants are adjusted, the said grants or either of them being at the same time claimed to have originated antecedent to such settlement of jurisdiction, shall on the petition of either party to the Congress of the United States, be finally determined as near as may be in the same manner as is before prescribed for deciding disputes respecting territorial jurisdiction between different States.

The United States in Congress assembled shall also have the sole and exclusive right and power of regulating the alloy and value of coin struck by their own authority, or by that of the respective States—fixing the standard of weights and measures throughout the United States—regulating the trade and managing all affairs with the Indians, not members of any of the States, provided that the legislative right of any State within its own limits be not infringed or violated—establishing and regulating post-offices from one State to another, throughout all of the United States, and exacting such postage on the papers passing thro' the same as may be requisite to defray the expenses of the said office—appointing all officers of the land forces, in the service of the United States, excepting regimental officers—appointing all the officers of the naval forces, and commissioning all officers whatever in the service of the United States—making rules for the government and regulation of the said land and naval forces, and directing their operations.

The United States in Congress assembled shall have authority to appoint a committee, to sit in the recess of Congress, to be denominated "a Committee of the States," and to consist of one delegate from each State; and to appoint such other committees and civil officers as may be necessary for managing the general affairs of the United States under their direction—to appoint one of their number to preside, provided that no person be allowed to serve in the office of president more than one year in any term of three years; to ascertain the necessary sums of money to be raised for the service of the United States, and to appropriate and apply the same for defraying the public expenses—to borrow money, or emit bills on the credit of the United States, transmitting every half year to the respective States an account of the sums of money so borrowed or emitted,—to build and equip a navy—to agree upon the number of land forces, and to make requisitions from each State for its quota, in proportion to the number of white inhabitants in such State; which requisition shall be binding, and thereupon the Legislature of each State shall appoint the regimental officers, raise the men and cloath, arm and equip them in a soldier like manner, at the expense of the United States; and the officers and men so cloathed, armed and equipped shall march to the place appointed, and within the time agreed on by the United States in Congress assembled: but if the United States in Congress assembled shall, on consideration of circumstances judge proper that any State should not raise men, or should raise a smaller number of men than the quota thereof, such extra number shall be raised, officered, cloathed, armed and equipped in the same manner as the quota of such State, unless the legislature of such State shall judge that such extra number cannot be safely spared out of the same, in which case they shall raise officer, cloath, arm and equip as many of such extra number as they judge can be safely spared. And the officers and men so cloathed, armed and equipped, shall march to the place appointed, and within the time agreed on by the United States in Congress assembled.

The United States in Congress assembled shall never engage in a war, nor grant letters of marque and reprisal in time of peace, nor enter into any treaties or alliances, nor coin money, nor regulate the value thereof, nor ascertain the sums and expenses necessary for the defence and welfare of the United States, or any of them, nor emit bills, nor borrow money on the credit of the United States, nor appropriate money, nor agree upon the number of vessels to be built or purchased, or the number of land or sea forces to be raised, nor appoint a commander in chief of the army or navy, unless nine States assent to the same: nor shall a question on any other point, except for adjourning from day to day be determined, unless by the votes of a majority of the United States in Congress assembled.

The Congress of the United States shall have power to adjourn to any time within the year, and to any place within the United States, so that no period of adjournment be for a longer duration than the space of six months, and shall publish the journal of their proceedings monthly, except such parts thereof relating to treaties, alliances or military operations, as in their judgment require secresy; and the yeas and nays of the delegates of each State on any question shall be entered on the Journal, when it is desired by any delegate; and the delegates of a State, or any of them, at his or their request shall be furnished with a transcript of the said journal, except such parts as are above excepted, to lay before the Legislatures of the several States.

ARTICLE X. The committee of the States, or any nine of them, shall be authorized to execute, in the recess of Congress, such of the powers of Congress as the United States in Congress assembled, by the consent of nine States, shall from time to time think expedient to vest them with; provided that no power be delegated to the said committee, for the exercise of which, by the articles of confederation, the voice of nine States in the Congress of the United States assembled is requisite.

ARTICLE XI. Canada acceding to this confederation, and joining in the measures of the United States, shall be admitted into, and entitled to all the advantages of this Union: but no other colony shall be admitted into the same, unless such admission be agreed to by nine States.

ARTICLE XII. All bills of credit emitted, monies borrowed and debts contracted by, or under the authority of Congress, before the assembling of the United States, in pursuance of the present confederation, shall be deemed and considered as a charge against the United States, for payment and satisfaction whereof the said United States, and the public faith are hereby solemnly pledged.

ARTICLE XIII. Every State shall abide by the determinations of the United States in Congress assembled, on all questions which by this confederation are submitted to them. And the articles of this confederation shall be inviolably observed by every State, and the Union shall be perpetual; nor shall any alteration at any time hereafter be made in any of them; unless such alteration be agreed to in a Congress of the United States, and be afterwards confirmed by the Legislatures of every State.

And whereas it has pleased the Great Governor of the world to incline the hearts of the Legislatures we respectively represent in Congress, to approve of, and to authorize us to ratify the said articles of confederation and perpetual union. Know ye that we the undersigned delegates, by virtue of the power and authority to us given for that purpose, do by these presents, in the name and in behalf of our respective constituents, fully and entirely ratify and confirm each and every of the said articles of confederation and perpetual union, and all and singular the matters and things therein contained: and we do further solemnly plight and engage the faith of our respective constituents, that they shall abide by the determinations of the United States in Congress assembled, on all questions, which by the said confederation are submitted to them. And that the articles thereof shall be inviolably observed by the States we respectively represent, and that the Union shall be perpetual.

In witness thereof we have hereunto set our hands in Congress. Done at Philadelphia in the State of Pennsylvania the ninth day of July in the year of our Lord one thousand seven hundred and seventy-eight, and in the third year of the independence of America.

The Constitution of the United States (1787)

We the People of the United States, in Order to form a more perfect Union, establish Justice, insure domestic Tranquility, provide for the common defence, promote the general Welfare, and secure the Blessings of Liberty to ourselves and our Posterity, do ordain and establish this Constitution for the United States of America.

Article. I.

Section. 1. All legislative Powers herein granted shall be vested in a Congress of the United States, which shall consist of a Senate and House of Representatives.

Section. 2. The House of Representatives shall be composed of Members chosen every second Year by the People of the several States, and the Electors in each State shall have the Qualifications requisite for Electors of the most numerous Branch of the State Legislature.

No Person shall be a Representative who shall not have attained to the Age of twenty five Years, and been seven Years a Citizen of the United States, and who shall not, when elected, be an Inhabitant of that State in which he shall be chosen.

Representatives and direct Taxes shall be apportioned among the several States which may be included within this Union, according to their respective Numbers, which shall be determined by adding to the whole Number of free Persons, including those bound to Service for a Term of Years, and excluding Indians not taxed, three fifths of all other Persons. The actual Enumeration shall be made within three Years after the first Meeting of the Congress of the United States, and within every subsequent Term of ten Years, in such Manner as they shall by Law direct. The Number of Representatives shall not exceed one for every thirty Thousand, but each State shall have at Least one Representative; and until such enumeration shall be made, the State of New Hampshire shall be entitled to chuse three, Massachusetts eight, Rhode-Island and Providence Plantations one, Connecticut five, New-York six, New Jersey four, Pennsylvania eight, Delaware one, Maryland six, Virginia ten, North Carolina five, South Carolina five, and Georgia three.

When vacancies happen in the Representation from any State, the Executive Authority thereof shall issue Writs of Election to fill such Vacancies.

The House of Representatives shall chuse their Speaker and other Officers; and shall have the sole Power of Impeachment.

Section. 3. The Senate of the United States shall be composed of two Senators from each State, chosen by the Legislature thereof for six Years; and each Senator shall have one Vote.

Immediately after they shall be assembled in Consequence of the first Election, they shall be divided as equally as may be into three Classes. The Seats of the Senators of the first Class shall be vacated at the Expiration of the second Year, of the second Class at the Expiration of the fourth Year, and of the third Class at the Expiration of the sixth Year, so that one third may be chosen every second Year; and if Vacancies happen by Resignation, or otherwise, during the Recess of the Legislature of any State, the Executive thereof may make temporary Appointments until the next Meeting of the Legislature, which shall then fill such Vacancies.

No Person shall be a Senator who shall not have attained to the Age of thirty Years, and been nine Years a Citizen of the United States, and who shall not, when elected, be an Inhabitant of that State for which he shall be chosen.

The Vice President of the United States shall be President of the Senate, but shall have no Vote, unless they be equally divided.

The Senate shall chuse their other Officers, and also a President pro tempore, in the Absence of the Vice President, or when he shall exercise the Office of President of the United States.

The Senate shall have the sole Power to try all Impeachments. When sitting for that Purpose, they shall be on Oath or Affirmation. When the President of the United States is tried, the Chief Justice shall preside: And no Person shall be convicted without the Concurrence of two thirds of the Members present.

Judgment in Cases of Impeachment shall not extend further than to removal from Office, and disqualification to hold and enjoy any Office of honor, Trust or Profit under the United States: but the Party convicted shall nevertheless be liable and subject to Indictment, Trial, Judgment and Punishment, according to Law.

Section. 4. The Times, Places and Manner of holding Elections for Senators and Representatives, shall be prescribed in each State by the Legislature thereof; but the Congress may at any time by Law make or alter such Regulations, except as to the Places of chusing Senators.

The Congress shall assemble at least once in every Year, and such Meeting shall be on the first Monday in December, unless they shall by Law appoint a different Day.

Section. 5. Each House shall be the Judge of the Elections, Returns and Qualifications of its own Members, and a Majority of each shall constitute a Quorum to do Business; but a smaller Number may adjourn from day to day, and may be authorized to compel the Attendance of absent Members, in such Manner, and under such Penalties as each House may provide.

Each House may determine the Rules of its Proceedings, punish its Members for disorderly Behaviour, and, with the Concurrence of two thirds, expel a Member.

Each House shall keep a Journal of its Proceedings, and from time to time publish the same, excepting such Parts as may in their Judgment require Secrecy; and the Yeas and Nays of the Members of either House on any question shall, at the Desire of one fifth of those Present, be entered on the Journal.

Neither House, during the Session of Congress, shall, without the Consent of the other, adjourn for more than three days, nor to any other Place than that in which the two Houses shall be sitting.

Section. 6. The Senators and Representatives shall receive a Compensation for their Services, to be ascertained by Law, and paid out of the Treasury of the United States. They shall in all Cases, except Treason, Felony and Breach of the Peace, be privileged from Arrest during their Attendance at the Session of their respective Houses, and in going to and returning from the same; and for any Speech or Debate in either House, they shall not be questioned in any other Place.

No Senator or Representative shall, during the Time for which he was elected, be appointed to any civil Office under the Authority of the United States, which shall have been created, or the Emoluments whereof shall have been encreased during such time; and no Person holding any Office under the United States, shall be a Member of either House during his Continuance in Office.

Section. 7. All Bills for raising Revenue shall originate in the House of Representatives; but the Senate may propose or concur with Amendments as on other Bills.

Every Bill which shall have passed the House of Representatives and the Senate shall, before it become a Law, be presented to the President of the United States; If he approve he shall sign it, but if not he shall return it, with his Objections to that House in which it shall have originated, who shall enter the Objections at large on their Journal, and proceed to reconsider it. If after such Reconsideration two thirds of that House shall agree to pass the Bill, it shall be sent, together with the Objections, to the other House, by which it shall likewise be reconsidered, and if approved by two thirds of that House, it shall become a Law. But in all such Cases the Votes of both Houses shall be determined by yeas and Nays, and the Names of the Persons voting for and against the Bill shall be entered on the Journal of each House respectively. If any Bill shall not be returned by the President within ten Days (Sundays excepted) after it shall have been presented to him, the Same shall be a Law, in like Manner as if he had signed it, unless the Congress by their Adjournment prevent its Return, in which Case it shall not be a Law.

Every Order, Resolution, or Vote to which the Concurrence of the Senate and House of Representatives may be necessary (except on a question of Adjournment) shall be presented to the President of the United States; and before the Same shall take Effect, shall be approved by him, or being disapproved by him, shall be repassed by two thirds of the Senate and House of Representatives, according to the Rules and Limitations prescribed in the Case of a Bill.

Section. 8. The Congress shall have Power To lay and collect Taxes, Duties, Imposts and Excises, to pay the Debts and provide for the common Defence and general Welfare of the United States; but all Duties, Imposts and Excises shall be uniform throughout the United States;

To borrow Money on the credit of the United States;

To regulate Commerce with foreign Nations, and among the several States, and with the Indian Tribes;

To establish an uniform Rule of Naturalization, and uniform Laws on the subject of Bankruptcies throughout the United States;

To coin Money, regulate the Value thereof, and of foreign Coin, and fix the Standard of Weights and Measures;

To provide for the Punishment of counterfeiting the Securities and current Coin of the United States;

To establish Post Offices and post Roads;

To promote the Progress of Science and useful Arts, by securing for limited Times to Authors and Inventors the exclusive Right to their respective Writings and Discoveries;

To constitute Tribunals inferior to the supreme Court;

To define and punish Piracies and Felonies committed on the high Seas, and Offences against the Law of Nations;

To declare War, grant Letters of Marque and Reprisal, and make Rules concerning Captures on Land and Water;

To raise and support Armies, but no Appropriation of Money to that Use shall be for a longer Term than two Years;

To provide and maintain a Navy;

To make Rules for the Government and Regulation of the land and naval Forces;

To provide for calling forth the Militia to execute the Laws of the Union, suppress Insurrections and repel Invasions;

To provide for organizing, arming, and disciplining, the Militia, and for governing such Part of them as may be employed in the Service of the United States, reserving to the States respectively, the Appointment of the Officers, and the Authority of training the Militia according to the discipline prescribed by Congress;

To exercise exclusive Legislation in all Cases whatsoever, over such District (not exceeding ten Miles square) as may, by Cession of particular States, and the Acceptance of Congress, become the Seat of the Government of the United States, and to exercise like Authority over all Places purchased by the Consent of the Legislature of the State in which the Same shall be, for the Erection of Forts, Magazines, Arsenals, dock-Yards, and other needful Buildings;—And

To make all Laws which shall be necessary and proper for carrying into Execution the foregoing Powers, and all other Powers vested by this Constitution in the Government of the United States, or in any Department or Officer thereof.

Section. 9. The Migration or Importation of such Persons as any of the States now existing shall think proper to admit, shall not be prohibited by the Congress prior to the Year one thousand eight hundred and eight, but a Tax or duty may be imposed on such Importation, not exceeding ten dollars for each Person.

The Privilege of the Writ of Habeas Corpus shall not be suspended, unless when in Cases of Rebellion or Invasion the public Safety may require it.

No Bill of Attainder or ex post facto Law shall be passed.

No Capitation, or other direct, Tax shall be laid, unless in Proportion to the Census or enumeration herein before directed to be taken.

No Tax or Duty shall be laid on Articles exported from any State.

No Preference shall be given by any Regulation of Commerce or Revenue to the Ports of one State over those of another; nor shall Vessels bound to, or from, one State, be obliged to enter, clear, or pay Duties in another.

No Money shall be drawn from the Treasury, but in Consequence of Appropriations made by Law; and a regular Statement and Account of the Receipts and Expenditures of all public Money shall be published from time to time.

No Title of Nobility shall be granted by the United States: And no Person holding any Office of Profit or Trust under them, shall, without the Consent of the Congress, accept of any present, Emolument, Office, or Title, of any kind whatever, from any King, Prince, or foreign State.

Section. 10. No State shall enter into any Treaty, Alliance, or Confederation; grant Letters of Marque and Reprisal; coin Money; emit Bills of Credit; make any Thing but gold and silver Coin a Tender in Payment of Debts; pass any Bill of Attainder, ex post facto Law, or Law impairing the Obligation of Contracts, or grant any Title of Nobility.

No State shall, without the Consent of the Congress, lay any Imposts or Duties on Imports or Exports, except what may be absolutely necessary for executing it's inspection Laws: and the net Produce of all Duties and Imposts, laid by any State on Imports or Exports, shall be for the Use of the Treasury of the United States; and all such Laws shall be subject to the Revision and Controul of the Congress.

No State shall, without the Consent of Congress, lay any Duty of Tonnage, keep Troops, or Ships of War in time of Peace, enter into any Agreement or Compact with another State, or with a foreign Power, or engage in War, unless actually invaded, or in such imminent Danger as will not admit of delay.

Article. II.

Section. 1. The executive Power shall be vested in a President of the United States of America. He shall hold his Office during the Term of four Years, and, together with the Vice President, chosen for the same Term, be elected, as follows:

Each State shall appoint, in such Manner as the Legislature thereof may direct, a Number of Electors, equal to the whole Number of Senators and Representatives to which the State may be entitled in the Congress: but no Senator or Representative, or Person holding an Office of Trust or Profit under the United States, shall be appointed an Elector.

The Electors shall meet in their respective States, and vote by Ballot for two Persons, of whom one at least shall not be an Inhabitant of the same State with themselves. And they shall make a List of all the Persons voted for, and of the Number of Votes for each; which List they shall sign and certify, and transmit sealed to the Seat of the Government of the United States, directed to the President of the Senate. The President of the Senate shall, in the Presence of the Senate and House of Representatives, open all the Certificates, and the Votes shall then be counted. The Person having the greatest Number of Votes shall be the President, if such Number be a Majority of the whole Number of Electors appointed; and if there be more than one who have such Majority, and have an equal Number of Votes, then the House of Representatives shall immediately chuse by Ballot one of them for President; and if no Person have a Majority, then from the five highest on the List the said House shall in like Manner chuse the President. But in chusing the President, the Votes shall be taken by States, the Representation from each State having one Vote; A quorum for this purpose shall consist of a Member or Members from two thirds of the States, and a Majority of all the States shall be necessary to a Choice. In every Case, after the Choice of the President, the Person having the greatest Number of Votes of the Electors shall be the Vice President. But if there should remain two or more who have equal Votes, the Senate shall chuse from them by Ballot the Vice President.

The Congress may determine the Time of chusing the Electors, and the Day on which they shall give their Votes; which Day shall be the same throughout the United States.

No Person except a natural born Citizen, or a Citizen of the United States, at the time of the Adoption of this Constitution, shall be eligible to the Office of President; neither shall any Person be eligible to that Office who shall not have attained to the Age of thirty five Years, and been fourteen Years a Resident within the United States.

In Case of the Removal of the President from Office, or of his Death, Resignation, or Inability to discharge the Powers and Duties of the said Office, the Same shall devolve on the Vice President, and the Congress may by Law provide for the Case of Removal, Death, Resignation or Inability, both of the President and Vice President, declaring what Officer shall then act as President, and such Officer shall act accordingly, until the Disability be removed, or a President shall be elected.

The President shall, at stated Times, receive for his Services, a Compensation, which shall neither be increased nor diminished during the Period for which he shall have been elected, and he shall not receive within that Period any other Emolument from the United States, or any of them.

Before he enter on the Execution of his Office, he shall take the following Oath or Affirmation:—"I do solemnly swear (or affirm) that I will faithfully execute the Office of President of the United States, and will to the best of my Ability, preserve, protect and defend the Constitution of the United States."

Section. 2. The President shall be Commander in Chief of the Army and Navy of the United States, and of the Militia of the several States, when called into the actual Service of the United States; he may require the Opinion, in writing, of the principal Officer in each of the executive Departments, upon any Subject relating to the Duties of their respective Offices, and he shall have Power to grant Reprieves and Pardons for Offences against the United States, except in Cases of Impeachment.

He shall have Power, by and with the Advice and Consent of the Senate, to make Treaties, provided two thirds of the Senators present concur; and he shall nominate, and by and with the Advice and Consent of the Senate, shall appoint Ambassadors, other public Ministers and Consuls, Judges of the supreme Court, and all other Officers of the United States, whose Appointments are not herein otherwise provided for, and which shall be established by Law: but the Congress may by Law vest the Appointment of such inferior Officers, as they think proper, in the President alone, in the Courts of Law, or in the Heads of Departments.

The President shall have Power to fill up all Vacancies that may happen during the Recess of the Senate, by granting Commissions which shall expire at the End of their next Session.

Section. 3. He shall from time to time give to the Congress Information of the State of the Union, and recommend to their Consideration such Measures as he shall judge necessary and expedient; he may, on extraordinary Occasions, convene both Houses, or either of them, and in Case of Disagreement between them, with Respect to the Time of Adjournment, he may adjourn them to such Time as he shall think proper; he shall receive Ambassadors and other public Ministers; he shall take Care that the Laws be faithfully executed, and shall Commission all the Officers of the United States.

Section. 4. The President, Vice President and all civil Officers of the United States, shall be removed from Office on Impeachment for, and Conviction of, Treason, Bribery, or other high Crimes and Misdemeanors.

Article III.

Section. 1. The judicial Power of the United States shall be vested in one supreme Court, and in such inferior Courts as the Congress may from time to time ordain and establish. The Judges, both of the supreme and inferior Courts, shall hold their Offices during good Behaviour, and shall, at stated Times, receive for their Services a Compensation, which shall not be diminished during their Continuance in Office.

Section. 2. The judicial Power shall extend to all Cases, in Law and Equity, arising under this Constitution, the Laws of the United States, and Treaties made, or which shall be made, under their Authority;—to all Cases affecting Ambassadors, other public Ministers and Consuls;—to all Cases of admiralty and maritime Jurisdiction;—to Controversies to which the United States shall be a Party;—to Controversies between two or more States;— between a State and Citizens of another State,—between Citizens of different States,—between Citizens of the same State claiming Lands under Grants of different States, and between a State, or the Citizens thereof, and foreign States, Citizens or Subjects.

In all Cases affecting Ambassadors, other public Ministers and Consuls, and those in which a State shall be Party, the supreme Court shall have original Jurisdiction. In all the other Cases before mentioned, the supreme Court shall have appellate Jurisdiction, both as to Law and Fact, with such Exceptions, and under such Regulations as the Congress shall make.

The Trial of all Crimes, except in Cases of Impeachment, shall be by Jury; and such Trial shall be held in the State where the said Crimes shall have been committed; but when not committed within any State, the Trial shall be at such Place or Places as the Congress may by Law have directed.

Section. 3. Treason against the United States, shall consist only in levying War against them, or in adhering to their Enemies, giving them Aid and Comfort. No Person shall be convicted of Treason unless on the Testimony of two Witnesses to the same overt Act, or on Confession in open Court.

The Congress shall have Power to declare the Punishment of Treason, but no Attainder of Treason shall work Corruption of Blood, or Forfeiture except during the Life of the Person attainted.

Article. IV.

Section. 1. Full Faith and Credit shall be given in each State to the public Acts, Records, and judicial Proceedings of every other State. And the Congress may by general Laws prescribe the Manner in which such Acts, Records and Proceedings shall be proved, and the Effect thereof.

Section. 2. The Citizens of each State shall be entitled to all Privileges and Immunities of Citizens in the several States.

A Person charged in any State with Treason, Felony, or other Crime, who shall flee from Justice, and be found in another State, shall on Demand of the executive Authority of the State from which he fled, be delivered up, to be removed to the State having Jurisdiction of the Crime.

No Person held to Service or Labour in one State, under the Laws thereof, escaping into another, shall, in Consequence of any Law or Regulation therein, be discharged from such Service or Labour, but shall be delivered up on Claim of the Party to whom such Service or Labour may be due.

Section. 3. New States may be admitted by the Congress into this Union; but no new State shall be formed or erected within the Jurisdiction of any other State; nor any State be formed by the Junction of two or more States, or Parts of States, without the Consent of the Legislatures of the States concerned as well as of the Congress.

The Congress shall have Power to dispose of and make all needful Rules and Regulations respecting the Territory or other Property belonging to the United States; and nothing in this Constitution shall be so construed as to Prejudice any Claims of the United States, or of any particular States.

Section. 4. The United States shall guarantee to every State in this Union a Republican Form of Government, and shall protect each of them against Invasion; and on Application of the Legislature, or of the Executive (when the Legislature cannot be convened), against domestic Violence.

Article. V.

The Congress, whenever two thirds of both Houses shall deem it necessary, shall propose Amendments to this Constitution, or, on the Application of the Legislatures of two thirds of the several States, shall call a Convention for proposing Amendments, which, in either Case, shall be valid to all Intents and Purposes, as Part of this Constitution, when ratified by the Legislatures of three fourths of the several States, or by Conventions in three fourths thereof, as the one or the other Mode of Ratification may be proposed by the Congress; Provided that no Amendment which may be made prior to the Year One thousand eight hundred and eight shall in any Manner affect the first and fourth Clauses in the Ninth Section of the first Article; and that no State, without its Consent, shall be deprived of its equal Suffrage in the Senate.

Article. VI.

All Debts contracted and Engagements entered into, before the Adoption of this Constitution, shall be as valid against the United States under this Constitution, as under the Confederation.

This Constitution, and the Laws of the United States which shall be made in Pursuance thereof; and all Treaties made, or which shall be made, under the Authority of the United States, shall be the supreme Law of the Land; and the Judges in every State shall be bound thereby, any Thing in the Constitution or Laws of any State to the Contrary notwithstanding.

The Senators and Representatives before mentioned, and the Members of the several State Legislatures, and all executive and judicial Officers, both of the United States and of the several States, shall be bound by Oath or Affirmation, to support this Constitution; but no religious Test shall ever be required as a Qualification to any Office or public Trust under the United States.

Article. VII.

The Ratification of the Conventions of nine States, shall be sufficient for the Establishment of this Constitution between the States so ratifying the Same.

The Word, "the," being interlined between the seventh and eighth Lines of the first Page, the Word "Thirty" being partly written on an Erazure in the fifteenth Line of the first Page, The Words "is tried" being interlined between the thirty second and thirty third Lines of the first Page and the Word "the" being interlined between the forty third and forty fourth Lines of the second Page.

Attest William Jackson Secretary

Done in Convention by the Unanimous Consent of the States present the Seventeenth Day of September in the Year of our Lord one thousand seven hundred and Eighty seven and of the Independance of the United States of America the Twelfth In witness whereof We have hereunto subscribed our Names,

G°. Washington
Presidt and deputy from Virginia

Delaware {
Geo: Read
Gunning Bedford jun
John Dickinson
Richard Bassett
Jaco: Broom
}

Maryland {
James McHenry
Dan of St Thos. Jenifer
Danl. Carrol
}

Virginia {
John Blair
James Madison Jr.
}

North Carolina {
Wm. Blount
Richd. Dobbs Spaight
Hu Williamson
}

South Carolina {
J. Rutledge
Charles Cotesworth Pinckney
Charles Pinckney
Pierce Butler
}

Georgia {
William Few
Abr Baldwin
}

New Hampshire {
John Langdon
Nicholas Gilman
}

Massachusetts {
Nathaniel Gorham
Rufus King
}

Connecticut {
Wm. Saml. Johnson
Roger Sherman
}

New York {
Alexander Hamilton
}

New Jersey {
Wil: Livingston
David Brearley
Wm. Paterson
Jona: Dayton
}

Pennsylvania {
B Franklin
Thomas Mifflin
Robt. Morris
Geo. Clymer
Thos. FitzSimons
Jared Ingersoll
James Wilson
Gouv Morris
}

Amendments to the Constitution

The Bill of Rights: A Transcription

The Preamble to The Bill of Rights

Congress of the United States
begun and held at the City of New-York, on
Wednesday the fourth of March, one thousand seven hundred and eighty nine.

THE Conventions of a number of the States, having at the time of their adopting the Constitution, expressed a desire, in order to prevent misconstruction or abuse of its powers, that further declaratory and restrictive clauses should be added: And as extending the ground of public confidence in the Government, will best ensure the beneficent ends of its institution.

RESOLVED by the Senate and House of Representatives of the United States of America, in Congress assembled, two thirds of both Houses concurring, that the following Articles be proposed to the Legislatures of the several States, as amendments to the Constitution of the United States, all, or any of which Articles, when ratified by three fourths of the said Legislatures, to be valid to all intents and purposes, as part of the said Constitution; viz.

ARTICLES in addition to, and Amendment of the Constitution of the United States of America, proposed by Congress, and ratified by the Legislatures of the several States, pursuant to the fifth Article of the original Constitution.

Note: The first ten amendments to the Constitution were ratified December 15, 1791, and form what is known as the "Bill of Rights."

Amendment I

Congress shall make no law respecting an establishment of religion, or prohibiting the free exercise thereof; or abridging the freedom of speech, or of the press; or the right of the people peaceably to assemble, and to petition the Government for a redress of grievances.

Amendment II

A well regulated Militia, being necessary to the security of a free State, the right of the people to keep and bear Arms, shall not be infringed.

Amendment III

No Soldier shall, in time of peace be quartered in any house, without the consent of the Owner, nor in time of war, but in a manner to be prescribed by law.

Amendment IV

The right of the people to be secure in their persons, houses, papers, and effects, against unreasonable searches and seizures, shall not be violated, and no Warrants shall issue, but upon probable cause, supported by Oath or affirmation, and particularly describing the place to be searched, and the persons or things to be seized.

Amendment V

No person shall be held to answer for a capital, or otherwise infamous crime, unless on a presentment or indictment of a Grand Jury, except in cases arising in the land or naval forces, or in the Militia, when in actual service in time of War or public danger; nor shall any person be subject for the same offence to be twice put in jeopardy of life or limb; nor shall be compelled in any criminal case to be a witness against himself, nor be deprived of life, liberty, or property, without due process of law; nor shall private property be taken for public use, without just compensation.

Amendment VI

In all criminal prosecutions, the accused shall enjoy the right to a speedy and public trial, by an impartial jury of the State and district wherein the crime shall have been committed, which district shall have been previously ascertained by law, and to be informed of the nature and cause of the accusation; to be confronted with the witnesses against him; to have compulsory process for obtaining witnesses in his favor, and to have the Assistance of Counsel for his defence.

Amendment VII

In Suits at common law, where the value in controversy shall exceed twenty dollars, the right of trial by jury shall be preserved, and no fact tried by a jury, shall be otherwise re-examined in any Court of the United States, than according to the rules of the common law.

Amendment VIII

Excessive bail shall not be required, nor excessive fines imposed, nor cruel and unusual punishments inflicted.

Amendment IX

The enumeration in the Constitution, of certain rights, shall not be construed to deny or disparage others retained by the people.

Amendment X

The powers not delegated to the United States by the Constitution, nor prohibited by it to the States, are reserved to the States respectively, or to the people.

Amendment XI

Passed by Congress March 4, 1794. Ratified February 7, 1795.

Note: Article III, section 2, of the Constitution was modified by amendment 11.

The Judicial power of the United States shall not be construed to extend to any suit in law or equity, commenced or prosecuted against one of the United States by Citizens of another State, or by Citizens or Subjects of any Foreign State.

Amendment XII

Passed by Congress December 9, 1803. Ratified June 15, 1804.

Note: A portion of Article II, section 1 of the Constitution was superseded by the 12th amendment.

The Electors shall meet in their respective states and vote by ballot for President and Vice-President, one of whom, at least, shall not be an inhabitant of the same state with themselves; they shall name in their ballots the person voted for as President, and in distinct ballots the person voted for as Vice-President, and they shall make distinct lists of all persons voted for as President, and of all persons voted for as Vice-President, and of the number of votes for each, which lists they shall sign and certify, and transmit sealed to the seat of the government of the United States, directed to the President of the Senate; — the President of the Senate shall, in the presence of the Senate and House of Representatives, open all the certificates and the votes shall then be counted; — The person having the greatest number of votes for President, shall be the President, if such number be a majority of the whole number of Electors appointed; and if no person have such majority, then from the persons having the highest numbers not exceeding three on the list of those voted for as President, the House of Representatives shall choose immediately, by ballot, the President. But in choosing the President, the votes shall be taken by states, the representation from each state having one vote; a quorum for this purpose shall consist of a member or members from two-thirds of the states, and a majority of all the states shall be necessary to a choice. [And if the House of Representatives shall not choose a President whenever the right of choice shall devolve upon them, before the fourth day of March next following, then the Vice-President shall act as President, as in case of the death or other constitutional disability of the President. —]* The person having the greatest number of votes as Vice-President, shall be the Vice-President, if such number be a majority of the whole number of Electors appointed, and if no person have a majority, then from the two highest numbers on the list, the Senate shall choose the Vice-President; a quorum for the purpose shall consist of two-thirds of the whole number of Senators, and a majority of the whole number shall be necessary to a choice. But no person constitutionally ineligible to the office of President shall be eligible to that of Vice-President of the United States.

Superseded by section 3 of the 20th amendment.

Amendment XIII

Passed by Congress January 31, 1865. Ratified December 6, 1865.

Note: A portion of Article IV, section 2, of the Constitution was superseded by the 13th amendment.

Section 1.
Neither slavery nor involuntary servitude, except as a punishment for crime whereof the party shall have been duly convicted, shall exist within the United States, or any place subject to their jurisdiction.

Section 2.
Congress shall have power to enforce this article by appropriate legislation.

Amendment XIV

Passed by Congress June 13, 1866. Ratified July 9, 1868.

Note: Article I, section 2, of the Constitution was modified by section 2 of the 14th amendment.

Section 1.
All persons born or naturalized in the United States, and subject to the jurisdiction thereof, are citizens of the United States and of the State wherein they reside. No State shall make or enforce any law which shall abridge the privileges or immunities of citizens of the United States; nor shall any State deprive any person of life, liberty, or property, without due process of law; nor deny to any person within its jurisdiction the equal protection of the laws.

Section 2.
Representatives shall be apportioned among the several States according to their respective numbers, counting the whole number of persons in each State, excluding Indians not taxed. But when the right to vote at any election for the choice of electors for President and Vice-President of the United States, Representatives in Congress, the Executive and Judicial officers of a State, or the members of the Legislature thereof, is denied to any of the male inhabitants of such State, being twenty-one years of age,* and citizens of the United States, or in any way abridged, except for participation in rebellion, or other crime, the basis of representation therein shall be reduced in the proportion which the number of such male citizens shall bear to the whole number of male citizens twenty-one years of age in such State.

Section 3.
No person shall be a Senator or Representative in Congress, or elector of President and Vice-President, or hold any office, civil or military, under the United States, or under any State, who, having previously taken an oath, as a member of Congress, or as an officer of the United States, or as a member of any State legislature, or as an executive or judicial officer of any State, to support the Constitution of the United States, shall have engaged in insurrection or rebellion against the same, or given aid or comfort to the enemies thereof. But Congress may by a vote of two-thirds of each House, remove such disability.

Section 4.

The validity of the public debt of the United States, authorized by law, including debts incurred for payment of pensions and bounties for services in suppressing insurrection or rebellion, shall not be questioned. But neither the United States nor any State shall assume or pay any debt or obligation incurred in aid of insurrection or rebellion against the United States, or any claim for the loss or emancipation of any slave; but all such debts, obligations and claims shall be held illegal and void.

Section 5.

The Congress shall have the power to enforce, by appropriate legislation, the provisions of this article.

Changed by section 1 of the 26th amendment.

Amendment XV

Passed by Congress February 26, 1869. Ratified February 3, 1870.

Section 1.

The right of citizens of the United States to vote shall not be denied or abridged by the United States or by any State on account of race, color, or previous condition of servitude—

Section 2.

The Congress shall have the power to enforce this article by appropriate legislation.

Amendment XVI

Passed by Congress July 2, 1909. Ratified February 3, 1913.

Note: Article I, section 9, of the Constitution was modified by amendment 16.

The Congress shall have power to lay and collect taxes on incomes, from whatever source derived, without apportionment among the several States, and without regard to any census or enumeration.

Amendment XVII

Passed by Congress May 13, 1912. Ratified April 8, 1913.

Note: Article I, section 3, of the Constitution was modified by the 17th amendment.

The Senate of the United States shall be composed of two Senators from each State, elected by the people thereof, for six years; and each Senator shall have one vote. The electors in each State shall have the qualifications requisite for electors of the most numerous branch of the State legislatures.

When vacancies happen in the representation of any State in the Senate, the executive authority of such State shall issue writs of election to fill such vacancies: *Provided,* That the legislature of any State may empower the executive thereof to

make temporary appointments until the people fill the vacancies by election as the legislature may direct.

This amendment shall not be so construed as to affect the election or term of any Senator chosen before it becomes valid as part of the Constitution.

Amendment XVIII

Passed by Congress December 18, 1917. Ratified January 16, 1919. Repealed by amendment 21.

Section 1.
After one year from the ratification of this article the manufacture, sale, or transportation of intoxicating liquors within, the importation thereof into, or the exportation thereof from the United States and all territory subject to the jurisdiction thereof for beverage purposes is hereby prohibited.

Section 2.
The Congress and the several States shall have concurrent power to enforce this article by appropriate legislation.

Section 3.
This article shall be inoperative unless it shall have been ratified as an amendment to the Constitution by the legislatures of the several States, as provided in the Constitution, within seven years from the date of the submission hereof to the States by the Congress.

Amendment XIX

Passed by Congress June 4, 1919. Ratified August 18, 1920.

The right of citizens of the United States to vote shall not be denied or abridged by the United States or by any State on account of sex.

Congress shall have power to enforce this article by appropriate legislation.

Amendment XX

Passed by Congress March 2, 1932. Ratified January 23, 1933.

Note: Article I, section 4, of the Constitution was modified by section 2 of this amendment. In addition, a portion of the 12th amendment was superseded by section 3.

Section 1.
The terms of the President and the Vice President shall end at noon on the 20th day of January, and the terms of Senators and Representatives at noon on the 3rd day of January, of the years in which such terms would have ended if this article had not been ratified; and the terms of their successors shall then begin.

Section 2.

The Congress shall assemble at least once in every year, and such meeting shall begin at noon on the 3d day of January, unless they shall by law appoint a different day.

Section 3.

If, at the time fixed for the beginning of the term of the President, the President elect shall have died, the Vice President elect shall become President. If a President shall not have been chosen before the time fixed for the beginning of his term, or if the President elect shall have failed to qualify, then the Vice President elect shall act as President until a President shall have qualified; and the Congress may by law provide for the case wherein neither a President elect nor a Vice President shall have qualified, declaring who shall then act as President, or the manner in which one who is to act shall be selected, and such person shall act accordingly until a President or Vice President shall have qualified.

Section 4.

The Congress may by law provide for the case of the death of any of the persons from whom the House of Representatives may choose a President whenever the right of choice shall have devolved upon them, and for the case of the death of any of the persons from whom the Senate may choose a Vice President whenever the right of choice shall have devolved upon them.

Section 5.

Sections 1 and 2 shall take effect on the 15th day of October following the ratification of this article.

Section 6.

This article shall be inoperative unless it shall have been ratified as an amendment to the Constitution by the legislatures of three-fourths of the several States within seven years from the date of its submission.

Amendment XXI

Passed by Congress February 20, 1933. Ratified December 5, 1933.

Section 1.

The eighteenth article of amendment to the Constitution of the United States is hereby repealed.

Section 2.

The transportation or importation into any State, Territory, or Possession of the United States for delivery or use therein of intoxicating liquors, in violation of the laws thereof, is hereby prohibited.

Section 3.

This article shall be inoperative unless it shall have been ratified as an amendment to the Constitution by conventions in the several States, as provided in the Constitution, within seven years from the date of the submission hereof to the States by the Congress.

Amendment XXII

Passed by Congress March 21, 1947. Ratified February 27, 1951.

Section 1.
No person shall be elected to the office of the President more than twice, and no person who has held the office of President, or acted as President, for more than two years of a term to which some other person was elected President shall be elected to the office of President more than once. But this Article shall not apply to any person holding the office of President when this Article was proposed by Congress, and shall not prevent any person who may be holding the office of President, or acting as President, during the term within which this Article becomes operative from holding the office of President or acting as President during the remainder of such term.

Section 2.
This article shall be inoperative unless it shall have been ratified as an amendment to the Constitution by the legislatures of three-fourths of the several States within seven years from the date of its submission to the States by the Congress.

Amendment XXIII

Passed by Congress June 16, 1960. Ratified March 29, 1961.

Section 1.
The District constituting the seat of Government of the United States shall appoint in such manner as Congress may direct:

A number of electors of President and Vice President equal to the whole number of Senators and Representatives in Congress to which the District would be entitled if it were a State, but in no event more than the least populous State; they shall be in addition to those appointed by the States, but they shall be considered, for the purposes of the election of President and Vice President, to be electors appointed by a State; and they shall meet in the District and perform such duties as provided by the twelfth article of amendment.

Section 2.
The Congress shall have power to enforce this article by appropriate legislation.

Amendment XXIV

Passed by Congress August 27, 1962. Ratified January 23, 1964.

Section 1.
The right of citizens of the United States to vote in any primary or other election for President or Vice President, for electors for President or Vice President, or for Senator or Representative in Congress, shall not be denied or abridged by the United States or any State by reason of failure to pay poll tax or other tax.

Section 2.
The Congress shall have power to enforce this article by appropriate legislation.

Amendment XXV

Passed by Congress July 6, 1965. Ratified February 10, 1967.

Note: Article II, section 1, of the Constitution was affected by the 25th amendment.

Section 1.
In case of the removal of the President from office or of his death or resignation, the Vice President shall become President.

Section 2.
Whenever there is a vacancy in the office of the Vice President, the President shall nominate a Vice President who shall take office upon confirmation by a majority vote of both Houses of Congress.

Section 3.
Whenever the President transmits to the President pro tempore of the Senate and the Speaker of the House of Representatives his written declaration that he is unable to discharge the powers and duties of his office, and until he transmits to them a written declaration to the contrary, such powers and duties shall be discharged by the Vice President as Acting President.

Section 4.
Whenever the Vice President and a majority of either the principal officers of the executive departments or of such other body as Congress may by law provide, transmit to the President pro tempore of the Senate and the Speaker of the House of Representatives their written declaration that the President is unable to discharge the powers and duties of his office, the Vice President shall immediately assume the powers and duties of the office as Acting President.

Thereafter, when the President transmits to the President pro tempore of the Senate and the Speaker of the House of Representatives his written declaration that no inability exists, he shall resume the powers and duties of his office unless the Vice President and a majority of either the principal officers of the executive department or of such other body as Congress may by law provide, transmit within four days to the President pro tempore of the Senate and the Speaker of the House of Representatives their written declaration that the President is unable to discharge the powers and duties of his office. Thereupon Congress shall decide the issue, assembling within forty-eight hours for that purpose if not in session. If the Congress, within twenty-one days after receipt of the latter written declaration, or, if Congress is not in session, within twenty-one days after Congress is required to assemble, determines by two-thirds vote of both Houses that the President is unable to discharge the powers and duties of his office, the Vice President shall continue to discharge the same as Acting President; otherwise, the President shall resume the powers and duties of his office.

Amendment XXVI

Passed by Congress March 23, 1971. Ratified July 1, 1971.

Note: Amendment 14, section 2, of the Constitution was modified by section 1 of the 26th amendment.

Section 1.
The right of citizens of the United States, who are eighteen years of age or older, to vote shall not be denied or abridged by the United States or by any State on account of age.

Section 2.
The Congress shall have power to enforce this article by appropriate legislation.

Amendment XXVII

Originally proposed Sept. 25, 1789. Ratified May 7, 1992.

No law, varying the compensation for the services of the Senators and Representatives, shall take effect, until an election of representatives shall have intervened.

PRESIDENTIAL ELECTIONS

Year	Number of States	Candidates	Parties	Popular Vote	% of Popular Vote	Electoral Vote	% Voter Participation
1789	11	**GEORGE WASHINGTON**	No party designations			69	
		John Adams				34	
		Other candidates				35	
1792	15	**GEORGE WASHINGTON**	No party designations			132	
		John Adams				77	
		George Clinton				50	
		Other candidates				5	
1796	16	**JOHN ADAMS**	Federalist			71	
		Thomas Jefferson	Democratic-Republican			68	
		Thomas Pinckney	Federalist			59	
		Aaron Burr	Democratic-Republican			30	
		Other candidates				48	
1800	16	**THOMAS JEFFERSON**	Democratic-Republican			73	
		Aaron Burr	Democratic-Republican			73	
		John Adams	Federalist			65	
		Charles C. Pinckney	Federalist			64	
		John Jay	Federalist			1	
1804	17	**THOMAS JEFFERSON**	Democratic-Republican			162	
		Charles C. Pinckney	Federalist			14	

Year	Number of States	Candidates	Parties	Popular Vote	% of Popular Vote	Electoral Vote	% Voter Participation
1808	17	**JAMES MADISON**	Democratic-Republican			122	
		Charles C. Pinckney	Federalist			47	
		George Clinton	Democratic-Republican			6	
1812	18	**JAMES MADISON**	Democratic-Republican			128	
		DeWitt Clinton	Federalist			89	
1816	19	**JAMES MONROE**	Democratic-Republican			183	
		Rufus King	Federalist			34	
1820	24	**JAMES MONROE**	Democratic-Republican			231	
		John Quincy Adams	Independent			1	
1824	24	**JOHN QUINCY ADAMS**	Democratic-Republican	108,740	30.5	84	26.9
		Andrew Jackson	Democratic-Republican	153,544	43.1	99	
		Henry Clay	Democratic-Republican	47,136	13.2	37	
		William H. Crawford	Democratic-Republican	46,618	13.1	41	
1828	24	**ANDREW JACKSON**	Democratic	647,286	56.0	178	57.6
		John Quincy Adams	National-Republican	508,064	44.0	83	

Year	Number of States	Candidates	Parties	Popular Vote	% of Popular Vote	Electoral Vote	% Voter Partici- pation
1832	24	**ANDREW JACKSON**	Democratic	688,242	54.5	219	55.4
		Henry Clay	National-Republican	473,462	37.5	49	
		William Wirt	Anti-Masonic	101,051	8.0	7	
		John Floyd	Democratic			11	
1836	26	**MARTIN VAN BUREN**	Democratic	765,483	50.9	170	57.8
		William H. Harrison	Whig			73	
		Hugh L. White	Whig	739,795	49.1	26	
		Daniel Webster	Whig			14	
		W. P. Mangum	Whig			11	
1840	26	**WILLIAM H. HARRISON**	Whig	1,274,624	53.1	234	80.2
		Martin Van Buren	Democratic	1,127,781	46.9	60	
1844	26	**JAMES K. POLK**	Democratic	1,338,464	49.6	170	78.9
		Henry Clay	Whig	1,300,097	48.1	105	
		James G. Birney	Liberty	62,300	2.3		
1848	30	**ZACHARY TAYLOR**	Whig	1,360,967	47.4	163	72.7
		Lewis Cass	Democratic	1,222,342	42.5	127	
		Martin Van Buren	Free Soil	291,263	10.1		
1852	31	**FRANKLIN PIERCE**	Democratic	1,601,117	50.9	254	69.6
		Winfield Scott	Whig	1,385,453	44.1	42	
		John P. Hale	Free Soil	155,825	5.0		
1856	31	**JAMES BUCHANAN**	Democratic	1,832,955	45.3	174	78.9
		John C. Frémont	Republican	1,339,932	33.1	114	
		Millard Fillmore	American	871,731	21.6	8	

Year	Number of States	Candidates	Parties	Popular Vote	% of Popular Vote	Electoral Vote	% Voter Participation
1860	33	**ABRAHAM LINCOLN**	Republican	1,865,593	39.8	180	81.2
		Stephen A. Douglas	Democratic	1,382,713	29.5	12	
		John C. Breckinridge	Democratic	848,356	18.1	72	
		John Bell	Constitutional Union	592,906	12.6	39	
1864	36	**ABRAHAM LINCOLN**	Republican	2,206,938	55.0	212	73.8
		George B. McClellan	Democratic	1,803,787	45.0	21	
1868	37	**ULYSSES S. GRANT**	Republican	3,013,421	52.7	214	78.1
		Horatio Seymour	Democratic	2,706,829	47.3	80	
1872	37	**ULYSSES S. GRANT**	Republican	3,596,745	55.6	286	71.3
		Horace Greeley	Democratic	2,843,446	43.9	66	
1876	38	Rutherford B. Hayes	Republican	4,036,572	48.0	185	81.8
		Samuel J. Tilden	Democratic	4,284,020	51.0	184	
1880	38	**JAMES A. GARFIELD**	Republican	4,453,295	48.5	214	79.4
		Winfield S. Hancock	Democratic	4,414,082	48.1	155	
		James B. Weaver	Greenback-Labor	308,578	3.4		
1884	38	**GROVER CLEVELAND**	Democratic	4,879,507	48.5	219	77.5
		James G. Blaine	Republican	4,850,293	48.2	182	
		Benjamin F. Butler	Greenback-Labor	175,370	1.8		
		John P. St. John	Prohibition	150,369	1.5		
1888	38	**BENJAMIN HARRISON**	Republican	5,477,129	47.9	233	79.3
		Grover Cleveland	Democratic	5,537,857	48.6	168	
		Clinton B. Fisk	Prohibition	249,506	2.2		
		Anson J. Streeter	Union Labor	146,935	1.3		

Year	Number of States	Candidates	Parties	Popular Vote	% of Popular Vote	Electoral Vote	% Voter Participation
1892	44	**GROVER CLEVELAND**	Democratic	5,555,426	46.1	277	74.7
		Benjamin Harrison	Republican	5,182,690	43.0	145	
		James B. Weaver	People's	1,029,846	8.5	22	
		John Bidwell	Prohibition	264,133	2.2		
1896	45	**WILLIAM MCKINLEY**	Republican	7,102,246	51.1	271	79.3
		William J. Bryan	Democratic	6,492,559	47.7	176	
1900	45	**WILLIAM MCKINLEY**	Republican	7,218,491	51.7	292	73.2
		William J. Bryan	Democratic; Populist	6,356,734	45.5	155	
		John C. Wooley	Prohibition	208,914	1.5		
1904	45	**THEODORE ROOSEVELT**	Republican	7,628,461	57.4	336	65.2
		Alton B. Parker	Democratic	5,084,223	37.6	140	
		Eugene V. Debs	Socialist	402,283	3.0		
		Silas C. Swallow	Prohibition	258,536	1.9		
1908	46	**WILLIAM H. TAFT**	Republican	7,675,320	51.6	321	65.4
		William J. Bryan	Democratic	6,412,294	43.1	162	
		Eugene V. Debs	Socialist	420,793	2.8		
		Eugene W. Chafin	Prohibition	253,840	1.7		
1912	48	**WOODROW WILSON**	Democratic	6,296,547	41.9	435	58.8
		Theodore Roosevelt	Progressive	4,118,571	27.4	88	
		William H. Taft	Republican	3,486,720	23.2	8	
		Eugene V. Debs	Socialist	900,672	6.0		
		Eugene W. Chafin	Prohibition	206,275	1.4		

Year	Number of States	Candidates	Parties	Popular Vote	% of Popular Vote	Electoral Vote	% Voter Participation
1916	48	**WOODROW WILSON**	Democratic	9,127,695	49.4	277	61.6
		Charles E. Hughes	Republican	8,533,507	46.2	254	
		A. L. Benson	Socialist	585,113	3.2		
		J. Frank Hanly	Prohibition	220,506	1.2		
1920	48	**WARREN G. HARDING**	Republican	16,143,407	60.4	404	49.2
		James M. Cox	Democratic	9,130,328	34.2	127	
		Eugene V. Debs	Socialist	919,799	3.4		
		P. P. Christensen	Farmer-Labor	265,411	1.0		
1924	48	**CALVIN COOLIDGE**	Republican	15,718,211	54.0	382	48.9
		John W. Davis	Democratic	8,385,283	28.8	136	
		Robert M. La Follette	Progressive	4,831,289	16.6	13	
1928	48	**HERBERT C. HOOVER**	Republican	21,391,993	58.2	444	56.9
		Alfred E. Smith	Democratic	15,016,169	40.9	87	
1932	48	**FRANKLIN D. ROOSEVELT**	Democratic	22,809,638	57.4	472	56.9
		Herbert C. Hoover	Republican	15,758,901	39.7	59	
		Norman Thomas	Socialist	881,951	2.2		
1936	48	**FRANKLIN D. ROOSEVELT**	Democratic	27,752,869	60.8	523	61.0
		Alfred M. Landon	Republican	16,674,665	36.5	8	
		William Lemke	Union	882,479	1.9		
1940	48	**FRANKLIN D. ROOSEVELT**	Democratic	27,307,819	54.8	449	62.5
		Wendell L. Willkie	Republican	22,321,018	44.8	82	
1944	48	**FRANKLIN D. ROOSEVELT**	Democratic	25,606,585	53.5	432	55.9
		Thomas E. Dewey	Republican	22,014,745	46.0	99	

Year	Number of States	Candidates	Parties	Popular Vote	% of Popular Vote	Electoral Vote	% Voter Participation
1948	48	**HARRY S. TRUMAN**	Democratic	24,179,345	49.6	303	53.0
		Thomas E. Dewey	Republican	21,991,291	45.1	189	
		J. Strom Thurmond	States' Rights	1,176,125	2.4	39	
		Henry A. Wallace	Progressive	1,157,326	2.4		
1952	48	**DWIGHT D. EISENHOWER**	Republican	33,936,234	55.1	442	63.3
		Adlai E. Stevenson	Democratic	27,314,992	44.4	89	
1956	48	**DWIGHT D. EISENHOWER**	Republican	35,590,472	57.6	457	60.6
		Adlai E. Stevenson	Democratic	26,022,752	42.1	73	
1960	50	**JOHN F. KENNEDY**	Democratic	34,226,731	49.7	303	62.8
		Richard M. Nixon	Republican	34,108,157	49.5	219	
1964	50	**LYNDON B. JOHNSON**	Democratic	43,129,566	61.1	486	61.9
		Barry M. Goldwater	Republican	27,178,188	38.5	52	
1968	50	**RICHARD M. NIXON**	Republican	31,785,480	43.4	301	60.9
		Hubert H. Humphrey	Democratic	31,275,166	42.7	191	
		George C. Wallace	American Independent	9,906,473	13.5	46	
1972	50	**RICHARD M. NIXON**	Republican	47,169,911	60.7	520	55.2
		George S. McGovern	Democratic	29,170,383	37.5	17	
		John G. Schmitz	American	1,099,482	1.4		

Year	Number of States	Candidates	Parties	Popular Vote	% of Popular Vote	Electoral Vote	% Voter Participation
1976	50	**JIMMY CARTER** Gerald R. Ford	Democratic Republican	40,830,763 39,147,793	50.1 48.0	297 240	53.5
1980	50	**RONALD REAGAN** Jimmy Carter John B. Anderson Ed Clark	Republican Democratic Independent Libertarian	43,901,812 35,483,820 5,719,437 921,188	50.7 41.0 6.6 1.1	489 49	52.6
1984	50	**RONALD REAGAN** Walter F. Mondale	Republican Democratic	54,451,521 37,565,334	58.8 40.6	525 13	53.1
1988	50	**GEORGE H. W. BUSH** Michael Dukakis	Republican Democratic	47,917,341 41,013,030	53.4 45.6	426 111	50.1
1992	50	**BILL CLINTON** George H. W. Bush H. Ross Perot	Democratic Republican Independent	44,908,254 39,102,343 19,741,065	43.0 37.4 18.9	370 168	55.0
1996	50	**BILL CLINTON** Bob Dole H. Ross Perot	Democratic Republican Independent	47,401,185 39,197,469 8,085,295	49.0 41.0 8.0	379 159	49.0
2000	50	**GEORGE W. BUSH** Al Gore Ralph Nader	Republican Democrat Green	50,455,156 50,997,335 2,882,897	47.9 48.4 2.7	271 266	50.4
2004	50	**GEORGE W. BUSH** John F. Kerry	Republican Democrat	62,040,610 59,028,444	50.7 48.3	286 251	60.7
2008	50	**BARACK OBAMA** John McCain	Democrat Republican	69,456,897 59,934,814	52.92% 45.66%	365 173	63.0

Candidates receiving less than 1 percent of the popular vote have been omitted. Thus the percentage of popular vote given for any election year may not total 100 percent.

Before the passage of the Twelfth Amendment in 1804, the electoral college voted for two presidential candidates; the runner-up became vice president.

ADMISSION OF STATES

Order of Admission	State	Date of Admission	Order of Admission	State	Date of Admission
1	Delaware	December 7, 1787	26	Michigan	January 26, 1837
2	Pennsylvania	December 12, 1787	27	Florida	March 3, 1845
3	New Jersey	December 18, 1787	28	Texas	December 29, 1845
4	Georgia	January 2, 1788	29	Iowa	December 28, 1846
5	Connecticut	January 9, 1788	30	Wisconsin	May 29, 1848
6	Massachusetts	February 7, 1788	31	California	September 9, 1850
7	Maryland	April 28, 1788	32	Minnesota	May 11, 1858
8	South Carolina	May 23, 1788	33	Oregon	February 14, 1859
9	New Hampshire	June 21, 1788	34	Kansas	January 29, 1861
10	Virginia	June 25, 1788	35	West Virginia	June 30, 1863
11	New York	July 26, 1788	36	Nevada	October 31, 1864
12	North Carolina	November 21, 1789	37	Nebraska	March 1, 1867
13	Rhode Island	May 29, 1790	38	Colorado	August 1, 1876
14	Vermont	March 4, 1791	39	North Dakota	November 2, 1889
15	Kentucky	June 1, 1792	40	South Dakota	November 2, 1889
16	Tennessee	June 1, 1796	41	Montana	November 8, 1889
17	Ohio	March 1, 1803	42	Washington	November 11, 1889
18	Louisiana	April 30, 1812	43	Idaho	July 3, 1890
19	Indiana	December 11, 1816	44	Wyoming	July 10, 1890
20	Mississippi	December 10, 1817	45	Utah	January 4, 1896
21	Illinois	December 3, 1818	46	Oklahoma	November 16, 1907
22	Alabama	December 14, 1819	47	New Mexico	January 6, 1912
23	Maine	March 15, 1820	48	Arizona	February 14, 1912
24	Missouri	August 10, 1821	49	Alaska	January 3, 1959
25	Arkansas	June 15, 1836	50	Hawaii	August 21, 1959

POPULATION OF THE UNITED STATES

Year	Number of States	Population	% Increase	Population per Square Mile
1790	13	3,929,214		4.5
1800	16	5,308,483	35.1	6.1
1810	17	7,239,881	36.4	4.3
1820	23	9,638,453	33.1	5.5
1830	24	12,866,020	33.5	7.4
1840	26	17,069,453	32.7	9.8
1850	31	23,191,876	35.9	7.9
1860	33	31,443,321	35.6	10.6
1870	37	39,818,449	26.6	13.4
1880	38	50,155,783	26.0	16.9
1890	44	62,947,714	25.5	21.1
1900	45	75,994,575	20.7	25.6
1910	46	91,972,266	21.0	31.0
1920	48	105,710,620	14.9	35.6
1930	48	122,775,046	16.1	41.2
1940	48	131,669,275	7.2	44.2
1950	48	150,697,361	14.5	50.7
1960	50	179,323,175	19.0	50.6
1970	50	203,235,298	13.3	57.5
1980	50	226,504,825	11.4	64.0
1985	50	237,839,000	5.0	67.2
1990	50	250,122,000	5.2	70.6
1995	50	263,411,707	5.3	74.4
2000	50	281,421,906	6.8	77.0
2005	50	296,410,404	5.3	77.9
2010	50	308,745,538	9.7	87.4

IMMIGRATION TO THE UNITED STATES, FISCAL YEARS 1820–2011

Year	Number	Year	Number	Year	Number	Year	Number
1820–1989	**55,457,531**	**1871–80**	**2,812,191**	**1921–30**	**4,107,209**	**1971–80**	**4,493,314**
1820	8,385	1871	321,350	1921	805,228	1971	370,478
1821–30	**143,439**	1872	404,806	1922	309,556	1972	384,685
1821	9,127	1873	459,803	1923	522,919	1973	400,063
1822	6,911	1874	313,339	1924	706,896	1974	394,861
1823	6,354	1875	227,498	1925	294,314	1975	386,914
1824	7,912	1876	169,986	1926	304,488	1976	398,613
1825	10,199	1877	141,857	1927	335,175		103,676
1826	10,837	1878	138,469	1928	307,255	1977	462,315
1827	18,875	1879	177,826	1929	279,678	1978	601,442
1828	27,382	1880	457,257	1930	241,700	1979	460,348
1829	22,520	**1881–90**	**5,246,613**	**1931–40**	**528,431**	1980	530,639
1830	23,322	1881	669,431	1931	97,139	**1981–90**	**7,338,062**
1831–40	**599,125**	1882	788,992	1932	35,576	1981	596,600
1831	22,633	1883	603,322	1933	23,068	1982	594,131
1832	60,482	1884	518,592	1934	29,470	1983	559,763
1833	58,640	1885	395,346	1935	34,956	1984	543,903
1834	65,365	1886	334,203	1936	36,329	1985	570,009
1835	45,374	1887	490,109	1937	50,244	1986	601,708
1836	76,242	1888	546,889	1938	67,895	1987	601,516
1837	79,340	1889	444,427	1939	82,998	1988	643,025
1838	38,914	1890	455,302	1940	70,756	1989	1,090,924
1839	68,069	**1891–1900**	**3,687,564**	**1941–50**	**1,035,039**	1990	1,536,483
1840	84,066	1891	560,319	1941	51,776	**1991–2000**	**9,090,857**
1841–50	**1,713,251**	1892	579,663	1942	28,781	1991	1,827,167
1841	80,289	1893	439,730	1943	23,725	1992	973,977
1842	104,565	1894	285,631	1944	28,551	1993	904,292
		1895	258,536	1945	38,119	1994	804,416
		1896	343,267	1946	108,721		

Year	Number	Year	Number	Year	Number	Year	Number
1843	52,496	1897	230,832	1947	147,292	1995	720,461
1844	78,615	1898	229,299	1948	170,570	1996	915,900
1845	114,371	1899	311,715	1949	188,317	1997	798,378
1846	154,416	1900	448,572	1950	249,187	1998	660,477
1847	234,968					1999	644,787
1848	226,527	1901–10	8,795,386	1951–60	2,515,479	2000	841,002
1849	297,024	1901	487,918	1951	205,717	2001–10	10,501,053
1850	369,980	1902	648,743	1952	265,520	2001	1,058,902
		1903	857,046	1953	170,434	2002	1,059,356
1851–60	2,598,214	1904	812,870	1954	208,177	2003	705,827
1851	379,466	1905	1,026,499	1955	237,790	2004	957,883
1852	371,603	1906	1,100,735	1956	321,625	2005	1,122,373
1853	368,645	1907	1,285,349	1957	326,867	2006	1,266,129
1854	427,833	1908	782,870	1958	253,265	2007	1,052,415
1855	200,877	1909	751,786	1959	260,686	2008	1,107,126
1856	200,436	1910	1,041,570	1960	265,398	2009	1,130,818
1857	251,306					2010	1,042,625
1858	123,126	1911–20	5,735,811	1961–70	3,321,677	2011	1,062,040
1859	121,282	1911	878,587	1961	271,344		
1860	153,640	1912	838,172	1962	283,763		
		1913	1,197,892	1963	306,260		
1861–70	2,314,824	1914	1,218,480	1964	292,248		
1861	91,918	1915	326,700	1965	296,697		
1862	91,985	1916	298,826	1966	323,040		
1863	176,282	1917	295,403	1967	361,972		
1864	193,418	1918	110,618	1968	454,448		
1865	248,120	1919	141,132	1969	358,579		
1866	318,568	1920	430,001	1970	373,326		
1867	315,722						
1868	138,840						
1869	352,768						
1870	387,203						

Source: U.S. Department of Homeland Security.

IMMIGRATION BY REGION AND SELECTED COUNTRY OF LAST RESIDENCE, FISCAL YEARS 1820–2011

Region and country of last residence	1820 to 1829	1830 to 1839	1840 to 1849	1850 to 1859	1860 to 1869	1870 to 1879	1880 to 1889	1890 to 1899
Total	128,502	538,381	1,427,337	2,814,554	2,081,261	2,742,137	5,248,568	3,694,294
Europe	99,272	422,771	1,369,259	2,619,680	1,877,726	2,251,878	4,638,677	3,576,411
Austria-Hungary	—	—	—	—	3,375	60,127	314,787	534,059
Austria	—	—	—	—	2,700	54,529	204,805	268,218
Hungary	—	—	—	—	483	5,598	109,982	203,350
Belgium	28	20	3,996	5,765	5,785	6,991	18,738	19,642
Bulgaria	—	—	—	—	—	—	—	52
Czechoslovakia	—	—	—	—	—	—	—	—
Denmark	173	927	671	3,227	13,553	29,278	85,342	56,671
Finland	—	—	—	—	—	—	—	—
France	7,694	39,330	75,300	81,778	35,938	71,901	48,193	35,616
Germany	5,753	124,726	385,434	976,072	723,734	751,769	1,445,181	579,072
Greece	17	49	17	32	51	209	1,807	12,732
Ireland	51,617	170,672	656,145	1,029,486	427,419	422,264	674,061	405,710
Italy	430	2,225	1,476	8,643	9,853	46,296	267,660	603,761
Netherlands	1,105	1,377	7,624	11,122	8,387	14,267	52,715	29,349
Norway-Sweden	91	1,149	12,389	22,202	82,937	178,823	586,441	334,058
Norway	—	—	—	—	16,068	88,644	185,111	96,810
Sweden	—	—	—	—	24,224	90,179	401,330	237,248
Poland	19	366	105	1,087	1,886	11,016	42,910	107,793
Portugal	177	820	196	1,299	2,083	13,971	15,186	25,874
Romania	—	—	—	—	—	—	5,842	6,808
Russia	86	280	520	423	1,670	35,177	182,698	450,101
Spain	2,595	2,010	1,916	8,795	6,966	5,540	3,995	9,189
Switzerland	3,148	4,430	4,819	24,423	21,124	25,212	81,151	37,020
United Kingdom	26,336	74,350	218,572	445,322	532,956	578,447	810,900	328,759
Yugoslavia	—	—	—	—	—	—	—	—
Other Europe	3	40	79	4	9	590	1,070	145

Asia	34	55	121	36,080	54,408	134,128	71,151	61,285
China	3	8	32	35,933	54,028	133,139	65,797	15,268
Hong Kong	9	38	33	42	50	166	247	102
India	—	—	—	—	—	—	—	—
Iran	—	—	—	—	—	—	—	—
Israel	—	—	—	—	—	—	—	—
Japan	—	—	—	—	138	193	1,583	13,998
Jordan	—	—	—	—	—	—	—	—
Korea	—	—	—	—	—	—	—	—
Philippines	—	—	—	—	—	—	—	—
Syria	—	—	—	—	—	—	—	—
Taiwan	—	—	—	—	—	—	—	—
Turkey	19	8	45	94	129	382	2,478	27,510
Vietnam	—	—	—	—	—	—	—	—
Other Asia	3	1	11	11	63	248	1,046	4,407
America	9,655	31,905	50,516	84,145	130,292	345,010	524,826	37,350
Canada and Newfoundland	2,297	11,875	34,285	64,171	117,978	324,310	492,865	3,098
Mexico	3,835	7,187	3,069	3,446	1,957	5,133	2,405	734
Caribbean	3,061	11,792	11,803	12,447	8,751	14,285	27,323	31,480
Cuba	—	—	—	—	—	—	—	—
Dominican Republic	—	—	—	—	—	—	—	—
Haiti	—	—	—	—	—	—	—	—
Jamaica	—	—	—	—	—	—	—	—
Other Caribbean	3,061	11,792	11,803	12,447	8,751	14,285	27,323	31,480
Central America	57	94	297	512	70	173	279	649
Belize	—	—	—	—	—	—	—	—
Costa Rica	—	—	—	—	—	—	—	—
El Salvador	—	—	—	—	—	—	—	—
Guatemala	—	—	—	—	—	—	—	—
Honduras	—	—	—	—	—	—	—	—
Nicaragua	—	—	—	—	—	—	—	—
Panama	—	—	—	—	—	—	—	—
Other Central America	57	94	297	512	70	173	279	649
South America	405	957	1,062	3,569	1,536	1,109	1,954	1,389
Argentina	—	—	—	—	—	—	—	—
Bolivia	—	—	—	—	—	—	—	—

Region and country of last residence	1820 to 1829	1830 to 1839	1840 to 1849	1850 to 1859	1860 to 1869	1870 to 1879	1880 to 1889	1890 to 1899
Brazil	—	—	—	—	—	—	—	—
Chile	—	—	—	—	—	—	—	—
Colombia	—	—	—	—	—	—	—	—
Ecuador	—	—	—	—	—	—	—	—
Guyana	—	—	—	—	—	—	—	—
Paraguay	—	—	—	—	—	—	—	—
Peru	—	—	—	—	—	—	—	—
Suriname	—	—	—	—	—	—	—	—
Uruguay	—	—	—	—	—	—	—	—
Venezuela	—	—	—	—	—	—	—	—
Other South America	405	957	1,062	3,569	1,536	1,109	1,954	1,389
Other America	15	50	61	84	407	371	763	432
Africa	—	—	—	—	—	—	—	—
Egypt	—	—	—	—	4	29	145	51
Ethiopia	—	—	—	—	—	—	—	—
Liberia	1	8	5	7	43	52	21	9
Morocco	—	—	—	—	—	—	—	—
South Africa	—	—	—	—	35	48	23	9
Other Africa	14	42	56	77	325	242	574	363
Oceania	3	7	14	166	187	9,996	12,361	4,704
Australia	2	1	2	15	—	8,930	7,250	3,098
New Zealand	—	—	—	—	—	39	21	12
Other Oceania	1	6	12	151	187	1,027	5,090	1,594
Not Specified	19,523	83,593	7,366	74,399	18,241	754	790	14,112

Total	8,202,388	6,347,380	4,295,510	699,375	856,608	2,499,268	3,213,749	6,244,379
Europe	7,572,569	4,985,411	2,560,340	444,399	472,524	1,404,973	1,133,443	668,866
Austria-Hungary	2,001,376	1,154,727	60,891	12,531	13,574	113,015	27,590	20,437
Austria	532,416	589,174	31,392	5,307	8,393	81,354	17,571	15,374
Hungary	685,567	565,553	29,499	7,224	5,181	31,661	10,019	5,063
Belgium	37,429	32,574	21,511	4,013	12,473	18,885	9,647	7,028
Bulgaria	34,651	27,180	2,824	1,062	449	97	598	1,124
Czechoslovakia	—	—	101,182	17,757	8,475	1,624	2,758	5,678
Denmark	61,227	45,830	34,406	3,470	4,549	10,918	9,797	4,847
Finland	—	—	16,922	2,438	2,230	4,923	4,310	2,569
France	67,735	60,335	54,842	13,761	36,954	50,113	46,975	32,066
Germany	328,722	174,227	386,634	119,107	119,506	576,905	209,616	85,752
Greece	145,402	198,108	60,774	10,599	8,605	45,153	74,173	37,729
Ireland	344,940	166,445	202,854	28,195	15,701	47,189	37,788	22,210
Italy	1,930,475	1,229,916	528,133	85,053	50,509	184,576	200,111	55,562
Netherlands	42,463	46,065	29,397	7,791	13,877	46,703	37,918	11,234
Norway-Sweden	426,981	192,445	170,329	13,452	17,326	44,224	36,150	13,941
Norway	182,542	79,488	70,327	6,901	8,326	22,806	17,371	3,835
Sweden	244,439	112,957	100,002	6,551	9,000	21,418	18,779	10,106
Poland	—	—	223,316	25,555	7,577	6,465	55,742	63,483
Portugal	65,154	82,489	44,829	3,518	6,765	13,928	70,568	42,685
Romania	57,322	13,566	67,810	5,264	1,254	914	2,339	24,753
Russia	1,501,301	1,106,998	61,604	2,463	605	453	2,329	33,311
Spain	24,818	53,262	47,109	3,669	2,774	6,880	40,793	22,783
Switzerland	32,541	22,839	31,772	5,990	9,904	17,577	19,193	8,316
United Kingdom	469,518	371,878	341,552	61,813	131,794	195,709	220,213	153,644
Yugoslavia	—	—	49,215	6,920	2,039	6,966	17,990	16,267
Other Europe	514	6,527	22,434	9,978	5,584	11,756	6,845	3,447
Asia	299,836	269,736	126,740	19,231	34,532	135,844	358,605	2,391,356
China	19,884	20,916	30,648	5,874	16,072	8,836	14,060	170,897
Hong Kong	—	—	—	—	—	13,781	67,047	112,132
India	3,026	3,478	2,076	554	1,692	1,850	18,638	231,649
Iran	—	—	208	198	1,144	3,195	9,059	98,141
Israel	—	—	—	—	98	21,376	30,911	43,669

Region and country of last residence	1900 to 1909	1910 to 1919	1920 to 1929	1930 to 1939	1940 to 1949	1950 to 1959	1960 to 1969	1980 to 1989
Japan	139,712	77,125	42,057	2,683	1,557	40,651	40,956	44,150
Jordan	—	—	—	—	—	4,899	9,230	28,928
Korea	—	—	—	—	83	4,845	27,048	322,708
Philippines	—	—	5,307	391	4,099	17,245	70,660	502,056
Syria	—	—	—	2,188	1,179	1,091	2,432	14,534
Taiwan	—	—	—	—	—	721	15,657	119,051
Turkey	127,999	160,717	40,450	1,327	754	2,980	9,464	19,208
Vietnam	—	—	—	—	—	290	2,949	200,632
Other Asia	9,215	7,500	5,994	6,016	7,854	14,084	40,494	483,601
America	277,809	1,070,539	1,591,278	230,319	328,435	921,610	1,674,172	2,695,329
Canada and Newfoundland	123,067	708,715	949,286	162,703	160,911	353,169	433,128	156,313
Mexico	31,188	185,334	498,945	32,709	56,158	273,847	441,824	1,009,586
Caribbean	100,960	120,860	83,482	18,052	46,194	115,661	427,235	790,109
Cuba	—	—	12,769	10,641	25,976	73,221	202,030	132,552
Dominican Republic	—	—	—	1,026	4,802	10,219	83,552	221,552
Haiti	—	—	—	156	823	3,787	28,992	121,406
Jamaica	—	—	—	—	—	7,397	62,218	193,874
Other Caribbean	100,960	120,860	70,713	6,229	14,593	21,037	50,443	120,725
Central America	7,341	15,692	16,511	6,840	20,135	40,201	98,560	339,376
Belize	77	40	285	193	433	1,133	4,185	14,964
Costa Rica	—	—	—	431	1,965	4,044	17,975	25,017
El Salvador	—	—	—	597	4,885	5,094	14,405	137,418
Guatemala	—	—	—	423	1,303	4,197	14,357	58,847
Honduras	—	—	—	679	1,874	5,320	15,078	39,071
Nicaragua	—	—	—	405	4,393	7,812	10,383	31,102
Panama	—	—	—	1,452	5,282	12,601	22,177	32,957
Other Central America	7,264	15,652	16,226	2,660	—	—	—	—

Region								
South America	15,253	39,938	43,025	9,990	19,662	78,418	250,754	399,862
Argentina	—	—	—	1,067	3,108	16,346	49,384	23,442
Bolivia	—	—	—	50	893	2,759	6,205	9,798
Brazil	—	—	4,627	1,468	3,653	11,547	29,238	22,944
Chile	—	—	—	347	1,320	4,669	12,384	19,749
Colombia	—	—	—	1,027	3,454	15,567	68,371	105,494
Ecuador	—	—	—	244	2,207	8,574	34,107	48,015
Guyana	—	—	—	131	596	1,131	4,546	85,886
Paraguay	—	—	—	33	85	576	1,249	3,518
Peru	—	—	—	321	1,273	5,980	19,783	49,958
Suriname	—	—	—	25	130	299	612	1,357
Uruguay	—	—	—	112	754	1,026	4,089	7,235
Venezuela	—	—	—	1,155	2,182	9,927	20,758	22,405
Other South America	15,253	39,938	38,398	4,010	7	17	28	61
Other America	—	—	29	25	25,375	60,314	22,671	83
Africa	6,326	8,867	6,362	2,120	6,720	13,016	23,780	141,990
Egypt	—	—	1,063	781	1,613	1,996	5,581	26,744
Ethiopia	—	—	—	10	28	302	804	12,927
Liberia	—	—	—	35	37	289	841	6,420
Morocco	—	—	—	73	879	2,703	2,880	3,471
South Africa	6,326	8,867	5,299	312	1,022	2,278	4,360	15,505
Other Africa	—	—	—	909	3,141	5,448	9,314	76,923
Oceania	12,355	12,339	9,860	3,306	14,262	11,353	23,630	41,432
Australia	11,191	11,280	8,404	2,260	11,201	8,275	14,986	16,901
New Zealand	—	—	935	790	2,351	1,799	3,775	6,129
Other Oceania	1,164	1,059	521	256	710	1,279	4,869	18,402
Not Specified	33,493	488	930	—	135	12,472	119	305,406

Region and country of last residence	1990 to 1999	2000 to 2009	2010	2011
Total	9,775,398	10,299,430	1,042,625	1,062,040
Europe	1,348,612	1,349,609	95,429	90,712
Austria-Hungary	27,529	33,929	4,325	4,703
Austria	18,234	21,151	3,319	3,654
Hungary	9,295	12,778	1,006	1,049
Belgium	7,077	8,157	732	700
Bulgaria	16,948	40,003	2,465	2,549
Czechoslovakia	8,970	18,691	1,510	1,374
Denmark	6,189	6,049	545	473
Finland	3,970	3,970	414	398
France	35,945	45,637	4,339	3,967
Germany	92,207	122,373	7,929	7,072
Greece	25,403	16,841	966	1,196
Ireland	65,384	15,642	1,610	1,533
Italy	75,992	28,329	2,956	2,670
Netherlands	13,345	17,351	1,520	1,258
Norway-Sweden	17,825	19,382	1,662	1,530
Norway	5,211	4,599	363	405
Sweden	12,614	14,783	1,299	1,125
Poland	172,249	117,921	7,391	6,634
Portugal	25,497	11,479	759	878
Romania	48,136	52,154	3,735	3,679
Russia	433,427	167,152	7,502	8,548
Spain	18,443	17,695	2,040	2,319
Switzerland	11,768	12,173	868	861
United Kingdom	156,182	171,979	14,781	13,443
Yugoslavia	57,039	131,831	4,772	4,611
Other Europe	29,087	290,871	22,608	20,316

Asia	2,859,899	3,470,835	410,209	438,580
China	342,058	591,711	67,634	83,603
Hong Kong	116,894	57,583	3,263	3,149
India	352,528	590,464	66,185	66,331
Iran	76,899	76,755	9,078	9,015
Israel	41,340	54,081	5,172	4,389
Japan	66,582	84,552	7,100	6,751
Jordan	42,755	53,550	9,327	8,211
Korea	179,770	209,758	22,022	22,748
Philippines	534,338	545,463	56,399	55,251
Syria	22,906	30,807	7,424	7,983
Taiwan	132,647	92,657	6,785	6,206
Turkey	38,687	48,394	7,435	9,040
Vietnam	275,379	289,616	30,065	33,486
Other Asia	637,116	745,444	112,320	122,417
America	5,137,743	4,441,529	426,981	423,277
Canada and Newfoundland	194,788	236,349	19,491	19,506
Mexico	2,757,418	1,704,166	138,717	142,823
Caribbean	1,004,687	1,053,357	139,389	133,012
Cuba	159,037	271,742	33,372	36,261
Dominican Republic	359,818	291,492	53,890	46,036
Haiti	177,446	203,827	22,336	21,802
Jamaica	177,143	172,523	19,439	19,298
Other Caribbean	181,243	113,773	10,352	9,615
Central America	610,189	591,130	43,597	43,249
Belize	12,600	9,682	997	933
Costa Rica	17,054	21,571	2,306	2,230
El Salvador	273,017	251,237	18,547	18,477
Guatemala	126,043	156,992	10,263	10,795
Honduras	72,880	63,513	6,381	6,053

Region and country of last residence	1990 to 1999	2000 to 2009	2010	2011
Nicaragua	80,446	70,015	3,476	3,314
Panama	28,149	18,120	1,627	1,447
Other Central America	—			–
South America	570,624	856,508	85,783	84,687
Argentina	30,065	47,955	4,312	4,335
Bolivia	18,111	21,921	2,211	2,113
Brazil	50,744	115,404	12,057	11,643
Chile	18,200	19,792	1,940	1,854
Colombia	137,985	236,570	21,861	22,130
Ecuador	81,358	107,977	11,463	11,068
Guyana	74,407	70,373	6,441	6,288
Paraguay	6,082	4,623	449	501
Peru	110,117	137,614	14,063	13,836
Suriname	2,285	2,363	202	167
Uruguay	6,062	9,827	1,286	1,521
Venezuela	35,180	82,087	9,497	9,229
Other South America	28	2	1	2
Other America	37	19	4	–
Africa	346,416	759,734	98,246	97,429
Egypt	44,604	81,564	9,822	9,096
Ethiopia	40,097	87,207	13,853	13,985
Liberia	13,587	23,316	2,924	3,117
Morocco	15,768	40,844	4,847	4,249
South Africa	21,964	32,221	2,705	2,754
Other Africa	210,396	494,582	64,095	64,228
Oceania	56,800	65,793	5,946	5,825
Australia	24,288	32,728	3,077	3,062
New Zealand	8,600	12,495	1,046	1,006
Other Oceania	23,912	20,570	1,823	1,757
Not Specified	25,928	211,930	5,814	6,217

— Represents zero or not available.

PRESIDENTS, VICE PRESIDENTS, AND SECRETARIES OF STATE

	President	Vice President	Secretary of State
1.	George Washington, Federalist 1789	John Adams, Federalist 1789	Thomas Jefferson 1789 Edmund Randolph 1794 Timothy Pickering 1795
2.	John Adams, Federalist 1797	Thomas Jefferson, Dem.-Rep. 1797	Timothy Pickering 1797 John Marshall 1800
3.	Thomas Jefferson, Dem.-Rep. 1801	Aaron Burr, Dem.-Rep. 1801 George Clinton, Dem.-Rep. 1805	James Madison 1801
4.	James Madison, Dem.-Rep. 1809	George Clinton, Dem.-Rep. 1809 Elbridge Gerry, Dem.-Rep. 1813	Robert Smith 1809 James Monroe 1811
5.	James Monroe, Dem.-Rep. 1817	Daniel D. Tompkins, Dem.-Rep. 1817	John Q. Adams 1817
6.	John Quincy Adams, Dem.-Rep. 1825	John C. Calhoun, Dem.-Rep. 1825	Henry Clay 1825
7.	Andrew Jackson, Democratic 1829	John C. Calhoun, Democratic 1829 Martin Van Buren, Democratic 1833	Martin Van Buren 1829 Edward Livingston 1831 Louis McLane 1833 John Forsyth 1834
8.	Martin Van Buren, Democratic 1837	Richard M. Johnson, Democratic 1837	John Forsyth 1837
9.	William H. Harrison, Whig 1841	John Tyler, Whig 1841	Daniel Webster 1841

President	Vice President	Secretary of State
10. John Tyler, Whig and Democratic 1841	None	Daniel Webster 1841 Hugh S. Legaré 1843 Abel P. Upshur 1843 John C. Calhoun 1844
11. James K. Polk, Democratic 1845	George M. Dallas, Democratic 1845	James Buchanan 1845
12. Zachary Taylor, Whig 1849	Millard Fillmore, Whig 1848	John M. Clayton 1849
13. Millard Fillmore, Whig 1850	None	Daniel Webster 1850 Edward Everett 1852
14. Franklin Pierce, Democratic 1853	William R. King, Democratic 1853	William L. Marcy 1853
15. James Buchanan, Democratic 1857	John C. Breckinridge, Democratic 1857	Lewis Cass 1857 Jeremiah S. Black 1860
16. Abraham Lincoln, Republican 1861	Hannibal Hamlin, Republican 1861 Andrew Johnson, Unionist 1865	William H. Seward 1861
17. Andrew Johnson, Unionist 1865	None	William H. Seward 1865
18. Ulysses S. Grant, Republican 1869	Schuyler Colfax, Republican 1869 Henry Wilson, Republican 1873	Elihu B. Washburne 1869 Hamilton Fish 1869
19. Rutherford B. Hayes, Republican 1877	William A. Wheeler, Republican 1877	William M. Evarts 1877

	President	Vice President	Secretary of State
20.	James A. Garfield, Republican 1881	Chester A. Arthur, Republican 1881	James G. Blaine 1881
21.	Chester A. Arthur, Republican 1881	None	Frederick T. Frelinghuysen 1881
22.	Grover Cleveland, Democratic 1885	Thomas A. Hendricks, Democratic 1885	Thomas F. Bayard 1885
23.	Benjamin Harrison, Republican 1889	Levi P. Morton, Republican 1889	James G. Blaine 1889 John W. Foster 1892
24.	Grover Cleveland, Democratic 1893	Adlai E. Stevenson, Democratic 1893	Walter Q. Gresham 1893 Richard Olney 1895
25.	William McKinley, Republican 1897	Garret A. Hobart, Republican 1897 Theodore Roosevelt, Republican 1901	John Sherman 1897 William R. Day 1898 John Hay 1898
26.	Theodore Roosevelt, Republican 1901	Charles Fairbanks, Republican 1905	John Hay 1901 Elihu Root 1905 Robert Bacon 1909
27.	William H. Taft, Republican 1909	James S. Sherman, Republican 1909	Philander C. Knox 1909
28.	Woodrow Wilson, Democratic 1913	Thomas R. Marshall, Democratic 1913	William J. Bryan 1913 Robert Lansing 1915 Bainbridge Colby 1920
29.	Warren G. Harding, Republican 1921	Calvin Coolidge, Republican 1921	Charles E. Hughes 1921
30.	Calvin Coolidge, Republican 1923	Charles G. Dawes, Republican 1925	Charles E. Hughes 1923 Frank B. Kellogg 1925

President	Vice President	Secretary of State
31. Herbert Hoover, Republican 1929	Charles Curtis, Republican 1929	Henry L. Stimson 1929
32. Franklin D. Roosevelt, Democratic 1933	John Nance Garner, Democratic 1933 Henry A. Wallace, Democratic 1941 Harry S. Truman, Democratic 1945	Cordell Hull 1933 Edward R. Stettinius, Jr. 1944
33. Harry S. Truman, Democratic 1945	Alben W. Barkley, Democratic 1949	Edward R. Stettinius, Jr. 1945 James F. Byrnes 1945 George C. Marshall 1947 Dean G. Acheson 1949
34. Dwight D. Eisenhower, Republican 1953	Richard M. Nixon, Republican 1953	John F. Dulles 1953 Christian A. Herter 1959
35. John F. Kennedy, Democratic 1961	Lyndon B. Johnson, Democratic 1961	Dean Rusk 1961
36. Lyndon B. Johnson, Democratic 1963	Hubert H. Humphrey, Democratic 1965	Dean Rusk 1963
37. Richard M. Nixon, Republican 1969	Spiro T. Agnew, Republican 1969 Gerald R. Ford, Republican 1973	William P. Rogers 1969 Henry Kissinger 1973
38. Gerald R. Ford, Republican 1974	Nelson Rockefeller, Republican 1974	Henry Kissinger 1974
39. Jimmy Carter, Democratic 1977	Walter Mondale, Democratic 1977	Cyrus Vance 1977 Edmund Muskie 1980

	President	*Vice President*	*Secretary of State*
40.	Ronald Reagan, Republican 1981	George H. W. Bush, Republican 1981	Alexander Haig 1981 George Schultz 1982
41.	George H. W. Bush, Republican 1989	J. Danforth Quayle, Republican 1989	James A. Baker 1989 Lawrence Eagleburger 1992
42.	William J. Clinton, Democratic 1993	Albert Gore, Jr., Democratic 1993	Warren Christopher 1993 Madeleine Albright 1997
43.	George W. Bush, Republican 2001	Richard B. Cheney, Republican 2001	Colin L. Powell 2001 Condoleezza Rice 2005
44.	Barack Obama, Democratic 2009	Joseph R. Biden, Democratic 2009	Hillary Rodham Clinton 2009 John Kerry 2013

Further Readings

Chapter 1

A fascinating study of pre-Columbian migration is Brian M. Fagan's *The Great Journey: The Peopling of Ancient America*, rev. ed. (2004). Alice B. Kehoe's *North American Indians: A Comprehensive Account*, 2nd ed. (1992), provides an encyclopedic treatment of Native Americans. See also Charles Mann's *1491: New Revelations of the Americas before Columbus* (2005) and *1493: Uncovering the New World that Columbua Created* (2011), and Daniel K. Richter, *Before the Revolution: America's Ancient Pasts* (2011). On North America's largest Native American city, see Timothy R. Pauketat, *Cahokia* (2010).

The conflict between Native Americans and Europeans is treated well in James Axtell's *The Invasion Within: The Contest of Cultures in Colonial North America* (1986) and *Beyond 1492: Encounters in Colonial North America* (1992). Colin G. Calloway's *New Worlds for All: Indians, Europeans, and the Remaking of Early America* (1997) explores the ecological effects of European settlement.

Laurence Bergreen examines the voyages of Columbus in *Columbus: The Four Voyages* (2011). For sweeping overviews of Spain's creation of a global empire, see Henry Kamen's *Empire: How Spain Became a World Power, 1492–1763* (2003) and Hugh Thomas's *Rivers of Gold: The Rise of the Spanish Empire, from Columbus to Magellan* (2004). David J. Weber examines Spanish colonization in *The Spanish Frontier in North America* (1992). For the French experience, see William J. Eccles's *France in America*, rev. ed. (1990). For an insightful comparison of Spanish and English modes of settlement, see J. H. Elliott, *Empires of the Atlantic World: Britain and Spain in America, 1492–1830* (2006).

Chapter 2

Two excellent surveys of early American history are Peter C. Hoffer's *The Brave New World: A History of Early America,* 2nd ed. (2006), and William R. Polk's *The Birth of America: From before Columbus to the Revolution* (2006).

Bernard Bailyn's *The Barbarous Years: The Peopling of British North America: The Conflict of Civilizations, 1600-1675* (2013) tells the often brutal story of British settlement in America during the seventeenth century. Jack P. Greene offers a brilliant synthesis of British colonization in *Pursuits of Happiness: The Social Development of Early Modern British Colonies and the Formation of American Culture* (1988). The best overview of the colonization of North America is Alan Taylor's *American Colonies: The Settling of North America* (2001). On the interactions among Indian, European, and African cultures, see Gary B. Nash's *Red, White, and Black: The Peoples of Early North America*, 5th ed. (2005).

A good overview of the founding of Virginia and Maryland is Jean and Elliott Russo's *The Early Chesapeake in British North America* (2012). For information regarding the Puritan settlement of New England, see David D. Hall's *A Reforming People: Puritanism and the Transofrmaiton of Public Life in New England* (2013). The best biography of John Winthrop is Francis J. Bremer's *John Winthrop: America's Forgotten Founding Father* (2003). On Roger Williams, see John M. Barry's *Roger Williams and the Creation of the American Soul* (2012)

The pattern of settlement in the middle colonies is illuminated in Barry Levy's *Quakers and the American Family: British Settlement in the Delaware Valley* (1988). On the early history of New York, see Russell Shorto's *The Island at the Center of the World: The Epic Story of Dutch Manhattan and the Forgotten Colony That Shaped America* (2004). Settlement of the areas along the Atlantic in the South is traced in James Horn's *Adapting to a New World: English Society in the Seventeenth-Century Chesapeake* (1994).

On shifting political life in England, see Steve Pincus, *1688: The First Modern Revolution* (2009). For a study of race and the settlement of South Carolina, see Peter H. Wood's *Black Majority: Negroes in Colonial South Carolina from 1670 through the Stono Rebellion* (1974). On the flourishing trade in captive Indians, see Alan Gallay's *The Indian Slave Trade: The Rise of the English Empire in the American South, 1670–1717* (2002). On the Yamasee War, see Steven J. Oatis's *A Colonial Complex: South Carolina's Frontiers in the Era of the Yamasee War, 1680–1730* (2004).

Chapter 3

The diversity of colonial societies may be seen in David Hackett Fischer's *Albion's Seed: Four British Folkways in America* (1989). John Frederick Martin's *Profits in the Wilderness: Entrepreneurship and the Founding of New England Towns in the Seventeenth Century* (1991) indicates that economic concerns rather than spiritual motives were driving forces in many New England towns.

Bernard Rosenthal challenges many myths concerning the Salem witch trials in *Salem Story: Reading the Witch Trials of 1692* (1993). Mary Beth Norton's *In the Devil's Snare: The Salem Witchcraft Crisis of 1692* (2002) emphasizes the role of Indian violence.

Discussions of women in the New England colonies can be found in Laurel Thatcher Ulrich's *Good Wives: Image and Reality in the Lives of Women in Northern New England, 1650–1750* (1980), and Mary Beth Norton, *Separated by Their Sex: Women in Public and Private in the Colonial Atlantic World* (2011). On women and religion, see Susan Juster's *Disorderly Women: Sexual Politics and Evangelicalism in Revolutionary New England* (1994). John Demos describes family life in *A Little Commonwealth: Family Life in Plymouth Colony*, new ed. (2000).

For an excellent overview of Indian relations with Europeans, see Colin G. Calloway's *New Worlds for All: Indians, Europeans, and the Remaking of Early America* (1997). For analyses of Indian wars, see Alfred A. Cave's *The Pequot War* (1996) and Jill Lepore's *The Name of War: King Philip's War and the Origins of American Identity* (1998). The story of the Iroquois is told well in Daniel K. Richter's *The Ordeal of the Longhouse: The Peoples of the Iroquois League in the Era of European Colonization* (1992). Indians in the southern colonies are the focus of James Axtell's *The Indians' New South: Cultural Change in the Colonial Southeast* (1997). On the fur trade, see Eric Jay Dolan, *Fur, Fortune, and Empire: The Epic Story of the Fur Trade in America* (2010).

For the social history of the southern colonies, see Allan Kulikoff's *Tobacco and Slaves: The Development of Southern Cultures in the Chesapeake, 1680–1800* (1986). On the interaction of the cultures of blacks and whites, see Mechal Sobel's *The World They Made Together: Black and White Values in Eighteenth-Century Virginia* (1987). On the slave trade, see William St. Clair's *The Door of No Return* (2007). African Americans during colonial settlement are the focus of Timothy H. Breen and Stephen Innes's *"Myne Owne Ground": Race and Freedom on Virginia's Eastern Shore, 1640–1676*, new ed. (2004). David W. Galenson's *White Servitude in Colonial America: An Economic Analysis* (1981) looks at the indentured labor force.

Henry F. May's *The Enlightenment in America* (1976) and Donald H. Meyer's *The Democratic Enlightenment* (1976) examine intellectual trends in eighteenth-century America. On the Great Awakening, see Frank Lambert's *Inventing the "Great Awakening"* (1999), and Thomas S. Kidd's *The Great Awakening: The Roots of Evangelical Christianity in Colonial America* (2007). The best biography of Edwards is Phillip F. Gura's *Jonathan Edwards: A Life* (2003).

Chapter 4

A good introduction to the imperial phase of the colonial conflicts is Douglas Edward Leach's *Arms for Empire: A Military History of the British Colonies in North America, 1607–1763* (1973). Also useful is Brendan Simms's *Three Victories and a Defeat: The Rise and Fall of the Fiurst British Empire* (2008). Fred Anderson's *Crucible of War: The Seven Years' War and the Fate of Empire in British North America, 1754–1766* (2000) is the best history of the Seven Years' War. For the implications of the British victory in 1763, see Colin G. Calloway's *The Scratch of a Pen: 1763 and the Transformation of North America* (2006). On the French colonies in North America, see Allan Greer's *The People of New France* (1997).

For a narrative survey of the events leading to the Revolution, see Edward Countryman's *The American Revolution*, rev. ed. (2003). For Great Britain's perspective on the imperial conflict, see Ian R. Christie's *Crisis of Empire: Great Britain and the American Colonies, 1754–1783* (1966). Also see Jeremy Black's *George III: America's Last King* (2007).

The intellectual foundations of revolt are traced in Bernard Bailyn's *The Ideological Origins of the American Revolution* (1992). To understand how these views were connected to organized protest, see Jon Butler's *Becoming America: The Revolution before 1776* (2000) and Kevin Phillips's *1775: A Good Year for a Revolution* (2012). On the first major battle, see Nathaniel Philbrick's *Bunker Hill: A Siege, a Revolution* (2013).

On the efforts of colonists to boycott the purchase of British goods, see T. H. Breen's *The Marketplace of Revolution: How Consumer Politics Shaped American Independence* (2004). For the events during the summer of 1776, see Joseph J. Ellis's *Revolutionary Summer: The Birth of American Independence*. Pauline Maier's *American Scripture: Making the Declaration of Independence* (1997) remains the best analysis of the framing of that document. The best analysis of why Americans supported independence is Thomas Slaughter's *Independence: The Tangled Roots of the American Revolution* (2014).

Chapter 5

Military affairs in the early phases of the Revolutionary War are handled in John W. Shy's *Toward Lexington: The Role of the British Army in the Coming of the American Revolution* (1965). The Revolutionary War is the subject of Gordon S. Wood's *The Radicalism of the American Revolution* (1991) and Jeremy Black's *War for America: The Fight for Independence, 1775–1783* (1991). John Ferling's *Setting the World Ablaze: Washington, Adams, Jefferson, and the American Revolution* (2000) highlights the roles played by key leaders.

On the social history of the Revolutionary War, see John W. Shy's *A People Numerous and Armed: Reflections on the Military Struggle for American Independence*, rev. ed. (1990). Colin G. Calloway tells the neglected story of the Indian experiences in the Revolution in *The American Revolution in Indian Country: Crisis and Diversity in Native American Communities* (1995).

Why some Americans remained loyal to the Crown is the subject of Thomas B. Allen's *Tories: Fighting for the King in America's First Civil War* (2010) and Maya Jasanoff's *Liberty's Exiles: American Loyalists in the Revolutionary War* (2011). A superb study of African Americans during the Revolutionary era is Douglas R. Egerton's *Death or Liberty: African Americans and Revolutionary America* (2009).

Carol Berkin's *Revolutionary Mothers: Women in the Struggle for America's Independence* (2005) documents the role that women played in securing independence. A superb biography of Revolutionary America's most prominent woman is Woody Holton's *Abigail Adams* (2010). A fine new biography of America's commander in chief is Ron Chernow's *Washington: A Life* (2010). The best analysis of the British side of the war is Andrew Jackson O'Shuaghnessy's *The Men Who Lost America: British Leadership, the American Revolution, and the Fate of Empire* (2013).

Chapter 6

A good overview of the Confederation period is Richard B. Morris's *The Forging of the Union, 1781–1789* (1987). Another useful analysis of this period is Richard Buel Jr.'s *Securing the Revolution: Ideology in American Politics, 1789–1815* (1972). David P. Szatmary's *Shays's Rebellion: The Making of an Agrarian Insurrection* (1980) covers that fateful incident. For a fine account of cultural change during the period, see Joseph J. Ellis's *After the Revolution: Profiles of Early American Culture* (1979).

An excellent overview of post-Revolutionary life is Joyce Appleby's *Inheriting the Revolution: The First Generation of Americans* (2000). On the political philosophies contributing to the drafting of the Constitution, see Ralph Lerner's *The Thinking Revolutionary: Principle and Practice in the New Republic* (1987). For the dramatic story of the framers of the Constitution, see Richard Beeman's *Plain, Honest Men: The Making of the American Constituion* (2009). Woody Holton's *Unruly Americans and the Origins of the Constitution* (2007) emphasizes the role of taxes and monetary policies in the crafting of the Constitution. The complex story of ratification is well told in Pauline Maier's *Ratification: The People Debate the Constitution, 1787-1788* (2010).

The best introduction to the early Federalists remains John C. Miller's *The Federalist Era, 1789–1801* (2011). Other works analyze the ideological debates among the nation's first leaders. Richard Buel Jr.'s *Securing the Revolution: Ideology in American Politics, 1789–1815* (1972), Joyce Appleby's *Capitalism and a New Social Order: The Republican Vision of the 1790s* (1984), and Stanley Elkins and Eric McKitrick's *The Age of Federalism: The Early American Republic, 1788–1800* (1993) trace the persistence and transformation of ideas first fostered during the Revolutionary crisis. The best study of Washington's political career is John Ferling's *The Ascent of George Washington: The Hidden Political Genius of an American Icon* (2009).

The 1790s may also be understood through the views and behavior of national leaders. See the following biographies: Richard Brookhiser's *Founding Father: Rediscovering George Washington* (1996), *Alexander Hamilton, American* (1999), and *James Madison* (2013), and Joseph J. Ellis's *Passionate Sage: The Character and Legacy of John Adams* (1993).

On the formation of the federal government and its economic policies, see Thomas K. McCraw's *The Founders and Finance* (2012). Federalist foreign policy is explored in Jerald A. Comb's *The Jay Treaty: Political Battleground of the Founding Fathers* (1970) and William Stinchcombe's *The XYZ Affair* (1980).

Chapter 7

Marshall Smelser's *The Democratic Republic, 1801–1815* (1968) presents an overview of the Republican administrations. Even more comprehensive is Gordon S. Wood's *Empire of Liberty: A History of the Early Republic, 1789-1815* (2010). The best treatment of the election of 1800 is Edward J. Larson's *A Magnificent Catastrophe: The Tumultuous Election of 1800* (2008).

The standard biography of Jefferson is Joseph J. Ellis's *American Sphinx: The Character of Thomas Jefferson* (1996). On the life of Jefferson's friend and successor, see Drew R. McCoy's. *The Last of the Fathers: James Madison and the Republican Legacy* (1989). Joyce Appleby's *Capitalism and a New Social Order: The Republican Vision of the 1790s* (1984) minimizes the impact of Republican ideology.

Linda K. Kerber's *Federalists in Dissent: Imagery and Ideology in Jeffersonian American* (1970) explores the Federalists while out of power. The concept of judicial review and the courts can be studied in Cliff Sloan and David McKean's *The Great Decision: Jefferson, Adams, Marshall, and the Battle for the Supreme Court* (2009). Liff Sloan and David McKean's *The Great Decision: Jefferson, Adams, Marshall, and the Battle for the Supreme Court* (2009). Milton Lomask's two volumes, *Aaron Burr: The Years from Princeton to Vice President, 1756–1805* (1979) and *The Conspiracy and the Years of Exile, 1805–1836* (1982) trace the career of that remarkable American.

For the Louisiana Purchase, consult Jon Kukla's *A Wilderness So Immense: The Louisiana Purchase and the Destiny of America* (2003). For a captivating account of the Lewis and Clark expedition, see Stephen Ambrose's *Undaunted Courage: Meriwether Lewis, Thomas Jefferson, and the Opening of the American West* (1996).

Burton Spivak's *Jefferson's English Crisis: Commerce, Embargo, and the Republican Revolution* (1979) discusses Anglo-American relations during Jefferson's administration; Clifford L. Egan's *Neither Peace Nor War: Franco-American Relations, 1803–1812* (1983) covers America's relations with France. An excellent revisionist treatment of the events that brought on war in 1812 is J. C. A. Stagg's *Mr. Madison's War: Politics, Diplomacy, and Warfare in the Early American Republic, 1783–1830* (1983). The war itself is the focus of Donald R. Hickey's *The War of 1812: A Forgotten Conflict* (1989). See also Alan Taylor's award-winnning *The Civil War of 1812: American Citizens, British Subjects, Irish Rebels, and Indian Allies* (2011).

Chapter 8

The best overview of the second quarter of the nineteenth century is Daniel Walker Howe, *What Hath God Wrought: The Transformation of America, 1815-1845* (2007). The classic study of transportation and economic growth is George Rogers Taylor's *The Transportation Revolution, 1815–1860* (1951). A more recent treatment is Sarah H. Gordon's *Passage to Union: How the Railroads Transformed American Life, 1829–1929* (1996). On the Erie Canal, see Carol Sheriff's *The Artificial River: The Erie Canal and the Paradox of Progress, 1817–1862* (1996). See also John Lauritz Larson's *Internal Improvement: National Public Works and the Promise of Popular Government in the Early United States* (2001).

Several books focus on social issues of the post-Revolutionary period, including *Keepers of the Revolution: New Yorkers at Work in the Early Republic* (1992), edited by Paul A. Gilje and Howard B. Rock; Ronald Schultz's *The Republic of Labor: Philadelphia Artisans and the Politics of Class, 1720–1830* (1993); and Peter Way's *Common Labor: Workers and the Digging of North American Canals, 1780–1860* (1993).

On the industrial revolution, see Charles R. Morris's *The Dawn of Innovation: The First American Industrial Revolution* (2013. The impact of technology is traced in David J. Jeremy's *Transatlantic Industrial Revolution: The Diffusion of Textile Technologies between Britain and America, 1790–1830s* (1981). On the invention of the telegraph, see Kenneth Silverman's *Lightning Man: The Accursed Life of Samuel F. B. Morse* (2003). For the story of steamboats, see Andrea Sutcliffe's *Steam: The Untold Story of America's First Great Invention* (2004).

The outlook of the working class during this time of transition is surveyed in Edward E. Pessen's *Most Uncommon Jacksonians: The Radical Leaders of the Early Labor Movement* (1967). Detailed case studies of working communities include Anthony F. C. Wallace's *Rockdale: The Growth of an American Village in the Early Industrial Revolution* (1978), Thomas Dublin's *Women at Work: The Transformation of Work and Community in Lowell, Massachusetts, 1826–1860* (1979), and Sean Wilentz's *Chants Democratic: New York and the Rise of the American Working Class, 1788–1850* (1984).

For a fine treatment of urbanization, see Charles N. Glaab and A. Theodore Brown's *A History of Urban America* (1967). On immigration, see Jay P. Dolan's *The Irish Americans* (2008) and John Kelly's *The Graves Are Walking: The Great Famine and the Saga of the Irish People* (2012).

Chapter 9

The standard overview of the Era of Good Feelings remains George Dangerfield's *The Awakening of American Nationalism, 1815–1828* (1965). A classic summary of the economic trends of the period is Douglass C. North's *The Economic Growth of the United States, 1790–1860* (1961). An excellent synthesis of the era is Charles Sellers's *The Market Revolution: Jacksonian America, 1815–1846* (1991).

On diplomatic relations during James Monroe's presidency, see William Earl Weeks's *John Quincy Adams and American Global Empire* (1992). For relations after 1812, see Ernest R. May's *The Making of the Monroe Doctrine* (1975). The campaign that brought Andrew Jackson to the White House is analyzed in Robert Vincent Remini's *The Election of Andrew Jackson* (1963).

Chapter 10

The best comprehensive surveys of politics and culture during the Jacksonian era are Daniel Walker Howe's *What Hath God Wrought: The Transformation of America, 1815–1848* (2007) and David S. Reynolds's *Waking Giant: America in the Age of Jackson* (2008). A more political focus can be found in Harry L. Watson's *Liberty and Power: The Politics of Jacksonian America* (1990). On the rise of urban political machines, see Terry Golway's *Machine Made: Tammany Hall and the Creation of Modern American Politics* (2014).

For an outstanding analysis of women in New York City during the Jacksonian period, see Christine Stansell's *City of Women: Sex and Class in New York, 1789–1860* (1986). In *Chants Democratic: New York City and the Rise of the American Working-Class, 1788–1850* (1984), Sean Wilentz analyzes the social basis of working-class politics. More recently, Wilentz has traced the democratization of politics in *The Rise of American Democracy: Jefferson to Lincoln* (2009).

The best biography of Jackson remains Robert Vincent Remini's three-volume work: *Andrew Jackson: The Course of American Empire, 1767–1821* (1977), *Andrew Jackson: The Course of American Freedom, 1822–1832* (1981), and *Andrew Jackson: The Course of American Democracy, 1833–1845* (1984). A more critical study of the seventh president is Andrew Burstein's *The Passions of Andrew Jackson* (2003).

On Jackson's successor, consult John Niven's *Martin Van Buren: The Romantic Age of American Politics* (1983) and Ted Widmer's *Martin Van Buren* (2005). Studies of other major figures of the period include John Niven's *John C. Calhoun and the Price of Union: A Biography* (1988), Merrill D. Peterson's *The Great Triumvirate: Webster, Clay, and Calhoun* (1987), and Robert Vincent Remini's *Henry Clay: Statesman for the Union* (1991) and *Daniel Webster: The Man and His Time* (1997).

The political philosophies of Jackson's opponents are treated in Michael F. Holt's *The Rise and Fall of the American Whig Party: Jacksonian Politics and the Onset of the Civil War* (1999) and Harry L. Watson's *Andrew Jackson vs. Henry Clay: Democracy and Development in Antebellum America* (1998). The outstanding book on the nullification issue remains William W. Freehling's *Prelude to Civil War: The Nullification Controversy in South Carolina, 1816–1836* (1965). John M. Belohlavek's *"Let the Eagle Soar!": The Foreign Policy of Andrew Jackson* (1985) is a thorough study of Jacksonian diplomacy. A. J. Langguth's *Driven West: Andrew Jackson and the Trail of Tears to the Civil War* (2010) analyzes the controversial relocation policy.

Chapter 11

Russel Blaine Nye's *Society and Culture in America, 1830–1860* (1974) provides a wide-ranging survey of the Romantic movement. On the reform impulse, consult Ronald G. Walter's *American Reformers, 1815–1860*, rev. ed. (1997). Revivalist religion is treated in Nathan O. Hatch's *The Democratization of American Christianity* (1989), Christine Leigh Heyrman's *Southern Cross: The Beginnings of the Bible Belt* (1997), and Ellen Eslinger's *Citizens of Zion: The Social Origins of Camp Meeting Revivalism* (1999). On the Mormons, see Alex Beam's *American Crucifixion: The Murder of Joseph Smith and the Fate of the Mormon Church* (2014).

The best treatments of transcendentalist thought are Paul F. Boller's *American Transcendentalism, 1830–1860: An Intellectual Inquiry* (1974) and Philip F. Gura's *American Transcendentalism: A History* (2007). For the war against alcohol, see W. J. Rorabaugh's *The Alcoholic Republic: An American Tradition* (1979) and Barbara Leslie Epstein's *The Politics of Domesticity: Women, Evangelism, and Temperance in Nineteenth-Century America* (1981). On prison reform and other humanitarian projects, see David J. Rothman's *The Discovery of the Asylum: Social Order and Disorder in the New Republic*, rev. ed. (2002), and Thomas J. Brown's biography *Dorothea Dix: New England Reformer* (1998).

Useful surveys of abolitionism include Seymour Drescher's *Abolition: A History of Slavery and Antislavery* (2009), James Brewer Stewart's *Holy Warriors: The Abolitionists and American Slavery,* rev. ed. (1997), and Julie Roy Jeffrey's *The Great Silent Army of Abolitionism: Ordinary Women in the Antislavery Movement* (1998). For the pro-slavery argument as it developed in the South, see Larry E. Tise's *Proslavery: A History of the Defense of Slavery in America, 1701–1840* (1987) and James Oakes's *The Ruling Race: A History of American Slaveholders* (1982). The problems southerners had in justifying slavery are explored in Kenneth S. Greenberg's *Masters and Statesmen: The Political Culture of American Slavery* (1985).

Chapter 12

Three efforts to understand the mind of the Old South and its defense of slavery are Eugene D. Genovese's *The Slaveholders' Dilemma: Freedom and Progress in Southern Conservative Thought, 1820–1860* (1992), William W. Freehling's *The Road to Disunion: Secessionists Triumphant, 1854–1861* (2007), and Walter Johnson's *River of Dark Dreams: Slavery and Empire in the Cotton Kingdom* (2013). Stephanie McCurry's *Masters of Small Worlds: Yeoman Households, Gender Relations, and the Political Culture of the Antebellum South Carolina Low Country* (1995) describes southern households, religion, and political culture.

Other essential works on southern culture and society include Bertram Wyatt-Brown's *Honor and Violence in the Old South* (1986), Elizabeth Fox-Genovese's *Within the Plantation Household: Black and White Women of the Old South* (1988), Catherine Clinton's *The Plantation Mistress: Woman's World in the Old South* (1982), Joan E. Cashin's *A Family Venture: Men and Women on the Southern Frontier* (1991), and Theodore Rosengarten's *Tombee: Portrait of a Cotton Planter* (1986).

John W. Blassingame's *The Slave Community: Plantation Life in the Antebellum South,* rev. and enlarged ed. (1979), Eugene D. Genovese's *Roll, Jordan, Roll: The World the Slaves Made* (1974), and Herbert G. Gutman's *The Black Family in Slavery and Freedom, 1750–1925* (1976) all stress the theme of a persisting and identifiable slave culture. On the question of slavery's profitability, see Robert William Fogel and Stanley L. Engerman's *Time on the Cross: The Economics of American Negro Slavery* (1974), and Edward E. Baptist's *The Half Has Never Been Told* (2014). Charles Joyner's *Down by the Riverside: A South Carolina Slave Community* (1984) offers a vivid reconstruction of one community.

Chapter 13

For background on Whig programs and ideas, see Michael F. Holt's *The Rise and Fall of the American Whig Party: Jacksonian Politics and the Onset of the Civil War* (1999). On John Tyler, see Edward P. Crapol's *John Tyler: The Accidental President* (2006). On the expansionist impulse westward, see Thomas R. Hietala's *Manifest Design: Anxious Aggrandizement in Late Jacksonian America* (1985), Walter Nugent's *Habits of Empire: A History of American Expansionism* (2008) and Richard White's *"It's Your Misfortune and None of My Own": A New History of the American West* (1991).

For the expansionism of the 1840s, see Steven E. Woodworth's *Manifest Destinies: America's Westward Expansion and the Road to the Civil War* (2010). The movement of settlers to the West is ably documented in John Mack Faragher's *Women and Men on the Overland Trail,* 2nd ed. (2001), and David Dary's *The Santa Fe Trail: Its History, Legends, and Lore* (2000).

Gene M. Brack's *Mexico Views Manifest Destiny, 1821–1846: An Essay on the Origins of the Mexican War* (1975) takes Mexico's viewpoint on U.S. designs on the West. For the American perspective on Texas, see Joel H. Silbey's *Storm over Texas: The Annexation Controversy and the Road to Civil War* (2005). On the siege of the Alamo, see William C. Davis's *Three Roads to the Alamo: The Lives and Fortunes of David Crockett, James Bowie, and William Barret Travis* (1998) and James Donovan's *The Blood of Heroes* (2012). An excellent biography related to the emergence of Texas is Gregg Cantrell's *Stephen F. Austin: Empresario of Texas* (1999).

On James K. Polk, see Robert W. Merry's *A Country of Vast Designs: James K. Polk, the Mexican War, and the Conquest of the American Continent* (2009). The best survey of the military conflict is John S. D. Eisenhower's *So Far from God: The U.S. War with Mexico, 1846–1848* (1989). The Mexican War as viewed from the perspective of the soldiers is ably described in Richard Bruce Winders's *Mr. Polk's Army: American Military Experience in the Mexican War* (1997). On the diplomatic aspects of Mexican-American relations, see David M. Pletcher's *The Diplomacy of Annexation: Texas, Oregon, and the Mexican War* (1973).

The best surveys of the forces and events leading to the Civil War include James M. McPherson's *Battle Cry of Freedom: The Civil War Era* (1988), Stephen B. Oates's *The Approaching Fury: Voices of the Storm, 1820–1861* (1997), and Bruce Levine's *Half Slave and Half Free: The Roots of Civil War* (1992). The most recent narrative of the political debate leading to secession is Michael A. Morrison's *Slavery and the American West: The Eclipse of Manifest Destiny and the Coming of the Civil War* (1997).

Mark J. Stegmaier's *Texas, New Mexico, and the Compromise of 1850: Boundary Dispute and Sectional Crisis* (1996) probes that crucial dispute, while Michael F. Holt's *The Political Crisis of the 1850s* (1978) traces the demise of the Whigs. See also Fergus M. Bordewich's *America's Great Debate: Henry Clay, Stephen A. Douglas, and the Compromise That Preserved the Union* (2012). Eric Foner, in *Free Soil, Free Labor, Free Men: The Ideology of the Republican Party before the Civil War* (1970), shows how events and ideas combined in the formation of a new political party. The pivotal *Dred Scott* case is ably assessed in Earl M. Maltz's *Dred Scott and the Politics of Slavery* (2007).

On the role of John Brown in the sectional crisis, see Robert E. McGlone's *John Brown's War Against Slavery* (2009). A detailed study of the South's journey to secession is William W. Freehling's *The Road to Disunion,* vol. 1, *Secessionists at Bay, 1776–1854* (1990), and *The Road to Disunion*, vol. 2, *Secessionists Triumphant, 1854–1861* (2007). Robert E. Bonner traces the emergence of southern nationalism in *Mastering America: Southern Slaveholders and the Crisis of American Nationhood* (2009).

On the Buchanan presidency, see Jean H. Baker's *James Buchanan* (2004). Maury Klein's *Days of Defiance: Sumter, Secession, and the Coming of the Civil War* (1997) treats the Fort Sumter controversy. An excellent collection of interpretive essays is *Why the Civil War Came* (1996), edited by Gabor S. Boritt.

Chapter 14

On the start of the Civil War, see Adam Goodheart's *1861: The Civil War Awakening* (2011). The best one-volume overview of the Civil War period is James M. McPherson's *Battle Cry of Freedom: The Civil War Era* (1988). A more recent synthesis of the war and its effects is David Goldfield's *America Aflame: How the Civil War Created a Nation* (2011). A good introduction to the military events is Herman Hattaway's *Shades of Blue and Gray: An Introductory Military History of the Civil War* (1997). The outlook and experiences of the common soldier are explored in James M. McPherson's *For Cause and Comrades: Why Men Fought in the Civil War* (1997).

The northern war effort is ably assessed in Gary W. Gallagher's *The Union War* (2011). For emphasis on the South, see Gallagher's *The Confederate War* (1997). A sparkling account of the birth of the Rebel nation is William C. Davis's *"A Government of Our Own": The Making of the Confederacy* (1994). The same author provides a fine biography of the Confederate president in *Jefferson Davis: The Man and His Hour* (1991). On the leading Confederate commander, see Michael Korda's *Clouds of Glory: The Life and Legend of Robert E. Lee* (2014). On the key Union generals, see Lee Kennett's *Sherman: A Soldier's Life* (2001) and Josiah Bunting III's *Ulysses S. Grant* (2004).

The history of the North during the war is surveyed in Philip Shaw Paludan's *A People's Contest: The Union and Civil War, 1861–1865,* 2nd ed. (1996), and J. Matthew Gallman's *The North Fights the Civil War: The Home Front* (1994). See also Jennifer L. Weber's *Copperheads: The Rise and Fall of Lincoln's Opponents in the North* (2006). The central northern political figure, Abraham Lincoln, is the subject of many books. See James McPherson's *Abraham Lincoln* (2009) and Ronald C. White, Jr., *A. Lincoln: A Biography* (2009).

The experience of the African American soldier is surveyed in Joseph T. Glatthaar's *Forged in Battle: The Civil War Alliance of Black Soldiers and White Officers* (1990) and Ira Berlin, Joseph P. Reidy, and Leslie S. Rowland's *Freedom's Soldiers: The Black Military Experience in the Civil War* (1998). For the African American woman's experience, see Jacqueline Jones's *Labor of Love, Labor of Sorrow: Black Women, Work and the Family, from Slavery to the Present* (1985). On Lincoln's evolving racial views, see Eric Foner's *The Fiery Trial: Abraham Lincoln and American Slavery* (2010). The war's impact on slavery is the focus of James Oakes's *Freedom National: The Destruction of Slavery in the United States, 1861-1865* (2013) and Bruce Levine's *The Fall of the House of Dixie* (2013). On the emancipation proclamation, see Louis P. Masur's *Lincoln's Hundred Days: The Emancipation Proclamation and the War for the Union* (2012).

Recent gender and ethnic studies include Nina Silber's *Gender and the Sectional Conflict* (2008), Drew Gilpin Faust's *Mothers of Invention: Women of the Slaveholding South in the American Civil War* (1996), George C. Rable's *Civil Wars: Women and the Crisis of Southern Nationalism* (1989), and William L. Burton's *Melting Pot Soldiers: The Union's Ethnic Regiments,* 2nd ed. (1998).

Chapter 15

The most comprehensive treatment of Reconstruction is Eric Foner's *Reconstruction: America's Unfinished Revolution, 1863–1877* (1988). On Andrew Johnson, see Hans L. Trefousse's *Andrew Johnson: A Biography* (1989) and David D. Stewart's *Impeached: The Trial of Andrew Johnson and the Fight for Lincoln's Legacy* (2009). An excellent brief biography of Grant is Josiah Bunting III's *Ulysses S. Grant* (2004).

Scholars have been sympathetic to the aims and motives of the Radical Republicans. See, for instance, Herman Belz's *Reconstructing the Union: Theory and Policy during the Civil War* (1969) and Richard Nelson Current's *Those Terrible Carpetbaggers: A Reinterpretation* (1988). The ideology of the Radicals is explored in Michael Les Benedict's *A Compromise of Principle: Congressional Republicans and Reconstruction, 1863–1869* (1974). On the black political leaders, see Phillip Dray's *Capitol Men: The Epic Story of Reconstruction through the Lives of the First Black Congressmen* (2008).

The intransigence of southern white attitudes is examined in Michael Perman's *Reunion without Compromise: The South and Reconstruction, 1865– 1868* (1973) and Dan T. Carter's *When the War Was Over: The Failure of Self-Reconstruction in the South, 1865–1867* (1985). Allen W. Trelease's *White Terror: The Ku Klux Klan Conspiracy and Southern Reconstruction* (1971) covers the various organizations that practiced vigilante tactics. On the massacre of African Americans, see Charles Lane's *The Day Freedom Died: The Colfax Massacre, the Supreme Court, and the Betrayal of Reconstruction* (2008).

The difficulties former slaves had in adjusting to the new labor system are documented in James L. Roark's *Masters without Slaves: Southern Planters in the Civil War and Reconstruction* (1977). Books on southern politics during Reconstruction include Michael Perman's *The Road to Redemption: Southern Politics, 1869–1879* (1984), Terry L. Seip's *The South Returns to Congress: Men, Economic Measures, and Intersectional Relationships, 1868–1879* (1983), and Mark W. Summers's *Railroads, Reconstruction, and the Gospel of Prosperity: Aid under the Radical Republicans, 1865–1877* (1984).

Numerous works study the freed blacks' experience in the South. Start with Leon F. Litwack's *Been in the Storm So Long: The Aftermath of Slavery* (1979). The Freedmen's Bureau is explored in William S. McFeely's *Yankee Stepfather: General O. O. Howard and the Freedmen* (1968). The situation of freed slave women is discussed in Jacqueline Jones's *Labor of Love, Labor of Sorrow: Black Women, Work and the Family, from Slavery to the Present* (1985).

The politics of corruption outside the South is depicted in William S. McFeely's *Grant: A Biography* (1981). The political maneuvers of the election of 1876 and the resultant crisis and compromise are explained in Michael Holt's *By One Vote: The Disputed Presidential Election of 1876* (2008).

Credits

Text Credits

Richard Breitman and Allan J. Lichtman: Excerpts reprinted by permission of the publisher from *FDR and the Jews* by Richard Breitman and Allan J. Lichtman, pp. 2, 6-7, Cambridge, Mass.: Harvard University Press, Copyright © 2013 by Richard Breitman and Allan J. Lichtman.

Leo Chavez: Excerpts from *The Latno Threat: Constructing Immigrants, Citizens, and the Nation, Second Edition*, by Leo Chavez. Copyright © 2008, 2014 By the Board of Trustees of the Leland Stanford Jr. University. All rights reserved. With the permission of Stanford University Press, www.sup.org

Paul Finkelman: Excerpts from "Jefferson and Slavery," in *Jeffersonian Legacies*, edited by Peter S. Onuf. pp. 181-183, 210-211. © 1993 by the Rector and Visitors of the University of Virginia. Reprinted by permission of the University of Virginia Press.

Nathan Glazer & Daniel Moynihan: From *Beyond The Melting Pot*, excerpts from pp. 12 - 14, 20, © 1963 Massachusetts Institute of Technology, used by permission of The MIT Press.

Gary B. Nash: Excerpts from "Social Change and the Growth of Prerevolutionary Urban Radicalism," by Gary B. Nash. From *The American Revolution: Explorations in History of American Radicalism*, by Alfred F. Young (ed.). Copyright © 1976 by Northern Illinois University Press. Used with permission of Northern Illinois University Press.

Jason Richwine: "The Congealing Pot," by Jason Richwine from National Review, August 24, 2009. © 2009 by National Review, Inc. Reprinted by permission.

Douglas L. Wilson: Excerpts from "Thomas Jefferson and the Character Issue," by Douglas L. Wilson. Originally published in *The Atlantic Monthly*, November 1992. Used by permission the author.

Image Credits

Chapter 1: p. 2: Library of Congress; **p. 2:** Collection of the New-York Historical Society; **p. 2:** bpk, Berlin/Kunstbibliothek, Staatliche Museen/Knud Petersen/ Art Resource; **p. 2:** North Wind Picture Archives/Alamy; **p. 2:** Abby Aldrich Rockefeller Folk Art Center Colonial Williamsburg; **p. 2:** Bettmann/Corbis; **pp. 4 & 5:** Bridgeman Art Library; **p. 4:** © British Museum/Art Resource; **p. 5:** The Granger Collection; **p. 6:** bpk, Berlin/ Kunstbibliothek, Staatliche Museen/Knud Petersen/Art Resource; **p. 9:** © British Museum; **p. 10:** Bettmann/Corbis; **p. 11:** Library of Congress; **p. 14:** Bettmann/Corbis; **p. 15:** © Richard A. Cooke/CORBIS; **p. 17:** MPI/Getty Images; **p. 19:** Bettmann/Corbis; **p. 25:** The Benson Latin American Collection, University of Texas; **p. 29:** The Royal Library of Copenhagen; **p. 34:** Bettmann/Corbis.

Chapter 2: p. 38: Bridgeman Art Library; **p. 43:** The Granger Collection; **p. 51:** The Granger Collection; **p. 53:** The Granger Collection; **p. 56:** Bettmann/Corbis; **p. 60:** The Granger Collection; **p. 64:** The Granger Collection; **p. 65:** Library of Congress; **p. 66:** The Granger Collection; **p. 68:** © British Museum/Art Resource; **p. 69:** The Swem Library, the College of William & Mary; **p. 73:** The Granger Collection; **p. 74:** Abby Aldrich Rockefeller Folk Art Center Colonial Williamsburg.

Chapter 3: p. 78: The Granger Collection; **p. 81:** The Granger Collection; **p. 82:** Connecticut Historical Society Museum; **p. 84:** The Granger Collection; **p. 85:** North Wind Picture Archive; **p. 86:** The Granger Collection; **p. 88:** The Granger Collection; **p. 94:** The Granger Collection; **p. 97:** Collection of the New-York Historical Society; **p. 100:** Library Company of Philadelphia; **p. 102:** Stock Montage/Getty Images; **p. 104:** The Granger Collection.

Chapter 4: p. 108: The Granger Collection; **p. 112:** Wikimedia Commons; **p. 118:** Library of Congress; **p. 119:** Collection of the New-York Historical Society; **p. 120:** The Granger Collection; **p. 129:** Library of Congress; **p. 131:** Library of Congress; **p. 132:** Library of Congress; **p. 133:** Library of Congress; **p. 136:** The Granger Collection; **p. 138:** The Granger Collection; **p. 140:** Courtesy of the Historical Society of Pennsylvania Collection, Atwater Kent Museum of Philadelphia; **p. 142:** National Archives; **p. 143:** North Wind Picture Archives/Alamy.

Chapter 5: p. 150: Private Collection/Photo © Christie's Images/ The Bridgeman Art Library; **p. 150:** The Granger Collection; **p. 150:** Collection of the New-York Historical Society/Bridgeman Art Library; **p. 150:** The Granger Collection; **p. 150:** © Francis G. Mayer/Corbis; **p. 150:** Private Collection/Photo © Christie's Images/The Bridgeman Art Library; **pp. 152 & 153:** Copyright American Philosophical Society; **p. 152:** Anne S.K. Brown Military Collection, Brown University Library; **p. 153:** The Granger Collection; **p. 154:** © Francis G. Mayer/Corbis; **p. 157:** US Senate Collection; **p. 160 (left):** Private Collection/Photo © Christie's Images/The Bridgeman Art Library; **p. 160 (right):** The Granger Collection; **p. 163:** The Granger Collection; **p. 166:** The Granger Collection; **p. 173:** Wikimedia Commons; **p. 175:** The Granger Collection; **p. 176:** Anne S.K. Brown Military Collection, Brown University Library; **p. 177:** MPI/Getty Images; **p. 181:** The Granger Collection; **p. 184:** The Granger Collection.

Chapter 6: p. 188: The Granger Collection; **p. 195:** Historical Society of Pennsylvania; **p. 196:** The Granger Collection; **p. 197:** The Granger Collection; **p. 201:** The Granger Collection; **p. 203:** The Granger Collection; **p. 206 (top):** Library of Congress; **p. 206 (center):** MPI/Getty Images; **p. 210:** Independence National Historical Park; **p. 211:** Courtesy of the Maryland Historical Society; **p. 212:** Historical Society of Pennsylvania; **p. 213:** The Granger Collection; **p. 217:** The Granger Collection; **p. 219:** Art Resource; **p. 220:** The Granger Collection; **p. 221:** National Portrait Gallery; **p. 222:** The Granger Collection.

Index